PETER THELLUSSON'S WILL OF 1797
AND ITS CONSEQUENCES ON CHANCERY LAW

Peter Thellusson's Will of 1797 and Its Consequences on Chancery Law

Patrick Polden

The Edwin Mellen Press
Lewiston•Queenston•Lampeter

Library of Congress Cataloging-in-Publication Data

Polden, Patrick
    Peter Thellusson's will of 1797 and its consequences on chancery law / Patrick Polden.
      p. cm.
    Includes bibliographical references and index.
    ISBN 0-7734-7237-1
    1. Thellusson, Peter, 1737-1797--Will. 2. Contested wills--England. 3. Equity--Great
Britain--History. I. Title.

KD1514.T49 P65 2002
346.4205'6--dc21

                                            2001054398

A CIP catalog record for this book is available from the British Library.

Front Cover: Picture no. A931144 BRODSWORTH HALL
The South front c1910 with Charles and Constance Thellusson on the steps.
Copy of historic photograph 90007321.
© *English Heritage Photo Library*

Copyright © 2002 Patrick Polden

        The Edwin Mellen Press   The Edwin Mellen Press
             Box 450   Box 67
         Lewiston, New York   Queenston, Ontario
        USA 14092-0450   CANADA L0S 1L0

                  The Edwin Mellen Press, Ltd.
                  Lampeter, Ceredigion, Wales
                UNITED KINGDOM SA48 8LT

Printed in the United States of America

To Anne

TABLE OF CONTENTS

ACKNOWLEDGEMENTS

For more than a decade this has been my equivalent of Spalding Gray's 'monster in a box', and at times it has seemed to fall under the curse of the court of Chancery whose ways it describes. It was begun in the reading room of the British Museum and in the old Public Record Office in Chancery Lane and over time it has grown to an unconscionable size, for which my only justification is the desire to provide something of interest to a variety of readers.

In the long course of making I have incurred a debt of gratitude to many people, too many to name individually, among them the staffs of many public libraries, archive repositories and record offices, particularly the Public Record Office. I am also indebted to several past and present staff at English Heritage. Thanks are also due to SLS publications for permission to include as chapter 9 material published as an article in the *Northern Ireland Legal Quarterly*. Lord Rendlesham was kind enough to answer some questions about the recent history of the family and I received great encouragement and assistance from Peter Thellusson.

My debt to Profession Brian Simpson will be immediately apparent, and among other scholars who have responded generously to my cries for help I would like particularly to acknowledge Professors Bill Cornish, Henry Horwitz and Keith Smith and Doctor David Grace. The many errors that remain are mine alone.

It has taken a great deal of patience and forebearance on the part of David Mathers and successive secretaries in the Law Department, particularly Amanda Crew, to convert the product of my untidy use of obsolescent technology into a presentable form. They will be very relieved to see it finally in print, as will my wife, to whom I owe the greatest debt of all for understanding and encouragement.

PREFACE

Death, though it comes to all of us, has never contrived to make itself fully acceptable in polite society, and to-day, as in the past, huge resources and much ingenuity is devoted both to postponing the event as long as long as possible, or, better still, to ensuring that, in spite of appearances, it never really happens at all. Lawyers have had little to do with the more far reaching schemes for the total abolition of death, but they have been much involved in devising mechanisms for the pursuit of a less ambitious alternative, posthumous immortality. There are many ways in which this aim can be pursued. One derives from the perception that although individuals come and go, the family to which an individual belongs is, in principle, capable of lasting into the indefinite future. It thus provides a vehicle whereby the dead can, in some mysterious sense, stay around too.

Much of the elaborate law of trusts, its limitations determined by a barely comprehensible body of legal doctrine called the rule against perpetuities, is parasitic upon this view of the family. Lawyers, who tend to go where the money is, have long catered for the desire of the wealthy to organise their affairs so as to ensure that the family endowment, and with it the family, is protected into the indefinite future both from the folly of the inevitable prodigal sons or daughters, and, even more threatening in the modern world, the ravages of taxation. Thus there exists a flourishing legal industry offering the wealthy what are known as "dynasty" trusts. Such trusts may take on weird forms. Thus in the U.S.A., under the complex law governing the valuation of gifts for taxation purposes, which rely on actuarial tables of life expectancy, "vulture" trusts have been devised, where the trust is made to endure for the lifetime persons selected because they are terminally ill, and thus certain to die early. Cruder devices include the surreptitious freezing of cadavers when death occurs at a moment which attracts an unwelcome high rate of tax, thus postponing the apparent date of death, and thereby protecting the family endowment.

The dynastic ambitions which exist today were perhaps even more prevalent amongst the wealthy in the past. Peter Thellusson, a wealthy eighteenth century merchant, together with his lawyers, came up with the idea of setting up a trust under which the income of his property should be accumulated for many years after his death. The period chosen was the lives of his living children and grandchildren; this could extend to somewhere near a century. Only then would his wealth be distributed to the family. His will carefully avoided any violation of the rule against perpetuities, which was, at that time, the only check on dynastic family trusts. Given prudent management, and compound interest, the fortune then available for distribution ought to have been vast; indeed if you took compound interest seriously the trust might absorb virtually the whole wealth of the country. But while the trust in one sense served to ensure the permanence of the Thellusson family, and with it Peter Thellusson's own immortality, in the not so short term, while the trust remained in force, it cut out the more immediate from the inheritance. It was good news for the unborn, but bad news for the living.

This book tells the story of Peter Thellusson's will, of the controversies to which it gave rise, and of the eventual outcome of the *Jarndyce v. Jarndyce* like litigation it provoked. This story has never been told before, except in the most superficial way. The immediate context is the world of the late eighteenth and nineteenth centuries, but the moral and political issues which were involved have a timeless quality. Why should individuals have a power to dispose of their property after they are dead? What limits should be placed on testamentary power? Should these limits be based on the idea that family members have moral claims to inherit? What precisely are their moral claims, and what is their basis? Where, if at all, does the public interest come into the picture? The story also has a significance for the understanding of the literature of the nineteenth century, much of which centres not simply upon the family as an institution, but upon its legal underpinnings. And, for

iv

those who derive a strange pleasure from the contemplation of the bizarre, there was surely never a more bizarre will than this. Ironically however, as it turns out, the testator has, in a way he surely never anticipated, achieved his object; he has now been given yet another an extra lease of life through this scholarly and entertaining book.

A.W.B. Simpson
University of Michigan Law School
June 2000

CHAPTER 1

'THE MOST FAMOUS WILL IN THE WORLD'

July 1797 found Britain at bay. Her main continental ally, the Austrian Empire, had been so battered by Bonaparte's armies that she had sued for peace. France was triumphant on land, and the fleet that stood between Britain and invasion had just been restored to a precarious obedience after paralysing mutinies; the ringleaders were now on trial for their lives. The Funds stood at their lowest point since Bonnie Prince Charlie reached Derby in the 'Forty-five and for the past six months the Bank of England had suspended cash payments. Confidence in William Pitt and his government had collapsed and at this low ebb in the nation's fortunes Edmund Burke, the embodiment of conservative resistance to the doctrines of revolution, had just died. Also dead, on the 22nd of the month, was Peter Thellusson, an enormously rich merchant and financier of Huguenot origin but a naturalised Englishman. He left a wife, three grown sons, three daughters, and a will.

Wills seldom make headlines nowadays. The few that do usually involve a shabby eccentric living in squalor who is revealed to have amassed a large fortune, or an elderly millionaire who has disinherited his family in favour of a recently acquired friend, servant or lover. Wills are public documents and the very rich usually desire privacy; this, as well as tax planning, dictates that their dispositions are usually made through lifetime trusts and gifts. It takes a family quarrel, a press investigation or a tax claim to uncover the arrangements of people like the Vesteys.[1] And because property is no longer a central concern of writers of novels or plays, wills and inheritance seldom figure in them except for that genre of English detective fiction which remains frozen in a never-never land of country houses and snug villages.

But in Peter Thellusson's day and for a hundred years afterwards it was quite otherwise. As Colin Watson wrote: `a measure of the importance attached to inheritance by the Victorian public is the frequency of its use as a motive, often the main motive in contemporary novels...The fiction of the period could almost be described as the fiction of probate.'[2] The writers of this fiction were not just Sheridan Le Fanu, Wilkie Collins and those who followed them down the dark paths of mystery and imagination, but great and serious novelists, for inheritance is central to two of Dickens' finest works - *Great Expectations* and *Bleak House* - and abounds in those of his more prolific contemporary Anthony Trollope, in *Cousin Henry* and *Mr. Scarborough's Family* for instance. Artists too found the reading of the will a compelling dramatic scene: the anxious and expectant family in deepest mourning, the hopeful retainers standing in the background and the family solicitor seated and composed, already possessed of the dead man's last secrets.[3] Writers exploited this dramatic potential.[4] In fiction disinheritance is commonplace and often accompanied by scathing aspersions on character; legacies are made subject to strict conditions, often demanding or forbidding marriage; large fortunes are bestowed upon mysterious persons and unsuspected liaisons come to light. Real life was always more sedate, less surprising. Most testators were as conventional in death as in life and the sensational, startling or merely eccentric will has always been a rarity. Nevertheless there was seldom a shortage of newsworthy ones; for instance, in the same year that Peter Thellusson died *The Annual Register* reported the death of Thomas Palmer esquire, who left a bequest to reward `the writer or writers of an essay or essays against the present cruel, detestable, and absurd practice of carrying on war, and to recommend the preservation of harmony among all the nations of the earth.'[5]

Of course the fame of such wills was usually fleeting, though it might be prolonged if the will was contested, particularly if there were sensational allegations of forgery, fraud or foul play. Such was John Marsden's will, recently the subject of an entertaining and instructive book by Emmeline Garnett, and the great Swinfen case, which involved not only a contested will but several other titillating elements.[6] More enduring fame has usually only resulted where the testator makes a public benefaction which leaves a lasting monument, like Guy's Hospital in London, or a scholarship or chair bearing his name.[7]

In the narrower world of the law some wills find an adventitious but lasting celebrity. They take their place in textbooks and treatises as examples of canons of construction or as cautionary tales about defects of form or costly mistakes in drafting. The overlap between wills which arouse even an ephemeral public interest and those of legal significance is small. The infamous Dr. Crippen has his place in the law books because he left his property (including that of the wife he murdered) to his mistress Ethel Le Neve, whom the law would not allow to inherit.[8] Some of the legally significant wills concerning the alleged undue influence of a spouse, lawyer, clergyman or favourite also had their brief glare of publicity.[9] But for lawyers the greatest will case in the twentieth century, generating long, complex litigation on vital points of law, is that of the wealthy recluse Caleb Diplock, who left all his estate on trust for `charitable or benevolent' purposes, a gift made void by the choice of the seemingly innocuous conjunction `or', rather than `and'. Yet Diplock's will is of no wider interest, for he disinherited only distant kin and there was nothing shocking to public morality in what he attempted.[10]

There are wills, but only a handful, which can also claim significance as the inspiration for literary works, and in even rarer cases the plaintiff's claim itself reads as though inspired by detective fiction; *Vane v. Vane* for instance might have been borrowed from an unused plot of Wilkie Collins.[11] The best known case of the former sort is that of the Suffolk miser William Jennens, who died only a year after Thellusson leaving an even bigger fortune which the latest in a long line of optimistic claimants were still attempting to wrest from the heirs in the twentieth century. The Jennens case is often said, with some plausibility, to have been the chief inspiration for *Jarndyce v. Jarndyce* in *Bleak House*, though it is sufficiently remarkable in its own right to merit a place in the testamentary hall of fame.[12]

Finally, there are a select few wills which have been of wider social, economic or political significance. They have either pointed the way to, or popularised, novel

3

ways of disposing of wealth, or probed the limits of the testamentary possibilities allowed by law. Cases of this sort were relatively abundant during the seventeenth century, as landowners and their conveyancers experimented with new and legally uncertain forms of family settlement, leading to the *Duke of Norfolk's Case*, in which Lord Nottingham pronounced the so-called 'modern rule against perpetuities'.[13] As the law became more settled they became fewer, but two stand out in the eighteenth century because in each case the Lord Chancellor of the day found the possibilities it suggested so alarming that he promoted legislation to ensure it remained unique. One was Thomas Guy's, which was probably the immediate impulse behind the Mortmain Act of 1736, the other was Thellusson's, the direct and avowed reason for Lord Loughborough's Accumulations Act of 1800.[14]

The claim of Peter Thellusson's will to be `the most famous will in the world'[15] rests on its uniquely falling within every one of these categories. The propertied Englishman of his time was allowed a rare degree of testamentary freedom and Thellusson flung down a deliberate challenge to law and society alike, flouting convention and pushing the bounds of the testamentary power to its limit. His will caused a public sensation because one of the largest mercantile fortunes of the day was removed from the grasp of his children, who were left with provisions which, while far from negligible, fell dismayingly short of what they had quite understandably expected. But while a mere disinheritance would have been a nine days' wonder, old Peter Thellusson ensured that his family would remain for two generations an object of public fascination by putting the bulk of his money out of reach to accumulate for a period measured by the lives of his living sons and grandsons, a period which might last anything up to a hundred years. This placed the family in an unprecedented and disturbing situation. Like some perverted tontine, it left some of them, who were themselves unable to enjoy any of the money, postponing by their continuing existence its distribution to those golden lads for whom it seemed destined. And since eminent men had calculated the ultimate yield from the accumulation at truly fabulous sums, for at least thirty years, until the myth

4

was exploded in 1833, the putative heirs were seen as the likely possessors of a princely inheritance. The will was therefore sensational and the sensation was a long lasting one.

But it was also a highly contentious will at law. As was only to be expected, the family fought to have the accumulation declared void, and so provoked the last serious attempt to narrow by judicial determination the liberal boundaries for the duration of property settlements which had been incrementally enlarged from the formulation of Lord Nottingham. With the defeat of that attempt the modern law of perpetuities was irrevocably set in the shape which tormented generations of lawyers and students with a world populated by such bizarre denizens as fertile octogenarians and sexually precocious toddlers.[16]

The Thellusson case also showed that the elaborate complex of legal rules which restricted the use of trusts to control property from beyond the grave had a gaping hole which an ambitious and unsentimental man could exploit. No-one much minded if the Thellusson brothers lost their inheritance, but the possibility of others following suit, with the prospect of a group of 'super rich' upstarts springing up like latter-day nabobs sometime in the next century, alarmed and affronted many establishment figures. The prospect was in some ways more appalling than the excessive charitable endowments which had led to the Mortmain Act, and it was immediately quelled by a statutory restriction subsequently copied in most of the major common law jurisdictions. The legislation remains on the statute book as a curious memorial to the ingenuity of one obscure merchant- a posthumous fame few men can claim.

The mark Peter Thellusson left on his own family was equally deep. To challenge the will they had to put the property into Chancery and once within that place it could not escape again until the whole trust came to an end. Peter's trustees still had the management of the trust. They took decisions on what lands to buy, what leases to grant, what rents to charge, but each decision, however minor, had to be sanctioned by the court; did a cottage need repair?; was timber ripe for felling?; was tithe payable? - each time the court must be asked. And every question it was asked cost money, for the fees of surveyors and land agents, solicitors and barristers, and above all in court fees. The campaign to reform Chancery which started up while the property was in its grip received an emphatic boost when it was disclosed in 1833 that the court had so 'sweated' the trust that the fabled accumulation had scarcely progressed at all. And nearly twenty years later, when Dickens came to present his devastating indictment of the court in *Bleak House*[17] there is little doubt, as George Keeton argued, that he had the Thellusson case in mind; hardly surprisingly for every lawyer knew it and practically everyone of note at the bar had been in it at one time or another.[18] The romantic stories linking the will to the hidden funds of French aristocrats which circulated after the will became public may also have been in Dickens' mind when he created Tellsons Bank in *A Tale of Two Cities*, for the similarity of the names is matched by some similarities in his description of their business.[19]

Other literary connections have been suggested, some rather implausible. It is difficult, for instance, to embrace the view that Peter Thellusson was the model for Eugene Sue's *Le Juif Errant* (1844-5)[20] or the inspiration for Samuel Warren's popular *Ten Thousand a Year*, although the latter starts with an unexpected inheritance descending on its vulgarian central character, Tittlebat Titmouse.[21] Amelia Edwards, however, in *Half a Million of Money*, does draw upon the idea of a massive accumulation fund, and though her knowledge of the law is decidedly shaky, the theme may well have been suggested by the publicity which accompanied the final stages of the Thellusson suit.[22] However, the one literary celebrity who is known to have been friendly with the family, George Augustus Sala, did not exploit the connexion. In a later generation John Galsworthy appropriately drew on Thellusson's device in making the will of his bourgeois archetype Timothy Forsyte, but embarrassingly for a sometime solicitor, he blundered sadly in his drafting and had to manufacture a distinctly inartistic correction in the sequel.[23]

In the event the trust endured for only sixty years, which were punctuated by quarrels within the family and between them and the trustees, leading to recurrent and expensive bouts of litigation. The will's description of the ultimate beneficiaries was not free from ambiguity and was not resolved by the original decision in favour of the will. Even after the claims derived through Peter's daughters were eliminated, uncertainties remained to set uncle against nephew, casting doubts on the financial prospects of each, embittering relations and leading to a final clash of forensic arms when the death of Peter's grandson Charles in 1856 brought the trust to an end.

By then everyone knew that the fabulous fortune was a chimera, that nearly sixty years of accumulation had not produced one million pounds let alone thirty. From being a public menace, Peter Thellusson had become a laughing stock, though writers then, and ever since, have seldom softened their verdicts on his scheme - it was 'posthumous avarice', he was 'spectacularly vindictive' and so forth. Few men have been so excoriated for what they did with their own money.

Quite apart from his will, Peter Thellusson was an interesting and important man. One of many Huguenots who have made their mark on English society,[24] his family connexions in France and Geneva and his membership of the 'Protestant International' of trade and finance, helped make his fortune and shape his aspirations. He and contemporaries like J.J. Angerstein, Lewis Tessier and Joseph Denison were the merchant princes of Augustan England, a class only now beginning to receive from historians the attention long bestowed on landowners and industrialists. Unfortunately, like most of them, Thellusson is frustratingly elusive. The surviving family papers tell us a good deal about the later history of the branch derived from his youngest son Charles, and the genealogy of the English Thellussons is treated in M. Girod de l'Ain's exhaustive account of the family,[25] but Peter's life and career has to be pieced together from fragments. I do not claim to have assembled all the fragments that exist. More information lurks in newspapers and court documents; in the records of institutions such as Lloyds and the Bank of England; in the unpublished correspondence and diaries of contemporaries[26] and the all too numerous published volumes which are unindexed. His role in the French Revolution (the subject of the most romantic stories) might be teased out from French archives, and a more painstaking and sophisticated analysis of his stock dealings could amplify our knowledge of his financial affairs.

But while it is not exhaustive, this book does provide an account of an extraordinary man and an extraordinary story, and just as Guy left his memorial in stone, so is there a tangible relic of the 'most famous will in the world' in Brodsworth Hall, built by one of the great-grandsons who inherited the shrunken pile of the great fortune. Thellusson's irrevocable act of audacious dynastic planning made him a byword for hubristic arrogance and folly. By the end of this book readers may be able to judge for themselves whether that reputation is deserved.

NOTES

1. G. Moffat, *Trusts Law: text and materials* (2nd edn., London, 1994), pp. 55-8.

2. *Snobbery with Violence* (London, 1971), p.20.

3. See for instance the reproduction on the cover of *Hanbury and Maudsley's Modern Equity* (13th edn., by J. Martin, London, 1989).

4. One of the most powerful is John Galt's Scottish novel, or 'theoretical history' as he preferred to call it, *The Entail* (1822).

5. *Annual Register* 39 (1797), Chronicle, 67.

6. E. Garnett, *John Marsden's Will* (London, 1998); H. Clayton, *The Great Swinfen Case* (London, 1980).

7. The oddest wills find their way into collections of curiosities. Thus Thellusson's has pride of place in J. Goldsmith and V. Powell-Smith's *Reader's Digest* publication, *Against The Law* (London, 1977).

8. *In the Estate of Crippen* [1911] P.108.

9. E.g. *Re Brocklehurst (deceased)* [1978] 1 All E.R. 767.

10. The last stage in the litigation is reported as *Ministry of Health v. Simpson* [1951] A.C. 251.

11. (1872) 8 Ch. App. 383.

12. W. Durston, The Real Jarndyce and Jarndyce, *The Dickensian*, 93 (1997), 27-33.

13. (1681) 3 Ch. Cas. 1.

14. See *infra*, Chapter 9.

15. A.G.Salmon, "The Most Famous Will in the World", *Solicitors' Journal*, 118 (1974), 544-7, 560-2.

16. For this development see A.W.B. Simpson, *Leading Cases in the Common Law* (Oxford, 1995), pp. 76-99.

17. *Bleak House* was published serially, beginning in 1852, but the Lord Chancellor depicted seems to resemble Lord Lyndhurst (1827-32, 1841-6).

18. G.W.Keeton, The Thellusson Will and Trusts for Accumulation, *Northern Ireland Legal Quarterly*, 21 (1970), 131-74.

19. *Ibid.*, at 138-9. It was published serially in *All The Year Round* in 1859, while the Thellusson case was in the House of Lords. The similarity in names is quite close, since the 'h' in Thellusson is silent.

20. Suggested by G. Girod de l'Ain in *Les Thellusson* (Paris, 1977), p. 326. The traveller Comte A.C. de la Garde, who met Charles Thellusson II in Brighton, remarked that 'Thelusson à sa

Majorité' would make a very dramatic novel centring on the heir to the vast fortune: *Brighton, Scenes Detachées d'un Voyage en Angleterre* (Paris, 1834), p.310.

21. Publication, in 1839, was pseudonymous. Warren was a barrister and later a master in Lunacy.

22. The book, published in 1865, opens with the will of Jacob Trefalden, a London merchant who has just (1760) died, worth half a million pounds. Trefalden's will neatly combines elements of Thellusson's with that of Thomas Guy.

23. Keeton, *Thellusson Will*, 140-2.

24. So many that in the recent account by R.D. Gwynn, *Huguenot Heritage* (London, 1985) he scarcely receives a mention.

25. *Les Thellusson.*

26. The dairy of Sir Charles Flint, for instance, was recently unearthed by Elizabeth Sparrow: *infra*, p. 261.

CHAPTER 2

THE THELLUSSONS

1. Calvin and Capitalism

In September 1704 a fourteen year old boy mounted a horse for the first time and left his home in Geneva for the house of his cousin Jean in Basle, the first stage of a long journey northwards, via other family connections in Frankfort and Cologne and down the Rhine to the house of a maternal uncle in Amsterdam. The boy was Isaac Thellusson and he was embarking on a decidedly unsentimental education in counting houses and warehouses, on exchanges and in markets, where he would put to practical use the algebra, arithmetic, accounting, navigation and Dutch he was to learn at Master Wynchel's school.

He was following a course which had become common among Protestant businessmen, a form of apprenticeship which at once initiated them into the mysteries of commerce and reinforced the family and business ties between their parents and their new masters. Many of these young men remained abroad, marrying into the host community and forming new partnerships, extending the 'Protestant International', the great network of Protestant firms located in the big commercial cities of Paris, Lyons, Geneva, Amsterdam and London. By their ready acceptance of each other's bills, their rapid and confidential exchange of information and their reliance on each other's probity, these families carved out a powerful position in many branches of international trade and above all in the mystery of foreign exchange.[1]

Young Isaac's adventure was unexpected and unsought. Inclination, aptitudes and temperament all seemed to mark this preternaturally sober and priggish boy for the priesthood, but his elder brother had just died of the smallpox, his father was wasting away and the family's money was wasting away with him. His mother had imbued him with the idea that his destiny was to restore the family name and fame: he became a Man with a Mission.[2]

This was not the first time the house of Thellusson had been faced with ruin. Any family which sought its livelihood from trade rather than land faced greater risks, even as it might hope for greater rewards. Thellussons had been merchants since the middle of the sixteenth century. Before that they had been minor landowners, indistinguishable from thousands of others, rising from modest beginnings in the neighbourhood of St. Symphorien-le-Cateau (now St. Symphorien-sur-Coise), some thirty miles south-west of Lyons, by the familiar route of good marriages, modest inheritances and shrewd land purchases. Noël de Thellusson (1480-1556) moved his wife, Jehan de Gouttes, and children to Lyons and his elder son Symphorien made the fateful decisions which determined their future.

Disdaining the life of a country squire despite the inheritance of the lordship of Thunes from an uncle, Symphorien plunged boldly into the making and marketing of silks and velvets, one of the first to profit from the secrets of their manufacture brought into France with royal encouragement by the Italian Turqeti. He also embraced the reformed religion expounded by John Calvin and the force of his own convictions enabled him to win over his parents, brother and strong-willed, devoted wife Françoise.[3] Fortunate in his marriage, with a large family and a successful business, and a considerable landowner as well, Symphorien Thellusson might well be more concerned, like any true Calvinist, with his prospects in the hereafter than on earth.

However, in 1572 the Huguenots of Paris were treacherously slaughtered in the massacre of St. Bartholomew's Day and the corporations of provincial towns were incited (superfluously in many cases) to emulation. Lyons, with a large and prosperous Huguenot minority, embarked on its own murderous purge and Symphorien was marked down as a victim. [4] His life was saved by the courageous actions of his wife's Roman Catholic family, who smuggled him into the citadel, leaving the mob to be confronted by an affecting tableau of a mother and her brood roused from sleep. These they capriciously spared and the next night Symphorien made an undignified and perilous exit from the town, hidden under bales of merchandise in a cart. He was safe but ruined, for hastily improvised attempts to safeguard his lands and chattels foundered on the faithlessness of supposedly trustworthy Roman Catholic associates. One nephew alone rose above temptation, rescuing a small sum of money and succouring Françoise and the children until they could safely join Symphorien in Geneva.[5]

Geneva, which had thrown out its bishop in 1536 and defied the Dukes of Savoy who claimed suzerainty, had long been a refuge for persecuted Protestants and now its citizens exerted themselves to cope with a much larger influx.[6] It was as congenial a refuge as the Thellussons could hope to find; orderly and peaceful, free of restrictions on the incomers' commercial activities and above all resoundingly Protestant. Calvin and Théodore Beza after him had transformed the city into 'the Protestant Rome', a city state where predestination was an article of faith, usury was legitimised and sobriety, diligence and restraint encouraged.[7] Immigrants introduced new trades and 'merchant bankers' like François Grenus and Théodore Tronchin appeared. These, perhaps, were the 'rational economic actors' imbued with the tenets of 'ascetic Protestantism' whom Max Weber postulated as embodying 'the Protestant ethic and the spirit of capitalism'[8] though the 'great capitalist manhunt'[9] has only succeeded in showing how elusive the quarry is. Men like Symphorien Thellusson have left little evidence to explain their activities through their religion or otherwise.[10]

However, Symphorien set about restoring his prosperity by the manufacture of velvets in association with a cousin in Lausanne and his brother-in-law at Basle and success soon enabled him to enlarge his house, incorporating one of the towers of the Corraterie and giving it the name 'la tour Thellusson'.[11] He was able to endow his children with large portions as they married, and though he could not break into the ranks of the ruling oligarchy who made up the syndics and council which governed the city[12] he married his offspring well, and in one case (Jean François) brilliantly.[13]

That was as well, for two sons frittered away their inheritance and brought ruin upon their father who, as guarantor of their marriage settlements, had to sell his business to his nephew Bastier at Basle to make good their defaults. He was now too old to begin afresh and died at seventy-nine in May 1597.[14]

His still vigorous widow was fortunate to have as her comfort the youngest child, Jean François, who shortly after his father's death married Marie de Tudert. He must have had considerable personal qualities for she, though bringing a small dowry, was linked by marriage to some of the great families in France and had an imposing lineage. Disgusted with his brothers' behaviour, Jean François set about reviving the family business in silks, velvets and armoisins and under skillful management it became profitable again. After ten years in partnership with his brother-in-law he was able to buy back the tour Thellusson and the restoration of the family name was signalled in 1637 when he and his sons were made 'bourgeois' of Geneva.[15] Like his parents, Jean François had many children but in both generations death carried most off in infancy and he was left with just two sons, Théophile (b.1611) and René (b.1616). In his time Geneva gradually lost much of its special character and religious vitality, but the Thirty Years' War which ravaged much of central Europe left the city untouched and its industries and commerce flourished.[16] Jean François died while the peace of Westphalia was being negotiated; he rashly put his head up a chimney which had caught alight and was killed by a piece of falling plaster. By his will he ordered his property to be divided equally between his sons.

René was described by his nephew Isaac (a severe critic) as 'une pauvre espèce d'homme; il n'y a rien a lui reprocher du côté d'honneur, mais il était sans ésprit ni talent [a poor sort of man; he could not be faulted on the score of integrity, but was without enterprise or ability].[17] He was a dealer in velvets while his brother Théophile took over most of his father's business. The brothers made a double marriage alliance with daughters of Théodore Tronchin, Beza's devoted disciple and residuary legatee, and this alliance was of the utmost value, for besides his personal

14

reputation Tronchin had important connections, notably with the rising banking firm of Mallet & Cramer, and his sons were well established in commerce at Lyons and in Geneva.[18]

René's eldest son Théophile (who was styled the younger because Théophile also called a son, born a year earlier in 1646, by the same name) started promisingly but in 1681 was declared bankrupt with suspicions of fraud which made him feel it expedient to take himself off to Holland. He became a clerk with the Huguenot bankers Huguetan and his sons Louis and Pierre, both lifelong bachelors, founded their own banking firm, 'Thellusson Brothers', which became very useful to Isaac Thellusson.[19]

René's elder brother Théophile died in his forties in 1684, leaving four sons and five daughters as well as a widow (her widowhood lasted thirty-two years). The daughters all made marriages that were respectable but no more than that, but the eldest son, Jean François, inherited the family manufacture of velvets and was prominent in city government, his rise assisted by a marriage to a daughter of the first syndic, Champeaunuye. Jean François however died in 1699 and his children, both daughters, soon followed him.

Théophile's youngest sons were both despatched to join their cousin Bastier in Basle as soon as they were in their teens. At least one remained there but never really prospered. Isaac Thellusson later wrote condescendingly that 'si la famille se soutenant, c'était en lui; mais il se contenta de se maintenir pour transmetre à son fils unique ce qu'il avait reçu de son père: [if the family managed to sustain itself, it was his doing; but he was content to hand down to his only son what he had received from his own father]'. In 1763 the male line died out entirely.[20]

Among Théophile's sons it was his namesake who had the most adventurous life. In his mid-twenties he left Basle for Lyons, took a wife (Jeanne Guiguer) and a partner and prospered for a while. Lyons and Geneva were closely linked in trade and were rivals in 'la grande fabrique [the great cloth manufacture]', in which the Thellussons were still engaged, but both were also prominent in the development of an international money market. Astride the trade routes from Italy and up the Rhône to Germany and the Low Countries, Lyons was perfectly situated for such a role and several Genevans, the Thellussons among them, made the transition from producers of textiles to middlemen, buying in goods from other centres besïdes Geneva and selling them at Lyons and elsewhere; it was not such a big leap from their putting out system which already involved them in loan transactions.

Those who had made the transition, and those who dabbled in the money markets, were better placed to withstand the severe slump which hit European trade, especially in luxuries such as silks and embellishments, in the last quarter of the seventeenth century, the result partly of demand slackened by Louis XIV's wearisomely regular wars. Marseilles and Lyons had already begun to feel the effects when Théophile Thellusson arrived.[21]

Louis however was not content to make war on other nations but extended his belligerence to the Huguenot members of his own, ratcheting up his persecutions from the curtailment of civil liberties to the infamous *dragonnades* and finally, in 1685, to the withdrawal of the Edict of Nantes, which had guaranteed Protestants freedom of worship. The Huguenots numbered about 10% of the people and included many of the most important businessmen.[22] Among them were the Tronchins, with whom the Thellussons had allied by marriage, and the extensive network of Guiguers and Tourtons, into which Théophile's marriage had brought him.[23]

For the Huguenots there was a stark choice between forcible conversion and clandestine flight- clandestine because the Sun King counted subjects among his treasure and would not release them voluntarily from their allegiance. They streamed across every friendly frontier, to England and Holland, to Germany, and of course to Switzerland and Geneva.[24]

Among some 4,000 refugees to whom Geneva gave long term succour was Théophile Thellusson. Though specific instructions had been given by the French monarch that the Swiss were not to be molested, he left Lyons as Symphorien had done a century before, though under less harrowing circumstances. Perhaps his banking venture was not thriving and he probably realised that the persecution would damage the prosperity of Lyons. Back in Geneva he took the rather strange decision to go into business as a dealer in iron goods, hammers and sickles. A few years on he undertook a more novel enterprise, being granted a twenty year monopoly to install the first covered 'bateaux-lavoirs [boat-laundries]' on the Rhône. Neither venture was a success. His son Isaac sternly attributed his father's failure to indolence rather than incapacity and it is evident that he was not unimaginative or unenterprising; but allowance should be made for the very changeable trading environment, which brought down abler men than him.[25] When the refugees came streaming in, Geneva was enjoying a deceptive boom in the luxury trades (now including watchmaking) and many hopeful businesses started up, only to collapse when trade fell away in the 1690s.

Théophile's brother Jean François was one who sought to profit directly from the Huguenot influx by setting up a new lacemaking factory employing a good many immigrants, and he probably did so despite the council's cautious unwillingness to antagonise the French by openly endorsing it.[26] But the wars and famines of the 1690s hit both brothers hard. Jean François died in 1699, Théophile in 1705, both leaving only small fortunes. Since the former left no sons, the retrieval of the family fortunes depended on Théophile's line. At forty-eight years old, his widow was fortunate to be able to remarry with her own daughter's father in-law, Abraham Mestrezat, one of the syndics. Only six of Théophile's twelve offspring survived infancy and of the three boys among those six, Jean died in 1697 aged eight and George Tobie, born in that same year, succumbed in 1703. One sister, Jeanne, died a spinster at thirty-three, but the others made fortunate matches, though in Henrietta's case not until the family was on the rise again. The name of Thellusson, after a century in Geneva, was one of note in a city where 'la richesse était beaucoup moins considereé que le nom [wealth counted for much less than lineage]',[27] but no family could sustain its position for long without money and, as his mother made clear, Isaac was being sent to Amsterdam to learn the secret of making it.

2. Isaac Thellusson: a Man with a Mission

In retirement at Geneva, Isaac Thellusson composed a memoir of his life and times. Prolix and flat in style, it offers a highly unreliable narrative of the public events in which the author was concerned, but does throw valuable light on his career and (unwittingly) his character.[28]

When the boy Isaac headed for Amsterdam there was no better school for an aspiring merchant or financier, the Dutch being acknowledged masters of commerce and the city the greatest financial centre of the age.[29] He was an apt pupil and after two years was sent to England to learn the language and something of English ways. Finding that Isaac Guiguer's household in London spoke exclusively in French, he had himself sent to Mr. Bidwell, a linen draper in Exeter, where he accomplished his purpose in six months.

In December 1707 he journeyed to Paris to join the banking concern of Jean Claude Tourton and Louis Guiguer.[30] His rise was rapid and unstoppable. Barely eighteen on arrival, such was his quickness, self-assurance and discretion that within a few months he had become a confidential clerk and, moving inexorably upwards through the very small hierarchy, he seized the opportunity presented in 1712 by the correspondence clerk's apoplectic stroke to gain the conduct of all its business.

His zeal was driven less by immediate rewards than by 'l'espérance d'être bientôt le maître [the hope of soon becoming the master'],[31] and he profited from increasing disharmony between the partners. Each looked to their cool, imperturbable managing clerk to deal with the other and before long the go-between was found to be indispensable. In 1715, when Guiguer decided to buy a mansion and live the life of a landowner, Thellusson's time had come. The firm was reconstituted as 'Thellusson et Cie' and the erstwhile clerk became a partner who brought no capital with him. By the time Guiguer abandoned commerce altogether Thellusson was able to put up a third of the capital for a fresh partnership with Tourton and for that input he would receive half the profits.[32]

Banking in France at that time could be highly profitable despite the parlous state of the French economy, distorted by almost incessant war and currency manipulations. War demanded huge loans to the state, which had not matched the more advanced systems of public credit and finance evolved by Holland and England. Instead it had to borrow from a small number of wealthy businessmen, merchants and shipbuilders with sufficiently long purses and diversified interests to enable them to bear long delays in repayment and fluctuations in the value of the securities they received.[33] Not a few were Huguenots, the best known being Samuel Bernard, whose grand schemes sucked in the Huguetans and their employee Théophile Thellusson.[34] So pivotal was Bernard's role that the state had to extricate him from his bankruptcy in 1709.

The Peace of Utrecht reduced the level of French borrowing, but it remained high in order to redeem, or at least service, the swollen national debt. A secret committee (the Visa) charged with finding a way out of this critical situation was fatally attracted to the plausible schemes of the Scottish projector John Law.

At the heart of Law's 'Système' was the Banque Générale, permitted to issue notes bearing the royal seal and closely modelled on the successful Bank of England and Bank of Sweden. The Banque, however, became inextricably intertwined with Law's other project, the Compagnie d'Occident, set up in 1717 to exploit the fabled wealth of the Americas. The Compagnie and its English counterpart the South Sea Company generated the first modern speculative boom (`bubble') and their share prices spiralled far beyond any realistic trading profits which might be generated. Law had let the genie out of the bottle and was helpless to restrain it. When the bubble burst the projector wisely fled to England, where the Drury Lane theatre put on a special performance of *The Alchemist* in his honour.

The bubble burst in England too, but though ministers fell and the financial structure tottered, it held firm around the Bank of England. In France, however, the renamed Banque Royale had been amalgamated with the Compagnie (now the Compagnie des Indes) in 1720 and state creditors had been receiving shares in the

Compagnie in lieu of government securities. Locked in the deadly embrace of the Compagnie, the Banque collapsed along with it, shattering the public finances.[35]

Those who had opposed Law when his star was in the ascendant now had their hour of triumph and among them, and not letting anyone forget it, was Isaac Thellusson. The youngest of the bankers summoned before the Parlement of Paris in 1718 to advise on currency measures, he spoke out so trenchantly that, if his own account is to be depended upon, he escaped a *lettre de cachet* only through the influence of D'Argenson, the leader of the anti-Law faction. Law made a vain attempt to charm the unimpressionable Swiss, who thenceforth provided most of the ammunition for Law's critics and made his one recorded joke, a rather grim one, at Law's expense.[36]

As he pointed out himself, Thellusson's consistent opposition to the Système earned him a reputation for shrewdness, but it was in fact attributable to simple fiscal conservatism. Thellusson was, it is true, quite astute enough to detect the flaws in the Scotsman's schemes, but when arguing against them he usually ended up opposing any regime based on credit which was not fully covered by specie deposits. His own creditworthiness stood high, he explained, because it was known that he never extended his credit beyond half-a-million livres. Law's schemes were disastrous for the public finances but if Thellusson had had his way there would have been no chance of breaking out of the old, unworkable system at all.

By his own account, Isaac remained austerely aloof from all the mania. He took credit for standing out: `tout le monde y gagnait et je n'y gagnait rien [everyone made money from it but I made nothing]', rather a curious boast for a banker. But this may be only literally true, for one enigmatic episode suggests that he may have used Tronchin's former valet, Dupin, as a stalking horse for his own speculations.[37]

However, even if he made no money from the Mississippi bubble, Thellusson gained enormously in reputation and credit and this was turned to good account. For a couple of years after Law's flight (itself something he could savour), he was a great man in the kingdom. The new finance minister, de la Houssaye, doted on him, opening all his designs to him, and besides the profit to be derived from advance knowledge, Thellusson gained directly by receiving the right to present to the Mint gold or silver coin for exchange at a specially favourable rate, a privilege confined to a handful of major bankers.[38]

His private affairs also prospered. By the time the partnership with Tourton expired in 1722 each partner reaped a profit of about 800,000l, a handsome return on 30,000l.[39] Not all his undertakings were so successful however. A partnership with J.J. Fenel and his own former bookkeeper Darius, probably designed to seize the new openings for trade with the Spanish colonies in America, was dissolved after only two of its five years. Thellusson blamed Darius, who ran the business, for not following his advice, but Thellusson was a difficult partner, overbearing, interfering and unaccommodating.[40]

A more successful venture, and a rare act of kindness, was in setting up two cousins in Amsterdam as a branch of his own business. Thellusson made very effective use of them to play the money exchanges and the large remittances sent to their bank were notable at a time when the stock market crash was causing most Amsterdam banks to suffer heavy withdrawals.[41]

A free agent and a wealthy man, thirty-two years old and in favour at court, Isaac decided it was time to marry. He left Paris for the first time since his arrival thirteen years before and, rejecting the chance of a rich widow in England, went on to Holland. At Leiden on 11th October 1722 he married Sarah Le Boullenger, ten years his junior. It was a typical match for the Huguenot banking set. Her father Abraham, a draper from Rouen, had left France after the Revocation and her mother Anne was the sister of a Dutch banker at Paris, Theodore van der Hulst. Sarah was the only child of that marriage and brought Isaac a dowry of some 70,000l., plus `grandes expectations d `heritages [great expectations of inheritance]', which later materialised in legacies totalling almost 100,000 florins.[42] But though the marriage was satisfactory in financial terms, it was not long before Isaac was on bad terms with his in-laws: evidently it was not just in business that he was hard to get along with.

In Paris he bought a palatial house, 'l'hotel de Bouligneus' which was later occupied by Necker, and he was soon deep in discussions on several projects with the aged chief minister Cardinal Dubois. The pride and hauteur that made him unpopular however were to face a humiliating and costly check.

On 24th October 1724 Jean Claude Tourton died. He was childless, and for several years he had been making property dispositions in conjunction with Thellusson aimed at depriving the cousins and nephews he detested, especially those who had apostasised to the Roman church. Now when his will was opened it was found that the unpopular foreign Protestant was the residuary legatee. Impervious to the indignation of the family and the dangers it posed, Thellusson complacently entered into his inheritance and had begun to distribute the small legacies when two Catholic nephews launched a suit to set the will aside.

Thellusson could have well afforded to compromise the suit, especially as he had already received great benefits from Tourton, but he stood out for his rights. Greed was probably not the leading motive (the residuary estate was in fact much smaller than the nephews put about, less than 250,000l), so much as loyalty to Tourton's wishes and his own self-righteousness. As with most will suits, few of the contestants came up smelling of roses.

Along with other grounds, the nephews impugned the privileges which enabled Genevans to inherit in France. This brought a Genevan delegation to Paris to plead their cause and its failure should have alerted Isaac to the way the wind was blowing.[43] His protectors at court were mostly dead or out of favour and Cardinal Fleury's regime was more Catholic than its predecessors. The law suit dragged through the courts until, in 1729, the confident opinions of Thellusson's lawyers were blown up by an adverse verdict. He was thunderstruck. Besides the hefty costs of the law suit it was revealed how powerless he was as a foreigner in France. The entry in his memoir is more enlightening than he intended: '[l]orsque j'ai perdu ce procès, je l'ai pris pour un signe que la volonté de Dieu n'était pas que je fuisse riche, et je n'ai plus songé qu'a la conservation de ce que j'ai [when I lost this law suit, I took it as a sign from God that it was not His will that I should become rich, and I thenceforth looked only to keeping what I had].'[44] A truly Christian resignation.

The affair of Tourton's will was a watershed in Thellusson's life. Henceforth he began to cultivate the establishment of Geneva with a view to creating a position for himself there. He was able to get himself elected in his absence to the council of two hundred and, in the course of a short visit (his first since he had left home more than twenty years before), bought a grand house next to the town hall in the sale of the effects of one of those ruined by speculation in Law's schemes. His great stroke, in 1730, was to have himself appointed the first Genevan minister to the court of France, for this, in addition to its intrinsic gratification, afforded him one of the few means whereby his sons, all born in Paris, could avoid forfeiting their claims to Genevan citizenship.[45]

The diplomatic duties were ceremonial and costly rather than demanding, so Thellusson was not distracted from business. However, to his surprise, fortune continued to desert him. While he was embroiled in the law suit his partners had begun taking a more independent line and when the term expired in 1728 he decided to form a new partnership which he could dominate.

He took in François Tronchin, the youngest son of a Genevan syndic with a famous name. Though the firm was styled Tronchin et Cie, the partnership, to run for six years from May 1729, was effectively financed by Thellusson, who was to have three-quarters of the profits and unusually dominant powers of management. His confidence that his name and reputation would enable him to poach the clients of his old partners (now Tourton and Baur) proved badly misplaced however, and though the partnership was successful enough for it to be renewed (on an equal profits footing) for a further six years, they were an ill-matched couple and conducted largely separate ventures.[46]

Thellusson's own operations included the traditional Genevan activities of money changing and remittances to the army, the brief war of the Polish Succession also offering the usual opportunities for speculations in grain and provisions. By his own account he turned down the more central role in war finance offered him by Fleury and his memoirs suggest that business no longer engaged his full attention.[47] Vanity and love of position, rather than the accumulation of wealth had been his ruling passion, and having made a substantial fortune he was not willing to devote his full energies to enlarging it.

By a portentious conjunction, Thellusson's term as ambassador coincided with a crisis in Genevan affairs. Oligarchic rule had generally been tolerated while the ruling families were perceived as relatively honest and disinterested, but as the bonds of religion slackened and the wealthy tended increasingly to be in international finance and trade rather than employers of labour in the manufactures, and as their culture became more `frenchified' and luxurious, class tensions grew and found a focus in the affair of Micheli du Crest, which set reformers of the government and tax systems (`michelistes') against conservative `negatifs'.[48]

No *negatif* was so intransigent as this absentee banker and in 1737, when the *michelistes* seemed to have the upper hand, he resolved on an intrepid stroke. Unauthorised, he sought an audience with Fleury and, giving a highly distorted account of the situation, besought French mediation. The citizens had already declined such offers from Berne and Zurich, fearing they would favour the *negatifs*, but this was an offer which could scarcely be refused even if, as Thellusson confidently expected, it resulted in the restoration of the old order.

In the event he was excluded from the negotiations and the imposed compromise was one he would never have willingly accepted. Ironically, he was fêted as the saviour of his country, feasted, thanked and given a special medal. Inasmuch as the mediation brought nearly thirty years of peace it was a distinct success, but Thellusson had given the French a foothold in Genevan affairs which would serve as a pretext for future interference. Nevertheless he revelled in public adulation, pomp and ceremony and the condescension of kings and princes. Fame was his spur and his desire was being gratified.[49]

A further opportunity came in 1738 when France fell victim to one of the crop failures which afflicted European countries and threatened the half million inhabitants of Paris with famine. As usual, a nation's ordeal was an individual's opportunity, but why Fleury should have resorted to Isaac Thellusson, for whom he had no affection, is a mystery. True, he had some reputation for honesty within the rather lax financial morals of the age, but he was no longer the precocious sage who had seen through Law but a middle- aged banker of conservative habits whose business was beset by wrangling with his younger partner.[50]

Still, however it arose, Thellusson was not going to let the chance slip and for the next three years the affair of the 'blés du roi[king's corn]' as it was known, was at the centre of his life. Along with Tronchin and d'Heguerty, a mysterious figure who claimed to have been the originator of the scheme, he conducted operations on a large scale, in wheat, barley, rye and rice, from Danzig, Palermo and Königsberg as well as the regular markets of Amsterdam, London and Marseilles; some even came from across the Atlantic via Philadelphia, but its re-export was forbidden by the British government so it had to be resold in Cork. More than 10 million livres were spent and relatives of both Tronchin and Thellusson were employed as agents- Thellusson Frères of Amsterdam alone made purchases to the sum of 1.32 million livres.

Even though it suffered a bad blow when Peter Flower, Thellusson's agent in London for twenty years, failed in 1740, his creditors receiving only fifteen pence in the pound, it was a profitable business.[51] Just how profitable would be difficult to establish. In the first place transactions for other parties were included in the accounts and the partners were not concerned with the niceties of accounting practice. In any event, there was one set of books for the King, showing the lawful commission of 2% and their allowances, and another set exhibiting an altogether less straightforward course of dealing which traversed the border between what was generally, if tacitly, seen as acceptable and the downright fraudulent. Government contracts were, and remain, an arena for contractors to match their wits with the Treasury.

But Thellusson went further. He kept secrets from his partners in the enterprise as well as its paymasters. When Tronchin subsequently asked their bookkeeper for the

25

cashbooks covering the 'blés du roi', he was told that Thellusson had kept all the important ones himself, so profits on sales of damaged goods, manipulation of exchanges etc. were effectively hidden.[52]

It is therefore no wonder that quarrelling broke out over the spoils and, like the law suit over Tourton's will, the dispute was lengthy, costly and bitter. The Thellusson-Tronchin partnership was dissolved in acrimony in October 1740 and Isaac took himself off to Geneva, leaving another Genevan banker, Ami Pictet, to settle accounts on his behalf. The law suit over the 'blés du roi' dragged on for so long that it became a notorious public embarrassment for Geneva and was finally put an end to by arbitration in 1748, Thellusson being obliged to pay Tronchin 48,500l. D'Heguerty's claims proved even more resistant to resolution: begun in 1741, the suit was apparently still in 'progress' in 1761, long after Isaac's death.

Neither the dubious practices they indulged in nor their unedifying wrangling over the profits should be allowed to obscure the service that Thellusson and his associates rendered to France in this affair. There was no reason to expect the Parisians to be generous in their verdict on an unpopular foreigner and even if some profits were concealed, their general level was no doubt guessed fairly accurately. Yet the relief operation was hailed as efficient, honest and relatively disinterested, devoid of the scandals which so often beset government contracts. The view was that Thellusson took his due and delivered the goods and Paris acknowledged his services in the ways he relished; a gold medal, a purse of 100 gold 'tokens' and two grand ceremonial receptions. The affair of the 'blés du roi' was a worthy climax to a notable career.[53]

It also marked Isaac's farewell to France. Though his affairs were long in the winding up, he left for Geneva in 1744 and abandoned active commercial pursuits, though he still made investments in promising enterprises. He was only fifty-four and with no sign of infirmity, but it was common for businessmen of that age to scale down their activities and his son will be found doing much the same.

What is more unusual in Thellusson's case is that he did not attempt to perpetuate a family business. Despite a lifetime of moneymaking, the spirit of commerce seems never to have entered his bloodstream and he had no desire to be the founder of a great banking house. It could have been done, for when they left France his sons Isaac Louis and George Tobie were seventeen and sixteen respectively, so a few years more would have seen them ready to assume responsibilities, while there were already cousins and in-laws able to take a part. Isaac's ambitions were different. He sought a patent of nobility from the King of Prussia, entitling him to a coat of arms of such complexity that when he wanted it carved in stone on the facade of his manor of Gara it had to be done in simplified form. The most plausible reason for turning to Prussia for what Louis XV would surely have granted is that suggested by one of Isaac's descendants, namely that this family, like many others, had assumed the precious particle `de', and when further researches showed their claim to nobility to be ill-founded, Isaac was too proud to have to seek by grace what he had assumed of right.[54]

Settled in Geneva, with his big town house and nearby château, Isaac began arranging the destinies of his numerous children. As befitted the eldest son of a noble house, Isaac Louis was bought a half company in the Swiss Guard, while George Tobie was packed off to Amsterdam for a commercial education in a banking house. Two of the daughters were rapidly married off in a joint ceremony. Her father's favourite, Ann Sarah, `a model of wisdom, modesty and piety', married Pierre Naville, a banker with business in London, bore him three children in as many years and died at twenty-four. Her younger sister Jeanne was matched with Jacques Pictet, a man of forty who had won her father's favour with his vigorous persecution of the *michelistes*; she lived to seventy-seven despite bearing eleven children. It was a distinguished alliance, for the Pictets were one of the oldest families in the city; Jacques became the English envoy to Geneva and the clan survives vigorously to this day, 'a typical example of a bourgeois family whose members held various official capacities in a tradition of solid, conscientious service to their native city'.[55]

The two other daughters both married in 1750 but Judith died after giving birth to her first child by her husband Bertran de Diesbach, from another patrician family. Elizabeth, the youngest, further consolidated links with the Genevan establishment through her marriage to Marc Conrad Fabri and by the marriage of a daughter of their eldest son the Thellussons subsequently acquired a distant kinship with the Lullins, the wealthiest of all the city's families.[56]

The two youngest sons, Pierre and Jean François, were still at home, probably growing restive under the dominion of their self-important, opinionated father. Isaac was under-occupied, for any expectations of playing an important role in public affairs were disappointed. Geneva honoured him and respected him, but except on matters of diplomacy and protocol it put him on a pedestal and left him there.

In truth he was something of an anachronism in the age of enlightenment. He had regarded his erstwhile partner's writing of a deservedly forgotten drama of Mary Queen of Scots as an act of unpardonable levity, but now the same François Tronchin was the cultivated man of the day, the collector of pictures and entertainer of Voltaire. Isaac collected nothing but the symbols of his own importance; a snuffbox presented by Louis XV in 1738 with his portrait by J.M. Lemaere and another given on Isaac's recall as *chargé d'affaires*, an elaborate, jewelled object worth 4,400l; a gold fishplate almost three feet long and inscribed with a suitably edifying message; a gold coffee pot with the arms of Geneva; the medal struck in his honour by Geneva in 1744 and weighing seven ounces- with no hint of irony, Isaac noted that this was without precedent, neither Calvin nor Beza having been so honoured. Truly there is something a little reminiscent of Mr. Sapsea of *Edwin Drood* in Isaac Thellusson in his retirement. One may be certain that every visitor had to undergo a detailed recitation of the circumstances surrounding all these artefacts.[57]

With little warning, on 2nd September 1755, Isaac was called from his estate at Champnel to render up his eternal accounts. He was sixty-five years old and left a substantial, but by no means spectacular fortune amounting to some 2.23 million livres, mostly in bankers' notes, plus modest estates and a quantity of unremarkable chattels. His daughters had been given dowries of 35,000 to 38,000l. and he took great pains to distribute his medals etc. among his sons. He went to his grave without abating his resentment against his brother-in-law Des Gouttes and his sister for taking the opposite side in the Micheli conflict. Even when Des Gouttes went bankrupt in 1753, quite blamelessly, Isaac would not lift a finger to help him. Hard as iron was Isaac Thellusson; self-righteous, unsympathetic and unattractive. Characteristically, his memoirs have very little to say of his wife and children but they would have been made fully aware of the nature of his mission and the exemplary way in which he had fulfilled it. Pierre Thellusson's father cast a long shadow.[58]

NOTES

1. W.C. Scoville, *The Persecution of the Huguenots and French Economic Development, 1680-1720* (California, 1960), pp. 151-3. H. Lüthy, *La Banque Protestante en France de la Révocation de l'Edit de Nantes à la Révolution*, 1961 edn., 2 vols.(Paris), contains a wealth of detail about the Protestant families and their networks. See also J.F. Bosher, Huguenot Merchants and the Protestant International in the Seventeenth Century, *William and Mary Quarterly*, 3rd s., 52 (1995), 77-102.

2. Ain, *Les Thellusson*, pp.36-44.

3. *Ibid.*, pp. 23-8.

4. According to S.L. England, 'the massacre at Lyons was one of the most bloody in all the provinces of France' (*The Massacre of St. Bartholomew* (London, 1938), p. 141). For context and analysis see N.Z. Davis, The Rites of Violence: Religious Riot in 16th Century France, in A. Soman (ed.), *The Massacre of St. Bartholomew: Re-appraisals and Documents* (The Hague, 1974), pp. 203-42.

5. Ain, *Les Thellusson*, pp. 27-8.

6. L.W. Spitz, *The Protestant Reformation* (New York, 1985), pp.204-8; J.C. Moerikofer (trans. G. Foux), *Histoire de Réfugiés de la Réforme en Suisse* (Neuchatel and Geneva, 1878), pp. 65-120. Geneva commemorates the coming of news of the massacre by a fast which has actually degenerated into a feast: R.M. Kingdon, Reactions in Rome and Geneva, in Soman, *Massacre of St. Bartholomew*, pp. 25-49.

7. Spitz, *Protestant Reformation*, 212-23; Moerikofer, *Histoire de Réfugiés*, 70-3.

8. M. Weber, *The Protestant Ethic and the Spirit of Capitalism* (1976 edn., trans. T. Parsons, London).

9. B.E. Supple, The Great Capitalist Manhunt, *Business History* 6 (1963-4), 48-62.

10. G. Marshall, *In Search of the Spirit of Capitalism* (London, 1982) pp. 100-17. Recent literature on the Anglo-Saxon fascination with Calvinism is reviewed by B. Nicollier de Weck, Calvin's Geneva, *Bulletin de la Société d'Histoire et d'Archéologie de Genève* 26 & 27 (1996-7), 57-74.

11. Ain, *Les Thellusson*, pp. 28-9.

12. A-E. Sayous, The Bourgeoisie of Geneva in the Age of the Reformation, *Economic History Review* 6 (1935-6), 194-200.

13. François and Susanne were married on the same day to siblings of the well known Pellisari family. Jean became a pastor and René married a daughter of the illustrious François Hotman,

'savant juriconsulte et homme d'état [learned jurist and statesman]', himself a refugee: Ain, *Les Thellusson*, p.28; Moerikofer, *Histoire de Réfugiés*, p.102.

14. Ain, *Les Thellusson*, pp. 28-30.

15. *Ibid.*, pp. 29-31. A 'bourgeois' was an outsider who had acquired citizenship; his children would be citizens. H. Lüthy, Une diplomatie ornée des glaces: la Representation de Genève à la Cour de France au XVIIIe Siècle, *Bulletin de la Société d'Histoire et d'Archéologie de Genève* 12 (1960), 9-42.

16. A-E Sayous, Calvinisme et Capitalisme: L'Experience Genevoise, *Annales de l'Histoire Economique et Sociale* 33 (1935), 225-44.

17. Ain, *Les Thellusson*, p.31.

18. For the Tronchins see Lüthy, *Banque Protestante*, vol. II, pp. 177-8; R. Stauffenegger, *Eglise et Societe: Genève au XVIIIe Siecle*, 2 vols.(Geneva, 1983-4).

19. Lüthy, *Banque Protestanate*, vol. I, pp. 151-2, 400; vol. II, pp. 203-4; Ain, *Les Thellusson*, p.31.

20. Ain, *Les Thellusson*, pp. 32-5. The quotation is at p.33.

21. Lüthy, *Banque Protestante*, vol. I, p.50; A-M. Puiz, Les Genevois de 1700, Ont-Ils une Opinion Economique?, *Bulletin de la Société d'Histoire et d'Archéologie de Genève* 15 (1972), 6-23, and Affaires et Politique: Recherches sur le Commerce de Genève au XVIIIe Siecle, *Société de l'Histoire et d'Archéologie de Genève, Memoires et Documentes*, 42 (1964), 392.

22. Scoville, *Persecution of the Huguenots*, pp. 1-55.

23. M. Natalis Rondot, *Les Protestants à Lyon au Dix-Septième Siècle* (Lyons, 1891), pp. 32-43; Ain, *Les Thellusson*, pp. 35-7.

24. Scoville, *Persecution of the Huguenots*, pp. 69-90, 98-113; E. Combe, *Les Refugiés de la Révocation en Suisse* (Lausanne, 1885).

25. Ain, *Les Thellusson*, pp. 36-7; Puiz, *Affaires et Politique*, pp. 392-4; Rondot, *Protestants à Lyon*, pp. 32-48.

26. Sayous, *Calvinisme et Capitalisme*, 235-7; Moerikofer, *Histoire de Refugiés*, pp.248-54; P. Bertrand, *Genève et la Révocation de l'Edit de Nantes* (Geneva, 1935), 96-172.

27. A-E. Sayous, La Haute Bourgeoisie de Genève, *Revue Historique* 180 (1937), 31- 57, at 35, quoting J.A. Galiffe, *Notices Généalogiques sur les Familles Genevois* (Geneva, 1829).

28. It has never been published, but was used extensively by Lüthy, *Banque Protestante*, and Ain, *Les Thellusson*.

29. V. Barbour, *Capitalism in Amsterdam in the Seventeenth Century* (edn. of 1963, Ann Arbor), esp. pp. 74-84, 130-41.

30.   Ain, *Les Thellusson*, p.44. It was an eventful voyage, encountering first a storm and then French privateers.

31.   Lüthy, *Banque Protestante*, vol.I, p.392.

32.   *Ibid.*, pp. 392-4.

33.   Scoville, *Persecution of the Huguenots*, pp.156-210. 34. Many Genevans, including the Mallets and Lullins, were tempted into this risky arena by the high profits: Sayous, *Haute Bourgeoisie*, 39-43; Puiz, *Les Genevois de 1700*, 6-23; S. Stelling-Michaud, Deux Aspects du Rôle Financier de Genève Pendant la Guerre de Succession d'Europe, *Bulletin de la Société d'Histoire et d'Archéologie de Genève* 6 (1935-6), 147-68.

35.   J. Cellard, *John Law et la Régence, 1715-29* (Paris, 1996).

36.   Lüthy, *Banque Protestante*, vol. I, pp. 394-6.

37.   *Ibid.*, vol.I, pp.399-400. The story gained currency - and was perpetuated by Voltaire- that the Genevans had shrewdly withdrawn their money before the crash, but the lavish outbreak of town house building in Geneva which prompted it was actually the result of the repatriation of capital which had been immobilised in the unfunded French debt: A-E. Sayous, L'Affaire de Law et les Genevois, *Revue d'Histoire Suisse* 3 (1937), 310-40.

38.   Lüthy, *Banque Protestante*, vol. I, pp. 400-4.

39.   *Ibid.*, vol. I, p.405. In the 18th century there were approximately 24 livres to the pound sterling.

40.   *Ibid.*, vol. I, pp. 402-3.

41.   *Ibid.*, vol. I, p. 400.

42.   Ain, *Les Thellusson*, pp. 46-7. A Dutch florin was worth just over 2 livres.

43.   Lüthy, *Banque Protestante*, vol.I, pp. 407-10; Ain, *Les Thellusson*, pp.48-50.

44.   Ain, *Les Thellusson*, p.49.

45.   *Ibid.*, pp.50-2.

46.   Lüthy, *Banque Protestante*, vol. I, pp. 404-5, 411-13.

47.   *Ibid.*, vol. II, pp. 186-94.

48.   Sayous, *Haute Bourgeoisie*, 39-47; Bertrand, *Genève et la Révocation*, pp.168-72.

49.   A. Corbaz, Isaac Thellusson et les Emigrés, and Micheli du Crest et Isaac Thellusson, *Bulletin de la Société d'Histoire et d'Archéologie de Genève* 4 (1917-18), 193-4;(1918-19), 279-80; Lüthy, *Banque Protestante*, vol. II, pp. 178-84.

50.   Lüthy, *Banque Protestante*, vol. II, pp. 194-6.

51.   In 1795 Thellusson's son was still involved in Chancery proceedings to recover a loan allegedly made to another Flower, Edward, in 1721: *Duroure v. Thellusson*, PRO C 12/657/12.

52. Lüthy, *Banque Protestante*, vol.II, pp. 197-201.

53. *Ibid.*, vol.II, p.201.

54. Ain, *Les Thellusson*, pp.53-6.

55. *Ibid.*, pp. 56-9, 74. The quotations (my translations) are from pp. 57 and 74.

56. *Ibid.*, pp. 57-9.

57. *Ibid.*, pp. 54-7, describes them in a minute detail which would have gratified Isaac.

58. H. Lüthy's character sketch in *Une Diplomatie Ornée de Glaces* is a fair and dispassionate one.

CHAPTER 3

MAKING THE FORTUNE

1. Citizenship

We know a good deal about Isaac Thellusson, but the son who was born Pierre but
called himself Peter left behind him no memoir and just a single portrait of himself
in middle age.[1] Scarcely a letter survives and no books of account or partnership
records are extant; he speaks to posterity only through the famous will, in which his
voice is distorted into twenty-three pages of interminable legalese.[2]

Peter Thellusson was not reclusive nor deliberately and unusually private, but
even among the rich a surprising degree of posthumous anonymity - increasingly
rare after Thellusson's generation - can be encountered. Men not educated at the
great schools, the universities and the inns of court, and who took to business rather
than the professions, often escape the standard works of reference.   If they
eschewed public life and polite society they will not be found in the memoirs of the
great, the gossip of the idle or the scheming of the politicians.   If they put their
money into trade not land, even their fortunes are often hard to trace; indeed, the
state itself did not possess the means to know with any exactness who the rich were
and how rich they were; only their wills, which could not be kept secret, might bring
them to the attention of the general public via the newspapers.[3]

In Thellusson's case even his date of birth has created a splendid confusion
among writers.   All are agreed that he was born at his father's house in Paris, in the
Rue Michel le Comte, on 27th June, but some say 1735,[4] others 1737[5] and M. de
l'Ain's exhaustive account of the whole family disconcertingly wavers between them,

once on the same page![6]   However, the Chancery bill which began the great law suit asserts confidently that the testator was in the sixty-first year of his age when, in April 1796, he drew up his will, and 1735 was the date produced for claims on the French annuities.[7] It also fits in better with the events of his life, for the age of majority in Geneva was twenty-five and Peter came to England - or more probably returned[8] - with his inheritance in 1760.

Within a few months of crossing the Channel this young man had taken three major decisions about his future; he became a British subject, married and entered into a business partnership; clearly Peter Thellusson did not lack self-confidence. Each of these decisions merits closer examination, though the information is pitifully meagre.

He certainly had no need to become a subject of King George III.   Many aliens were settled permanently who had not troubled to do so and it was not part of the traditional pattern of the `international houses' Isaac had been most anxious for his sons to have Genevan citizenship despite their French upbringing and his bachelor cousins traded for twenty years in Amsterdam without ever becoming Dutch.   There were some disadvantages to being an alien in England, but the inability to own freehold land was a minor inconvenience to a young merchant with his fortune still to make, and the trades which were closed to him were not those in which Thellusson was likely to wish to engage. On the whole (and with one major exception still to be discussed) the disabilities were few.[9] Most taxes fell impartially on subject and alien alike; aliens might sue in the courts to enforce their contracts and prove in bankruptcy to recover their debts; except for enemy aliens it was even uncertain whether the crown could expel them from the kingdom by the prerogative power.[10]

For many aliens the biggest obstacle to citizenship was the cost.   Like divorce, naturalization could be obtained only by the expensive means of a private act of Parliament, though a sort of `halfway house' by means of letters patent of denization was available more cheaply. A 'general act' creating a cheaper and simpler procedure had been passed in 1709 for Protestants but was quickly repealed and similar bills failed in 1747, 1748 and 1751.[11]

As this suggests, Englishmen had an ambivalent attitude to foreign immigrants. They might be welcomed and succoured as persecuted fellow Protestants with useful skills but when their numbers or their concentration in particular areas made them conspicuous, when their success in business threatened native artisans, manufacturers or merchants, or when their favour at court created jealousy among politicians and courtiers, then the latent xenophobia which lurked so near the surface of English life found ready expression. It was strikingly manifested in the controversy over the ill-fated Jew Bill of 1753, and the war with France in 1756 did nothing to diminish it.[12] The Act of Settlement (1700) barred even naturalized aliens from public office and election to the House of Commons and by a statute of 1715 these prohibitions were expressly introduced into all naturalization acts; even so humble an office as that of a constable of one of the wards of the City of London would still be beyond Peter Thellusson,[13] but he may perhaps have already been looking to the future and to his children's position rather than his own.

Individual naturalization bills were hardly ever opposed however, and parliamentary procedures were adapted so that they could pass swiftly and without disturbing more important public business. Several aliens were allowed to petition jointly for leave to bring in a bill, so reducing the costs of printing, parliamentary agents etc., and others could subsequently be given leave to add their names.[14] So it was in Thellusson's case. On 1st December 1760 he and John Dolignon petitioned the Commons for leave to introduce their bill and after the first reading Peter Anthony Planché was allowed to add his name. By the 10th the bill had completed all its stages in the House of Commons and its progress in the Lords, where Christian Poppé had his name added, was equally swift, with the third reading on 17th December and the royal assent on the 23rd.[15]

Of the three others naturalized with Thellusson, Dolignon was born at Crécy but bore the name of a family which was already settled here. He is probably the wine merchant of the same name who died in Mincing Lane in 1776 and almost certainly the man who became executor to Thellusson's partner Anthony Fonblanque.[16]   Peter Planché was an East India merchant[17] whose family kept up at least a social connexion with the Thellussons[18] and Christian Poppé was a Hamburg merchant who in 1768 was trading from Sam's Coffee House in Exchange Alley.[19]   Taken together, they probably form a fairly representative group of foreign merchants in Georgian England.

2. The Partnership with the Fonblanques

In coming to London to make his fortune Peter Thellusson chose a favourable place at a very auspicious time. For one thing there were few artificial barriers to the incomer, guild restrictions having been swept away and most of the monopolies of the great trading companies broken. In the banking sector the Bank of England was the only permitted joint-stock bank, but it had no monopoly over the issue of notes or other banking functions.[20]

This freedom did not spring from any government adherence to the philosophy of *laissez-faire*. Adam Smith did not publish *The Wealth of Nations* until 1776, and governments still adhered to the belief of their Stuart forbears in `a general assumption that government had a necessary role in attempting to ease the problems afflicting the economy by interfering with natural market mechanisms',[21] particularly to attain a favourable balance of trade. Mercantilist regulation distorted colonial economies into postures which complemented the mother country's rather than competing with it, (a straitjacket which was already irking the American colonists), and a central plank in the regulation of commerce was the Navigation Acts which sought to give English shippers an advantage over their competitors.[22]

Whatever its merits as an economic doctrine, even Adam Smith acknowledged that mercantilism aided producers and marketers of goods. Commercial men also benefitted from a benevolent tax regime. Governments struggled to bridge the gap between the produce of the chief instrument of direct taxation, the Land Tax, and a national debt regularly swollen by wartime expenditure, and their resort to indirect taxation, particularly the regressive and notoriously unpopular excises, left the profits of business largely unscathed.[23] Peter Thellusson's was the last generation to have a whole lifetime of moneymaking unhindered by an effective tax upon incomes, which entered the world just as he departed from it.

Furthermore, Englishmen who had made a fortune were now able to keep it pretty secure without tying it up in land purchases as their forbears had had to. Like their Dutch counterparts they could now place their surplus in the Funds, where it would yield a steady interest and could be withdrawn instantly at need.[24] Men like Alexander Pope's father, who retired from business with a hoard of gold and silver upon which he drew for the rest of his life,[25] became eccentric rarities. Public confidence in the Funds was underlined by the court of Chancery's insistence that with the exception of some land mortgages, they alone were a suitable investment for trustees.[26]

In this climate some men became very rich from next to nothing, their inspiring stories later collected by Fox-Bourne as a counterpart to Samuel Smiles' lives of industrialists and engineers. These were men like William Miles, who 'walked into Bristol with three-halfpence in his pocket, and...so well did he succeed that in 1795, when his son...proposed to marry a daughter of the Dean of Lismore, he was rich enough to hand him a cheque for £100,000'.[27] Even more spectacular was the rise of Joseph Denison of Leeds, so poor when he came to London that he could not read yet who, after begging a situation in a counting house, 'by unabated industry and the most rigid frugality', eventually ended by employing his former master as a clerk and died in 1806 leaving more than a million pounds in land and money.[28]

Peter Thellusson of course, with his £12,000 and his family connections, started with plenty of advantages and an obvious opportunity to enter international trade. This had become less risky now that the trade routes were charted, piracy rare and insurance well developed, but vessels still miscarried, buyers defaulted, markets glutted and unreasonable panics swept the exchanges. Moreover it was a century plagued by recurrent wars and Thellusson came to England in the midst of the latest, the Seven Years' War. War may not have been damaging to the nation's economic progress but it certainly added to the hazards of trade and capriciously made or marred merchant fortunes.[29]

Thellusson's first major business decision was whether to trade as an individual or to become a partner. There was really no third way, for the `Bubble Act' 1720 had made any form of incorporation difficult and expensive and in the absence of limited liability the consequences of business failure were very serious.[30]

English law provided creditors with powerful weapons to get at a debtor's property and the debtor's prison was a grim backcloth to enterprise, available even on mesne process to extract repayment from the debtor, his family or his friends.[31] But while the law proceeded on the assumption that the debtor was culpable rather than unfortunate, it also recognised that businessmen were different. As Blackstone explained:

`that set of men are, generally speaking, the only persons liable to accidental losses, and to an inability to pay their debts, without any fault of their own...Trade cannot be carried on without mutual credit on both sides: the contracting of debts is therefore here not only justifiable but necessary. And if by accidental calamities, as by loss of a ship in a tempest, the failure of brother traders, or by the non-payment of persons out of trade, a merchant or trader becomes incapable of discharging his own debts, it is his misfortune and not his fault.'[32]

For this reason traders alone were accorded the privilege of being adjudged bankrupt and this in some measure `served as a curious form of surrogate for corporate limited liability'.[33] Unpleasant as it was, it did wipe the slate clean and gave a man a second chance. Walter Boyd, for instance, gazetted in 1800 after the crash of the great house of Boyd, Benfield & Co., still died worth more than £200,000.[34]

English partnerships were usually `small and unstructured',[35] often lacking a formal partnership deed, which could make their existence a matter of dispute, particularly when one of the alleged members was insolvent.[36] The bitter recrimination and dispute that marked the dissolution of the Boyd-Benfield partnership underlined the need to choose partners carefully, for the ill-developed law of partnership made each partner liable to the full extent of his private fortune for all partnership debts and each was regarded as the agent for the other in contracts. The partnership deed might impose restrictions on their powers and liabilities *inter se*, but third parties without express notice of them were not bound.[37] No wonder, then, that a sort of `family capitalism' remained common, and many merchants took for partners their own kin.[38] Not that this always had happy results; the famous banker Thomas Coutts had to prise his brother James out of the firm when he began to exhibit the first signs of insanity and George Warde Norman had the more common experience of finding his brother so feckless and oversanguine as to threaten the solvency of their timber trading concern. Even the Baring brothers' partnership was dissolved in 1777 after working out badly.[39]

Thellusson chose as his partners a Huguenot family called Fonblanque. Well respected in their native Languedoc, they had suffered bitterly from Louis XIV's persecutions and Count Grenier de Fonblanque had sent two sons, Jean and Antoine, to England for a Protestant education. John was naturalized in 1748, and though the brothers are shown separately in business in 1758 they were in partnership by 1760 and linked also in marriage, to Eleanor and Ann respectively, daughters of another merchant, Thomas Bagshaw.[40] John had children but they were still infants when he took sick in November 1760, dictated a deathbed will and died, presumably quite young. He had enough confidence in his brother's business skills to see the firm as the best way of providing for his family, directing that his half share, £5,000, should remain in the firm for eight years, with Eleanor as his successor as partner, receiving half the profits.[41] It was at this juncture that Peter Thellusson joined forces with the Fonblanques, contributing £5,000 of his own and acquiring a one - third share in the business. What the business consisted of is not readily apparent, since directories of the period for the most part describe them simply as merchants and the partnership books have long since disappeared.[42]

For most firms of this era it is only by indirect means that even a fragmentary view of their activities is possible, and then usually only by a very laborious trawl through newspapers and the records of corporations etc. Fortunately, in this case the partnership accounts became one of the matters in a Chancery suit, and for that purpose Thellusson supplied a list of bad debts still outstanding some years after its dissolution, along with the last payments and receipts, which gives a useful idea of the range of its operations.[43]

The debts range from the insignificant (16s 3d due from Thomas Bagshaw, the Fonblanques' late father-in-law) to the very substantial; £504 19s 1d from Thomas Bourget of London; £528 16s 10d from Louis Lermac of Martinique; £435 16s 6d from Layrel Sauvage of Calais; £451 12s 9d from Jean Testas at Guadeloupe; £481 7s 11d from Le Maistres Frères at Hamburg. The receipts and payments are mostly very small apart from the repayment in full of £1,488 2s 11d by the Chevalier Desure and Lyaune Dufasa, both of the Grenadines. The geographical spread is considerable; debts were due in Bremen, Dunkirk, Florida, Uddenville and Bordeaux; payments were received from Waterford, Madrid, Paris and for 'a watch sent to East India'. The risks of trade are evident in the dividends received from the bankruptcies of Richard Doulton, Patrice Joyes & Son, John Kearman and Godfrey Nokes.[44]

The West India connection was obviously substantial, for in Peter's answer to the Chancery bill he defended his slowness in winding up the firm partly on the ground that large assets were tied up there.[45] Opportunities for profit in that quarter were varied and extensive. Unlike their French counterparts the English planters established a near monoculture based on sugar on progressively larger plantations. Except in Barbados the whites came not to settle but to make a rapid fortune and enjoy it back in England, where absentee planters' extravagance and vulgarity made them a target for satire and derision.[46]

This conspicuous consumption had to be paid for by loans, since although sugar was in great demand it grew slowly and made only one crop a year, which, having to be part-processed into molasses or muscovado, was not ready for shipping until the new year. The long round trip, often via Ireland and/or the American colonies, could barely be completed within a year, so planters were dependent upon borrowing against the next crop.[47] Most of this lending was done by London merchants and bankers, sometimes in conjunction with purchases of the sugar and/or the provision of shipping, otherwise by straightforward loans, generally secured by mortgages on the plantations.[48]

This was a profitable investment but a risky one. Absentees left their affairs in the hands of agents (often other planters) on a commission basis which invited short-term exploitation, and even those who remained in the islands tended to neglect capital investment. As a class they showed little interest in increasing the efficiency of their operation, bought slaves with careless profusion and lounged down the road to ruin in the insouciant expectation that their near monopoly and the prevailing high prices would go on for ever.[49] The island courts were notoriously and sometimes quite blatantly biased in favour of planter-debtors[50] and the plantations were in any case a doubtful security, wearing out through over-cultivation, difficult to manage from 3,000 miles away and hard to sell when the potential buyers were so few.[51] It is therefore no wonder that Fonblanque and Thellusson had bad debts in the West Indies, but the 1760s were generally good years and they probably did well on balance.

Peter's particular contribution to the partnership was to bring agency work for the French houses, especially his brother's. George Tobie had begun in business earlier and his success had been spectacular. He was taken up by Isaac Vernet, a childless Paris banker looking to retire from the day-to-day running of a very profitable and reputable bank. Vernet was just then discovering the impressive talents of one of his young employees, Jacques Necker. Necker was also Genevan and by the fortunate marriage of Jacques' father into one of the old established families of Geneva, the rather impecunious Neckers had already achieved some prominence in that city. Vernet was so impressed by Necker and Thellusson that in 1756 he gave them control of the bank, gradually increasing the frequency of his own absences until in 1761 he went into permanent retirement at Geneva. When they first received this extraordinary mark of confidence Necker was just twenty-four and Thellusson twenty-eight, but by the time they dissolved their partnership in 1770 they had proved the soundness of Vernet's judgement. In the bank's prosperity Necker was no doubt the driving force but Thellusson, level-headed, well-connected, prudent and urbane, pulled his weight, and his presence in Paris was invaluable to the younger brother striving to make his mark in London, not least as a source of capital.[52] The other family connexion who was particularly useful was Pierre Naville, a Genevan who had married Peter's eldest sister Ann Sarah in 1745 and who was long established in business in London.[53]

For the rest, it looks as though Fonblanque and Thellusson took on anything that seemed likely to be profitable, operating both in partnership and individually. They were certainly engaged in marine insurance, since they insured a cargo of indigo from Sto. Domingo to France in 1763, Thellusson for £165, Fonblanque for £135, and refused payment when the ship was taken as a prize.[54] But their progress was halted by Anthony's untimely death in November 1766.[55] The partnership still had more than a year to run, but there was no adult able to take Fonblanque's place, his only son, the youngest of five children, being still a baby.[56] Since Eleanor was probably a sleeping partner, Thellusson was effectively running things on his own and after a year or so he carted off the books from Tower Street to his own place of business in Philpot Lane.[57] The inevitable delays in liquidating West India assets delayed the process of splitting the assets into three equal shares, but it had been largely completed within six years. Meanwhile, a year after the partnership expired Thellusson and its chief clerk John Cossart had formed a new one, evidently intended to operate as a continuation of the firm.[58]

Apart from a minor dispute over an apprentice who was taken on for 100 guineas shortly before the end of the partnership- 'on trial only' Thellusson maintained- the distribution seems to have gone smoothly enough, but in November 1773 a bill was filed in Chancery on behalf of Anthony's children by their aunt

Elizabeth Bagshaw. This sought to have accounts taken, a receiver appointed and Anthony's estate distributed according to the terms of his will.[59]

As in many Chancery suits, it is impossible to accept the bill at face value. All proceedings had to be couched in adversarial terms, postulating a genuine dispute and real wrongdoing, but the fact of the matter in many instances was simply that the construction of a document- a will or a partnership deed- was uncertain.[60] The problem for executors, trustees or partners anxious to carry out their duties was that even if they took legal advice and acted upon it, their actions could be challenged many years later and money or property claimed from them personally. This was a particularly dangerous possibility where, as so often with testamentary and settlement cases, some of the potential beneficiaries were infants or persons still unborn, since there was no way of securing a consent or agreement which would debar them from later resorting to law.

The court of Chancery justified its uncompromising stance on the ground that it was always open to an executor etc. who had doubts to seek the court's ruling, and this was an open invitation to do so, since the costs of any reasonable request would be directed to be paid out of the estate. In this case therefore, it may have been just a precaution that the executors, faced with some uncertainties about Anthony's will, sought also to remove any sum which might form part of Anthony's estate from Thellusson's hands, lest he go bankrupt and it vanish into his bankruptcy.

That, however, does not explain why it was seven years after Anthony's death when the suit was launched, nor why it was brought by the children not by the trustees. And if the suit was an amicable one, it is surprising that it followed the wearisome and costly course of procedural delays which put back the main hearing before Lord Chancellor Bathurst until March 1778. Was there real bad blood between Thellusson and the Fonblanque family?

Outside the records of the suit there is only one piece of information known to me, and that of very questionable accuracy. In the diary of Joseph Farington is an entry for 24th July 1803:

45

`The father of Counsellor Fonblanque was connected in trade with one of the Houses so formed- and he took into Partnership also, the late Mr. Thellusson...By his connection with Fonblanque, old Thellusson laid the foundation of his great fortune. Fonblanque dying left his share of the business to be carried on for the benefit of his widow, in conjunction with Thellusson, but the latter, managed to get the whole concern into his own hands.'[61]

`Counsellor Fonblanque' was John Fonblanque's son and namesake. He made a name as an equity lawyer and, when the political career he sought among the Whigs came to nothing, leaving him poor and out of favour, he had to revert to his legal practice. Though better known for his learning than his practice, he became in due course a respected legal writer, senior queen's counsel and `father of the English bar'.[62] The story he told Farington is plain wrong on one count- John senior was dead before Thellusson became a partner- and, possibly through Farington's fallible recollection, very vague on others. John was a young boy when these events occurred and probably heard them from his mother. It is likely that as Thellusson's wealth grew, so did the envy of the Fonblanques whom he had distanced in the race. It is a story often to be heard when successful men are being talked about and it fitted neatly into the prevailing view of Thellusson as a monster of avarice and ruthless ambition to insinuate that he had got his start by cheating widows and orphans.

The law suit however tells a different story. If Eleanor Fonblanque did feel cheated, she did not express it in her testimony, for by her answer to the bill she refused to join in bringing an action against Thellusson, hoping to settle the accounts by an `amicable arrangement'.[63] Having no major interest in Anthony's will she was peripheral to the main action. The more likely hostility is between Anthony's widow Ann and Thellusson. Relations between the partners must have been cool, for Anthony preferred Cossart to Thellusson as executor and left the latter only £20 for a mourning ring, with no expression of regard.[64]

One guess may be hazarded. The Fonblanque widows (who were sisters) both remarried after a few years, Eleanor to Charles Maxwell in 1766, Ann to Thomas

Maxwell Adams in 1770, and both husbands came from prominent Barbados families-a further indication of the importance of West India trade in the firm.[65] If either or both of the men wanted to run the Fonblanque business they would have found that many customers had been annexed by Thellusson and Cossart (and the loss of Cossart's experience would itself be a blow), and if they did trade- the name of Fonblanque remains in London directories until at least 1781- it would have been under a considerable handicap. This would be consistent with the allegation in the bill that `the said Peter Thellusson and John Cossart in order to enlarge and preserve their engagement in trade have permitted large sums of money to remain abroad or at home in the hands of persons who had corresponded with them and who had formerly dealt with [Fonblanque and Thellusson]':[66] in other words, they bribed the customers by not putting pressure on them to pay their old debts.

Unfortunately this suit, like so many in Chancery, runs into the sand. When it finally came to a preliminary hearing, in March 1777, Thellusson was ordered to pay into court £1,000 which he admitted holding, while Master Holford took the accounts.[67] A year later the Lord Chancellor heard the cause, made decisions on the contentious clauses of Fonblanque's will, and ordered a final account to be drawn by Master Eames. There is no trace of reports by either master, and beyond a motion in 1782 to have the decree entered *nunc pro tunc* there are no further proceedings; presumably the accounts were settled out of court.[68]

The figures produced in the suit give some idea of the success of the venture, though they do not reveal what drawings the partners allowed themselves out of the profits. Each invested £5,000 and in all Thellusson paid over £14,393 to John's trustees before the suit was launched, with a further £1,000 following. He retained a few hundred pounds to meet possible liabilities arising out of the partnership or from Anthony's private dealings in marine cargo and fire insurance for which it might also face claims. That makes a yield of roughly 18% on the original sum at compound interest, or 30% p.a. simple interest, which is in line with estimates of commercial profits generally.[69] Dealings of this sort would make Thellusson a wealthy man, but not one of the `plums'.[70]

3. The Partnerships with Cossart

Thellusson's partnerships with John Cossart lasted in all for twenty-three years and because they did not end acrimoniously less is known about them. If, as has been claimed, Cossart was a member of an old Amsterdam house with strong West Indian connections,[71] it is odd that he should have spent a dozen years as a chief clerk and that in all his partnerships with Thellusson he held only a 1/16th share. Moreover, there is nothing in his will to suggest that he was not native born and the name is not uncommon in England at this time.[72] He seems, at all events, to have been just the partner for Thellusson, hardworking, tractable and essentially subordinate.

As for what the partnership did, its foundation was probably the same two elements as its predecessors, the West India trade and the links with France. The scale of the Caribbean operations can be seen from two transactions which ran into difficulties. They lent £7,000 to the owners of the Windmill estate(580 acres) on Montserrat in 1772 and in the same year the Fourmilliers, owners of the Bacolet estate (384 acres) on Grenada, borrowed £12,855.[73] In each case the purpose seems to have been to raise annuities for younger sons, a regular practice and one which often burdened estates disastrously. It may be significant that these were among the ceded islands, attractive to lenders because of their virgin soils, more diversified economies and freedom from a duty on Caribbean produce shipped to England. To meet their demand for capital investment all restraints on interest rates were lifted in 1774 and money poured in.[74]

The ceded islands prospered - sugar exports from Grenada peaked in 1774, having trebled in a decade- but the islands depended upon the North American colonies for most staple goods and when the Prohibitory Act of 1776 all but closed that trade the effects were shattering.[75] The war with the French which followed, sending shipping rates soaring and shrinking continental demand, had an effect which was 'traumatic and permanently devastating'.[76] No island fared worse than Grenada, which had gone in for coffee in a big way and suffered from a recession in the German economy. Next an army of voracious ants rampaged across the island and were only wiped out by a further natural calamity in the form of a hurricane. The French landed in 1779 and by the time they decamped after the Peace of Versailles Grenada was ruined and lenders found their loans hard to recover.[77] Their Grenada loan turned out very badly for Thellusson & Cossart but most of their Caribbean enterprises were probably profitable.

The firm also had dealings with the American colonies, as shown by the import of 303 hogsheads of tobacco in 1775, probably for re-export, which is unlikely to have been an isolated transaction.[78] British merchants with heavy involvement in the colonies were naturally big losers from the rebellion, especially those who, unlike their Dutch rivals, granted long credits to tobacco planters and, in some instances, showed a surprising laxity in tendering or even calculating the loan accounts.[79] Since Thellusson & Cossart are not to be found in the final, very ungenerous, settlement of outstanding accounts under the Jay Treaty of 1794 it may be inferred that America was probably only a sideline for them.

Other activities can be fleetingly glimpsed from disputes at law. Thus in 1776 they, along with John Aubert, were sued over a quantity of ginseng, parts of which had gone mouldy and for which Joseph Middleditch had paid £,1474. 5s.[80] In 1782, along with Aubert and Howard Simeon, they sold £4,742 17s of cotton (its origin unfortunately not stated) through an agent to William Shepherd.[81] Selling of a range of goods on commission was therefore certainly one facet of the business.

They were also active both as brokers and underwriters in insuring ships and cargoes. The network of underwriters who were members of Lloyds had created a highly developed market and though it became precarious in wartime operators like J.J. Angerstein, with ample capital, still made money, for if losses were heavy (especially in the dreadful year of 1780), premiums were high.[82] English rates were nevertheless very competitive, so many French merchants and shipowners preferred to insure in London, and since French commerce with their colonies expanded hugely over the century this could be a very profitable line.[83]

It was also a traditional Huguenot business and when the French East India Company's monopoly was lifted the international houses immediately mobilised their resources to fit out costly and risky, but potentially lucrative, expeditions to the China Seas and Malabar Coast. Thellusson & Cossart were involved in insuring them. In 1776 they arranged cover for the *Duc de Fitzjames* and *L'Aimable Victoire* in London for £2,920 on a voyage financed mostly through Jean Texier at Amsterdam. In the previous year, when Marck and Lefevbre had fitted out the *Sevère*, three policies had been taken out; 35,000l. from Dolier et Cie of Marseilles, 4,700 marcs de banque from Poppé, Chapeaurouge et Cie in Hamburg and £2,100 with Thellusson and Co., a truly international venture.[84]

London underwriters still considered themselves within the law in insuring enemy property against capture, a practice not definitively ruled to be unlawful until 1794,[85] and besides themselves insuring French vessels, Thellussons acted as agents for French merchants. This led to appearances as plaintiff in several law actions arising from the West India trade. The firm recovered £300 from Fletcher on three ships out of Sto. Domingo for Bordeaux laden with sugar and muscovados, two of which were captured and the third sunk. By suffering judgment by default the insurer was held to have admitted the claim and as a result a second claim under a similar policy also succeeded and that insurer, John Walter, was driven by such reverses out of insurance and into founding *The Times* newspaper.[86]

Other reported actions involving the firm turned on a question of great significance during the American war, the point at which an insured voyage was deemed to have commenced. Great sums depended upon the outcome of the series of cases in which Lord Mansfield settled the principles; £100,000 was said to be riding upon *Bond v.Nutt*,[87] and Thellusson's action against Fergusson was also a test case.[88] He was successful, but twenty other underwriters refused to accept the outcome, which necessitated further actions;[89] even then one stubborn underwriter persisted until Mansfield sternly insisted that 'at last there must be an end to litigation' before capitulating.[90]

Thellussons had to sue Fergusson on other policies, this time insuring *The Hero* voyaging home from Grenada.[91] As these law suits show, Thellusson was making good use of his French connections and was one of the major players in marine insurance. Like most big merchants, he also had shares in some of the ships in which his goods were transported. This was a declining practice and Schroders were unusual in owning ships outright,[92] but one year (1787) taken at random, shows that Thellusson held a share in both *The Bordeaux Packet* and *The London Packet*.[93]

Peter still had a long way to go before he could rival the achievements of his brother in Paris. The bank of Thellusson and Necker was one of the biggest in France and although both partners ostensibly retired from the direction early in the 1770s, Necker in pursuit of his ambitions to direct the public finances, Thellusson to indulge his leisure, they continued to hold 13/16ths of the capital of Germany, Girardot et Cie as it was thenceforth known. Louis Necker, Jacques' brother, and Thellusson's brother-in-law, Jean Girardot de Marigny, were officially in charge.[94] Vernet had left his young partners a solid, established clientele of foreign investors in the French revenues, most of them Dutchmen, and commission on their receipts was a routine, reliable and substantial source of revenue- except when the clerk in charge decamped with the proceeds, as happened on one occasion.[95] Peter Thellusson's agency for this large firm must have contributed handsomely to his accumulation of portable property.   From the limited evidence of their activities, Thellusson and Cossart look to be typical of many London merchants of their time. Specialisation in particular commodities was becoming commoner, though there were still generalists like William Braund, who with neither warehouse nor stock of his own plunged into whatever speculation took his fancy.[96] An increasing number made one branch of trade the foundation of their business but dabbled in others as occasion arose. John Thornton, the great Russia merchant who died in 1790, was one of these, whose prim and proper son and partner Henry found his 'occasional and sometimes large speculations in any articles which happened to take his fancy' too disturbing for his comfort.[97]

Thornton was in a long tradition of merchants who combined their trading ventures with sporadic forays into `pure' finance, while bankers and financiers were seldom inhibited from making occasional ventures in merchandising. It was regarded as something unusual in fact when Nathan Rothschild achieved `outstanding success... by speculation; he never interested himself in anything much beyond bills, bonds and bullion. He repudiated his early career interest in merchanting, he missed out on English railways and he avoided all industrial business.'[98] Thellusson was more like Thornton than Rothschild, but almost all these City men were happier to risk their money in distant islands than in the nascent industrial revolution in England. Thellusson's one truly speculative venture that can be partially discerned, again through the distorting mirror of a Chancery suit, was in alum. It looks as though a group of producers in the north-east of England attempted to concert a price ring in 1769 and treated with Lord Mulgrave to procure his output for the next few years and so keep it off the market. Thellusson got wind of this and himself made an agreement with Mulgrave with a view to reselling to the combination for a quick profit.[99] The transaction seems to have foundered but it illustrates Thellusson's eye for the main chance and willingness to risk enterprises M. Lüthy calls `scabreuses' [dubious].[100]

It is also likely that he went in for pure speculation in the Funds- what one contemporary called `domestic bubbling'.[101] To ascertain the extent of his speculations would require the sort of detailed scrutiny of his holdings recently undertaken for a group of merchants by David Hancock, though his conclusion is that it was surprisingly limited in scale and that for the most part money was put into the Funds primarily to await other opportunities for profit.[102] Thellusson's personal holdings certainly grew steadily however. His balances in Bank stock show substantial dealings from about 1780 onwards, with bigger balances during the later stages of the American war (probably reflecting the difficulty of finding productive trading ventures) than later in the decade.[103] Dealings in East India stock, very modest in the

52

1760s, had risen to £10,400, with an end of year balance of £4,400; at the beginning of 1787 the balance was £15,755.[104] By this time he was clearly becoming a rather wealthy man.

By the end of the 1780s there was a notable change in emphasis among the international houses of the Huguenots and English merchants, away from commodity trading and into the developing world of commercial services. As usual the Dutch led the way, seduced (in the eyes of disapproving and pessimistic commentators) by the lure of foreign government loans and stock exchange gambling from the increasingly competitive staple trades on which Dutch prosperity was founded.[105] In England the motive may have been as much social as economic, for as wholesale trading was less inimical to gentility than retail, so financial services were perceived as less contaminated by the stigma of `trade'.[106] Banking and stockbroking were perhaps also easier to combine with the semi-leisured existence characteristic of a gentleman than a merchant's way of life; no- one would have called Henry Thornton an idler, but he seldom found it necessary to spend more than four hours a day at work and usually less.[107] This shift from commodities into money often took place over two generations, as with the Fonnereaus, who forsook the linen trade for government finance, but some made the transition directly, such as Sir Richard Glyn, drysalter turned banker.[108] And apart from the handful of big government contractors who could make a fortune in wartime, it was in finance rather than trade that the really big money was increasingly being made.

NOTES

1. Reproduced in E.L.S. Horsbrugh, *Bromley* (London, 1929), facing p. 182, and Ain, *Les Thellusson*, facing p.225.

2. PRO PROB 11/1294, f.574.

3. The records of the Legacy Duty provide, from 1809, the starting point for W.D. Rubinstein's study of the rich, *Men of Property: the very rich in Britain since the Industrial Revolution* (London, 1981).

4. E.g. *D.N.B.*, vol.XIX, p.589; *Complete Peerage*, vol. X, p.765; *Burke's Peerage* (106th edn, 1999); Lüthy, *Banque Protestante*, vol. II, p. 204; J. Foster, *The Peerage, Baronetage and Knightage* (1882 edn., London).

5. E.g. E. & E. Haag, *La France Protestante* (2nd edn., Paris, 1877-88), vol. 9, pp.364-5; A. Corbaz, *Dictionnaire Historique et Biographique de la Suisse*, vol. 6 (Neuchatel, 1932); E. Walford, *Great Families* (1890 edn., London).

6. *Les Thellusson*, p. 59, facing p.225, p.326.

7. PRO C 12/241/27; PRO T 78/66.

8. According to Lüthy, *Banque Protestante*, vol.II, p.204, he first came to England to study.

9. S. Lambert, *Bills and Acts: Legislative Procedure in Eighteenth Century England* (Cambridge, 1971), p.32; W.S. Holdsworth, *A History of English Law* (3rd edn., London, 1944), vol. 9, pp.91-5.

10. Holdsworth, *History of English Law* (2nd edn., London, 1937), vol. 8, p.237, 3rd edn., vol.9, pp. 95-6; P. Polden, John Reeves as Superintendent of Aliens, *Journal of Legal History* 3 (1982), 31-51, at 32-3.

11. Denization remained a prerogative after it had been established in the time of Coke and Bacon that only a statute could make a naturalised subject: Lambert, *Bills and Acts*, pp.77-8.

12. Lambert, *Bills and Acts*, pp.78-83.

13. *R v. de Mierre* (1771) 5 Burr. 2788.

14. Lambert, *Bills and Acts*, pp.31-9.

15. *House of Commons Journals* 28 (1760), 902, 958, 964, 968-9, 972; *House of Lords Journals* 30 (1760), 23-4.

16. *Gents. Mag.* 6 (1736), 356; 46 (1776), 531; *Mortimer's Universal Directory* (London, 1763); W.A. Shaw, *Naturalizations and Denizations,1700-1800* (Manchester, 1923), p.161.

17. *Mortimer's Universal Directory* (1763); *Baldwin's New Complete Guide* (London, 1768). Planche and Jacquery figure as merchants trading with France in the law suit of *Planche v.*

Fletcher (1779) 1 Doug. 252.

18. The will of Peter Thellusson's wife (PRO PROB 11/1805, f.136) contains a small bequest to a Miss Planché and was witnessed by Mary Planché. One member of the family introduced porcelain manufacture to Derby and in the next generation James Robinson Planché achieved some celebrity as a dramatist, stage designer and finally as Somerset Herald: D.C. Agnew, *Protestant Exiles from France in the Reign of Louis XIV* (London, 1874), vol.II, p.490.

19. *Baldwin's Complete New Guide* (1768). He was born in Bremen.

20. C. Wilson, *England's Apprenticeship* (London, 1963), pp.269-71; P. Mathias, *The First Industrial Nation* (2nd edn., London, 1983), pp.148-59.

21. Wilson, *England's Apprenticeship*, p.76.

22. *Ibid.*, pp.76-84, 163-8; R. Davis, *The Rise of the English Shipping Industry* (London, 1962), pp. 304-14; L. Sawer, The Navigation Acts Revisited, *Economic History Review* (2nd s.) 45 (1992), 262-84.

23. This was a contemporary perception, see e.g. Sir J. Sinclair, *History of the Public Revenue of the British Empire* (3rd edn., 3 vols., London, 1803-4), vol III, p.241, but P.K. O'Brien, The Political Economy of British Taxation, 1660-1815, *Economic History Review* (2nd s.) 41 (1988), 1-32, argues that the regressive character of wartime taxation has been exaggerated.

24. N. Rogers, Money, Land and Lineage, the Big Bourgeoisie of Hanoverian London, *Social History* 4 (1979), 437-54, at 448-50; C. Wilson, *Anglo-Dutch Commerce and Finance* (Cambridge, 1941).

25. Quoted in C.P. Kindleburger, Financial Institutions and Economic Development, *Explorations in Economic History* 21 (1984), 103-24 at 112. See also R. Grassby, English Merchant Capitalism in the Late Seventeenth Century, *Past and Present* 46 (1970), 87-107.

26. M.J. Chesterman, Family Settlements on Trust, in D. Sugarman and G.R. Rubin, *Law, Economy and Society, 1750-1914* (Abingdon, 1984), pp. 124-167, at 157-67.

27. H.R. Fox-Bourne, *English Merchants* (2 vols., London, 1866), vol. I, p.16.

28. *Ibid.*, pp.216-7.

29. Wilson, *England's Apprenticeship*, pp.52-65, 160-85, 263-87; A.H. John, War and the English Economy, 1700-63, *Economic History Review* (2nd s.) 7 (1955), 329-44.

30. W.R. Cornish and G. de N. Clark, *Law and Society in England, 1750-1950* (London, 1989), pp. 246-51; P.L.Davies (ed.), *Gower's Principles of Company Law* (6th edn., London, 1997), pp.19-36. The minimal use of devices to create limited liability seems to have been due more to a lack of desire for it than to any obstacles made by the Act: R. Harris, The Bubble Act:

Its Passage and its Effects on Business Organization, *Journal of Economic History* 54 (1994), 610-27.

31.   Cornish and Clark, *Law and Society*, pp.226-37; J. Cohen, The History of Imprisonment for Debt, *Journal of Legal History* 3 (1982), 151-71.

32.   Quoted in Cohen, *Imprisonment for Debt*, at 160-1.

33.   *Ibid.*, at 160.

34.   S.R. Cope, *Walter Boyd, A Merchant Banker in the Age of Napoleon* (Gloucester, 1983), pp. 156-73.

35.   J.M. Price, Transaction Costs: A Note on Merchant Credit and the Organization of Private Trade, in J.D. Tracy (ed.), *The Political Economy of Merchant Empires* (Cambridge, 1991), 276-97 at 292.

36.   One such instance led to a suit in Chancery by Thellusson Brothers in 1800, against William Hipkins, allegedly a partner in a Birmingham firm: PRO C 12/268/38.

37.   This is an oversimplification of a complex legal issue. See E.H. Scammell and R.C. I'Anson Banks, *Lindley and Banks on Partnership* (16th edn., London, 1990), pp.249-319.

38.   *Business History* 35 (no.4), (1994), especially G. Jones and M.B. Rose, Family Capitalism, 1-17; P.J. Cain and A.G. Hopkins, Gentlemanly Capitalism and British Expansion Overseas (part one), *Economic History Review* (2nd s.) 39 (1986), 501-25.

39.   R.M. Robinson, *Coutts, the History of a Banking House* (London, 1929), pp. 11-25; Norman Mss KAO U310/C144, pp. 432-5; P. Ziegler, *The Sixth Great Power. Barings, 1762-1929* (London, 1988), p.24.

40.   There is a mystery about the Fonblanque brothers. Jean was certainly naturalized in 1748 and had a brother Antoine. An Anthony Fonblanque was also naturalized in 1748, but he is described as the son of Francis, by Mary (Shaw, *Naturalizations and Denizations*, pp.149, 159). The only family history is the sketchy and unreliable introduction to *The Life and Labours of Albany Fonblanque* (London, 1874), by his nephew E.B. Fonblanque. Presumably Jean's brother Antoine was not naturalized, which is curious, and the other Anthony was not a close relation.

41.   PRO PROB 11/860, f.424. He was buried at St. Dunstan-in-the-East on 13th January (*Registers of St. Dunstan-in-the-East*, London, 1956-7, p.168).

42.   An exception is *Mortimer's Universal Directory* (1763), which lists them as 'flemish merchants'. Fonblanque (*Albany Fonblanque*) calls them bankers, but is unlikely to be right.

43.   *Fonblanque v. Thellusson*, PRO C 12/89/5, C 12/94/21.

44.   *Ibid.*

45.   PRO C 12/83/13.

46.   L.J. Ragatz, *The Fall of the Planter Class in the British Caribbean, 1763-1833* (New Haven, 1928), pp. 1-34, 43-56; R.B. Sheridan, *Sugar and Slavery, An Economic History of the British West Indies* (Cambridge, 1974), pp.447-86. Ragatz (at p.39) describes the chief characteristics of life on the plantations as 'a democratic spirit, an openness of life, hospitality, a tendency to view financial obligations lightly, an intense individualism and lack of public spirit, conservatism and a striking measure of ostentation'.

47.   Davis, *Rise of English Shipping*, pp.278-82.

48.   Ragatz, *Fall of the Planter Class*, pp. 54-60. The London sugar bakers also exercised a 'quasi-banking function': D.W. Thoms, The Mills Family: London Sugar Merchants of the 18th Century, *Business History* 11 (1969), 3-10.

49.   F. W. Pitman, *The Development of the British West Indies, 1700-63* (New Haven, 1917), pp.335-53; R. Pares, *War and Trade in the West Indies, 1739-63* (Oxford, 1936), pp.216-26.

50.   The legislature of Grenada passed an anti-mortgagee measure in 1774: R.P. Devas, *The History of the Island of Grenada* (Grenada, 1964), p.68.

51.   Pitman, *Development of British West Indies*, pp.130-2; Ragatz, *Fall of the Planter Class*, pp. 51-4, 111-15.

52.   Lüthy, *Banque Protestante*, vol. II, pp.228-37. Peter still owed his brother £6,000 when George Tobie died in 1776.

53.   *Ibid.*, p.204; Ain, *Les Thellusson*, p.57; F. Crouzet, *Britain, France and International Commerce* (Aldershot, 1996), p.256.

54.   *Villion v. Thellusson* (1770) PRO C 12/891/13. Underwriters in marine insurance were not permitted to form partnerships for that purpose.

55.   PRO PROB 11/942, f.51. He made his will on 24th September and died on 9th November.

56.   PRO C 12/94/21. The son, John Anthony, died in 1774, aged ten.

57.   Order of 7 Mar. 1778, PRO C 33/449(2), f.671.

58.   *Ibid.*

59.   PRO C 12/89/5. The size of the premium is an indication that the firm was as yet by no means one of the most prestigious. Leading merchants could ask £500: Rogers, *Big Bourgeoisie*, 444.

60.   See H. Horwitz, *Chancery Equity Records and Proceedings 160-1800* (London, 1995). The classic description of a Chancery bill is by Lord Bowen, Progress in the Administration of Justice During the Victorian Period, *Select Essays in Anglo-American Legal History*, 3 vols., 1968 reprint (London), 517-59 at 524-5.

61.   K. Garlick, A.M. McIntyre and K. Cave, *The Farington Diaries*, 16 vols., (New Haven and

London, 1978-84), vol 6, p.2088.

62. *D.N.B.*, vol. VII, p.365; *House of Commons, 1790-1820*, vol. II, p.783.

63. Order of 7 Mar. 1778, PRO C 33/449(2), f.673.

64. PRO PROB 11/924, f.451.

65. *Gents. Mag.* 40 (1770), 344; 37 (1767), 382; V.L. Oliver, *Caribbeana*, 6 vols. (London, 1910-19), vol. V, p.290.

66. Order of 7 Mar. 1778, PRO C 33/449(2), f.671.

67. PRO C 33/447(1), f.255.

68. Proceedings can be followed in PRO C 33/441, 443, 445, 447, 449 and 451.

69. R.B. Westerfield, *Middlemen in English Business, 1660-1760* (New Haven, 1915), p. 373. Where the books of businesses do survive they often display such 'woeful ineptitude or lack of interest in profit measurement' that the owners may have had little idea of its profitability until the final winding up: J.R. Edwards, *A History of Financial Accounting* (London, 1989), p.79.

70. A personal fortune of £100,000: P. Earle, *The Making of the English Middle Class* (London, 1989), p.14.

71. Lüthy, *Banque Protestante*, vol. II, p.237.

72. As examples, Isaac Cossart (d.1792) was head of the East India Company's private trade warehouse (*Gents. Mag.* 62 (1797), 678), Abraham was an elder of the French church in London in 1703, Henry was agent to the Moravian Brethren in 1767 and John secretary to the Corporation for preserving the Port of Dublin in 1816 (*British Library Index to Mss*).

73. Report of 30 Jul. 1814, PRO C 38/1091.

74. Ragatz, *Fall of the Planter Class*, pp.122-3, 142-72; *Journal of Interdisciplinary History* 1987, especially B.L. Solow, Capitalism and Slavery, 711-36.

75. *Ibid.*, S.H.H. Carrington, The American War of Independence and the British West Indies Economy, 823-50.

76. *Ibid.*, 826.

77. Ragatz, *Fall of the Planter Class*, pp. 37-42, 59-60, 134-6, 156; Devas, *Grenada*, pp.103-52.

78. *Joshua Johnson's Letter Book, 1771-4*, ed. J.M. Price (London, 1979).

79. K.A. Kellock, London Merchants and the pre-1776 American Debts, *Guildhall Studies*, vol.I, no.3 (1974), 109-49; J.M. Price, Joshua Johnson in London, 1771-5. Credit and Commercial Organization in the British Chesapeake Trade, in A. Whiteman, J.S. Bromley and P.M.G. Dickson (eds.), *Statesmen, Scholars and Merchants: Essays in Eighteenth Century History, presented to Dame Lucy Sutherland* (Oxford, 1973), 153-80.

80. J. Oldham, *The Mansfield Manuscripts and the Growth of English Law in the Eighteenth*

Century (2 vols. Chapel Hill, 1992), vol. I, pp.321-2.

81.   *Ibid.*, pp.378-9.

82.   C. Wright and C.E. Fayle, *A History of Lloyds* (London, 1926), pp.155-7; H.E. Raynes, *A History of British Insurance* (London, 1948), pp.161-89.

83.   O. Petré-Grenouilleau, *Les Negoçes Maritimes Français, XVIIe-XXe Siècle* (Paris, 1997), pp.116-24.

84.   A.C.Carter, Financial Activities of the Huguenots in London and Amsterdam in the mid-eighteenth Century, in *Getting, Spending and Investing in Early Modern Times* (Amsterdam, 1975), pp.91-106; Lüthy, *Banque Protestante*, vol.II, pp.442-5.

85.   Raynes, *History of British Insurance*, pp. 165-71. The case was *Furtado v. Rogers* (1794) 3 Bos. & Pul. 191.

86.   *Thellusson v. Fletcher* (1780) 1 Doug. 315.

87.   Cowp. 601, also subjoined to *Thellusson v. Fergusson* (1780) 1 Doug. 360 at 367; Wright and Fayle, *History of Lloyds*, p.155.

88.   (1780) 1 Doug. 360 at 366n.9, 367.

89.   *Thellusson v. Staples* (1780) 2 Doug. 438.

90.   *Thellusson v. Fergusson* (1780) 1 Doug. 360. These were part of a series of cases in which Lord Mansfield magisterially systematised the law on marine insurance, enabling Park to write *A System of the Law of Marine Insurance* (1786), in which the Thellusson cases are featured.

91.   1 Doug.360 at 370n. Insurers had to be litigious as there were many frauds, but it was claimed on their behalf that they were often very generous in cases of honest or careless mistakes: Raynes, *History of British Insurance*, p.185. Defending a later action brought by Thellusson and others as assignees of an insolvent firm, Bartholomew Huber alluded to the underwriters' 'liberal way of thinking, and...the interest which the generality of underwriters have to deal generously with eminent brokers who can easily make up to them (by giving them good risks to sign) their facility in settling losses and averages which if scrutinized with rigour could not legally be inforced against them.' (PRO C 12/1743/33).

92.   S.P. Ville, *English Shipowning During the Industrial Revolution* (Manchester, 1996), pp.1-5; R. Roberts, *Schroders: Merchants and Bankers* (London, 1992), p.10.

93.   PRO BT 107/8.

94.   Lüthy, *Banque Protestante*, vol.II, pp.230-2, 398-405.

95.   Ain, *Les Thellusson*, p.116.

96.   L.S. Sutherland, The Accounts of an Eighteenth Century Merchant, in A. Newman (ed.), *Politics and Finance in the Eighteenth Century; for Lucy Sutherland* (London, 1984),

pp.366-85.

97.   Thornton's diary, quoted in the introduction by F.A. Hayek to Thornton's *Enquiry into the Nature and Effects of the Paper Credit of Great Britain* (1802, edn. of 1939, London). For a similarly venturesome provincial merchant and banker (Arthur Heywood) see G. Chandler, *Four Centuries of Banking* (vol. I, London, 1964), pp.181-7.

98.   S.D. Chapman, *The Rise of Merchant Banking* (London, 1984), pp.4, 18.

99.   *Gilbert v. Thellusson*, PRO C 12/694/13.

100   Lüthy, *Banque Protestante*, vol.II, p.237. Francis Baring also came unstuck with a speculation in soda ash in 1774: Ziegler, *Sixth Great Power*, p.20.

101   Thomas Mortimer, quoted in D. Hancock, `Domestic bubbling': eighteenth-century London merchants and individual investment in the Funds, *Economic History Review* (2nd s.) 47 (1994), 679-702.

102.   *Ibid.*, 700-1.

103.   Bank of England Stock Ledgers AC 470-502.

104.   East India Company Stock Ledgers L/AG 14/5/13-27.

105.   Carter, *Financial Activities of the Huguenots*; Wilson, *Anglo-Dutch Commerce*; J.C. Riley, *International Government Finance and the Amsterdam Capital Market, 1740-1815* (Cambridge, 1980), pp.24-30.

106.   Cain and Hopkins, *Gentlemanly Capitalism*, 512-19.

107.   Thornton, *Enquiry into Paper Credit*, p.26. See also Rogers, *Big Bourgeoisie*, 448-50.

108.   Agnew, *Protestant Exiles*, vol. II, p.399; R. Fulford, *Glyns, 1753-1953* (London, 1953), p.3.

CHAPTER 4

FOUNDING A FAMILY

1. Marriage and Children

On 6th January 1761 Thellusson married a girl of solidly English family. Since he had become a British subject only a few days earlier it is possible that her parents had wanted some re-assurance that the young foreigner had a firm intention to settle in this country. Peter was twenty-five, his bride twenty-one, both their ages and the differential being well within the normal range for merchant marriages.[1] It is, nevertheless, a surprising match in some ways. The marriages of his father and brothers fitted comfortably into the orthodox pattern for the leading Genevan families. Isaac's wife came from a Dutch commercial background but her father was a French Huguenot.[2] Isaac's eldest son Isaac Louis married Henriette Bernard, daughter of one of the few Genevans who both made and kept a fortune in the madness of the Mississippi speculation, and after she died in childbirth a year later, he wed Julie Pleydel, daughter of a Genevan banker based in Marseilles. George Tobie's wife was Marie Jeanne Girardot de Vermenoux, who allied the Thellussons to the French Protestant community of the south and west, her family specialising in the timber and wool trade.[3]

Ann Woodford however was as quintessentially English as her name suggests. When her eldest brother Ralph received a baronetcy the family hoped to claim descent from Woodfords of great antiquity and renown, but even the indefatigable researchers in the Heralds Office could not plausibly bridge the gap between the Woodfords of the distant romantic past, with their broad acres in the east midlands, and unglamorous Matthew Woodford, born in the reign of Charles II and the progenitor of the new baronet's line.[4]

Matthew was a successful clergyman in a modest way (his own father was a clergyman from Salisbury) who became sub-dean and prebendary of Chichester cathedral. He had a son, also Matthew, and this son greatly improved the family fortunes by successfully wooing Mary Brideoak, one of the co-heiresses in a family which boasted a recent bishop of Chichester and an archdeacon who had been active in Southampton, where the Woodfords were living. Bishop Brideoak had been an ardent royalist and by this union of two clerical families the Woodfords inherited a small collection of artworks and memorabilia of the civil war period.[5]

Matthew II was not a clergyman and whatever trade he pursued in Southampton, he was able to combine it with being the political agent of Hans Stanley,[6] the town's most prominent citizen and Member of Parliament. The marriage of Matthew and Mary was happy and fruitful: with the same fine symmetry that Peter Thellusson's own union was to show, three sons and three daughters grew to adulthood and with textbook planning for their advancement the sons were placed respectively in the diplomatic service, the church and the army.

Hans Stanley, known for his self-proclaimed expertise in foreign affairs, was probably influential in starting the eldest, Ralph Sherer, born c. 1735, in the diplomatic line. Ralph went as secretary to the Earl of Bristol first to Savoy - Sicily and thence to Spain, staying in Madrid until December 1761 when the two nations went to war.[7] The second son, yet another Matthew, pursued the placid, leisurely life of an Augustan clergyman; from Winchester College he went on to Oxford to become a Doctor of Divinity, then held an Oxfordshire living until 1767 when he returned to his native Hampshire.[8] The youngest, John, a captain in the Guards, married an heiress, the curiously named Mary Emperor from Norfolk, the only daughter of an old county family whose arms bore the Imperial eagle.[9] Ralph also married in due course but both of Ann's sisters lived as spinsters and Matthew died a bachelor, an uncommonly high proportion of unmarried children. [10]

There could hardly be a more marked contrast between the Woodfords and the Thellussons, whose names are locked in an enduring embrace by the famous lawsuit. The one was native, provincial and clerical, climbing the social ladder through the professions with the helping hands of influential patrons. The other was immigrant, cosmopolitan and metropolitan, taking the path of commerce and finance. Peter must have been confident in his abilities and in his existing business contacts to ally with a family which was neither very wealthy nor especially useful to him in business. When and where he met his wife, how long their courtship was and what financial settlement accompanied the marriage are quite unknown.[11]

The newly wedded couple may have lived initially above Peter's place of business, first in Lime Street and then in Philpot Lane,[12] for merchants had traditionally lived above their counting houses, workshops and warehouses. It made practical sense, reducing the risk of fire and theft, facilitating the conduct of business and the supervision of apprentices and workmen and eliminating the need to journey to and from work through the unpleasant and often dangerous streets.[13]

Philpot Lane was certainly convenient for business. In the heart of the City, just off Fenchurch Street and barely 100 yards long, it slopes down to Eastcheap. The counting house has long gone, victim of Victorian redevelopment which in its turn has yielded first to the bombs and then to the bulldozers. There is nothing distinguished there, nor any hint of the old City, but it is appropriately overshadowed by the lowering tower block which houses a latter day giant of merchant banking, Kleinwort Benson. Close to the Bank, to the Stock Exchange, to the Custom House, in the heart of the business quarter, but also close to the unembanked, unhealthy river, the counting house was a place for business rather than family life.

But social habits were changing. The desire for, and the feasibility of, social segregation and more gracious living grew among the business class and after the end of the Seven Years' War a new phenomenon began to be remarked upon - the active merchant who removed his dwelling from his place of work and commuted between them.[14] John Cornwall, whose daughter married Thellusson's heir, was one such, a

Russia merchant with a house in Duchess Street, off Portland Square. Others preferred to house themselves north or east of the City and Thellusson was among them, leasing one of the properties of the Cass charity around Grove Street, probably from as early as 1765.[15]

By 1778 he was wealthy enough to embrace another option now open to the big bourgeoisie, also in imitation of their social superiors, the purchase of a villa or small country house outside the metropolis as a weekend and summer retreat. The villages which now form the cores of the outer London suburbs are sprinkled with dwellings that met this growing partiality for *rus in urbe*. Middlesex and Essex were the most favoured directions (John Cornwall had his in Hendon), but from London bridge, quite close to Philpot Lane, north-west Kent was open to the City and Peter Thellusson bought a large plot of land at Plaistow, a hamlet just to the north of the much bigger settlement of Bromley.[16] For his architect he chose Thomas Leverton, largely forgotten nowadays but well known in his time, much influenced by the Adam brothers and believed to be the designer of Bedford Square, which was even then being laid out.[17]

Leverton designed a charming house for Thellusson, which stood in ninety-six acres of grounds and was soon surrounded by large hothouses. One of the few personal details we have of the owner is his delight in growing exotic fruits in these hothouses, for the traveller Henry Meister wrote: `It was early in the month of August [1790] that I went to dine with Mr. Thellusson at his country house nine miles from London. I never saw finer fruit than was brought in with the desert [sic]; pine apples, peaches and grapes, the most delicious that can be imagined...I can assure you I never tasted finer fruit at Paris. It is true that the hothouses of Mr. Thellusson are spoken of as the finest in the Kingdom.'[18]

Bromley was too far from the City for convenient commuting on horseback, as the roads leading from it were very bad and highwaymen were not yet unknown; the mother of George Warde Norman was robbed at gunpoint at the foot of Chiselhurst Hill in 1793 and Bromley common remained a wild place until its enclosure in 1822. Nevertheless, it was becoming a popular retreat; the Bishop of Rochester had just rebuilt his episcopal palace there; Thomas Raikes, a deputy governor of the Bank, came to live at Freelands and William Pitt the younger acquired Hollwood House, where young Norman recollected being taken to see him by Thellusson's son.[19] The building of Plaistow, then, marked a stage in the metamorphosis of the Thellussons from rootless foreign bankers to English gentlemen.

By the time the new house was built however, Peter and Ann's older children were almost grown up. The first, Peter Isaac, arrived on 1st October 1761. A second son, George Woodford, followed on 2nd March 1764,[20] and a third, Charles, on 2nd February 1770, punctuated by two babies who must have died in infancy, (Hannah, 1765 and John, 1768).[21] The three sons were then followed by three daughters: Maria in 1771, Anne in 1774 and Augusta Charlotte in October 1776. Unless there were later stillbirths or infant deaths unrecorded, Ann ceased childbearing rather early.[22]

As the children grew, their education had to be attended to. Predictably, girls' schools are poorly documented, so it is not known whether the Thellusson girls attended one of the numerous `academies' and boarding schools where they could learn those `accomplishments' in the fine arts and in performing music which would (it was hoped) gratify lovers and husbands and assist them to pass the long hours of their enforced idleness.[23]

Schools for younger boys were also plentiful, but the quality was as variable as might be expected in the absence of any checks or controls and many parents of substantial means preferred to employ a tutor rather than to entrust them to a school.[24] For older boys - at least, for those of Anglican families - there were, of course, the `public schools', while nonconformists had their own `dissenting academies', which offered an education better suited to the business world than could be obtained anywhere else in England.[25] A `public school education' in the eighteenth century was an altogether less civilised and orderly affair than it became in the many schools which followed the model introduced by Dr. Arnold at Rugby in the 1840s, and boys came and went irregularly, often for shorter periods and from more diverse backgrounds. They came also in much smaller numbers; in 1746 Harrow had sunk to only 46 pupils.[26]

One of the most distinctive characteristics of the Victorian public school might already be discerned: an extraordinarily narrow syllabus totally dominated by the study of the classics. It was perhaps a suitable education for a gentleman, but for a man of business it was a doubtful benefit, if not downright pernicious, since it fostered the disparagement of all the avocations of commerce as unworthy of the attention of an educated man.[27] To send a son to a public school was a decision to flirt with, if not embrace, its values, and that is why Peter Thellusson's decision to send each of his sons to Harrow is significant.

Harrow was not an obvious choice. Westminster had the best reputation for learning and that is where John Woodford sent his eldest son. Other Woodfords had gone to Winchester for geographical reasons and there seems no particular logic in choosing Harrow, though it was improving its reputation, cultivating the Whig nobility but quite happy to accept the Thellussons and their like too.[28] Peter Isaac and George went up together in 1774, the one at thirteen, the other just ten, and both stayed for only two years. Their father cannot have been too dissatisfied with what was on offer, for in 1785 he sent Charles there, aged fifteen, though he stayed only for a year. These brief, and in George's case surely premature, sojourns at boarding school are puzzling. Even if Peter was abroad at that time it is unlikely that Ann went too, since she gave birth to a daughter in 1774, and if the original intention was that they should stay longer, there is nothing to explain what changed it.[29] Significantly, there is also no evidence that the pattern of previous Thellusson generations and of the international houses generally in sending the sons abroad for a year or two to learn the business with relatives or associates was followed, though were plenty of connexions available for it.

66

2. Matchmaking

In view of the grand dynastic scheme embodied in his will, it is natural to examine the marriages which Peter's children made, particularly his sons', for earlier signs of what he had in contemplation, but a good deal of caution is necessary in doing so. It would be wrong to assume that he was a patriarchal despot, able to command his family's obedience and eager to arrange their affairs. Old Isaac had been just such a man, unable to brook opposition or to sympathise with different dispositions, but Peter was a different man and England was another country.

Historians offer widely differing interpretations of English family life in the eighteenth century, but they are mostly in agreement that patriarchy - in the crude sense of the father and head of the family exercising a despotic power over its members - was at a relatively low ebb.[30] England was unusual in permitting a boy over fourteen and a girl over twelve to enter a valid marriage, though Hardwicke's Marriage Act of 1753 made the purported marriage of a person under twenty-one without the consent of parents or guardians void. This belated reinforcement of parental authority was of very limited effect because the law of Scotland was not altered, so that elopement to Gretna Green came into fashion.[31]

A more effective restraint was the power which fathers had to impose financial sanctions on the child who married without consent. It was a strong weapon, especially in the case of daughters, but it was often difficult for parents to maintain their displeasure in the face of a *fait accompli*, as the case of John Scott, the future Lord Chancellor Eldon, and his wife Elizabeth Surtees shows.[32] Parents, it seems, did not usually claim the right to arrange their children's marriages. Rather they claimed the right to encourage eligible suitors and to veto unsuitable ones. Likewise the children claimed the right to veto and the right to encourage, and the balance of power varied in each case according to family circumstances and personalities.[33] This being so, the most we can say of the marriages of the Thellusson boys is that they had Peter's acquiescence and probably his approval. They cannot be treated as evidence of his own designs for the family.

Curiously, all the sons' marriages are much more the sort to be expected than Peter's own, since the families of all three brides had a background in commerce which the Woodfords seemingly lacked. The eldest son was the first to marry, in 1783. His bride was Elizabeth Eleanor Cornwall, from a merchant family in Hull which had risen to local eminence in the person of William, who died in 1716/7. William's only surviving son, also William, had at least ten children by three marriages, one of them to a daughter of Samuel Watson, through whom the Cornwalls were linked with another rising Hull family, the Thorntons.[34]

Both the Cornwalls and the Thorntons (and probably the Watsons too) were Russia merchants, a rather specialised trade in which London merchants were active, but in which the east coast ports, especially Newcastle and Hull, exploited their location and the expansion of manufacturing in their hinterlands to claim a sizeable share. The trade was of national importance because as well as linens and flax, iron and naval stores, especially masts from Riga, were imported in large quantities and Britain's naval power depended on an assured supply. Following the Anglo-Russian commercial treaty of 1734 trade "began to expand at a pace unmatched for a time, by that of any other area"[35], bringing great prosperity to the merchants involved. John Thornton was able to give away £2 - £3,000 a year out of the fortune he inherited and enlarged and still left £600,000 when he died in 1790, and if the Cornwalls were not quite in that league, they were certainly prosperous. The two families were already linked in business and later had in their counting house young Henry Thornton, who became one of the leading lights of the `Clapham Sect'.[36] Cornwall and his partner Godfrey Thornton married sisters, Susanna and Jane respectively, the co- heiresses of Stephen Peter Godin, also in the Russia trade as an insurance broker.[37]

On his marriage to Susanna, John Cornwall bought an old mansion house at Hendon, much favoured as a rural retreat,[38] and and the couple raised one son and seven daughters. The son, John, and one of the daughters, Mary Ann, married into the Gardner family while another daughter married the banker Edward Gale (later Boldero), a connexion of the Gardners by marriage. Most of the other daughters found the charms of rising lawyers irresistible. The eldest, Rebecca, married John Simeon, a Chancery lawyer and already recorder of Reading since the age of twenty-three; Susanna picked out Samuel Heywood, son of a Liverpool banker and a common law practitioner on the northern circuit, while Augusta took as her husband James Stanley, another Chancery lawyer; all three men will re-appear in later chapters.[39]

Elizabeth Eleanor, twenty-two when she married Peter Isaac Thellusson, was the third daughter, and in terms of family connexions it was a desirable match. The bride's father was now a Bank of England director, as were Godfrey and Samuel Thornton, whose family described themselves as `all City people and connected with merchants, and nothing but merchants on every side',[40] and were a rising force in the City. A boy (Peter Henry) was soon born to Elizabeth, only to die four months later, but in September 1785 a second son, John, was born, and after an anxious interval (there must be the possibility of miscarriages or unrecorded births) further children began to arrive with impressive regularity: Frances (July 1790), George (May 1791), Henry (July 1792) and Caroline (October 1793). The three sons made the senior branch of Peter's descent as secure as anything might be in an uncertain world.[41]

The middle son, George Woodford, was twenty-six before making a match that was highly suitable. Alone among Peter's sons, he married into a family of Huguenot origin as well as mercantile background. The Fonnereaus were from La Rochelle and in 1693, when the persecutions became intolerable, young Claude Fonnereau was sent to England.[42] He prospered mightily as a merchant in the `nearby trades', specialising in the importation of linens from Hamburg and making an immense fortune. Claude married twice[43] and invested part of his fortune in the purchase of lands in Edmonton and in Suffolk. When he died in 1740 the construction of his will gave rise to several disputes which might have served as a warning of the dangers of testamentary complexity.[44] Claude's fourth son, Zachary Philip, had a large family to support. His two eldest sons, Philip and Martyn, both became MPs and Philip made a good catch in the marriage market, the heiress of Mundon in Hertfordshire, a pleasant, modest estate bought by a prosperous London mercer, Rogers Parker in 1715. From Philip's marriage came four children, of whom the only son died young and childless. The eldest daughter, Elizabeth Mary, was claimed at a tender age by a rising West India merchant George Hibbert; her sister Isabella had a long life as a spinster, and George Thellusson married the youngest, Mary Ann, when she was twenty-two.

In terms of connexions it was a solid, rather than a brilliant marriage, for the great Fonnereau fortune, dispersed among several sons, some of whom themselves produced large families, gradually seeped away and somehow the family came to much less than they had promised, another thing that may have given George's father food for thought. Although for several generations Fonnereaus were MPs, they never made any impact in political life,[45] and while Martyn was a Bank director and several of the family are listed in the London directories as merchants, they seem not to have been great figures in the City.[46] The senior branch were respectable landed gentry with a penchant for becoming clergymen, but even in Suffolk they never made much of a splash.[47]

In one crucial respect George's marriage did not prove an immediate success. Mary Ann soon conceived but the first child was a girl, named after her mother, and when a second child followed four years later it proved to be another girl, so that when Peter made his momentous will it was uncertain whether he would have a grandson in this line.[48]

There was the same uncertainty in the case of his youngest son Charles, but that was to be expected since he had been married for little over a year. His wife was Sabine Robarts, her faintly exotic christian name taken from her mother, who was from the Irish family of Tierney. The rise of the Robartses in the City almost parallelled that of the Thellussons but they proved to have more staying power.

Abraham (1701-61), an army officer, married the only daughter of Samuel Wildey of Stepney and their second son, Abraham II, born in the year of the 'Forty Five, was Sabine's father.[49] The Robarts' mercantile activities are even harder to follow than Thellusson's, but by 1781 Abraham II was a director of the Royal Exchange Assurance Company and in 1786 he became a director of the East India Company in the City interest. He was also a West India factor, but it was the formation of the large and successful banking firm of Robarts, Curtis, Were, Hornyold and Berwick in 1792 that really marked him out as one of the City élite.

At the general election of 1796 Robarts came in for Worcester and held it for the remaining twenty years of his life, a loyal and silent supporter of William Pitt despite the fact that his brother- in- law George Tierney, with whom he was on affectionate terms, was one of Pitt's most outspoken opponents and even went to the lengths of fighting a duel with him in 1798. Abraham II had married Tierney's sister in 1774 and they had at least nine children. The eldest son, Abraham Wildey, was not born until 1780 and the likelihood is that Sabine was the eldest of the five girls. It might be expected that the other Robarts children would also make good marriages, but in fact most are surprisingly obscure.[50]

Peter Thellusson also had daughters to marry and the eldest, Maria, was soon off his hands, married in July 1792 at only twenty. It was a rather different match from those of the sons and gave the Thellussons a distant but valuable social link with the aristocracy and with Pitt's ministry. Maria's husband was Augustus Phipps, who had been at Harrow with her brothers and was then thirty years old. From school Augustus had gone first to Lincoln's Inn and then, presumably deciding that the law did not suit him, to St. John's College, Cambridge, where he took his M.A. in 1785. Now, to give him an income sufficient for his marriage, he had been made a commissioner of Excise, which was perfectly compatible with a leisured mode of existence.[51]

Augustus' parents were both dead. His father Constantine, who had been created Baron Mulgrave in the Irish peerage, died in 1775 and a few years later

Augustus had the shock of finding his mother dead in her bed. The barony had devolved upon their eldest son, Constantine John, but he had no sons and when he died a few months before Augustus' wedding the English barony obtained in 1790 became extinct. The Irish barony and the estates in Yorkshire passed to Augustus' eldest brother and the new Lord Mulgrave was much in favour with the government. An alliance with the Phippses was therefore a very good one.[52]

Marriages within the propertied classes contracted with parental approval were invariably accompanied by a financial settlement. Negotiations took place against a legal backdrop in which a wife, a *feme couverte* in the law's terminology, was for all practical purposes unable to call anything her own and was at the mercy of her husband even for the necessities of life, though the common law imposed on him a duty to house and feed her.[53] Therefore one of the main objectives of the bride's father in the marriage settlement was to ensure that the common law position was improved by contract, lest he find himself saddled with a daughter separated from an intolerable husband who retained control of her property.[54] The contingency of widowhood had also to be provided for, since the common law provision, in the form of dower, was unpopular with landowners,[55] and both families had further to be satisfied that the settlement made adequate provision for the children of the marriage, particularly for daughters and younger sons.

On the whole, the groom's father's anxieties were more straightforward. Brides were a source of ready money or land, money which was often needed to pay off mortgages or other debts, to finance the marriage of the other children or to enlarge the family's estates. Heiresses, and girls with large portions, were eagerly sought and few thought it indelicate for the *Gentleman's Magazine* to include the bride's fortune in its wedding announcements. The groom's father knew there would be a price to be paid for this windfall and wanted to get the most satisfactory bargain.[56]

The marriage settlement was by this time a complex arrangement, still being refined by developments in equity such as the restraint upon anticipation (known as

`Lord Thurlow's Equity'[57]), and the study of settlements can reveal a good deal about social values that are not openly articulated; about the relative value placed on sons and daughters and the position of widows and about the strategic role of marriage in dynastic and estate planning and the nature of family life. Not surprisingly, they have been extensively studied. Equally unsurprisingly there has been vigorous argument over their interpretation, but it has focused chiefly on the settlements made by substantial landowners, both because until the nineteenth century land was still the biggest source of wealth and power and because the affairs of landowners are much better documented than those of businessmen.[58]

Conclusions drawn from marriage settlements alone also create a distorted picture of family provision and inter-generational wealth transfer, for variations and augmentations often resulted from wills made by parents and collateral relations; moreover as the amount of `portable property' grew these dispositions became more important. We are still rather ill-informed about the financial side of bourgeois marriages, for few of their marriage settlements have been studied,[59] and unfortunately, of the four Thellusson children who married in their father's lifetime the only settlement that survives is Maria's, who married into an aristocratic family.[60]

Maria was given £12,000 as her marriage portion. Augustus had received his portion on coming of age and with his salary and their life interest under the settlement the couple would be quite comfortably placed. The settlement has few unusual features, except that Maria's jointure took the form of rent from Augustus' chambers in New Square, Lincoln's Inn, a `flying freehold' rare in England.[61] The portions fund for their younger children was likely to produce about £7,500 each and if (as turned out to be the case) there were no children and Augustus should outlive Maria, he would receive half of the settled fund absolutely, the other half for life with a remainder to her two sisters; if she survived him, she would receive it all absolutely.

Much less is known about the sons' settlements. The will of Peter Isaac's father-in-law John Cornwall shows that he treated all his daughters alike, giving them each a portion of £10,000 - £5,000 on marriage and a further £5,000 at his death.[62] In

Peter Isaac's own will he left his wife £2,400 per annum charged on land, with the right to occupy their country house rent free until the heir came of age and enough household articles to furnish another house when she left it. He also gave her a life interest in £20,000 3% consols (£600 per annum) with power to appoint £2,000 among his children. Peter Isaac's younger children were to receive sums ranging from £20,000 down to £12,000 (probably reflecting advancements already made) and any later born child was to have £10,000, all these provisions in satisfaction of their entitlements under the marriage settlement, which must therefore have been £10,000 or less. These are lavish sums, too lavish in fact, for they just about exhausted his estate.[63] With almost £3,000 p.a. as a widow Elizabeth was receiving notably generous treatment.[64]

Very little is known about George's settlement. Philip Fonnereau settled £200 Irish annuities in the 1776 tontine on each daughter to her separate use and by his will exercised a power of appointment under his own marriage settlement to provide them with £4,000 as well as an equal share in his residue.[65] When George died he left his wife a life interest in his entire realty, which was not very substantial, and his residuary personalty absolutely, giving portions of £5,000 to each of his two children and his wife a power of appointment.[66] Since George, like all his siblings, had £12,000 from his father, it seems probable that the settlement was entirely conventional.

Charles also had £12,000 to go into the settlement. His wife Sabine predeceased him, and her father's will settled £8,000 on Sabine's children, but this was evidently not in furtherance of the marriage settlement and there is too little evidence for any plausible reconstruction.[67]

There is nothing unorthodox or surprising in what we know of these settlements. Peter Thellusson was perfectly fair to his children and it is likely that the £12,000 portions deliberately echo what he had received from *his* father. The daughters were treated as well as the sons and Peter Isaac, who married first, when his father's fortune was still moderate, fared no worse than Charles, who married in

1795. When these marriages took place the in-laws must have felt reasonably hopeful that there would be large further gifts to the children in Thellusson's will and that they would be distributed fairly as between siblings of the same sex.

NOTES

1.   Earle, *Making of the English Middle Class*, pp.181-5; E.A. Wrigley and R.S. Schofield, *The Population History of England, 1541-1871* (London, 1981), pp.422-3.

2.   *Supra*, P. 21.

3.   Ain, *Les Thellusson*, pp.82-4; Lüthy, *Banque Protestante,* vol.II, pp.232-4. George Tobie's marriage contract is summarised in G. Antonetti, *Une Maison de Banque a Paris. Greffulhe, Montz et Cie* (Paris, 1963), annexe 1.

4.   J.F. Crosthwaite, *A Brief Memoir of Major-General Sir J.G. Woodford* (2nd edn., London etc., 1883), pp.1-3.

5.   J.B. Burke, *Extinct and Dormant Baronetcies* (London, 1844), p.579 *sub* Woodford of Carleby; G.E.C., *Complete Baronetage*, p.274; J.S. Davies, *A History of Southampton* (Southampton, 1883), pp.342-3; will of Sir Ralph Woodford, PRO PROB 11/1748, f.682.

6.   *House of Commons, 1754-90*, vol.III, pp.468-72; A. Temple Patterson, *A History of Southampton, 1700-1914* (Southampton, 1966), p.61.

7.   D.B. Horn, *British Diplomatic Representatives, 1689-1789* (London, 1932), pp.5, 72, 125, 135; Pares, *War and Trade in the West Indies*, pp.557-95.

8.   *Alumni Oxonienses, 1715-1886*, vol. IV, p.1603; M. Woodford to Earl of Buckinghamshire, 8 Feb. 1767, *Report of the Historical Manuscripts Commission on the Manuscripts of the Marquis of Lothian preserved at Blickling Hall, Norfolk* (London, 1905), p.276. From 1789 he was rector of Chilbolton, a preserve of deans and prebendaries with good hunting and fishing on the Test: *V.C.H. Hampshire*, vol.3 (London, 1923), p.405.

9.   Crosthwaite, *Memoir of Sir J.G. Woodford*, p.2.

10.   Curiously, Sophia seems to have vanished from the record books, but see Mary Woodford's will, PRO PROB 11/124, f.293.

11.   See *infra*, pp. 133-4

12.   Disparagingly described in *The Times* (5 Jul. 1859) as `a dingy little back parlour behind the Bank'. John Baker referred to it as Philpot Corner (P.C. Yorke (ed.), *The Diary of John Baker* (London, 1931), p.394) and there is an engraving of it in the Soane Museum.

13.   G. Rudé, *Hanoverian London, 1714-1808* (London, 1971), pp.1-20; Earle, *Making of the English Middle Class*, pp.205-39.

14.   `The commuting City gent had arrived': Rogers, *Big Bourgeoisie*, p.450; Rudé, *Hanoverian London*, pp.16-17. It was not yet a general practice among bankers: D. Hardcastle, *Banks and Banking* (London, 1842), p.21.

15.   W. Robinson, *The History and Antiquities of the Parish of Hackney* (2 vols., London, 1842), vol. I, p.206; *V.C.H. Middlesex* vol. 10 (Oxford, 1995), p.88. His short-lived daughter Hannah was baptised at St. John's, Hackney in 1765.

16.   Rudé, *Hanoverian London*, pp.56-8; ; order of 26 Apr. 1806, PRO C 33/554, f.482.

17.   Horsburgh, *Bromley*, pp.181-7; H.M. Colvin, *A Biographical Dictionary of British Architects, 1600-1840* (3rd edn., New Haven and London, 1995), pp.612-4. Leverton designed a bank (since demolished) in Lombard Street for Robarts Curtis & Co. in 1796. Abraham Robarts' daughter married Thellusson's son Charles and he must have visited Plaistow.

18.   H. Meister, *Letters Written during a Residence in England* (London, 1799), p.51.

19.   P. Norman, Notes on Bromley and the Neighbourhood, *Archaeologia Cantiana* 24 (1900), 139-60.

20.   The printed copy of George's evidence to the enquiry into East India patronage in 1809 records him as saying that he was born on the 22nd and Emperor Woodford on the 2nd, but the dates have probably been transposed: *PP* 1809 (91) II, p.500.

21.   In the case of Hannah the mother is not mentioned in the transcript but it is assumed that the child was Peter and Ann's.

22.   The menopause tended to arrive at about forty: L. Stone, *The Family, Sex and Marriage in England, 1500-1800* (1979 edn., London), p.68.

23.   Stone, *Family, Sex and Marriage*, pp.228-33. One school in Queen Square, Bloomsbury was known as `the Ladies' Eton': Robinson, *Coutts*, pp.41-2.

24.   Schools might be injurious to health. John Woodford's two younger boys were removed from Dr. Valpy's well known school at Reading when one had a bad hand which was dangerously neglected: Crosthwaite, *Memoir of J.G. Woodford*, app.,n.1.

25.   Mathias, *First Industrial Nation*, p. 142, though compare P. Langford, *A Polite and Commercial People* (Oxford, 1989), pp.84-7.

26.   J. Chandos, *Boys Together* (Oxford, 1969), p.30-47.; *V.C.H. Middlesex*, vol. I, (Oxford, 1969), pp.299-302.

27.   Harrow, for example, had no specialist mathematics teacher until 1839 and even under Dr. Butler (1860-85), `the curriculum was practically the same as it had been in 1615': E.D. Laborde, *Harrow School, Yesterday and Today* (London, 1948), pp.48-9.

28.   Laborde, *Harrow School*; P.M. Thornton, *Harrow School and its Surroundings* (London, 1885), pp.121-83.

29.   W.T.J. Gun (ed.), *The Harrow School Register, 1571-1800* (London, 1934). Anne was baptised on 19 October. Peter had been in Geneva in September 1773: *Journal of the R.H. William Hervey for 1755 to 1814* (Bury St. Edmunds, 1906), p.240.

30.   K. Wrightson, The Family in Early Modern England: Continuity and Change, in S. Taylor, R. Connors and C. Jones (eds.), *Hanoverian Britain and Europe. Essays in Memory of Philip Lawson* (Woodbridge, 1998), pp. 1-22.

31.   D. Lemmings, Marriage and the Law in the Eighteenth Century. Hardwicke's Marriage Act of 1753, *Historical Journal* 39 (1996), 339-60.

32.   H. Twiss, *The Public and Private Life of Lord Chancellor Eldon* (3rd edn., 2 vols, London 1846), vol.I, pp.50-62.

33.   Stone, *Family, Sex and Marriage*, pp.270-320.

34.   Lord Liverpool and C. Reade, *The House of Cornewall* (Hereford, 1908), pp.255-8.

35.   Davis, *Rise of English Shipping*, p.219, and see G. Jackson, *Hull in the Eighteenth Century* (Oxford, 1972), pp.194-7.

36.   H. Thornton, *Enquiry into Paper Credit*, introduction, pp.13-15; *D.N.B.*, vol. LVI, pp.301, 306; E.M. Howse, *Saints in Politics, The Clapham Sect and the Growth of Freedom* (Toronto, 1952), pp.15-28. Cornwall lived to eighty-seven and his will (PRO PROB 11/1336, f.91) suggests very substantial wealth.

37.   For the Godins see W.M. Acres, Directors of the Bank of England, *Notes and Queries* 179 (1940(2)), 118 *sub* Thornton, Godfrey; *V.C.H. Middlesex*, vol. V (Oxford, 1976), p.160; Liverpool and Reade, *House of Cornewall*, p.258.

38.   D. Lysons, *The Environs of London*, vol.III (London, 1795), p.7.

39.   Liverpool and Reade, *House of Cornewall*, p.258.

40.   Ms. recollections of Marianne Thornton, quoted in Thornton, *Enquiry into Paper Credit*, introduction, p.11.

41.   *Complete Peerage*, vol. X, p.765.

42.   Agnew, *Protestant Exiles*, vol.II, pp.399-400. The best depiction of their complicated family tree is in J.E. Cussans, *A History of Hertfordshire* (3 vols., Hertford, 1870-81), vol. VI, pp.178-80.

43.   His second wife, whom he married when he was sixty-one, was probably the widow of another Bank director, Clement Boehm, and brought him £10,000: *Gents. Mag.* 8 (1738), 324.

44.   *Fonnereau v. Fonnereau* (1745) 3 Atk. 115, 645; *Doe d. Fonnereau v. Fonnereau* (1780) Doug. 487. Lord Mansfield's judgment in the latter illustrates the judges' tendency to give effect to the testator's presumed intention unless positively prevented by rules of law.

45.   *House of Commons, 1754-1790*, vol.I, pp.378, 382, 445-9. The Fonnereaus held Aldeburgh as a pocket borough but also sat for the notoriously venal borough of Sudbury. They earned a reputation as `Swiss' [i.e. mercenaries] and Zachary Philip (Mary Ann's grandfather) never

spoke in debate in his twenty-seven years in the House. He and Thomas were rewarded with a lucrative victualling contract and were big subscribers to government loans.

46. Acres, *Directors of the Bank of England*, 97, 118.

47. Burke, *Landed Gentry* (1846), p.425. They do not appear at all in J. Bateman, *The Great Landowners of Great Britain and Ireland* (4th edn., rep. Leicester, 1971).

48. Mary Anne was born on 6th Nov. 1791, Georgiana on 6th Oct. 1795.

49. Abraham I became a coal merchant in Stepney, perhaps taking over the business of his father-in-law, and also had a share in the new ferry at nearby Ratcliffe. The bequests in his will (PRO PROB 11/869, f.368) suggest a man of quite modest means. The youngest of the three sons, George, went into trade at Beverley and Hull. Some information on the Robarts and Tierney families is in H. R. Phipps, *Notes on the Phipps and Phip Family* (Lahore, 1911).

50. *House of Commons, 1790-1820*, vol. II, p.434. Two daughters died in their teens in July 1793 (*Gents. Mag.* 63 (1793), 675). Abraham's will (PRO PROB 11/1387, f.636) mentions four unmarried daughters and three sons. The eldest son married a Wilkinson, possibly the daughter of the big merchant John Wilkinson of Lothbury.

51. *Alumni Cantabrigienses, 1752-1900*, vol. V, p.117. The Excise post brought in £975 p.a and in 1804 (when his father was in the cabinet) he became Assistant Paymaster for Gibraltar, a sinecure worth £547 10s.

52. *Complete Peerage*, vol.IX, pp.392 (Mulgrave), 639 (Normanby); Phipps, *Notes on Phipps Family*, pp.70-105.

53. R. E. Megarry and H.W.R. Wade, *The Law of Real Property* (5th edn., London, 1984), pp.1020-4; O.R. McGregor and L. Blom-Cooper, *Separated Spouses* (London, 1970), pp.1-10.

54. A.L. Erickson, Common Law v. Common Practice: the use of marriage settlements in early modern England, *Economic History Review* (2nd s.) 48 (1990), 21-39, suggests that this was the chief object of most settlements.

55. H.J. Habbakuk, *Strict Settlement and the Estates System* (Oxford, 1994), pp.8-9.

56. The importance of heiresses and the need to endow daughters with substantial marriage portions has been the subject of much historical debate; Habbakuk, *Strict Settlement* and E. Spring, *Law, Land and Family. Aristocratic Inheritance in England, 1300-1800* (Chapel Hill and London, 1993) are recent contributions.

57. Megarry and Wade, *Law of Real Property*, pp.1021-3. It was designed to prevent husbands from coercing their wives into giving them access to the capital settled to the wife's `separate use'. A particularly scandalous example of this was the starvation and confinement of the Countess of Strathmore by her husband Mr. Bowes, reported in the *European Magazine* 13

(1788).

58.   For these controversies see *infra*, pp. 128-31.

59.   The detailed study by L. Bonfield, *Marriage Settlements, 1601-1740: the Adoption of the Strict Settlement* (Cambridge, 1983), deals with landed families. Earle, *Making of the English Middle Class*, pp.179-204, and A.L. Erickson, *Women and Property in Early Modern England* (London and New York, 1993), have much interesting material.

60.   Report of 13 Jun. 1805, PRO C 33/538, f.773.

61.   A freehold estate confined to an upper floor of a building has been rare in England because the land law has offered no effective means of providing the necessary rights of support, access etc. The law, however, takes care of its own; Lincoln's Inn freeholds are regulated by a private Act of 1860.

62.   PRO PROB 11/1336, f.91.

63.   PRO PROB 11/1469, f.920, and see *infra*, pp. 226-7.

64.   The standard ratio of a jointure to a wife's portion was 1:10. According to Habbakuk, (*Strict Settlement*, p.86), it tended to absorb 20% of gross income.

65.   PRO PROB 11/1285, f.84.

66.   PRO PROB 11/1387, f.210.

67.   PRO PROB 11/1387, f.636.

CHAPTER 5

A TALE OF THREE CITIES

1. Peace

`It was the best of times; it was the worst of times ...' With these well known words
Charles Dickens opens *A Tale of Two Cities*, setting in motion a story which switches
between London and Paris in the years before and during the French Revolution.[1] But
for the Thellussons on either side of the English Channel there was no ambiguity. In
material terms at least, it was unquestionably the very best of times.

In Paris George Tobie had found banking so profitable that he was able to
retire in his early forties and was now able to devote himself to spending money
rather than making it. He is the most attractive figure among all the Thellussons in
this story, for despite his commercial success he left a spotless reputation and if he
spent lavishly on his own wardrobe he was also a discerning patron and collector.
Having first assembled a fine collection of silverware he then turned his attention to
paintings and drawings, acquiring pictures by Poussin, Vernet, Fragonard, Watteau
and Vouwermans and well over four hundred prints, mostly of very high quality.
This cultivated man was more thoroughly at home in Paris than his father had ever
been. For while old Isaac had always felt himself a foreigner in France, cut off from
his hosts by religion, nationality and his austere temperament, his son was French in
all but name, although he remained a Protestant and prudently kept Genevan
citizenship. Besides his town house in Paris he had an estate at Marnes, not far from
Versailles, the counterpart to his brother Peter's villa at Plaistow; like other *nouveaux
riches* he had also bought a seigneurie, Biere and Berolle in the high Aubonne. He

81

was preparing to retire to his *chateau* in 1776 when death called him to a more permanent lodging at the early age of forty-eight.[2]

Country life held no charms for his widow, eager to make her mark in Parisian society, so she promptly sold Marnes to the king and picked out a huge plot of land on the fashionable Chausse d'Antin, where she employed the architect Ledoux to build a mansion for her. He was the wrong choice for `une habitation commode et jolie, moitié mondaine, moitié rustique, mais ayant l'air plutôt modeste d'une retraite que l'apperance d'un riche hôtel [a comfortable and pretty residence, part urban, part rural, but with the air more of a retreat than a grand town house]', for his visions were on the grandiose scale and instead of 400,000 which was expensive enough, she eventually paid more than 2 millions for a white elephant of a house, peculiar to look at and uncomfortable to live in. Sadly, the chastened owner did not live long enough to inhabit it. Jeanne Marie had a phobia of contagious diseases and demanded to be vaccinated against the smallpox. Vaccination was novel and dangerous and she succumbed to its effects.[3]

Both George Tobie and his wife died in middle age, but they left three healthy sons to carry the name and to further the family integration into the mainstream of French aristocratic life. The sons also kept their nationality, and their religion too (though they wore it lightly), but there was little to distinguish them from their French contemporaries. Paul Louis, the eldest, flirted briefly with commerce but his brothers never gave it a thought and all entered the king's service as commissioned officers. Part of George Tobie's wealth went to transform his twenty-seven year old eldest son from a mere Swiss seigneur to the splendid Marquis de Thellusson de Franconville, and he so enjoyed his bachelor life that he put off marrying and securing the line.[4]

The middle brother, Jean Isaac, was the first to wed. A lieutenant in the Swiss Guard from the age of eighteen, he was still only twenty-three when he married the seventeen year old Louise Rilliet. No match could have been more suitable, for the Rilliets had been one of the five great families in Geneva before the

Huguenots arrived and had fully maintained their position ever since. The bank of Lullin Frères et Rilliet was one of the most successful and cosmopolitan of all the Protestant international firms and Louise's father, wealthy in his own right, was married to Antoinette Marguerite Julien, daughter of a Parisian banker. Jean Isaac paid out half a million livres for the estate of Sorcy, close to Joan of Arc's birthplace Domrémy and carrying with it the old and honourable title of Comte de Sorcy as well as a recently refurbished and comfortable *chateau*.[5] The youngest of the three sons, Pierre Germain, joined his eldest brother in Schomberg's regiment. The lands and title of Baron de Coppet, an estate midway between Geneva and Nyon, had been bought for him by his mother in 1780, but her building schemes soon compelled it to be sold again and it was snapped up by Necker, recently resigned and wanting a retreat to sulk in.[6]

The French Thellussons had thus abandoned commerce and in Geneva their two uncles were also living the lives of *rentiers*. The head of the family, Isaac Louis, seigneur of Gara, lived much as old Isaac had done in his retirement, successively a member of the two hundred, a councillor and finally a syndic from 1785 to 1789. He had five children by two wives and one of his descendants became the wife of the great linguistic scientist Ferdinand de Saussure, but he had only one son, Isaac George, who vanishes from the record after 1794, the last of the Thellussons of Geneva.[7]

The youngest of old Isaac's sons, Jean François, was an unambitious and typical `capitaliste de Geneve',[8] drawn like so many Genevans to the *rentes viagères*, which gave him a dangerously large stake in the *ancien régime* of France.

A *rente viagère* is an annuity sold for a capital sum and payable during the continuance of one or more lives, differing from a tontine in that it is not linked to the survival of persons other than those nominated by the buyer. Both tontines and *rentes* are self-amortising and therefore superficially attractive to governments in search of loans, but in the more advanced financial systems of Britain and Holland they had fallen out of favour, displaced by the perpetual, redeemable annuity which offered greater flexibility.[9] Even those countries however, occasionally resorted to them as expedients, and 100 Genevans subscribed £100,000 to the Irish tontine of 1779, Peter Thellusson acting as agent for their bankers.[10] In France, however, tontines and *rentes* became increasingly important. Necker was already familiar with *rentes*, since he and George Tobie had raised a large loan for the Prince de Conti in this way, and when Necker became finance minister he resorted to them again and again.[11]

Necker's specious promise that a war could be waged without financial hardship made heavy borrowing unavoidable but successive ministers consistently offered *rentes* on prodigal terms, based either on a single, undifferentiated average life expectancy or a series of very broad age/life expectancy bands, allowing the purchaser to nominate any life he chose.[12] As long as men, Peter Thellusson among them, were content to buy modest *rentes* on their own lives or those of young relations, there was little harm to the treasury (though a misanthrope like Jean Claude Tourton was enabled to invest his great fortune in *rentes* on his own, waning life and so disinherit his posterity), but issues `sans distinction d'âge [undifferentiated by the age of the holder]' were not taken up on that basis alone.[13]

In the Age of Enlightenment rational, scientific curiosity was abroad. Public health was improved by vaccination, pioneered by Théodore Tronchin in Geneva, and the accumulation of data on mortality enabled actuarial tables to be refined and life insurance to become a more soundly based art. Genevan financiers exploited both these advances to plunder the French treasury through the `*trente immortelles* [thirty immortals]'; they would buy, say, thirty *rentes* in their own name but each secured on a different life chosen from a group of Genevan maids procured by advertisement and selected to embody the best combination of health, age and family longevity. The *rentes* were then sold in blocks which gave each purchaser a fraction of every *rente* so that he spread his risk, receiving his annuity in full until the first of the *immortelles* died and then in a progressively diminishing proportion. He need have no anxiety about proving the continued existence of his `lives', for they were local celebrities. The bankers dealt (for a fee) with the obstructive French bureaucracy and the *rentes* even became marketable securities. Genevans like Jean François Thellusson were so entranced by the elegance of the scheme and the certainty of profit that in this last decadent phase of their republic this once prudent people became almost frenzied in their desire to acquire *rentes*.[14]

The English Thellussons, of course, were also deeply concerned for the stability of the French monarchy and for amicable relations between the two great powers. Pitt's commercial treaty of 1786 had been good for trade, especially for the English, whose superiority in insurance and shipping won them the lion's share.[15] The last of Peter Thellusson's partnerships with John Cossart expired at the end of 1791 and he retired, his sons succeeding to the business under the style of Thellusson Brothers. Both the old and the new firm engaged in dealings in a variety of goods and services. Two law cases show them at work in shipping sugar cargoes, although they are known only from the reports of Espinasse, a byword for inaccuracy, and very sketchily at that. They fared badly before Lord Kenyon in both, losing their claim to a total rather than a partial loss on a cargo sent from Ostend to Havre and failing in their claim arising out of the wreck of the *Ami*, voyaging in the other direction; part of her cargo was salvaged and sold at three months' credit, but by settlement day the livre had plummeted against the pound and Thellussons unsuccessfully demanded the difference from the insurers.[16]

The firm was also deeply involved in the hyperactive Paris money market. A great speculative boom had developed in the 1780s, encouraged by the government's huge loans and intensified by the creation of joint stock companies by professional speculators, whose securities were 'created, manipulated and attached like pieces on a speculative chess board.'[17] Paris sucked in great quantities of foreign capital. The Dutch deserted London, worried by the large national debt disclosed through the openness of England's public accounting and dazzled by the *comte rendu* [account delivered], Necker's conjuring trick, which suggested that the French state was financially healthy.[18] *Agiotage* (speculation on shares) and *arbitrage* (speculation on the rate of exchange) reached new heights, with Parisian bankers playing a leading part in both, along with a new breed of *agioteur*, reckless and rootless. The old `family capitalism' found little difficulty in adapting to new games[19] and foreign investors could take a hand too, either by joining *sociétés en participation* and sharing the profits of speculation or simply by acting as agents for clients wanting to invest in Paris (placing their money, remitting their dividends) and playing the money exchanges.[20]

Peter Thellusson had never been averse to a bit of speculation in the Funds. He had `joué immensement [speculated enormously]' in one murky episode of 1769 - 70 when De Guines, the French ambassador, had mingled secret diplomacy with even more secret speculations, though that time the speculators were losers, and in 1778 he was Emmanuel Haller's London agent in a `projet ... vaste, immense, je dirois presque effrayant [a project...vast, tremendous, I should say almost frightening]' of which no details are known.[21] Now he was involved with some of the biggest players on the Paris exchange and although we shall never know how big his own stake was, nor how large his profits, it is plain that he was an important figure. The firm was, for instance, the principal London correspondent of J.L. Grenus, with whom it concerted at least one bear operation, and who kept his nerve and continued his increasingly dangerous activities in the menacing atmosphere of Paris in 1792.[22]

Even more important were Greffulhe, Montz et Cie, whose books have fortunately survived. Ultimate successors to Thellusson, Necker et Cie, they included Haller (`l'une des éminences grise de la spéculation [one of the hidden masters of speculation]'[23]) and a domineering newcomer Louis Greffulhe, a self-made man in the mould of old Isaac Thellusson, `brusque, authoritaire, plein de confiance en soi et de fierté [blunt, masterful, full of self- confidence and pride]'.[24] After quarrelling with their agents, the Anglo-Dutch firm of Robert Muilman, in the spring of 1790, they transferred their business to Thellussons, related by marriage to their third partner, J-M. Montz.[25] The ill-fated Dutch firm of

86

Vandenyver et Fils was another important connection,[26] and there were others whose involvement in the *arbitrage* was born of necessity rather than desire, such as the banker Perregaux, whose main line of business lay in changing for money for English milords on their trips to France.[27] Altogether the stake of the English Thellussons in the *ancien régime* must have been substantial.

2. Revolution

Self-interest alone would have inclined all branches of the Thellusson family to be opposed to a revolution in France. Opinion in England, which had for the most part been condescendingly approving when it looked as though something along the lines of her own Glorious Revolution was in prospect, and which in any case welcomed anything which weakened her formidable neighbour, soon began to crystallise into doctrinaire support or opposition, the doctrines being supplied by Edmund Burke's *Reflections on the French Revolution* for the defenders of order and tradition and by Thomas Paine's *Rights of Man* for the friends of liberty. Predictably Burke's clarion call against the contagion of democratic and atheistic doctrines appealed more to the Thellussons, as to the City generally, than Paine's stark logic and radical ideas.

As the revolution gathered momentum the bankers became increasingly unpopular in France. The foreign money that had poured into Paris flooded out again, obliging the government to issue a paper currency (the *assignats*) to cover the shortage of specie.[28] The *assignats* rapidly depreciated as peasants hoarded coin and investors sold out (Peter Thellusson disposed of most of his *rentes* to the speculator Eugène Delassert in 1790[29]) and at last even the more venturesome bankers left off playing the exchange and started to salt away their gains; Greffulhe, Montz, for instance, had bought £64,000 of Bank and East India stock through Thellussons by May 1792 and during the following year sent at least two million lt. across the Channel. By August 1792 the Paris banks had ceased lending and the Bourse closed after the September massacres.[30]

Besides their own money, the banks were also the channel for the export of money and chattels by emigrants. Many Frenchmen went abroad in the summer of 1789, shrewdly judging that a temporary absence from home might be agreeable and politic. Events soon decided many to prolong their absence, and they were joined by others at each landmark on the road to the Terror, beginning with the King's botched flight to Varennes (20th-21st June 1791) and ending with the Law of Suspects (17th September 1793) and the decree establishing the Revolutionary Government (4th December).

At first emigration was legal, but the first restrictions were imposed after Varennes, toughened shortly afterwards, and emigrants were first commanded to return, then forbidden to do so on pain of death.[31] But laws did not deter those who feared that if they stayed their heads would roll and many thousands became exiles, from the highest in the land, the princes of the blood and the king's own brothers, to some of the lowest, fugitive priests and servants to the nobility. They went everywhere, and many of them came to England, either directly or via the Low Countries ahead of the advancing armies of the Republic. It is reckoned that 25,000 at one time or another endured our weather, our food and our phlegmatic temperament with varying degrees of fortitude and gratitude. Few stayed on - Fanny Burney's husband the Comte d'Arblay is a well-known exception - and few Englishmen were disappointed when their uninvited guests departed, for those that were not Papists were often republicans, those who received charity were not always so obsequiously grateful as the donors wished and those who hated the Republic could not always pretend dismay at the success of French armies.[32]

The poverty of most of the refugees was inevitably a source of embarrassment and friction. Even Louis XVI's younger brother the Comte d'Artois spent months living in Edinburgh Castle courtesy of George III but besieged and harrassed by an army of creditors who compelled him to keep house, while lesser mortals found themselves in much worse straits.[33] No doubt some Englishmen exploited their necessitous state and profited from the turmoil in France, and it is said that among the latter were the Thellussons.

One of the strangest parts in the tale of Peter's will is the story that his fortune was founded largely on the money of guillotined Frenchmen and that the will was his attempt to do right by the heirs of these headless ghosts. This is the story as told by Edward Fournier in 1864:

`Beaucoup d' émigres avaient apporté tout ce qu'ils avaient pu sauver de naufrage de leur fortune. A plusieurs, il rendit plus qu'il n'avait reçu tant il avait de douleur à voir dans la misère des gentilshommes français; mais à d'autres, faute des réclamation, il ne put rien restituer ... M. Thélusson se trouvait donc être ainsi pour de fortes sommes une sorte de dépositaire à perpétuité. La tâche peut pas semblé incommode à certaines consciences; mais M. T, qui était l'honnêteté même, la trouve gênante pour lui et pour les siens. Ne pouvant s'y soustraire, il l'accepta. C'est en vue de la responsabilité, qui malgré lui grevait sa fortune, qu'il fit le testament don't les dispositions ont toujours été si mal expliqueés.

Il voulut que le plus grande partie de sa fortune restât intacte pendant une longe suite d'années, afin que la restitution des sommes qui pouvaient être reclammeés s'effectuat sans peine et sans débat, et pour ainsi dire à bureau ouvert, comme s'il eût toujours été vivant; et non point, comme on l'a dit, afin que sa fortune, déjà considérable, devînt des plus énormes par l'accumulation des interêts capitalisés.

[Many emigrants had brought with them all they had been able to save from the wreck of their fortunes. To some, he had returned more than they had deposited, so grieved was he at the wretchedness of these French gentlemen; but to others, in default of their reclaiming their property he had been unable to restore anything. Mr. T. thus found himself to be a sort of perpetual repository of large sums. This role would not have troubled some consciences, but Mr. T., always the most honest of men, was embarrassed by the circumstance for himself and his family. Being unable to renounce it, he accepted it. It was in view of this responsibility, which was an unsought encumbrance on his fortune, that he made the will whose terms have always been given the wrong explanation. He wanted the greatest part of his estate to be kept intact for a long term of years, so that the restitution of those deposits which might be reclaimed could be accomplished without hardship or dispute, as it were an open drawer such as he always kept in his lifetime, and not as it is asserted, so that his already large fortune should be enlarged by the accumulation of capitalised interest.]'[34]

Now this story contains two separate assertions; first that Thellusson was the repository of much property still unclaimed when he came to make his will; second that he disinherited his sons in order to keep property safe for the rightful owners. The second allegation will be considered later, but the first can be dealt with now. Fournier gives no source for this story, which can be found in the *Law Magazine* for 1838 thereafter in Haydn's *Dictionary of Dates* and other works but I cannot trace it back further than that in any English publications which would have been available to him.[35] That is not to say, however, that it is untrue, for some such stories were circulating within a few years of Peter's death and thanks to Joseph Farington they are preserved. His diary entry for 24th July 1803, containing the accusation about the Fonblanque partnership, goes on:

`The present Thellussons, the Sons, are supposed to have become possessed of vast sums, in consequence of remittances having been made to them during the Revolution by Frenchmen, who being afterwards guillotined, or in some cases destroyed no Claimants have appeared. This caused Frank Chalie at an entertainment, to propose "The Guillotine" as a toast to one of the Thellussons as one of their best friends.'[36]

Some years later, in an entry for 25th January 1811, Farington records remarks by David Pike Watts:

`during the French Revolution very great property came to Mr. Thelusson [sic] from France at various times, manifestly from various persons, who not daring to risk their names being known, only put marks upon the Packets, which were to be claimed whenever corresponding marks should be produced. By the Guillotine, or by some other means, these persons were destroyed, so that little was claimed. This property, however, it is supposed [he] did not think himself entitled to call his own till a longer period shall have passed and therefore he has removed the possession of it to a distant time to give claimants, if there are any, time to come forward.'[37]

It is this second version that corresponds to Fournier's, though the diary was not published until sixty years after Fournier wrote. But though these entries are evidence of near contemporary rumours about the Thellussons' role, they are still only rumours, and rumour may be malicious as well as merely false, for the Thellussons certainly had their enemies.

The fact that no such rumours have been noted about any other English banker or merchant may suggest, what Brydges asserted, that it was through Thellussons that 'most of the great remittances to and from the Continent were conveyed'[38], and Dickens' Tellsons Bank, `a French house and an English house'[39] would certainly have been in a position to become the main conduit for secret emigrant deposits. Furthermore the very essence of the story told by Watts is that these transactions were secret and meant to leave no trace.   In September 1792 the National Assembly forbade the export of money or precious metals and what had been a thriving part of the business of the Perregaux, Vandenyvers, Boyd-Ker and others dried up - or rather, went underground.   Both the profit motive and loyalty to their clients tempted bankers to make clandestine remittances, disguised as legitimate transactions or kept wholly from view. Lüthy describes how some of the papers seized at Montz's house in 1793:

`avec leurs pages maquilleés, lacéreés, aux noms arrachés, rendus illisibles, substitué ou remplacés par des sigles, aux lieux et dates falsifiés après coup, font sentir l'atmosphere sinistre dans laquelle s'opèrent les affairs de banque à l'approche de la Terreur.

[with their pages faked and torn, with names erased, made unreadable, disguised or replaced by signs, with places and dates falsified after the event, give off a whiff of the sinister atmosphere in which banking operations were conducted on the eve of the Terror.']⁴⁰

These papers included letters to Peter Thellusson, and no doubt he acted also in concert with the Vandenyvers and others, but that does not make him unique. There were plenty of other financiers in London with French connections - David André, Van Nottens and Bourdieu, Chollet et Bourdieu are examples - and there is no obvious explanation why Thellusson should have become *the* repository for emigrant money. Boyd, Ker et Cie, which did have offices in Paris and London, is a better model for Tellsons, but the will made the Thellusson family notorious and invited ingenious explanations.⁴¹

In fact it is surprising how few mentions Thellussons receive in the histories of the emigration and in the best known memoirs of emigrants.⁴² They took no part in the movement to relieve the French clergy which was headed by Burke and Eardley Wilmot, and though Peter Isaac was on the Committee for the Relief of Refugees both Laity and Clergy, formed in September 1792, along with the family friend George Norman, its activities are less well recorded than Wilmot's Committee.⁴³

It has also been suggested that when Pitt proposed to raid the unclaimed dividends at the Bank, Thellusson was among the most forceful protestors because some belonged to emigrants. It seems, however, that many belonged to creditors under assignments in bankruptcy. As merchant bankers Thellussons regularly found themselves acting as assignees, and that, along with the concern of the trading community at the risk to investor confidence Pitt's action posed, is quite sufficient to explain their opposition.⁴⁴ They did, however, feature in one dramatic episode of the Revolution. Thieves stole Madame du Barry's jewels while she was at a ball, fled to England to sell them, found themselves unmasked and fled again. She began the tedious and expensive process of recovering the jewels from the custody of an English bank, making four visits to London in all, each one quite open and public and taking every precaution against being considered an emigrant, yet she ended out of pocket and still bereft of her jewels.⁴⁵

The visit of such a celebrity was naturally a cause for junketing among the exiles and Thellusson was one who gave a dinner in her honour. Given that her travels were watched with intense suspicion by government agents, it was folly on her part to help the emigrant Duc de Rohan-Chabot remove his money from France. Thus compromised, and her lover de Brissac having already become a victim of the mob, she would have done well to stay in London but she went home, was arrested and after the usual travesty of a trial, guillotined.[46] Among her papers was a letter from P.I. Thellusson asking to be put in funds to prosecute her law suit, either via Geneva or Berne: with unconscious prevision of his family's own experiences at law he wrote, `dans tous les pays lès procès coûtent; mais, celui-ci, ils sont ruineuses[in every country law suits are expensive, but here they are ruinous]'.[47]

The luckless Vandenyvers went to the guillotine with their most illustrious client, victims of a vendetta on the part of the prosecutor Héron (himself a failed banker in Marseilles), who exploited the paranoia of the Terror and the stored up hatred of the people for the *agioteurs* and bankers. Much of the information against her was collected by her implacable and unhinged pursuer George Grieve, who had once been articled to Peter Thellusson.[48]

As the Vandenyvers' fate shows, bankers had become violently unpopular with the revolutionary regime. A few years earlier the Comte de Bruny had railed against the ramp of the international moneymen:

`without allegiance, without bond, it has all countries for fatherland, or to speak better it has none, it governs them all as far as it can; and since M. Necker especially, it intrudes upon us considerably in administrative affairs and even substitutes itself for the service of *la finance*.'[49] These attacks intensified as the *assignats* plummeted. One critic blamed the state of the finances on a `Club of 1789', naming Vandenvyers along with Greffulhe, Montz, Boyd et Ker, Grenus, Haller and Mallet, and while the Vandenyvers were in prison Fabre d'Eglantine denounced `les banquiers cosmopolité de Paris [the international bankers of Paris]' to the Convention as agents of Pitt.[50] Those who were still in France and could make their escape did so - Grenus to Switzerland, Boyd to England - while others like Montz were imprisoned. The Terror did not destroy international banking but it brought down the old order, shattering the `Protestant International' which had dominated it for a century.[51]

As a result, whatever gains they may have made from emigrant deposits, Thellussons suffered badly from the loss of large parts of that network of contacts, correspondents and connections on which their international dealings depended, as well as putting a stop to the direct trade between England and France.

The Terror came very close to depriving them of their French kinsmen as well. The Thellusson brothers had prudently resigned their commissions in 1790 but otherwise made no attempt to accommodate themselves to the new regime, presumably relying on their Swiss nationality and the fact that they were no longer in business to keep them from harm. But in the Terror it was not enough to be passive and neutral: the fearsome Law of Suspects put everyone at risk of `incivisme' and none more so than *ci-devant* aristocrats with relations in enemy countries. At the end of October 1793 Paul Louis and Pierre Germain were arrested at Dormans, an estate on the Marne which they had bought together in 1790, and taken to La Force. Paul Louis was a childless widower, his wife Amélia de la Frete, daughter of the receiver-general of taxes for Lorraine, having recently died after three years of marriage, and Pierre Germain was still unmarried.[52] The third brother, Jean Isaac, was taken up at the same time, with his wife and three children, Aimeé (born 1788), Antoinette-Marguerite-Jean (`Jenny' for short) born on Christmas Eve 1790 and a boy, Amable, barely three months old. Jean Isaac's parents-in-law were imprisoned with them, all on the pretext that a cousin, Girardot de Vermenoux, had emigrated, but really as part of a general round up of bankers and their relatives.[53] As they languished in La Force watching others come and go, occasionally to freedom, more often to the scaffold, they must have regretted not joining Peter's family in England.

The coup of Thermidor which ended Robespierre's reign of terror probably saved them from death, for all the representations of the Genevan envoy on their behalf had been ineffective until then. Surprisingly, they chose to stay in France where, despite considerable losses, they were still men of fortune. Paul Louis soon remarried, in August 1795 to Amicie Augustine, a daughter of the Marquis de Coulaincourt.[54] When Pierre Germain followed suit his choice may have raised some eyebrows in the family. Jeanne Rosalie de Reghat had divorced her first husband, the emigrant Count de Lascaris de Vintimille, in December 1793, despite which she had been arrested, tried, condemned and just given her final haircut for the guillotine when the Terror ended. She had something of a reputation for `moeurs legères'[lax morals], hardly unusual in republican France, and was pregnant when they married in October 1796, delivering the first of their four daughters before the year ended.[55]

So, precariously, the Thellussons survived the revolution in France and by and large maintained their social position. The Genevan branch however, was less fortunate. The tide of revolution rolled in upon Geneva, where Rousseau had prepared the way, and in 1794 Jacobins swept away the old oligarchy, driving its leading notables into exile. Jean François Thellusson was among them, and his was an impoverished exile, for payment of his French annuities had ceased. What happened to Isaac Louis and his son is not clear: he was an elderly man by this time and perhaps they kept out of the way at Gara, though his son-in-law Micheli was sentenced to death in his absence.[56] By the end of the eighteenth century however, the Thellussons of Geneva were at a very low ebb.

3. War

In January 1793, a few days after the French had killed their king, they went to war with England and the Long War, as it came to be called, lasted, with two short interludes, until Waterloo eighteen years later.

War with France was bad news for a house with major interests in the West

Indies and in trade with France. Ships they had insured, like the *Malabar*, carrying a French cargo from the Ile de France to Toulon, were detained when they put into ports of nations at war with the Republic[57] and agency business for French traders was wiped out.[58] Fortunately they still had a wide spread of activities; one law suit of 1792, for instance, shows that the house had advanced at least £13,000 to a Wiltshire clothier, John Ainslie of Devizes.[59]

The war cost Britain dear in money as well as men, for as well as raising funds for her own armies and navies she became the paymaster to her continental allies on an unprecedented scale, not so much Napoleon's 'nation of shopkeepers' as a nation of moneylenders. Low taxation, especially of property, was almost a constitutional right in eighteenth century England. No Chancellor dared raise the Land Tax, the chief instrument of direct taxation, above its accepted 'wartime' level of 4/- in the £ and even with all the indirect taxes and imposts upon conspicuous consumption that Pitt managed to impose, it was inevitable as well as traditional that large loans must immediately be raised, especially as peacetime economies had left the armed forces in no condition for fighting.

Granted the assumption which Pitt and most informed observers shared, that the war would be a short one, an extensive resort to loans was a perfectly defensible strategy. If taxes old and new could be made to yield 30% of the embattled country's needs that would be enough, or so it was thought, to service the growing national debt and prove that the present generation had borne its share of the burden which it would pass down to its successors.[60] Even though foreign investment in the Funds had largely dried up there were ample savings waiting to be tapped. A Chancellor of the Exchequer might in theory issue a direct invitation to the public to subscribe to his loan, publishing the terms and accepting those who came forward until it was filled up, but not since William III's time had that approach actually been tried, for the disadvantages were very real. It was administratively burdensome to have to deal directly with numerous individuals; there was the risk of subscribers defaulting; the Chancellor would have to guess what terms he should offer; and, most serious of all,

96

if he guessed wrong he might fail to find enough takers and so give the public credit a shock that would shake its very foundations.

Not surprisingly, Chancellors preferred to deal through intermediaries, the loan contractors. The contractors were consortia of City men - merchants, bankers, bill brokers, stockjobbers - headed by a single individual, and the Chancellor might either deal with a single consortium direct or, as he usually preferred, might make his requirements known - the amount he sought and the stocks he would offer in exchange - and invite tenders, thereby injecting an element of competition.[61]

However, when Pitt sought to raise a modest loan of £4½ million to finance a war which had begun barely a year after he had airily declared that 'there never was a time in the history of this country, when, from the situation of Europe, we might more reasonably expect fifteen years of peace, than we may at the present moment',[62] conditions were distinctly unpropititious. A sudden downturn in trade, largely the result of an over-extension of credit to merchants trading overseas, had sent the Funds plummeting, bankruptcies soaring, and country banks and many merchants plunging deep into trouble.[63] The City greeted the Chancellor's offer with no enthusiasm. Only one group was prepared to deal and that was the Thellussons and their friends. Pitt's attempts to drum up some competition were vain and the terms of the loan naturally reflected the weakness of his position, for he was unable to persuade the contractors to take 4 or 5% stock instead of the 3% consols that they always preferred and had to offer them £138-16s of stock for every £100 lent, a rate of £4-3s-4d%. Since Pitt was severely criticised in Parliament for these terms and made only a lame defence, it may be thought that the Thellussons struck a very good bargain, but they took a big risk under the prevailing circumstances and if they did make more than the 4% profit that was usually deemed fair they deserved it.[64]

In fact the contractor's game was always a risky one. His group had to be prepared to pay over the loan in large instalments at rather short intervals by banker's draft. In exchange they received subscription receipts ('scrip') for the stock which they were allotted and these could be sold on the market; indeed being only partly paid for they were cheap to deal in and therefore popular with speculators, though towards the end of the loan period, as more instalments were paid, they became more expensive and rather less attractive. The contractor's profit came from selling the scrip at a higher price than he had paid and this required him to exercise careful judgment about market trends, for if he held onto his allocation too long in the hope of a rise he might find himself unable to shift it at any profit at all, as eventually happened disastrously to Walter Boyd.[65]

Most of the contractor's group usually preferred to limit their speculation by making up a list of persons who agreed in advance to take part of their allocation. The proportion retained by the principal varied widely, with bankers often anxious to oblige their customers by offering them a chance to participate in the loan while merchants and jobbers usually preferred to keep a higher proportion for themselves. Outside the contractor's own lists, some stock was always reserved for the directors of the Bank of England and their chief cashier, Abraham Newland, who made his fortune by this means.

The loan for 1794 was much bigger (£11 million), there was competition and Thellussons were outbid by a consortium led by Godschall Johnson. But they were still very keen to be involved in public finance and soon became caught up in the ambitious projects of Walter Boyd. Boyd was a *parvenu* in the world of international finance and the first stage of his career had been abruptly ended by the revolution in France, which forced him to flee and ruined his bank, Boyd, Ker et Cie of Paris.[66] Setbacks never daunted Boyd, who was resilient, full of self-confidence, a born taker of calculated risks, in fact the very antithesis of the London banker of the old school, that 'man of serious manners, plain apparel, the steadiest conduct and a rigid observer of formalities'.[67]

Boyd lost no time in establishing a banking house in London, using capital supplied by his new partner Paul Benfield. Benfield was not a man many would have cared for as a partner - an arrogant nabob with a disreputable past and an unlikeable character - but he was a man with ready money who was content for the most part to give Boyd his head and count the profits.[68]   Soon Boyd was approached by the Austrian government to raise a loan on the London money market and Thellussons were willing to put up some of the money.   It looked a reasonably good risk but the French advanced into the Netherlands even as the negotiations were being concluded and the very day after the Emperor signed the loan agreement his troops were routed at the battle of Turcoing, imperilling the only real security for the loan, the revenues of the Austrian Netherlands. The whole thing stalled and Thellussons pulled out, selling at a 4% loss.[69]

There was no rupture with Boyd, who needed all his backers. He did not abandon the project and eventually, at the end of the year, reached an agreement with Pitt by which his group would undertake the Austrian loan along with a new British one, a total borrowing of £22 million.   The powerful consortium he assembled for this purpose dominated the loan business during the next three years and besides the Thellussons included Robarts, Curtis & Co., the Goldsmid brothers (perhaps the first specialist bill brokers), the merchant firm of John and George Ward and three sets of stockjobbers, Rawson Aislabie, E. P. Salomons and Solomon Salamons.[70] Boyd himself was prepared to take on almost anything which would entrench their position and by accommodating the government in some rather unorthodox financial transactions he laid a strong claim to Pitt's favour and support.[71]

Three successive loans were awarded to Boyd's group, establishing the practice that the loan contractors of one year had a prescriptive right to the next loan if it was launched within the year, while they still had substantial holdings of stock on their hands; given the scale of war expenditure, including huge subsidies to the continental allies, the government usually needed more than a yearly loan. Naturally this monopoly of lucrative opportunities created great jealousy among those excluded from the magic circle, and Pitt provoked particular anger by seriously mishandling the 1796 loan, first encouraging tenders then allowing himself to be persuaded by Boyd that the existing contractors should be given preference. The other would-be contractors forced the setting up of a Commons select committee, whose 'report exposed some of the *arcana* of the loan business to the public gaze.[72] It showed for example the make up of the `lists' for each member of the consortium and the proportion of the loan to be found by each member: Boyd Benfield £5,709,000, Robarts Curtis and Goldsmids £2,977,000 each, Thellussons £1,141,000, E. P. Salomons £1,711,000, S. Salomons and Wards each £685,000, Rawson Aislabie £342,000.

It would be unwise to infer from the fact that Thellussons were not among the biggest contributors that their resources were correspondingly modest, since merchants were always likely to have a wider range of other commitments than more specialised financial houses. Moreover the house and the family kept the greater part of their allocation: £430,000 was in Peter's own name, £445,000 in those of George and Charles, of which the firm held £400,000. The other £266,000 (only 23% of the total) was for fifteen others, including the sons of John Cossart, who were down for £2,000 (the smallest sum on the list), the banker I.L. André (£5,000), Charles Teissier (£5,000) and the firm of Cornwall, Smalley (£50,000).[73]

It is impossible to assess the profitability of the loan business but it certainly *was* profitable. Both the Goldsmids and Robarts Curtis are said to have made their fortunes in it, and the clamour from the disappointed would-be bidders reflects their expectations.[74] The controversial 1796 loan may well have been the most profitable of all, for Pitt thoughtlessly gave further ammunition to his critics by choosing the day following the loan agreement to deliver a message from the king indicating willingness to enter peace negotiations, with the entirely predictable result that the loan premium shot up from seven to thirteen percent. There was also a strong suspicion that the Commissioners for the Reduction of the National Debt had altered their own operations in such a way as to suit the interests of the contractors.[75]

If the 1796 loan is any guide, Peter was still actively involved in that side of business. It was his list, and the bulk of the £1,141,000 that had to be found was split almost evenly between him and his sons. He was known to be a very wealthy man himself and the prominence of the family and the firm in loan contracting in addition

100

to their more familiar leading place in international trade had cemented their reputation as one of the great City houses.[76] Peter Thellusson had achieved great things with his modest initial capital: it now remained for him to ensure that they did not die with him.[77]

NOTES

1. Published in 1859.

2. Ain, *Les Thellusson* pp.113 - 22.

3. *Ibid.*, pp.123 - 5.

4. *Ibid.*, pp. 127 - 8.

5. *Ibid.*, pp.131 - 40.

6. *Ibid.*, pp.130, 283 - 4.

7. *Ibid.*, pp.83 - 111.

8. Lüthy, *Banque Protestante*, vol.II, p.528, and *cf.* p. 495. M. Girod de l'Ain ignores him completely, referring to Isaac's nine children but listing only eight (*Les Thellusson*, pp.57 - 9). Others, e.g. Haag, *France Protestante*, vol.9, pp.364-5, confuse him with Isaac Louis.

9. Riley, *International Government Finance*, pp.35 - 40.

10. Lüthy, *Banque Protestante*, vol.II, p.511; R.M. Jennings and A.P. Trout, *The Tontine: from the Reign of Louis XIV to the French Revolutionary Era* (Homewood, Ill., 1982), pp.61-9.

11. Lüthy, *Banque Protestante*, vol.II, pp.464 - 590.

12. *Ibid.*, vol.II, pp.469 - 72.

13. Necker has his defenders (e.g. D. Harris, French Finances and the American War of Independence, *Journal of Modern History* 48 (1976), 233-58 at 242- 3) but Riley's verdict that `France paid returns that exceeded any reasonable estimate of what was necessary' (*International Government Finance*, p. 174) seems convincing.

14. Lüthy, *Banque Protestante*, vol. II, pp.474 - 92; Jennings and Trout, *The Tontine*, pp.57-61; D.R. Weir, Tontines, Public Finance and Revolution in France and England, *Journal of Economic History* 49 (1989), 95-124. The Genevan investment in *rentes* (1763 - 88) was 130 million lt.

15. J. Ehrman, *The Younger Pitt*, vol. I (London, 1969), pp.483 - 92.

16. *Thellusson v. Fletcher* (1793) 1 Esp. 73; *Thellusson v. Bewick* (1793) 1 Esp. 77.

17. G.V. Taylor, The Paris Bourse on the Eve of the French Revolution, 1781-1789, *American History Review* 67 (1961-2), 951-72, at 972.

18. Riley, *International Government Finance*, pp. 36 - 40, 52 - 6, 90 - 4.

19. Taylor, *Paris Bourse*; Antonetti, *Une Maison de Banque*, pp. 57 - 83, 143-50. The most detailed studies are by J. Bouchary, *La Marché au Changes de Paris à la Fin du XVIII Siècle* (Paris, 1937) and *Les Manieurs d'Argent à Paris à la Fin du XVIIIe Siècle* (3 vols., Paris, 1939-43).

20. Lüthy, *Banque Protestante*, vol. II, pp.414 - 17, 622.

21. Bouchary, *La Marché au Changes*, pp.65-75. Operations were also concerted with Poppé in Hamburg, probably a relation of the Christian Poppé naturalised with Thellusson.

22. Lüthy, *Banque Protestante*, vol. II, p.625. 23. Antonetti, *Une Maison de Banque*, p.36. Greffulhe's rise as a clerk in an Amsterdam counting house over which he gradually won complete control echoes Fonblanque's complaint about Thellusson.

24. *Ibid.*, pp.99 - 102.

25. Bouchary, *Les Manieurs d'Argent*, pp.143 - 73.

26. Bouchary, *La Marché au Changes*, p. 37.

27. J. Lhomer, *Le Banquier Perregaux et sa Fille la Duchesse de Raguse* (1926 edn., Paris). The English firm of Herries & Co. established themselves in Paris in 1787 to play this same role.

28. The *assignats* were 'a necessary instrument in the administrative revolution' detected by J.F. Bosher, *French Finances, 1770 - 95, from Business to Bureaucracy* (Cambridge, 1970), at p. 273. They became legal tender in April 1790 and the sole currency in April 1793. More than 40 billions were issued and as they became worthless many *rentiers* were ruined. M.D. Bordo and E.N. White, A Tale of Two Currencies: British and French Finance during the Napoleonic Wars, *Journal of Economic History* 51 (1991), 303-16.

29. Lüthy, *Banque Protestante*, vol.II, pp. 558 - 9.

30. Bouchary, *La Marché au Changes*, pp. 67 - 8; Antonetti, *Une Maison de Banque*, pp. 209 - 20. For a glimpse of Thellusson's involvement in other speculations se G. Morris, *A Diary of the French Revolution* (1939 edn, New York), vol. I.

31. J.L. Vidalenc, *Les Emigrés Français, 1789 - 1825* (Caen, 1963), pp.20 - 33.

32. In addition to Vidalenc, there is a modern account by M. Weiner, *The French Exiles* (London, 1959). E. Wilkinson, *The French Emigrés in England, 1792 - 1802* (Oxford B. Litt thesis, 1952) is the most detailed study of the emigrants in England. See also K. Carpenter, *Refugees of the French Revolution: Emigrés in London, 1789-1802* (Basingstoke and London, 1999).

33. Some of the shifts they were reduced to are described in L. Saint-Ogen, Les Métiers de l'Emigration, *Nouvelle Revue* 32ns (1905), 315 - 24.

34. *Chroniques et Legendes des Rues de Paris* (Paris, 1864), pp. 308 - 10.

35. *Law Magazine* 14 (1838) pp.38-44. See also 'NHR' in *Notes & Queries* (1859) 2nd s., vol. 8. Neither gives a source.

36. *The Farington Diary*, vol. VI, p.2088. The source was M. Barroneau, of Huguenot stock. Chalie's father had business dealings with Thellusson (East India Company Stock Ledger L/AG/14/J/23 f. 849; Bank of England Stock Ledger AC 27/502 p. 2145).

37. *Ibid.*, vol.XI, p. 3860. Watts was uncle to John Constable. He had been clerk to the great wine merchant Ben Kenton, a charity boy made good, who died leaving legacies to twenty-four

London charities and £200,000 to Watts. Kenton's daughter had died `of a decline' when he discouraged Watts' suit to her and he made it up to Watts in this way.

38. Sir E. Brydges, *The Biographical Peerage of Ireland* (London, 1817), *sub* Rendlesham.

39. *A Tale of Two Cities* (1970 edn., London), p.54. See also pp. 83, 242, 264.

40. Lüthy, *Banque Protestante*, vol.II, p.634.

41. When the British government wished to send money abroad for counter-revolutionary activities they used Boyd Benfield rather than Thellussons: E. Sparrow, *Secret Service. British Agents in France 1792-1815* (Woodbridge, 1999), pp.55-6.

42. The standard older histories are unrevealing on this point. There are references in the *Memoirs* of H.P. Danloux, pp. 199, 271, 280; others are cited in Keeton, *Thellusson Will.*

43. Wilkinson, *French Emigrés*, pp. 117 - 52. The Thellussons did not even subscribe to the clergy relief fund (PRO T 93/8).

44. Sir J. Clapham, *The Bank of England, a History* (2 vols., Cambridge, 1944), vol. I, pp.187-91; J. Hoppit, *Risk and Failure*, p.39. Lists of dividends long unclaimed are in *HL Sessional Papers* vol.81, no.4284. The only Thellussons who feature are deceased members of the Amsterdam branch as owners of South Sea stock.

45. The numerous biographies of the du Barry all cover this episode, and C. St. André, *Madame du Barry* (Paris, 1909) prints some of the documents.

46. The proceedings are detailed in J. Bouchary, *Les Manieurs d'Argent*, pp. 147 - 64.

47. Printed in St. André, *Madame du Barry*, at p.470. Grieve scrawled across the letter `C'est un des plus forts banquiers de Londres, neveu de Thellusson ancien avoué de Necker, et grand ennemie de la Révolution [He is one of the biggest bankers in London, nephew of Thellusson, former partner of Necker, and a great enemy of the revolution]'. It would be unwise to read much into his description since he denounced indiscriminately all those connected with du Barry.

48. J.G. Alger, *Englishmen in the French Revolution* (2nd edn., London, 1889), pp.185-6; *Gents. Mag.* 60, (1790), 1216.

49. Taylor, *Paris Bourse*, at 964. The firms involved in the royal finances were, for the most part, quite distinct from the sort of bankers Bruny had in mind: J. Bouvier and H. Germain-Martin, *Finances et Financiers de l'Ancien Régime* (Paris, 1964), pp.114-26; G. Chaussinand-Nogaret, *Gens de Finance au XVIIIe Siècle* (Paris, 1972).

50. Bouchary, *La Marché au Changes*, pp.66, 74 - 5.

51. Antonetti, *Une Maison de Banque*, p. 60; Lüthy, *Banque Protestante*, vol. II, pp. 727 - 33.

52. Ain, *Les Thellusson*, p.128.

53. *Ibid.*, pp. 140 - 6.

54. *Ibid.*, pp. 128 - 30.

55. *Ibid.*, pp. 283 - 4.

56. Lüthy, *Banque Protestante*, vol. II, p.204. Micheli's son Jules was at Brodsworth in 1794: *Hervey Journals*, p.406.

57. *Thellusson v. Cosling* (1803) 4 Esp. 266. *Thellusson v. Bell, The Times*, 22 Dec.1802, seems to be the same suit.

58. In `*The Rebecca'* (1804) S.C. Rob. 102, George Thellusson can be seen making a belated and unsuccessful effort to enforce a bottomry bond, an action he had begun in 1792 as agent of M. Guerin of Marseilles.

59. *Hanson and others v. Thellusson* (1793), PRO C 12/957/31.

60. P.K. O'Brien, *English Government Revenue, 1793 - 1815* (Cambridge University D.Phil., 1967); P. Mathias and P.K. O'Brien, Taxation in Britain and France, 1715 - 1810, *Journal of Economic History* (1976), 601 - 40; Ehrman, *The Younger Pitt*, vol.I, pp. 247 - 56, 273 - 5.

61. O'Brien, *English Government Revenue*, examines the loans in detail. The terms, but not always the contractors, are in J.J. Grellier, *The Terms of All the Loans* (London, 1812) and W. Newmarch, *The Loans Raised by Mr. Pitt during the First French War, 1793 - 1801* (London, 1855).

62. Ehrman, *The Younger Pitt*, vol.II, p.52.

63. Sinclair, *History of the Public Revenue*, vol.II, pp. 135 - 48 and appendix p.61; T.S. Ashton, *Economic Fluctuations in England, 1700 - 1800* (Oxford, 1959), especially pp. 132 - 4, 168 - 9; J. Hoppit, Financial Crises in 18th Century England, *Economic History Review* (2nd s.) 39 (1986), pp.39 - 58. Twenty-three country banks failed and Pitt had to arrange an unprecedented advance of £5 million in exchequer bills to tide needy merchants over the crisis.

64. Newmarch, *Loans Raised by Pitt; Parl. Reg.* 35 (1793) (H of C), cols. 156 - 63.

65. Report of the Select Committee into the Circumstances of the Loan, *House of Commons Journals* 51 (1797), 309: The loan process is described in S.R. Cope, The Goldsmids and the Development of the London Money Market during the Napoleonic Wars, *Economica* (ns.)9 (1942), 180 - 206 and The Stock Exchange Revisited, *Economica* (ns.)45 (1978), 1 - 21.

66. Cope, *Walter Boyd*.

67. Hardcastle, *Banks and Bankers*, p.22.

68. Cope, *Walter Boyd*, pp.37 - 41.

69. *Ibid.*, pp.46 - 59; K. Helleiner, *The Imperial Loans* (Oxford, 1965), pp.12 - 13.

70. Cope, *Walter Boyd*, pp.57 - 9.

71. *Ibid.*, pp.71 - 80.

72. *Ibid.*, pp.80 - 91; *Select Committee Report, 1797.*

73. *Select Committee Report, 1797* qq. 432 - 9, 461 - 5 and appendix 2. There is no mention of

the eldest son, Peter Isaac, although he was a partner in the firm. Perhaps he was trying to emphasise to Pitt his withdrawal from its operations (see *infra*).

74. Cope, *Goldsmids*, 191; J. Francis, *Chronicles of the Stock Exchange* (London, 1855), p.180.

75. Cope, *Walter Boyd*, pp.86 - 8.

76. Their bookkeeper, Henry Churchill, subscribed £40,000 to the 1796 loan and the firm was said to have made a profit of £83,000 in 1795 : *Farington Diary*, vol.8, p.3082.

77. Peter's own reputation was such that as late as 1880 he was referred to (misleadingly) in a speech to the American Bankers' Association as 'the great English private banker': F. Redlich, *The Molding of American Banking* (reprint, 1968, New York and London), p.402 n.88.

CHAPTER 6

PROPERTY, POLITICS AND PEERAGE

1. Property

Thellusson was only fifty-six and in good health when he retired from the family firm in 1791, but according to what he later told his sister, he had only kept working for as long as he did to ensure his family's prosperity.[1]

Winding up a partnership was often a very slow process, especially when the business was to be continued, which is why John Cossart, who was also retiring, very sensibly gave his sons authority to make a negotiated settlement if one had not been concluded in his lifetime.[2] There had been no distribution of profits during the seven year term and Peter was allowed his share on a calculation of monies due to the firm, undertaking to repay the proportion attributable to debts that turned out to be uncollectable.[3]

His retirement from active participation in the firm certainly did not mean that he lost interest in business ventures, and apart from his role in tendering for the loans, he was also in the sugar refining business, as is apparent from his will, which gave to George Lear and William Handasyde twenty-five guineas apiece for a ring 'if they shall still be in partnership with me at the time of my death.'[4] The Lears were second generation refiners and George Lear and Company was operating from Great Garden Street, Whitechapel in 1781. By 1791 Lear had been joined by Handasyde at Brewhouse Lane, Wapping. Handasyde's name disappears soon after 1800 but two distinct concerns, Lear & Co. and George Lear, continued at the Wapping and Whitechapel addresses respectively.[5] Lear, grandfather of the landscape artist and comic versifier Edward Lear, was a prosperous man by then, with a house at Leytonstone in Essex and a daughter married to the eldest son of the big banker William Curtis. By 1811 the Wapping establishment had become Lear, Curtis & Co., the Whitechapel one Lear and Cobden, and so they remain until a final appearance (but strangely as Lear and Handasyde) in 1821.[6] Thellusson's role in the firm, chiefly providing capital, ended soon after he made his will; a few months afterwards Lear & Handasyde gave him a bond for £49,000, presumably representing his share of the profits, and this was gradually paid off down to the end of 1802.[7] He may well have had other interests which do not show up in directories, and from which he disengaged himself some time before making his will.

Thellusson probably spent his retirement rather quietly, at Plaistow and in Yorkshire. He had no ambition to go into society, apparently no interest in sport or the fine arts, no desire to figure strongly in politics or church affairs. But he was certainly not withdrawing from this world to prepare his soul for the next, for he told his neighbour William Wells, a shipbuilder and art collector with a house at Bickley, that he would give £200,000 to be restored to youth, even as a hackney coachman.[8] What his money *could* buy was country estates for his sons, and he had already made at least two unsuccessful bids, one (in 1789) of £29,000 for a house near Bath, the other for a Yorkshire mansion belonging to the Duke of York. The king had bought Thornville Royal, `a superb structure' dominating the hamlet of Aston Mauleverer, near Knaresborough, for his second son out of the revenues of the bishopric of Osnabruck, which had been accumulating during his minority. Like his elder brother, Frederick was a prodigal and usually unsuccessful gambler who must have found Thellusson's offer (reportedly £105,000) tempting, but he refused it, only to sell to Colonel Thornton not long afterwards.[9] Whether Thellusson was particularly attracted to Yorkshire, a county with which his family had no connection, or whether he was simply on the lookout for suitable estates wherever they were located is not clear, but he did buy a Yorkshire estate a few years later.

Not far from Doncaster is the village of Brodsworth. According to the historian of the district it was

'one of the most picturesque and beautiful of the many villages situated in this limestone tract. The ground is broken and uneven. In such a spot a hall, a church, a parsonage and a group of neat and cleanly cottages, must always have formed a pleasing picture of an English village, of dependance, protection and comfort. But the natural beauties have been aided by the hand of taste while Brodsworth was the seat of the noble house of Kinnoul.'[10]

The Kinnouls were scarcely rooted in the place, having only bought it in 1713, and the ninth earl (1758 - 87) spent little time there. He was for many years the political drudge of the Pelhams and after the Duke of Newcastle resigned in 1762 Kinnoul spent his unaccustomed leisure in planting thousands of trees on his Scottish estate and indulging his taste for classical literature.[11] Brodsworth became the country home of his younger brother, made archbishop of York a few months before Newcastle lost his command of patronage, and it was the taste of this 'sensible, worldly man, but much addicted to his bottle' that enhanced the beauties of mansion and grounds. The ninth earl being childless, the archbishop's son succeeded to the earldom in 1787 and whether he was short of money (despite marrying the daughter and co-heiress of a lord mayor) or whether Brodsworth was superfluous to requirements, he sold it ('one of the largest properties ever disposed of together') and into Hunter's Augustan Eden glided the rich foreigner Peter Thellusson.[12]

According to Francis Hargrave it cost him £140,000 and over the next few years Thellusson was busy trying to enlarge it by small purchases.[13] Brodsworth seems to have been intended for his heir, even though Peter Isaac had already set himself up with an estate in Suffolk, and other estates were being sought for the younger brothers. By their accounts he was touchingly anxious to find the right places; one that would let Charles indulge his passion for hunting, one where George could fish; touching, but perhaps also discomforting, a little reminiscent of John Jarndyce presenting Esther with a Bleak House of his own choosing.[14]

In fact Peter did not succeed in making further purchases, although in 1795 he tried to buy Park Place, Henley from Lady Aylesbury. Made picturesque with stones from Reading Abbey, it was a favourite meeting place for Gray, Hume and old Horace Walpole, who snobbishly wrote that `I am not sorry that Thellusson has withdrawn - Lord Malmesbury [another would- be buyer] I hope is no banker and does not propose to buy the most beautiful villa in England to make money of it'.[15]

This unfulfilled intention to purchase two more mansion houses left Thellusson's personal estate fortuitously larger than he intended it to be.

2. Parliament

Thellusson, not being a natural born subject of His Majesty, was debarred from sitting in the House of Commons, but there was nothing to prevent his sons from doing so if they wished, and even from a purely business standpoint the right of franking letters which an MP possessed was worth something; in the 1790s forty banker - MPs were reckoned to save £30,000 a year in this way and abuse of the franking privilege had to be curbed by statute after `a long and desultory conversation [in which] almost every member present repeatedly delivered his sentiments'.[16] It was then limited to ten letters sent and fifteen received a day, still a useful perquisite. Other material rewards were less obvious. An MP was advantageously placed to obtain directorships with the Bank, the East India Company and the insurance companies, and he was better able to seek favours from ministers, whether posts in the public service for relations, government contracts for his firm or honours for his family. Plenty of merchants and bankers found it worthwhile to become MPs, though a few, driven there in the first place by vanity, quickly got bored with the whole business. Among 558 members who made up the House of Commons elected in 1796 were 114 merchants, bankers and industrialists, no fewer than 66 of them describing themselves as bankers, including many of the leading houses - Robarts Curtis and the Smiths for example.[17] To judge from the record, few were motivated by strong political convictions.

110

Thanks to the smallness of the electorate in some constituencies and the understandable venality of many voters in the larger ones, anyone with money could become an MP in the unreformed House of Commons.[18] Pitt had introduced moderate reform bills in 1782 and 1783 but whatever prospect of success existed, and it was slender enough, was dashed by the progress of the revolution in France; William Windham caught the mood of most MPs with his rhetorical question: `what would recommend you to rebuild your house in the hurricane season?'[19], and the house was promptly barred and shuttered against the rather feeble tempests the reformers could whistle up.

Until Curwen's Act of 1809 it was even possible for `pocket boroughs' to be openly advertised for sale in the newspapers, so it was not difficult for Peter Isaac Thellusson to find himself a seat at Midhurst, a classic `rotten borough' described by the radical T. H. B. Oldfield:

`This is a borough, which has the privilege of sending two members to parliament, although there is not a single house standing within the limits of it. The right of election is in one hundred and twenty burgage holds, the situation of which is distinctly marked at present by the position of a large stone upon each of them. There is no part of the town of Midhurst built upon these tenures; they were the property of the late Lord Viscount Montagu, who made, at the time of an election, a temporary assignment of a part of them, either to some of his domestics or particular friends, for the purpose of having those members returned that he should nominate.'[20]

The Montagu trustees had sold the borough to Lord Egremont for 40,000 guineas and for an unknown sum Peter Isaac was able to procure the seat held by Egremont's dissolute brother Charles Wyndham, being returned on 17th January 1795.[21]

It is unlikely that the new member had any political philosophy beyond that of most businessman-MPs, which was to support Pitt's government except when it trod on commercial toes, and to do so mostly in silence unless he had particular expertise in the subject under debate. Thellusson however soon had to make himself heard, because his brother George had become involved in a political row.   The controversy was the sad and sordid aftermath of a brilliant feat of arms, the capture of Martinique in 1794 by a combined military and naval operation directed by Sir Thomas Dundas, Sir Charles Grey and Sir John Jervis.   The rich town of St. Pierre, its warehouses stuffed full of island produce, had fallen almost without resistance and the commanders made arrangements for prize money for the deserving troops, marines and sailors in lieu of plunder.[22]

These arrangements, and particularly two proclamations issued in May 1794, were strongly attacked by the West India planters and merchants as going beyond the scope of those adopted during previous rounds of the favourite war game of filching sugar islands. They feared that this would present the French with an irresistible temptation to retaliate in kind on English islands when they were in the ascendant - which given the havoc wrought by disease upon the English forces and the reluctance of the British government adequately to reinforce them was all too likely to occur. The Judge- Advocate General, Sir William Scott, advised that the proclamations *were* indeed unjustifiable and to the great disgust of the commanders they were rescinded, but that was not the end of the story.[23]

Sir Charles Grey's son was a rising Whig politician and Jervis too had friends who would not let his treatment pass unnoticed, but in any case the West Indians were not satisfied and pressed for a more public disavowal of the commanders' actions through a motion for papers.[24]   In the discussion that followed Grey attacked a memorandum presented by George Thellusson as chairman of a meeting of the owners of confiscated property: `who that Mr. Thellusson is he did not know, but his memorandum breathed nothing but direct and positive falsehood'. Peter Isaac weakly defended his brother but when he tried to get the affidavit of a French merchant, Malespine, placed before the House on 2nd June as a prelude to the debate on a motion officially condemning the proclamations, it became apparent that the West Indians had overreached themselves.[25]

For once Pitt and Fox were united against them in `a situation inexpressibly ludicrous',[26] since the commanders had made an effective counter- attack, alleging that behind the complaints lay the discreditable self-interest of British merchants with investments in Martinique threatened by the confiscations and composition. Malespine's character was strongly impugned. Sheridan told the House that G. W. Thellusson 'had been grossly imposed upon',[27] Grey renewed his attack, and all Peter Isaac could say was that his brother 'merely acted as an agent, and was not responsible for the character of Mr Malespine unless it had been notoriously bad; the contrary was the fact, his reputation was good'.[28] The West Indians' petition was voted down by 57 to 19 (the three Smiths, Curtis, William Manning and Thellusson all in the minority) and George was left looking decidedly foolish.[29]

There is nothing to suggest that the Thellussons had a vested interest of their own in Martinique, and they seem to have avoided the disastrous entanglement in Sto. Domingo that embroiled some British businessmen[30] but they undoubtedly suffered when Grenada was devastated by an insurrection in 1795 which was estimated to have resulted in losses of £2.5 to £4.5 million to planters, investors and merchants.[31]
1796 saw a general election, but even by contemporary standards it was a quiet one, with only sixty-six contests.[32] Peter Isaac needed a new seat, since Egremont had sold Midhurst to the Smiths, who would use it in their quest for a peerage, and he asked the Treasury for assistance. They pointed him in the direction of Malmesbury, a snug little place in Wiltshire with 1,000 inhabitants but only thirteen voters, the franchise being confined to the corporation. These votes were controlled by one of the odder borough patrons, an apothecary called Dr. Edmund Wilkins, receiver-general of taxes for the county and consequently a supporter of the government of the day. The disfranchised assistant burgesses put up a candidate and petitioned hopelessly against their exclusion from the poll, but Peter Isaac and Samuel Smith, another of the banking family, became what were quaintly termed 'paying guests' of the remarkable apothecary.[33]

This time all the Thellusson brothers were electioneering. Charles, only twenty-five, contested Evesham, a good chance but no certainty, for this was no pocket borough. Sir John Rushout, bart. was patron `partially', i.e. he could hope to return himself or another as one member, but with 700 electors there was no real management and a candidate must depend upon demagoguery, personal charm or, much the most persuasive, money. In 1790 the opposition had succeeded through Thomas Thompson in capturing one seat, probably at a cost of several thousand pounds, and Thompson and Rushout now stood again. In a sharp contest Thellusson topped the poll with 315 votes to Thompson's 267 and Rushout's 248: only 830 votes were cast in all, compared with 1,199 in 1790 but it must still have been quite a costly affair.[34]

The hardest contest, however, was reserved for George, who rashly accepted the role of a ministry- backed candidate for Southwark, one of the sitting members having prudently retired. It was an internecine contest in that he was related by marriage to both of the other candidates; Henry Thornton was a distant connection through Peter Isaac's wife and George Tierney's sister was married to Abraham Robarts, Charles Thellusson's father-in-law. Thellusson was on good terms with both, having provided Tierney with some modest investments, as Tierney's opponents did not fail to point out, but `Citizen' Tierney was a formidable candidate for such a constituency. Southwark had one of the largest borough electorates in the country, strongly tinged with radicalism, and apart from 1790 elections were invariably contested and usually expensive.[35] Financed entirely by public subscription, campaigning on a slogan of `peace and reform against war and corruption' and supported by the leading radical organisation of the day, the notorious London Corresponding Society, Tierney was a vigorous and confident orator, certainly far better on the platform than either of his City merchant opponents, who combined informally against him. Thornton's position was also strong, both as a sitting member and as having a track record of independence and support for peace. Thellusson was known to be the government's man and shrewdly attended to local issues, opposing the Wapping Dock Bill which threatened Southwark's prosperity. Four days of noisy, boisterous, thoroughly `Eatanswill' polling among an electorate

114

of over 2,000 'scot and lot' voters left Tierney trailing badly, with only 976 votes to Thornton's 1,584 and Thellusson's 1,373, though he had many more 'plumpers', i.e. votes for him alone, where the elector declined to use his second vote.[36]

But in these elections the poll was not always the end of the story. Petitions against the return, alleging unlawful treating, bribery and other misdemeanours, were common, and Tierney promptly challenged Thellusson's election, sensibly ignoring any violations on the part of Thornton, whose reputation as one of the 'Saints', incorruptible and pure, was unassailable.[37] The select committee charged with investigating the petition reported on 12th November in favour of Tierney, finding that Thellusson had violated the Treating Act (7 Will. III c.4) and the standing orders of the House and that his election was void.[38] A new writ was ordered and battle was joined afresh between the two candidates, but Tierney clearly felt that his best chance of success lay in an election committee rather than on the hustings, for after three days he conceded the poll and launched another petition. This time he alleged, *inter alia*, that Thellusson had hired prize fighters to 'obstruct the Poll, and ..., by their outrageous conduct, intimidate quiet and well-disposed Persons from attempting to vote'; that he had suborned the marshal of the king's bench prison to let many of his jailed and disfranchised debtors out to vote and that 'gross and scandalous bribery' had been practised.[39]

Tierney acted as his own counsel, and very ably too. The outcome was sarcastically recorded by Charles Abbot:

'the Southwark election Committee came this day to a most absurd determination. They 1st resolved that Mr. Thellusson having treated within Statute of W & M at his preceding Election for this Parliament was *ineligible* upon this second Return- 2ndly that Mr. Tierney his *opponent was duly elected*; and 3rdly that Mr. Thellusson's defence was not *frivolous and vexatious. Id Est* 1st That the Statute which only vacates the very return on which the treating took place, extends to all subsequent elections, 2nd that this ineligibility was *so notorious* to the Electors, as to make their votes thrown away which were given to him. 3rd That Mr. Th. being

115

notoriously *ineligible* nevertheless *did not know of his own ineligibility occasioned by his own treating*, for else his defence to the Petition must have been *frivolous and vexatious.*[40]

Thellusson himself got up a petition with 1,150 names pointing out the unfairness of an election conducted on the assumption that (as the returning officer had publicly declared) a candidate was eligible to receive votes only for these votes, a majority, to be then held void and the loser declared elected, a distant echo of John Wilkes' Middlesex election of 1769.[41]   His petition was unsuccessful and after barely a month as an MP, during which he had spoken only to deny any knowledge of having spirited away a key witness to prevent his giving evidence,[42] George found himself out of Parliament and heavily out of pocket; he was particularly unfortunate in having had the expense of fighting two elections and two petitions and all for nothing.   Moreover he probably felt that Tierney had been guilty of some rather sharp practice himself, for an election petition had to be presented within fourteen days after the return was made, and according to Thornton it was common to delay paying any 'treating' bills until the risk of a petition was past. Thellusson, however, was said to have paid his, relying on Tierney's intimation that he would not petition, though this is difficult to reconcile with the press reports.[43]   All in all, the Southwark election was a sorry business, and the 'quiet seat' in the Isle of Wight that George had lined up failed to materialise.

3. Peerage

Even setbacks like the Southwark election could be turned to advantage.   In the middle of George's misfortunes Pitt received a letter from Peter Isaac Thellusson, transmitted rather unwillingly by William Windham, his Secretary at War. Starting from the first election it continues:

'before however we again embark on this troubled Ocean, it behoves our family well to consider its own private situation, its public duty and those future

116

prospects of honor and advancement which are laudable objects in us all, and which by blending the general good with the individual interest gives to the one dignity and to the other zeal.

My father's fortune is certainly very large, our own not inconsiderable and is increasing but great as they may be, they will not bear unperceived frequent contested Borough Elections. Our Public duty I trust we have hitherto fulfilled towards the State to the very utmost limits of that which even exaggerated expectation could require, compatible with our profession and situation in life.

You are acquainted with the future prospects of Honor and advancement we have formed and have had the goodness in some degree to interest yourself in them and to think if it is judged advisable to confer such distinctions on mercantile men, we have least as good pretensions as those who have obtained them.

The claims of Parliamentary influence; the exertions to insure to the Country persons of Property and character, well affected to its laws and constitution as its Representatives, form one of the acknowledged claims to the honors of the Peerage. We are already possessed of two, were yesterday and may be tomorrow of three seats in our own family. We have also another seat offered us which we are willing to fill by any person of consideration whom administration wish to recommend. But surely the exertions and enormous expense go beyond the duties imposed upon us towards the State and must be looked upon as a bold and volunteering spirit in its defence. To look forward to some end and fruit of such exertions, to obtain some reasonable assurance that they are attainable cannot I trust be called trafficking by bargain or Sale. Our good wishes to Government are well known. We shall not be more or less attached to it whether we obtain or not our ends. But we may reasonably confine ourselves to zealous duty not encountering unreasonable difficulties. If therefore any *reasonable* assurances of this object of our wishes be given to us we are again willing to strain every nerve on the election. If not Mr. Tierney must walk over the course and my brother will take a quiet seat for a Borough in the Isle of Wight.

Without comparing our pretentions to the honor we solicit with those of Lord Eardley or of the two last persons in our line who have lately obtained it I trust you will not deem it vain here to say, that our family was ennobled above 400 years ago, was driven from France by the Edict of Nantes, and has ever since filled in Switzerland the very first offices in the Magistracy, the Army and the Diplomatic line. My father being a younger son settled with a handsome fortune in this country. By his industry and his abilities he has increased it, and has proved himself a worthy member of the community.

Since the year 'ninety he has completely left trade and resides the greatest part of the year on his Estate in the country. My continuing in business is uncertain. I am daily investing my fortune in land and certainly my eldest son will not be brought up to trade.

If you think that the favour I ask is not unreasonable and that the moment is not an improper one for obtaining a firm assurance that within some *reasonable* period I may look forward to it, I shall feel myself under even greater obligations if you will forward this letter to Mr. Pitt and obtain his decision on it as on that must depend the conduct we have now to hold.

I flatter myself that even in the City, barring that envy which allways follows the successful, it would not be an unpopular measure. I will not judge of Popularity by the reports of designing and malevolent men. I will take criterion from effects and will ask whether an election for the Borough by a large majority, one for the East India Direction carried against every effort of Ministerial and Presbyterian influence, and a preponderating influence in the City of which Mr Lushington and Mr Curtis can give proofs, is evidence or not of popularity.[44]

Now if there was one sort of request a Prime Minister detested it was a request for a peerage. Offices of state, after all, were finite in number and previous engagements could always be pleaded, while pensions and grants were usually made only under well established circumstances. But Parliament had no control over the prerogative to create peers and there was no constitutional or practical limit on their

118

number, nor any formal qualification which might debar applicants. Since most applicants claimed to be supporters of government, and almost all were men of some influence and position, they could not be brushed aside with too much brusqueness, but neither could they readily be given their wish.

In the nineteenth century Pitt had the reputation of having been liberal with his recommendations for peerages and more, of having changed the whole character of the peerage by massively enlarging it and by systematically infiltrating commercial and `middle class' men; he `scorned and snubbed [the nobility], and flooded their blue blood with a plentiful adulteration of an inferior element.'[45] Disraeli popularised this view: in Medina's graphic words, `[h]e made peers of second-rate squires and fat graziers. He caught them in the alleys of Lombard Street and clutched them from the counting houses of Cornhill'.[46] But as so often happens, the bold, clear outline breaks up under the historian's microscope. The squires and graziers are there, though not all second rate, but the denizens of Lombard Street and Cornhill are scarcely to be found. Pitt certainly enlarged the peerage substantially, for in 1800 there were 267 against only 189 in 1780, and new creations in the last twenty years of the century, 94 in all, far exceeded the rate for earlier decades. But then the county's population had been rising rapidly, and its prosperity growing too, while the Hanoverian monarchs had been so reluctant to sanction new creations that for much of the century the peerage had barely increased at all.[47]

The composition of the peerage *did* change in Pitt's time, notably by the great increase in Scotsmen and Irishmen receiving peerages of Great Britain, but the new peers were overwhelmingly members of aristocratic families, with only a sprinkling of men whose services in the armed forces, diplomatic corps or the law demanded recognition or whose political influence commanded it.

The separate peerage of the kingdom of Ireland was, however, less highly esteemed (indeed sometimes disparaged) and was of a more mixed and less exclusive character.[48] Even so, for a merchant, a banker or an industrialist the heavenly peerage was a distant and almost unattainable vision. Writing in 1798 to *The Gentleman's*

Magazine `Acis' set out to prove, *contra* Citizen Tom Paine, that the British aristocracy was open to talents, and along with soldiers, sailors and lawyers he cited four men from `trade' as proof: Lords Caledon, Huntingfield, Eardley and Carrington.[49]   Of these four, Caledon is the rare case of an ennobled nabob, who spent prodigiously on buying estates in Ireland on his return from India, and Huntingfield and Eardley were both sons of foreigners who had become famous in the middle of the century for their wealth, and in particular, for their immense participation in the national debt. Sampson Gideon was a Portuguese Jew to whom George II refused a baronetcy on religious grounds, giving it to his thirteen year old son instead.   The son inherited half-a-million pounds, held £200,000 in government stock, was a county MP and in 1789, changing his name to Eardley, obtained an Irish barony. Joshua Vanneck was the greatest of the Dutch financiers who settled in England and, being a Protestant, he *was* made a baronet in 1781. His son, MP for Dunwich, was made Baron Huntingfield in July 1796, an encouraging portent for the Thellussons.[50]

Much more encouraging however, was the metamorphosis of Pitt's friend Bob Smith into Baron Carrington in June 1796, for Smith was a banker, one of the great firm of Smith, Payne & Smith.   Pitt explained to the Irish viceroy Lord Camden that it was Smith's reward for bringing in several members at the general election, but he evidently expected Camden to be surprised, and it was rumoured that he had had a hard task persuading the king to agree.   It is the Carrington peerage that is usually cited as evidence for Disraeli's jibe, but `the eyebrows raised at his elevation suggest not a new class entering the peerage, but the extreme fastidiousness which still prevailed.'[51] Eyebrows were certainly raised and Windham left Pitt in no doubt that by opening the door to Smith he had exposed himself to solicitations from the Thellussons and their like, of which this would be the first of many:

`[y]ou have opened the door - I will not say how wisely - but `to shut' will `exceed your power' ... The fact is that to the whole of the business I am so ill-inclined as to be a very bad intermediate agent. My goodwill to the object is only conditional: *if* such things are to be; if this door, now as I think unhappily opened, is still to let in persons of the description in question, there is then no conscience of aiding one person, with equal pretensions, instead of another.'[52] Windham was probably right. So far as is known, neither Peter nor his sons had previously asked for a baronetcy or even a knighthood and here they were seeking a peerage. True they had broad acres in Yorkshire and Suffolk[53]; true Peter was no longer in the firm and Peter Isaac was disengaging from active business and promising to keep his heir out of `trade'; true they were very wealthy; but none of this made their claims persuasive. However, if Bob Smith with his handful of rotten boroughs and the family bank could aspire to a peerage, why could not Peter Isaac Thellusson, with one brother in the Commons alongside him and another battling at great expense to defend a seat for the government? Where was the difference? They held quantities of stock, had been regularly among the loan contractors, had an international reputation and were firm supporters of the government.

Windham spoke to Pitt and to the Duke of Portland, Home Secretary and the leader of the Whigs in the cabinet, about the matter.[54] Pitt's answer to the claim has not survived, but obviously it was not discouraging, or George would scarcely have plunged back into the fray at Southwark. It must have fallen short of a definite promise however.

The interesting thing is whether the fate of the application had any influence on Peter's will. The will pre-dated the letter and it is even possible that Peter Isaac acted without consulting, perhaps without even telling, his father, but that seems unlikely. The letter itself clearly shows that these pretensions were already well known to ministers and that Peter Isaac, and presumably his father, believed that they were attainable through a combination of land and parliamentary seats. If the peerage was Peter's aim for his sons, and it was seen to be accessible in this way, then perhaps he had a longer perspective than his heir did, seeing that it might be eventually be taken by storm if he endowed his descendants with so much land that they might claim a coronet almost as of right.

NOTES

1. *Thellusson v. Woodford*, PRO C 12/241/27.

2. PRO PROB 11/1231 f.193.

3. General report, 9 Jul. 1819, PRO C 38/1192 f 184. ff.

4. PRO PROB 11/1294, f.574. Participation in the sugar industry was common among Glasgow's colonial merchants: T.M. Devine, *The Tobacco Lords* (Edinburgh, 1975), pp.35-7.

5. Both George and Henry Lear were based at Blackfriars between 1768 and 1774. Lear and Handasyde both signed the merchants' `Loyal Declaration' in December 1795.

6. *The Post Office Directory* 1821. *Gents. Mag.* 72 (1803), 1805 notes the marriage. *The Morning Herald* (24 Jul. 1797) reported a breach of promise action brought by Miss Williams (aged 35) against a Mr. Handasyde at the Guildhall; he was 50 years old and `a man of considerable property', who may have been Thellusson's ex-partner.

7. *General report*, schedule I.

8. P.I. Thellusson to W. Windham, 12 Nov. 1796, PRO PRO 30/8/182, f.174; *Farington Diary*, vol. XIII, p.4448 (19 Jan. 1814).

9. *The Times*, 4 Sept. 1789; R. Fulford, *Royal Dukes* (London, 1948), pp.34 - 6; A. Aspinall (ed.), *The Correspondence of George, Prince of Wales, 1770-1812* (8 vols., London, 1963-71), vol.I, p.251 n.

10. Rev. J. Hunter, *South Yorkshire, a History of the Deanery of Doncaster*, (2 vols., London, 1823-31), vol.I, p.314.

11. *Complete Peerage*, vol. VII, pp.318 - 26.

12. *Ibid.*; Hunter, *South Yorkshire*, vol. I, pp.315 - 6.

13. *Juridical Arguments and Collections*, vol. II (London, 1799) app. I. *The Morning Herald*, 28 Jul. 1797, puts it at only £40,000, *Gents. Mag* .67 (1797), 708, more plausibly has £92,000 with £20,000 spent on improvements and additions.

14. PRO C 12/241/27.

15. To Mary Berry, 6 Nov. 1795: W.S. Lewis (ed.), *The Correspondence of Horace Walpole* (46 vols., Oxford, 1937-83), vol.XII (1944), p.176; *V.C.H. Berkshire*, vol.III (London, 1923), p.162.

16. *Parl. Reg.* (2nd s.) 41 (1795), cols. 39-40, 51-67, 179-83, at col. 67; *House of Commons, 1754 - 90*, vol.I, p.197. See also the debate on Sir B. Hammet's conduct, *Woodfall's Debates* 3 (1795), pp.4-10.

17. *House of Commons, 1790 - 1820*, vol. I, pp.318 - 26. See also I. R. Christie, *British Non-Elite*

MPs, 1715-1820 (Oxford, 1995).

18. A modern account is F. O'Gorman, *Voters, Patrons and Parties, the Unreformed Electoral System of Hanoverian England* (Oxford, 1989).

19. T. Amyot (ed.), *Speeches in Parliament of the Rt. Hon. William Windham* (3 vols., London, 1812), vol.I, p.192. J. Cannon, *Parliamentary Reform, 1640 - 1832* (Cambridge, 1973) is a modern account.

20. *History of the Boroughs of Great Britain...* (London, 1792) vol.III, pp. 43 - 4. George Tierney drew heavily on this avowedly propagandist work for a publication of his own in 1793 but was careful to omit several borough owners who were Whig friends of his: Cannon, *Parliamentary Reform*, pp. 111 -12.

21. *Complete Peerage*, vol. V, pp.35 - 8; *House of Commons, 1790 - 1820*, vol.II, pp.422 - 4.

22. M. Duffy, *Soldiers, Sugar and Seapower* (Oxford, 1987), pp.100-13.

23. *Ibid.; House of Commons Sessional Papers*, 96 (1794-5) nos. 4537 - 41.

24. *Parl. Reg.* (2nd s.) 41 (1795), cols.225 - 43.

25. *Ibid.*, cols. 236 - 7, 457 - 8.

26. Sir J. Fortescue, *A History of the British Army* (13 vols., London, 1899-1930), vol.IV(1), p.378.

27. *Parl. Reg.*(2nd s.), 41 (1795) col. 499.

28. *Ibid.*, col.457.

29. *Ibid.*, cols.457-9, 461 - 502; *House of Commons Sessional Papers* 96 (1794-5), 4537-41.

30. C.L. Lokke, London Merchant Interest in the St. Domingue Plantations of the Emigres, 1793-1798, *American Historical Review* 43 (1937-8), 795-802.

31. Duffy, *Soldiers, Sugar and Seapower*, pp.141-56 and War, Revolution and the Crisis of the British Empire, M. Philp (ed.), *The French Revolution and English Popular Politics* (Cambridge, 1991), 118-45.

32. *House of Commons, 1790 - 1820*, vol.I, pp.141 - 51.

33. *Ibid.*, vol.II, pp.397 - 8, 422 - 4. Paul Benfield had to vacate Malmesbury in 1792 after supporting the opposition.

34. *Ibid.*, vol.II, pp. 432 - 4.

35. *House of Commons, 1754 - 90*, vol.II, pp.387 - 8; *House of Commons, 1790 - 1820*, vol.II, pp.384 - 7.

36. H.K. Olphin, *George Tierney* (London, 1934), pp.25 - 7. Olphin's thesis, on which the book is based, has a slightly fuller account.

37. Thornton was elected in 1782 despite refusing to pay the customary bribes. Tierney was an experienced petitioner, having won Colchester that way in 1789 after a tied vote, losing it

next year to another Thornton despite an unsuccessful petition. The elections ruined his finances: Olphin, *George Tierney*, pp.17 -18.

38.   *Ibid.*, pp.27 - 32. Since Grenville's Act of 1770 these committees were generally impartial and Thellusson's violations are not in doubt.

39.   *Ibid.*, pp.34 - 8; *Parl. Reg.* (2nd s.) 51 (1796-7), cols.243 - 4, 336 - 7. Tierney successfully presented the election as a David and Goliath contest between his own appeals to voters' intelligence and the City merchant's gross bribery and intimidation, and this is the version accepted by his biographer. Thellusson's bribery, conducted through his agent Peter Cossart (brother of his father's late partner), was on a large scale but he certainly had no monopoly of intimidation, for Tierney enlisted the `support' of many unenfranchised workmen. Nor, as Tierney admitted, were Thornton's hands (or at least those of his agent) quite clean, since money was spent quite freely on their part. A report on the election by Cossart is in Southwark Public Library.

40.   Lord Colchester (ed.), *The Diaries and Correspondence of Charles Abbot, Lord Colchester*, (3 vols., London, 1861), vol.I, pp.80 - 1. Abbot had refused to be Thellusson's nominee on the Committee: Abbot's diary, PRO PRO 30/9/31, f. 374.

41.   *House of Commons Journals* 52(1796), 296 - 7. There was a good deal of merit in the petition, especially since the decision in the Southwark case contradicted an earlier one on a Norwich election.

42.   *Parl. Reg.* (2nd s.) 51 (1796-7), cols. 293 - 6.

43.   *Ibid.*, cols. 617 - 22 (Henry Thornton). Thellusson was said to have engaged to spend up to £10,000 on the election and Olphin (p. 35) suggests his outlay must have come close to that amount.

44.   P.I. Thellusson to Windham, 12 Nov. 1796, PRO PRO 30/8/182 f. 174 ff.

45.   Lord Rosebery, *Pitt* (London, 1891), pp.276 - 7.

46.   *Sybil or The Two Nations* (1926 edn., London), p.19 (the page heading is `A Plebeian Aristocracy'). *Cf.* 'A.F.A.' in *Gents. Mag.* 84, (1814), 30 - 2: `he considered a Coronet a feather, which was light payment for any favour, without caring on whose head it fell'.

47.   J. Cannon, *Aristocratic Century: the Peerage of Eighteenth Century England* (Cambridge, 1984), pp.12 - 33; G.C. Richards, The Creation of Peers Recommended by the Younger Pitt, *American Historical Review* 24 (1928-9), 47 - 54; M.W. McCahill, Peerage Creations and the Changing Character of the British Nobility, 1750 - 1830, *English Historical Review* 96 (1981), 259 - 84; W.C. Lowe, George III, Peerage Creations and Politics, 1760-84, *Historical Journal* 35 (1992), 587-609.

48.   Cannon, *Aristocratic Century*, pp.16, 28 - 31.

49. *Gents. Mag.* 68 (1798), 1035.

50. *Complete Peerage*, vol. II, pp.485 - 7; V, pp.1 - 2; VI, pp. 674 - 5.

51. Cannon, *Aristocratic Century*, p.23.

52. Windham to Pitt, 15 Nov. 1796, PRO PRO 30/8/330, f.328.

53. Peter Isaac had bought the estate of Sir George Wombwell in 1786 for £51,400.

54. Entries of 23 Jun., 4 Jul. 1796, Mrs. H. Baring (ed.), *Diary of the Rt. Hon. William Windham, 1784 - 1810* (London, 1866), p.339.

CHAPTER 7

PETER THELLUSSON'S WILL

1. Law and custom

Peter Thellusson made his last will on 2nd April 1796- one day earlier and one would have suspected him of an otherwise unrevealed sense of humour. He used the firm of Ward, Dunnett and Greaves, located in Soho Square, in the heart of the Huguenot community, and it was witnessed by Townley Ward and two of his clerks. Peter may have deliberately chosen to use a firm which did not usually act in Thellusson affairs, and his sons ensured that it did not ever do so again.[1]

When he made the will Peter seemed to be in good health and had every hope of seeing out the century. He probably expected to make alterations to the will, since he was busy making land purchases and by an inconvenient rule of common law only those lands already in the testator's ownership when a will was made passed under it. The will's complexity makes it certain that it was not the product of impulse or haste, and the novelty of its scheme certainly required specialist professional advice, but curiously, although rumour pointed strongly to the well-known conveyancer Henry Atherton as its draftsman, his role has never been definitely established.[2]

In order to appreciate the sensation created by the will, it is necessary to understand something of what the law permitted a man to do with his property through his will and what social custom suggested he ought to do with it. The striking feature of the law at that period is the minimal restraints it imposed. The time had been when a widow was entitled to half the personalty (one third if there were children) and the children to one third, leaving only half or a third at his free disposal,[3] but these restraints fell away with the authority of the ecclesiastical courts which had enforced them. Their last stronghold was in the City of London, but in 1724 Walpole's City Elections Act gave City freemen full testamentary power.[4]

As for land, where the power to devise had first been granted by the Wills Act 1540, the remaining limitations were removed at the Restoration, leaving the heir at law, who had long been vulnerable to a lifetime conveyance, now at the mercy of a testamentary disposition as well.[5] Apart from the obstacles to `perpetuities',[6] an eighteenth century property owner had practically complete freedom to choose the recipient of his property. Between 1660 and the timid Inheritance (Family Provision) Act 1938,[7] there were only two significant statutory curbs placed on this freedom; one was the Accumulations Act 1800, enacted directly in response to Peter's will, the other the Mortmain Act 1736.

Mortmain as understood in the middle ages was the grant of land to corporations, usually ecclesiastical, which had an artificial legal personality but were practically immortal. Such grants were objectionable to feudal lords, and to the crown, both as depriving them of certain feudal dues and as removing land from circulation into the greedy maw of abbeys and cathedrals, and they were controlled by legislation which, by the 1730s, had degenerated into a mere taxing mechanism. The 1736 bill had a somewhat different target. It sought to annul any gift of land (or money earmarked by the donor for land purchase) which was directed to a charitable use unless it was made at least twelve months before the owner's death and by a deed subscribed by two witnesses. The reports contain four arguments put forward in its support.[8] One, which resurfaced in the controversy over Thellusson's will, was that huge endowments to corporations might distort the land market, and coupled with this is the curious assertion that:

`any man who has in his own person a particular right to a land-estate, which he may transmit to his posterity, will be more daring and active in defence of that right against a foreign enemy, and more jealous of arbitrary power by which that right can be made precarious, than we can suppose any man will be, who has a right in the lands only as a lessee, or as a member of a corporation.[9]

Second, it was argued that `a man's heirs-at-law have some sort of natural right to succeed after his death, at least to his land estate, unless they have forfeited that natural right by some sort of unnatural behaviour'.[10] The right to disinherit is not questioned, but it is not to be used arbitrarily or unjustly and in particular it should not be exercised in the shadow of death under the influence of a designing clergyman. There is a strong undercurrent of anti-clericalism in the debates, forcefully expressed by Lord Chancellor Hardwicke, who saw the clergy of the established church as *ex officio* ambitious for their order and insinuating in their methods.[11]

The other arguments focused upon the effects of endowing charitable institutions such as hospitals. `Large and improvident alienations and dispositions made by languishing and dying persons' were a social menace, encouraging `laziness, idleness and extravagance'[12] by a lavish and indiscriminate provision.[13] The fourth argument was simply an antagonism to `the prevailing madness of perpetuating one's memory, by leaving a large estate to some body politic', and from a reference to `that delirious ambition of erecting a palace for beggars, and having his name engraved with gilded letters above a superb portico',[14] it can be inferred that the target was Thomas Guy, whose will directing the munificent endowment of the eponymous hospital, had recently been republished.[15] Guy's modest and traditional almshouses in his native Tamworth were the acceptable face of posthumous charity: a hospital which looked for all the world like the London residence of a Whig grandee was vulgar self-glorification.

The arguments over the Mortmain Bill are instructive. Testamentary freedom was not to give a licence to disinherit the heir without good cause, and even philanthropic endowments might, if too ostentatious, be disapproved. There were few testamentary rules, but they were buttressed by conventions.

The first convention was that a man of property ought to make a will. This social imperative had been much stronger in the middle ages when to die intestate (unless death swooped unexpectedly) was disgraceful, but even in the nineteenth century writers still urged it as a quasi-religious duty although the Statutes of Distribution had long provided a reasonably satisfactory basis for dividing personal property.[16] Even so, then as now, will-making was the exception rather than the rule except among the gentry and the very wealthy.[17] But if will-making was a duty, what distribution should be made? The question is not easy to answer, first because the will was often only the last in a series of dispositions- on children coming of age and marrying, entering business etc.- which need to be seen in their totality and often cannot; secondly because social expectations changed over time and differed between social classes.

There was, in England as in most western European countries, a tension between two models of inheritance, one of equal division among children (at least of the same sex), the other favouring one child, usually the eldest son, at the expense of the rest.[18] Whichever prevailed, however, it was universally accepted that provision should be made for the widow. There was room for considerable variation in the amount- in England it usually fell well short of the one-third suggested by dower or custom- and it was commonly provided in the form of an annual income rather than a capital sum, avoiding inconvenient sales or mortgages and enabling it to be reduced or cancelled if she remarried; such provisions were not usually intended to discourage remarriage so much as to reflect the widespread view that a widow's new husband should not benefit at the expense of her children.[19]

Primogeniture was the common law rule for inheritance of land, but the Statute of Wills enabled landowners to modify it and to obtain more flexibility in making provision for their families; the statute also had the effect of strengthening their control over the children where no lifetime settlement had yet taken place.

The classical form of settlement, the so-called strict settlement, which had emerged after the Restoration, was a modified form of primogeniture, which (where there was an eldest son) denied the other children any proportionate share in the family's wealth, giving them however a capital sum with which to launch themselves into the world or, in the case of girls, into marriage. The eldest son, as heir, gained control of the estate but his ownership was limited to his own lifetime with a following remainder to his own eldest son in tail and successive remainders in tail to the male cadet branches to provide against a failure of heirs in the senior line. This `aristocratic model' was widely adopted- albeit with innumerable variations- among the landed gentry and was usually brought into operation by settlements on marriage or coming of age and only refined and adapted by will.[20] However, where a man made his fortune in trade, as Peter Thellusson had, he might well wait and establish the settlement by will. The logical culmination of the family's metamorphosis from *parvenu* foreign merchants to English landowners would have been for Peter's will to settle the bulk of his estate on Peter Isaac and his heirs male.

But what if a man held a poor opinion of his eldest son? Nothing in law prevented his being passed over in favour of a younger son and disinherited, *in extremis* cut off with the proverbial shilling. Disinheritance probably occurred more often in literature than in life, though it certainly did happen.[21] There was no lack of despotic fathers nor of unfilial sons, the royal family setting a deplorable example over several generations, but in public opinion the heir's conduct must go beyond imprudence and youthful rebelliousness to justify disinheritance. Mere incompetence in managing affairs, falling short of actual imbecility, would not do so except where a business formed a major part of the inheritance and demanded application and intelligence.[22] The presumptive right of the heir to inherit was not lightly to be displaced, for that inflicted a social disgrace upon him as well as financial hardship.

Short of disinheritance, the risk that his extravagance or incompetence would ruin the family might be lessened by several devices. The strict settlement itself was one means, limiting his ownership to a life interest, and common law rules about `waste' prevented a life owner from exploiting natural resources to the detriment of his successors,[23] but there were other ways besides. In particular his inheritance might be postponed until he was more mature, to twenty-five or thirty, and a possibility conveyancers had recently begun to explore was what became known as the protective, or spendthrift trust.[24]

Outside the gentry the strict settlement probably did not gain much currency, nor perhaps did landowners wish it to do so. After all, partible inheritance tended to diminish personal fortunes which might rival their own, would produce more heiresses for the marriage market and would go to reinforce important social distinctions.

It seems that the usual inclination of parents in western Europe has been to treat their children equally (at least within each sex) in terms of inheritance even where the consequences are manifestly `inefficient' in sustaining the family as an economic and social unit, as where the repeated subdivision of a peasant holding pushes the family towards the margin of existence. Primogeniture, and other discriminatory forms of inheritance, while not `unnatural', do seem to represent a departure from the norm.[25]

Unfortunately we know relatively little about the inheritance patterns of the men of business and commerce in Hanoverian England. Studies of London's big businessmen in a slightly earlier epoch suggest that they mostly departed from the `custom of London' and there are some signs of a shift towards the `aristocratic model'.[26] A century later, it was certainly adopted by some of the very wealthy; for example, Sir Richard Glyn was removed from the contamination of trade in this way and his younger brother, who went into the family banking business, in turn left elaborate instructions for his heir to establish a landed dynasty.[27] The practice, however, seems not to have been general. To give just a few examples from the families already encountered; John Thornton (d.1790) made an equal division of the part of his estate intended for his sons, as did Z.P. Fonnereau (d.1778) and George Hibbert (d.1837).[28]

Of course, when a man died with both broad acres and a sizeable personal fortune, he could combine the two modes, as Claude Fonnereau (d.1740) did, settling lands on his eldest son *inter vivos* and dividing his personalty equally among all of the sons. Similarly, Abraham Robarts (d.1816) gave the realty to his eldest son outright and shared out the personality equally.[29] On the basis of very limited information, it seems safe to suppose that Peter Thellusson might, without causing surprise or incurring criticism, have divided the bulk of his estate equally among his children, or among his sons.[30]

This latter, indeed, is what the sons claimed in their Chancery bill they had been led to expect: `at sundry different times and upon various occasions between the time of the date and execution of his...will and the time of his death [he] declared it to be his intention to give a large fortune to each of his...three sons'.[31] However, his land purchases, which were still incomplete when he died, might suggest that Peter had in mind to provide an estate for each son, big enough to yield the rents needed to sustain the full expense of a country house establishment,[32] and entailing these estates would have been the obvious mode of reconciling the competing demands of equal treatment and family endowment.

One last arrangement would have been entirely legitimate but unusual and daring. Peter's father-in-law Matthew Woodford (d.1767) left his residue:

`to my most dearly beloved wife Mary Woodford in full trust and confidence that she will never do any act to the prejudice of my children and that at my decease she will dispose of it among them all with that prudence and discretion I have always found in her and in such proportions as each of them by their dutiful behaviour and sober and virtuous life may deserve and that she will make no other distinction or difference among them but as they fail in their duty and good behaviour.'[33]

Woodford's was a small inheritance, Thellusson's a huge one, but few men with any property seem to have been prepared to entrust it to their wife in this way.

It is clear, then, that Thellusson had a very wide legal and social freedom to dispose of his fortune, the chief social constraint being that it was not deemed acceptable to choose a younger son to inherit the bulk of it simply because he seemed the most likely to manage it well. Essentially the choice seemed to be between dividing it equally among the sons and trusting that one or more would use it wisely enough to perpetuate and enhance the family's fame, and concentrating it in the eldest and his male heirs. Only when the will was opened did a third way appear.

2. The Contents of the Will

Peter Thellusson died at his house at Plaistow on 21st July 1797, some fifteen months after making his will and a month after his sixty-second birthday. Since the will gave directions for his burial in the vault of Brodsworth church it seems he already regarded it as the family seat. It was not a sudden death. His doctor's bill came to £65 and by the desire of the family the apothecaries Child and Roberts were paid £100 'for their great and long attendance on the testator during his last illness',[34] but in that illness he made no changes to his will, although it was common and easy to do so by codicil.

Peter directed that his funeral be conducted 'in a very plain and decent manner'. The funerals of landed proprietors were often affairs of great and ceremonious pomp,[35] but reading the wills of those connected with the great law suit, it is striking how many contain similar directions to Thellusson's. There is William Tatnall (d.1826) wishing to be buried 'in as private a manner as decency will permit'; Samuel Heywood (d.1828) was to be buried 'without pomp or parade in that simple manner which behoves a contrite and repentent sinner' and Abraham Robarts(d.1816) thoughtfully required 'only a hearse with four horses and one coach and four and with such of my own servants as may be living with me at the time of my decease but I do not desire any of my friends or relatives to attend me to the grave as I have too often experienced the melancholy task imposed upon myself'.[36] Zachary Fonnereau went further: the body was to be interred by daylight within four days of his decease in the parish where he died, without pallbearers or any attendants other than one or two of his clerks or servants, no part of his house to be hung with black and the total costs not to exceed £40.[37]

In Peter Thellusson's case the costs were greatly inflated by the charges for transporting the body to Yorkshire, and the undertaker's bill came to £660 19s, further small sums being laid out for mourning dress and a guinea for ringing the knell at Bromley church.[38]

The reading of a will is a favourite scene for novelists and dramatists, but some of the wills of this period were so lengthy and unintelligible to laymen that it has to be presumed that the contents were summarised rather than read in full. One hopes Peter's was among them, for it would have taken more than an hour and a half to read aloud at normal speed. Did his family have any idea of the contents? Almost certainly they did not. That is what they claimed of course, but better evidence is Peter Isaac's letter to Windham making the peerage claim, written in November 1796 and giving no hint that anything unusual was in contemplation.[39] Their complacency was to be rudely shattered.

After directions for his burial and the customary instruction to pay his debts, the testator turned to the important matter of appointing executors and trustees. This was a matter where the law gave an unfettered discretion and though in a normal case one might expect at least one of his sons to be nominated, that would plainly be inappropriate in view of what he planned. Having no near relatives in England he turned to his kin by marriage, but his choice from within this group is surprising. He passed over Sir Ralph Woodford and chose his brother Matthew, the elderly archdeacon of Winchester, and rather than the third brother-in-law, Colonel John Woodford, chose his son Emperor John Alexander. For the third trustee he chose James Stanley, brother-in-law to Peter Isaac's wife. [40]

There is a neatness about this selection, comprising as it does representatives of the church, the law and the army, but it is curious that he wanted no-one with any business experience. There was no shortage of successful men of business among his connections; Abraham Robarts was an eminent banker; another of the Cornwall sisters had married a banker's son and there were Fonnereaus still in trade. George Hibbert, a West India merchant married to another of the Cornwall girls, was named in the will, but only as 'reserve', to act if any of the others should be dead before the will came into effect.[41] The will next made provision for Ann, the testator's widow. She was to have the right to live at Plaistow and her main provision was the income from £22,000 Bank stock and £600 long annuities, totalling £2,140 p.a. She was also given a power of appointment by will over £3,300 of the Bank stock, exercisable in favour of the children. If she remarried her income would be reduced to £685 p.a.[42]

When she made her own will, Ann acknowledged this to be a generous provision.[43] She had to renounce her claim to dower, but it would have fallen well short of what the will offered in substitution so that was no hardship. Without knowing what marriage portion she brought it cannot be known how her provision compared with the 10 to 15% of the dowry which seems to have been common,[44] but it is likely to have comfortably exceeded it. Her father had had six children to provide for and, to put it at its very highest, he would not have been worth more than £100,000; her sisters seem to have been of very moderate means and brother Matthew was by no means rich. Considered in the light of Peter's fortune of more than £500,000 in personalty, yielding at least £15,000 p.a., her income may not seem much- it certainly fell well short of the custom of London- but by the standards of the time it was quite generous.

Peter had also to provide for three daughters, one married and (Augusta Charlotte) still legally an infant. Maria had already received £12,000 on her marriage and her sisters were to have the same amount provided that they married with the consent of their mother and the executors, or such of them as were still alive. Posthumous supervision of daughters' marriage choices was common and unremarkable, the *quid pro quo* of a dowry which was guaranteed rather than left in the discretion of the mother or trustees, and probably intended in part to deter fortune hunters. If one of Peter's daughters married without consent she would have only £2,000 and her other legacies would also be sharply reduced; filial disobedience was to be penalised but not so severely as to amount to naked coercion; if the penalty were exacted, the unclaimable portion would fall into the residue.

The rest of the daughters' provision came from two sources. The first was the property enjoyed by their mother during widowhood, which was to be divided among the children after her death, save where she had exercised her power by giving away the permitted portion in her will. From this each daughter would have £1,500 Bank

136

stock and £200 long annuities, together worth £312 10s. p.a. They only had access to the income, but could dispose of the investments by will. Once again, if they married without consent, they would lose the stock and half the annuities.[45] Their other inheritance comprised several annuities, but only one, £100 on Maria's life in the Irish tontine of 1777, was then being paid. Six French annuities, also on various combinations of the girls' lives, would only become valuable if the French government resumed payments.[46]

The daughters could have little complaint. Their portions would not make them great heiresses but they were handsomely endowed by most standards. However, they stood to gain considerably if the will were overturned. The Statutes of Distribution would then operate to give their mother one-third of the personalty, the balance of perhaps £400,000 being divided equally among the six children, who would be required to bring into hotchpot (that is, deduct from their share), advances received in their lifetime from their father. Since the sons had all received considerable advances, the daughters' shares would considerably exceed what they were given in the will.

What of the testator's own brothers and sisters? Two brothers were dead but the eldest, Isaac Louis, and the youngest, Jean François, were living, and George Tobie and the deceased sisters Ann Sarah and Judith had left issue.[47] Yet Peter chose to remember only his younger brother, Jean François, and the daughters of his sisters Jeanne Pictet and Elisabeth Fabri. Perhaps he felt the others were already rich enough, but the Pictets and Fabris were wealthy families too, and he offered no explanation for discriminating in this way. £1,000 was set aside, the interest to be paid to Jean François for life and the capital then to be divided equally, half for the Pictet girls in equal shares, half for the Fabris likewise.

Relations by marriage were not forgotten. Peter had a soft spot for the mettlesome younger sons of his brother -in-law Colonel John Woodford, and left 100 guineas for each of them to be laid out in the Funds, payable at twenty-one together with accumulated interest, but to be available to the trustees for their `promotion, advancement or benefit' if the trustees thought it desirable. He felt it necessary to 'expressly order that no part of the said sums...shall be in any manner subject to the control or management or disposition of the father of my said Nephews as I mean and intend such legacies as marks of my esteem for them and to be applied for their benefit and advantage'. Perhaps Colonel John's financial affairs were not quite so healthy as might be wished.[48] There were also small legacies to servants in the usual form, half a year's wages if they had been in his service for at least two months, and mourning rings for various more distant kin and his partners in the sugar refinery. In common with most of the wills examined in connection with the suit, there were no charitable bequests,[49] nor any to former clerks or employees.[50]

Thus far there is nothing unusual about the will. But what was he going to do for his three sons? There were family heirlooms to be apportioned, mostly relics of their grandfather. George would have the picture of old Isaac already hanging at Brodsworth; Charles a gold watch made by Mudge and three seals mounted on gold; all the rest- the picture of Isaac by Rigaud and his wife's by Largillière; the gold seal with the family arms; the precious gold snuffbox of Louis XV with the picture of his son;[51] a copy in silver of Isaac's gold medal from the city of Geneva; the large silver coffee pot and salver also presented by the grateful citizens, and sundry family pictures- all went to Peter Isaac as the new head of the English branch of the family.

In every other respect the sons were treated alike. When their mother died they would each have the option of purchasing Plaistow, exercisable in order of seniority, and those of them who remained in the family business for at least six years would share equally in the proceeds of the sale of the premises in Philpot Lane at the end of that period. They received cash too; £7,600 each plus a small annuity in the French funds or, in Charles's case, in the Irish tontine. These cash payments augmented previous gifts, bringing the total to £23,000 each. That much they got, and to their dismay, it was all they got.

So what was to happen to the rest of Thellusson's property, to his land at Brodsworth and his extensive holding in the Funds, believed to be worth more than

138

half-a-million pounds? It was to be held by his trustees and they were to invest the personal property, not as usual in government securities or land mortgages but in land itself, freehold or copyhold[52] (not more than a quarter of the total being copyhold) but not leaseholds or life estates. They were given wide powers of management over both these and existing landholdings and were directed to complete any contracts for further purchases made by the testator before his death, but in choosing lands to buy they were given no guidance. The lands, of course, would yield rents and other income and these would be put into government securities until convenient land purchases could be made, so that at any time there would be a fund inexorably accumulating to finance further purchases.

And for how long was this accumulation to continue before the property was freed from the trusts?

`during the natural lives of my sons Peter Isaac Thellusson, George Woodford Thellusson and Charles Thellusson, and of my grandson John Thellusson, son of my said son Peter Isaac Thellusson and of such other sons as my said son Peter Isaac Thellusson now has or may have, and of such issue as my grandson John Thellusson may have, and of such issue as any other sons of my said son Peter Isaac Thellusson may have and of such sons as my said sons George Woodford Thellusson and Charles Thellusson may have and of such issue as such sons may have as shall be living at the time of my decease or be born in due time afterwards'.

In plain language, the accumulation was to end on the death of the last survivor of persons in the following categories:

1.   Peter's own three sons;

2.   Those of his grandsons who were already born or conceived at the date of his death and

3.   The issue of the grandsons in (2) or of other grandsons who had predeceased Peter and who were themselves born or conceived in his lifetime.

In fact the number of `measuring lives' was quite small, for Peter died when his eldest grandson, John, was only twelve, so that class 3 was empty. Class 2 consisted of Peter Isaac's three surviving sons, John, George and Henry, and the only son of Charles, named after his father. However, when Peter died Peter Isaac's wife was pregnant and in the following February she gave birth to twin boys, William and Frederick, who also qualified as measuring lives.[53] In all, therefore, nine persons had to die before the accumulation ended. In diagrammatic form:

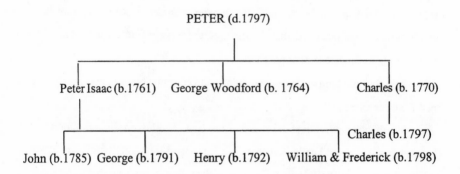

PETER (d.1797)

Peter Isaac (b.1761)   George Woodford (b. 1764)   Charles (b. 1770)

Charles (b.1797)
John (b.1785) George (b.1791)   Henry (b.1792)   William & Frederick (b.1798)

And what was to happen to the property at the end of this period? It would be divided into three equal portions, as nearly as might be, one apiece to the `eldest male lineal descendant then living' of each of Peter's sons, who would receive it in tail male, with successive remainders in the usual strict settlement form to `the second, third and fourth and all and every other male lineal descendant then living, who shall be capable of taking as heir male of any of the persons to whom a prior estate is hereby directed to be limited of [each son]'; a maze of further remainders and cross-remainders covered the contingencies of a failure of male issue in any of the possible lines of inheritance, so that each third would be kept intact as long as there were any male issue of the parent branch and when that branch failed, it would be divided equally between the current tenants in tail of the other branches and made subject to their respective limitations. It was also made a condition of anyone taking an interest in the residue that he should bear the name Thellusson or forfeit his inheritance.[54]

The possibility of inheritance by females was entirely eliminated, for instead

140

of the conventional ultimate remainder to the testator's right heirs, he directed that in the event of a complete failure of male lineal descendants of his sons, the estates were to be sold and the money paid to the Crown to the use of the sinking fund for the discharge of the national debt.[55]

The precise terms used to direct the division of the trust fund, particularly the expression `eldest male lineal descendant' were to cause endless legal argument, but the general thrust of the will is clear enough: to create three separate entailed estates, but not immediately, nor following a single life interest (which was common) but after a lengthy period during which the property could only grow, expenditure being limited to the cost of management. The children and grandchildren Peter Thellusson knew were irrevocably excluded from sharing in the great bulk of his wealth; his treasure was to be piled up for persons yet unborn and undreamt of. Such was Peter Thellusson's will.

3. Reactions to the Will

Why did Thellusson do such a thing? He will have been told that he was treading on dangerous ground at law[56] and he must have known he would be condemned by the world at large as well as by his own family? He must have guessed the reaction, else why did he insert in the will this passage?

`As I have earned the fortune which I now possess with industry, I trust and hope that the legislature will not in any manner alter my will or the limitations thereby created but permit my property to go in the manner in which I hereby dispose of it.'[57]

We simply do not know. The will offers no direct explanation and he seems to have kept his intentions to himself. One explanation already mentioned is that he wished to provide against claims to sums deposited by French emigrants, but this is implausible. After all, what deposits could be reclaimed from the estate? They could only have been ones made with Peter personally or with the firm before his retirement in 1791. His possessions included no unaccountable jewellery or valuables and those who managed to export their money early in the revolution mostly got themselves out as well. Moreover, if that was his motive, and he wished to conceal it, he could more simply have had recourse to a secret or half-secret trust.[58] And in all the vilification in the press and the arguments in court this explanation was never hinted at.[59]

To prove a negative is always difficult, but the strongest argument here is the utter disproportion between the end desired and the means adopted. By 1796 the Terror was well past and several years must have elapsed since any deposits were made. The amount unclaimed by depositors, even with interest, is unlikely to have exceeded £200,000, for Peter was certainly wealthy in his own right, so to set aside thrice that and keep a huge fund in existence for perhaps a hundred years to that end would be absurd. Furthermore, it would be illogical to invest that fund in land, the least liquid of assets. And the fact is that despite all the notoriety of Thellusson's will and the great pile of money no such claims materialised. An advertisement for creditors was placed in the *Moniteur* as well as English newspapers, but no French claimant proved.[60]

Of course, it is arguable that Thellusson's concern was not his personal obligations but those of the firm. However, it is unlikely that big claims were outstanding against the old partnership and by depriving the sons of access to the money he would in fact have created problems for them if there were big emigrant claims against the current one. It is a fine, romantic tale, but it does not add up.

Contemporaries were puzzled by the will and sought precedents. *The Craftsman* cited Sir John Webb's as being `dictated in some degree by the same spirit that actuated [Thellusson], having quarrelled with his daughter',[61] while *The Saint James' Chronicle* and *The Gentleman's Magazine* alluded to the will of `Vulture' Hopkins, but more in point of legal similarity than motivation.[62] None could offer an explanation.

The will does in fact provide one clue, for in it Peter says:

`the provision which I have made for my three sons, and the very great success they have met with, will be sufficient to procure them comfort; and it is my earnest

142

wish and desire, that they will avoid ostentation, vanity and pompous shew; as that will be the best fortune they can possess.'

This passage has roused the indignation of commentators ever since Hargrave described it to the judges as 'endeavouring to palliate this cruel disposition by satirical insinuations against his three sons, at the same time tending to injure their credit as merchants and in some degree to detract from the esteem of them as men',[63] and it is indeed a very peculiar injunction.

After all, Peter had seemingly not discouraged them from the outlay necessary to get themselves into Parliament.[64] He was seeking to bestow country houses upon them which would tempt them to a leisured and expensive way of life, and it is assumed that he did not disapprove the peerage application. There may have been quarrels about extravagance, for some of the sons were disposed that way, and naturally these would not be admitted. Even so, there is no reason to doubt that Peter had been an affectionate father.[65] Furthermore, it has not escaped notice that, while the sons were to eschew ostentation, Peter's remoter descendants were to be put in a position where they could avoid it only be heroic self-denial: for 'what could a great peer, with a great castle and a great fortune, do but be splendid and idle?'[66]

The same implicit mistrust of his sons crops up elsewhere in the will, in the direction that they profit from the sale of the counting house only if they remain in business, and if they should all have given it up within six years ('which I most earnestly pray and hope to God will never be the case'), it should fall into the residue. Yet if his eldest son knew of his father's wishes it is odd that he claimed to be withdrawing from business, and what is known of the youngest suggests he took little part in the firm.[67] Peter's brother George Tobie had retired from banking as soon as he was rich enough and Peter's own retirement while still hale and hearty scarcely suggests an addiction to wealth accumulation. It was also hardly prudent to tie men to business who preferred a life of leisure; commerce in the 1790s was not for the *dilettante*.[68]

In fact it is difficult to reconcile what Peter did either with his own actions or with what the family (whose testimony, if suspect, is at least uncontradicted) claimed he had led them to expect. They said that only ten days before his death he asked Peter Isaac to get a private tutor for John, praising his talent, predicting a great future for him and saying, `I have taken care of him'; yet all John received was a French annuity of £150 p.a. and currently worthless.[69]

Was it all humbug? Did he intend all along to disappoint them? Was there, as de Lolmé averred, a will in the same terms made at least six years earlier found among his papers?[70] When he prowled the corridors at night (according to a very doubtful family tradition), was he hesitating over his will or laughing at a cruel jest?[71] All that can be said is that nothing in his life suggests he was a dissembling hypocrite and one is left to wonder whether something had happened in the months before he made the will to make him distrust his sons' prudence.

Of course, the family had to present the will as inexplicable and irrational. They could not claim that the testator had lost his reason- he was doing business with evident sharpness a few days before he died- but had to stigmatise his conduct as harshly as decency allowed. In a moment of inspiration their counsel Francis Hargrave came up with the phrase `posthumous avarice', which has attached itself to Thellusson's will ever since. It was picked up by John de Lolmé in the second edition of his book,[72] used by the compiler of the *Parliamentary Register* in describing Lord Loughborough's bill,[73] and later found its way into Holdsworth's *History* and other standard works.

The phrase was particularly damning because misers were celebrated characters whose grotesque obsessions were regularly exhibited in the public prints. Readers of *Our Mutual Friend* will remember Noddy Boffin's descent into (feigned) avariciousness, sending Silas Wegg to scour the bookstalls for tales of misers.[74] Some of the most infamous were Thellusson's contemporaries. Jemmy Taylor, the Southwark stockbroker, was buried in the cathedral there having accumulated £100,000. John Elwes of Suffolk, who had managed in middle age to combine traits of a miser and a gambler before the former prevailed, died in 1789, probably worth more than Thellusson.[75] Elwes' neighbour William Jennens, said to be the richest commoner of the day, lived frugally in an unfinished mansion and died in 1798, his affairs giving rise to litigation that outlasted the Thellusson case.[76] These, and others like William Fuller, always 'arrayed in an old crimson velvet cap, and a suit of clothes for which no wandering jew would have offered him half-a-crown without being the loser',[77] were public characters, and Hargrave's epithet went to make Thellusson one of their contemptible company.[78]

He was not a miser though, and even Hargrave conceded that 'though he was for many purposes rather a slave to wealth than a possessor of it; yet neither in his stile of living, nor in the management of his family and domestic concerns did he usually condescend to that coarse, vulgar and ungentlemanly sordidness that some misers practise.'[79] Nor was he obviously eccentric. He is frequently accused of 'inordinate ambition, vanity and avarice',[80] but if he was vain he was vain for his posterity, not for himself. There was to be no public monument like Guy's, to keep his name before the public, and if wanting to aggrandise his family was vain few of the great families could escape censure. Peter was not vain as his father had been; on the contrary he was personally unassuming. Nor is it fair of a recent writer to term the will 'spectacularly vindictive':[81] no-one was left impoverished, no child singled out for unfair treatment. Thellusson was not avaricious, not vindictive, but he was audaciously and breathtakingly ambitious for his posterity.

At this juncture we should recall that his father had been cast as the restorer of the family's fortunes and, as Peter had heard *ad nauseam* in his youth, had triumphantly fulfilled his destiny. Through his efforts and that of his sons the family had become great in the small community of Geneva, opulent and aristocratic in France and wealthy in England. Then the French Revolution had come, and when Peter made his will Geneva was a jacobin republic and France an unstable, fermenting place where his nephews, though released from prison, were living in relative obscurity. If the Thellussons were to become renowned it would have to be through the English branch.

Renown meant broad acres and a title, or better still several titles. The *sine qua non* was a country estate and Brodsworth was such. On the foundation Peter had laid his sons might by diligent and shrewd application to business so expand the family fortune that their claim to a peerage would ultimately be irresistible. But did they have those qualities? That may have been the question nagging at their father in the months before he made his will. Boyd had a gambler's disposition and was leading his consortium into bigger and riskier commitments. It must be possible that Thellusson *père* grew alarmed at Thellusson *fils'* sanguine approach to business, and if he remained determined to treat them all alike he may have come to fear that his money, split three ways (say, £250,000 each) might rapidly be dissipated in rash speculations and mismanagement. All his toil might end with the family again lapsing into obscurity.[82]

And how could it be prevented? Not by a strict settlement, protective trust or similar device, for they only went to curb extravagance without increasing wealth. He needed a strategy to insure against the failings of a generation. If his sons, starting out with a good deal more than he had had from his father, continued to prosper, then so much the better, but what was required was an inexorable accumulation of untouchable income which would reach such a level that only a Chandos or a Buckingham could run through it.[83] Posthumous ambition, not posthumous avarice, is the likeliest key to the will.

Given the desire, it is easy enough to see how he hit upon the means. It would not be from English precedent, for the two well known accumulations, Webb's and Lady Denison's, fell short of what he envisaged.[84] A more widely publicised example was Benjamin Franklin's will. Franklin's extraordinary range of talents and achievements made him one of the most celebrated figures of the Enlightenment, and when he died in 1790 he left 1,000 dollars each to Boston and Philadelphia for a scheme under which loans at interest to young artisans would finance an accumulation for a hundred years, after which part of the money would be spent on public works and the balance accumulated for a further century, when it would be distributed for public purposes. Franklin calculated that this second accumulation would come to 4,061,000 dollars.[85] Less well known, but possibly familiar to Thellusson through his Dutch contacts, was the much older accumulation of 150 years directed by Jacob Pereyra of Amsterdam, at the end of which 1,000 guilders was to be used to endow a charity and the rest divided among his descendants, who were to be advertised for.[86]

Probably, though, Thellusson had no need of such models to inspire what another writer called his *mania accumulandi*.[87] Although there was nothing novel in the use of compound interest in financial calculations, the late eighteenth century provided unusually favourable conditions for it. To be successful an accumulating fund at compound interest needs a stable economy, a secure source of investment and a low level of taxation upon income. Given such conditions its long term potential is awesome and struck some observers as almost magical. Dr. Richard Price's example was particularly well known:

`ONE PENNY, put out at our Saviour's birth to five per cent compound interest, would before this time, have increased to a greater sum, than would be contained in A HUNDRED AND FIFTY MILLION EARTHS, all solid gold, but if put out at *simple interest*, it would, in the same time, have amounted to no more than seven shillings and fourpence halfpenny.'[88]   Price helped persuade Pitt to introduce the famous sinking fund in 1786, a giant accumulation devoted to the purpose of reducing, or at least containing, the national debt. The weakness of the scheme was that it predicated a regular surplus of income over expenditure and it became discredited when a prolonged war meant that the sinking fund was only serviced, in effect, by borrowing at the market rate (often a very high one) in order to redeem stocks which carried lower rates of interest.[89]   However, all public finances which stand upon a large funded debt depend ultimately upon sustaining the confidence of creditors in the integrity and capacity of the state to honour its obligations and the existence of the sinking fund undoubtedly helped to sustain that confidence over a period of unusual difficulty. Moreover it made accumulation familiar and acceptable as a financial device.

Peter Thellusson was also more familiar than most of his adopted countrymen with the tontine. It was probably more natural for Thellusson to conceive of using persons simply as 'measuring lives' than it would have been for most settlors and it is his special familiarity with accumulations and tontines that may well have given his testamentary thoughts their peculiar twist.[90]

By their own account the family were stunned by the terms of the will and when they recovered it is said that one of the sons took up a pistol and fired at his father's portrait, as if to counter posthumous avarice with posthumous parricide.[91] But appearances had to be maintained and proprieties observed. Peter was duly interred beneath the chancel in Brodsworth church but either no memorial was put up or, less probably, it was replaced with a joint memorial when his widow was laid to rest beside him. The inscription is distinctly cool- 'erected out of filial piety and respect by their affectionate children'- and no doubt they did not urge the executors to disregard his wish for a plain funeral.[92]

The newspapers quickly got wind of what had happened, one juxtaposing the news of his death with the piquant announcement that 'Coleman's play *The Heir at Law* now reigns with triumph and permanency in the public favour'.[93] Since 'human interest' stories were seldom given much space in the newspapers of that time, one would not expect to find even the most sensational will of a man hardly in public life given much prominence, but most summarised the will, in some cases inaccurately; thus *The Oracle* averred that the Yorkshire estate was to be sold and the purchaser obliged to take the name of Thellusson, the accumulation becoming the property of his first grandson to reach the age of twenty-three.[94] All were agreed that the will was 'one of the most extraordinary ever made' and that it was 'the subject of general conversation'.[95] Within a few days it was being used in a satirical joke against politicians[96] and, as we have seen, unflatteringly compared with that of the notorious 'Vulture' Hopkins. It was also rumoured from the first that the will would be contested, and *The Gentleman's Magazine*, which had initially assured readers that it would not, hastily changed its tune when it received fuller details from the family's

148

lawyers.[97]

NOTES

1.   The firm, which in 1793 comprised Townley Ward, Jonathan and Robert Dennett and William Greaves, had offices in Henrietta Street (*British Directory*, 1793, p.391) and later set up in the City as well. Their bill for making the will, £38 18s 6d, was not paid until 1806 : *General report*. By coincidence, Townley Ward is buried in Aldenham church, amid the Thellusson estates : R. Clutterbuck, *A History of Hertfordshire* (3 vols., London, 1815-27), vol.I, p. 141.

2.   Eldon doubted whether he was the draftsman: Keeton, *Thellusson Will*, 149.

3.   Holdsworth, *History of English Law* (5th edn., reprint of 1966), vol.III , pp. 534-56; C. Shammas, English Inheritance Law and its Transfer to the Colonies, *American Journal of Legal History*, 31 (1987), 145-63.

4.   H. Horwitz, Testamentary Practice, Family Strategies and the Last Phases of the Custom of London, 1660-1725, *Law and History Review* 2 (1984), 223-39.

5.   S.F.C. Milsom, *Historical Foundations of the Common Law* (2nd. edn., London, 1983) pp. 200-39; A.W.B. Simpson, *An Introduction to the History of the Land Law* (2nd edn., Oxford, 1986), pp. 173-90.

6.   On these see *infra*, pp. 160-71.

7.   Superseded by the Inheritance (Provision for Family and Dependants) Act 1975. These statutes give the court power to order provision for claimants out of an estate rather than creating any protected portions.

8.   *Parl. Debs.* vol.14 (1736-7), cols. 1-60; *Parl. Hist.* vol.9 , cols. 1110-56. G. Jones, *A History of the Law of Charity, 1532-1827* (Cambridge, 1969), pp. 106-30; J.C.D. Clark, *English Society, 1688-1832* (Cambridge, 1985), pp. 304-5.

9.   *Parl. Debs.* vol.14 (1736-7), col.14. Arguments in these sources are summarised and not attributed.

10.   *Ibid.*, col. 20.

11.   *Ibid.*, cols. 16-17, 37-8. It was probably Hardwicke who said that if devises by will had been permitted in the middle ages, 'we should never have had a reformation, nay, I doubt much if we should have had a lay owner of an estate in England.'

12.   *Ibid.*, cols. 44-56, and *cf.* the preamble to the statute, 9 Geo II c.36.

13.   Jones, *History of Law of Charity*, pp. 106-12; M.J. Chesterman, *Charities, Trusts and Social Welfare* (London, 1979), pp.35-7. The two universities and three great public schools, which successfully petitioned for exemption, were described as 'the only public foundations which

are either useful or necessary in this kingdom': *Parl. Debs.* vol.14 (1736-7), cols. 1-7.

14.   *Ibid.*, cols. 40, 57.

15.   *D.N.B.*, vol. XXIII, p.390. The will went through several editions. Guy, although frequently bracketed with misers, was only parsimonious, not avaricious. When the infamous `Vulture' Hopkins visited him to learn the secrets of economical living, Guy began his demonstration by extinguishing the only candle that lit the room: H. Wilson, *Wonderful Characters* (London, 1821), vol.I, pp.19ff.

16.   *Ex inf.* Ms. A. Real.

17.   Estimates suggest that 5-10% of property owners left wills in the mid-19th century: D.R. Green and A. Owens, Metropolitan Estates of the Middle Class, 1800-50: Probates and Death Duties Revisited, *Historical Research* 70 (1997), 294-311, at 296. P. Lovelass's *The Law's Disposal of a Person's Estate, who dies without Will or Testament* (London, 1785) sold 1,500 copies within a few weeks. It is estimated that one adult in three leaves a probated will today: J. Finch *et al.*, *Wills, Inheritance and Families* (Oxford, 1996), p.32.

18.   J. Goody, J.E. Thirsk and E.P. Thompson, *Family and Inheritance: Rural Society in Western Europe, 1200-1800* (Cambridge, 1976), especially J. Thirsk, The European Debate on Customs of Inheritance, 1500-1700, pp. 177-91.

19.   Provision for widows in England has produced both literature and controversy in some abundance. For discussion of two recent contributions see J.V. Beckett, Family Matters, *Historical Journal* 39 (1996), 249-56.

20.   Cannon, *Aristocratic Century*, pp.132-7. The legal aspect of strict settlements is treated in more detail *infra*, pp. 161-4. A useful introduction is J. Saville and B. English, *Strict Settlement, a Guide for Historians* (Hull, 1983).

21.   One instance occurred in the Codrington family, into which Arthur Thellusson married, see *infra*.

22.   Earle, *Making of the English Middle Class*, pp. 186-8, bears out its rarity even among that group.

23.   `Waste' covered actvities such as mining and felling timber. For a notorious example of the need for such restraints see the happenings at Raby Castle described in *Vane v. Lord Barnard* (1716) 2 Vern. 738.

24.   See *infra*, pp. 226-8.

25.   *Family and Inheritance*, 10-37 (J. Goody), 177-91 (J.E. Thirsk), 192-337 (J.P. Cooper).

26.   Horwitz, *Testamentary Practice*; R. Grassby, English Merchant Capitalism in the late 17th Century: the Composition of Business Fortunes, *Past and Present* 46 (1970), 87-107. But see L. Davidoff and C. Hall, *Family Fortunes: Men and Women of the English Middle Class,*

1780-1850 (London, 1987), pp. 205-7 for the continuing dominance of partible inheritance in the provinces.

27. Fulford, *Glyn's*, pp.68-70.

28. PRO PROB 11/1198, f.534; 11/1044, f.318; 11/1889, f.27.

29. *Doe d. Fonnereau v. Fonnereau* (1780), 2 Doug. 487; PRO PROB 11/1587, f.636.

30. Claims are made for an `aristocratic-bourgeois fusion' in the early 19th century, an example being the economist David Ricardo: F.M.L. Thompson, `Life after Death': how successful nineteenth century businessmen disposed of their fortunes, *Economic History Review* (2nd s.) 43 (1990), 40-59.

31. *Thellusson v. Woodford*, PRO C 12/241/27.

32. G.E. Mingay, *English Landed Society in the Eighteenth Century* (London, 1963), p.1, suggests a great landlord needed an income of £5 to 6,000 p.a. c.1790.

33. PRO PROB 11/934, f.469.

34. *General report*, 2nd schedule.

35. J.S. Curle, *The Victorian Celebration of Death* (Newton Abbot, 1972), suggests a gentleman's funeral in the mid-19th century cost £100. Earle, *Making of the English Middle Class*, pp.312-14, notes that some middle class funerals were also lavish.

36. PRO PROB 11/1715, f.465; 11/1747, f.648; 11/1827, f.86. Other instances include Sir Ralph Woodford (d.1828), John Cornwall, the 3rd Baron Rendlesham, George Hibbert, John Cossart, Anthony Fonblanque and Matthew Woodford.

37. PRO PROB 11/1044, f.318.

38. *General report.*

39. *Supra*, pp. 114-16.

40. For these see *supra*, pp. 209-12.

41. PRO PROB 11/1295, f.574.

42. On the growth of such clauses see B.J. Todd, The Remarrying Widow- a Stereotype Reconsidered, in M. Prior (ed.), *Women in English Society, 1500-1800* (London, 1985), pp. 54-92.

43. PRO PROB 11/1805, f.136.

44. Habbakuk, *Strict Settlement*, p.86.

45. Dividends on Maria's stock were to be paid to her separate use, Augusta's accumulated until she came of age, with £200 p.a. available to the trustees for her benefit until then. The daughters also shared out Peter's harpsichords and pianofortes.

46. The value of a tontine could be very considerable. The banker John Martin (d.1870) was among the last survivors of the 1777 one and was receiving £3,891 10s 2d a half year when

he died: J.B. Martin, *The `Grasshopper' in Lombard Street* (London, 1892), p.100.

47. Ain, *Les Thellusson*, pp.127-32, 138-47, 282-4; Haag, *La France Protestante*, vol.9, pp.364-5.

48. Colonel Woodford died in Scotland. No will was proved in England.

49. Earle, *Making of the English Middle Class*, pp.316 -18, remarks on the surprising rarity of charitable bequests among his London businessmen.

50. It is difficult to know what was usual. Abraham Robarts was quite generous to his clerks (PRO PROB 11/1587, f.636) while William Fuller's obituarist drily noted `legacies to faithful clerks and servants, who all fared hard in his service...we hear not': *Gents. Mag.* 70 (1800), 289.

51. According to Salmon, *Most Famous Will in the World*, the snuffbox became the subject of Chancery proceedings in the 1960s.

52. For this distinction see *infra*, pp. 267-8.

53. In fact William was born on the 16th, Frederick on the 17th. This is the version given in the copy of the baptismal register in PRO TS 15/1801, but most printed sources, presumably following *Gents. Mag.*, give the 6th and 7th.

54. A precaution against any of his prospective heirs being tempted to adopt another name as a condition of an inheritance. For such an instance in the case of Anne Thellusson's husband William Lukin, see *infra*, p. 320.

55. Sir Joseph Jekyll, a former Master of the Rolls, left a large quantity of stock to his wife for life and then to the use of the sinking fund (PRO TS 18/342), but the next of kin had it set aside by Parliament `on the plea of dotage': L.M. Hawkins, *Memoirs, Anecdotes, Facts and Opinions, Collected and Preserved by Laetitia-Matilda Hawkins (London, 1824), vol.II*, p.323.

56. Hargrave's ms. note on his copy of the printed report of *Thellusson v. Woodford* throws some interesting light on two earlier ventures into this legal *terra incognita*. In framing the Duke of Norfolk's settlement the conveyancer Booth had given an express warning to his client that he was on doubtful ground, while the eminent lawyers who drew up the will at issue in *Duke of Marlborough v. Godolphin* (1759) believed their handiwork transgressed the rules, and were proved right: *Observations...on the Bills against Trusts of Accumulation* (London, 1801), p.109.

57. I know of no instance where Parliament did this, but it is said that Lord Foley's will, which disinherited his sons for gambling, was almost overturned: J. Timbs, *A Book of Modern Legal Anecdotes* (London, 1874), p.47.

58. In a secret trust the will makes a seemingly unconditional gift, but is subject to trusts

previously agreed by the recipient; in a half-secret trust the recipient is shown as a trustee but the terms of the trust are not disclosed by the will.

59.   Hargrave, who was closest to the family, mentions it neither in his *Juridical Arguments* nor in his commentary on the bill.

60.   Report of 23 Mar. 1803, PRO C 38/913.

61.   12 Aug. 1797.

62.   *St. James's Chronicle*, 25-27 Jul. 1797; *Gents. Mag.* 67 (1797), 708.

63.   *Juridical Arguments and Collections* (London, 1799), vol. II, p.16.

64.   For these expenses see *supra*, pp. 109-14.

65.   Farington heard that 'a few days before his death he said to a friend of William Wells, that he hoped that when he (the friend) should see his end *approaching*, he would have to say what he (Thelusson[sic]) could: " That he had the comfort of excellent sons".' *Farington Diaries*, vol.9, p.3436 (17 Apr. 1809).

66.   W.M. Thackeray, *The Four Georges* (1855, edn. of 1995, Stroud), p.67. See also Hunter, *South Yorkshire*, vol.I, p.317.

67.   *Supra*, p. 115.

68.   Compare what Francis Baring wrote: 'the posterity of a Merchant, Banker etc., particularly when they are young, abandon the pursuit of their predecessors as beneath them, or they follow it by agents without interfering themselves, which is only a more rapid road to ruin.': to W. Bingham, 6 Jan. 1803, quoted in Ziegler, *Sixth Great Power*, p.445.

69.   Hargrave, *Judicial Arguments*, vol.II, p.11.

70.   J. de Lolmé, *Observations on the Power of Individuals to prescribe, by Testamentary Dispositions, the particular Uses to be made of their Property...*(London, 1798), p.37n.

71.   *The Times*, 25 May 1859.

72.   *Observations*, p.47, though he also alleges that Thellusson was 'living somewhat expensively' (p.2).

73.   *Parl. Reg.* (3rd s.) vol.12 (1800), col.77.

74.   G.F. Young, Noddy Boffin's Misers, *The Dickensian* 43 (1946-7), 14. Langford, *Public Life and the Propertied Englishman,* p.11 notes the fascination they exerted.

75.   They feature in, *inter alia*, F.S. Merryweather, *Lives and Anecdotes of Misers; or the Passion of Avarice Displayed* (London, 1850), at pp. 95, 129.

76.   See *supra*, p. 3.

77.   [R.S. Kirby], *The Wonderful and Scientific Museum or, Magazine of Remarkable Characters* (London, 1803), vol.III, p.27.

78.   Kirby's and Merryweather's collections, and others such as Wilson, *Wonderful Characters*

were largely based on obituaries etc. which had appeared in the *Gentleman's Magazine* and elsewhere.

79. *Juridical Arguments*, vol.II, app.1.

80. J.F. Thellusson, *A Treatise on the Thellusson Act etc.* (London, 1842), p.24.

81. *House of Commons, 1790-1820* , vol.V, p.362.

82. 'T', Life of Lord Alvanley, *Law Magazine* 19 (1838), 38-44 had heard this 'on good authority'.

83. These are the most spectacular cases of aristocratic ruin. For Chandos see Cannon, *Aristocratic Century*, p.127; for Buckingham see F.M.L. Thompson, The Fall of the Grenvilles, 1844-48, *Huntingdon Library Quarterly*, 19 (1956), 154-90.

84. See *infra*, pp. 174-5.

85. De Lolmé, *Observations*, pp. 36-7. Some of Franklin's calculations proved over-optimistic: C. Van Doren, Benjamin Franklin (New York, 1938), pp.761-4; J. Warren, Trusts for Accumulation of Income and Wealth: the Wills of Benjamin Franklin and Peter Thellusson, *Proceedings of the Massachusetts Historical Society*, 66 (1941), 346-56.

86. *Law Times* 34 (1859-60), 241.

87. Hargrave, *Treatise on the Thellusson Act*, p.57.

88. Quoted in Ehrman, *The Younger Pitt*, vol. I, p.261.

89. E.L. Hargreaves, *The National Debt* (London, 1930); Ehrman, *The Younger Pitt*, vol.I, pp.260-9.

90. See *supra*, pp. 81-2. Note Hargrave's remark that `a future Mr. Thellusson will be encouraged to *tontine* upon the conjunction of trusts of accumulation and executory devise to the utmost stretch of such latitude', *Juridical Arguments*, vol.II, p.156.

91. Ain, *Les Thellusson*, p. 326.

92. Hunter, *South Yorkshire*, vol. I, p.321.

93. *The Morning Herald*, 24 Jul. 1797.

94. 27 Jul. 1797.

95. *The St. James' Chronicle*, 25-27 Jul. 1797. Similar expressions can be found in, *inter alia*, *The Times, The General Evening Post, Bell's Weekly Messenger, The Craftsman, The London Chronicle* and *The True Briton*, as well as *The Scots Magazine* and *The European Magazine*.

96. *The True Briton*, 1 Aug. 1797.

97. 67 (1797) 624, 708, 747.

CHAPTER 8

THE FIRST ROUND IN THE GREAT LAW SUIT

1. Preliminaries

The decision to contest the will being taken, the ponderous machinery of the law was set in motion. In March 1798 two bills were presented to the court of Chancery; in one the Thellusson family prayed that the provisions of the will directing the accumulation and ultimate division of the bulk of the estate be declared contrary to law and void, leaving the property to be distributed according to the laws of intestacy; in the other the executors desired that the trusts be upheld and their administration decreed. Answers were filed in June and the case came on for hearing before the Lord Chancellor in Lincoln's Inn Hall on 23rd November, perhaps in the `implacable November weather' in which *Bleak House* opens, with the court of Chancery `at the very heart of the fog'.[1]

No fewer than six counsel had been retained by the family. Sir James Mansfield was the leader by seniority rather than talent, no better than `a good average lawyer',[2] a failed politician who eventually became a judge. In support was a younger, more gifted man, William Grant, soon to become Solicitor- General and then a highly esteemed Master of the Rolls. The third counsel was Francis Hargrave, less eminent as a forensic lawyer but famous for his erudition, displayed so impressively in his edition of the property lawyers' classic text, *Coke upon Littleton*. Hargrave, who above all others is responsible for the received view of Peter Thellusson's will, gave the family the first legal opinion and now devilled for the leaders, providing them with a copious magazine of learning from which to select their ammunition.[3] The other three counsel on this side were Samuel Compton Cox, soon to become a master in Chancery, Robert Greenhill, who inherited a baronetcy and changed his name to Russell, and John Lodge Hubbersty, later recorder of Lancaster. All were experienced, capable men.

They faced equally formidable opposition. Despite the fact that its only interest in the proceedings was the very remote chance that the sinking fund might benefit, the Crown called out its law officers and a junior, John Campbell; they paid no heed to Hargrave's rather questionable suggestion that they should not exert themselves too vigorously in defence of a morally odious will.[4] The law officers, Sir John Scott and Sir John Mitford, were lawyers of the highest quality, who became Lord Chancellors of England and Ireland respectively as Lords Eldon and Redesdale. The trustees briefed Arthur Piggott and Edward King, who are less well known to posterity, and for the infant grandsons - whose peculiar situation was held to require separate representation - appeared a rising man at the Chancery bar, Thomas Manners Sutton, a polished and graceful speaker, Solicitor- General in 1803, a baron of the Exchequer in 1805 and Lord Chancellor of Ireland for twenty years from 1807. With eleven of the best lawyers to argue before him, the Lord Chancellor would not lack expert assistance, but as soon as Mansfield had completed the opening of the family's case he interrupted, declaring that it was a case of great importance and singular novelty and that he wished to have the assistance of common law judges.[5] This was quite a common proceeding, which helped to ensure that Chancery judges would not reach conclusions on difficult points of common law which their brethren on the common law side would decline to support; it thereby mitigated the practical inconvenience of the institutional separation of law from equity. For further assistance the Chancellor summoned the Master of the Rolls, and the hearing was delayed until 5th December so that Sir Soulden Lawrence, a judge of the King's Bench, and Sir Francis Buller of the court of Common Pleas, might attend. At times during the hearing they must have wished themselves back in their own courts, for the plaintiffs gave Hargrave his head and his argument spanned three days, dwarfing in length and erudition all the other speeches.

The legal arguments deployed in the suit were basically of two kinds. Some centred on the meaning to be ascribed to certain words and phrases in the will; on the interpretations contended for on behalf of the family, these would make the trusts void as breaking the permitted bounds of testamentary dispositions or would render them too uncertain to be understood and enforced at all. The other arguments were premised on the will being given the interpretation most favourable to the testator's grand design, and alleged that the design itself transgressed the rules of property law and was therefore void; these latter arguments are of greater significance in the development of the law.

2. Questions of Construction

Three questions of construction were raised, but one was disposed of very briskly. It was contended that the wording of the direction to the trustees to accumulate funds and use them to purchase estates required the accumulation to be continued until the lands were in fact purchased, even though that might protract the period of the accumulation beyond the legal limit. Hargrave alone advanced the argument and evidently with little hope of success, for as the Master of the Rolls observed, a similar objection might be made whenever there was a direction to accumulate for the purchase of land and it was fanciful to suppose that the testator intended the accumulation to continue beyond the end of his carefully chosen perpetuity period.[6]

The second point of construction had more substance but it led counsel for the family onto very unfavourable ground. The clause describing the persons whose lives are to measure the accumulation read thus:

`the natural lives of [1] my sons Peter Isaac Thellusson George Woodford Thellusson and Charles Thellusson and of [2] my grandson John Thellusson son of my said son Peter Isaac Thellusson and of [3] such other sons as my said son Peter Isaac Thellusson now has or may have and [4] of such issue as my grandson John

Thellusson may have and [5] of such issue as any other sons of my said son Peter Isaac Thellusson may have and [6] of such sons as my said sons George Woodford Thellusson and Charles Thellusson may have and [7] of such issue as such sons they have *as shall be living at the time of my decease or born in due time afterwards.*`

The underlined phrase is capable of governing either the whole sentence or only the last of the seven descriptions of persons it contains. If it is restricted to the last, then classes three to six inclusive are each capable of including persons not living at Peter's death, and the possibility that such a person might be the last survivor among the measuring lives would take the accumulation beyond the legal limits and render it void. Given that two constructions were possible, how should the court choose between them? This was where the family's difficulty arose, for the most basic, fundamental and overriding rule of construction in wills is that the court should endeavour to give effect to what it considers to be the testator's intention:[7] `for this purpose', said Lord Mansfield, `words of limitation shall operate as words of purchase; implications shall supply verbal omissions; the latter shall give way; every inaccuracy of grammar, every impropriety of terms shall be corrected by the general meaning, if that be clear and manifest'.[8] Such had been the rule in the ecclesiastical courts, which applied the Roman civil law, and although the broad highway of intention had become narrowed and obstructed by outgrowths of precedent from the thickets of English case law, it remained open to testamentary traffic.

Such cases sometimes gave the courts great difficulty, especially where the testator had made his own will, either in wholly inartistic language or, even worse, larded with half-comprehended legal terms. In this case, though, there was a professionally drawn will and the adoption of one construction, so far from giving effect to the testator's intentions, would bring his whole scheme crashing to the ground. It is another rule that if a will can be plausibly read in such a way as to make its dispositions valid rather than void, then that reading should be adopted,[9] so what the family had to argue was that there were cases, of which this was one, where a less generous approach should be adopted, cases in which the failure of the testator's purpose should be accepted with indifference if not satisfaction. What are these cases? Those where:

'as the design most evidently is to use the indulgence given to testators for very different purposes, this testator is not entitled to any assistance in the execution of that design.... He says, he will defraud the law, if he can, under the cover of its own rules.... If the Court is bound to say, that attempt is lawful, there is no rule calling upon the Court as a duty, if he has executed it insufficiently, to interfere, and aid him in making the disposition more complete'.[10]

But this approach tends to circularity. The court's aim is to ascertain and, if possible, give effect to the testator's intention, unless the intention is seen to be one which the court disapproves, in which case it will turn its back on the intention it has inferred and set to construing the will as though it had no knowledge of it.

That course failed to commend itself to the judges. The Master of the Rolls, Sir R.P. Arden, made a point of repudiating most emphatically

'a most novel and dangerous rule of construction... that a will is to be affected on account of the unmeritorious object in the view of the testator. It was very ably and ingeniously, but not, I think, solidly, contended, that, whatever may be the rule as to wills in general, the Court ought to endeavour to defeat the object of this will as unworthy of the countenance of a Court of Equity; and that it is the rule of the Court to adapt the construction of a will to the view of the merit of the intention. If it is supposed, that the intention is to be collected in a different manner as to a will, that meets with the approbation of the Court, and a will that the Court disapproves, I deny that. I know only one general rule of construction, equally for Courts of Equity and Courts of Law, applicable to all wills; which the Courts are bound to apply, however they may condemn the object; the intention is to be collected from the whole will taken together. Every word is to have its effect. Every word is to be taken according to the natural and common import: and if words of art are used, they are to be construed according to the technical sense, unless upon the whole will it is plain, the testator did not so intend.[11]'

This is surely the better approach, if only because there is real practical difficulty in operating different rules of construction according to a preliminary decision whether the will is one the court approves or not. The court has only a very imperfect and partial knowledge of the testator's motives and the circumstances of his family and besides, as Lord Justice Knight Bruce said in a later case, 'a testator has the right to be capricious if he chooses'.[12] Testamentary freedom is not, as Hargrave suggests, 'an indulgence' to be withheld if the court disapproves the manner of its exercise, but a right guaranteed by law.

Without the court's willingness to depart from the basic rule of construction, it was obviously unlikely that arguments based on mere grammar would carry enough weight. The maxim *ad proximum antecedentem fiat relatio, nisi impediatur sententia* was freely quoted for the family,[13] sounding much more authoritative for being in Latin, but to call it 'a rule of grammar, of law and of common sense'[14] was stretching it somewhat and Hargrave's researches yielded only citations from the *Maxims* of Noy and Wingate and Finch's *Discourse* and a scattering of applications in decided cases which, significantly, did not include any on wills. His opponents felt sure enough of their ground to be dismissive: 'in the construction of a will it is ridiculous to talk of grammatical rules, if the Court is possessed of the real intention',[15] and the judges agreed, Buller making the telling point that in the original will the whole phrase is in parentheses, strengthening the supposition that it is to be read as a whole.[16]

The last point on construction had more in it than either of the others, but as the lawyers probably realised, it could and would be side-stepped by the court. In the description of the persons who were ultimately to take the accumulated residue Thellusson repeatedly used the phrase 'eldest male lineal descendant then living' of each of his sons. Unfortunately the phrase was capable of three different meanings: first, the eldest son of the eldest son - an entail as it were; second, the eldest male of any branch tracing descent exclusively through males; third, the eldest male claiming descent through *any* child of one of Peter's sons.

162

Obviously, if the court was completely unable to determine which was Peter's meaning, it must hold the disposition void, and so it was argued.[17] Several of the judges thought that the question was by no means difficult,[18] but strictly speaking neither the prayer of the family nor that of the trustees required it to be answered; the latter merely required the trusts to be executed, and the great accumulation could be started up without resolving the question of ultimate entitlements which, after all, might never cause a problem, since the same individual might fit each of the competing interpretations.

Hargrave had to admit that `it is certainly the duty of a Court of Justice to give effect to last wills, and it is difficult to annul them for uncertainty'.[19] Once again his citations, though extensive, only served to confirm his admission, for he was scarcely able to point to any reported case where the beneficiaries of a will or trust were described in explicit language only demanding a choice among possible interpretations and where the court had refused to make a choice.[20] Since each of the possible interpretations of `eldest male lineal descendant' would yield a perfectly clear result, it would be a perverse and cowardly decision to decline to adopt any of them.

Predictably the court evaded a decision on the point, though indicating that the correct interpretation was that there was, in effect, an entail limited to males on each of Peter's sons so that descent should be traced always through the senior male line.[21] However, the court was perfectly prepared to launch the trust with its great accumulation onto uncharted seas to a destination which might become perfectly clear during the voyage or might remain obscure to the end. In fact it probably could not make a definitive pronouncement, for any decision it reached would be vulnerable to subsequent challenge on the footing that it was unnecessary for the purposes of deciding the question directly before the court and therefore merely an *obiter dictum* of no binding effect.

The consequences of leaving the description of the ultimate beneficiaries unresolved, however, were unfortunate. When the original judgment was given the end of the accumulation was remote and none of the adult parties to the suit (except the Crown) had any possibility of inheriting the fortune if the will were upheld. But with the will upheld and the definition of the `eldest male lineal descendants' left open, there might well come a time when members of the Thellusson family had conflicting personal interests in the resolution of that question. If the fund reached the dizzy heights that were predicted it would require considerable strength of character in a prospective claimant to remain on terms of friendship with a rival, especially if neither was in affluent circumstances, and to the family tensions created by fortunes depending on the deaths of the unfortunate kinsmen who were `measuring lives' would be added those generated by the rival interpretations of the will.

3. The Arguments on the Rule against Perpetuities

The arguments based on construction then, were unsuccessful. Others, of wider import, were based on the law governing future interests and settlements, a branch of legal learning which by this time had become luxuriant in its growth, complex in its substance and esoteric in its reasoning to a degree almost unparallelled in English law.[22]

Arrangements made by a landowner in his own lifetime to direct the inheritance of his estates further than an immediate gift, either by using an entail or a succession of life estates or some combination of the two, were hedged about with a formidable range of obstacles. `Contingent remainders'- that is, estates[23] whose owner was unidentified when the settlement was made, had become particularly vulnerable, especially during the seventeenth century, when some judges, most famously Chief Justice Coke, conceived an antipathy towards `perpetuities' and persecuted them through the application of general `rules' of doubtful validity and even more doubtful necessity. There was a `rule against double possibilities', a `rule against remote possibilities' and a `rule against remainders to the issue of unborn persons', and these were undoubtedly conceived as `rules against perpetuities'.[24] What is more, even those contingent remainders which were undoubtedly valid enjoyed a precarious existence, since in many cases they were liable to deliberate destruction by the owner of a preceding estate in possession. The complex interaction of rules governing seisin and merger of estates and the quirky operation of medieval conveyancing made possible this `artificial destruction', which remained a blot upon the land law until well into the nineteenth century.[25] The learning surrounding contingent remainders grew to be prodigious and arcane but formed an effective, if somewhat indirect, barrier to perpetuities in the broader sense of that term, arrangements determining ownership of land over a long period of time.

At common law it was not possible to pass land by will, and attempts to circumvent that unpopular restriction through the creation of `uses' were severely curtailed by Henry VIII's Statute of Uses. The statute was so violently unpopular with landowners that in 1540 the right to devise land, subject to restrictions, was conceded by another Act, the Statute of Wills. Each had the effect of allowing the creation of estates unknown to the common law and on one crucial point both statutes were silent. Were these dispositions to be subject to the common law rules and void if they did not comply with them? Were they to form a new class wholly exempt from the common law's restrictions? Was there some intermediate position? Such estates (known as `executory' interests and devises because their effect is not immediate) caused much difficulty in the seventeenth century.[26]

If executory interests were not subject to the rules which governed common law contingent remainders - and the first cases upon the Statute of Uses suggested they were not[27]- then the policy which now firmly rejected `perpetuities' could easily be circumvented. Ultimately the law crystallised in the fatuous rule in *Purefoy v. Rogers*.[28] Thenceforward any executory disposition was to be examined for conformity with the common law rules governing remainders and if it did not on the face of it necessarily break them it was made subject to them, and to all the hazards of accidental and deliberate destruction from which they suffered. However, if the disposition *ex facie* failed the examination then the contingent remainder rules had no application to it at all! Thus paradoxically the most `dangerous' forms of executory disposition escaped to wreak their mischief unhampered.[29]

Perplexed judges grappled with these novel forms of property, often with unhappy results. Several early seventeenth century cases treated executory devises indulgently,[30] and later attempts to whittle down the effect of those cases produced a body of law distinguished neither by logic nor consistency, a thicket into which none but the most acute and well informed conveyancer could venture with any safety.[31] Then to compound this complexity the use, which the Statute of Uses had sought narrowly to restrict, re-appeared in the transparent disguise of the trust. Once the Crown's feudal revenue interest in inheritance, which had demanded the Statute of Uses in the first place, ceased, the unabated and widespread desire to create uses for quite unexceptionable purposes was allowed to be met by devious but convenient means; the 'use upon a use', a device rejected in the Statute's heyday, was successfully resurrected, the Statute by-passed and reduced to such an enfeebled condition that, as Lord Hardwicke said, it did no more than add three words to a conveyance.[32] The revival of the use/trust now opened up yet another medium for the creation of long settlements, threatening to generate its own set of perpetuity rules different again from those governing entails, legal contingent remainders and executory interests.

Fortunately 'out of the welter the vision and strength of Lord Nottingham was able to extract a general rule'.[33] It was one of the finest achievements of this great Lord Chancellor to create a single rule encompassing all limitations, irrespective of the mode employed, a rule which drew a clear boundary between legitimate settlements and perpetuities in the wider sense.[34] The opportunity came to him in 1681, when he had to pronounce upon the validity of a series of dispositions whereby the Howard family sought to deal with the problem which arose from the unfortunate fact that the son and heir to the dukedom and estates was insane. Nottingham called in the heads of the three common law courts to advise him, only to reject their unanimous view that the scheme was void.[35] He went through the motions of reconciling his own views with the existing case law which stood in his way, but 'the truth is that Lord Nottingham's rule ... was an innovation, and only the barest shreds of authority for the doctrine could be dragged out of the earlier cases which he reviewed'.[36] Even then Nottingham's rule was almost strangled at birth by his successor Lord Keeper North, but it was rescued by the House of Lords, which evidently recognised its virtues.[37]

What Nottingham sought for was a rule which would bring executory trusts and devises, whether of freehold or terms of years, within the bounds of what could be legitimately achieved through the manipulation of common law estates, but without unnecessarily narrowing their scope or subjecting them to the technicalities which enmeshed common law contingent remainders. He identified a perpetuity as `the settlement of an estate or an interest in tail, with such remainders expectant upon it as are in no sort in the power of the tenant in tail in possession to dock by any recovery or assignment, but such remainders must continue as perpetual clogs upon the estate'.[38] Through a gift to an eldest son for life, with remainder in tail to *his* eldest son, it was possible to restrain alienation of the fee simple for the lifetime of the eldest son, plus the minority of the grandson if he was still a minor when his estate fell into possession upon the death of his father, and Nottingham took up the position that provided a remainder would vest within that period - the lifetime of a person already living and a minority thereafter - the mischief of a perpetuity would be avoided. This mischief he identified in rather curious terms: `such [perpetuities] do fight against God, for they pretend to such a stability in human affairs as the nature of them admits not of, and they are against the reason and policy of the law, and therefore not to be endured'.[39]

In the *Duke of Norfolk's Case* all the gifts involved were to living members of the same generation, but in argument the Chancellor was pressed with the need to establish a clear line between good and bad gifts and replied: `Where will you stop if you do not stop here? [i.e. if you allow this gift]. I will tell you where I will stop: I will stop wherever any visible inconvenience doth appear'.[40] The line Nottingham probably wished to draw was between sensible responses to real and present family situations and hubristic schemes to protect family estates from all conceivable unfavourable contingencies.[41] What he had produced, however, was a test based solely on remoteness of vesting, though his *dictum* left it open for argument that the outer boundary could be adjusted to deal with any unforeseen mischiefs.

This rule became known, not very felicitously, as 'the modern rule against perpetuities'[42]. It did not and could not replace the mass of existing rules but rather added to them, albeit in a form which was simple and elegant. But to describe it as a rule *against* perpetuities is apt to mislead, for it did in fact *permit* landowners to create settlements which might endure for relatively long periods with greater security from legal challenge than had hitherto been the case.[43]

The form which such settlements usually took is the so-called strict settlement, which has already been mentioned. It seems to have become *the* characteristic settlement in Charles II's reign and its popularity was such that when in 1740 the House of Lords had to take a crucial decision on the effectiveness of a key element in the strict settlement, whether the so-called 'trustees to preserve contingent remainders' had vested interests, Chief Justice Willes, advising the House, openly adverted to policy considerations:

'Surely, it is much less evil to make a construction, even contrary to the common rules of law (though I think this is not so) than to overthrow I may say 100,000 settlements; for it is a maxim in laws, as well as reason, *communis error facit jus*.'[44]

Most landowners seem to have been satisfied with the strict settlement. On its face it was a disappointing device for the would-be dynast, since it allowed his grandson to break the entail at twenty-one,[45] but in practice it had the potential for self-renewal. If the grandson reached twenty-one while his father, the life tenant, was still alive he would be offered a handsome allowance as a bribe to enter into a re-settlement which reduced him to a life tenant in remainder, with remainder to *his* eldest son in tail, so perpetuating the settlement for another generation.[46] The combination of financial and social pressures seems to have worked well enough for there to have been few attempts to seek alternative forms of settlement, and when a

168

blatant attempt to achieve something more ambitious did come along, as in *Duke of Marlborough v. Godolphin*[47], the judges were perfectly willing to strike it down; there is no sense however of any battle between the courts and settlors.

Perhaps because the judges no longer felt the need to maintain a suspicious vigilance towards settlements, they began to apply the rule against perpetuities in a literal, rather than a purposive way. In particular, there seems to have developed a confusion between remoteness of vesting and alienability, and the view became established that so long as the fee became *alienable* no later than the length of a minority (twenty-one years) after the death of the grantee, the rule was satisfied. Inasmuch as the cases in question gave rise to no 'mischief' on this benevolent extension of the *Duke of Norfolk's Case* they are defensible, but as a body of precedent in a court of equity which was becoming increasingly prone to apply precedents rigidly, they led Nottingham's rule down the slippery slope to a discreditable and almost unintelligible formula. An equally significant development, not much regarded at the time, was the decision in *Madox v. Staines*[48] that the rule applied to settlements of pure personalty as well as realty and leaseholds, although the policy that land should not be kept off the market does not apply with equal force to chattels and scarcely at all to money.

The Thellusson will presented the judges with their last real chance to reverse the trend which was making Lord Nottingham's rule into a formula divorced from reality, a danger vividly illustrated by Lord Kenyon's decision in *Jee v. Audley*.[49] If executory devises and trusts were to be judged good or bad solely on whether vesting must occur within the lifetime of *some* person or persons alive at the date of the gift and twenty- one years thereafter, then settlements could be framed which were likely to last for considerably longer than any at common law, while others which were perfectly innocuous and most unlikely to exceed the 'perpetuity period' would fail because of fanciful and grotesque possibilities which inhered in them through draftsmen's oversights.[50] Thellusson was exploiting the latitude of Nottingham's rule as few had done before him and counsel for the family would claim that he had overstepped the bounds.

They based this claim on several distinct grounds. The first turned on the number of lives by which the vesting of the estates was to be measured and the basis of their selection. Hitherto all the reported cases other than the difficult and controversial *Humberston v. Humberston*[51] had involved a suspension of vesting during the life of one person, or at most two or three, and those persons usually enjoyed a prior gift themselves or were intimately connected with the remaindermen; even in *Hopkins v. Hopkins,*[52] which broke new ground with three lives, there was a gift limited in succession to the sons of the three daughters of a living person.

It was argued that in view of the pernicious tendency of the Thellusson will the court should decline to go beyond that established limit but without necessarily marking the outer boundary, since in this case Nottingham's 'visible inconvenience' had become apparent. If this will were allowed, future settlors might contrive much wider classes of lives, perhaps wholly unrelated to the beneficiaries, chosen simply to ensure the greatest chance of a really long perpetuity period; all the MPs, all the deans and chapters, all the royal family now living might be selected.[53] As this argument implicitly acknowledges, Thellusson had *not* extended and abused the established formula as blatantly as he might have done. His 'lives' were nine but they were all directly connected with the ultimate beneficiaries and even without going outside his own family he might have easily have increased the probable length of the period by including the lives of his daughters and of his children's daughters living at his death; after all, a man so well acquainted with the *trentes immortelles* of Geneva knew that women tend to outlive men.[54]

The challenge to Thellusson's will on the basis of numbers and relationships failed, partly because the spectre of 'royal lives' clauses was too remote and insufficiently alarming to persuade the court not to follow logic and precedent. The logic was clear, for it had been said in *Scattergood v. Edge* that 'let the lives be never so many, there must be a survivor, and so it is but the length of that life; for Twisden used to say, the candles were all lighted at once'.[55] If the length of a human life, and twenty-one years thereafter, constituted no perpetuity problem, then it was a matter of indifference whether there were one life or many, since the rule was now considered to be a rule about *possibilities* only. Suppose, it was said in argument for the trustees, a testator had nominated the fabulously long-lived Old Parr or Jenkins alone, that would have suspended vesting for longer than any hundred other lives he might have chosen. Mansfield's reply that 'the law looks to what usually happens in the common course of affairs; and does not consider it worthwhile to advert to such rare instances'[56] was mere assertion, and assertion that was barely reconcilable with *Jee v. Audley.*[57]

Moreover, the logic was uncomfortably closely linked to common law principles for Hargrave's liking. If Lord Nottingham's rule was based on analogy with what might be done at common law without creating a perpetuity, then there was nothing wrong with using multiple lives; for a common law limitation of life estates successively to twenty living persons followed by a fee tail to an unborn person would be perfectly valid and this was merely the same thing by way of executory devise, the only difference being that the 'lives' had no estate themselves.[58] Nor could it be plausibly argued that the 'measuring lives' must be confined to prospective beneficiaries, for that proposition was incompatible with established case law.[59] Counsel for the family had no intelligible principle to put forward for limiting the *number* of measuring lives, and when they argued for a close causal connection between them and the beneficiaries they were handicapped by the fact that in the instant case the connection *was* close. By adopting either of the arguments the court would have made the rule less simple and logical but also less prone to absurdity, and by adopting the second they might still have pronounced in favour of Thellusson's scheme. All that *Thellusson v. Woodford* accomplished was to publicise and confirm the legality of concocting artificially elongated perpetuity periods by employing multiple lives.[60]

There was another argument that the selection of lives transgressed the rule, and this one focused on the inclusion of unborn children. The phrase in the will 'or born in due time afterwards' expressly provided for their inclusion among the `measuring lives', so that the perpetuity period was in effect enlarged at the beginning by the time necessary to establish whether any such children would be born, while the description of `eldest male lineal descendant then living' included children *en ventre sa mère*[in the womb] by implication, so extending the period at its end.

Two separate points were taken on this. The first was that an unborn child could not be used as a life in being for the purposes of the rule except where it was capable of taking a benefit itself, so that its inclusion merely as a measuring life, by creating the possibility that it might be the last survivor of those lives and that vesting might therefore be delayed beyond the permitted perpetuity period, would infringe the rule. The second point was that such a `double allowance' at the beginning and the end of the perpetuity period had never been countenanced and took it beyond the accepted limits.[61]

The legal position of an unborn child is necessarily anomalous and creates awkward problems in a variety of contexts. There is therefore nothing inherently implausible in arguing that if the law of property treats an unborn child as a living person for some purposes, it does not follow that it should do so for all purposes. Counsel for the family sought to show that the existing law included an unborn child in categories such as `children', `issue' and `descendants' where it was to its benefit, but not otherwise; hence it followed that it *must* be included at the end of the accumulation period, where beneficial entitlements were involved, but could not count as a life in being when chosen as a measuring life: `there is no case in which such a child has been considered in existence, where it is no benefit to him to be so considered. The rule has never gone farther'.[62]

This rule was said to have been derived from the civil law and applied by Lord Hardwicke in a series of cases, achieving an independent existence in equity from the time of *Beale v. Beale*, in which Hardwicke had stated that `equity should consider such child, in order to its being provided for'.[63] By contrast, to include unborn children as lives in being under Thellusson's will would actually prejudice their interests, since

172

they would then be excluded from benefitting under the trusts of the will, whereas to declare the trusts void was to give them a chance of inheriting through their fathers.

However, counsel for the trustees could cite instances in which unborn children had the legal status of persons without receiving any benefits. In particular they might be vouched to warranty under the authority of Coke himself, while by the civil law they might be made heirs or executors. It was contended that for the most part the cases turned on the intention of the donor and did not establish any clear cut distinctions between instances of benefit and others.[64] Mansfield made some attempt to explain away the `curious' case of vouching but had mainly to rely on the general argument that `every particular instance showing, that a child *en ventre* is to be considered in being for particular purposes, proves that it is not to be so considered for all purposes'.[65]

There was however more recent and unfavourable authority which confronted counsel for the family. Loughborough himself had sent *Long v. Blackall* to the judges of the King's Bench for their opinion whether a devise over on the death of a child yet unborn was valid and they had certified that it was.[66] Hargrave could scarcely hope to persuade the common law judges that their solemnly delivered opinion was wrong, but he suggested that from the brevity and terms of the certificate it had not been fully argued or properly considered and was therefore open to re-examination.[67]

Neither of the family's arguments persuaded the court. Buller gave a trenchant, slightly sarcastic rebuttal to the first, about the status/capacity of an unborn child. `Such a child has been considered a non-entity. Let us see, what this non-entity can do. He may be vouched in a warranty, though it is for the purpose of making him answer over in value. He may be an executor. He may take under the *Statute of Distributions*.... He may take by devise. He may be entitled under a charge for raising portions. He may have an injunction, and he may have a guardian'.[68]

Furthermore, admitting that in most of the cases the issue had been whether the unborn child was intended to be within the scope of a limitation and therefore able to benefit, `there is no reason for so confining the rule. Why should not children *en ventre sa mère* be considered generally as in existence? They are entitled to all the privileges of other persons. In this case it is enough to say, such a child is capable of having an estate given to him, and consequently to another person for his life. The infant is not hurt, nor is the Law transgressed, by giving the interest to a third person any more than by giving it to the infant himself'.[69]

Buller and the other judges do fail to answer one of the arguments: the infant *is* hurt in this case, for by including Peter Isaac's twins among the measuring lives they are debarred from any benefit under the will, *and* by holding that their inclusion is lawful the will itself is sustained. This however, would be presumably answered by the argument that Thellusson never intended them to take the benefit, so the prejudice is in fact illusory.

That left the second point, that to incorporate gestation periods at beginning and end was to go beyond the accepted formula. Authority for the inclusion of gestation at the end was so firmly settled by *Stephens v. Stephens*[70] that the contrary was unarguable, and the case of a possible double extension seemed to be covered by *Long v. Blackall*.[71] Hargrave attacked the latter on several grounds. The first was that the `boasted analogy between strict legal entail by estates for life with remainders over and the irregular but permitted entail by executory devise will be destroyed; and entail by executory devise will continue property unalienable for a longer time than can be effected by entail through the medium of remainders.'[72]

He exaggerates somewhat by describing this as `a vast extension of executory devise whereby the boundary becomes in effect extended to a generation beyond lives in being'.[73] There is, he explains, a fundamental difference between allowing the period of gestation at the end, which only adds nine or ten months to the perpetuity, and allowing an unborn life at the beginning, which adds the whole of that life, thereby contradicting Lord Kenyon's statement in *Long v. Blackall*, `that the rules respecting executory devises have conformed to the rules laid down in the construction of legal limitations'.[74]

Almost as an afterthought, Hargrave contends that even if *Long v. Blackall*[75]

174

`should be deemed the most conclusive precedent for allowing time for the birth of a posthumous child twice, it will not reach this will[76], since unlike that case, where the purpose of the testator was `laudable and meritorious', on which account the judges might feel it their duty to do all in their power to save the will, this one was `unmeritorious and even unnatural'.[77] None of the judges was much impressed by the argument. It was predictable that Buller would feel obliged to defend the King's Bench from the imputation of want of thoroughness:

`in my opinion it does not deserve that imputation. Though the immense quantity of business, that passes through that Court goes almost beyond the bounds of comprehension, I, who sat there near twenty years can say, it is not treated in that manner. I know, the habit of that Court's to deliberate upon the papers as soon as they are delivered. Whoever reads what was said by one of the Judges in that case must feel, that he was fully master of the subject and gave full scope to every thing, that could be said; though his sentiments were expressed in few words.'[78] Notwithstanding that he considered that the question properly belonged to the common law judges, the Master of the Rolls went over the ground with scrupulous care and agreed with him. Hargrave's reasoning was thought fallacious; if an unborn child was to be taken as a life in being then he was equated with other lives without a distinction and the length of the perpetuity period was not *ipso facto* increased by his inclusion: it began before he was born and would end on his death only if he were the last survivor of the measuring lives.[79]

There was however an argument which was not put which is of some interest, and that is the argument about evidential certainty. With a gift by will to `the children of Mr. X' there is no difficulty (if we exclude the possibility of his wife's adultery) in establishing, once he has died, who they are, for if he is to have posthumous issue unmistakable signs of pregnancy will be apparent at most within a few months. It is otherwise however in a gift by will `to the children of Mr. X on the death of the last survivor of my sons and grandsons living at my death', if we define the benefitted class as including children *en ventre sa mère* when the testator dies. Suppose that at the date of my death none of the wives of my sons exhibits signs of pregnancy, but that within a few months afterwards, one does: how are we to know (and how could it be known in the state of medical science in 1800) whether the conception predated my death? The parents themselves might not know! Neither in *Thellusson* nor any other English case I am aware of is this question considered: was it perhaps too delicate to be asked? It could be solved pragmatically by a rule of thumb presumption that any live birth between x and y weeks after the settlor's death is to be conclusively taken to be a child conceived before his death, but in *Jee v. Audley*[80] the court of King's Bench had refused to make the common course of nature its guide. There seems a plausible case for arguing that where lives are being used purely to measure the perpetuity period they do not and must not include those of children *en ventre sa mère*.

4. The Argument upon Accumulations

The last argument open to the family, and perhaps the strongest, was to concentrate on the accumulation direction itself and to argue that there is a material distinction between providing that the use and enjoyment of property or the income it produces shall move from one person to another -the situation governed by the rules against perpetuities - and the suspension of any beneficial enjoyment of property, a much stronger exercise of dominion, and that in view of the difference the courts had both the power and the duty to be much more jealous of the latter and to circumscribe it more narrowly.

Some telling points could be made in favour of this argument. First, 'an entail precluding enjoyment is wholly unknown':[81] at common law it was impossible to divorce ownership of an estate in land from enjoyment of its fruits, the divorce which is the very essence of a trust. Yet the rule against perpetuities was framed so to as permit for executory devises and trusts what could be done at common law by way of one or more life estates vested in persons in being, followed by estates in tail in remainder which might only be barred when they vested in possession in an adult tenant in tail - in other words the strict settlement. There was no such compelling need for coherence and consistency in the case of accumulations.

Second, the mischief to be apprehended was different and perhaps more serious. The mischief of an unbarrable entail was that land or capital was rendered effectively inalienable whatever the circumstances of family. The original concern, in Nottingham's time, was on the ill-effects this might have on the family if its circumstances changed, but in the next century the emphasis shifted to the disturbing influence long settlements might have on the land market. Accumulations permitted the income from property as well as the capital to be tied up and could be objectionable because (a) they might be intended ultimately to place in the hands of one or two persons a vast fortune, creating over-mighty subjects and (b) if they became widespread they would tend to distort the economy by obliging investments of large sums to be made in land, the Funds or whatever other object the settlor had directed.[82]

But suppose the evil to be admitted, was it was not too late to remedy it by judicial action? It could not be contended that the device was novel. Hargrave had to admit that it had `by some means insinuated itself'[83] and rightly traced it to the directions given in cases of infancy and lunacy, while Mansfield acutely linked it to the coming of settlements of personal property.[84] They argued however that the cases were few, that they had not received thorough judicial consideration, that there was no widespread practice which would be deranged by any alteration in the law, and that there was therefore no serious objection to restricting accumulation to the limits already covered by decided cases.

Accumulations had indeed come in by the back door, and are intimately associated with the development, as yet little studied, of a managerial role for trustees in addition to their custodial one.[85] Medieval feoffments to uses had quite regularly imposed active duties on feoffees, who might for example be empowered to mortgage, lease or sell lands and hold the proceeds of such capital transactions for the *cestuis que use*. Such `active uses' were explicitly recognised in the Statute of Uses and excluded from being executed, though that in itself suggests that the draftsman regarded them as comparatively insignificant.[86] Where the property enfoeffed was land, however, the utmost duty of a trustee would usually be to account for the rents and profits he had received and at least in the absence of an express direction by will, it remained arguable until the eighteenth century that a solvent executor or trustee charged with holding money on trust might invest the money and retain the profit for himself.[87] However, it had become well established that when a will or trust deed which gave a benefit to an infant or a lunatic was brought into Chancery the court would direct the property to be accumulated for his benefit even if no express direction to that effect was found in the instrument.[88]

Express directions were probably unusual but were already in progress under three well known wills. Mr. Shepherd, of Exning in Cambridgeshire, was the sort of character who usually inhabits examination papers, for as Lord Hardwicke drily noticed, `if the testator had studied to lay a foundation for all the questions that could arise on such an estate in account of equity, he has done it effectually, for there is hardly a point upon limitations over or resulting trusts in this court but there is a foundation for it in this will some time or other.'[89] Essentially, Mr. Shepherd left his residuary realty and personalty in equal shares to the children of his bastard daughter Frances Gibson, then an infant, with remainders over in default. Out of the rents and profits arising in the meantime certain annuities were directed to be paid, but the balance was not specifically appropriated and the heir sought to claim it. Following *Stephens v. Stephens*[90] it was decided that an executory devise of residue *tout court* includes the interim profits, to the exclusion of the heir, and the Lord Chancellor directed that the surplus after payment of the annuities be invested in South Sea annuities in the name of the Accountant-General and the annual produce re-invested; the accumulation would continue during the whole lifetime of the daughter if she had no children, and even in the events that happened, it had to continue for at least twenty-one years. Frances (Lady Irwin as she had become) was still alive in 1798 and the will was a celebrated one at the Chancery bar.[91]

Shepherd's was not an accumulation expressly directed by a settlor, but Lady Denison's was. Her will had been in court in 1787, 'with much prejudice against it'.[92] She had two very young nieces and directed that her residue be invested in land and the rents and profits of her existing estates, plus those investments, be accumulated until the elder niece should have a second son and he should reach twenty-one, with other limitations in default of those events. She directed that when the son became twenty-one the whole lot be conveyed to him 'and the heirs male of his body...'. The will was arranged so as to comply with the rule against perpetuities, but the accumulation would be likely to last for a very long time. For that reason, apparently, it was contested before Lord Kenyon but he reluctantly upheld it, and the accumulation was in progress.[93]

Even more recent was the will of Sir John Webb. Webb had three bastard sons, James, John and Frederic, and for each of them he set apart land which his trustee, Arrowsmith, was to manage for them in conjunction with a steward/agent, a relation of Webb. The income from each estate was to be invested and used for the maintenance and education of a son until he was twenty-one, who would then receive £1,200 p.a. until he was twenty-five, when the whole property and accumulated surplus became his for life with remainders in tail male. Webb's biggest estate, in Gloucestershire, was devised to Arrowsmith on trust (after various payments) until Webb's granddaughter Lady Barbara Ashley should be twenty-one or until her marriage if it took place sooner, while his Dorset estates were for Arrowsmith to hold and accumulate the income during the lives of Barbara and her mother Lady Shaftesbury, and on the death of the survivor to hand over to certain of Barbara's children.[94]

Webb's will has a number of interesting features. First, anticipating a contest 'he declared, that if his daughter or granddaughter or any of their issue should institute any suit against his trustee, his heirs, executors and co., or molest or disturb them in the execution of any of the trusts, he revoked the several devises or bequests to them';[95] this attempt to oust the court's jurisdiction would clearly have been void.

Second, Arrowsmith's burdensome task was to be rewarded with 5% of the gross rental of realty and profits of personalty until each beneficiary successively became absolutely entitled. This was the same allowance the court gave to agents managing lands and is a rare early example of a trustee receiving, in effect, a management fee. What is equally interesting in the light of what was to happen on the Thellusson estates is that in 1802, a few years after the will was upheld, a quarrel came before the court over the trustee's attempt 'to keep up an establishment of pleasure' on the estates.[96]

The one case in which Chancery had declared void a trust for accumulation did not help the family's cause very much. An eminent conveyancer and 'very able lawyer' named Bradley had died in 1790 leaving a will in which he directed an accumulation of income from stocks and annuities to commence three years after his death and to continue until 1860. For the first twenty years £500 p.a., for the rest of the term £1,000 p.a., and thereafter in perpetuity the whole sum was to be

'applied in the purchasing of such books, as by a proper disposition of them under the following directions may have a tendency to promote the interest of virtue and religion and the happiness of mankind; the same to be disposed of in Great Britain or any other part of the British dominions: this charitable design to be executed by and under the direction or superintendency of such persons and such rules and regulations, as by any Decree or Order of the High Court of Chancery shall from time to time be directed on that behalf.'[97]

Lord Thurlow struck this down and left his successors lamenting the absence of a report of his reasons, for it seemed even to Eldon, who greatly respected Thurlow, an ungenerous and dubious denial of charitable status, apparently on the ground that it was too vague.[98] Counsel in *Thellusson* suggested tentatively that Thurlow's decision exemplified a robust attitude to trusts that were essentially abuses of the testamentary power and that the accumulation itself was objectionable, but had to concede that the point had not been raised.[99] Bradley's will does suggest however that

180

the potential of compound interest was beginning to be appreciated.

Express directions to accumulate then, were novel but emergent, a significant part of the increasing sophistication of trusts and extension of the functions of trusteeship. There must have been other instances, though it is unlikely that there were any involving large fortunes which did not somehow find themselves in Chancery. Lady Denison's case had worried the court; Sir John Webb's will had been upheld, but only by the Master of the Rolls; now here was Peter Thellusson directing a vaster, longer accumulation. Could nothing be done? Should nothing be done?

Counsel for the trustees contented themselves with arguing that although express accumulations were relatively new, the notion was familiar in and out of court. It was regularly to be found in the wills of West India planters for the purpose of discharging incumbrances and was done as a matter of course whenever there was no adult beneficiary in possession and able to claim the profits of a trust fund. It was not therefore something new and alarming and there was no reason to regulate it by creating new, judge-made law.[100]

The common law judges were actually less impressed with the dangers of accumulation than their Chancery colleagues. Buller said that all the cases that had been cited as showing that accumulation directions could be held void only went to prove their validity,[101] while Lawrence addressed the policy issues directly. It was a novel objection to a legal device that it might enable a man to acquire a vast fortune, and it could hardly be made a sensible foundation for a whole doctrine; as to the mortmain tendency, the money would not be locked away but circulated - a direction to hoard, rather than to invest and accumulate, would be pernicious.[102] Arden and Loughborough were more uneasy and the former rested his answer wholly on Lady Denison's case. With sound logic he rejected the pragmatic view that one could say that because Kenyon upheld an accumulation for two lives, that might be made the *ne plus ultra* of accumulation. Loughborough regarded the question, outside of Lady Denison's case, as 'wholly new' but found that it had never been stipulated that profits should be beneficially allocated during a perpetuity period and was not willing to introduce such a rule this late in the day.[103]

The argument for tighter restrictions on accumulations is not so forceful as one would expect. Hargrave in particular allowed his dislike of executory devise in general to obscure the novelty and objectionableness of this new device. Indeed, Hargrave's *tour de force* was not well suited to the needs of his clients. The judges grew impatient with his repeated attempts to put down executory devises as

`not a genuine, antient, branch of our law, but an indulged superinduction to it; not a regular production of our general system, but an excrescence; not a strictly regular species of intail, but a permitted, irregular, mode of settlement; not a legitimate offspring of our Common Law, but a privilege gradually insinuated into our jurisprudence'.[104]

For Hargrave the 250 years since the Statute of Wills was all recent history, a postscript to the land law as set forth in *Coke upon Littleton,* and he seems to have been making a doomed effort to re-assert the primacy of the common law of real property and to put the upstart doctrines and devices which had their origin in equity back into a subordinate place. It was all a little unrealistic, a little `academic' and not very effective. Worse, by its length and amplitude it may have obscured the thrust of the family's case, which should have emphasised the differences between devises proper, firmly governed by the modern rule against perpetuities, and the still new and essentially different device of the accumulation. Buller swept aside all Hargrave's antique erudition with dismissive and wounding briskness:

`As a matter of history or curiosity an inquiry into the origin of the rule may be the amusement of a leisure hour: but it will not afford any assistance in the decision of a Court of Justice'.[105]

It is unlikely however, that the outcome of the case turned on the skill of counsel on one side or the other, for the judgments make it only too clear that the family faced an uphill struggle. There seems little difference between the approach of the common law judges and those of the Chancery, and Buller in particular found little merit in the case against the will. Two related points emerge as being decisive.

182

The first is that the only objection to executory devises is that they tend to a perpetuity and that tendency is restrained by the rule laid down by Lord Nottingham, which ensures that an executory devise cannot render property inalienable for longer than can be achieved through common law. Nottingham himself defined the `visible inconvenience' in that way and consequently his rule might and should be applied consistently and rigidly, for nothing which conforms to it can create a mischief - or at least, such a mischief as judges may correct. The exclusive concentration on alienability as the criterion, despite the fact that in an increasing number of cases, the subject matter was personal property of the most interchangeable kind, and the disappearance of any reference to the purpose of the rule in protecting families against inflexible settlements is striking and obviously unfavourable to any argument based on the adverse effects of the will on the family.

The second point is the sheer emphasis on the immutability of judge-made rules and the binding nature of precedent. It is not a common law judge but the Master of the Rolls who insists:

`the doctrine that has been contended for....[is], that in every case the Court is not to look for a general rule, but for particular instances, in which the rule has been acted upon; and is to go no farther. There is no such rule. It is contrary to the first principles of judicial determination, and would vest a most dangerous power in the Judges, which no Judge would wish to possess. The Judges are to decide the law, not to make the law. If an inconvenience arises, the legislature, not the Judges, must apply the remedy'.[106]

Equity had once been criticised for being `a roguish thing, for law we have a measure, know what to trust to. Equity is according to the conscience of him that is Chancellor, and as it is larger or narrower so is equity.'[107] At the end of the eighteenth century, however, the doctrines of equity had become so well settled that its judges denied themselves any power to adjust them to meet cases where they produced an unsatisfactory and perhaps dangerous result, even when the doctrines were barely a century old. The Lord Chancellor, plainly sympathetic to the family, described the will as `unkind and so illiberal' but lamented that `it is not for me to make a new law; and without making a new rule I do not know what to do'.[108]

This combination made the family's case hopeless. It also marked a decisive point in the development of the rule against perpetuities. The fullness of the arguments, the extent of the property involved and the obvious importance of the issues meant that the court had to confront the workings of the rule as it had evolved in the case law and consider whether its stealthy extension ought to be halted, perhaps reversed, and failing that, whether it was adequate to serve also as the outer limit for accumulations. The judges' unwillingness to adapt or complicate the simple formula of a life in being (including lives *en ventre sa mère*) and twenty-one years (including gestation at that end too), when added to the earlier refusal, in *Jee v. Audley*,[109] to circumscribe the possibilities which governed the rule, ensured that the rule became detached from common sense and received a remorseless, mechanistic construction that ultimately discredited the law.[110]

NOTES

1. PRO C 12/241/27; *Bleak House*, p.50.

2. E. Foss, *The Judges of England* (9 vols., London, 1848-64), vol. VIII, pp.332-4.

3. Hargrave, *Juridical Arguments*, vol.II, appendix I.

4. *Ibid.*

5. *Ibid.*, 'advertisement'; *Thellusson v. Woodford* (1799) 4 Ves. Jun. 227 at 237.

6. *Thellusson v. Woodford* (1799) 4 Ves. Jun. 227 at 328.

7. C.H. Sherrin *et al.*, *Williams' Law Relating to Wills* (7th edn., London, 1995), vol. I, pp. 513-62; J.B. Clark and J.G. Ross-Martyn, *Theobald on Wills* (15th edn., London, 1993), pp. 199-211; A.J. Hawkins and E.C. Ryder, *The Construction of Wills* (London, 1965).

8. *Chapman v. Brown* (1765) 3 Burr. 1626 at 1634-5.

9. *Williams' Law Relating to Wills*, vol.I, pp.427-8.

10. *Thellusson v. Woodford*(1799) 4 Ves. Jun. 227 at 239.

11. *Ibid.*, at 320. *Thellusson v. Woodford* is one of the leading authorities for this proposition.

12. *Hart v. Tulk* (1852) 2 De G.M. & G. 300 at 315.

13. *Thellusson v Woodford* (1799) 4 Ves. Jun. 227 at 240, 268.

14. *Ibid.*, at 240. References to arguments for the family are from Hargrave's argument unless otherwise stated.

15. *Ibid.*, at 295. The report does not identify the arguments of individual counsel.

16. *Ibid.*, at 325.

17. *Ibid.*, at 283-5.

18. *Ibid.*, at 326, 328, 343. Buller however, said the will was 'expressed in a blundering way' (326).

19. *Ibid.*, at 283.

20. *Ibid.*, at 283-4. It is of course otherwise where the words do not define the class of beneficiaries with 'sufficient practical certainty' to enable the testator's wishes to be carried into effect. Even in the context of discretionary trusts, however, the leading modern case, *McPhail v. Doulton* [1971] A.C. 424, suggests that the courts will strive hard to avoid such a finding.

21. *Ibid.*, 326, 328 (Buller and Arden).

22. There are good modern accounts in Milsom, *Historical Foundations of the Common Law*, pp. 166-242, Simpson, *History of Land Law*, pp. 81-102, 173-240, and Bonfield, *Marriage Settlements, 1601-1740*, pp. 1-81.

23.   In the language of the land law an estate describes the duration of a grant of land.

24.   Simpson, *History of Land Law*, pp.216-17; Megarry and Wade, *Law of Real Property* (2nd edn., London, 1959), pp. 214-22. P. Bordwell, Alienability and Perpetuities, *Iowa Law Review* 22 (1936-7), 437-460; 23 (1937-8), 1-23; 24 (1938-9), 1-65, 636-59; 25 (1939-40), 1-31, 708-36, remains a valuable account of the subject of future interests and attributes the coinage `perpetuity' to Sir Francis Bacon.

25.   Bonfield, *Marriage Settlements*, pp. 31-2; Bordwell, *Alienability and Perpetuities*, vol. 24, 649-59. Seisin had an elusive and changing meaning but for many purposes it was tantamount to a right to possession enforceable at common law.

26.   Milsom, *Historical Foundations*, pp. 216-29; Simpson, *History of Land Law*, pp. 191-207.

27.   Simpson, *History of Land Law*, pp.196-8, 218.

28.   (1671) 2 Wms Saunders 380.

29.   Milsom, *Historical Foundations*, pp. 225-30; Megarry and Wade, *Law of Real Property*, pp. 218-20.

30.   Notably *Manning's Case* (1609) 8 Co. Rep. 946, *Lampert's Case* (1612) 10 Co. Rep. 466 and *Pells v. Brown* (1620) Cro. Jac. 590.

31.   Simpson, *History of Land Law*, pp.219-23; Milsom, *Historical Foundations*, pp. 230-3.

32.   Simpson, *History of Land Law*, pp.199-207; Milsom, *Historical Foundations*, pp. 233-9.

33.   Milsom, *Historical Foundations*, p. 233.

34.   D.E.C. Yale, Lord Nottingham's Chancery Cases, *Selden Society*, 72 (1954), lxxiii-xci; H. Barry, The Duke of Norfolk's Case, *Virginia Law Review* 23 (1937), 538-68; G.L. Haskins, Extending the Grasp of the Dead Hand: Reflections on the Origins of the Rule Against Perpetuities, *University of Pennsylvania Law Review* 126 (1977), 19- 46.

35.   (1681) 3 Ch. Cas 1, at 14-26.

36.   Simpson, *History of Land Law*, pp. 227-8.

37.   3 Ch. Cas. 1.

38.   *Howard v. Duke of Norfolk* (1681) 2 Swans. 455 at 460.

39.   3 Cas. in Ch. 31.

40.   *Ibid.*, 49.

41.   Simpson, *Legal Science and Legal Absurdity*, at 77-8.

42.   See Bordwell, *Alienability and Perpetuities*, vol. 22, 437-40 for a discussion of how a policy became a rule.

43.   This point is emphasised by recent writers on settlements, e.g. Haskins, *Dead Hand*, and Chesterman, *Family Settlements on Trust*, pp.124- 67.

44.   *Dormer v. Parkhurst* (1741) Willes 327.

186

45.   By a device known as the common recovery, see Simpson, *History of Land Law*, pp. 125-37.

46.   How often is debated. The arguments are summarised by J.V. Beckett, *The Aristocracy in England, 1660-1914*(Oxford, 1986), pp. 58-66.

47.   (1759) 1 Eden 404.

48.   (1727) P. Wms. 421. The arguments are given more fully in *Maddock v. Staines* 3 Bro. P.C. 109. The significance of this case is pointed out by Chesterman, *Family Settlements on Trust*, at p.141.

49.   (1787) 1 Cox Eq. 324. As Simpson points out (*Legal Science and Legal Absurdity*, pp. 96-8), it did not acquire the status of a `leading case' until long afterwards.

50.   This is precisely what did happen: see e.g. *Ward v. Van der Loeff* [1924] A.C. 653; *Re Gaite's W.T.s* [1949] 1 All E.R. 459; *Re Dawson* (1888) 39 Ch. D. 155; *Re Frost* (1889) 43 Ch. D 246.

51.   (1716) 1 P. Wms. 332. It involved a series of life estates which clearly broke the rules but Lord Chancellor Cowper directed a settlement to be drawn *cy-près*, that is giving effect to the settlor's intentions as nearly as the law allowed. C. Fearne, *An Essay on the Learning of Contingent Remainders* (10th edn., by J.W. Smith, London, 1844), vol. I, pp. 205-6.

52.   (1734) Atk. 581. Discussed in *Thellusson v. Woodford* at 246, 288-9, 298, 303; Fearne, *Contingent Remainders*, p.10. It was a devise to trustees on trust for B for life, then to his first and other sons successively in tail male, remainder to the future sons of C successively for life, with divers other remainders and an ultimate gift over to D. B died before the testator and none of the remainders vested before the testator's death.

53.   *Thellusson v. Woodford* (1799) 4 Ves. Jun. 227 at 277-80, 301-3.

54.   *Supra*, p. 82. The prophecies of counsel were to be fulfilled much later, when the descendants of Queen Victoria began to turn up in deeds and wills, sometimes in undignified juxtaposition with grants of drainage and sewerage rights, and it would be interesting to know whether the learned conveyancers who popularised these `royal lives' clauses in their precedent books took the idea from these very suggestions. They were not put in print, however, until it had been definitively ruled that wide and arbitrary selections of lives could only be challenged on the grounds that they posed unreasonable difficulties in ascertaining when the perpetuity period expired. In *Re Villar* [1928] Ch. 471, the court took a generous view even on that question, though by then the `lineal descendants of Queen Victoria' chosen by the testator numbered about 120, including the scattered refugees of the continental ruling families liquidated during and after the Great War. See J.H.C. Morris and W.B. Leach, *The Rule Against Perpetuities*,(2nd edn., London, 1964), pp. 61-2.

55.   (1687) 1 Salk. 229; 1 Eq. Cas. Abr. 190. Twisden said this in *Goring v. Bickerstaffe* (1662)

Pollexf. 31.

56.   *Thellusson v Woodford* (1799) 4 Ves. Jun. 227 at 302.

57.   (1787) 1 Cox Eq. 324. `I am desired to do in this case something which I do not feel at liberty to do, namely to suppose that it is impossible for persons in so advanced at age and John and Elizabeth Jee to have children; but if this can be done in one case it may be done in another; and it is a very dangerous experiment, and introductive of the great inconvenience to give a latitude to such sort of conjecture': *per* Lord Kenyon MR at 324.

58.   *Duke of Norfolk's Case* (1681) 3 Ch. Ca. 29. *Cf. Robinson v. Hardcastle* (1786) 2 Bro. C.C. 22 at 30, where Lord Chancellor Thurlow says a man may appoint 100 or 1,000 trustees and direct the survivor to appoint a life estate without a perpetuity.

59.   E.g. *Goodman v. Goodright* (1759) 2 Burr. 873. See *Thellusson v Woodford* (1799) 4 Ves. Jun. 227 at 244 for argument on the point.

60.   Henry Bengough (who made his will in 1818, see *Bengough v. Edridge*, 1 Sim. 173) was among the first to push this permissiveness to its limits; he used the lives of *twenty eight* named persons and the will was finally upheld in the House of Lords in *Cadell v. Palmer* (1833) 7 Bligh N.S. 202. It is discussed by Fearne, *Contingent Remainders* (appendix 8), W.D. Lewis, *A Practical Treatise on the Law of Perpetuity* (London, 1843) and J.C. Gray, *The Rule Against Perpetuities* (4th edn., by R. Gray, Boston (Mass.), 1942), s. 216-8. The Real Property Commissioners were also unable to find any workable limitation on the number or connectedness of the lives (3rd report, *PP* 1831-2 (484), XXIII at pp.69-71).

61.   *Thellusson v. Woodford* (1799) 4 Ves. Jun. 227 at 271-6.

62.   *Ibid.*, at 241.

63.   1 P. Wms. 244; *Thellusson v. Woodford* (1799) 4 Ves. Jun. 227 at 242.

64.   *Thellusson v. Woodford* (1799) 4 Ves. Jun. 227 at 293-5. *Reeve v. Long* ((1694) 1 Salk. 247), was pertinent here: all the judges had agreed that a contingent remainder under a strict settlement did not by necessary implication include an unborn child, and when that decision was reversed by the House of Lords, Lord Somers being the only lawyer to participate in their decision, a statute was passed confirming the Lords' view but in the process tacitly acknowledging that it was wrong in law.

65.   *Thellusson v. Woodford* (1799) 4 Ves. Jun. 227 at 308.

66.   (1797) 7 Term Rep. 100.

67.   *Thellusson v. Woodford* (1799) 4 Ves. Jun. 227 at 273-6.

68.   *Ibid.*, at 322.

69.   *Ibid.*, at 323.

70.   (1736) Cas. Temp. Talb. 228.

71.   (1797) 7 Term. Rep. 100.

72.   *Thellusson v. Woodford* (1799) 4 Ves. Jun. 227 at 275.

73.   *Ibid.*

74.   *Ibid.*, at p.276.

75.   (1797) 7 Term Rep. 100.

76.   *Thellusson v. Woodford* (1799) 4 Ves. Jun. 227 at 276.

77.   *Ibid.*

78.   *Ibid.*, at 323-4.

79.   *Ibid.*, at 334-7.

80.   (1787) 1 Cox Eq. 324.

81.   *Thellusson v. Woodford* (1799) 4 Ves. Jun. 227, Hargrave at 245.

82.   *Ibid.*, at 245-7, 280-2.

83.   *Ibid.*, at 281.

84.   *Ibid.*, at 306.

85.   Chesterman, *Family Settlements on Trust*, pp.145-50.

86.   Simpson, *History of Land Law*, p. 195; Milsom, *Historical Foundations*, pp. 235- 6.

87.   Chesterman, *Family Settlements on Trust*, pp. 157-8.

88.   For the early cases see Hargrave, *Treatise Upon the Thellusson Act*, ch.2.

89.   *Gibson v. Lord Montfort* (1750) 1 Ves. Sen. 485 at 489. See also *Gibson v. Rogers* (1750) Amb. 93 and *Shepherd v. Ingram* (1764) Amb. 448.

90.   (1736) Ca. Temp. Talb. 228.

91.   *Thellusson v. Woodford* (1799) 4 Ves. Jun. 227 at 306.

92.   *Ibid.*, at 286 (counsel for the trustees).

93.   *Ibid.*, at 286-7, 338-9; Hargrave, *Treatise upon the Thellusson Act*, pp.54-5. It is in the registrar's book for 1786 as *Harrison v. Harrison*.

94.   *Thellusson v. Woodford* (1799) 4 Ves. Jun. 227 at 287; Hargrave, *Treatise upon the Thellusson Act*, p.55.

95.   *Webb v. Earl of Shaftesbury* (1802) 7 Ves. Jun. 481 at 484.

96.   *Ibid.* For further litigation, see 6 Mad. 100, 3 Myl. & K. 599.

97.   Reported as a note to *Brown v. Yeall*, 7 Ves. Jun. 50.

98.   *Attorney-General v. Stepney* (1804) 10 Ves. Jun. 27; *Morice v. Bishop of Durham* (1805) 9 Ves. Jun. 399 at 406.

99.   *Thellusson v. Woodford* (1799) 4 Ves. Jun. 227 at 266, 281-2.

100.   *Ibid.*, at 286-90.

101.   *Ibid.*, at 320-1.

102.   *Ibid.*, at 316-7.

103.   *Ibid.*, at 338-9, 341.

104.   *Ibid.*, at 262.

105.   *Ibid.*, at 319.

106.   *Ibid.*, at 332.

107.   F.M. Pollock (ed.), *The Table Talk of John Selden*, (London, 1927), p.43.

108.   *Thellusson v. Woodford* (1799) 4 Ves. Jun 227 at 340-1.

109.   (1787) 1 Cox Equity 324.

110.   Gray, *Rule against Perpetuities*, s. 190. *Cadell v. Palmer* (1833) 1 Cl. & Fin. 372, which settled the few points on perpetuities left unresolved after *Thellusson v. Woodford*, tends to receive more prominence, perhaps because the first monographs on perpetuities and accumulations (by Lewis and Hargrave) appeared shortly afterwards. But the Real Property Commissioners appreciated the significance of *Thellusson (3rd Report*, 1832) and the arguments in *Cadell* were almost exclusively technical.

CHAPTER 9

THE THELLUSSON ACT

As a judge, the Lord Chancellor had been unable to follow his inclination to strike down Peter Thellusson's will, but as a cabinet minister he was able to ensure that no-one else would evade the wholesome restraints on the power of the dead. Within months of the judgment he laid before Parliament a bill `to prevent the effects of posthumous avarice'[1] and after it received the royal assent on 28th July 1800 no-one might `settle or dispose of any real or personal property...in such manner that the rents, issues, profits or produce thereof, shall be wholly or partially accumulated' for any period longer than :

(1) the grantor's life;

(2) twenty-one years from the grantor's death;

(3) the minority or respective minorities of any persons living or *en ventre sa mère* at the grantor's death; or

(4) the minority or respective minorities of the person or persons who would under the terms of the disposition directing the accumulation, be entitled to the income produced by that property if he, she or they were of full age.[2]

Two further alternative periods were added in 1964[3] but the basic structure of the Act has not been changed in 200 years. Several exceptions were introduced during the bill's passage; for heritable property in Scotland;[4] for wills made before the Act by testators who were not still alive and with testamentary capacity one year after its passage; for `directions touching the produce of timber or wood upon any lands or tenements';[5] and, most important, for accumulations directed towards the payment of debts or as provision for the grantor's children or children of anyone taking an interest under the instrument; these, however, must still comply with the rule against perpetuities.[6]

As an interference with property rights and as an immediate response to an unpalatable judicial decision this measure is highly unusual.[7] Loughborough was not attempting to overthrow by legislation the will he had been forced to uphold (as Thellusson had feared might happen), so why was he so eager to shut the stable door after the horse had bolted? Why not at least await the outcome of the appeal to the House of Lords? He must have believed that trusts of accumulation were so pernicious that they must be curbed, and that any delay would result in other wills or deeds of the same sort being made. Both propositions warrant closer examination.[8]

Amidst all the vituperation directed at Thellusson's will it is often difficult to pin down the precise nature of the objection. Take Hargrave, for example, who describes it as:

'a cruel and deceitful testamentary disposition: which aims not only to overwhelm the most near, most affectionate, most unoffending relatives, by an unnatural proscription, merely for the sake of an outrageous and eccentric vanity; but by an abuse of the act of willmaking, to over-reach the laws of this country and to pervert some of its most wise and convenient rules for regulating the enjoyment and transmission of property, with instruments of mischief to the whole community.'[9] Which is not much help.

But as originally drafted the Executory Devises Bill had a preamble which began:

'Whereas attempts and devices have lately been made to carry such accumulations to their utmost extent, and there is reason to apprehend that the same will be repeated and become frequent: and, whereas while such accumulations are carried on, the property subject thereto is wholly lost to individuals, to the great inconvenience of private families; *and such accumulations may be prejudicial to the community at large...*' Hargrave proposed to elaborate on the underlined phrase by substituting 'and both the property itself, and the produce thereof, are wholly taken out of commerce to the great detriment and injury of the community at large.'[10]

192

This suggests two objections, one economic, the other social. Loughborough claimed that the only objectors among the leading conveyancers to whom he had circulated the bill were two who dissented 'on a principle of political economy'. They held that a big accumulation might be advantageous to the state but the Chancellor asserted that, on the contrary,

'a fortune in circulation, even if spent in luxuries, waste and dissipation, did more good to the public, and afforded more emulation to industry, and better encouragement to arts and manufactures than any useless accumulation of money could do.'[11]

The argument that the fund is taken out of circulation had been advanced at the trial and was rebutted then by Sir Soulden Lawrence, as Francis Burton was to do in the Commons, by pointing out that accumulation is not hoarding (despite the picturesque metaphor that Peter Thellusson 'locked his treasure in a mausoleum and flung the key to some remote descendant yet unborn'[12]), for its very essence is investment.[13] Of course, the form of the investment may be restricted or prescribed, but that is a feature of trusts in general and few were prepared to follow John de Lolmé in arguing that trusts themselves were pernicious.[14] Even though accumulations earmark capital as well as income for investment, their number would have to be very large before their effect in limiting the purchase of consumer goods was significant.

Furthermore, the court of Chancery insisted that, in the absence of an unambiguous express authorisation, trust funds should be invested only in land mortgages or government securities and this helped to secure a captive market for the latter.[15] The consequence that trust funds were seldom available as a source of venture capital was not found objectionable.

The social argument, that it was a wrongful deprivation of families' and individuals' right to income, was also weak. After all, accumulation trusts were simply one more mode of disinheritance, howbeit exotic and novel; since instances of disinheritance far more absolute and harsh than Thellusson's were reported every year, there was no logic in singling out this one for special restraint.[16]

Unfortunately the debates on the bill, held in a thin house at the end of the session, are only sketchily reported.[17] However, Lord Hawkesbury represented it as simply an extension of the restrictions on entails which existed *'lest too great a mass of property should be in the possession of the individual to the danger and injury of the State*,[18] and it is significant that the bill's few opponents treated this as the only argument worth taking seriously. William Windham feared it would 'very sensibly counteract the views of those who wished to become the founders of great families, which was the leading object of many, and had been encouraged from the commencement of all states and societies, at least in Europe',[19] while for R.J. Buxton 'it was necessary that the bulk of the people should be very poor, in order to render them laborious; that the lower ranks should have but little property in order to excite their industry; and that there should be some extremely rich, to supply the state in cases of imminent exigency, and advance schemes of enterprises which required capital'.[20]

Since the only division ended 50 to 3 in favour of the bill, it seems that Hawkesbury's view commanded wide support. The alarmist position was no doubt fuelled by Dr. Morgan's well publicised calculation of the produce of the Thellusson accumulation at somewhere between £19 and £38.4 million, a stupendous sum at that time.[21]

But granted that such a result *might* be achieved, nevertheless, since it must be done at the expense of a man's own children, by means branded 'cruel, unnatural and absurd,[22] anxiety lest others were prepared to brave the vituperation directed at Thellusson implies belief in a whole class of miserly, eccentric and megalomaniac demi-millionaires. This point was made by the bill's opponents: 'no man could continue to accumulate such a fortune, without being callous to all the natural feelings which bind man to man and without being actuated by wild ambition, fruitless and absurd'.[23] But Loughborough averred that 'it was astonishing what ideas and practices obtained, and to a considerable extent, among those who took occasion to dispose of property in that sort of way', and he alleged that several leading conveyancers had received instructions to draw up a will like Thellusson's.[24]

Loughborough was probably tapping into a widespread unease at the growing wealth and influence of moneyed men, particularly bankers and City merchants. Jealousy of the *nouveaux riches* is constant on the part of the not-so-*nouveaux* rich, and most of all among the previous generation of *nouveaux riches*, now safely within the castle and anxious to pull up the drawbridge. Old Horace Walpole, snobbishly aghast at Thellusson's bid for Park Place, is a classic example.[25]

`The theme...is the most hackneyed in the history of landed society'[26] and pervaded the eighteenth century. Tensions between landed and business wealth and between old and new money had been very pronounced at its beginning, aggravated by the xenophobia which fed upon William III's Dutchmen, and distaste for the City and `Dutch finance' remained an article of faith within the Tory party during its long years in opposition.[27] Financiers were never likely to be popular with squires and farmers and at times particular opprobrium was also directed at contractors and stockjobbers,[28] but merchants, including those who traded overseas, attracted less hostility and received generally favourable, or at least neutral, treatment from poets, playwrights and novelists until the appearance of the `nabobs' in George III's reign.

The nabobs were not very numerous but their sudden intrusion into county and London society, where some of them flaunted their riches with the same vulgar ostentation as West India planters, was startling. Knowledge that their gains were often ill-gotten, the booty of a plundered land, and especially the revelations which emerged during the interminable impeachment proceedings against Warren Hastings, led to a more general questioning of business ethics and gave merchants a less flattering image.[29] City men were now richer, more numerous and more visible than ever before, the wealthiest of them in banking, foreign trade and stockjobbing. It has been estimated that roughly a thousand families were engaged in big business or high finance, and while in the seventeenth century £20,000 was a considerable personal fortune, by 1800 £100,000 was no longer quite out of the ordinary.[30] No wonder the country gentlemen found them disturbing.

Far from challenging the established political order, most commercial men were resolute, if frequently critical, supporters of Pitt, their interests closely bound up with the huge borrowing which funded the war. But their wealth enabled them, if they chose, to enter politics, and therein was seen a potential danger.[31] As we have seen, Pitt's peerage creations, especially Bob Smith, were disquieting and the Thellussons' ambitions in that direction were notorious. The Smiths had crashed the peerage partly through their control of Parliamentary seats, now the Thellussons were following suit.[32] This was a prospect to dismay peers and gentry alike. A handful of rotten boroughs might be the road to the peerage down which a train of bankers and brokers would pass, and if, like the Thellussons, their progress was funded by an accumulation directed at land purchases, their huge estates would come to dominate the countryside as well. Hostile reaction to the will from that perspective is quite understandable.[33]

Moreover, the ultimate beneficiaries of a big accumulation would be so wealthy as to be impervious to the normal methods of political control, so besides their power almost to command a peerage as the price of their support they could upset the delicate business of managing the Commons. Their sudden ascent to positions of influence would set them apart from the 'organic' growths represented by the great landed families, embedded in their counties, centres of an established nexus of authority and obligation. Burke's 'great oaks of the constitution' might find themselves overshadowed by these alien plantations, shallow-rooted and unprincipled. A measure to prevent that possibility, even one involving curbs on testamentary freedom, could count on a sympathetic hearing.

But emulators of Peter Thellusson might have less overweening ambitions. Whatever his motives, he had hit upon a device which might have had a perfectly rational appeal for men in his situation, men who had made fortunes by their own exertions and were anxious to secure their family's wealth and enhance their social status. The strict settlement went some way towards this but had serious drawbacks. First, it only preserved the capital fund without enlarging it, since all the income not allocated as jointures, portions and other burdens was at the disposal of the tenant for

196

life; second, it could be broken within a relatively short time; third, it discriminated among the sons, giving the eldest sole charge of the family's finances. The idea of posthumous accumulation might be especially attractive to men who had worked relentlessly and lived frugally to create fortunes. Old habits die hard, the fear that idle and extravagant sons would fritter away painstakingly amassed riches was common, and primogeniture was unpalatable. Thellusson offered a solution. A man with a quarter of a million might make sufficient provision for his children to live in reasonable affluence whilst still putting say, £100,000 into an accumulation for his grandchildren or great-grandchildren. In this way he would avoid favouring one child above another, would reduce the temptation for his son(s) to give up business, yet would insure against their incompetence or misfortune ruining the family by setting up the remorselessly growing fund.

So if, as Loughborough claimed, conveyancers reported ominous interest in trusts of accumulation, it may well have owed less to the existence of 'posthumous avarice' on an unsuspected scale than to a perfectly rational desire to find a settlement structure more closely aligned to the needs of a tiny but important section of the community. Fears that the device could also serve more dangerous ends may have been less plausible but were not wholly imaginary. And if this is so, the Thellusson Act was not 'rushed through Parliament in a panic ... at a time when people had an almost superstitious fear of the power of compound interest'[34], but was a deliberate check on a rational but objectionable development.

Since the whole purpose of the Act was to *prevent* recurrences of Thellusson's will it is difficult to know how far Loughborough's anxieties were justified.[35] The question can only be approached obliquely. On the hypothesis that wealthy men, determined to found a dynasty and commanding the services of the most ingenious conveyancers of the day, might either seek out loopholes in the Act or in some other way stretch the law to its limits, we may scan their wills for signs of such devices, and we may also examine the reported cases in which the Thellusson Act was invoked to see what sort of dispositions were challenged.

197

The first approach would be laborious, given the lack of reliable evidence for persons dying before 1809, but a small experiment has been made using three groups; a tiny group identified in the *Gentleman's Magazine* as `for many years, in the commercial world, proverbial for their immense accumulations';[36] the twelve `half-millionaires' who died between 1809 and 1825;[37] and those whose obituaries in the *Annual Register* from 1797 to 1809 suggest personal wealth of more than £200,000.[38]

Their wills range from the simplest, all property being given to the widow,[39] to the inordinately complex,[40] and while there is a bias towards partible inheritance there are several who concentrated their wealth upon one individual.[41] Usually the next generation received personal property outright, but Samuel Galton, a Birmingham gunmaker who died in 1799 worth £200,000, left his land to his son for life, with remainders to his eldest and subsequent grandsons successively in tail and the residue of his personalty to be accumulated until the youngest grandchild reached twenty-four, each grandchild receiving a capital sum as they attained that age.[42] Others also directed large accumulations for grandchildren or nephews, but the case which comes closest to Thellusson's occurs outside these groups. Augustine Pentheney, `a miser of the most perfect drawing that Nature has ever given to the world' died in an obscure Dublin lodging house in 1811 having made £300,000 in Antigua and Santa Cruz, a worthy successor to his uncle and patron Peter `Big Brogues' Gaynor. Pentheney had numerous relations but considering them unqualified to manage a fortune (and having given them no opportunity to learn) he left all his money - with the exception of a £4 annuity to a faithful servant - to a rich family in the West Indies at the end of an accumulation of fourteen years.[43] There were others not quite so rich who were prepared to pass over the claims of their nearest relatives in favour of more distant kin or no kin at all[44] and others still upon whom no-one had any claims.[45]

The second set of wills (and a handful of deeds) examined is those against which the Act was invoked. From the 1820s onwards, it generated considerable litigation, enough for J.F. Hargrave to devote a substantial treatise to it, and the cases he cites, and others from the 1840s and 1850s make up a corpus of over sixty.[46] Of course, the number of cases is not a reliable guide to the number of testators who tried to evade the statute, since ignorance and carelessness on the part of the testators and their advisers were more likely to bring a will into court than deliberate efforts at evasion. Indeed, the very first time the statute fell to be construed, in its application to the will of Charlotte Matthews, Lord Eldon remarked that `the sort of case before me was not, I believe,  much in the contemplation of the legislature',[47] and his implicit criticism of its language - `not very similar to any other Act, with either enabling or restraining clauses'- was echoed by his successors in less measured terms.[48] It is easy to find other instances of innocuous provisions snared, or at least clutched at, by the Act, among them, by a nice irony, a deed by Lord Loughborough's widow.[49] But like the rule against perpetuities, the Thellusson Act was also inefficient, for while it ambushed the unwary it left escape routes open to the crafty; furthermore, whereas an unsuccessful attempt to escape the rule against perpetuities could bring down the whole trust, it was established very early on that an excessive accumulation was void only as to the excess,[50] so there was little deterrent to experimentation.

Eldon had been opposed to the bill at the outset[51] and indications in early cases that the judges were disposed to construe it benevolently meant that a determined emulator of Thellusson would certainly find conveyancers willing to test out the Act.[52] There were three main possibilities, using portions, `dancing trusts' and disguised accumulations respectively, and if any of these is found in combination with a substantial fund it may be a case of deliberate avoidance.

The exclusion of portions from the Act was marked out as its weakest point by the great authority Richard Preston, who predicted that `by this means all the mischiefs of the Thellusson will could be reproduced'.[53] The judges were certainly exercised by the difficulty of defining a portion for this purpose and the case of *Beech v. Lord St. Vincent* shows that a portion *could* be used to produce a big fund.[54]

Beech died in 1828, leaving large estates in the midlands in strict settlement and a big personal fortune. Trustees were to accumulate £2,000 p.a. for twenty-one years or during the lifetime of his son, whichever proved to be the longer, holding the fund as portions for the son's own younger children. The direction was unsuccessfully challenged at the end of twenty-one years, when the fund amounted to £41,536-9s-1d in 3% consols; since Beech's son was then only thirty-seven and had as yet but one child of his own, it might easily have lasted as long again. Clearly there was no upper limit on the size of the fund which was to accumulate, nor its ultimate produce and although decisions in the 1850s made it clear that, whatever contortions judges might get themselves into in trying to define a portion, they would not countenance a big accumulation up to an unspecified amount for ultimate division, until then it was at least arguable that a testator might legitimately make small gifts or annuities to his children and living grandchildren with the residue accumulating for the grandchildren and great-grandchildren.[55]

Another device was the 'dancing trust of accumulation'[56] using the fourth period, 'the duration of the minority or respective minorities only of any person or persons who under the limitations of the instrument directing the accumulations would for the time being, if of full age, be entitled to the income directed to be accumulated'.

This was intended to cover the common arrangement of a gift to A for life and then to such of his children as attain twenty-one, the income from each one's prospective share accumulating during his minority, but Eldon himself pointed out that it could be manipulated to provide an accumulation of forty years in favourable circumstances.[57] In fact this period was ultimately given a rather narrow interpretation but once again, it was not immediately apparent that this would be so.[58]

The third possibility was to disguise an accumulation by not directing it expressly but either leaving it to be implied through the normal practice of Chancery or actively dressing it up as a charge or something similar. Do the reported cases suggest that the wealthy still hankered after posthumous accumulations, resorting to

200

avoidance devices to achieve them?

Many cases can be eliminated simply on the basis of the small size of the fund concerned. This is not always clear from the report, especially where it concerns a residue or rents and profits of unspecified value, but it is often possible to get a rough idea from obituaries and other sources, and by dismissing those which involved an initial fund of less than £50,000 the 'dangerous' ones are reduced substantially.[59] If we also set aside those where the accumulation period was not likely to exceed thirty years[60] we are left with only a small number. A few of these are eccentric, like Sir John Lombe's accumulation for the purpose of building a 'copy cat' mansion which, in the event, his heir objected to,[61] while others are simply muddled, like John Oddie's will, 'an instrument so mysteriously constructed that one is agreeably surprised to find the four judges before whom it has been brought for exposition arriving at only three different conclusions upon it'[62].

Only a handful look as though they are within the real mischief of the Act. One of them, under the will of Thomas Eccleston, who died in 1809, was a complicated series of trusts to settle property 'so far as the rules of law and equity ... would admit', involving continuous, unbroken accumulations during minorities which conflicted with the Act; however it seems to have been designed not so much to expand the property as to preserve it and ensure a just and equal distribution.[63] John Thomas's will (1824) also foundered by requiring accumulation during minorities other than those permitted by statute; he gave only annuities to his nephews and the funds ultimately to their eldest sons, so he is a possible candidate.[64] There is also the case of Robert Lowndes, who created one of the biggest accumulations recorded - £184,984 consols plus other stock- by a 'dry period' of twenty years from his death, to be followed by a life interest for his son with remainder to his nephew; this displays such a lack of faith in his son that one wonders how long he would have protracted it but for the Act.[65]

However, the only two cases which have usually been regarded as manifestations of the *mania accumulandi* arise out of the wills of Joseph Wildsmith and Thomas Shaw Hellier. Wildsmith was excoriated by J.F. Hargrave: 'the life annuity given by the testator to his children amounted to mere paupers' allowances, doled out in weekly payments to individuals, whose children would be overwhelmed with wealth'.[66] He was a carpet manufacturer who died in 1804, giving one guinea a week to each of his sons and his daughter; subject thereto the whole estate was to accumulate until the death of his last surviving child for the benefit of their children and those of his late daughter Mary Ann Maceroni.   Only when Elizabeth, who outlived her brothers, died in 1834 was the will contested and Lord Langdale MR, holding that the accumulation should rightfully have ended after twenty-one years, ordered immediate distribution.[67] However, the clear residue of Wildsmith's estate in 1834 was still only £12,411-18s-6d in 3% consols, hardly enough wealth to overwhelm even one child.[68]

The second case concerns the Helliers, owners of profitable ironstone quarries in Staffordshire which the unmarried Sir Samuel Hellier had left along with the bulk of his estate, to his friend the Reverend Thomas Shaw.[69] Shaw (now Shaw-Hellier) died in 1812, leaving his lands in trust for his grandson Thomas, giving his eldest son James (Thomas's father) £400 p.a., his younger son Theophilus and his married daughter Mary £100 p.a. each, and directing the balance to be invested for accumulation in favour of his present and future grandchildren during either the lifetime of his last surviving child or twenty-one years from his own death, whichever was the longer.   There would then be a further 'charge' on the estate sufficient to produce £30,000 in fifteen years; this charge would last twenty years and the fund would then finally be divided among those grandchildren who reached twenty-one.

This has all the hallmarks of a deliberate and professional attempt to squeeze the utmost length out of the Act and it was sufficiently plausible to give the judges a great deal of trouble, but they finally decided to regard the 'charge' as a direction to accumulate, void under the Act.[70] Mary, the last surviving child, had died in 1831 and the distribution finally took place after the House of Lords had concluded a costly and prolonged law suit.[71]

202

The argument from silence is always suspect and if the case law does not suggest that there were many wealthy men anxious to follow Thellusson's lead, it does reveal that some were prepared to confine their children's inheritance to mere annuities, passing the capital down to the next generation.[72] Both sets of wills also suggest a readiness to experiment. The Act may have discouraged the rich from pursuing the goal of impregnable family fortunes by accumulations, but it only deflected their concern with spendthrift heirs into other legal channels. The decade which opened with the Accumulations Act was also marked by the emergence of the spendthrift or protective trust. This takes the form of an immediate gift of property which is subject to automatic forfeiture if the donee attempts to charge it as security for a debt, commits an act rendering him liable to bankruptcy proceedings or otherwise encumbers it; upon forfeiture the property vests in trustees upon discretionary trusts whose permitted beneficiaries include the former owner and his family. It was a useful weapon to settlors in the perpetual battle to prevent improvident heirs from falling into the clutches of unscrupulous creditors. The implicit aspersion on the donee's character was embarrassing, but because it only defended family wealth from creditors' claims, the protective trust was not considered objectionable by the propertied classes. It received the *imprimatur* of Lord Eldon in *Brandon v. Robinson* and one of its earliest exponents, as we shall see, was Thellusson's own eldest son Peter Isaac.[73]

Loughborough and his supporters probably exaggerated the threat from accumulations, but if it is arguable that Parliament acted precipitately in passing the legislation, it is more than arguable that it has been kept on the statute book long after any danger has passed. It has been altered three times in its history, never very substantially, and the first changes actually went to add a further restriction. In the 1880s the sharp fall in farm rentals experienced by many landowners finally persuaded them to abandon the strict settlement which had served their interests so well for two hundred years. The Settled Land Act of 1882 undermined its legal basis by enabling a tenant for life to sell the settled property and transfer the beneficial interests in the trust from the land to the purchase money.[74] As a postscript, private members' bills were introduced a few years later to facilitate the break up of accumulation trusts where the fund was invested in land, and though they went too far for the House of Lords,[75] Lord Salisbury's government introduced a short bill confining directions to accumulate by investing in land to the fourth period under the 1800 Act.

Appearing late in the session and badly mishandled, the bill was given a rough passage by the former Lord Chancellors Herschell and Selborne[76] from which it emerged even shorter, shorn of any objectionable features and practically useless.[77] It is ironical that this `check [on] a particularly loathsome manifestation of posthumous avarice'[78] - the very one which Thellusson had indulged in - should have its origin in a concern lest trustees be obliged to invest in land when it was a drug on the market and a hopeless investment, rather than any fear of a plutocratic monopoly of land ownership.

In the same year the Thellusson Act acquired a colourless official title under the Short Titles Act and in the 1920s lost its distinctive identity entirely when swallowed up by the Law of Property Acts, which also made minor relaxations in its substance.[79] Surprisingly, however, it re-emerged with its old senior partner as the Perpetuities and Accumulations Act 1964,[80] a belated implementation of the Law Reform Committee's fourth report, on the rule against perpetuities. That report proceeded from a questionable premise: `the necessity for placing some time limit on the vesting of future interests,... we take to be beyond argument', and a single paragraph embodied its endorsement of the continuing need for a separate restriction on accumulations.[81] Accordingly, the restriction remained, eased by the addition of two new alternative accumulation periods.[82]

There was by then a clear trend in other common law jurisdictions against a distinct restriction on accumulations. Sundry American states and most jurisdictions in Canada and Australia had introduced such statutes,[83] for fear of a latter day Thellusson crossed the oceans of the world. As one scholar wrote, `[h]ad not this will

204

come up for a hearing under the circumstances that surrounded it, I venture to assert that there never would have been any legislation against accumulation as such.'[84] He concluded that the main result had been that `the moment you have a separate rule for accumulations with a shorter permissible period, the volume of litigation on the subject increases enormously',[85] and in the United States at least, the inconvenience created by the very occasional long accumulation which cannot be struck down either as a perpetuity or on some other ground seems nowadays to be regarded as too slight to justify the existence of restrictions so productive of costly litigation.[86] Australian states seem to have come to a similar conclusion and it may be that, as Peter Thellusson's adopted home was the first to react to his will, so it will be the last to retain safeguards against a repetition. How unnecessary the safeguards are is suggested by the fact that while Morris and Leach in 1962 devoted one-eighth of their book to accumulations, Maudsley's 1979 study needed only one-sixteenth; in fact since the 1964 Act there have been only two reported cases and in the last two decades none at all.[87] Nor has either book had a new edition.

In this century the preoccupations of the very rich have included the desire to shield themselves from taxation and they have sometimes found trusts for accumulation useful in that exercise. A particularly inventive instance came to light in the late 1970s, when the notoriously secretive and immensely wealthy Vestey family unwillingly exposed some of their affairs to the public gaze. The Thellusson Act, which passed into law a few months before the Act of Union, had never applied to Ireland and neither the republic nor Northern Ireland seems to have felt the want of it.[88] The Vesteys exploited this by constructing extremely flexible discretionary trusts under the law of Northern Ireland, utilising the full amplitude of the common law perpetuity period and providing for lengthy accumulations of income.[89] When the frustrated Inland Revenue at length resorted to draconian assessments on the beneficiaries under anti-avoidance provisions aimed at offshore trusts, the family was compelled to challenge them in court. The judges found the arbitrary powers that earlier judicial interpretations of the law had given the taxman infinitely more disturbing than the Vesteys' anti-avoidance devices.[90]

The Vesteys came in for a barrage of press criticism,[91] but although no family member had any entitlement to the fund, it was not for any disinheritance, nor for any alleged threat to the social fabric. Simply, they were criticised (quite justifiably) for their unwillingness to pay their fair share of taxes. The Vesteys exhibited only the banality of the very rich, not a sinister design for aggrandisement and the revelation that in the absence of a restriction accumulations might be utilised for tax avoidance did not lead to any suggestions for curbs in Ireland. The remedy was just one more move in that 'undignified game of chess' between the Revenue and the tax specialists.[92]

It was therefore rather surprising that when the Law Commission again reviewed perpetuities in the 1990s they initially suggested that there was still a need for distinct provisions against accumulations despite fiscal measures which protect the public at large from the anti-social impact of 'posthumous avarice' and the Variation of Trusts Act and Inheritance (Provision for Family and Dependants) Act which protect the family from its more immediate consequences.[93] However the final report concluded that 'there is very little reason nowadays for the rule against accumulations. It should be abolished except in relation to charitable trusts.'[94] After two centuries Peter Thellusson's ghost may cease to haunt the statute book.

1. *Parl. Reg.* (2nd s.)12 (1800), col.77. The first draft was entitled `An Act for declaring illegal in future all Trusts and Directions whereby the Profits or Produce of Real or Personal Estate shall be accumulated... for an Undue Period of Time.': F. Hargrave, *Observations on the Bill Against Trusts of Accumulation* (London, 1801), appendix 1. The *Journals* call it the Executory Devises Bill (though it extended to deeds as well).

2. 39, 40 Geo. III c. 98 s.l. I have paraphrased the periods.

3. (1) a term of twenty-one years from the making of the disposition and (2) the duration of the minority or respective minorities of any person or persons in being at that date (Perpetuities and Accumulations Act 1964, s.13). The reduction of the age of minority to eighteen in 1969 while leaving intact the twenty-one year periods in the Act makes those periods arbitrary.

4. Repealed by the Entail Amendment Act 1848, s.41.

5. Explained by Hargrave, *Treatise upon the Thellusson Act*, pp.206-7.

6. *House of Commons Journals* 55(1799-1800), 703; *House of Lords Journals* 42(1799-1800), 546, 550; Hargrave, *Observations*, appendix 3.

7. D. Lieberman, *The Province of Legislation Determined* (Cambridge, 1989), draws attention to the dramatic increase in public Acts through the eighteenth century (see especially pp. 13-28). However, only a small number concerned the law of land or wills. The lists in J. Hoppit and J. Innes (eds.), *Failed Legislation* (London, 1997) do not alter this picture.

8. I know of no record of cabinet discussions on the bill, but Pitt's ministry was in disarray, its leading figures preoccupied with a disastrous war. The Chancellor, who was mistrusted by his colleagues, may have hoped to curry royal favour, since the King was notoriously opposed to any dilution of the peerage. Loughborough helped bring down the ministry a few months later by leaking its proposals for Roman Catholic relief to the King, only to be hoist with his own petard when the Seals were given to Sir John Scott instead. To general astonishment he nevertheless continued to attend cabinet meetings until plainly told he must not. Lord Campbell, *Lives of the Lord Chancellors*, vol. VI (London, 1847), pp.292-330; P.Mackesy, *War without Victory* (Oxford, 1984), pp.185-201; R. Willis, Pitt's Resignation in 1801, *Bulletin of the Institute of Historical Research* 44 (1971), pp.239-57.

9. Hargrave, *Juridical Arguments*, vol. II, p.3.

10. Hargrave, *Observations*, appendix 1.

11. *Parl. Reg.*(2nd s.) 12 (1800), col.77.

12. Morris and Leach, *Rule against Perpetuities*, p.267.

13. *Thellusson v. Woodford*, 4 Ves. Jun. 227 at 318; *Parl. Reg.* (2nd s.) 12 (1800), cols. 373-4. Francis Burton (`the blind senator') was MP for Oxford and a bencher of Lincoln's Inn.

14. *Observations on the Power of Individuals...*, p. 19.

15. G.W. Keeton, *Modern Developments in the Law of Trusts* (Belfast, 1971), pp.45-55.

16. For example, *Wilkinson v. Adams*, as noticed in *Gents. Mag.* 83 (1813), 279: `nearly a million pounds sterling in estates is confirmed to three illegitimate children of the late Mr. Wilkinson, ironmonger, to the exclusion of his nephew who had been brought up as his heir, resided with him and managed his business upwards of thirty years without any salary. Mr. Wilkinson became acquainted with the mother of the children in one of his visits to London, where she acted as a servant, and after he had attained his seventieth year'.

17. *The Parliamentary Register* and *The Senator* (1st series, vols. 25-6) are my sources; there may also be newspaper reports.

18. *Parl. Reg.* (2nd s.) 12 (1800), col. 184. My italics.

19. *Ibid.*

20. *Ibid.*, col. 140. Robert John Buxton, a Norfolk squire, was MP for Great Bedwyn.

21. Hargrave, *Treatise upon the Thellusson Act*, pp.5-7.

22. See Keeton, *Thellusson Will*, for a selection of abusive epithets.

23. R.J. Buxton, *Parl. Reg.* 12 (1800), cols. 280-1.

24. *Parl. Reg.*(2nd s.) 11 (1800), cols. 56-7, echoed by the Master of the Rolls at col.184.

25. See *supra*, p. 108.

26. Langford, *Public Life and the Propertied Englishman*, p. 40.

27. On the earlier period see H. Horwitz, The `mess of the middle class' revisited: the case of the big bourgeoisie of Augustan London, (1987) 2 *Continuity and Change*, 263-283.

28. H.V. Bowen `The Pests of Human Society': Stockbrokers, Jobbers and Speculators in mid-18th Century Britain, *History* 78 (1993), 38-53; J. Brewer, *The Sinews of Power: War, Money and the English State, 1763-83* (London, 1989), pp.208-10.

29. J. McVeagh, *Tradefull Merchants, the Portrayal of the Capitalist in Literature* (London, 1981), pp.83-100; J. Raven, *Judging New Wealth: Popular Publishing and Responses to Commerce in England, 1750-1800* (Oxford, 1992).

30. L.D.Schwartz, Income Distribution and Social Structure in London in the Late Eighteenth Century, *Economic History Review* (2nd s.) 32 (1979), 250-9; R. Grassby, The Personal Wealth of the Business Community in Seventeenth Century England, *Economic History Review* (2nd s.)23 (1970), 220-34. According to Rubinstein's figures (*Men of Property*, pp. 26-37), the annual average of probated estates (comprising personal property alone) exceeding £100,000 in the quinquennium 1809-14 was 16.5, i.e. more than 80 persons died with at least that much.

The figure for the previous four quinquennia, embracing most of Peter Thellusson's contemporaries, would have been lower but even taking it at 50, that means that almost 300 persons, very rich by the standards of their day, died during the Long War.

31. The place of commercial men and their influence upon Augustan society is vigorously debated. Good expositions of the different positions are Clark, *English Society, 1688-1832* and P. Langford, *A Polite and Commercial People* (Oxford, 1989).

32. *Supra*, p. 118.

33. There has been some disagreement over the extent to which the very rich in the 19th century did in fact enter landed society (see e.g. F.M.L. Thompson, Business and Landed Elites in the Nineteenth Century, in F.M.L. Thompson (ed.), *Landowners, Capitalists and Entrepreneurs, Essays for Sir John Habbakuk*, (Oxford, 1994), pp. 139-70 and W.D. Rubinstein, Businessmen into Landowners: the Question Revisited, in N. Harte and R. Quinault (eds.), *Land and Society in Britain, 1700-1914: Essays in Honour of F.M.L. Thompson* (Manchester, 1996), pp. 90-118), but it seems safe to assume that in 1800 it was expected that they would usually wish to do so.

34. Morris and Leach, *Rule Against Perpetuities*, p. 303.

35. The usually sceptical Jeremy Bentham, writing about the Treason Forfeiture Bill, was impressed enough to ask, `Do you reach the future Thellusson with his 18 millions of consols?- the *single* Thellusson who will have stuff enough in time to make half-a-dozen Dukes of Orleans?': to C. Abbot, 26 Jun. 1799, J.R. Dinwiddy (ed.), *The Correspondence of Jeremy Bentham*, vol. VI (1798-1803), (Oxford, 1984).

36. 81 (1811), 667: Thellusson himself, along with Joseph Denison, William Fuller, Sir Francis Baring and Lewis Tessier, who died in 1811, `the last of that standing, unless Mr. Coutts were included'.

37. F.M.L. Thompson, Life After Death: how successful 19th century merchants and businessmen disposed of their fortunes, *Economic History Review* (2nd s.) 46 (1990), 40-59.

38. I have also added a few mentioned in Rubinstein, *Men of Property*.

39. E.g. Thomas Coutts (PRO PROB 11/1654, f.130) and the eminent Hamburg merchant Christopher Strotthoff (PRO PROB 11/1354, f.137).

40. E.g. John Langston's will of forty-eight sheets (PRO PROB 11/1531, f.130).

41. The most dispersed estate in the group is probably Abraham Newland's, who had no close relations (PRO PROB 11/1470, f.936). Examples of concentrations are Thomas Quinton (*Annual Register* 48 (1806), 508) and Robert Drummond (PRO PROB 11/1403, f.19).

42. PRO PROB 11/1330, f.655. This accumulation would have infringed the Act. There is an account of the Galtons by B.D.M.Smith in *Business History*, 1967, 132-50. The son, Samuel, forsook the business to go into banking and left £300,000 at his death in 1832.

43. *Gents. Mag.* 81 (1811) 187. I have not seen his will and his career would certainly repay investigation. Unlike Thellusson, however, he was unmarried, for 'his wife was the public purse and his children guineas'.

44. E.g. the solicitor Albany Wills, who left between £70- and £80,000 to Lady Bailey and her son in strict settlement, passing over his sister's needy children (*Annual Register*, 42 (1800), 64) and Sir P.C. Ewins, who cut off his son with £40 p.a., leaving, it was said, £500,000 to a distant relation who in the event predeceased him (*Annual Register* 49 (1807), 549).

45. Like Christopher Barber, the Calcutta merchant who could think of no heir to his fortune: *Annual Register* 41 (1799), 64. Presumably men in this condition often died intestate, like William Pulteney, supposed to be the richest commoner then living: *Annual Register* 47 (1805), 549.

46. He was Francis Hargrave's nephew. The later cases are taken from Morris and Leach, *Rule Against Perpetuities*. The earlier work of H. Randell, *An Essay on the Law of Perpetuities and on Trusts of Accumulation* (London, 1822) mentions none not in Hargrave.

47. *Griffiths v. Vere* (1803) 9 Ves. Jun. 127 at 132.

48. *Ibid.* Examples of later criticisms are in *Tench v. Cheese* (1855) 6 De G. M. & G. 453 (Cranworth LC) and *Shaw v. Rhodes* (1835) 1 My. & Cr. 135 (Brougham LC).

49. *In re Lady Rosslyn's Trust* (1848) 16 Sim. 391. Loughborough, created Earl of Rosslyn in 1801, died in 1805, his widow in 1826.

50. *Griffiths v. Vere* (1803) 9 Ves. Jun. 127; *London v. Simson* (1806) 12 Ves. Jun. 295. 'A more consistent and complete series of decisions on the operation of any clause in an Act of Parliament can scarcely be found', Hargrave, *Treatise*, p.144.

51. He only refrained from outright opposition 'out of deference to those great characters who framed it': *Parl. Reg.* (2nd s.)12 (1800), col. 140; see also *Senator*, 26 (1800), col. 1627.

52. Hargrave, *Treatise*, p.140.

53. *Ibid.*, p.203. *Cf.* Randell, *Perpetuities*, p. 227.

54. (1850) 3 De G. & Sm. 678.

55. Hargrave, *Treatise*, pp.199-203, reflects the uncertainty which prevailed in the 1840s. The judgments in *Burt v. Sturt* (1853) 10 Hare 415 and *Edwards v. Tuck* (1853) 3 De G.M. & G. 40 really closed off this avenue of escape, the former distinguishing *Barrington v. Liddell* (1852) 2 De G.M. & G. 480 as 'essentially within the spirit of the Act' (*per* Page Wood VC at 420). *Barrington, Beech* and the doubtful pair of *Middleton v. Lash* (1852) 1 Sm. & G. 61 and *St. Paul v. Heath* (1865) 13 L.T. 271, are the only successful attempts to use the portions exception.

56. *Per* Lord Eldon LC in *Marshall v. Holloway* (1818) 2 Swanst. 432 at 448.

57. Hargrave, *Treatise*, pp.118-140.

58. *Ibid.* Sir John Leach VC's decision in *Haley v. Bannister* (1819) 4 Madd. 275, followed in *Ellis v. Maxwell* (1841) 12 Sim. 554n, was criticised by Hargrave and by Thomas Jarman, A *Treatise on Wills* (London, 1844), pp.267-8 and was finally departed from in *Re Cattell* [1907] 1 Ch. 567.

59. Examples of very small accumulations are *In re Lady Rosslyn's Trust* (1843) 16 Sim. 391, *Williams v. Nixon* (1840) 2 Beav. 472 and *Jones v. Maggs* (1852) 9 Hare 605.

60. E.g. where the accumulation is to cease when a named living person reaches twenty-five (*Crawley v. Crawley* (1835) 7 Sim. 427); is for the life of the testator's widow (*Miles v. Dyer* (1837) 8 Sim. 330); until his son reaches forty-five (*Williams v. Nixon* (1840) 2 Beav. 472), or during the lifetime of Mary Jacob (*O'Neill v. Lucas* (1838) 2 Keen 313).

61. *Lombe v. Stoughton* (1841) 12 Sim. 304.

62. *Oddie v. Brown* (1849) 4 De G. & J. 179, *per* Knight Bruce LJ at 189.

63. *Scarisbrick v. Skelmersdale* (1849) 17 Sim. 187. Eccleston was a celebrated agricultural improver: *Annual Register* 51 (1809), 700.

64. *Wilson v. Wilson* (1851) 1 Sim. (N.S.) 288.

65. *Gorst v. Lowndes* (1841) 11 Sim. 434. Lowndes, who came from a family of Cheshire landowners, was eighty-five when he died (*Gents. Mag.* 90 (1820), 89), so it is not surprising that his son never lived to enjoy even his limited ownership, dying in 1840.

66. *Treatise*, p.35.

67. *Eyre v. Marsden* (1838) 2 Keen 564.

68. PRO C 33/884, f.886.

69. *V.C.H. Staffordshire*, vol XX (Oxford, 1984), p.204.

70. *Shaw v. Rhodes* (1836) 1 My. & Cr. 135, affirmed by the House of Lords in *Evans v. Hellier* (1837) 5 Cl. & F. 114. This case illustrates the inconvenience of the institutional separation of law and equity: see Hargrave, *Treatise*, pp.77-84.

71. The accumulated fund in court in 1830 stood at over £98,000: PRO C 33/821, f.1892.

72. E.g. *Haley v. Bannister* (1819) 4 Madd. 275; *Burt v. Sturt* (1853) 10 Hare 415; *Turner v. Turner* (1831) 4 Sim. 430; *Porter v. Fox* (1834) 6 Sim. 485.

73. (1811) 18 Ves. Jun. 429. For the development of the protective trust see Moffat, *Trusts Law*, pp.264-76.

74. A. Underhill, Changes in the English Law of Real Property in the Nineteenth Century, *Select Essays in the History of Anglo-American Law* (London, 1968 reprint), vol.III, pp.673-722.

75. *Parl. Debs.* (4th s.) 3 (1892), col. 1742 (Sir Richard Webster).

76. As Roundell Palmer, Lord Selborne had appeared in the later stages of the Thellusson saga,

211

from 1852 onwards.

77. *Parl. Debs.*(4th s.) 3, cols.1737, 1742-3; 5, cols. 562-3, 1542, 1889-95.

78. Morris and Leach, *Law of Perpetuities*, p.272.

79. Law of Property Act 1925 (15 & 16 Geo. V c.20), ss. 164-66.

80. Only ss.13-14 deal with accumulations.

81. Cmnd.18 of 1957, paras.4 and 55.

82. One of the new periods opened up significant tax-saving possibilities: R.H.Maudsley, *The Modern Law of Perpetuities* (London, 1979), pp.205-6.

83. Morris and Leach, *Rule against Perpetuities* lists them at pp.268-70.

84. L.M. Simes, *Public Policy and the Dead Hand* (Ann Arbor, 1955), p.88.

85. *Ibid.*, pp.99-100.

86. Maudsley, *Perpetuities*, 200-2. A spectacular American case is *Holdeen v Ralterree*; 292 F 2d 338 (2d Cir. 1961).

87. The only ones cited in the 1998 Law Commission report are *Re Earl of Berkeley* [1968] Ch. 744 and *Re Dodwell & Co. Ltd's Trust Deed* [1979] Ch. 361.

88. Oddly enough the 1892 Act did apply to Ireland.

89. The 1942 trusts, which became the subject of the litigation, are set out in Walton J's judgment: [1979] Ch. 177 at 187-91. There was an earlier (1921) settlement of substantially the same property.

90. *Ibid.* On appeal to the House of Lords ([1980] A.C. 1148), they overruled their own decision in *Congreve v. I.R.C.* (1948) 30 TC 163.

91. See e.g. Moffat, *Trusts Law*, pp.55-8.

92. Lord Morton of Henryton's well-known phrase, from his speech in *Chapman v. Chapman* [1954] A.C. 429 at 468. The move was Finance Act 1981 s.45.

93. Consultation paper no. 133, 1993; see C.T. Emery, *Modern Law Review* 57 (1994), 203-10.

94. The Variation of Trusts Act 1958 allows the court to consent on behalf of the infant, lunatic and unborn *cestuis que trust* to variations proposed by the trustees or adult beneficiaries, extending the scope of the rule in *Saunders v. Vautier* (1841) 4 Beav. 115, under which the *cestuis que trust* may if unanimous, put an end to a trust, including a trust for accumulation.

95. LC 251 (HC 579 of 1998), para. 7, with discussion in parts IX and X.

CHAPTER 10

IN THE SHADOW OF THE WILL: THE FIRST GENERATION

1. Woodfords and Thellussons

The Lord Chancellor's judgment upholding the will was given on 20th April 1799, and came as no surprise, for even leading counsel for the family had initially thought it valid.[1] An appeal to the House of Lords was the only recourse left, and although it offered little prospect of success the Thellussons can hardly be blamed for going on to the end.

Their hopes were kept alive for an unusually long time because of inordinate delays in getting the case heard by the peers, whose judicial functions at this time still had to be fitted into their Parliamentary timetable. This became increasingly difficult as the number of Scottish appeals waiting to be heard expanded, and the Irish Act of Union, by returning Irish appeals to Westminster, made things worse. Since the Lord Chancellor's presence on appeals was indispensable, it was particularly unfortunate for litigants that a steady expansion of judicial business coincided with the tenure of Lord Eldon, whose painstaking mastery of every aspect of a case frequently paralysed his capacity to decide it.[2]

However, Loughborough's unregretted unseating from the Woolsack meant that at least the Thellussons would not experience the Gilbertian situation of the Chancellor rehearing the case *de novo* in order to test the correctness of his own solemnly pronounced judgment.[3] Meanwhile the trusts of the will had to be brought into operation and the Thellussons' relations with the Woodfords, who had the trusts in their keeping, became all important. James Stanley, Peter Isaac Thellusson's brother-in-law, had also been named as a trustee.. Trusteeship, however, is a burdensome office and not one which can be forced upon a person. An unwilling nominee may disclaim the position provided he has not already involved himself in the administration of the trust and Stanley decided that he wanted nothing to do with it. This suggests that Thellusson had not taken his intended trustees into his confidence, presumably wanting to keep his secret and counting on their sense of family obligation to make them accept the duty. It was not uncommon for testators to do so,[4] but this was a very unusual and controversial trust and it is interesting that Thellusson did not feel it worth following Sir John Webb's example of offering the trustees a percentage of the trust income as an incentive.[5]

Stanley may well have been chosen because he was a lawyer, for nothing suggests he was especially close to the family. A younger son of a Lancashire clergyman, he was admitted to Lincoln's Inn in 1782 and made a success of the Chancery bar, becoming in due course a master in Chancery and steward of the Marshalsea.[6] The will gave the other trustees the power to appoint a replacement but there was no necessity for a third and with the appeal pending both Woodfords and Thellussons preferred to leave things to Matthew and Emperor.

The Woodfords had been doing rather well for themselves. Ralph had a relatively undistinguished career as a diplomat but excelled in London society, where his polished manners made him a favourite of ladies' drawing rooms. He was rather a surprising choice to be the commissioner to negotiate a commercial treaty with Spain in 1784 and his involvement in this negotiation, and others with Sweden and the kingdom of the Two Sicilies, continued intermittently until 1793.[7] The negotiations never did yield an agreement but they earned Woodford a baronetcy as Sir Ralph Woodford of Carlby in Lincolnshire, a distant hamlet in an unfashionable county with which he had no known connection and which probably saw very little of him.[8] He passed the uneventful evening of his life in London and Cheltenham, marrying his daughter to the son of the big London banker Sir John Hammet, placing his only son in a snug place at the War Office and dying in 1810, far from rich and

214

without making a will.[9]

Ralph's brother Matthew pursued a placid bachelor existence as archdeacon of Winchester and in time his unmarried sisters also came to live in the cathedral close. Mary's will refers to his `numberless kindnesses and indulgences', which included interposing to dissuade their mother from discriminating against her and Sophia in her distribution of money under a power given her by her late husband. He was already in his early sixties when the Thellusson trust began and could not be expected to take a very active part in it from the cloistered calm of Winchester.[10]

The only active trustee therefore was Emperor Woodford. His father John- the youngest of the three brothers- had been an officer in the Grenadier Guards, a handsome and dashing figure, but also a real solder who had learned his trade under Wolfe, whom he idolised.   In the years of peace he was a fashionable man-about-town, a widower whose exemplary bearing when his house in St. James's Square burned down with all his possessions made a good impression. Of three sons, one joined the navy and drowned off Newfoundland and another also died young, but the gallant officer - now a colonel - remarried and started a second family.[11]

This time he married into the highest society, to Susan, dowager Countess of Westmorland, a widow of thirty-two, and whatever her Fane and Gordon kinfolk might think, it did save them a jointure and Woodford was unquestionably a gentleman.[12] The marriage underwent an early test of a most unusual kind. Susan's brother Lord George Gordon was a wild and erratic youngster whose eccentricities grew more noticeable and dangerous as he got older, coalescing into an obsessive hatred for Roman Catholicism which passed the bounds of reason and finally triggered an explosion of mob violence in London. The Gordon riots convulsed the capital in the summer of 1780 and at their height it was Colonel Woodford who had to order his troops to fire on the mob; once that became known his own household became a target and only the prompt action of a servant saved him from being homeless a second time.[13]

It was the last time Woodford saw fighting of any sort but he had the gratification of seeing all his surviving sons join the army. The two boys of his second marriage, Alexander (b.1782) and John (b.1785) could hardly wait to get into uniform and into battle. The elder had a commission while still at Winchester, joined his regiment at seventeen, embarked on the Duke of York's disastrous Helder expedition and was wounded and reported dead; in fact he was taken prisoner, his captivity solaced by the attentiveness of his Dutch cousins the Reesens until he was exchanged for General D'Oyley. John also went abroad at the first opportunity, to Brunswick with the Duke of Gloucester (`Silly Billy'), who made him an ensign in the Guards at fifteen.[14] These two spirited boys were great favourites with their uncles and aunts and were their father's pride and joy. His own rather half-hearted attempts to contest his native Southampton as a ministerialist in 1784 and 1790 had come to nothing - though he was always popular there - and he was happier with the task of organising volunteer forces in Scotland as Lt. Colonel of the North Fencible Highlanders. Having lived just long enough to see the boys launched in the army he died in 1800 and was buried in Holyrood's royal chapel.[15]

Their half- brother Emperor had been a favourite of Peter Thellusson and like a brother to his near contemporary George, though he no doubt exaggerated in claiming to have been `the adopted son of his [George's] father'.[16] He also started out as a soldier. After three years at Westminster he became a cornet in the 10th Dragoons and by dint of several exchanges he was a captain in the 17th Foot when the war began, yet he went onto the half-pay list almost immediately, clearly having some other career in mind.[17] An ardent royalist, he had made Burke's acquaintance in 1791 and in due course became a protégé of the great alarmist. Although there was little to be gained while the Whigs were in increasingly disunited and dispirited opposition, the realignment of parties brought about by the French Revolution worked in Woodford's favour. Burke failed to get him sent as governor to the penal colony in New South Wales[18] but in 1794 Burke's wing of the Whig party formally made a junction with Pitt and one of their cabinet posts was given to Burke's friend William Windham, who became Secretary at War.

At this time the organization of the army was marked by a 'total failure to provide unity of responsibility and direction',[19] being designed as much to ensure that the army did not become a threat to liberty at home as to secure the efficient conduct of wars abroad. The Secretary at War's job was essentially mundane. He authorised all troop movements at home, handled the army's legal and disciplinary business and oversaw expenditure on pay, clothing and stores; he was a civilian watchdog on army spending, who had to explain and justify the army budget to Parliament. It was a second-rank ministry and Windham was only in the cabinet because of the political circumstances of his appointment.[20]

Burke soon solicited Windham on Woodford's behalf, describing him as 'a young man of very great honour, and great good nature; as well as of excellent talents and much activity',[21] and he was quickly found employment. The English expeditionary force to the Low Countries included several regiments of French emigrants which had been taken into the service, a troublesome, anomalous and temperamental body which required special treatment.[22] Woodford was appointed assistant commissary and paymaster to them, and later chief inspector, and he spent a trying couple of years on the Continent, chivvied from pillar to post by the French armies, 'never certain of my residence for twenty four hours together'[23] and needing the utmost tact and patience with the royalist regiments, whose terms and conditions of service gave rise to constant disputes. He returned home in September 1796 to continue his duties under the style of chief clerk to the newly created foreign department, exercising, he was to claim, 'with regard to the Foreign Corps the same powers as the Under Secretary at War does to the English troops.'[24]

Woodford's prospects looked bright. He was sufficiently in the minister's confidence to be trusted with secret service money, of which he spent almost £6,000, probably under the direction of the Alien Office.[25] He was also a close enough friend of Burke's to be tapped for a loan of £2,000 by that great, but impecunious man. When he had a serious operation at the end of 1796 Burke despaired of him, but Woodford recovered and it was Burke who died not long afterwards.[26] He must have seemed a safe choice as trustee.

It was probably through Woodford that Peter Thellusson's daughter Anne met her future husband, William Lukin. William, eldest son of the dean of Bath and Wells, was the grandson of Robert and Sarah Lukin. After Robert's death Sarah had remarried with William Windham (1717-61) and it was their son who became Secretary at War. The only son of an only son, whose father died when he was still a boy, Windham remained a bachelor for so long that his friends felt he would never marry and because of his isolation his contacts with his half- brother's family were unusually close. He was particularly fond of the boy William, who was perhaps named after him.[27] William Lukin went to sea at twelve - not an unusually tender age in that unsparing century - and Windham used his influence to get him a naval commission when war came. He was a favourite visitor at Felbrigg, Windham's seat in Norfolk, where his uncle tried to teach him geometry and in return the nephew went electioneering for him in the boisterous Norwich election of 1796.[28]

William is a Hornblower figure whose naval career went ahead promisingly, from sloop to frigate, then to the 64 gun ship of the line *Standard* and so to his own ship, the 32 gun *Thames*.[29] Prospects were good for young officers in wartime, with rapid promotions and prize money always on the cards, but for the men who manned the leaky wooden walls, in many cases involuntarily as victims of the impress service, war only added the hazards of battle to the `price of Admiralty'. In 1797 their discontents broke out into mutinies at the Nore and Spithead and it says much for Lukin's popularity that the *Thames* was the first Spithead ship back on duty even though it was awaiting convoy for the dreaded West Indies.[30] Lukin survived that voyage and after taking part in Sir James Saumarez' action off Gibraltar early in 1801 came home on leave to marry Anne Thellusson.

Peter's will required the consent of the trustees and the girl's mother if she was to have her marriage portion. Lukin was duly approved, and Anne was married from the house at Plaistow.[31] Both bride and groom had further expectations, rather faint in Anne's case, as depending on the will being overturned on appeal, but strong in

William's. Three years earlier Windham (then forty-eight) had startled everyone by quietly marrying Cecilia Forrest,[32] the daughter of a deceased admiral, but no children had yet been born and in conjunction with Anne and William's settlement Windham made a will naming William his heir.[33] By the time the settlement was finally approved by the court of Chancery some of its provisions had been overtaken by events, for William and Anne already had two sons and two daughters.[34]

Anne's younger sister had beaten her to the altar. Augusta came of age shortly after her father died and in March 1798 married Thomas Champion de Crespigny, some thirteen years her senior.[35] The Crespignys were Huguenots long settled in England and allied to the Fonnereaus of Suffolk, and Augusta's husband was already a distant kinsman through her brother George's marriage to Mary Ann Fonnereau.[36]

Thomas's father Philip was an uxorious man, marrying four times and having at least four sons and five daughters by his various wives.[37] In Parliament first for Sudbury then for Aldeburgh, he supported North and subsequently Fox, his hauteur earning him the nickname 'God Almighty'.[38] But though proud, he was much less wealthy than his brother Claude, who had married a great heiress, Mary Clarke, and later acquired a baronetcy.[39] Thomas had been at Cambridge, taking the degrees of Bachelor and then Doctor of Laws so that he might be eligible to practise, like his father, in the cosy backwater of Doctors' Commons. The family had a house (Ufford Park) near Sudbury and in time Thomas set about reviving the family's political fortunes in the borough, joining with Windham in defeating ministerial candidates at the 1790 general election. However the rupture in the Whig party split their alliance, Thomas stepping down at the next election and devoting himself to his duties in the East Suffolk militia.[40]

Augusta's marriage settlement was broadly similar to Anne's but since Thomas' expectations were different from William Lukin's, there are significant variations; in particular, if Augusta survived him with fewer than three children, the trustees of the settlement were to raise £6,500 for her benefit.[41] That melancholy contingency came about more quickly than anyone had expected, for Thomas died following a short illness after less than eighteen months of marriage, leaving his young widow with a daughter, Augusta Anne.[42] The connection between the Thellussons and the Crespignys therefore proved to be transitory and although the senior branch of the Crespignys were minor celebrities[43] and the junior, which continued to prosper, lived close to Rendlesham, the families appear to have had nothing more to do with each other.

Augusta's position as a young widow was, in material terms, very pleasant. She had an ample income and a good position and needed to feel no undue haste to remarry, something which she deferred until she was almost forty and her daughter was herself of marriageable age. Her portrait in middle age[44] shows a stoutly built woman of strong but not unpleasing features, certainly not one who would go short of suitors, so we can infer that she had found a widow's life agreeable.

With all her children now married, Peter's widow lived alone at Plaistow until she took pity on a young orphan, Sophy Dixon, and brought her into the household. Ann's health deteriorated and her long and ultimately fatal illness was all the harder to bear because she grudged medical expenses that ate into her small and carefully nurtured capital. She was not a mean woman but had been saving most of her income to pass on to her children as a small compensation for their disinheritance.[45] Her sister Sophia nursed her devotedly until the end came on 18th January 1805 and the will she left is a poignant document. It contains no direct reproaches to her 'kind and indulgent husband' but her firm refusal to use the power he had given her to appoint £5,500 Bank stock selectively, 'thinking it would be injustice to show any partiality when I think [my children] all equally entitled to my love and affection', and her pride in her sons, who were 'in that affluent way of business that I am sure they will be content with the blessings of an affectionate mother whose ardent wish is for a continuance of the prosperity to them and their children' make it clear that her sympathies were all for the deprived children. The will itself, muddled and homemade, was not effective to pass her real estate, a small piece of land at Plaistow bought with £1,652 lent by the trustees, which accordingly went to Peter Isaac as the

220

heir.[46] Admitted to probate with the will was a letter in which Ann exhorted her sons to ensure that Sophy Dixon learned a useful trade under `some good woman'.[47]

Ann Thellusson died happy in the belief that her sons were all doing well, but in reality the firm was going downhill fast. When Peter made his will it was not only prosperous but very highly esteemed, for Lord Kenyon alludes to the holder of a bill of exchange `seeing the name of Messrs Thellusson on it, which is equal to the Bank of England, as they were Gentleman of the first Character and Reputation'.[48] Yet a few years later City opinion as recorded by the indefatigable Farington noted the eminence of Barings, while `Thellusson's might have been of more consideration, but they have been losers by speculation and have not conducted themselves as to be esteemed: their Bond is looked upon to be of more value than their Word'.[49] In the close, private world of merchant banking the loss of reputation for complete integrity, so secure in Peter's day, was immensely damaging and very difficult to recover.[50]

What had been happening in the six years since Peter died? When the partnership of Thellusson Brothers expired at the end of 1798 a new one was formed. All the brothers stayed in the firm- they stood to lose their share of the sale of the Philpot Lane premises if they did not- but Peter Isaac was trying to distance himself from trade to further his peerage claims and Charles seems to have taken little part in the business.[51] The firm was probably too big for a single active partner to cope with, hence the decision to admit a new partner, William Mitchell, but who he was, why he was chosen, and what share he had in the business all remain unclear.[52] He was about thirty-five and probably belonged to one of several families of that name which were active and successful in the West Indies;[53] he may possibly have been already in the office as a chief clerk and was almost certainly wanted for his personal qualities and perhaps family connections rather than for any capital he might bring.

Even in the early 1790s the French house of Greffulhe, Montz had singled out Thellussons as exceptional among English houses in rivalling its own lax bookkeeping,[54] and the new partnership certainly failed to live up to the standards of profitability, and apparently of conduct, set by its predecessors. The evidence is mostly negative. When Boyd Benfield crashed, leadership of the rump of their loan consortium was taken up by Robarts Curtis not Thellussons, who never again figured prominently in the loan business.[55] This may suggest that Peter was right to mistrust his sons' capacities, but they faced great difficulties owing to the collapse of the twin pillars upon which their prosperity had been built. The French trade was gone and with it all the business from the French houses, an immense loss for it was a `closed circuit' which the Huguenots had dominated.[56] And the West India trade was in deep depression.

The last great burst of prosperity for the planters and merchants came in the late 1790s, with production from Santo Domingo, `the Queen of the Antilles', virtually halted and the seas relatively clear of privateers. However, even that was not shared by islands like St. Vincent and Grenada which had suffered from rebellion, and it was threatened by competition from the islands taken from the French. With enormous credits given by lenders in London and Glasgow, West India paper became very important in the money market but the Hamburg crisis in 1799 brought down several big houses and shook others. Optimism revived by the return of most islands in the Peace of Amiens proved illusory as increasing duties in Britain, the closure of continental markets by Napoleon and the success of the slavery abolition campaign plunged the West India trade into a deep and prolonged recession. Merchants were much better placed than planters to cope with these difficulties and George Hibbert and William Manning[57] are examples of those who did, but it called for sound judgment, foresight and a degree of good fortune. A law suit, *Thellusson v. Shedden*[58], shows that the firm was still active in the islands but it may be significant that Thellussons were not among those summoned to give evidence to the Commons committee which heard in exhaustive detail the plight of the West Indians.[59]

Given the eclipse of one of its branches of business and the hazards of another, it would not be surprising if the attractions of `pure finance', speculation on the bill and bond market, had exerted an increasing appeal for the Thellussons, especially as it held out the prospect of rapid gains to partners who had no real interest in commerce and whose lifestyles were geared to the expectation of a large inheritance. They may well have burned their fingers in the tense months when Addington strove to keep the fragile peace he had made without putting England at the mercy of Napoleon, whose appetite for conquest now seemed insatiable; at a crucial stage the Thellussons and other City firms were predicting peace and if they played the markets accordingly they would have lost heavily.[60] Playing the money markets was a very risky game and at least the Thellussons were never ruined like Walter Boyd or the Goldsmids.[61] All the same, their fall from grace was rapid, and one would dearly like to know the facts behind Barroneau's allegation that they were no longer trusted.[62]

At all events the profits which came to be shared out at the end of the partnership were obviously disappointing. Charles dropped out, Peter Isaac offered his second son George in place of himself and as Thellusson and Nephew the business continued, no longer in Philpot Lane but at Old Jewry, a shadow of its former self.[63]

2. Battle Rejoined

There is a gap of six years and two months between the Chancellor's decree in *Thellusson v. Woodford* and the hearing of the appeal in the House of Lords. It was spread over five days, but the appellants had no new arguments to deploy.[64] They dropped the contention that the reference to the 'eldest male lineal descendant' made the disposition too uncertain to be upheld, but persevered with most of the others which failed them in the court of Chancery. In the light of Buller's dismissive remarks, Hargrave was not called up to renew his erudite display of legal history,[65] and Charles Butler, the learned editor of Fearne's *Contingent Remainders* and a leading light in the relief movement for the refugee Roman Catholic clergy, replaced him. The oral arguments were delivered by Mansfield and Samuel Romilly for the appellants, the law officers (Perceval and Manners Sutton) for the Crown, Sir Arthur Piggott, Richards, Cox and Alexander for the various respondents,[66] and on their conclusion the Lord Chancellor put questions to the judges which were in essence the same ones put by Lord Loughborough in 1799.

It took two years to extract the judges' opinions. During this time the Master of the Rolls, Lord Alvanley, had died and been succeeded by Sir James Mansfield, who had represented the family, and Baron Hotham had resigned and been replaced by Manners Sutton. No fewer than six judges attended from King's Bench and Common Pleas - headed by Lord Ellenborough, the former Attorney-General, now Lord Chief Justice - and the Chief Baron of the Exchequer, Sir Alexander MacDonald, gave the collective opinion of the three Exchequer barons.

Once more both the judges and the Lord Chancellor showed themselves impervious to arguments based on the pernicious nature of the will or its mischievous example, from which the passing of the Accumulations Act had drawn much of its sting. It was difficult to contend that any real harm might come from permitting even so large an accumulation if it must remain a solitary curiosity rather than a dangerous tendency, while as far as perpetuities *simpliciter* were concerned, the law already sanctioned a duration which might be a century or so and would not now recoil at devices calculated to increase the probability of it lasting so long. The *number* of lives, and their *connection* with the ultimate devisees, could not form a satisfactory long-stop to Lord Nottingham's rule because neither could be converted into a test which clearly met the mischief of very long suspensions and would necessarily be arbitrary and illogical. The other invitation put up by the family, that the court should be astute to detect, what was found here, a `fraud upon the rule', i.e. its use for an illegitimate purpose, and if convinced that such was the settlor's intention could set it aside, was foredoomed, despite the frail analogy with unconscionable conveyances. The judges were unanimous and Eldon was also able to invoke the known views of other great lights of the law, Lords Kenyon and Thurlow, formidable buttresses to his own opinion.[67]

The decision in the main law suit immediately necessitated recourse to the court on another, subsidiary point. Whatever the level of skill the draftsman had shown in dealing with the accumulation, he certainly nodded when directing what went into the residue, in which Peter wanted to include all the purchases of land he was making.[68] So leisurely was the pace of Georgian conveyancing and so tricky the investigation of titles that months usually elapsed between the agreement for the purchase and the conveyance which gave effect to it. When he made the will Peter had an outstanding agreement for lands at Thorpe-in-Balne near Brodsworth and, contemplating further purchases, he provided that such contracts should be carried into execution by his trustees and the lands held on the trusts of the residue. Between the making of the will and his death three further contracts were made; 770 acres at Amotherby for £21,000; Yellots Farm (60 acres) for £1,050 and Newton Hanzard, 802 acres at £9,600; the first two are close to Brodsworth but the last is in Durham, many miles from his other properties and presumably just looked a bargain.[69] The difficulty about giving effect to the will's directions for these properties was that the Statute of Wills only permitted devises of land which the testator already owned when making the will, so that while the testator (and his executors) could be compelled in equity to complete contracts to buy land, those purchases would not pass under the last will, but would descend instead upon the heir-at-law.[70] However, the injustice this rule might create was mitigated by the equitable doctrine of election, whereby if a person (A) is given a benefit under a will which also purports to dispose of his (A's) property to another, A is required to choose between receiving the benefit or renouncing it and keeping his own property.[71] In July 1806 the Solicitor-General (Romilly) for Peter Isaac argued that election had no application to this case, while Martin and Buller for the trustees, the Attorney- General (Piggott) for the Crown and Alexander, for the grandchildren, all sought to have it applied, forcing Peter Isaac to make the choice between the lands and the legacies.[72]

The doctrine can be carried back centuries, but has been treated by Lord Hardwicke as originating in *Noys v. Mordaunt*[73] and because will making was enmeshed in technicalities which frequently trapped the unwary, it became the subject of a whole group of cases around this time.[74] From these cases there emerged a doctrine so far removed from the apparently simple proposition from which it derives that it is nowadays criticised as having become 'technical and refined, and an uncertain instrument of equity in the broad sense. A supportable basis for the doctrine in its developed form is ... hard to find.'[75]

Thellusson v. Woodford[76] played a modest part in settling the doctrine. It had never previously been applied to defeat the claim of an heir at law to real property and this application was resisted on the ground that, since the will could not be read as a devise of the lands in question, neither should it be looked at for guidance as to the testator's intentions. Instances where the will was formally defective or where the testator was an infant were cited in support,[77] and an attempt was also made to confine election to cases where the testator *knows* that the property is not his to dispose of, a view which had recently been espoused by the Lord Chancellor of Ireland in a case not yet reported.[78] On the other side it was contended that the general principle was clear and that the will might be examined unless it was inoperative either by reason of the testator's legal incapacity or defective execution; the principle is that 'a man shall not take a benefit under a Will ... and at the same time disappoint the provision of that instrument',[79] and this in turn is an expression of a broader principle 'that it is against conscience in claiming the benefit of an instrument, to set up a legal right to disappoint the claims of other persons under the same instrument'.[80]

The Lord Chancellor, Erskine,[81] delayed giving judgment for five months and then did so 'with some reluctance; considering the Will as dictated by feelings, not altogether consistent with convenience'.[82] It seemed to him a clear case of election based upon an implied condition that the heir would not take both the property expressly and validly given to him and hold onto the land fortuitously his by the testator's mistake. In Erskine's view this 'plain simple principle' was only hedged about with later qualifications explicable by considerations of public policy.[83] Peter Isaac was therefore put to his election between the three estates and his pecuniary and other legacies.

He had already made his choice, an easy one since the value of the lands was at least £32,000 and comfortably exceeded the legacies,[84] but he was not prepared to abide by the Chancellor's verdict and appealed to the House of Lords, causing a further delay in settling the question. He still held the lands at his death, though since they were inconveniently distant from his Suffolk estates he had been negotiating for the trust to buy them from him, and his will required them to be sold.

The trustees for their part sought to recover the legacies on the footing that the election had already taken place, but accounts between the trust and Peter Isaac's estate were complicated by mortgages, rent charges, rents and the terms of his mother's will. The trustees of his will insisted on continuing with the appeal,[85] which did not come on until June 1813 and is reported only in summary form.[86] Romilly and Bell emphasised the special favour which the common law shows to the heir but the Lords - in effect Lord Eldon - needed little persuasion to uphold Erskine's judgment.[87]

In due course the pecuniary legacy of £7,600 (with interest at 4% from the date of Peter's death), his share of the proceeds of the sale of Philpot Lane and all the `heirlooms' so carefully particularised in the will had to be handed over by Peter Isaac's trustees.[88] The costs of this venture into litigation, however, like the main election, were taken out of the residue.

3. 'The Oldest Peer'

Peter Isaac was a well known figure in society, with a rented town house in Dover Street, the very heart of the fashionable quarter, where he gave splendid entertainments.[89] He is almost certainly the subject of this anecdote: `One or two of the Brothers Thellusson have made themselves remarkable by the splendour of their entertainments - the Duchess of Gordon, being struck at one of them with the costly magnificence before her said in her sarcastic way to her Host - "What would your entertainments have been if your Father had not disinherited you?".'[90]

His lavish parties did not make him popular; his craving for a peerage was too blatant and his personal qualities evidently if obscurely dislikeable; still, he was not a thin-skinned man and persevered. The road to the peerage lay through the House of

Commons and when a general election came around in 1802 all three brothers sought seats. Charles topped the poll at Evesham, where his considerable expenses including the cost of fighting off a petition from the Whig nabob whom he had defeated.[91] Peter Isaac and George ventured into Henry Holland's stronghold at Okehampton and were narrowly beaten by the votes of 30- odd new freeholders hastily brought down from London;[92] they petitioned but George was never lucky with petitions and while his elder brother bought his way in at Castle Rising, probably paying about £5,000 for the privilege,[93] George found himself still without a seat until August 1804, when he came in for the 'insignificant village' of Tregony.[94]

In the unsettled decade which followed the fracture of Pitt's seemingly impregnable coalition in 1801, anyone who could command two or three votes might extract considerable advantages from insecure ministries.[95] The Thellussons do not seem to have acted in concert; perhaps like the Duries of Ballantrae in Stevenson's novel they tried to keep a brother in each camp, for whereas Peter Isaac put himself firmly behind Pitt when the ex-minister decided to displace his successor Henry Addington, Charles was still counted as a 'doubtful Addingtonian' and at another time was listed among the 'Prince's friends'. George, though he later flirted with the Whigs, was definitely Pitt's man and that must have weighed with the minister when Peter Isaac claimed his peerage.[96]

The promise he wrung out of Pitt was for an Irish peerage, less prestigious than an English one and frequently used as a staging post, as in the case of the Mulgraves.[97] When Pitt decided to bring to an end the separate Irish Parliament and unite the kingdoms the position of the Irish peers presented the same problem as their Scottish counterparts before the earlier Union, *viz.* that the House of Lords would never consent to admit them *en bloc* to membership. It was resolved the same way: a body of representative peers, to be elected by and from the Irish peers for the lifetime of a Parliament, would sit in the Lords, the rest being eligible for election to the Commons.[98]

Inducing the Irish Parliament to vote itself out of existence took great perseverance and political skill, especially on the part of the young Chief Secretary, Lord Castlereagh, but it also took bribery and corruption on an heroic scale. Irish peers feared that after the Union similar tactics would be used to secure the return of pro-government representative peers of English origin and as a safeguard they secured an undertaking that for as long as the size of the Irish peerage exceeded 100 no more than one new peerage would be created for every three that became extinct.[99] Thellusson scanned the newspapers daily for the deaths of Irish peers without sons to carry the title, the men who stood between him and his goal rather as he stood unwillingly between his grandchildren and their fortune. After one false dawn the death of Lord Holmes opened up a vacancy and in October 1805 Thellusson's name went before the King for approval, much to the disgust of some of Pitt's followers.[100] The delighted recipient could not wait for the patent to be drawn up before getting his coach decorated with his new coat of arms, so his agitation when Pitt fell critically ill before the patent could be executed can be imagined. In the gloomy days while Pitt lay dying with the third coalition in ruins after the battle of Austerlitz, London society found some light relief in contemplating the spectacle of `the oldest peer' running frantic after his patent.[101] The execution of the patent, 1st February 1806, was almost the last act of Pitt's ministry, and it solemnly invested the alien merchant's son with the dignity of the barony of Rendlesham in the county of Suffolk in the peerage of Ireland, with a coat of arms supported by two improbably ferocious greyhounds and the family motto, in which he probably saw no trace of irony, *Labore et Honore*.

The new peer promptly gave up his town house, the lease having almost expired, for he wished to live in the country. His picture collection, fifty-eight paintings mostly purchased through a single dealer, was sold by auction and it is a reflection either of his lack of discrimination as a collector or changing public tastes that they made only £8,700, having cost him nearly £14,000.[102] He probably felt the need to retrench, for he was no longer in business, his family was large and his way of life costly. Peter Isaac and Elizabeth had a facility for producing sons, and although Henry died in 1800 aged seven, six others were still alive when their father

229

received his peerage, namely John (20), George (15), the twins (7), Edmund (baptized Edward)(6) and Arthur (5). Frances, the elder of the daughters, died in 1807, leaving Caroline (born in 1782) alone of her sex among her horde of brothers.[103]

As befitted his social standing and expectations the eldest son, John was sent to Eton and went up to St. John's College, Cambridge in 1802, the first of the family to go to university. George also went to Eton and so, after their father's death, did William and Arthur, but neither Frederick (William's twin) nor Edmund seems to have been sent away to school; Frederick had a lifelong speech impediment but why Edmund was not given a public school education is not clear.[104]

Rendlesham was evidently anxious to retain his seat in the Commons, though he made a poor figure there. His opposition to the Talents ministry effectively barred him from defending Castle Rising, which was a Treasury borough, at the 1806 general election and a canvass at Seaford was too discouraging to proceed to a poll so he was out of the Commons for a year until he found a home in one of the rottenest of Cornish rotten boroughs, Bossiney, `a very small dirty village and inhabited only by the lowest class of people', with nine or ten voters and no contests.[105]

His interests certainly lay in Suffolk where he assiduously stocked his woods and coverts with game. A contemporary wrote:

`He possesses an estate, famous for the abundance of its game, as the Duke of York can testify... Rendlesham Hall is ... one of the most fashionable residences in the kingdom. Of late years it has become the scene of much splendid hospitality and has been visited by several branches of the royal family. The neighbourhood abounds with game, and the number of pheasants, partridges and hares killed there, astonishes the sportsman, while the philosopher is disgusted by the unnecessary waste of animal life'.[106] In this generation at any rate, the Thellussons tended towards sport rather than philosophy.

Lord Rendlesham was in the prime of life and in September 1808 he prepared the Hall for a visitor whose presence would afford particular gratification, no less a personage than the exiled King of France. Louis XVIII had arrived off Yarmouth,

230

unbidden and unannounced, obliging the dismayed British government to admit him in the uncomfortable awareness that it would be impotent to get rid of him again. The glamour of even exiled royalty ensured this fat, lugubrious Bourbon a steady flow of visitors at Gosfield Hall in Essex, put at his disposal by the Marquis of Buckingham, who regarded his own family as the next thing to royalty.[107] On 16th September Lord Rendlesham rode out with Lord Chatham, Pitt's indolent elder brother,[108] to bang away at some unoffending wildlife and suddenly fell dead from his horse.[109] He was forty-six years old, and the second of the nine lives had expired after just eleven years of the accumulation. His wife Elizabeth lived as a widow for fifteen months, but according to one knowledgeable acquaintance she never got over his death, `which was considerable remarkable, as he was not a man likely to have excited such affections'.[110]

Peter Isaac left a will which contains unexpected features, although the basic provisions are wholly conventional.[111] Out of his personalty his widow was to have £20,000 in the 3% Consols for life, with power to appoint it by deed or will among their children, and in default to be shared among their children equally when they reached twenty-five; she also received various chattels (the usual household items) and £2,000 absolutely. The younger sons were to receive sums ranging from £10,000 for any yet unborn to £16,000 for George, these legacies to be invested until they reached twenty-one so that they would produce a roughly equal figure in each case; George however would only be paid if his share of the profits of Thellusson & Nephew, in which he was a partner, fell short of his £16,000. The girls (Frances was still alive when the will was made) received £20,000 each, all the childrens' portions being in satisfaction of their claims under their parents' marriage settlement. The residue, evidently not expected to be large since the bequests (which also included £300 to each executor/trustee), totalled over £130,000, was to be invested in land to be held on the trusts of his realty.[112]

These trusts took the form of the basic strict settlement. However, it was, as we have seen, open to a settlor who mistrusted the capacity or character of his eldest son to impose safeguards on this imprudence. There were three principal means of doing so; first, by postponing his right to receive the income from the trust property until some age beyond the age of majority, twenty-five being the commonest; secondly, by requiring him to obtain the consent of the trustees and/or his mother to any marriage on pain of forfeiting some part of his property; thirdly, by means of a protective trust.[113]

Remarkably, Peter Isaac imposed all three forms of restraint on John. Until he reached thirty- one he was to have no right to income, only to a sum not exceeding £1,500 and payable at the trustees' discretion; moreover if *at any age* he married without the consent of his mother (while she lived) and the trustees he was to be paid only £400 per annum plus whatever the trustees thought proper for `the maintenance, advancement, education or other use or benefit of any issue which he may have'. And if, once having got his hands on the income, he should `charge mortgage sell or otherwise dispose of the rents issues and profits ... or any part thereof by way of anticipation or agree or attempt so to do or shall commit or permit any act whereby if this clause had not been inserted the said rents issues and profits would have vested or become payable to any other person', then the protective trusts would spring into operation.

Peter Isaac made it insultingly plain that he did not trust his son and heir, and compounded the insult in the devises to the other sons, for though they also contain the protective trust, they do not impose any restriction on marriage and they make the income payable in full at twenty-five, giving the trustees a full discretion to pay some or all of it earlier. The testator says nothing to explain this harsh and discriminatory approach and it is all the more notable in a man who had suffered a humiliating snub through the will of his own father. John was twenty-one when the will was made, but as a young an army officer he had already exhibited a worrying tendency to contract debts.[114] Nonetheless, this powerful exercise of patriarchal power created a potentially explosive situation within the family.

Rendlesham's trustees therefore had a burdensome and delicate task, but none of them disclaimed it. He had chosen his brother George and a more distant relation, the husband of his wife's sister Susan, Samuel Heywood, together with William Manning, a great West India merchant and MP for Evesham. Heywood and Manning were middle- aged, shrewd and capable men, well able to resist the importunities of an impecunious heir, and it is perhaps significant that Peter Isaac passed over his youngest brother Charles and all the Woodfords.[115]

The executors immediately met with trouble from an unexpected quarter, the Thellusson trustees, or rather Emperor Woodford, for although there were two other trustees by this time,[116] it was Emperor who ran the trust. According to George Thellusson, `having proposed to himself to go and live down at Butley, which is the estate adjoining to my brother's property, he sent gamekeepers and persons down, and took it from my nephews'.[117] Woodford had been so obliging hitherto that the family had got into the habit of looking on the whole intermingled property as all of a piece and his abrupt and tactless decision to use Butley himself set them by the ears. Whatever the merits of the case, it was astonishingly foolish of Woodford to alienate some of his most useful and influential friends, for he now had need of friends as never before.

4. The Fall of Emperor Woodford

Woodford's promising career in the public service had somehow stalled. Obliged to leave the War Office when Windham resigned in 1801, he had lived on his half- pay and a sort of pension which made it up to £300 p.a.[118] When the foreign department he had headed was revived in 1804 it was not restored to him, but was given to his young cousin Ralph; if he tried for other government posts he was unsuccessful, and he evidently had no desire to compete with younger men in the army. Not having married, he had no family to support, but his means fell short of his tastes, especially after a fire in 1802 in which he lost over £1,000, so he must have been very disappointed when Windham and his party rejected Pitt's offer of coalition in 1804.[119]

By that time what had been a cloud on the horizon was fast filling his sky. It took the form of the Audit Office and their demand for his War Office accounts. Every civil servant who handled public money had eventually to face the Audit Office, there to produce the vouchers which authenticated and authorised his disbursements.[120] Since the public auditors laboured with tedious slowness even in peacetime, and were completely overwhelmed by the increase in government activity in wartime, he might have to retain these vouchers for many years and often in a state of some anxiety, for discrepancies were common. The audit of War Office accounts, with all its dealings with individual regiments and agents, was spectacularly in arrears, but however slowly the Audit Office moved, it advanced ponderously towards the day of reckoning.[121]

Woodford had good reason to fear that day, for his accounts could not hope to pass the auditors. Windham was the last minister to have worried himself about such niceties as accounts, for he was a man of large views and men of large views seldom set much store by accounting. The attitude of the minister infected the people who worked under him, especially those who were in confidential situations and were friends or relatives - and not a few of Windham's friends and relations were found places in the War Office.[122] Windham was indignant at the shabby treatment he felt the government accorded to the French refugees and it was a short step from putting his hand in his own pocket for them to putting his hand - via Woodford - into the money kept for office expenses, let alone the secret service money.[123] Windham's own estates were subjected to `profligate mismanagement'[124] and his indifference to his own finances extended to the public purse which he held. He sent Woodford abroad, utterly inexperienced in the management of money and with negligible supervision, to deal with royalist officers made unscrupulous by want and sharp-witted purveyors of provisions, and neither then nor afterwards took any care to see how he had performed his task. It would have been remarkable if for the period of Woodford's continental service there were no gaps and deficiencies in his vouchers.

But the position was much worse than that. For one thing Woodford and his assistant Richard Gardiner had no vouchers at all, nor accounts of any sort, covering their dealings on the exchanges- or if they had they were not ones they cared to produce; when changing sterling into local currencies they had simply pocketed the profits `as though they were merchants trading on their own account rather than public servants'.[125] What vouchers they had for their other dealings were few, unspecific and hopelessly inadequate and Woodford must have realised this, since before quitting office he persuaded Windham to give verbal instructions to another of Windham's relations, a certain Captain Foy of the Artillery, to carry out an audit of his accounts. Foy had no obvious qualifications for the task, which was perfunctorily performed and rejected by the Audit Office.[126]

Woodford fought a rearguard action for as long as possible but by 1806 it was clear that he would have to face the music, although it was equally clear that at the current rate of progress it would not be for some years.[127] Unfortunately for him, however, the state of the War Office accounts attracted attention in Parliament. Robert Lukin, Windham's half- brother, was a bigger target than Woodford, £1,524,630 having passed through his hands as agent for the foreign corps without proper accounts being presented, and the opposition seized on this as a stick to beat Windham, who now held the more important position of Secretary for War.[128] A Commission of Military Enquiry was set up by statute to investigate a whole range of possible abuses and soon they too were on Woodford's trail.[129]

Any sympathy one may feel for Emperor Woodford is quelled by a document among Windham's papers.[130] It is a report by the government's law officers dated 30th May 1805 on a pamphlet published by a man named Poole, who charged that Woodford and Gardiner had been in league with one Devaux to commit frauds in the supply of provisions to the troops and that at least some of the profits had been salted away in stock held in the names of Gardiner and another man in trust for Devaux and Woodford. Poole's claims fell short of the proof required to launch a prosecution but the law officers found they created a `strong presumption ... that Mr. Devaux, Mr. Woodford and Mr. Gardiner acted in concert together, for the purpose of diverting a part of the allowance made by Government, particularly the Rations of Forage, from the proper Channel; and that the benefit derived from this Practice was immediate to Devaux, and was probably communicated in part by him to Woodford and Gardiner.'[131] No wonder Windham did not re-employ Woodford.

After skulking at Butley on the plea of ill-health, Woodford was examined by the commissioners on 5th August 1808 and must have known that their report would blast his hopes of resuming a public service career.[132] What is more, he had £461,000 to account for and might expect to have to find some of the unvouched sums out of his own pocket. Parliament meanwhile was hunting bigger game, no less than the Commander- in- Chief, the Duke of York. Allegations that the Duke's mistress, Mary Anne Clarke, was able to procure and sell commissions from her royal protector gave the Opposition an unmissable opportunity to vex the Government and on the first day of 1809 a succession of unpleasant creatures was pulled from beneath their stones and exposed to public gaze.[133] Not surprisingly the 7th Report of the Commissioners for Military Enquiry, containing their findings on Woodford and presented to the Commons on 20th January, fell rather flat in the context of this drama, and luckily the 9th Report, which appeared with it, was full of the 'regular and unchecked system of peculation'[134] audaciously conducted by the commissary general for Jamaica, Valentine Jones, which far surpassed Woodford's modest efforts. The commissioners were relatively mild in their censures,[135] but some of the press made up for it with withering sarcasm at the expense of Windham and all his connections and it cannot have been a pleasant experience for them to read either the report or the comments on it.[136]

Much worse was to follow. Among the disreputable specimens examined in the search for evidence against the Duke was Jeremiah Donovan, who disclosed that among the places in which he had trafficked were East India cadetships and writerships. This was not germane to the business in hand but the House was prepared to follow any trail where it scented corruption and the very next day a select committee was formed to investigate these abuses of East India patronage.[137]

236

John Company was one of the greatest sources of patronage outside the cabinet, sending forth a score of young men every year as writers and cadets; though they had to pass an examination to show their fitness they were not chosen by competition, rather the directors had the nominations in rotation.[138] This was indeed one of the main attractions of a directorship, though it meant they were pestered and solicited without mercy by relatives, friends and total strangers. Money was offered and money accepted and the abuses grew so notorious that in 1798 the Company's new charter contained an oath to be taken by each director within ten days after his appointment, 'not directly or indirectly to take any prerequisites, emolument, fee, present or reward ... or any promise for any... or in respect of the appointment or nomination of any person or persons to any place or office in the gift or appointment of the Company'. For the director there was no penalty, but a Court of Directors' resolution prescribed dismissal for the appointee. India House at this time was full of intrigue and bitterness and the whole issue got caught up in partisan politicking; an investigating committee set up in 1798 was not reappointed after close voting in 1801 and proposed stronger penalties were dropped as being probably unlawful.[139]

Trafficking in Company posts still went on- indeed men like Donovan and Shee advertised them in the press- but George Woodford Thellusson by his own account suspected nothing when Emperor Woodford approached him for one nomination after another. Why should he? Woodford was an intimate friend, with no stain on his character, and George was so unsuspecting that when a City friend mentioned a recent instance of corruption, he and another director decided to investigate, a brave thing to do since he was up for re-election shortly.[140]

He soon regretted it:

'On Saturday, as I had been at my counting house, I was returning and coming through Lombard Street, when I was accosted by Mr. Emperor John Alexander Woodford, who is my first cousin and trustee under my father's will to all his property: I was surprised at Mr. Woodford's speaking to me, as ever since my brother's death he and I have been on terms of the greatest hostility, on account of his treatment, as I conceived, of my brother's family; he said that he was an undone man, or something to that effect, and I told him that certainly he must know that he was, in my opinion, for we could never speak more; he then told me he was going to Mr. George Hibbert, who is my brother-in-law, to communicate something to him concerning me. He said, I must see you, do you dine at home? I told him I did not know, that I did not want to see him; he said "I know you do dine at home, for I have called at your house, and I must see you to-night at eight o'clock, we must not be seen together now." I was surprised; and he then said, you remember the Writership, I told him yes, I remember three that I have given you, and I have seen the return that I have met with for it. He mentioned Mr. Donovan's name; at that moment I thought I should have fallen down, I pushed him away from me, and told him not to speak to me any more, that I must go directly to the India House ... I met a relation of mine passing by, my uncle, who had come to town and who does not very often come to town; I ran on to the India House, and could not speak to him; I feared that he should think I was really crazy, and I wrote a letter of apology to him ..."[141].

Of the three posts Woodford had solicited from Thellusson he had sold two to a shady attorney called Gabriel Tahourdin and, indirectly down this greasy chain, to Donovan, pocketing £3,000 each time, and had given Tahourdin the third in exchange for the promise of a living for his cousin Sherer, a promise he afterwards commuted for a similar sum.[142] Tahourdin had a very distant connection with the Woodfords, his brother being a curate to the old archdeacon, and he had been trying to interest Emperor in some Hampshire estates for the trust, or so at least their story went. Emperor gave Tahourdin to understand that he was on the lookout for a seat in Parliament, believing that he was the sort of factotum who picked up such knowledge; he was in some haste, for there was a general election in the offing and as an MP he might be able to gain some sinecure or pension to help discharge his debts. Tahourdin was a wily bird; yes, something might possibly be done if Emperor had something to offer, something like East India patronage for instance. A more cautious, or less desperate man, would have recognised the danger and drawn back. Emperor had no influence at India House but Tahourdin knew, as all lawyers did, of his connection with Thellusson.[143]

For George Thellusson the whole thing was a complete humiliation. The enquiry he had urged turned chiefly upon his own patronage and although he was absolved of corruption sceptical observers were unconvinced and to those who were he appeared a fool, the dupe of his former friend.[144] To Woodford's credit he did his very best both in public and in a letter to J.J. Angerstein, the chairman of Thellusson's re-election committee, to exonerate him, but as far as the election was concerned, he stood no chance; the Company's shareholders condemned him emphatically at the poll.[145]

Woodford's plight was now desperate. His involvement in the sale of offices was not illegal but a man is known by the company he keeps and Tahourdin and Donovan were very low company indeed; he was also a man known to have abused the trust of his best and oldest friend. Windham demanded to know if *his* name had ever been made use of to further corrupt ends, and was himself in difficulties in the Commons, having to defend himself against the pretty plain conclusion of the commissioners that he had been lax with the public purse and the insinuations of his political foes that his own relatives, the Lukins, Disneys and Woodfords, had been the beneficiaries of his laxity.[146] On 25th April 1809 Woodford at last delivered his accounts, such as they were, to the Audit Office; four days later the shady Devaux put in an explanation of his part in these events of long ago and at the beginning of May, Emperor Woodford fled the country. George Hibbert was entrusted with letters and excuses and alone knew of his departure; according to Woodford 'he concurred in my wishes to be abroad just now. All my other friends have advised strongly the measure.' To Windham he darkly hinted that 'I am sure if I had staid my head would have failed [and] I might have done worse,' and in a hollow gesture asked for his half-pay to be commuted and invested in the Funds to meet any disallowance in his accounts.[147]

It was a bad time for an Englishman to go abroad, with the French controlling most of Europe, and it is perhaps surprising that he did not go to the United States. Instead he began in Madeira, from which he wrote sententious nonsense, admitting his guilt but excusing it by `the success of others [in] the Practices which time has sanctioned; `had I lived in better times', he claimed, `I had been a better man'.[148] From there he drifted to Rio de Janeiro where `I pass my time in idleness and sauntering'.[149] He never did come home and died in Bordeaux in 1817.[150]

This was the man Peter Thellusson chose to be the trustee of his millions! This man who cheated the public and deceived his best friend, and his brother, an old man and hardly wordly wise, were to choose the land purchases, appoint receivers of rents and oversee the application of the rents to their rightful purposes. Of course, it does not follow that the man who played fast and loose with public funds could not be trusted with private money: few then regarded the two things as comparable at all. But consider the temptation and opportunities for Woodford in his desperate days had the will not gone into Chancery. Until uncle Matthew died there needed to be only the two of them and Matthew would never question his cousin's integrity. The income from the trust fund was payable to no-one, so who would notice if money was borrowed from it for short term exigencies? True there were solicitors necessarily involved and no fraud could have lasted very long without their connivance, but all the same, the risk would have been considerable. Whatever the price of Chancery, it did secure the property from plunder by its guardians.

5. George and Charles

George Woodford Thellusson was an unlucky man. While his brothers had sons he had only two daughters; his wife was only twenty-seven when she had Georgiana but no more children followed and George had to reconcile himself to having no male heir. Others in that not uncommon situation adopted a nephew (as Windham did), a distant cousin or even a stranger, but George's position was peculiarly cruel, since he was barred from any share in the great fortune himself and - except on a very strained construction - for his posterity.

He was also the unlucky one in politics. The Southwark election was a costly fiasco and when he did get into Parliament he had to spend heavily to keep his seat and gained nothing from it. It was he who kept the family business going only to find it inexorably slipping into a decline, and then to crown it all he had the bitter experience of quarrelling with the great friend of his childhood and finding that his trust had been betrayed and his friendship exploited,[151] to the ruin of his position at India House and his humiliation in the public prints. Worse, a reputation for credulity and unsound judgment was disastrous in the London business world and probably hastened the firm's rapid decline, which was accelerated by losses arising out of the failure of the Liverpool brokers Lowndes and Bateson in that city's financial crisis of 1810.[152]

But there was an another side to George, which found expression in architecture. He had leased a small house at Otterspool, not far from Watford, and in 1799 found that in the nearby parish of Aldenham a substantial estate was on the market. This was Wall Hall, and as with many estates in the area it had proved a popular purchase for London merchants for a long time past. The latest of them, Samuel Vandenwall, had settled it by his will in 1771 and the house had then been let, for the Neates, who were the beneficiaries under the settlement, preferred their estates in Berkshire. Now Thomas Neate was willing to sell.[153] It cost George £24,000, much of which he had to borrow from the trustees of his marriage settlement, but that was only a beginning.[154] He clearly intended Wall Hall to form the core of a large group of estates, both his own and those of the Thellusson trust, and as a preliminary step set about enclosing the last open part of Aldenham common and redeeming his land tax.[155] The house was transformed from an undistinguished Georgian 'oblong box' into a Gothick fantasy, 'Aldenham Abbey', turreted and battlemented, a house in which to read the novels of Mrs. Radcliffe by the light of a guttering candle.[156] Later writers poured scorn on the 'architectural sham', reserving their especial displeasure for the use of old tombstones from the local churchyard to create mock ruins, and this romantic streak would have confirmed his father's worst fears about his sons.[157]

Money soon became a problem for George. In 1804 he was asking the trust to lend him £30,000 for his business on the security of the Aldenham estate (said to be worth £2,000 p.a.), and within a year he was offering to sell the whole lot (920 acres) to the trust at £98,153; perhaps the firm's speculations had already taken their toll.[158] The trust did not want to be saddled with another mansion house, especially one so peculiar, and in the end George kept Wall Hall but sold all but the seven acres around the house for £72,395.[159]

George's sister Maria Phipps had leased Otterspool and not far away was the home of George Hibbert, Mary Ann Thellusson's brother-in-law.[160] George Woodford was receiver for the Hertfordshire trust estates and, unfortunate to the end, was engaged in a dispute over some extravagant repairs he had commissioned when he went down to Rendlesham for the Christmas of 1811. On 30th December, a seemingly healthy forty- seven year old, he went out shooting and within a few yards of the very spot where his brother had died three years earlier, fell dead of an apoplectic fit.[161] He was buried at Rendlesham, not by his own wish but probably because of the difficulties of transporting the body a hundred miles in the depths of winter, and for the convenience of the family, still gathered in Suffolk.[162]

His death was financially untimely and he knew it, for less than a year earlier he had made a will in which he anxiously requested his partner Mitchell (whom he made one of his executors) 'to use his utmost exertions to recover as much as possible of the considerable debts owing to my several partnerships'.[163] To the surprise of those outside his circle, his personal property was proved at less than £15,000 (excluding gifts of £1,000 and household goods to his wife), but even so the legacies could not be paid for several years as claims for debts exceeded his available assets.[164]

Like Lord Rendlesham's estate, though to a much lesser extent, George's testamentary affairs were held fast in Chancery tentacles until claims against him by the trust (over his receivership, the West India estates and the old partnership) and

242

counterclaims by his own estate against the trust could be resolved, but whatever the outcome of these tangled accounts there was no disputing that George had died comparatively poor and that his widow and children could not hope to maintain their previous standard of living.[165]

It is not surprising therefore that Wall Hall was now sold as quickly as possible, and that although Mary Ann was empowered to keep it for life, she preferred living off the invested proceeds of the sale and her jointure. The property fetched £28,406[166] and was bought by one of those figures who seems to step right out of fiction - not Dickens this time but the pages of Jane Austen. In *Persuasion* (1818) the egregious Sir Walter Kellynch has to let Kellynch Hall to Admiral Croft, lamenting that naval officers are `all knocked about, and exposed to every climate, and every weather, till they are not fit to be seen'. Sir Charles Morice Pole, the purchaser of Wall Hall, was just such a man.[167]

Georgiana Thellusson got married in 1813[168] and some time afterwards Mary Ann and her unmarried daughter, having first occupied Blackbirds Farm,[169] returned to Otterspool. Otterspool has a spring with mildly medicinal properties which had given it a fleeting vogue and enabled the house to be let as an inn/ hotel until Thellusson took a thirty year lease from the owner in 1798.[170] He had sublet it to Maria and her husband Augustus Phipps, perhaps the most engaging couple in the story. Childless but sociable, artistic and thoroughly amiable, they feature regularly in Farington's diaries,[171] where we can hear Augustus describe the light duties of a Commissioner of Excise.[172] Farington himself taught Maria drawing and George Dance promised to sketch her. We can sympathise with Augustus when he found S.T. Coleridge `oppressive in company', be curious when Maria criticises J.M.W. Turner and enjoy Northcote's view of Augustus: `He is like a Boy ... who disregards quality and pretension and plays about with constant good humour'.[173]

Augustus Phipps died in 1826 at their town house in Portland Place, in his sixty- fourth year.[174] Maria outlived him by eight years and left legacies to over forty relatives, friends and servants, requesting Earl Mulgrave to pass on various pictures, books and other articles to the persons with whose names she had methodically labelled them. Like her husband, she was sixty- three years old.[175]

Death had been walking abroad among the Thellussons to grim effect. Between Trafalgar and Waterloo scarcely a year passed without the death of someone intimately connected with the great law suit.[176] Most of the deaths were from natural causes but the war claimed one victim. In June 1813 Wellington's army engaged Napoleon's brother Joseph, the puppet King of Spain, in the battle of Vittoria, putting him to flight with the loss of 8,000 men, his artillery and a great wealth of plunder. The British army suffered 5,000 fatalities and among them was George Thellusson, Peter Isaac's second son, an officer in the 11th Light Dragoons temporarily attached to the 16th.[177] He was only twenty-five and unmarried but he had made his will before embarking for Spain, bequeathing all that he might be entitled to under his father's will or marriage settlement to Eliza Maria, the third daughter of Walter Parry Hodges of Dorchester.[178] It looks as if George, like his elder brother John, had found a sweetheart while in the army.

Charles, the youngest of Peter's sons, is also the most elusive. Inactive in business and probably as a politician, though he somehow contrived to `render himself obnoxious' to the electors of Evesham,[179] he was the owner of a modest property in Kent, (probably on the Surrey borders, since his younger children were baptised in Addington church),[180] but seems to have formed the intention to settle in the neighbourhood of Evesham, for in June 1802 he bought Bengeworth from the Rushouts for £31,000, most of it provided on mortgage by the trust. Two years later, however, the property was sold in lots; as with his brother George, one wonders whether Charles's finances had taken a hit.[181] There is no evidence that he made any further efforts to find a country estate and later on he passed much of his time at Brodsworth. In addition to Charles, born in old Peter's lifetime, he had two sons, Alexander and Thomas Robarts, born in 1800 and 1801 respectively, and one daughter Adeline Maria, born in January 1803; Sabine's childbearing stopped at an early age, which was a good thing in view of her husband's lack of thrift.

244

Oddly, the three boys were each sent to a different public school; Charles to Eton, Alexander to Harrow and Thomas to Rugby. Their father-in-law Abraham Robarts was still a director of the East India Company and a career in the Company's service was in prospect for both younger sons, the groundwork being laid for Alexander by transferring him to the Company's new college at Haileybury. His father was a widower by then, Sabine having died at Brighton in the winter of 1814,[182] and like his brothers he died unexpectedly in middle-age, at his beloved Brodsworth on 2nd November 1815, aged just forty-five.[183] Charles left a short will, made just after his wife's death, and since all his children were still minors, he appointed his father-in-law and a friend, John Mansel of Cosgrave, Northants, trustees for them.[184] Charles junior inherited the realty, farm animals and equipment and household effects, the personal estate being divided among all the children who should live to be twenty-one or (in the case of Adeline) should marry at a younger age with the consent of her guardians (the trustees, her grandmother and aunt Maria Phipps). Meanwhile their shares were to be invested with the usual powers of maintenance and education. The personal estate was sworn at less than £16,000,[185] which hardly left the younger children with much of a prospect and, as we shall see, even the heir would find his patrimony woefully inadequate.

NOTES

1.   Hargrave, *Juridical Arguments*, vol.II, 'advertisement'.

2.   R.Stevens, *Law and Politics: the House of Lords as a Judicial Body* (London, 1979), pp.6-16.

3.   See *infra*, pp. 219-20.

4.   This remained true throughout the century; see evidence to the Committee on Trusteeship, *PP* 1895 (248), XIII.

5.   *Webb v. Earl of Shaftesbury* (1802) 7 Ves. Jun. 481, *supra*, p. 175.

6.   *Gents. Mag.* 80 (1810), 392.

7.   For nearly ten years (1763-72) he was resident minister to the Hanse towns at Hamburg, then briefly envoy extraordinary to Denmark: Horn, *British Diplomatic Representatives, 1660-1789*, pp. 5, 72, 125, 135.

8.   G.E.C., *Complete Baronetage*, p. 274; Burke, *Extinct and Dormant Baronetcies*, pp. 579-80.

9.   *Gents. Mag.* 80 (1810), 290; *PP* 1809 (91) II, p.18; PRO PROB 6/186. His personal estate was sworn under £1,500.

10.   PRO PROB 11/1246, f.293. According to G.W. Thellusson, Emperor 'had the whole management': *PP* 1809 (91) II, p.211.

11.   Crosthwaite, *Memoir of Sir J. G. Woodford*, pp. 3-8; *The Letters and Journals of Lady Mary Coke* (reprint, Bath, 1970), vol.II, p.21; Burke, *Extinct and Dormant Baronetcies*.

12.   *Complete Peerage*, vol.XII pt.2, pp.575-6; Sir J.B. Paul, *The Scots Peerage* (9 vols., Edinburgh, 1904-14), vol.IV, p.555.

13.   J.P. de Castro, *The Gordon Riots*, (London, 1926), pp.98-102; Walpole to Lady Ossory, 7 Jun. 1780, *Horace Walpole Correspondence*, vol.XXXIII, pp.183-6.

14.   Crosthwaite, *Memoir of Sir J.G. Woodford*, pp.5-10 and app. 1.

15.   Temple Patterson, *History of Southampton, 1700-1914*, pp.61, 66; *House of Commons, 1754-90*, vol.I, p.299; PRO PROB 6/176.

16.   Woodford to J.J. Angerstein, 6 Apr. 1809, BL Add.Mss. 37,951, f.198. His aunt Thellusson stood as his godmother: Crosthwaite, *Memoir of Sir J.G. Woodford*, p.17.

17.   E. Burke to W. Windham, 17 Aug. 1994, *The Windham Papers* (2 vols., London, 1913), vol.I, p.227.

18.   A. Cobban and R.A.Smith (eds.), *The Correspondence of Edmund Burke* (9 vols., Cambridge 1958-78), vol.VI, p.223, vol.VII, pp.462-3. His correspondence with Burke began in February 1791.

19.   R.K. Glover, *Peninsular Preparation* (Cambridge, 1963), p.14.

20. *Ibid.*, pp.34ff. The Secretary at War should not be confused with the Secretary *for* War, created in 1794 and subsequently combined with the Secretaryship for Colonies. Windham held that post in the Talents ministry (1806-7).

21. Burke to Windham, 17 Aug. 1794: *The Windham Correspondence*, vol.I, p.213.

22. C.T. Atkinson, Foreign Regiments in the British Army, 1793-1802, *Journal of the Society for Army Historical Research* 21 (1942), 175-81; 22 (1943), 2-14.

23. 7th Report of the Commission of Military Enquiry, *PP* 1809 (3) V, app.1, q.4. The campaign can be followed in A.H. Burne, *The Noble Duke of York* (London, 1949).

24. *Seventh Report of the Commission of Military Enquiry*, app.2, q.17. Both the *Annual Register* 52 (1810), 203-5 and *The Times*, 31 Mar. 1809, waxed sarcastic about this unconstitutional ˋsecond under secretary of state'.

25. Woodford to Windham, 5 Mar. 1801, BL Add Mss 37,851, f.144 gives an account of his dealings and advice on future disbursements.

26. He also helped with Burke's emigrant school at Penn. *Burke Correspondence*, vols. VIII, IX, *passim*; *Windham Papers*, vol.II, pp.33, 56.

27. The best accounts of Windham are by R.W. Ketton Cremer in his introduction to *The Early Life and Diaries of William Windham* (London, 1930) and *Felbrigg: the Story of a House* (London, 1962).

28. There is correspondence in 37,912-13, and in 37,914, f.55 is Windham's letter to Lord Chatham seeking preferment for him (August 1793). See also *The Diary of William Windham, passim*.

29. J. Marshall, *Royal Naval Biography* (12 vols., London, 1823-30), vol. I pt. 2; W.R. O'Byrne, *A New Naval Biography* (3 vols., London, 1849), vol. III, p.1309. For the Lukin family see Sir A. Tudor-Craig, *The Romance of Melusine and de Lusignan* (London, 1937).

30. R. Wells, *Insurrection, The British Experience, 1795-1803* (Gloucester, 1983), pp.79-109.

31. *Gents. Mag.* 71 (1801), 571.

32. *Windham Papers*, vol.I, pp.74-5; PRO PROB 11/1514, f.446. Cecilia had waited 27 years to be asked, Windham having first been enamoured of her elder (married) sister Bridget Byng.

33. Heads of the settlement in BL Add Mss 37,919, f.265 do not differ significantly from the final version in PRO C 33/538, f.833. It has no unusual features save for elaborate provision for the unlikely eventuality of Anne receiving a windfall from her father's estate.

34. Order of 13 Jun. 1805, PRO C 33/538, f. 833.

35. *Gents. Mag.* 68 (1798), 352.

36. *House of Commons, 1754-1790*, vol.II, p.275; *House of Commons, 1790-1820*, vol III, p.529.

37. According to *House of Commons, 1790-1820*, vol.III, p.529 and *Alumni Cantabrigienses*,

1752-1900, vol.II, p.190, Thomas was the second son, but the codicil to his father's will (PRO PROB 11/1538, f.226) suggests he was the eldest.

38. *House of Commons, 1754-1790*, vol.II, p.275.

39. E. Lodge, *The Peerage, Baronetage, Knightage and Companionage* (81st edn., London, 1912), vol.I, pp.582-4.

40. *Alumni Cantabrigienses, 1752-1900*, vol.II, p.190; *House of Commons, 1790-1820*, vol.II, pp.74-7, 529.

41. Order of 13 Jun.1805, PRO C 33/539, f.889. The settlement was altered after being engrossed but before being executed.

42. He died on 1st August: *Gents. Mag.* 69(1799), 722. He left no will and since Augusta renounced her right to administer his estate, sworn at under £2,000, it was left to a creditor to take out letters of administration, PRO PROB 6/175.

43. *Public Characters of 1805*, p. 187. There is some information about the family in later years in Sir C. Champion de Crespigny, *Fifty Years of a Sportsman's Life* (rev. edn., London 1925).

44. Reproduced in Ain, *Les Thellusson*, facing p.225.

45. Will dated 7 Feb.1804, PRO PROB 11/1805, f.136.

46. *Ibid.*; order of 21 Dec.1808, PRO C 33/567, f.230. The will was attested by only two witnesses and the Statute of Frauds 1677 required three for real property.

47. There is an oddity here. The doctrine of incorporation by reference, which allows the inclusion of other documents with the will, requires the letter to be already in existence when the will is made. The will does refer to such a letter, but the one incorporated postdates the will.

48. *Bish v. Thellusson, The True Briton*, 22 Jul. 1797. The action concerned a bill for £25 accepted by Thellussons who, presumably by some incompetence at their office, were now called upon to pay for a second time. They lost the case.

49. *Farington Diary*, vol.VI, p.2059, entry of 19 Jun. 1803.

50. S.D. Chapman, *The Rise of Merchant Banking* (London, 1984), pp.70-81.

51. *Supra*, p. 115.

52. In 1800 Mitchell was living at the house of Mrs. Orde: *Danloux Journal*, p.437. He died at 45, Norfolk Street on 25 Jul. 1834, aged 71, PRO TS 18/1501.

53. Neither William Mitchell, receiver-general for Jamaica and a vastly wealthy plantation owner (died 1823) nor his brother David, a prosperous London merchant, is known to have a son of this name. Another possibility is that he was descended from William, Secretary to the East India Company, who died in 1790, *Musgrave's Obituaries* (Harleian Society publications, vols 44-49, London, 1899-1901), vol. III, p.207.

54. Antonetti, *Une Maison de Banque*, p.90.

55. They were, however, participants in a loan engagement for £20 million under the leadership of Sir Francis Baring in 1806: *NRA Report 41369 (Northbrook MSS)*.

56. Lüthy, *Banque Protestante*, vol.II, pp.318-20.

57. Ragatz, *Fall of the Planter Class*, pp.204-330; S.G. Checkland, Finance for the West Indies, 1780-1815, *Economic History Review* (2nd s.) 20 (1957-8), 461-9.

58. (1806) 2 Bos. & Pul. (N.R.) 228. This was an action on an insurance policy covering the *Mary,* Jamaica to London, which was captured and then re-taken and the cargo sold by the Admiralty Court to cover salvage and expenses.

59. *PP* 1807 (65) III.

60. T. Grenville to Lord Grenville, 12 May 1803, *Report on the Manuscripts of the Hon. J.B. Fortescue preserved at Dropmore*, vol.VII (London, 1910), p.167.

61. For Boyd see *supra*, pp. 96-7. The Goldsmids' successful career in government finance ended in disaster and personal tragedy as both brothers committed suicide, Benjamin in 1808, Abraham in 1810: *Gents. Mag.*78 (1808), 373, 451; 80 (1810), 382; Cope, *Goldsmids.*

62. In 1801 an accusation of perjury was brought against George Thellusson by one Copinger, a shipowner. He charged that Thellusson had falsely sworn to ownership of the vessel *The Guardian*, which the Copinger brothers had mortgaged to Thellusson brothers. In *R. v. Thellusson*, before a special jury, Thellusson employed no fewer than four lawyers who were then or subsequently celebrated (Erskine, John Scott, Gibbs and Scarlett) and was vindicated, the mortgage having fallen into arrears, thereby vesting the ship in the lenders. He promptly sued Copinger for malicious prosecution and was awarded £1,000 damages. Since Copinger was in gaol for debt it is unlikely he ever received the money: *Thellusson v. Copinger*, 3 Esp. 616; *The Times*, 27 Feb., 4 Mar., 23 Apr., 4 Jun.1801.

63. *Post Office Directories*, 1811-13.

64   According to the highly unreliable Sir Egerton Brydges, there was vigorous lobbying on the part of the appellants: *The Autobiography, Times, Opinions and Contemporaries of Sir Egerton Brydges* (2 vols., London, 1834), vol.II, p.15.

65. Butler, Mansfield and Romilly signed the appellants' printed case; the trustees' was signed by Piggott and N. Ridley; the infants' by Manners Sutton, Cox, G. Thomson and R. Richards; the Crown's by Law, Perceval and Campbell.

66. Hargrave, *Juridical Arguments*. II, `advertisement'.

67. *Thellusson v. Woodford* (1805) 11 Ves. Jun. 113.

68. The clause is reproduced in *Thellusson v. Woodford* (1806) 13 Ves. Jun. 206 at 209-10.

69. The purchases are described in Master Cox's report of 14 May 1812, PRO C 38/1055. An

earlier report (20 May 1806, PRO C 38/958) incorporates some pre-contract correspondence, including letters of Peter Thellusson.

70.   In *Thellusson v. Woodford* (1799) 2 Ves. Jun.at 427 this rule is said to have been established in *Bunder v. Cooke,* Fitz. 225, Holt 236.

71.   The principle is not confined to wills. It has been invoked in lengthy and costly litigation arising out of the desolation of a South Sea island by phosphate extraction: *Tito v. Waddell (no. 2)* [1977] Ch. 106.

72.   *Thellusson v. Woodford* (1806) 13 Ves. Jun. 209.

73.   (1706) 2 Vern. 581. Both G. Spence, *The Equitable Jurisdiction of the Court of Chancery* (2 vols., London, 1846-9), vol.II, p.585, and Swanston (note to *Dillon v. Parker* (1818) Swanst. 359) discuss the earlier history of the doctrine.

74.   In the works listed in n.75 below thirty-six cases between 1790 and 1822 are cited.

75.   Hanbury, Maudsley and Martin, *Modern Equity* (15th edn., London, 1997), pp.852-9. See also *Halsbury's Laws of England* (4th edn.), vol. XVI (1992), paras. 837-56 and G.W.Keeton and L.A. Sheridan, *Equity* (2nd edn., London, 1976), pp. 277-88.

76.   (1806) 13 Ves. Jun. 209.

77.   E.g. *Hearle v. Greenbank* (1749) 1 Ves. Sen. 298.

78.   *Moore v. Butler* (1805) 2 Sch. Lef. 249 at 267.

79.   *Thellusson v. Woodford* (1806) 13 Ves. Jun. 209 at 218.

80.   Keeton and Sheridan, *Equity*, p. 276.

81.   Even Erskine, though he was Chancellor for only 13 months in the 'Ministry of all the Talents' could not escape having to grapple with the Thellusson case. According to Campbell (*Lives of the Lord Chancellors*, vol.VI, at p.571) this decision was 'the great boast of his Chancellorship'.

82.   *Thellusson v. Woodford* (1806) 13 Ves. Jun. 209 at 221.

83.   *Ibid.*, 220-4.

84.   Order of 27 May 1807, PRO C 33/553, f.658.

85.   Orders of 21 Dec.1808, 11 Feb. 1811: PRO C 33/567, f.230; C 33/584, f.553.

86.   *Lord Rendlesham v. Woodford* (1813) 1 Dow. 249. Arguments are summarised but the Lords' speeches are not reported, only the decision. Eldon's own notes are likewise confined to the arguments.

87.   Erskine had based his judgment on an implied condition in the will and this line of reasoning, by analogy with express conditions, leads to the conclusion that the donee should forfeit the entire gift if he rejects the condition. It was not until Eldon's judgment in *Tibbets v. Tibbets* (1821) Jac. 317 that it became accepted that the appropriate basis was compensation, not

250

forfeiture.

88.   Order of 11 Aug. 1813: PRO C 33/602, f.1449.

89.   One such entertainment is described at length in *Bell's Weekly Messenger*, 3 Jun. 1804. It was a masquerade of the most sumptuous kind, of `a splendour and brilliancy scarcely equalled on any similar occasions'. Among the 800 guests were the Prince of Wales and other members of the royal family, a duke, two duchesses, a marquis, two marchionesses, three earls, eight countesses, nine other peers and twenty-seven titled ladies. Peter Isaac was got up first as a dowager, then as a jockey, and the Prince foreshadowed his famous Scottish tour by dressing as a highlander.

90.   *Farington Diary*, vol. VI, p.2089, 24 Jul. 1803.

91.   *House of Commons, 1790-1820*, vol.II, pp.432-3.

92.   *Ibid.*, vol.II, p.115. The architect Smirke and his two sons were among those sent down to vote against Thellusson: *Farington Diary*, vol.V, p.797, 13 Jul. 1802.

93.   *House of Commons, 1790-1820*, vol. II, p.288.

94.   *Ibid.*, vol.II, pp.85-7; J. Wilson, *Biographical Index to the Present House of Commons* (1806 edn., London), pp.537-8.

95.   There were six ministries in the decade after Pitt's resignation in January 1801.

96.   *House of Commons, 1790-1820*, vol.V, pp.360-4; D.E. Ginter (ed.), *Voting Records of the British House of Commons, 1761-1820* (London, 1995).

97.   Cannon, *Aristocratic Century*, pp.28-31, 87-8.

98.   G.C. Bolton, *The Passing of the Irish Act of Union* (Oxford, 1966), pp.197-207.

99.   T.W. Moody and W.E.V. Vaughan (eds.), *A New History of Ireland* (Oxford, 1986), vol.IV, pp.365-7.

100   *House of Commons, 1790-1820*, vol.V, pp.362-4; C. Long to Pitt, 29 Oct.1805, P.I.Thellusson to Pitt, n.d. and 6 Oct. 1805, PRO PRO 30/8/189, f.259; 30/8/183, ff.170-3.

101   *House of Commons, 1790-1820*, vol.V, p.364. He was called `the oldest peer' because he acted as a peer before the creation.

102   *Farington Diary*, vol.VII, pp.2784, 2789, 2796 (Jul. 1806).

103   Affidavit of A.W.Robarts, PRO TS 33/6; PRO TS 18/1501; *Gents. Mag.*77 (1807), 689.

104   H.E.C. Stapylton (ed.), *Eton School Lists,1791-1850* (London, 1864); *Alumni Cantabrigienses, 1752-1900*, vol.VI, p.197.

105   *House of Commons, 1790-1820*, vol.II, pp.45-6; Oldfield, *History of the Boroughs*, vol.III, p.209.

106   Wilson, *Biographical Dictionary of the House of Commons* (1808 edn., London), p.75. The Duke of York was a regular visitor: *V.C.H. Suffolk*, vol.II (London, 1907), p.368.

107   P. Mansel, *Louis XVIII* (London, 1981), pp.137-69; G.O. Rickword, Exiled Royalties in Essex, *Essex Review* 49 (1940), 190-7.

108   By another account, with Chatham's son: *Examiner*, 17 Sep. 1808.

109   Rickword, *Exiled Royalties* preferred to *Gents. Mag.*78 (1808), 861, which places it at Gosfield. One (later) account says death was caused by the bursting of his gun: *Sharpe's Genealogical Peerage of Great Britain and the British Empire* (3 vols., London, 1833) vol. III. He was buried in Rendlesham church.

110   *Farington Diary*, vol.X, p.3598(11 Feb. 1810). She seems to have died intestate.

111   PRO PROB 11/1489, f.20, made on 18 Apr.1806.

112.   It was assumed that he was much wealthier than he really was. Wells said he left £400,000: *Farington Diary*, vol.IX, p.3422 (19 Mar. 1809).

113   The modern form is described in Underhill and Hayton, *The Law of Trusts and Trustees* (London, 1995), pp.181-5.

114   *Infra*, pp. 310-11.

115   For Heywood and Manning see *infra*. Lady Rendlesham did not prove the will.

116   French Laurence was appointed in August 1806 and R.J. Woodford took the place of his late uncle Matthew in February 1808.

117   Report of the Select Committee on Corrupt Practices in the Appointment of Writers and Cadets in the East India Company, *PP* 1809 (91) II, p.211.

118   *Seventh Report of Commission of Military Enquiry*, p.5.

119   Windham to Mrs. Crewe, 21 Sep. 1802, *Windham Papers*, vol.II, p. 196. The house was the one probably in Pall Mall where he had a sumptuous library: *Gents. Mag.* 82 (1812), 645.

120   J.E.D. Binney, *British Public Finance and Administration, 1774-92* (London, 1958), pp.189-218.

121   *Seventh Report of the Commission of Military Enquiry*; P.J. Harling, *The Waning of 'Old Corruption': the Politics of Economical Reform in Britain, 1779-1846* (Oxford, 1996), pp.73-8.

122   Among Windham's relations employed at the War Office were Robert and J.W. Lukin, W. Disney and H.J. Forrest. E.H. Budd, a celebrated sportsman and a relative of Windham's solicitor, and Samuel Cossart, possibly a relation of Thellusson's deceased partner, were also on the payroll.

123   *Seventh Report of the Commission of Military Enquiry*, at p.5.

124   T.H. Budd to Windham, 29 Dec. 1806, BL Add. Mss 37918, f.139.

125   Woodford claimed that when the rate was in favour of the pound he gave credit for it in his accounts, but given the state of his accounts that hardly helped: *Seventh Report of the*

Commission of Military Enquiry, p.11.

126   *Ibid.*, pp. 12-13 and appendix 14 (B). Foy's explanation in BL Add. Mss 37918, f.218. Foy was the husband of Mary Lukin, daughter of the dean.

127   His memorial to the Treasury (Jun. 1806, BL Add. Mss. 37851, f.218) was rejected, but by August 1808 the auditors had still made no progress with his examination: *Seventh Report of the Commission of Military Enquiry*, pp. 12-13.

128   Woodford to Windham, 8 Jun. 1806, BL Add. Mss. 37851, f.185; *Parl. Debs.* vol.7 (1806), cols. 614-18. Lukin had done remarkably well out of the war, for in addition to his £900 salary as chief clerk, he had made £4,822 in fees in 1796 alone: *PP* 1797, HC 13, Finance Committee, 19th Report, appendixes, O3, Q9.

129   Among the big defalcations which came to light were those of George Villiers, paymaster of marines, and Joseph Hunt, treasurer of the ordnance: Harling, *Waning of 'old corruption'*, pp.133-5.

130   BL Add. Mss. 37851, f.183.

131   *Ibid.*

132   *Seventh Report of the Commission of Military Enquiry*, pp. 40, 63.

133   Burne, *Noble Duke of York*, pp.287-316; D. Gray, *Spencer Perceval* (Manchester, 1963), pp.193-205; Fulford, *Royal Dukes*, pp.53-63.

134   *Annual Register* 51 (1809), 263-5.

135   E.g. in their description of Woodford's proceedings on the Continent: `It appears therefore on the whole, that those checks and precautions, which are usually adopted in the cases of Officers entrusted with such large powers in money transactions, were not observed in his case.'(p.12). One of the commissioners was S.C. Cox, the Chancery master with oversight of the Thellusson trust.

136   E.g. *The Times*, 1, 3 Mar.1809; *The Annual Register*, 263-5; *The Examiner*, 2 Apr. 1809. The decision to allow Ralph Woodford to retire through bad health (aged 26) on half his salary also came in for criticism.

137   *Parl. Debs.* vol. 12 (1809), cols. 488-505. For Donovan, Tahourdin etc. see J.M. Bourne, *Patronage and Society in Nineteenth Century England* (London, 1986), pp.82-3.

138   Thomas Love Peacock's performance in this examination earned the accolade, `nothing superfluous and nothing wanting'.

139   *Report of the Select Committee on Corrupt Practices*, pp. 8-10; C.N. Parkinson, *War and Trade in the Eastern Seas, 1793-1813* (1966 edn., London), pp.367-72; B.R. Misra, *The Central Administration of the East India Company, 1773-1834* (Manchester, 1959), pp.402-13.

140   *Report of the Select Committee on Corrupt Practices*, p.40.

141   *Ibid.*, pp.18-19.

142   *Ibid.*, pp. 19-20, 38-9. Tahourdin was of Huguenot ancestry (Agnew, *French Protestant Exiles*, vol.II, p. 258) and also turns up in some rather murky theatrical business: H.B. Baker, *The London Stage* (2 vols., London, 1889), vol.I, p.193.

143   *Report of the Select Committee on Corrupt Practices*, pp.19-33.

144   Thellusson had also given a Madras nomination to Arthur Denny at the solicitation of Johan George, the husband of his wife's milliner, who sold it. Other directors, among them Robert Thornton, had also been imposed upon in this way: *Ibid.*, pp.1-6.

145   BL Add. Mss. 37851, f.198 (6 May 1809); *Farington Diary*, vol.IX, p.3437, 18 Apr. 1809 (and compare the sceptical view on p.3471). Seven candidates stood for six places and Thellusson trailed the sixth by nearly 400 votes. His being 'thrown out of the direction' in this way was long remembered at India House: Report of the Select Committee on the Affairs of the E.I.C., *PP* 1832 (735-I) IX, q.88 (P.Auber).

146   *The Times*, 31 Mar.1809, made great play with Woodford's appearance in the two reports coming so close together.

147   4 May 1809, BL Add. Mss. 37851, f.222 .

148   *Ibid.*, f.232, 9 Jul.1809.

149   *Ibid.*, f.235, 2 Dec. 1809.

150   Crosthwaite, *Memoir of Sir J.G. Woodford*, 2. There are letters concerning his will in Newdegate Mss (Warwicks. CRO) CR764/237.

151   'I lived with him as my brother; we were brought up as children together; he was born the 2nd of March and I the 22nd, we had never been separated till that time, but were in the habits of closest intimacy as if we were brothers, and never, till my brother's death, had I a word of dispute with Woodford all my life. I looked upon him as my brother.' *Report of the Select Committee on Corrupt Practices*, p.501. The birth dates seem to be transposed.

152   Thellussons had played a leading part in persuading the Treasury to assist in an unsuccessful rescue package and Mitchell was accused of misleading the Bank as to the firm's solvency: *Mair v. Thellusson*, PRO C 13/2471. Some of the fallout from the failure can be followed in *Denison v. Richardson, Denison v. Mair* (1811) 14 East. 291, 622.

153   W. Page, *A History of the Manor of Wall Hall in Hertfordshire* (1902); E.J. Connell, *Hertfordshire Agriculture, 1750-1860* (M.Sc. Econ., London, 1966). Harris Neate, his father, was a West India merchant.

154   Herts. CRO D/EWh includes documents of title; 26183-5 has some correspondence about the purchase.

254

155   Herts. CRO d/EWh/T3 contains the inclosure award (7 Jul. 1803) and land tax redemption (March 1801).

156   *V.C.H. Hertfordshire.*, vol.II (London, 1908), p.426; Cussans, *History of Hertfordshire*, vol.I, pp.243-5, 260-76.

157   Cussans, *History of Hertfordshire*, vol.I, p.243. Sir Nikolaus Pevsner (*The Buildings of England, Hertfordshire* (2nd edn., with B. Cherry, London, 1977), p.67) is terse and unenthusiastic. Though the gardens were laid out by Humphrey Repton the architect of the `Abbey' is not mentioned. It is pictured opposite p.326 in W. Brigg (ed.), *The Parish Registers of Aldenham, 1660-1812* (St.Albans, 1910).

158   Order of 20 Jan.1804, PRO C 33/528, f. 237.

159   Order of 2 Apr. 1805, PRO C 33/537, f.371.

160   Page, *Wall Hall*.

161   *Gents. Mag.* 81 (1811), 661; Norman diary, KAO U310 F69 f.153.

162   PRO TS 18/1501.

163   PRO PROB 11/ 1529, f.48, made on 31 Jan. 1811.

164   PRO IR 26/559; *Farington Diary*, vol.XI, p.4141 (8 Jun. 1812).

165   *Farington Diary*, vol.XII, p.4220 (19 Oct. 1812), where Lady Beaumont suggests that they had `been accustomed to live sumptuously at an expence of perhaps £10,000.'

166   Herts. CRO D/EWh/T2. £15,000 of the money was left outstanding on a mortgage which was assigned to the bankers Harman and Meade in 1814.

167   P.20 (World's Classics edn., Oxford, 1930); *D.N.B.*, vol.XVI, p.19. Perhaps Pole was attracted by the proximity of the former Admiralty secretary, William Marsden.

168   See *infra*, p. 324.

169   *Hervey Journals*, p.503 (7 Aug.1812). They kept only two female servants: *Farington Diary*, vol.XII, p.4220.

170   Page, *Wall Hall*, insertion at p. 80 with print; Herts. CRO D/EWh/ T6.

171   Especially vols. VII to IX. They also make several appearances in the *Hervey Journals*.

172   Though he claimed that `they have much duty and are underpaid' (at £1,070 p.a.): *Farington Diary*, vol. XII, p.4420 (5 Sep. 1813).

173   *Ibid.*, vol. VII, p.2796, vol.IX, p.3298, vol.VII, p.2749-50.

174   *Gents. Mag.* 96 (1826), 476; PRO PROB 11/1712, f.286.

175   *Gents. Mag.* 104 (1834), 330; PRO PROB 11/ 1837, f.587. She was generous to servants and left £50 to the doorkeeper at the Excise Office.

176   1807, Frances Thellusson and Matthew Woodford; 1808 Lord Rendlesham; 1809, his wife Elizabeth; 1811, George Woodford Thellusson; 1813, George Thellusson; 1814, Maria, wife

of the 2nd Lord Rendlesham, and Sabine, Charles Thellusson's wife; 1815, Charles.

177   *Gents. Mag.* 83 (1813), 74.

178   PRO PROB 11/1567, f.210. She married another soldier, who rose to be Lt. Gen. Sir William Maxwell Wallace KH: J. Hutchins, *History and Antiquities of the County of Dorset* (3rd edn., 4 vols., London, 1861-73), vol.IV, p.460.

179   *House of Commons, 1790-1820*, vol.IV, p.460.

180   *The Parish Registers of Brodsworth, 1538-1813* (Yorkshire Parish Register Society, Wakefield, 1937), p.153.

181   *V.C.H. Worcestershire*, vol. III (London, 1906), pp.400-2.

182   *Gents. Mag.* 84 (1814), 412.

183   *Ibid.*, 85 (1815), 637.

184   PRO PROB 11/1576, f.49.

185   PRO IR 26/688.

CHAPTER 11

IN CHANCERY: MANAGING THE FUND

1. The Execution of the Will

Before the trusts of the residue could come into operation Peter's estate had to be administered, all his property gathered in and all his debts, funeral and testamentary expenses and legacies discharged. In this case, as in many others, the same persons were appointed executors and trustees and the point of transition between the two, which might be significant for several reasons, is not always easy to detect, for the law held that it took place automatically on completion of the winding up of the estate. The absence of any formalities for the transition meant a saving in costs, but where administration took place out of court awkward questions might be left unanswered.[1]

The family took the unusual step of allowing Hargrave to make public the main assets of the estate, presumably hoping to attract sympathy for their cause.[2] He showed them as follows:

Realty

Brodsworth   £140,000 or £3,500 p.a.

Plaistow   £25,000

Philpot Lane £10,000

Personalty

3% Consols   £396,458 8s   7d

3% Imperial Annuities   £113,388 9s 10d

Bank stock	£21,000
East India stock	£14,125
4% Consols	£36,005 11s 1d
South Sea stock	£2,500
5% Loyalty loan	£3,000
Irish 5% stock	£15,000
Hudson's Bay stock	£2,500
Long Annuities	£900
Irish annuity	£712
East India bills	£24,000
Lear and Handyside's bond	£49,000
Other debts	£56,000
Cash at bank	£5,500

The nominal value of all these items exceeds £900,000 and with the personal chattels it nears £1,000,000. But of course the nominal value of the stocks and their real market value are two very different things and even Hargrave, anxious to inflate the residue, put the gross estate at only £721,000, the residue at £600,000. This £600,000 formed the basis for Morgan's calculations,[3] which have ever since been the yardstick against which the actual performance of the trust has been measured. Morgan however had to work with three imponderables - the initial capital, the annual yield and the length of the accumulation- and a significant error in any of them would badly distort his calculations.

In fact, taking the stocks at the values quoted at Peter's death, they would have fetched about £370,000.[4] The Funds were low and might be expected to rise to some extent, but the executors needed to sell stock quickly to pay debts, expenses and legacies.[5] When the administration had been completed, the trustees could not delay their forays into the land market, so it would not be reasonable to value his stocks at much more than £400,000. We can add, however, some £95,000 in dividends received between July 1797 and the end of 1802, by which time the bulk of the stocks in the residue had been transferred to the Accountant-General of the court of Chancery.[6]

Turning to the other elements in the personal estate, the East India bills produced almost £25,000 and Exchequer bills (ignored by Hargrave) £4,500, while Lear and Handyside's bond yielded £46,000. Hargrave had estimated the other debts at £56,000 but in fact they fell well short even allowing for about £3,000 finally certified as irrecoverable.[7] Part of the gap is presumably to be attributed to the debts secured on the Grenada plantation, originally £17,000 but climbing rapidly. Money at the bank was also over-estimated, amounting to no more than £855 with the London bankers Smith, Payne & Smith, and £200 with Cook Childers of Doncaster, plus loose cash totalling less than £450; like most City men Thellusson took care to put his money to productive use and never left much lying idle with his bankers or in his pocket.[8]

The real property was as Hargrave describes it. Plaistow could not be sold until Ann died and events proved that valuations of £25,000 for Plaistow and £10,000 for Philpot Lane were optimistic, for they actually fetched no more than £20,300.[9] Brodsworth never was sold and the Yorkshire estates yielded an average of £5,550 per annum gross down to 1804; deducting annual payments averaging £1,800 per annum out of the realty and what was spent on repairs etc. (an average of £650), Hargrave's estimate of £3,500 a year is rather higher than the true net rental.[10]

What the executors received down to 1805 can therefore be roughly summarised thus:

Dividends	£95,000
Lear & Handyside	£46,000
East India bills	£25,000
Exchequer bills	£4,500
Other debts	£4,000
Cash	£1,500
Rent etc. (net)	£22,000
	£198,000

Receipts from the sales of stock are not easy to summarise. Some was transferred direct to legatees, other stocks were purchased out of the receipts shown above and the majority was in any case transferred to the Accountant- General in 1802. Most (£180,000) was then in Consols which stood at 68.[11]

Out of this gross estate various claims had to be met by the executors. First there would be funeral expenses, including the cost of mourning. The bills for this ranged from £660 for the undertaker (John Robins) down to the single guinea paid to John Dunn for tolling the knell at Bromley church, and it is an interesting perspective on the plain funeral that Peter had requested, and which in the circumstances one would have thought his family more than ready to provide, that the overall cost was £1,100. Then there were debts owing to creditors of all sorts. Household bills were numerous but mostly small, with the notable exception of an impressive £381 worth of wine from J. & J. Cossart, sons of his former partner. Plaistow, however, was a continuing drain on the estate as long as Ann lived, the outlay on repairs and maintenance being more than £1,000 in the first two years, and then another £3,000 in a thorough restoration programme in 1802. In all, at least £5,000 was spent on the house and in clearing up household bills.[12]

There were also commercial creditors. Even without the statutory newspaper advertisements, the publicity surrounding the will made it likely that creditors would put in their claims in good time, but few came in whose existence was not already known to the executors and as the list shows, several were in fact members of his own family:[13]

Balances due on promissory notes:

Brown, Collinson and Tritton	£1,000
Assignees of J. T. Vaughan	£500
Balance of the account of J. F. Thellusson	£852 15s
Dividends on Imperial Annuities in Peter's name not belonging to J. F. Thellusson	£99

Balance of the account of Peter's nephews at Paris	£1,419 16s 3d
Dividends on East India stock for Baillie du Crinsol	£451 3s 6d
Executors of Edward Cleaver, debt proved	£73 10s
Executors of Edward Coxe	£71 18s 2d
Trustees of Rabone and Crinsoz	£4,511 7s 6d
Emperor Woodford, balance of his account	£5,171 9s 4d
	£14,010 19s 9d

As late as 1819 one debt, claimed by the executor of Marie Michelle Nöuel de Vieuxchatel for £900 3% consols of dividends since 1794, remained outstanding. There had also been more substantial claims, totalling £21,555, by Peter's own sons as partners in Thellusson Brothers, but these were withdrawn and the final settlement of accounts between the estate and the various Thellusson partnerships, made with Charles's executors, involved only a modest payment.[14]

Naturally there were also debts due to lawyers. Besides Ward, Dunnett and Greaves, who had made his will, and Jenner and Bust, the proctors who had handled the probate, Peter had employed the London firm of Coore and Hubbersty for conveyancing and other work and also Winter, Kayne and Maynard, each of whom were owed nearly £400; in all £940 was paid for legal work *not* undertaken in connexion with the law suit. And of course a much bigger sum (£31,773) had to be paid to complete the three land purchases for which Peter had contracted and which led to litigation with his eldest son.[15] The executors had also to meet a variety of other expenses- £25 to Jules Micheli for putting his accounts in order, subscriptions to the Middlesex Hospital and shirts for the poor, £189 to Peter Isaac for going to Geneva to fetch his grandfather's bust and so forth[16]; they also had to pay income tax, a novelty which sorely tried them, and redeemed the land tax on the Yorkshire properties.[17]

Then there were Peter's legacies to pay. Some were very small; half a year's wages to nine servants scarcely made a dent in the estate, nor did the 300 guineas which were Matthew and Emperor's rather inadequate recompense for their trouble, nor the 105 guineas invested in the Funds for his Woodford nephews. £1,000 had to be remitted to his brother in Switzerland and the various annuities in the French funds and Irish tontine made over to their new owners, but the only really substantial legacies and bequests were to his own widow and children. Advancements made in Peter's lifetime reduced the amount that had to be found, but even so Imperial annuities had to be sold at 49-1/3, an illustration of the depressed state of the market. Using 1797 values, the legacies totalled between £80,- and £90,000, not negligible but still only between 10 and 15% of the gross estate.[18]

George Thellusson, however, received additional payments which are especially interesting in the light of what was to follow. Peter had promised to underwrite his son's expenses in the Southwark election and more than £8,600 had been paid on account. At the end of 1803 Woodford paid George another £2,700 although, as he admitted, only £1,200 was covered by vouchers collected by the election agent Cossart. Woodford readily trusted to Thellusson's airy assurances that it would be simpler to produce the rest *en masse* rather than piecemeal as they came to hand and in the event they never were produced. Quite properly the Master refused to allow the undocumented £1,500 but when Woodford died the trustees persuaded the Master to interpret the clause in the will restricting trustees' liability to `wilful default' generously enough to cover these election expenses; there was, in the circumstances, nothing to be gained by taking a hard line.[19]

The residue available for land purchases was therefore much smaller than the £600,000 on which Morgan calculated, and some of it was actually lent out on mortgage, authorised by the will for purposes of temporary deposits. All the sons benefitted in this way; Peter Isaac had £50,000 in 1799, George £6,000 a few months later and Charles £21,000 in 1802 to buy Bengeworth, all at 5%; both Charles and George repaid their loans in good time. Small advances were made to Emperor Woodford on the security of a house at Vauxhall and to the widow for the purchase of a small piece of land adjoining Plaistow. These accommodations underline the cosy relationship which initially existed between the trustees and the family.[20]

2. The Trustees of the Will

The law prescribed neither a maximum nor a minimum number of trustees and even a sole trustee was perfectly legitimate, though often practically inconvenient.[21] However, the will called for three trustees and, as has been seen, one of them declined to act. In fact for all practical purposes Emperor Woodford was in sole charge and it was obviously unnecessary to replace Stanley until it had finally been determined that the trusts were valid. The obvious choice as third trustee was George Hibbert, who had been nominated to take the place of any named trustee already dead when the will took effect, and it is possible that he was approached and declined.[22] However, Woodford may have preferred someone better placed to serve his own interests as well as those of the trust and his choice fell upon Dr. French Laurence.[23]

There could certainly be no objection to Laurence, for this son of a Bath watchmaker had made himself one of the leading civilian lawyers of the day, with a large practice in Admiralty and Doctors' Commons. He had entered the House of Commons in 1796 under the patronage of the Whig grandee Earl Fitzwilliam but he proved to be a colossal bore, whose oratory became `a sort of dinner bell to most of the House, even to those of his own Party'.[24] Undeterred by the discouraging effect produced by his unprepossessing appearance and turgid delivery, he compelled grudging respect for his learning and for the principled consistency with which he supported Windham's tiny `war party' in good times and - more often - bad. Above all, he was the living repository of Burke's doctrines, which he absorbed completely, his mind becoming `so dominated by the influence of Burke as almost entirely to have parted with its independence'.[25] Windham had been battling, vainly as things turned out, to get Laurence a place in the new ministry, the `Talents', and to make one of his most valuable connexions a trustee would obviously do Woodford no harm at all.

About a year later old Matthew Woodford died and was replaced by another of the family, Sir Ralph's son, Ralph James, a youthful War Office functionary with nothing to recommend him other than his family name.[26] Emperor continued to run the trust more or less single- handed and in the midst of his row with the Thellussons following Peter Isaac's death, Laurence died unexpectedly.[27] This time Emperor's nominee was far from distinguished, another War Office crony called William Disney, an obscure Irishman with a brother rising fast in the army but whose own talents lay rather in collecting profitable regimental agencies, in which he was no doubt assisted by being Mrs. Windham's brother-in-law.[28] Suspecting that he was merely Woodford's stooge, the Thellussons objected to his appointment and put up as their own candidate the celebrated property lawyer Charles Butler; however, despite Butler's obvious superiority, the Master rightly ruled that in the absence of any evidence that Disney was unsuitable, he should ratify the trustees' choice since it was to them that the testator had entrusted the power of selection.[29] Almost uniquely in this great law suit, there was no appeal against the Master's decision.

Within a few months one Woodford (Emperor) had gone abroad to escape his creditors[30] and in 1812 the other (now Sir Ralph) sailed for Trinidad as a remarkably young governor, though he did not retire from the trust.[31] In fact it was only when Sir Ralph sailed that Emperor offered to stand down[32] and why the Thellussons had not sought to get rid of him before is unclear; perhaps it reflects the leaderless state of the family after the deaths of the two eldest sons. When Emperor did go however, Disney soon followed and his explanation was far from conventional and highly revealing. He claimed to have `acted without ever having interfered in any patronage under the trust [although when he] consented only at the behest of Emperor Woodford he was assured that a considerable patronage would attach to a trust of such importance but on a late occasion when a receiver was appointed in the place of

264

George Woodford Thellusson deceased and when [he] proposed his brother-in-law to be such receiver and such proposal was refused [he] discovered that the patronage of the trust, particularly that of naming receivers of the rents of the trust estates, was confined to the branches of the Thellusson family'.[33]

Disney was lucky not to be ordered to pay the costs of his application to retire, but the family were probably grateful just to see the back of him.[34] The two new trustees were very different characters. One was the younger of Peter's soldier-nephews, John George, who had been following his brother Alexander round the battle grounds of Europe as British forces scrabbled for a foothold on the Continent. He was with Sir John Moore on the grim retreat to Corunna, where he suffered a foot wound that kept him chafing at home for eighteen months before he could return to the peninsula, though by way of consolation he found himself the recipient of a handsome £10,000 legacy from the wealthiest and most notorious of rakes, the Marquis of Queensberry ('Old Q').[35]

The other new trustee had risen in the public service by a very different route. Charles Flint was a Scotsman, son of a king's messenger who died in 1793 shortly after Charles had been taken into the Foreign Office, where his fortunes quickly became bound up with those of William Wickham. Flint was sent out to join Wickham on his mission to organise an 'underground war' against the French Republic and they spent several years prowling its eastern frontiers fomenting intrigues and plots, usually ineffective but vastly infuriating to the French. When the success of the French armies drove them out, Wickham found himself in charge of the Alien Office in London, where he and Flint presided over an unprecedented collection of secret files on foreigners and probably Englishmen too.[36] After the Peace of Amiens their collaboration in secret service business entered its third and last phase, with Wickham Chief Secretary to the Lord- Lieutenant of Ireland and Flint running his small London office. Flint stayed in post when Wickham resigned and in 1812 was knighted when standing proxy for Sir Henry Wellesley at the installation of Knights of the Bath.[37] It was probably his friend Sir Ralph Woodford who recommended him as a trustee,[38] for he had no direct link with the Thellusson family, and with one Woodford in Trinidad and the other on active military service Flint was to be effectively in charge of the trust for the next twenty years.

3. Administering the Trust Properties

Brodsworth and Plaistow

Even before they entered the land market, the trustees found themselves owners of several properties, though most of them were directed to be sold as soon as practicable or at a specified time. Brodsworth alone was expected to remain in the trust and the big house posed something of a problem. Thellusson had ordered the furniture sold except what the trustees `shall think necessary to be kept for the purpose of receiving any of them, or my sons who shall choose to go and spend a little time there occasionally', and a few years later, when John Shaw was sent to report on the state of the house, he found it riddled with dry rot and needing extensive repairs.[39] The Master agreed to a modest establishment costing £286 10s a year, with an allowance of just £15 a week (limited to twelve weeks a year) whenever one of the sons should be staying there, though for a few years the house had little appeal, the furniture and fittings growing dilapidated as they did in the less favoured country seats of great magnates.[40]

Then in 1810, Charles, who had hitherto gone there only occasionally, asked that the length of the permitted visits be increased to practically half the year and the servants be considerably augmented to an establishment costing almost £800 a year. He was plainly intent on making Brodsworth his country home and the trustees and the Master, while accepting the enlarged establishment, jibbed at the extended term of residence; even so, Charles persuaded them to authorise nearly £5,000 for refurbishment and did in fact spend much of the rest of his life there, attracted by the excellent shooting.[41] After his death its cost was to become a major bone of

266

contention.

The counting house in Philpot Lane was to be sold after six years or earlier if the sons abandoned the business; by doing so they became entitled to share the proceeds but the eldest stood to lose his share if the court's decision on the doctrine of election went against him and to avoid a delay until the distant day when his appeal could be heard, it was agreed that his share should be held in the court.[42] The auctioneer John Robins, who did profitable business for the trust, bought it for £3,000 and Peter Isaac's share duly fell into the residue.[43]

Peter's villa at Plaistow, with its famous hothouses and nearly 100 acres of grounds, was formally handed over to the widow in October 1797. Profits of cultivation were never likely to cover the running expenses of the house and none of the sons wanted to exercise their option to buy it, so when Ann died it was put up for sale. However, when the drawer marked `Title Deeds to Plaistow' was opened it was empty, and it transpired on investigation that the only bundle which had been seen in it after Thellusson's death had related to Philpot Lane; in other words, the trustees had neglected their fundamental duty of securing the title to trust property. Enquiries of Gregg and Corfield, the solicitors who had acted for Thellusson when he bought the house, proved fruitless and advertisements offering a handsome reward for the missing deeds brought no response.[44]

All that could be done was to make arrangements for a possessory title to be documented and to let the property while that ripened into something marketable. Thomas Maltby agreed to take it for five years at £400 a year and to spend the £500 needed to put it back into good repair, undertaking to cultivate it `according to the best and most approved method of husbandry of the neighbourhood'. When his lease ran out the house was auctioned to the Hon. Hugh Lindsay for £15,800, about £5,000 short of the value with a proper title; the furniture was sold separately for £1,545. No attempt was made to hold the trustees liable for the difference, perhaps because lawyers for the family did not consider they could prove that the breach of duty had actually caused the loss, but more probably because the original trustees were by then either dead or gone abroad.[45]

Exasperatingly, the conveyance had no sooner been signed than the deeds were discovered - Gregg & Corfield had had them all along. What followed was an expensive absurdity: the solicitors refused to hand them over to Lindsay without the trustees' consent, and they were advised by counsel `sanctioned as they understood by the opinion of the Master' not to give their consent while there was a chance of impeaching Lindsay's title, which would have been an outrageous act.   Lindsay therefore filed a bill against solicitors and trustees alike and after two years got judgment, with costs to be paid by the trustees.   Reasonably enough, the Vice-Chancellor accepted their plea that the trust should pay and a further £142 came out of the fund along with the trustees' own costs.[46]   There was, it may be thought, a good case in negligence, bailment or breach of contract against Gregg and Corfield, and trustees are obliged by law to pursue any course of action remorselessly, but nothing seems to have been done.[47]   As a pleasing postscript, Plaistow Lodge was bought a few years afterwards by Walter Boyd, Thellusson's sometime partner in the public loans and now restored to prosperity, but despite the better title he gave only £17,000.[48]

The West Indian Property

Of all Peter's inheritance it was the West Indian interests which proved the most troublesome.   When he made his will he still owned an interest in the Windmill Hill plantation on Montserrat, arising out of default on a loan made by the partnership of Thellusson and Cossart in 1772, but a few months later he cut his losses and sold it to the banker Harman for £5,700.[49]   The sale did not quite liquidate his involvement since the partners had bound themselves to pay several annuities charged on the plantation. Thellusson had purchased £250 Long Annuities for the partnership to help meet these and similar annuities in Grenada; ownership of that stock, and liability for annuities, were now split between the estates of the two deceased partners in the proportion of 15:1, a final distribution of stock waiting therefore on the expiry of the annuitants' lives, a kind of feeble echo of the great accumulation itself.[50]

There remained a 384 acre plantation on Grenada called Bacolet. The owner, Peter Fourmillier, had borrowed money from Thellusson & Cossart in the early 1770s and by 1787 the debt had risen to £17,500, in addition to which substantial annuities were charged on his plantation. Fourmillier's widow and the partners then agreed a salvage plan, the term of the mortgage being extended and further advances made on condition that she would use part of the advance to buy eighteen more slaves (which would also become part of the security) and would make over all the reserves and produce except rum to the mortgagees to service their debt and the annuities.[51]

But the planters of Grenada were having a wretched time. They missed out on the Indian summer most islands enjoyed while Sto. Domingo was virtually out of commission through slave revolts, because a rising of their own slaves, and a particularly bloody and threatening one at that, damaged property, ruined crops and decimated the labour force.[52] In fact, despite the purchase of another ten slaves in 1797 Bacolet was badly short of its proper complement, so the area under cultivation shrank and output declined.[53] The resumption of war in 1803 destroyed the last chance of prosperity for Grenada, for having missed the fat years it experienced in full the lean years which followed. The closure of European markets by Napoleon's Continental System coincided with a steady rise in competition from sugar growers in the east, and in Cuba and Brazil, which drove prices so far down that by 1807 most estates were running at a loss and those which came onto the market did not even fetch enough to pay their owners' debts. The West Indian interest used all its might to force Parliament first into an enquiry then into action, but neither the closure of the malt distilleries in England nor other measures halted the decline.[54]

The planters and their allies lost a more momentous battle when the slave trade was abolished in 1807 and for plantations like Bacolet which were already short of labour, that turned the screw even tighter; war with the United States in 1812 was just one more blow. All this time the produce of Bacolet had been sold to service the

Thellusson mortgage and the annuities but in the whole period from 1797 to 1821 it yielded less than £1,000 a year.[55]

Under the circumstances it is difficult to see why no attempt was made to unload this doubtful asset and one can only presume that the trustees were still hoping that better times lay ahead, that the West Indies would recover and that the inexorably rising mortgage debt would ultimately be discharged in full. At any rate it was not until 1814 that they sought to initiate decisive action.[56]

It soon transpired that to put the plantation back into good running order would be expensive. Only forty-two negroes worked a plantation needing three times that number, and many of them were worn out and incapable of hard work.[57] Only 130 acres were in productive use, the buildings were ruinous and one expert reckoned it would take £10,000 to put it in condition. The trustees proposed to spend £7,000 (mostly on negroes and livestock) to make it saleable at a price which would discharge the mortgage, now standing at £47,000. It was also thought necessary to bring foreclosure proceedings, since the existing title would not get full market value.[58]

It took four years for the Master's report on these proposals to emerge and by that time the brief burst of optimism about West Indian prospects which had surfaced in 1814 had evaporated. The mortgage now stood at £83,000 and the most optimistic of the views presented reckoned seventy-five negroes as the minimum needed for viability, others putting it as high as 200. At current prices the seventy-five would cost £6,000, to which rebuilding and repairs would add a minimum of £6,500 and cattle and mules perhaps another £2,000.[59]

The alternative, to cut losses and put the plantation on the market in its existing state, looked equally unattractive. Remittances were only £800 and declining - one expert wrote, `with their strength it is a matter of surprise how they can manufacture *one* hogshead of sugar'[60]- the market was depressed and even with a good title it was worth no more than £6 or £7,000. What is more John McWilliam (`reckoned among ye foremost in his profession')[61] warned that a foreclosure suit would be expensive -

'a Chancery suit is a very costly proceeding in all countries but in this country is ruinously so as I too well know and have felt'- and uncertain, since it might lead planters claiming an interest in the equity of redemption to make a contest, who at present felt their claims not worth pursuing.[62] McWilliam, however, was anxious to persuade the trust to invest more in the island rather than quitting, so his evidence should be treated with caution.

Since it was obvious that there was no point in throwing good money after bad, everyone approved the Master's recommended sale, but the auction was a disaster, with the highest bid a derisory £1,200 and the property having to be bought in at the reserve.

In truth a buyer could almost name his own terms and when William Le Blanc offered £3,000 on condition that the annuities (now £180 p.a.) were paid by the trust, it was felt best to close with him.[63] Humphreys passed his final accounts and was duly discharged and as a dispiriting postscript to the whole ill- fated business 'through some mistake in the Accountant-General's office the whole of ye dividends [from the Long Annuities set aside to pay the annuities] were laid out so that there is now no cash to pay the half-year's annuities new due'[64]; every mistake in Chancery cost money to put right.

In effect, nearly £90,000 of mortgage debt had to be written off, for Ann Fourmillier was long since dead and her heirs were evidently not worth pursuing. It is obvious with hindsight that the plantation should have been sold much earlier, or at least that the options should have been thoroughly examined well before 1814, certainly when the Abolition Bill passed in 1807. If Hibbert had become a trustee he might have done something and if there had been beneficiaries receiving trust income they would probably have demanded action; as it was the passivity of the court and the inactivity of the trustees combined to cause a bigger loss than was necessary.

4. Land Purchases

Thellusson had given his trustees no guidance towards the purchase of the lands in which his fortune was to be sunk beyond stipulating that they must not be leasehold and that no more than a quarter might be copyhold. Copyhold land remained liable to various burdens in favour of the lord of the manor in which it was situated, the most regular and important being the fine or premium which each new tenant of the manor had to pay on entry, whether he acquired the land by inheritance or by purchasing it from the owner. Since fines were sometimes considerable - £575-5s-9½d had to be paid for the 182 acres of Rendham Rookery Farm, purchased in 1815, and £332 for the Hill Farm Estate in 1826 -[65] the cost of copyhold incidents was naturally reflected in the land market, where it generally sold for five years' rental less than freehold.

There were also complications and uncertainties. Often enough the same farm formed part of several manors, as was the case with Otley Farm, where entry fines had to be paid to the manors of Monewdon, King's Hall and Overhall in Otley, and it was often hard not only to distinguish which fields were subject to which manor but even which were freehold and which copyhold; in at least two cases the Thellusson trustees got the purchase price abated when the mixture could not be unscrambled.[66] The legal and managerial inconveniences attending copyholds however did not always outweigh the desirability of particular fields in purely farming terms and in Herftfordshire and Suffolk, where copyhold was still a common tenure, appreciable quantities of copyhold land were bought for the trust.

Nothing indicated where the trust lands were to be situated. The uncompleted contracts Peter had negotiated were for purchases in the North Riding of Yorkshire and Durham, plus a small plot near Brodsworth, but they were now to belong to his heir, whose own estates were in Suffolk. Since the other sons had just bought estates in Buckinghamshire and Worcestershire respectively, there was much to be said for a strategy which would assemble blocks of land around their homes and

Brodsworth; there would then be no need to acquire large houses to serve as management centres, the costs of running the estates would be less than if they were widely scattered, and the integration of the trust estates with those which the lucky beneficiaries had inherited, or stood to inherit, from their own fathers, would be greatly facilitated. The only serious obstacle was that if it became clear that the trust was spending its great resources in those areas, prices would be driven up.

It seems clear that the sons' own wishes were influential. George, though he persuaded the trust to buy Wall Hall, (apart from the mansion house), and Peter Isaac went looking for suitable purchases in their respective counties while Charles quickly sold Bengeworth again and evidently saw his own sons' future in the Yorkshire estates. Essentially, until the quarrel following Peter Isaac's death, the trust's purchases were guided by Peter's sons.[67] Perhaps because there was not enough land available in those districts to absorb the funds they had at their disposal, the trustees made bids for several large estates in other parts of the country. Sir Roger Salisbury's, on which they were in effect gazumped, was in Buckinghamshire, but near Aylesbury, well to the north of Wall Hall ; in fact Canons Park, whose owner wanted too high a price, was closer although in the next county. It looked as though Lord Charles Spencer's 800 acres around Thame would become the nucleus of another block, but he could not make a good title and that too fell through.[68] In the end they bought a more modest midland estate, at Southam in Warwickshire, and fitfully expanded from there.[69] Shortly afterwards Lord Rendlesham's death afforded an opportunity of restoring the uncompleted purchases to the trust. They were not ideal, inconveniently far from Brodsworth and, in the case of Newton Hanzard, badly mismanaged, but buying them would simplify recovering the large mortgage debt due from Rendlesham's estate, which could not be met out of his liquid assets.[70]

In about thirty years, down to 1834 when the management of the trust was effectively removed from them, the trustees spent almost three-quarters of a million pounds (£734,000) in buying 22,500 acres of land, an average price of £33 per acre. It was scattered over seven counties, with over 9,100 acres in Suffolk, 4,100 in the home counties, 6,000 in Yorkshire, 2,500 in the midlands and 800 in Durham.[71] The copyhold formed well under one quarter of the whole, but was a sizeable proportion in Suffolk; for instance on three farms purchased in 1815, it formed only 12 acres out of 183 on Pytches, but 89 out of 107 on Cuttings' and 142 out of 162 on Lackford's;[72] it was also significant in the home counties, but the precise acreages are hard to determine, not least because they were so inextricably mixed on the ground.

These purchases represented more or less continuous activity in the market, often on a very small scale, rather than occasional purchases of big estates. There were over seventy transactions in all, with a mean acreage of less than 100 acres. The biggest outlays in fact were on the first estates acquired, George's Wall Hall and Butley Abbey, which Peter Isaac had snapped up with a view to reselling to the trust.[73] After that there were only a handful costing more than £20,000; a bundle of Suffolk farms, also acquired through Peter Isaac, for £33,800 (1807); Southam for £25,000 (1808); Bilham and Roe Farms for £32,500 (1810); £34,500 and £20,000 respectively for the re-purchase of Newton Hanzard and Amotherby in 1812 and £23,020 for Park Manor and other parts of the Duke of Marlborough's Hertfordshire estates at auction in 1819.[74] Quite often, in any event, bids for substantial properties were not accepted, like those of £48,000 for Canons Park, £43,000 for Payne's lands at Frickley, near Brodsworth, and £28,500 for the Letheringham Estate at Wickham Market.[75] Sometimes, as in the case of North Weston (£52,500), a bid was accepted but foundered on the title.[76] Large, ready-made estates in the right areas were difficult to find, for there were always enough aspiring country gentlemen in the market to keep prices up and strict settlement played its part in enabling established families to hang on to the core of their patrimony.[77] Where an estate was sold as a unit the price could be inflated by the inclusion of a mansion which the trust did not want and in the many cases where they were auctioned piecemeal - like Marlborough's and the Duke of Devonshire's Wetherby - local farmers might bid above market value for plots of special value to their own holding.[78]

So the characteristic purchase made by the trust was not an estate but a farm or

274

group of farms, ranging in size from twenty acres to 300 but usually between 100 and 250. In addition, however, they followed the orthodox precepts of the experts of the day (which only repeated the conventional wisdom of shrewd farmers down the centuries) in trying to pick up scraps of land intermixed with their own fields, which improved their balance of arable and pasture, summer and winter grazing etc. or which generally made holdings more compact and easy to manage efficiently.[79] Only in the midlands, where this sort of activity is notably absent, were the farms more or less discrete units; elsewhere the map of ownership was often as much a patchwork as the map of tenures or cultivation, complicated by rights of common, especially grazing, replete with wasteful duplication of buildings and economically incoherent. While tenant farmers often lacked the capital or the security of tenure to undertake programmes of consolidation and rationalisation, the trust did so enthusiastically. They paid £1,700 for some cottages and a few acres at Patchetts Green, Aldenham in 1809,[80] £300 above the open market value, because it was meadow land that would enhance the letting value of a large farm; a few years on they bought and demolished several cottages on Edge Row Farm to put a stop to the depredations of their owners[81] and in 1829 paid £9,500 for lands mingled with their own, which they considered especially valuable as they included open field strips which might then be enclosed.[82] Transactions of this sort, and there were also several which did not come to fruition,[83] show that the trust had regard not only to putting together manageable blocks of land but, within those blocks, was seeking to create compact and attractive farms.

This is important because, as we shall see, accusations that the trust was chronically mismanaged gained wide currency.[84] Of course, they are not rebutted simply by showing that the trustees' purchasing strategy was rational, unless it can also be shown that they did not pay extravagant prices for land and that what they bought was not subject to encumbrances that ought to have been discovered. Unfortunately it is very difficult to establish what the `true price' for a particular piece of land was. It is obvious that there can never be a single market price for a given acreage of land as there can for interchangeable commodities such as company shares, government stocks and bonds and manufactured produce. Each plot has unique characteristics, the volume of transactions is comparatively low and non-commercial motives among prospective buyers exert a much more significant influence than on most goods (works of art excepted), so the land market is bound to be a curious and imperfect one. Indeed, as some nineteenth century commentators indignantly and perplexedly remarked, there was no market at all in an institutional sense, which seems to have created few problems for those engaged in land dealings but has given headaches to historians seeking to reconstruct the movement of prices.[85]

For land values did not, of course, remain constant, neither did they fluctuate in an arbitrary way but rather rose and fell in a broadly inverse ratio to the price of the Funds. Depression in the Funds, loss of confidence in trade and industry, meant more money seeking the haven of land - safe as fields if not yet safe as houses.[86] The inflexibility of Peter Thellusson's directions obliged the trustees to buy land whether on a rising or falling market, using rents which had been lodged in the 3%s pending a suitable purchase, so that in bad times stock had to be sold at a low price to buy land at a high one.[87] The price of land was usually calculated by a multiple of the gross rental and expressed as x years' purchase, for only thus could any degree of uniformity be imposed on the infinitely varying value of plots in different locations and on different soils. This figure, discounted for copyholds at a standard rate, was never uniform but provides a useful rough and ready guide.

The best available reconstructions suggest the following:[88]

1785 - 94   27½ years
1790 - 99   27 years
1795 - 1804 27 years
1800 - 09   27½ years
1805 - 14   28 years

After the war there was a slump, prices slipping as low as twenty-three years in the early 1830s before picking up again.[89]   These figures must be used with considerable

276

caution, concealing as they do significant regional and annual fluctuations, but when set against the prices paid by the trust they do seem to give some ammunition to its critics. Masters' reports, the best source for its purchases, do not always show the basis on which the price was calculated, and many of the purchases, especially in Suffolk, are complicated by the inclusion of freehold and copyhold within the same transaction, but in Yorkshire and the home counties the trust seems to have been paying thirty years' purchase quite regularly even after 1815, and seldom below twenty-eight; thus at auctions in 1825 and 1826 respectively two properties in Buckinghamshire, the 242 acres of Hill Farm and the 432 of Woodwicks, cost thirty years' purchase, so did the Red House estate in Yorkshire in 1833.[90] Prices in Suffolk were consistently, though not invariably, lower in the war years (the copyhold element perhaps distorting the figures) but surprisingly, so far from declining, seem afterwards to have risen; two purchases in 1826 for example were taken at thirty years, a third at twenty-eight.[91] The sample is too small and the figures too unreliable to indict the trustees for extravagance, but this does lend weight to the suspicion that the trust did not always drive such a hard bargain as other buyers.

There is nothing very surprising in that of course. After all, it was not their own money[92] and none of the trustees had any worthwhile experience of farming or estate management: they were soldiers, clergymen, civil servants, politicians, lawyers - but not a landowner among them. Large sums were spent on purchases arranged by Peter's sons - £223,375, around 30% of the total- and Peter Isaac at least was not a man to be backward in spending his own money, still less other people's money that *should* have been his.[93] Still, the trustees always had independent professional advice. For well over twenty years John Shaw of Bedford Square was their surveyor, also looking out for possible purchases and negotiating on their behalf. Shaw was a respected professional who no doubt acted honourably, but he was paid 1% on the purchase price of each completed transaction (only ½% if it proved abortive) and so had a vested interest in high prices.[94] That shrewd and eminent publicist William Marshall counselled the employment of a local man as well as `a man of more general knowledge' to ensure that the asking price was a proper one but Shaw seems to have been trusted to do the job alone, which saved the expense of a second valuer.[95]

There remained, of course, the control exercised by the master by whom all expenditure had to be approved, and there is one instance of Master Cox rejecting the negotiated price, the vendor being persuaded to settle for less;[96] Chancery supervision may have been costly but it was not negligible. Furthermore, the fact that negotiations often fell through because the trustees would not meet the asking price suggests that they were not a really soft touch. That happened at least a dozen times before 1809 and in some instances big purchases were involved, as when the trustees refused to bridge the gap between the £43,000 they offered for the Frickley estates and the £44,875 the owner demanded.[97]

The purchase of land in pre-Victorian England was a decidedly risky enterprise.[98] The vendor had to prove that he or persons through whom he derived his title to the land had enjoyed seisin for at least sixty years past and the evidence for this was contained in the title deeds in which transactions affecting the title were recorded.[99] It was the task of the purchaser's solicitor to examine these documents, pithily described by Lord Wensleydale as `disgusting to touch, difficult to read and impossible to understand', and to confirm that they revealed no weakness and no undisclosed third party rights.[100]

The perusal of the deeds was but the first step in `the conveyancers' stately saraband',[101] which progressed circumspectly through requisitions and replies, further requisitions and more replies until, if the replies were satisfactory, the conveyance could at last be drawn up and solemnly executed.[102] And all too often there *were* defects, or at least doubts, calling perhaps for the opinion of a more eminent conveyancer on some abstruse or controversial point, or to haggling over an abatement of the price, the exclusion or inclusion of parcels of land or negotiations with third parties to settle their claims. So little faith had the courts in the soundness of titles that they developed the aberrant and anomalous rule in *Bain v. Fothergill*, which deprived a purchaser whose vendor could not provide the title he had contracted to deliver of all damages except the cost of investigating the title.[103]

Defects in titles were of various kinds. Among the commonest was the most basic of all - the inability to identify boundaries and parcels precisely and certainly from the elaborate but imprecise descriptions in the deeds and the colourful but inaccurate sketch maps which often went with them.[104] Others involved the presence of unexpected encumbrances - trusts and settlement, mortgages and rentcharges, tithes and easements. The risks associated with land purchase were formidable and the costs substantial.[105]

One of the few advantages of being in Chancery was that titles had to pass the master's scrutiny, as well as the trust solicitor's. Apart from the North Weston purchase, which went off altogether, there are several cases in which the price was lowered because of the inclusion of copyhold or an unadvertised encumbrance,[106] while one contract gave rise to a law suit. 289 acres at Pigburn, all mixed up with the trust lands at Brodsworth and therefore highly desirable, were offered for sale in 1802 at £7,875 by J. L. Hubbersty, a London lawyer.[107] The Thellussons must have been eager to have it, for at that time the appeal against the will was still pending and the trustees were not actively in the land market, but Hubbersty went bankrupt before completion and in the muddle of his affairs conveyancing counsel reported that no good title could be made out by his assignees.[108] There the matter rested until 1811 when a fresh agreement was made with Hubbersty, his wife and his assignee, one Vernon Berks, this time at £11,000. Now the mortgagee who held the deeds refused to co-operate because Hubbersty had started an action against him to set aside an annuity he claimed and things stalled until Master Cox recommended a bill in Chancery against Berks to compel disclosure of the deeds.[109] It was July 1814 before a good title was established and June 1817 before the purchase was completed, further delays arising from the mortgagee's death and the last-minute claim of an undisclosed trust in favour of Mrs. Hubbersty.[110] Pigburn finally did become part of the trust estates but the price must have been inflated significantly by legal fees.[111]

What is more, all the officious care of Chancery did not prevent the trust falling foul of claims in tithe. As well as being universally unpopular with farmers and (because it tended to drive down rents) with landlords, and particularly with dissenters,[112] it was also highly uncertain, for not all land and not all crops were tithable. Former monastic lands were not, so when the rector of Hooton Pagnell claimed tithe on the Bilham estate, the trustees were disappointed when their researches showed that it did not form part of the lands of Welbeck Abbey.[113] However, in many parishes tithes for some or all crops had been commuted into a *modus*, a fixed payment which usually bore little relation to the real value of the tithe. *Moduses* were permanent but even where they were not established it was common to find that a clergyman had compounded for a fixed sum for a period of years and the tithe payers usually claimed that this *was* a *modus*.[114]

The position was complicated by the division of tithes into the great or rectorial tithe and the small or vicarial one, the former usually comprising tithes of corn, hay and wood, the latter everything else; but as with other aspects of tithe, the division turned on local custom and was often unreliable. Farmers artfully exploited these distinctions and tithe owners who attempted to collect their tithes in kind met with every kind of obstruction.[115]

In view of the obstacles and hostility encountered in collecting their due, it is not surprising that many tithe owners welcomed enclosures which substituted for their tithes a plot of land which could be farmed or leased but those who still owned tithes were making increasingly determined attempts to extract their full value and take their share of the increasing profits of agriculture. In particular, tithes which had been allowed to lapse were reclaimed and *moduses* were challenged in the courts. Whether these challenges succeeded depended on the strength of the legal case and the relative financial strength and determination of the parties.[116]

The two actions in which the trustees became involved illustrate this clearly. When they bought the Bilham estate the price had been reduced by £500 because the *moduses* respecting tithes were not convincingly sustainable and the doubt proved well founded within a few months when the rector of Hooton Pagnell filed a bill in the Exchequer against the tenants (whose leases were guaranteed tithe free). The trustees were advised that their defence was doubtful but the law's expense and delays induced Warde, who was being pressed by his creditors, to offer to sell the tithes for £1,000, well below their value.[117]

Moduses on two Warwickshire farms bought in 1819 proved equally vulnerable to a challenge, this time from the new vicar. The vicarial tithe was claimed on all but corn and hay and the moduses, paid for many years, were only £3-12-6 and £1-12-10½. Just how derisory they were is evident when the terms of the compromise made in 1825 are considered: the vicarial tithes were leased for twenty-one years at £30 and £15 p.a. respectively.[118]

On the whole, given the sale and spread of their purchases, the trust probably got off lightly in terms of titles, though defects could of course become 'sleepers', awakened only when a sale was under consideration.

NOTES

1. Some are still unanswered, see C.V. Margrave-Jones, *Mellows: The Law of Succession* (5th edn., London, 1993), pp. 319-26 and E.C. Ryder, Re King's Will Trusts, a Re-assessment, *Current Legal Problems*, 29 (1976), 60-73.

2. *Gents. Mag.* 68 (1798), 1082.

3. Hargrave, *Juridical Arguments*, vol. II, appendix 2. For the details of the calculations see R.R. Powell, *Materials for a Course in Future Interests and Non-Commercial Trusts* (New York, 1929), p.759 n.1.

4. Stock prices are from the *Gentleman's Magazine* for the nearest day to Peter's death.

5. The normal rule, in the absence of any direction in the will, is that general legacies must be paid within a year of the testator's death ('the executor's year'), after which they carry interest: *Wood v. Penoyre* (1807) 13 Ves. Jun. 325a, 333-4.

6. *General Report.*

7. *Ibid.*

8. In fact as late as 1850 Smith's Bank paid into court £449, a hitherto undiscovered balance in Thellusson's favour: PRO C 33/994, f.1137.

9. *Infra*, pp. 262-4.

10. *Juridical Arguments*, vol.II, app.2.

11. Order of 14 Aug. 1802, PRO C 33/519, f.810.

12. *General Report.*

13. *Ibid.*

14. Order of 24 Dec. 1818, PRO C 33/661, f.625.

15. *General Report.* For the purchases see *supra*, pp. 220-2.

16. *General Report.* 17. Orders of 18 Jun. 1801 (PRO C 33/515, f.734), 23 Dec. 1802 © 33/522, f.91) and *General Report.* Income tax was introduced in 1798, withdrawn in 1802 and reimposed in a more effective form in 1803.

18. *General Report.*

19. *General Report*; report of 27 Jan. 1821, PRO C 38/1232. For the election, see *supra*, pp. 112-14.

20. *General Report.*

21. This remains the case. Provisions in the Law of Property Act 1925 make two or more trustees of land necessary if it is to be sold, leased or mortgaged.

22. For Hibbert's connection with the Thellussons by marriage see *supra*, p. 67. He joined a firm

of West India merchants as a young man from Lancashire and remained with them for fifty years, becoming in time the head of the concern and one of the leading men in that branch of trade, chairman of the West India Committee, agent for Jamaica and a skilful and respected lobbyist in their interest as MP for Seaford (1806-12). Acknowledged to be `remarkable for candour and placidity of temper', he raised a large family, dividing his time between Munden and a house at Clapham which contained a notable collection of botanical specimens. His library was one of the finest in the land but his best monument was the West India dock which he had a great share in bringing about. *D.N.B.*, vol. XXVI, p.343; J.H. Markland, *A Sketch of the Life and Character of George Hibbert* (London, 1837).

23. Laurence was appointed trustee on 2nd August 1806.

24. *House of Commons, 1790-1820*, vol. IV, p.387.

25. *D.N.B.* vol.XXXII, p.203. There is an unflattering description of his personal habits in *The Farington Diary*, vol.IV, p.29.

26. Matthew died on 30th September. Ralph was appointed on 24th February 1808, aged about twenty-four.

27. On 27th February 1809. His will (PRO PROB 11/1494, f.213) makes no mention of the Woodford or Thellusson families.

28. His brother Sir Moore Disney (1766? - 1846) is in the *D.N.B.*, vol.XV, p.100 and was about to distinguish himself in the retreat from Corunna. Disney was appointed on 8th May but had been proposed in March.

29. Report of 8 May 1809, PRO C 38/992.

30. See *supra*, pp. 234-5.

31. When the first baronet died on 20th September 1810, his son was already in Madeira: PRO PROB 6/186.

32 Woodford offered the conventional explanation that he was obliged to live abroad for his health: order of 26 Feb. 1812, PRO C 33/591, f.671.

33. Order of 27 May 1812, PRO C 33/593, f.861.

34. A trustee has no right to retire from a trust but since an unwilling trustee is likely to be a bad trustee, the court almost invariably allows him to do so, penalising him in costs where he cannot show good cause. Disney was a trustee of some of Windham's estates (PRO PROB 11/1514, f.446) but disappeared into obscurity, meriting no obituary in the *Gentleman's Magazine*, nor leaving any will I have been able to trace.

35. Crosthwaite, *Memoir of Sir J. G. Woodford*, pp.10-16.

36. *Burke's Landed Gentry* (1952) p.876; H. Mitchell, *The Underground War Against Revolutionary France* (Oxford, 1965); E. Sparrow, The Alien Office, 1792-1806, *Historical Journal* 33 (1990),

361-84 and *Secret Service*, p.57.

37. Wellesley was the brother of Arthur, Duke of Wellington, for whom Flint acted as private secretary when the Duke was in England.

38. Woodford's will, PRO PROB 11/1748, f.682.

39 Report of 16 May 1804, PRO C 33/536, f.98.

40. Order of 10 May 1810, PRO C 33/577, f.881. A similar situation arose at Gosfield: J.V. Beckett, Gosfield Hall: a country estate and its owners, 1715-1825, *Essex Archaeology and History* (3rd s.) 25 (1994), 185-92.

41. Report of 27 Jan. 1812, PRO C 38/1055. Charles described himself in his will as `of Brodsworth': PRO PROB 11/1576, f.49.

42. *Supra*, p. 222.

43. Orders of 27 May 1807 (PRO C 33/553, f.658), 22 Dec. 1809 © 33/575, f. 167).

44. Orders of 29 Mar. 1806 (PRO C 33/544, f.482), 22 Jan. 1807 © 33/551, f.158).

45. Orders of 22 Jan. 1807 (PRO C 33/551, f.158), reports of 13 Dec. 1811, 27 Feb. 1812, C 38/1039, 1055.

46. Order of 4 Jul. 1815, PRO C 33/618, f.1535.

47. In *Re Brogden* (1888) 38 Ch. D 546, the Court of Appeal held that only a well-founded belief that an action would be unprofitable justifies failure to pursue legal remedies.

48. Cope, *Walter Boyd*, p.171. Its last private owner was the famous sportsman Lord Kinnaird. It became a school in 1896.

49. Order of 25 Apr. 1814, PRO C 33/608, f.746; *General Report*, schedule 1.

50. The Montserrat annuities originally amounted to £550 p.a. but by 1814 they were reduced to £300.

51. Order of 25 Apr. 1814, PRO C 33/608, f.746.

52. Ragatz, *Fall of the Planter Class*, p.220; Devas, *Grenada*, pp. 103-52.

53. Order of 25 Apr. 1814, PRO C 33/608, f.746.

54. Ragatz, *Fall of the Planter Class*, pp. 286-330; *PP* 1807 (III) (65).

55. Ragatz, *Fall of the Planter Class*, pp.346-8; *House of Lords Sessional Papers* 1833 vol. 11, (92) p. 833; Ambrose Humphreys' accounts in PRO C 38. Remittances were made by the manager to George Thellusson for the family firm until his death and there was some difficulty in unravelling his accounts: order of 25 Jul. 1818, PRO C 33/652, f.1665.

56. It is probably coincidental that Sir Ralph Woodford had taken up his post in Trinidad by then, for there is no evidence that he played any part in this decision.

57. Order of 25 Apr. 1814, PRO C 33/608, f.746. There had been 121 slaves in 1772.

58. Order of 5 Jul. 1814, PRO C 33/610, f.1282.

59. Order of 25 Jul. 1818, PRO C 33/652, f.1665.

60. *Ibid.*, affidavit of William Burke.

61. *Ibid.*, affidavit of the manager, G. Munro.

62. *Ibid.*, McWilliam's affidavit. Courts in the islands were notorious for their bias towards indebted planters.

63. Order of 25 Jul. 1820, PRO C 33/676, f.1728.

64. Order of 14 Aug. 1822, PRO C 33/700, f.1671. Sale had been delayed because Le Blanc tried to insist on seeing the mortgagor's title, which had been specifically excluded in the contract and had to be threatened with a decree of specific performance before he would complete: Order of 4 Aug. 1821, C 33/689, f.1866.

65. Reports of 19 Nov. 1816, 8 Jul. 1827, PRO C 38/1110, C 38/1382.

66. Orders of 20 Jul. 1829 (PRO C 33/790, f.1761), 24 Feb. 1808 © 33/559, f. 313).

67. See *supra*, p. 269.

68. Reports of 3 Feb. 1809 (PRO C 38/1006), 20 Dec. 1810 © 38/1023).

69. Order of 13 Aug. 1808, PRO C 33/562, f.1337.

70. Order of 27 May 1812, PRO C 33/594, f.1286. Rendlesham had offered the three parcels of land to the trust shortly before his death.

71. These figures are drawn from the masters' reports in PRO C 38 and orders based upon them in PRO C 33. The acreages are given in round numbers because of omissions and imprecisions in these sources, and the total of money spent cannot be reconciled with the figure of £677,015-15s-10d given to Parliament in 1833 (*House of Lords Sessional Papers* 1833 Vol. XI (92)).

72. Order of 24 Feb. 1815, PRO C 33/616, f.521.

73. About 913 acres for £72,395 and 4,042 acres for £51,000 respectively. The high price for Wall Hall reflects the value of the manor of Aldenham which was included in the sale: orders of 2 Apr. 1805 (PRO C 33/537, f.371), 27 Jul. 1803 © 33/523, f.771).

74. Orders of 24 Jul. 1807 (PRO C 33/553, f.771), 13 Aug. 1808 © 33/562, f. 1337), 11 Jul. 1810 © 33/577, f.1045), 27 May 1812 © 33/594, f.1286), 27 Apr. 1819 © 33/662, f.943).

75. Report of 3 Feb. 1809, PRO C38/1006; report of 24 Jul. 1815, C38/1109.

76. Order of 21 Jun. 1810, PRO C 33/577, f.825.

77. The availability of estates naturally varied widely both geographically and over time. There are useful discussions in *Economic History Review* (2nd s.) 27 (1974) by C.M. Clay, The Price of Freehold Land in the later 17th and 18th Centuries (pp.173-89); B.A. Holderness, The English Land Market in the 18th Century: the Case of Lincolnshire (pp.557-76) and D. Rapp, Social Mobility in the 18th Century: the Whitbreads of Bedfordshire, 1720-1815 (pp. 380-9). Also

J.V. Beckett, The Pattern of Landowners in England and Wales, 1660-1800, *Economic History Review* (2nd s.) 37 (1989), 1-22 and W.O. Aydelotte *et al.*, Country Houses and their Owners in Hertfordshire, 1540-1789, in L. Stone and J.C. Fawtier Stone, *The Dimensions of Quantitative Research in History* (Princeton, 1972), 56-123.

78. Order of 27 Apr. 1819, PRO C 33/662, f.943; R.W. Unwin, A Nineteenth Century Estate Sale: Wetherby, 1824, *Agricultural History Review* 23 (1975), 116-38.

79. *Cf.* the painstaking accumulation of Sir John Griffin Griffin described in T.D. Williams, A Pattern of Land Accumulation: the Audley End Experience, 1762-97, *Transactions of the Essex Archaeological Society* (3rd s.)11 (1979), 90-110, and see also T.W. Beastall, A South Yorkshire Estate in the Late 19th Century, *Agricultural History Review* 15 (1967), 40-4.

80. Order of 3 Aug. 1807, PRO C 33/554, f.1073.

81. Order of 17 Mar. 1818, PRO C 33/650, f.815.

82. Order of 5 Nov. 1828, PRO C 33/777, f.2594.

83. E.g. report of 24 Apr. 1826, PRO C 38/1349.

84. See *infra*, pp. 347-50.

85. F.M.L. Thompson, The Land Market in the Nineteenth Century, *Oxford Economic Papers* 9 (1957), 285-300; J.V. Beckett, Landownership and the Land Market, *Agrarian History*, vol. VI, (1750-1850), pp.546-64.

86. Clay, *Price of Freehold Land*. R.C. Allen, The Price of Freehold Land and the Interest Rate in the 17th and 18th centuries, *Economic History Review*. (2nd s.)41 (1988), 1-32, argues against any 'positional premium' in the price of land arising from social demand but this is rebutted by A. Offer, Farm Tenure and Land Values, 1750--1950, *Economic History Review* (2nd s.)44 (1991), 1-20 and G. Clark, Land Hunger: Land as a Commodity and a Status Good, England 1500-1910, *Explorations in Economic History* 35 (1998), 59-82.

87. Clay, *Price of Freehold Land*, 185-6, makes this point about other would-be merchant buyers. For the price differential between land and Consols see Offer, *Farm Tenure and Land Values*, fig.2.

88. Clay, *Price of Freehold Land*, table 1, p. 174.

89. Thompson, *Land Market*, 35-6.

90. Orders of 4 Nov. 1826 (PRO C 33/749, f.970), 6 Aug. 1827 © 33/760, f.1646), 7 Jun. 1833 © 33/852, f.1927).

91. Orders of 8, 29 Jul. 1826 (PRO C 33/748, ff.1570, 1641), 26 Jun. 1827 © 33/759, f.1301).

92. This seems not to have made the trustees of Guy's Hospital noticeably more generous: B.E.J. Trueman, Corporate Estate Management: Guy's Hospital Agricultural Estates, 1726-1815, *Agricultural History Review* 28 (1980), 31-44.

286

93. The fact that the House of Lords specifically requested to know how much was spent on this was suggests that it was regarded with suspicion: *House of Lords Sessional Papers* (1833) XI (92).

94. Shaw had been in practice for seven years when the trustees sent him to report on the repairs needed at Brodsworth in 1804. It was the start of a lucrative connection which ended only with his death in 1834. In that time he received almost £10,000, an average of more than £300 p.a. *House of Lords Sessional Papers* (1833) XI (92); PRO C 38/975, 1658; PRO C 33/536, f.98. Shaw and his son John were also surveyors to Christ's Hospital: P. Eden, *A Directory of Land Surveyors etc* (Folkestone, 1975).

95. W. Marshall, *On the Landed Property of Great Britain* (London, 1804), pp.6-8.

96. Order of 15 Mar. 1815, PRO C 33/616, f.665.

97. Report of 29 Jul. 1815, PRO C 38/1109.

98. For an account of 'the old conveyancing' see Holdsworth, *History of English Law*, vol. VII (2nd edn., 1966 reprint, London), pp.353-400.

99. Sixty years was the minimum period which conveyancers found acceptable, probably because it virtually ensured that all better (i.e. older) claims would be barred by the Statutes of Limitations. The courts gave judicial approval to it by ruling that a purchaser who had made no express stipulation for a longer title could not refuse to carry out a contract where the vendor showed sixty years.

100 By this time it was claimed that settlements, Inclosure Acts etc. had swollen the size of abstracts of title, which usually went back a century: J. Tyrell, *Suggestions sent to the Commissioners appointed to inquire into the Laws of Real Property* (London, 1829), p.173.

101 The phrase of Buckley J., *Re Stone and Saville's Contract* [1962] 1 W.L.R. 460 at 465.

102 Systematic treatises on conveyancing began to appear in the early 19th century, notably E.G. Sugden, *The Law of Vendors & Purchasers* (London, 1805) and R. Preston, *Essay on Abstracts of Title* (London, 1818-24); a glance at either is enough to reveal the intricacies of the dance. Nevertheless, landowners were generally unenthusiastic about proposals for title registration: J.S. Anderson, *Lawyers and the Making of English Land Law, 1832-1940* (Oxford, 1992).

103 (1874) 1 L.R.H.L. 158. The rule, which had already fallen into marked disfavour with the judiciary, was finally abolished by the Law of Property (Miscellaneous Provisions) Act 1989 (c.34).

104 Conflicts between verbal descriptions and plans were not uncommon and gave rise to a considerable body of case law explored, down to 1914, by the House of Lords in *Eastwood v. Ashton* [1915] A.C. 900.

105 Underhill, *Changes in the Law of Real Property*, pp.673-719. In Offer's view (*Farm Tenure and*

Land Values), legal costs were one of the disincentives to purchases of land by tenant farmers.

106   E.g. reports of 3 Feb. 1809 (PRO C 38/1046), 23 Feb.1822 © 38/1251).

107   Order of 19 Aug. 1803, PRO C 33/523, f.736.

108   Order of 12 Feb. 1811, PRO C 33/583, f.361.

109   Order of 20 Jan. 1812, PRO C 33/591, f.360. *Woodford v. Berks* may be followed in C 33/591-639.

110   Order of 1 Apr. 1816, PRO C 33/627, f.937.

111   It was also costly in terms of repairs to the property: report of 28 Apr. 1818, PRO C 38/1170.

112   E.J. Evans, *The Contentious Tithe* (London, 1976), pp. 1-66.

113   *Ibid.*, pp. 16-26; report of 23 Feb. 1818, PRO C 38/1170.

114   Evans, *Contentious Tithe*, pp. 18-20.

115   *Ibid.*, pp.21-6. Some leased their tithes: A.W.Purdue, An Oxford College, Two Parishes and a Tithe-Farmer: the Modernisation of Tithe Collection, *Rural History* 8 (1997), 1-19.

116   Evans, *Contentious Tithe*, pp. 42-66.

117   Orders of 11 Jul. 1810 (PRO C 33/577, f.1045), 3 Apr. 1811 © 33/584, f. 430), 10 Feb. 1812 © 33/591, f.518), 15 Jul. 1825 © 33/736, f.1881).

118   Orders of 1 Jul 1826 (PRO C 33/748, f. 1822), 30 Apr. 1827 © 33/758, f. 923).

CHAPTER 12

IN CHANCERY: MANAGING THE ESTATES

1. The Management Structure

From the reign of `Farmer George' onwards the management of many landed estates became more professional, more ambitious and more effective than ever before. The key figure in this development was the land agent, whose profession evolved out of the stewards of earlier centuries through a phase in which attorneys frequently acted as agents to the point where fully fledged land agents, trained on a big estate and knowledgeable in farming techniques, working full time for one large estate owner or several smaller ones, became common.[1] Men like the celebrated James Loch, who worked *inter alia* on the Leveson-Gowers' vast estates in the midlands, are essentially creatures of the nineteenth century, though a few progressive landlords, like Thomas Coke of Holkham, were employing them at an earlier date. Most were still content to use an attorney who could draw, interpret and enforce their leases, keep rudimentary accounts and defend and promote their legal interests.[2] The trust began operating during a transitional period in estate management, when the desirability for the great estates to be run as businesses was becoming widely recognised, the owner exercising a more or less active supervision as his temperament and other interests dictated and being supported by a functionally specialised hierarchy comprising a core of permanent, full-time employees supplemented by part time and casual labour. The Duke of Northumberland's huge estates, with their headquarters at Alnwick Castle, were a model enterprise of this kind, but not a typical one.[3] The keeping of accounts ranged from the sophisticated to the primitive, not always in accordance with the size of the estate, and because the concentration of authority which progressives advocated also enlarged the scale on which frauds and embezzlement could be practised, there were plenty of landowners who preferred a more diffused style of management; after all, the Holkham steward made £100,000 out of *his* venal practices and compelled Coke to a Chancery suit to get rid of him.[4]

A landowner, of course, was free to arrange the management of his estates in the way that best suited him and if he chose to take no personal interest that was his business. Trustees could not so easily delegate their responsibilities to others, for they remained at risk if the beneficiaries suffered any loss, whether from positive fraud on the agent's part, from his insolvency or from his neglect to collect all monies due. The rule that a trustee must perform his trust personally was obviously not to be taken literally.

Agents must be employed and Chancery acknowledged as much in cases of `legal or moral necessity',[5] but the scope for delegation was narrowly drawn.[6] Agents might be employed to do ministerial work but not to take decisions; they might collect the rents but not choose the tenants; buy and sell stock but not choose which stock was to be bought and sold; experts might propose but the trustees must dispose and be able to justify their dispositions.[7] And even the ministerial work of the agent must be vigilantly supervised; the collector and the banker must not be allowed to retain money or negotiable securities longer than strictly necessary and must be called regularly to account.[8] Equity judges were not always indulgent to trustees and there were plenty of cases to make a man think twice about assuming a trust or, if he did so, dispose him to be ultra-cautious in carrying it out.[9] After all, however enterprising and diligent the trustee, he stood to gain nothing since all profits must accrue to the beneficiaries, no rule in equity being more rigidly adhered to than that a trustee must not take any profit from his trust beyond what the settler had expressly authorised.[10]

To encourage their chosen executors and trustees to assume the responsibilities, settlors began to insert into wills and settlements clauses relieving them of liability for losses that were not occasioned by their own `wilful default' but rather by the fraud or misfortune of fellow trustees or agents and it is no surprise to find this one in Peter Thellusson's will:

`they...shall be chargeable only every one of them with and for his own receipts, payments, accounts and wilful defaults only and not otherwise and shall not be accountable for any sum or sums of money other than such as shall actually come to his or their own hands respectively by virtue of this will notwithstanding their joining in receipts for the sake of conformity nor with any loss or damage which may happen ...without his or their respective wilful default...'[11]

The clause is in common form and also places a restriction on deposits with private bankers which probably echoes the rash of failures that had taken place in 1793. The security which these clauses afforded was, however, more apparent than real, for the judges usually construed them ungenerously, sometimes to the point of making them quite ineffective.[12] No wonder trustees tended to be prudent and conservative.

Once a trust was in Chancery, however, the position was changed. Against the costs that afflicted it and the tedious process of the masters' office may be set the facility to propose bolder management in those cases, such as the Thellusson trust, where there was land to be managed, not just Consols and mortgage money to be looked after. The accumulation encouraged long term planning and grand, even grandiose projects whose rewards might be long deferred. No party had a vested interest in short term profit since the only real choice lay between improving the trust estates and augmenting them. What schemes might one of the day's great improvers, Sir John Sinclair, Thomas Coke, Arthur Young or William Marshall have confronted Master Cox with?

Sadly, neither Emperor Woodford nor his successors showed any interest in agriculture and if initiative was forthcoming it must be from their agents. Initially they employed a lawyer, T.W. Budd of Budd & Hayes, paying him £150 a year to manage the Brodsworth property,[13] but once the first new purchases were made, the sons were mollified by being appointed receivers of rents in their respective counties.[14] Since they took 5% of the gross rental it was a potentially valuable perquisite, though none of them lived long enough to profit greatly, even Charles, the last survivor, never clearing much above £500 p.a. This arrangement had some advantages. The sons knew their locality, the elder two having estates of their own from which they could administer those of the trust. They all had some business experience and the percentage gave them an incentive to improve the rentals of the estates. On the other hand, none knew much about farming (though they seem to have known plenty about shooting), none was exactly prudent with his own money and they had no personal interest in the long term. While he owned the Newton Hanzard estate, Peter Isaac's determination to exact the highest rent, against the advice of his own surveyors, had very bad results,[15] while George spent extravagantly on building and repairs on the trust estates in Hertfordshire.[16] Damage from any imprudence on their part was, of course, limited by the court's supervision and their own short lifespans but they were not the men to make the best of the property.

On Peter Isaac's death the trustees chose Francis Whishaw, a surveyor from Gloucestershire without any known connection with the family or trustees; he may well have been a crony of Emperor's, so making plausible William Disney's hopes of getting *his* nominee installed when George died.[17] John, the second Lord Rendlesham, was passed over both times, the second time in favour of George Hibbert, one of George's executors and a Hertfordshire landowner himself, but both receiverships came back into the family later.[18] John *was* appointed when Whishaw died, although he was by then in Italy and notoriously unfitted for any active business,[19] and when Hibbert retired through old age it was rather surprisingly in favour of Henry Hoyle Oddie I, father of George's son-in-law; since the Oddies had just been worsted in a law suit against the trust, this may have been a peace offering.[20] Charles's receivership, however, left his side of the family for good on his death, the Yorkshire estates being put in charge of his executor John Christopher Mansel, an army friend of the Woodford brothers who owned land in Northamptonshire,[21] while the midlands was given to William Lukin, Anne Thellusson's husband.[22] Charles's own sons were too young to be candidates and even when the eldest (Charles) was struggling against mounting debts to raise a family, no-one proposed that either Mansel or Lukin should make way for him; perhaps by that time the necessary sureties would not have been easy to find.

The choice of receivers to succeed the sons indicates clearly enough that they were not intended to be active in running the estates. The man who mostly nearly corresponds to the land agent is John Shaw, the London surveyor, who must have spent a good deal of his time on trust affairs, and perhaps he earned his rewards. There is however one undertaking which looks extravagant - the production of a comprehensive set of plans and terriers to furnish the detailed information he argued was necessary for the efficient running of the estates. He may well have been right, for Marshall certainly recommended such things,[23] but even Marshall might have balked at what Shaw came up with. The finished product was lavish and splendid, comprising a whole series of plans, with each field numbered, and its tenure and tithe liability noted, along with terriers listing acreage and crops, all handsomely bound in vellum. But they took him fifteen years and cost not far short of double the £1,125 that had been originally approved: this, perhaps, was carrying long term planning too far.[24]

Shaw was not actually resident on the trust estates, nor were the receivers or the trustees themselves. There was a resident bailiff in Yorkshire, John Ives, and the Brodsworth household included a steward,[25] but there is no evidence for equivalents elsewhere, so perhaps the most respectable tenants actually collected the rents and acted as local representatives for the absentee landlords, or perhaps local lawyers or surveyors were used.[26] Local valuers were used to confirm and elaborate Shaw's testimony when abatements of rent were under consideration and when leases were being drawn up;[27] the bailiff on the Rendlesham estates was consulted on occasion[28] and Rendlesham's London solicitor, J.H. Benbow, as well as Budd, can be found taking a part in the running of the estates.[29] Finally, in the early 1830's, full- time woodreeves were taken on as Shaw recommended.[30] On the whole, however, the picture that emerges is of a rather improvisatory structure, lacking in coherence and continuity, and certainly not comparable to the most advanced estates.

2. Enclosures and Improvements

It was the Age of Improvement and the Improvement *par excellence*, which left the most lasting mark on the landscape and the people, was the enclosure of open fields, commons and waste. Enclosure was a continuous process, so much so that by this time few open fields remained in some of the counties where the trust held land, in Suffolk and Herts. for instance;[31] but it was not a uniform process either chronologically or geographically and the last great burst of enclosing under private acts of parliament took place during the Napoleonic Wars.[32] Enclosures are a powerful element in the mythology of the English rural past, and it is a double myth: the economic myth that enclosure was pre-eminently a matter of changing land use and farming patterns, of modernising agriculture at a stroke, and the social myth that it `was fatal to three classes: the small farmer, the cottager and the squatter'.[33] Modern scholarship, as it does so often, dissolves the firm outlines of this picture without bringing a truer one into focus.[34]

George Woodford Thellusson had already instigated the enclosure of Aldenham common,[35] but the only venture the trustees made was at the very heart of their estates, in Brodsworth itself. Only about one- quarter of the fields in the parish were still open when Napoleon was driven out of France - 394 acres out of 1,962 - but the common comprised a further 380 acres. The trust held two- thirds of the land and the rights of common, having removed the only other significant lay landowner by buying Pigburn. Sir John Copley's lands on nearby Scarsby intruded into the parish but they could be excluded from the enclosure proposals.[36] The vicar's glebe

294

however amounted to 170 acres and the dean and chapter of York cathedral, as owners of the great tithe (already leased to the trustees) might expect a substantial allotment in lieu.[37] Getting rid of the tithe and consolidating the estate seem to have been the trustees' chief motives in seeking an enclosure act, for they offered Master Cox no estimates of higher rents or plans for better cropping beyond some rather generalised disparagement of the state of the open fields.[38] It was all very straightforward, with no vocal opposition and no major difficulties, and the trustees got 320 acres out of it, parts of which they immediately exchanged for more conveniently located plots.[39] It was a costly business - £5,900 11s 9d in all, excluding any fencing, ditching and building- and at £18 an acre it is very much on the high side, reflecting the rising cost of the procedure and the high proportion (305 acres) allotted to the dean and chapter, which had to be paid for by the other owners.[40] It is impossible even to guess how profitable the enclosure was in the long term, but since it was undertaken right at the tail of the boom, as corn prices fell and cultivation began to shrink back from the margins which it had encroached upon, it must have taken many years to pay for itself.

Another species of `improvement' which writers like Marshall and Nathaniel Kent urged upon landlords was the drainage of wetlands, first by ridge and furrow, later by tile drains and finally from the 1840s by pipe drains.[41] It was not until the post-war depression that their advice was widely followed and whereas enclosure was generally profitable, the returns on capital spent in draining heavy soils usually proved disappointing, so it may be as well that the trustees and their agents were not enthusiasts and that the only instance of money spent on inland farms is a modest £250 on tile drains for New Farm, on the cold midland clay.[42] However, they owned lands in Suffolk which were washed by the North Sea and by the tidal rivers Deben and Butley, some of them liable for charges to keep the sea walls and sluices in repair[43] and in 1811 the trustees put proposals before the Master for a joint enterprise with the Marquis of Hertford, who owned the opposite bank, to embank the Butley. At that time `the trust lands are only fit to turn a few sheep upon in the interval of the tides, are let at a very low rent and the rest of such lands called the Ooze by and close to the ... river are covered with slime and mire from the continual overflow thereof and ... totally unproductive.[144]

The cost was estimated at £3,000 however and Shaw's report, suggesting only a precarious and doubtful gain, was so discouraging that they did not persevere and made no further suggestions for land reclamation.[45] Some years later they supported a private bill promoted by Sir W. B. Cooke to embank the River Don to protect the adjacent lands from flooding. Some 500 of the 8,000 acres concerned belonged to the trust and since its contribution to the very hefty cost of the venture (£10,000) was to be a modest £625, the court's sanction was obtained with a minimum of fuss and delay.[46] All in all then, the trust's spending on drainage was very modest indeed.

3. Repairs

In addition to these `pure' improvements, landlords also spent more or less freely on maintaining and enhancing the fabric of the estate buildings. To the frustration of scholars, they seldom distinguished between capital and recurrent expenditure, making it very difficult to discover how much of their outlay represented capital investment.[47] The most imposing and conspicuous building was usually the mansion house, and one landowner after another discovered about architects' estimates what the French Thellussons had learned of Ledoux's, that they were often wholly unrealistic. The trust built no mansions, but Brodsworth had to be repaired and furnished.[48]

Some of those who spent lavishly on their own houses were niggardly when it came to the farm buildings.[49] At the other extreme were estates like the Duke of Bedford's at Woburn and Coke's at Holkham, though some Holkham farm buildings were more impressive than functional and did not meet the exacting scientific prescriptions of the experts, who laid down admirable principles which were seldom followed.[50] During the Long War landowners made considerable efforts to shift the burden of repairs onto their tenants and the balance of legal obligations varied widely, but what counted for more than legal rights was economic muscle. Whatever tenants might have agreed, it was all too clear that in bad times they could not and would not perform their obligations, and a few years' neglect could raise the cost of repairs astronomically; thus, £4,000 had been taken off the purchase price of Smog Oak Farm (Herts.) for repairs but they were not carried out until 1812, by which time rising labour costs and the effect of weather had nearly doubled the cost.[51] Furthermore, to attract desirable tenants and keep satisfactory ones it was often necessary to put farmhouses and outbuildings into repair, so we should expect to find heavier expenditure in the period of depression after Waterloo.

The trustees had an early experience of the cost of delay. In 1808 George Thellusson set to work as receiver in repairing and improving Bathers Green and Aldenham Place farms, which he had sold to the trust a few years earlier, transforming Bathers Green by three double barns, stables, cattle sheds, pigsties, cartsheds, a granary and more besides. Nearly £2,000 had been spent, with £940 still needed, when the Master pulled him up short, being `of the opinion that the said repairs, alterations and improvements made on Bathers Green Farm were to a much greater amount than ought to have been made and therefore were not proper and necessary to be made or for the benefit of the trust estate'.[52] They certainly far exceeded the £1,267 allowed off the price on account of disrepair and although Thellusson disputed the Master's report he was still allowed only £1,500 on the £1,965 9s 10d he had spent without authorisation.[53] That may have acted as a salutary restraint against the extravagant spending to which a trust with no life owner in possession might be particularly prone, and similarly when one of the Suffolk tenants claimed £1,200 for emergency repairs, £500 was disallowed as being `ornamental'.[54]

Substantial sums *were* spent in order to make the farms attractive for leasing, but some projects were dropped when the depression hit rents, notably a full scale rearrangement and reconstruction programme at Amotherby costed at £5,890 and

£900 worth of repairs to the Thorp estate. Delays on another Yorkshire farmhouse, the grandly styled Pigburn Hall, left it 'in too ruinous a state of condition to be repaired with advantage',[55] and a new one had to be built, but spending in Yorkshire was generally modest. The compact, modern midlands and home counties farms fared better. Byfield, bought in 1829, was immediately given a new farmhouse and at the same time the 300 year old farmhouse at Woodwicks in Hertfordshire was replaced. The total cost was over £2,000 and although a London builder had to be got in to do it, he still underquoted the famous Thomas Cubitt by almost £300.[56]

In most cases the rebuilding was part of schemes to regroup farms or improve their layout, as at Rendham Rookery, where the woes of the tenant had been echoed in the buildings, barns being 'so much sunk in the earth as to be injurious to the corn kept therein.'[57] A few years later, when the Suffolk receiver was having great difficulty in finding good tenants, several farms were given a major building programme costing £2,735, which had to include labourers' cottages. These were 'dreadfully ill provided for' in this part of Suffolk, one farmhouse being 'occupied by several families in a close and loathsome state so much so that he had a consultation with the parish officers as to what was to be done with them to enable the workmen to proceed with the repairs ... [he] saw no remedy for the evil but by making provision on every farm for the accommodation of its own labourers'.[58] With the labouring poor in this condition it comes as no surprise that Henry Ashford's farm was burned down by incendiaries in that same year and had to be rebuilt.[59]

On the whole the impression created is that the trust eschewed grandiose schemes and that after 1814 it had no master plan. Advantage was taken of occasions when repairs were needed anyway to make improvements but there was no rolling programme and probably no attempt at an overview of the estates' condition and needs.

In all, the spending on repairs and rebuilding which I have located,[60] including Brodsworth but not Plaistow, comes to the following:

Yorkshire	£12,777
Suffolk	£10,305
Home Counties	£6,876
Midlands	£2,957
	£32,915

Because the estates were constantly growing and because of the way in which the receivers' accounts were arranged, it is very difficult to calculate the proportion of the gross rental which this represents and the figure would not, in any case, be very meaningful in the case of such an unusual landlord. What the trust had to do, in essence, was to strike a balance between spending income on adding to the estates and spending it on maintaining and improving the existing ones so as to produce more revenue for the purchase of new estates, and that required a sophistication in their accounting and in their deliberations which is unlikely to have occurred.[61]

5. Leases and Tenancies

The trustees began their work at a time when the apostles of improvement were insistent that one of the keys to prosperity was the substitution of leases of seven, fourteen or twenty- one years for tenancies at will or from year to year;[62] `the improvements which have been wrought in England', wrote Arthur Young, `have been almost totally owing to the custom of granting leases'.[63] The logic sounded persuasive. Without the security of a lease behind him a farmer could not be expected to make the substantial capital investments, in drainage, buildings and livestock, that were needed to bring his farm to the perfection their prescriptions promised, while the appeal to landlords lay in the higher rents that they would be able to charge and, perhaps, in the transfer of capital expenditure to the tenant in exchange for his enhanced security. Longer leases also introduced a greater legal formality into the landlord- tenant relationship, usually embodying husbandry covenants designed to compel improvements in crop rotation and farm management.[64]

In fact the publicists greatly exaggerated the advantages of leases over traditional forms of tenure, but their adoption remains one of the touchstones of a progressive estate and the trust was eager to convert the miscellany of arrangements which prevailed on the lands they acquired into a uniform basic lease, subject to variations dictated by the character of the land and the size of the farm.[65] At first this had to be done piecemeal when the opportunity arose. Thus Shepherd's Farm, near Rickmansworth, bought in 1806, was quickly let for a fourteen year term at 350 p.a., and in 1809 the tenant of the 243 acre Langley Hall Farm agreed to exchange his existing lease, due to expire in 1812, for a twenty-one year lease at £270 p.a. subject to all the usual covenants as to good husbandry and to a penalty of £20 an acre if he ploughed up pasture.[66]

But tenants were not always so obliging. Samuel Gross, who rented a large farm of over 2,000 acres at Butley in Suffolk, was an independent man with a freehold of his own. When Rendlesham bought Butley for the trust in 1804, Gross had just been promised a new twelve year lease at £400 by the previous owner but had to settle for just four years at the same rent. In 1809 Rendlesham was prepared to renew it for fifteen years at £470 but after his death the trustees sent in valuers who came up with much higher figures. Gross claimed to have spent over £2,000 on improvements, and to have leased out his freehold farm on the basis of Rendlesham's assurances of reimbursement and security. He even appeared before the Master in person but would pay no more than £750 for five years. Since the trustees had already had an offer matching their terms -sixteen years at £978 - Gross was turned out.[67]

In 1814 the trustees decided on a determined push to put all their farms on long leases, including those in the north which were mostly on tenancies at will and would need substantial repairs before good tenants could be persuaded to take them on leases imposing repairing duties. The wartime farming boom was at its height, there was no shortage of potential tenants and the trustees, naturally taking the long view, obviously felt it advantageous to negotiate a high and stable rent while reducing their own repairing and management obligations. A dozen leases in Suffolk and the home counties were approved, all on broadly similar terms - that is, fourteen years, rent payable every six months, with the usual reservation of fishing, game and timber to the lessor, covenants to practise what was considered good husbandry in that district, to do repairs (but with the lessor to provide the timber and pay half the workmen's bills), not to assign or underlet without consent and, as with the earlier leases, to pay a £20 an acre penalty for ploughing up pasture.[68]

However, before some of these leases had even been executed, and before any real progress had been made with those in the midlands and the north, the end of the war and the precipitous fall in food prices transformed the position, the move to leases was rapidly abandoned and some of the remaining tenants at will threw up their farms.[69]   In common with other landlords, the trustees seem to have abandoned the long lease because they could not in practice enforce rents which were out of line with prices and could seldom find good tenants willing to accept farms on onerous terms; in a buyer's market the farmers' preference for yearly tenancies reasserted itself, although the position on the trust estates was confused,   as new purchases brought with them tenants holding under a wide assortment of terms and conditions.

It probably made little difference, certainly less than was once supposed.   In practice good, or even halfway decent, tenants enjoyed *de facto* security and other than Gross none was turned off by the trust simply to obtain a higher rent.[70] In theory, tenants of an estate in the hands of trustees *were* vulnerable since the trustees' duty to their beneficiaries was clear and unsentimental - to maximise their investment with regard neither to personal preference nor even to common morality: gazumping for trustees is rather a duty than a disgrace.[71] Nevertheless, there was no real danger that these trustees would be brought to book if they were less than ruthless in their management and even the court showed itself generous with the trust fund on occasion.

Adam Brown, lessee of Aldenham Place Farm and Patchetts Green Farm (nearly

400 acres in all) was a model tenant, whose improvements added £5,000 to the value of the farms, but his heavy outlay only made him more vulnerable to the fall in prices and after eight years he was nearly £2,500 in arrears; distress warrants were issued and the arrears recovered, Brown gave up his lease on the promise that his unfortunate situation would be brought to the court's notice, and he was given £300 as a modest consolation.[72] Such treatment was not only generous but also politic and on the whole even Sir John Caird, a great critic of short tenancies, admitted that they worked well enough.[73]

Apart from Samuel Gross, only one tenant on the estates had a serious grievance and he was treated leniently. The Yorkshire farmers, tenants at will though they were, had the benefit of the custom of `tenant right' - that is, the right to be compensated by their successor for the value of unexhausted improvements. It was confined to south Yorkshire, Lincolnshire and parts of south-eastern England until put on a statutory basis in 1883, and although capable of being manipulated by an unscrupulous occupier it did give tenants an incentive to improve their farms.[74] Every now and then the valuation of the improvements made by a neutral umpire dissatisfied one party or the other but few went so far as Thomas Hicks, who in 1814 was displaced as yearly tenant of land at Thorp and offered £396 compensation; he left his last year's rent unpaid and before he was thrown into York Castle for other debts (£100 borrowed from Charles Thellusson among them) he committed serious depredations to the land and assaulted his successor Fretwell, who was encouraged and indemnified by Charles Thellusson in bringing actions against Hicks, with the net result that the trust had to pay over £300 to Fretwell for his losses and expenses.[75]

After the war the trust seems to have abandoned its attempt to rationalise the estate leases in favour of *ad hoc* negotiation, a reflection of landlord weakness in this era of lower prices and farming bankruptcies. It was sensible to do so, for it was one thing for a Coke to impose uniformity on compact farms under his direct supervision, quite another for trustees to do so over a scattered and growing holding run from a distance by receivers with no conspicuous qualifications. Diversity of

302

tenure in such circumstances had real practical merits.

6. Timber

The days in which the old rhyme that `from Blacon Point to Hillbree, a squirrel may jump from tree to tree'[76] had any truth were long gone. By Thellusson's day England had become `a land of park, copse, plantation, and - in many parts - of hedgerow timber ... with singularly little forest, natural or cultivated'.[77] But the woods and copses still covered three million acres in Gregory King's estimation, and were a vital economic resource both to the nation and the individual landowner. Ships of the line and merchantmen needed their hearts of oak and were using them up at an unprecedented rate, though they had to rely on the softwood forests of North America and the Baltic for masts and deals.[78] The law recognised the value of timber (which it restrictively defined as oak, ash and elm at least twenty years old) to an estate by restraining life owners from committing `waste', i.e. felling it for their own profit, unless specifically authorised by the settlor,[79] but it was not only the stately trees of the great parks that had their value - Burke's description of the Whig grandees as the `great oaks of the constitution' was a vivid and apt metaphor- but humbler growths in coppices and hedgerows besides. Despite the decline in the use of wood as fuel for charcoal burning and the inroads which sea coal made into the domestic and industrial fuel market, demand for wood remained strong, artificially buoyed up by import duties. A host of specialised trades - in baskets, brushes and brooms, clothespegs, crates, hop poles, hoops and fences - made the scientific exploitation of woodland profitable and in some cases made forestry more rewarding than renting the land to a farmer; on the Duke of Bedford's estates in the home counties the profits of timber and other wood made up 24% of his total income from the land, although more often large landowners resorted to timber sales as an *ad hoc* expedient to finance capital expenditure or to pay off debts.[80] It was a resource not to be neglected and the will had empowered the trustees to cut and sell timber from time to time.

An order to this effect was made by the court in 1808,[81] but it was more than twenty years before a plan for the management of the estate timber was settled. The fault was not really in the trustees, for the Master had been asked to approve the preparation of one in 1813; unfortunately it became bound up with John Shaw's mapping project and his separate report on timber did not see the light of day until 1830, a long delay even by Chancery standards.[82]

Some of the woods, like the extensive ones round Brodsworth, were already being managed profitably,[83] and at intervals felling was ordered on other parts of the estates, though some of it was to facilitate repairs and it is not possible to make up an accurate account.[84] Neglect, however, could be costly, as with a plantation at Edge Row (Herts.) which cost over £150 to restore to good condition.[85] New plantations were begun, notably at the northern outlier at Newton Hanzard in 1818, comprising more than 2,700 trees on 121 acres of cold, wet soil, extended by a further sixty-three acres in 1830.[86] As well as yielding saleable wood, plantations offered shelter and helped to anchor loose soils, this being the main justification for plantations in Suffolk which were 'of light soil and ... parts thereof were of an inferior quality called sheep walks and other parts thereof were nearly barren and were greatly exposed to the influence of the sea winds from which the crops frequently suffered considerable damage and were occasionally entirely destroyed.'[87]

The leases authorised the landlords to take land for this purpose and in 1819 and again in 1825 they did so, covering several hundred acres of exposed sheepwalk and grazing with trees.[88] By the time the estates were finally divided between the two successful claimants they included over 2,000 acres of woodland (over 7% of the total acreage), most of it in the north and in Suffolk, and sales of timber were yielding a handsome profit.[89]

7. Rents

The trust began operations in the midst of `a golden age for landlords'[90]. Rents were rising rapidly, a windfall to some landlords though others had earned it through their investment in enclosures, drainage and buildings. Farm rents rarely compared favourably with the profits from land mortgages and other, riskier investments[91], but on some estates the rise during the war years was spectacular and overall it averaged perhaps 90 - 100%.[92] The trust took advantage of the situation when it could, but as we have seen it was only in 1814 that any general review of leases and rents was attempted and if what happened in Samuel Gross's case is typical,[93] then the new rents were set at levels close to the market rate.

Wartime prosperity for farmers peaked in 1813 and by 1815 there was widespread distress and impoverishment, at least in the corn growing areas, though this was not immediately reflected in rent movements - Holkham rents, for example, reached a peak in 1820 that they did not approach again until 1833.[94] Landlords throughout England were faced with pleas for rents to be reduced or abatements granted, and their response naturally varied according to their perception of the tenants' means, the likely duration of the crisis, the desirability of retaining their tenants, their own financial circumstances and sense of social obligation. On the Thellusson estates the matter came to a head early, for in February 1816 the trustees petitioned the Vice- Chancellor to let them lay before the Master proposals: `since the leases were granted a great depression hath taken place in the price of corn, cattle and every article of agricultural produce and in consequence thereof several of the tenants have made repeated applications ... for a reduction in their respective rents alleging that it will be impossible for them to meet their present rents and that unless a considerable reduction is made therein their ruin will be the inevitable consequence`.[95]

The remissions which were sanctioned were on the generous side. Rents in Suffolk were reduced by 25%, in the midlands by 23%, in Yorkshire by 21% and in

Hertfordshire by 15%, making an overall reduction of just over 20%.[96] The reductions were to run from Michaelmas 1816 for two years, but by the end of 1820 it was clear that things had not improved in Suffolk and the home counties, though the lack of petitions from the other areas suggests that in line with national trends, prices on the clay soils of the midlands and in south Yorkshire had recovered sufficiently for tenants to find the rent, or perhaps their rents had not been raised so high in the first place.[97] Both in 1821 and again 1824 the tenants in the southern counties had to be given abatements: 23% and 20% in Herts., 16% and a remarkable 34% (distorted perhaps by one or two big farms) in Suffolk.[98] Suffolk tenants alone were given another year at 20% in 1825,[99] but although there was no blanket remission for the Hertfordshire tenants, it is plain that many of them too were having a struggle. Besides the sad case of Adam Brown,[100] the tenant of Theobald Street Farm, paying £190 p.a., became insolvent with heavy loss to the trust, two others refused even the lower rents they were offered and tenants of most of the bigger farms (now usually held on yearly tenancies) won substantial reductions- Old Parkbury Farm £600 to £500, Smog Oak £500 to £450, King's Langley from £270 to £230.[101] To put the decline in perspective however, it is worth recording that the tenant of King's Langley had originally held a lease at £180 p.a., which had been raised by 50%.[102] There was really no alternative for the trust when 'it might be difficult to find new tenants of capital and respectability to take the farms and much additional expense would be incurred as new tenants mostly require considerably sums to be expended in alterations and improvements of buildings'.[103]

Judging from the rather limited evidence of what happened elsewhere, the treatment of the trust's tenants looks been rather generous, but it is unlikely that this reflects a lax or indifferent management, for all the reductions had been recommended by receivers who had a vested interest in maximising their receipts or with the advice of competent and sometimes disinterested surveyors. Events in Hertfordshire certainly do not suggest a cosseted tenantry and the Suffolk abatements have to be seen in the light of East Anglia's particularly bad social conditions.

The rate of return on the trust estates cannot readily be estimated. The estates themselves grew steadily from year to year and the rent roll rose accordingly, but the way in which receivers' payments into court are recorded do not make calculation easy. In 1833 Parliament was given a gross rental of £24,165 5s 10d, including £1,430 3s 11d casual profits, and an average figure for net profits of £14, 207 over the previous twenty-five years.[104] The crudest of calculations yields a gross return of 3.5% and a net of 2.1%. The first accords closely with Beckett's suggested figure, but the latter is significantly lower, perhaps reflecting a higher level of management expenses, outlay on buildings and repairs and, of course, legal costs. The last item alone, totalling £44,922, averages £1,500 a year or more than 0.2% of the total outlay.[105] In the light of these figures, however, and with the important exception of Brodsworth Hall itself, it would be difficult to substantiate severe criticisms of the management of the estates.

NOTES

1. B. English, Patterns of Land Management in Yorkshire, 1840- c.1880, *Agricultural History Review* 32 (1984), 29-48; Beckett, *Landownership and the Land Market*, 590-6; F.M.L. Thompson, *English Landed Society in the Nineteenth Century* (London, 1971), pp.3-134; D. Spring, *English Landed Estate in the Nineteenth Century* (Baltimore, 1963).

2. E. Richards, `The Leviathan of Wealth': West Midlands Agriculture, 1800-50, *Agricultural History Review* 22 (1974), 97-117; Beckett, *Landownership and Land Market*; Spring, *English Landed Estate*, pp. 3-20, 55-68; Thompson, *English Landed Society*, pp. 175-83.

3. Thompson, *English Landed Society*, pp. 169-72; see also the detailed account of the Duke of Bedford's estates in Spring, *English Landed Estate*, pp.20-54.

4. Thompson, *English Landed Society*, pp. 153-6. Other examples of dishonest agents are given in English, *Patterns of Land Management*, though Spring's verdict is generally favourable (*English Landed Estate*, at p.134).

5. *Ex p. Belchier* (1754) Amb. 219. `Moral' necessity seems to be equated with accepted business practice.

6. See Lord Hardwicke in *Knight v. Earl of Plymouth* (1747) 1 Dick. 120 at 126-7.

7. Thus, in the early case of *Attorney-General v. Scott* (1750) 1 Ves. Sen. 413, it was legitimate for trustees to authorise a proxy to sign the presentation of a clergyman on their behalf but not to cast their vote.

8. *Townley v. Sherborne* (1633) J. Bridg. 35 (collection of rents); *Knight v. Earl of Plymouth* (1747) 1 Dick. 120 (entrusting money to a reputable banker).

9. E.g. *Doyle v. Blake* (1804) 2 Sch. & Lef. 231, and see the characteristic judgment of Lord Eldon in *Chambers v. Minchin* (7 Ves. Jun. 195), delivered in May 1802 after 16 months of cogitation, in which he declared that a clear rule was preferable to uncertainty `however I may lament the consequences in this case' and that `if a trustee trusts an attorney, he must abide by the effect of that confidence' (at 200, 196).

10. Laid down by King LC in *Keech v Sandford* (1726) Sel. Cas. t. King 61 and followed ever since, even in hard cases such as *Protheroe v. Protheroe* [1968] 1 W.L.R. 519.

11. Very similar clauses are founded in most of those wills examined for this study which set up trusts.

12. See e.g. *Underwood v. Stevens* (1816) 1 Mer. 712.

13. *General Report.*

14. Reports of 1 Feb., 4 and 10 Jul., 1805, PRO C 38/944.

15. Order of 27 May 1812, PRO C 33/594, f.1286.

16. See *infra*, pp. 292-3.

17. Report of 16 Aug. 1810, PRO C 38/1023.

18. Report of 12 Mar. 1812, PRO C 38/1055.

19. Report of 21 Jan. 1817, PRO C 38/1129. Whishaw died in November 1816. Two of the Pole family stood as sureties for him.

20. See *infra*, pp. 325-7.

21. Report of 15 Mar. 1816, PRO C 38/1129. John Christopher Mansel was born in 1771 and educated at Rugby. He joined the army and at the battle of Le Cateau in 1794 his father was killed and himself saved from death by a French officer and taken prisoner. He was released in 1795. It is not clear how he made Charles Thellusson's acquaintance but he became one of Charles's sureties in 1809 and subsequently the guardian of his son Thomas: F.P. Statham, *A History of the Family of Maunsell* (2 vols. in 3, London, 1917-20), vol. II, pp. 327-30.

22. Report of 24 Feb. 1816, PRO C 38/1129.

23. *On the Landed Property of England*, pp. 363-70.

24. Several copies were made, one of which is in the Suffolk Record Office as HB 416. The scheme was authorised in 1814 (PRO C 33/610, f.1309) and in 1830 Shaw deposed vaguely that 'the magnitude of the undertaking together with some unforeseen difficulties in its progress have tended to procrastinate its completion', which was something of an understatement. Elaborate projects of this sort were in vogue: A.S. Bendall, *Maps, Land and Society, A History...* (Cambridge, 1992), pp.77-138 and D.H. Fletcher, Mapping and Estate Management in the Early Nineteenth Century *Archaeologia Cantiana* CIX (1993), 85-109.

25. Orders of 10 May 1810 (PRO C 33/577, f.881), 21 Dec. 1816 © 33/637, f.303).

26. Such arrangements were common: see *supra*, n.1.

27. E.g. Order of 7 Aug. 1832, PRO C 33/839, f.2776; report of 20 Jul. 1832, C 38/1545; orders of 11 Jul. 1810 © 33/577, f.833), 22 Dec. 1820 © 33/685, f.231).

28. Order of 11 Jul. 1810, PRO C 33/577, f.833.

29. Orders of 21 May 1818 (PRO C 33/651, f.1167), 21 Dec. 1829 © 33/801, f.515).

30. Report of 16 Mar. 1831, PRO C 38/1514.

31. See the maps in G.E. Mingay, *Enclosure and the Small Farmer in the Age of the Industrial Revolution* (London, 1968), after p. 42.

32. A million acres of common and waste were enclosed under acts of parliament between 1793 and 1815, facilitated by the General Enclosure Act 1801 (41 Geo. III c. 109).

33. J.D. Chambers and G.E. Mingay, *The Agricultural Revolution, 1750-1880* (London, 1966), at p.88, quoting the Hammonds.

34. A great deal has been written about enclosure. G.E. Mingay, *Parliamentary Enclosure in England. An Introduction to its Causes, Incidence and Impact, 1750-1850* (London, 1997) offers a good summary.

35. The enclosure award, July 1803, can be seen in Herts CRO, D/Ewh/T3, together with a copy of the Act.

36. PRO C 38/922; Orders of 15 Mar. 1815 © 33/616, f.583), 21 Mar. 1817© 33/639, f.836). The Master's report of 9th August 1804 referred to an intended enclosure bill but nothing seems to have come of it, perhaps because of the difficulties over Pigburn.

37. Order of 15 Mar. 1815, PRO C 33/616, f.583. Tithe owners usually received between 14 and 25% of the enclosed land: Mingay, *Parliamentary Enclosure*, p.47.

38. Order of 15 Mar. 1815, PRO C 33/616, f.583. According to J. Chapman, The Extent and Nature of Parliamentary Enclosure, *Agricultural History Review* 35 (1986), 25-35, the more usual motive in this phase was the reclamation of waste.

39. Orders of 21 Mar. 1817 (PRO C 33/639, f.836), 23 Dec. 1817 © 33/648, f.287).

40. Orders of 25 May 1815 (PRO C 33/616, f.909), 20 Dec. 1815 © 33/625, f.254), 7 May 1816 © 33/627, f.789), 21 Jul. 1817© 33/641, f.1578). Estimates of costs vary - see *Agrarian History*, vol. VI, pp.603-4. Subsequent costs might easily come to as much again.

41. *Agrarian History*, vol. VI, pp. 599-600, 604-7; Thompson, *English Landed Society*, pp. 247-53.

42. Order of 24 Dec. 1818, PRO C 33/661, f.427.

43. E.g. Orders of 5 Aug. 1819 (PRO C 33/665, f.1773), 21 Dec. 1825 © 33/744, f.281 (Peyton Hall Farm, sea wall repairs estimated at c.£50 p.a.).

44. Order of 23 Dec. 1811, PRO C 33/591, f.485. Hertford's estate is described in A. Jobson, *Victorian Suffolk* (London, 1972), pp.45-6.

45. Report of 10 May 1813, PRO C 38/1072.

46. Orders of 14 May, 13 Jun. 1827, PRO C 33/758, f.991, C 33/759, f.1174.

47. B.A. Holderness, Landlords' Capital Formation in East Anglia, 1750-1870, *Economic History Review* (2nd s.) 25 (1972), 434-47.

48. See *supra*, p. 262. Many instances of architects' optimism are to be found in J. Franklin, *The Gentleman's Country House* (London, 1981) and M. Girouard, *The Victorian Country House* (Oxford, 1971, see index *sub* "Wealth").

49. Sir J.Caird, *English Agriculture in 1850-51* (London, 1852), pp.490-3. The Leveson-Gowers seem to be an example: J.R.Wordie, Rent Movements and the English Farmer, 1700- 1839, *Research in Economic History* 6 (1981), 193-243.

50. R.A.C. Parker, *Coke of Holkham* (Oxford, 1975), pp. 94-5, 154-5; Spring, *English Landed*

310

Estate, especially pp. 44-53. Samuel Whitbread the elder was another who spent heavily on rebuilding: Rapp, *Social Mobility*, 384-5. For expert prescriptions see N. Harvey, *A History of Farm Buildings in England and Wales* (London, 1970), pp. 73-80.

51. *Agrarian History*, vol. VI, pp. 599-607; order of 27 May 1812, PRO C 33/593, f.977.

52. Order of 11 Aug.1810, PRO C 33/578, f.1278. Thellusson's executors had to make good the balance: order of 26 Jul. 1813, C 33/601, f.1153.

53. Report of 25 Jan. 1814, PRO C 38/1090.

54. *Ibid.*

55. Order of 21 May 1818, PRO C 33/651, f.1194.

56. Orders of 12 Jun. 1830, 19 Jul. 1831, PRO C 33/804, f.1742, C 33/822, f.2336.

57. Order of 30 Jun. 1823, PRO C 33/713, f.1873, Shaw's affidavit.

58. Report of 15 Aug. 1829, PRO C 38/1449, Shaw's affidavit.

59. Order of 2 Apr. 1829, PRO C 33/788, f.1021. This is the only recorded incident of incendiarism or machine breaking on the trust estates. There had been serious disturbances in Suffolk in 1816, and again in 1822 and incendiarism remained a frequent occurrence. Woodbridge (the market town for the trust estates) had a riotous tradition but the famous `Swing' riots of 1830 passed it by. A.J. Peacock, *Bread or Blood* (London, 1965); P. Muskett, The East Anglian Riots of 1822, *Agricultural History Review* 32 (1984), 1-13; E.J. Hobsbawm and G. Rudé, *Captain Swing* (London, 1970); J.E.Archer, *"By a Flash and a Scare"* (Oxford, 1990).

60. Using PRO C 33 and C 38. Parliament did not call for returns on expenditure in the debates on the estate bill in 1833. These figures cover the period 1797-1834.

61. *Agrarian History*, vol. VI summarises the scanty evidence from other estates at pp. 601-7.

62. A tenancy at will is determinable by either party upon giving notice, though the tenant may re-enter to harvest crops he has sown. A tenancy from year to year is determinable by six months notice expiring on the anniversary of its commencement.

63. Quoted in Chambers and Mingay, *The Agricultural Revolution, 1750-1880*, at p. 46.

64. In fact husbandry covenants on most estates seem to have been principally defensive in nature, seeking to guard against tenants' misdeeds rather than to compel them to practise enlightened farming: *Ibid*, pp. 46-7; *Agrarian History*, vol. VI, p. 614,

65. Ironically, by the time the trust made this decision, the popularity of the lease was already on the wane and this tendency to lag behind current trends may have been one to which corporate and trust estates were prone: *Agrarian History*, vol. VI, pp. 612-3.

66. Orders of 4 Nov. 1807 (PRO C 33/559, f.1071), 30 May 1810 © 33/577, f.848).

67. Order of 11 Jul. 1810, PRO C 33/577, f. 833; report of 28 Mar. 1810, C 38/1022. Gross was

still farming in Alderton in the 1830s: S.W. Martins and T. Williamson, Labour and Improvement: agricultural change in East Anglia, c.1750- 1870, *Labour History Review* 62 (1997), 275-95.

68. Order of 22 Dec. 1814, PRO C 33/616, f.586, giving full details of the leases. Mary Woodford's, for example, 14 years at £240 p.a., contained a covenant that she would use the 'best and most improved method of husbandry of ye county [Herts.]'. It must be doubtful whether such general terms would have been enforceable at law.

69. Orders of 12 Jun. 1816 (PRO C 33/628, f.1923), 18 Jul. 1818© 33/653, f.1744). It is typical of Anthony Trollope's father that he should have taken on a long lease just before prices fell: A. Trollope, *Autobiography* (1980 edn., Oxford), p. 11.

70. J.A. Perkins, Tenure, Tenant Right and Agricultural Progress in Lindsey, 1780-1850, *Agricultural History Review* 23 (1975), 1-22; *Agrarian History*, vol. VI, p. 615. Offer, *Farm Tenure and Land Values*, who emphasises landlord power, nevertheless acknowledges that tenant turnover was low.

71. *Buttle v. Saunders* [1950] 2 All ER 193. The obligation was affirmed by the House of Lords' judgment in the Mineworkers' Pension scheme case, *Cowan v. Scargill* [1984] 2 All ER 750.

72. Order of 29 Nov. 1825, PRO C 33/744, f.157.

73. *English Agriculture in 1850-51*, pp.504-9.

74. Perkins, *Tenure, Tenant Right and Agricultural Progress*, 9-22; *Agrarian History*, vol. VI, pp. 616-17.

75. Orders of 26 Jul. 1815 (PRO C 33/618, f.1533), 21 Apr. 1817 © 33/638, f.781).

76. S.T. Bindoff, *Tudor England* (London, 1950), p.9.

77. E.J.T. Collins, The Coppice and Underwood Trades, in *Agrarian History*, vol. VI, pp. 485-501 at p. 501, quoting Sir John Clapham.

78. R.G. Albion, *Forests and Sea Power* (Cambridge, Mass., 1926) remains the classic study. See also *Agrarian History*, vol. VI, pp. 64-72.

79. The range of 'timber' was expanded by local custom to include, for example, beech in Buckinghamshire. Megarry and Wade, *Law of Real Property* (5th edn.), pp. 96-100, summarises a branch of the law which nowadays has an esoteric ambience, with its references to estovers, botes and dotards. There is much learned judicial discussion in *Honywood v. Honywood* (1874) L.R. 18 Eq. 306.

80. *Agrarian History*, vol. VI, pp. 508-9, 625-6.

81. Order of 2 May 1808, PRO C 33/560, f.623.

82. Orders of 11 Aug. 1813 (PRO C 33/602, f.1335), 12 Jun. 1830 © 33/804, f.1778).

83. Order of 29 Mar. 1806, PRO C 33/544, f.407.

84. See e.g. report of 29 Apr. 1825, PRO C 38/1323 (timber valued at £892.15s).

85. Order of 4 Jul. 1815, PRO C 33/618, f.1537.

86. In 1818 the trees to be planted included larch, oak, ash, Spanish chestnut, Scotch fir, spruce, silver fir, mountain ash, beech, elm and sycamore. Reports of 31 Jan.1818, 27 Jan. 1830, PRO C 38/ 1170, 1484.

87. Order of 16 Aug. 1825, PRO C 33/737, f.1951.

88. *Ibid.*

89. Report and Division of the Thellusson Estates, Suffolk RO HB 416/F1.

90. Wordie, *Rent Movements*, at 224.

91. Samuel Whitbread, for example, made only 4% on his land against 12% on the brewery: Rabb, *Social Mobility*. According to Beckett, *Pattern of Landownership*, the gross return was 3½%, net 2½%, but as Beckett writes elsewhere (*Agrarian History*, vol. VI, p. 619), the problem of distinguishing landowners' gross incomes from net incomes, especially in relation to rents, is almost intractable. For a recent attempt showing higher net returns (3 to 31/2%) see Clark, *Land Hunger*, table 3.

92. M.E. Turner, J.V. Beckett and B. Afton, *Agricultural Rent in England, 1690-1914* (Cambridge, 1997), pp.51-2 and figs. 8.1 and 8.2 on pp.149-50.

93. *Supra*, pp. 295-6.

94. *Agrarian History*, vol. VI, pp.621-3.

95. Order of 6 Mar. 1816, PRO C 33/626, f.558.

96. Report of 19 Aug. 1816, PRO C 38/1129.

97. Just as rental variations around the country were appreciable (*Agrarian History*, vol. VI, pp.623-4) so was the impact of the depression, which was especially serious in cereal gowing areas: A.R. Wilkes, Adjustments in Arable Farming after the Napoleonic Wars, *Agricultural H.R.* 28 (1980), 90-104; Chambers and Mingay, *Agricultural Revolution*, pp.124-31.

98. Reports of 20 Dec. 1821 (PRO C 38/1232), 7 Feb.1824 © 38/1298).

99. Report of 14 Feb. 1825, PRO C 38/1323.

100. *Supra*, p. 297.

101. Report of 20 Jul. 1832, PRO C 38/1545.

102. Order of 30 May 1810, PRO C 33/577, f.848.

103. Order of 7 Aug. 1832, PRO C 33/839, f.2776. Both the Leveson-Gower estates, where rents had been raised too high, and those of the Grenvilles at Gosfield experienced similar problems: Wordie, *Rent Movements*, 209; Beckett, *Gosfield Hall*, 185-92.

104. *House of Lords Sessional Papers*, (1833) XI (101) 839.

105. By the time the matter was brought before Parliament, they were considerably higher, see *infra,*, pp. 348-9.

CHAPTER 13

THE SHADOW OF THE WILL: THE SECOND GENERATION

1. The Senior Branch

The first Baron Rendlesham left seven children, six of them male. Only two boys were old enough to be earning their living, John and George, both in the army. John, the heir, was twenty-three but for inheritance purposes his father's will had prolonged his infancy to thirty-one, facing his executors (William Manning[1], Samuel Heywood[2] and George Woodford Thellusson) with the task of looking after the interests of an overgrown 'infant' who chafed at his extended dependency as well as those of the younger children.

One of John's father's fears- that he would make an unsuitable marriage- soon proved well founded. Within a year, and far away in Malta, the new head of the family took a wife who had neither fortune nor connections to recommend her. The trustees seem to have given their consent, probably with misgivings, for the match, although unequal, was certainly not disgraceful. Maria Andalusia Dickens was just eighteen, and having been raised on the dreary and claustrophobic Rock of Gibraltar, where her father was an officer of engineers, had accompanied him to Malta, the *casus belli* of the war of 1803, where he was commander-in-chief.[3] John's love match was sadly brief, for Maria was consumptive and in the summer of 1814 had a fatal attack, though she remained mercifully unaware that she was dying until her end was very near. Flaxman was commissioned to furnish her memorial in the little church at Rendlesham, inscribed with verses of shuddering sentimentality.[4]

John was a childless widower at twenty-nine and a handful for his trustees.

When his uncle died, the others chose as his replacement George Norman, a wealthy timber importer and a neighbour when the family had lived near Bromley, probably in the hope that he might be a restraining influence. In fact it only made things worse, for the grieving widower started paying court to Norman's daughter Charlotte and took umbrage when his attentions were discouraged. The Normans had some reason for their attitude, as their son's description of Rendlesham's way of life shows:

'I suppose that he never kept an engagement exactly in his life, nor ever breakfasted or dined at the appointed hours. When he could do exactly as he liked, he would be in bed half the day, and stay up half the night. He was a very free liver in all ways, and owed probably his early death to his want of prudence.'[5]

Norman's last visit (admittedly when Rendlesham was a widower) involved him in 'a week of hard going. The hardest indeed I ever went through. Shooting all day, a late and long dinner with much wine, then billiards and grog for half the night.'[6]

This was the man who might have inherited the bulk of the Thellusson fortune: a Regency peer, hard shooting, hard drinking, extravagant, mildly eccentric; by no means stupid or dull but seemingly without any intellectual or political interests and devoid of the habits of methodical application that business demanded. It is easy to see why his father, mistrusted by *his* father, mistrusted him in turn, but what cannot be known is how far his constitutional laziness was aggravated by being denied responsibility for his own property.

In his search for a second wife John had better success among his Suffolk neighbours. In the village of Leiston, which now cowers in the shadow of the Sizewell reactors and which was already untypical in housing Garrett's farm machinery factory, is a picturesque old abbey, then owned by a retired London merchant, William Tatnall.[7] Tatnall had no son but two daughters, the elder already married to a local landowner;[8] now the younger, Ann Sophia, barely eighteen, became Lady Rendlesham. Tatnall was solidly prosperous but not among the first rank even in the county. John however had already shown his indifference to the marriage market and was content with another wife with a modest fortune.[9]

Furthermore, John had just come into his inheritance at last, but the vultures descended immediately for their pickings. As several Chancery bills reveal, John had been borrowing and not from the most reputable lenders (indeed Emperor Woodford's nemesis Tahourdin crops up in this connection) and, so he claimed, without using a solicitor. Disguised sales, of jewellery, port, shares in the Russell Institution, even a house in Hampstead, were the means of evading the protections for expectant heirs and the usury laws.[10] Inevitably John found himself cheated and dunned, but like most Chancery suits, those against him did not get very far; no doubt actions were compromised and no doubt his credit was dearly bought.[11] These vexations must have increased the attractions of the Continent, now open again to the English, and he was soon off abroad. His daughter Emily was born at Coligny, just outside Geneva, where they may have been visiting his relations,[12] and although a second girl, Sophia Maria Andalusia, was born in England,[13] they were in Florence for Ann's third pregnancy. The wait for a son was causing great anxiety and there was relief and rejoicing when a boy was born on 8th July 1821.[14]

John had bought the house in the Casa Lorenzani, suggesting that he contemplated regular visits if not permanent residence, and one happy event was closely followed by another, the wedding of his sister Caroline and Charles Boulton at the English ambassador's house.[15] With the birth of Charles Thellusson's son back in England a few months afterwards, all seemed to be going well, but John's baby, Frederick Adolphus, first became ill with teething, then developed whooping cough which quickly proved fatal. The family coachman kept vigil over the tiny body for two nights before it was taken for burial in the English cemetery at Leghorn, resting among the forlorn company of Britons who had gone south in a vain hope of fighting off consumption.[16] Though George Warde Norman (roaming France and Italy in a desperate search for distractions from his own mental disturbance) found the Rendleshams' mode of living little changed- his host still abed at noon- the couple were distracted by their loss and before long they returned to England to live quietly at Rendlesham.[17]

They had no more children and not much money either. Only the east wing of the big house was occupied[18] and the distribution of John's father's estate caused family tensions. Two of his brothers were dead by then, first George in battle and then Edmund at sea. A midshipman on H.M.S.*Tiber*, he and two companions had gone ashore on a blustery March day in 1818 to see the great tragedian Edmund Kean perform in Portsmouth and returning in a wherry they were overwhelmed by a large wave just as they reached the mouth of the harbour; all three, along with the boatman and his boy, were drowned.[19] This left the twins, who came of age in 1819, Arthur, two years younger, and Caroline. All were understandably impatient for their portions, but the trustees had found the estate a difficult one to handle. First there was the appeal against the Chancellor's decree in the matter of Rendlesham's duty to elect between the benefits of his father's will and the post-testamentary land purchases, the failure of which depleted the estate.[20] Then they had to repay the £50,000 loan from the trustees of Peter's will, with accrued interest, and to restore some items of Ann's property from Plaistow.[21] The general report in *Thellusson v. Woodford* was delayed until 1819, partly because the deaths of George Woodford and Charles hindered the unscrambling of the complex intertwined accounts of the various partnerships.[22]

Rendlesham had been counting on a handsome credit balance but in the end, when bad debts had been written off and a fund set aside to meet obligations which might yet materialise, the later partnerships were found to be unable to meet what was due to the earlier, and Rendlesham's estate netted less than £5,000.[23] The upshot was that Rendlesham's lavish legacies, which even on a sanguine calculation must have come close to exhausting his personal property, comfortably exceeded what the trustees had at their disposal.[24] In this situation, which is common enough, the law sensibly directs that all the legacies abate in proportion unless the testator has clearly indicated an order of priorities.[25] It was equally firmly established, though here the reasoning is much more technical, that recourse might not be had to real property to make good deficiencies in personalty, so that except for his own legacy of £2,000, John did not stand to suffer.[26] Not surprisingly, the disappointed legatees were keen to scrutinise the accounts closely and questioned various charges for the children's maintenance, argued over interest payable on legacies and agitated other doubtful points. Eliza Hodges and her husband began a suit for payment of George's legacy (made over to her in his will[27]) and now a joint approach from John's siblings raised the spectre of yet more litigation, which this time would not be financed by the great accumulation. John, although 'backed in my claims, by the opinion of the cleverest lawyers of the day'[28] was conciliatory and a settlement was knocked together which gave the legatees about 70% of their claims.[29]

This episode may suggest a marked lack of family harmony but John's notorious lack of business sense makes the suspicions understandable and, Caroline possibly excepted, they were none of them in easy circumstances. William had taken holy orders after Cambridge and in 1825 was given the trust's living at Aldenham; his twin Frederick was a soldier on half- pay, but there were few prospects in the peacetime army; Arthur, just down from Brasenose, had no occupation at all.[30]

Despite the income from the Rendlesham estates and the receivership of the trust's Suffolk estates,[31] John was perennially hard up and it was well for his wife that her father's death in 1826 left her with independent means,[32] for John had ruefully acknowledged in his will that he was unlikely to have property worth disposing of;[33] when his obituarist described him as ' a man of simple tastes, averse to ostentation, and living in the bosom of his family'[34], he might have added that the simple tastes were to some extent forced upon him.

Prosperity is relative of course and the Rendleshams, even in their reduced state, lived in comfort in surroundings of some splendour, the first baron having created a 'princely residence' in full- blown Gothick style, a facade of 180 feet flanked by hothouses at either end and principal rooms of impressive dimensions.[35] The house was fit for a great magnate but John could not afford to be one and took himself off again, to Paris this time.

Rendlesham Hall lacked just one thing- fire insurance. As the last of the handful of servants was preparing to go to bed on 5th February 1830, she noticed a light in the conservatory. Soon the great bell was clanging urgently, but when the fire engine from Wickham Market arrived it could not raise a head of water. It probably made no difference, for it was soon apparent that the house was doomed and onlookers turned to salvaging the contents. They did quite well, rescuing plate, deeds, books and prints, saving the orange and lemon trees and protecting most of the outbuildings. They had to work fast, for within two hours of the alarm the roof caved in, the bell itself melted and flames shot upwards in great columns. When day broke Rendlesham Hall was a smoking shell.[36]

In an age when fire was a constant hazard and insurance readily available at a reasonable price, John's lapse was inexcusably foolish. Now, even if he wished to come home, he could not afford to rebuild the mansion.[37] Having nothing to return to except the reproaches of his brother William (now his heir), he stayed in Paris, his constitution undermined by loose living, and died at Auteuil on 3rd July 1832.[38] Like his father and uncles, he was only in his mid-forties. His body was brought home for interment at Rendlesham, the coffin carried by sixteen poor servants as he had directed.[39] His widow never remarried, living in town, at her house in Grafton Street, until her death in 1856.[40] Only thirty-five years had elapsed since the great trust had come into being and with John's death six of the nine candles had already been snuffed out, leaving only the twins and their cousin Charles of the nine lives.

William, the elder twin and third Lord Rendlesham, seems to have been a rather colourless man, a problem even for his obituarists.[41] As well as being rector of Aldenham he was a magistrate, one of those `squarsons' so detested by radicals, but made little mark on church or state.[42] His marriage was thoroughly conventional, his wife, Lucy Pratt, being the daughter of a Norfolk squire.[43] There had been Pratts in Norfolk since Henry VIII's time and this branch had their home at Ryston with an outlying estate in Suffolk. Lucy was one of ten children and to judge from the marriages made by the others, a peer, even a rather impecunious one, was something of a catch.[44] She brought him £7,500,[45] but after seven years of marriage there was still no heir; indeed since the next generation was represented only by Arthur's seven year old son, Arthur may have begun to dream of succeeding to the title himself.

Although William was comparatively poor, he soon abandoned his original intention of remaining in the Aldenham living until he had saved enough to rebuild the Hall.[46] He spent at least some of his time in the best Parisian society,[47] but was at Rendlesham in September 1839, probably for some shooting, when he had an apoplexy which proved fatal.[48] He was forty-one and childless. The modest property he left was to be divided between his brothers and sister after his wife's death, she having £4,000 outright and the rest for life. He was buried, as he sought, in the family vault.[49]

This left a second dowager for the estate to sustain, a burden which some families found crippling.[50] Luckily Lucy's jointure was only £375 p.a., and in the event it had to be paid for little over a year, ceasing when she remarried with Stewart Marjoribanks, MP for Hythe,[51] a wealthy shipowner who had been a neighbour of theirs in Hertfordshire. He was elderly and there were no children.[52] Most of their time was spent in his constituency, at the newly developed resort of Folkestone, but Lucy died at Bushey Grove, not far from Aldenham, in 1854.[53]

And so, unexpectedly, Frederick inherited the title. Because of a speech defect he had been educated at home, was content to remain on the army's half-pay list and had lived mostly abroad in the house John had bought in Florence.[54] He showed no impatience to be married and may have done so at last only when it seemed likely that William would have no heir. His wife, Eliza Charlotte Duff, was a thirty-two year old widow with several young children.[55] Daughter of a big London banker, Sir George Beeston Prescott, bart.,[56] she had married the only son of General Sir James Duff, whose death left her comfortably off.[57] The wedding, in September 1838, was at fashionable St.George's, Hanover Square and a daughter, Ann Blanche, was born shortly before Frederick inherited the title.[58]

When Eliza became pregnant again they went south for the winter, and in the same Florence house where John's son and heir had passed his brief existence, Eliza bore a boy, Frederick William Brook, heir to the barony and to half the fortune.

Happily history did not repeat itself, but although the child lived his mother did not long survive their return to England, passing away on the last day of 1840.[59]

Frederick surprised everyone. Nothing in his upbringing or adult life had prepared him for the part of country landowner and his speech impediment and poor health were serious handicaps. Nevertheless, if John had been the epitome of the Regency peer, Frederick became the model of a Victorian squire, sober, responsible and hard-working. It was symptomatic of the new regime at Rendlesham that he restored the family's links with George Warde Norman, now a leading man in the Bank of England and a weighty authority on currency questions. Norman came for the shooting, but if there were all night sessions at Rendlesham now they were more likely to feature serious talk on the day's big issues than grog and billiards.[60]

What is more, Frederick entered the House of Commons, where no Thellusson had sat for thirty-five years. When one of the Conservative members for East Suffolk died early in 1843, he was persuaded to stand and won a sharp contest with the Liberal R.S. Adair by 2,952 votes to 1,818. As the number of votes suggests, this was not one of those snug boroughs his father's generation preferred but a county seat, much more prestigious, but (despite the Reform Act) expensive too.[61]

In the House, Frederick made occasional speeches despite his handicap and was anything but lobby fodder. Indeed for Conservatives there were hard choices to be made as Peel led his party in a direction which affronted their most deeply cherished ideas and prejudices. Peel's earlier betrayal over Roman Catholic emancipation had not been forgotten and his disregard for Anglican susceptibilities surfaced again in his support for proposals to increase the endowment of the Maynooth seminary. But of much deeper concern to landowners was their justified suspicion that he was willing to jettison the cornerstone of agricultural protection, the Corn Laws.[62]

Peel had become a convinced free trader long before the Irish famine forced his hand, but he could not convert the majority of his party. The Suffolk electorate was staunchly protectionist and Rendlesham shared their convictions, opposing the repeal that Peel carried only with Whig support and taking part in the retribution exacted under the leadership of that improbable pair, Lord George Bentinck and Benjamin Disraeli. In the election of 1847 he was returned unopposed in tandem with a local landowner, Sir Edward Gooch, and he continued to sit and vote with the Conservatives until his death.[63]

Protectionists were not all obscurantists or traditionalists, and Rendlesham, like many others, was a keen promoter of improvements in farming. Ever ready to subscribe to societies for the encouragement of scientific farming, he was equally enthusiastic about measures to promote habits of industry and thrift among the labouring poor,[64] and if some of these projects are tainted with class interest, the same can scarcely be said of his involvement in the unrewarding and laborious affairs of the county lunatic asylum. The pauper lunatics had no votes, paid no rents and, Lord Shaftesbury and a few others apart, attracted little interest among the higher orders. Until Sir George Onisophorus Paul's Act of 1808, they had been left to the mercies of private asylums and a few charitable institutions which were not much better and sometimes (like the infamous Bedlam) worse.[65] Paul's Act was permissive, empowering counties to levy a rate to support an asylum, and though Suffolk's was not among the first, it soon became one of the biggest.[66] Abuses abounded in the asylums and though Shaftesbury's labours brought forth Acts of 1842 and 1845, giving the Lunacy Commissioners a supervisory role, local notables still had an important part to play. Rendlesham gave unstintingly of his time and put to good use his 'remarkable talent for arithmetical calculations', especially in an inquiry which was mounted near the end of his life.[67]

In fact there is a good deal to admire in the fourth baron. He was one of the earliest subscribers to the British Archaeological Association,[68] perhaps stimulated by his residence in Italy. His invariable courtesy towards those of opposite views won general approval and it is pleasing to find him calling his step-daughter simply 'my daughter Louisa'.[69] But his health remained poor and he had just one son to continue the line. Moreover because of the existence of a rival claimant, Frederick's brother Arthur, that one young life, if it lasted long enough, threatened to create an unpleasant family quarrel when the suit finally ended.

Arthur's hopes of the title had been blighted by the birth of Frederick's heir and he seems to have become a rather disagreeable man. He never took up a profession and could afford a leisured existence because he married a wealthy wife.[70] Caroline Anna Maria Codrington came from another family which had been sundered by a disinheritance, perpetrated by the second baronet on his son and heir. The penniless heir, deprived of lands but not the title, embarked on an adventurous, rather *louche*, life in France while the favourite nephew, Christopher, Caroline's father, who had supplanted him, lorded it at Dodington. When the disgraced baronet produced a son, Christopher disputed its legitimacy, claiming the title himself and refusing to climb down even when the verdict went against him. For sixty years there were two baronets, one with a recognised title but no money, the other rich and respectable but with an indefensible claim.[71] Marrying the bogus baronet's daughter only heightened Arthur's ambitions and it enabled him to give his own son, Arthur John Bethell, an education befitting those aspirations.[72]

2. Peter's Daughters

Old Peter Thellusson's daughters outlived his sons by more than twenty years. With their marriage settlements made and their portions handed over to their trustees,[73] it might be thought that they at least would stay out of Chancery, but it drew Thellussons irresistibly. The bone of contention this time was a deduction of £1,771 5s from the £12,000 they were each to have under the will. The deduction, representing £1,000 East India stock Peter had put into their names shortly after the will was drawn, had been approved by the Master and not until 1818 did the daughters petition for the balance (with accrued dividends) on the ground that the deductions were improper.

They sought to justify this stale claim by the discovery of an unexecuted codicil among the papers of the solicitor, Townley Ward, who had drawn the will.[74]

Nothing was ever final in Chancery and the daughters' declaration that their receipts for the money had not been intended to preclude further claims was scarcely even contested. The only question was whether their claim to the unpaid sums was persuasive. The basis for the deduction was the maxim that 'equity leans against double portions'; that is, a father is presumed to intend to treat all his children alike in the matter of financial provision. One application of this presumption is known as ademption, whereby a legacy is diminished or replaced by a lifetime gift made after the execution of the will,[75] and by Eldon's day it was firmly embedded in the law, though Thurlow for one regretted that it had gained acceptance.[76] To claim both legacy and gift, the donee must demonstrate that the donor did indeed intend a double portion, relying either on the terms of the donations themselves or extrinsic evidence;[77] even mere 'gossipy conversation' was admissible,[78] the judge deciding what weight it ought to bear, but given the highly unsatisfactory means of obtaining and recording evidence in Chancery, Thurlow's unease had some justification.[79]

In finding against the daughters Master Cox had leaned heavily on entries in a ledger kept by their father which plainly described each transfer as 'to be accounted as part of what I bequeath to her by my will',[80] and when their exceptions were heard by the Vice-Chancellor he rejected their attempt to exclude the ledger from evidence.[81] Two arguments were advanced on the daughters' behalf; first, that the outright gift of stock was not *ejusdem generis* [of the same nature] with the legacies, which were given on conditions and subject to being settled in case of marriage; second, that as the codicil explicitly ordered the advances to be deducted from the legacies, the fact that Peter had declined to execute it indicated that he had changed his mind.[82]

Such arguments might have troubled the cunctative Eldon but they made no impression on the impetuous Leach:[83] indeed, the second rather undermined the first, for since Townley Ward's books explained the non-execution of the codicil as occasioned by the wish to include Thellusson's impending purchase of Amotherby, the terms of the codicil actually reinforced the evidence of the ledger. In the light of

325

this actual evidence, the otherwise plausible argument from the divergent nature of the gifts could hardly be sustained. Though Maddock found it worth reporting, the case is of little importance in the development of legal doctrine and it is suggestive of the flimsiness of the daughters' case that they did not trouble to appeal, even though Leach's judgments were notoriously hasty. What it does offer is a tantalising glimpse of the lost ledger, with its `accounts of his pecuniary transactions in the way of loans, purchases and sales of stock, discount, yearly profits and loss, Dr. and Cr. account with sundry persons, a particular of the payments for his house expenses, and a general statement of his property'.[84]

Even a little money would have been welcome to Anne and her husband William, with twelve children rapidly approaching the ages when they must find careers or husbands. William had left the navy by now and was impatient to play the country squire, but his position was delicate, for while Windham's widow lived she had the right to occupy Felbrigg and though preferring the more sociable atmosphere of Bath, she was understandably touchy over her nephew's unconcealed eagerness to set about improving the old house.[85] By the time she died,[86] William (now Windham by royal licence[87]) found his income would not stretch to the ambitious schemes he had laid with his architect Donthorn, a disciple of Wyatville. It was probably as well, for whatever their architectural merits, the workmanship of the more modest alterations that were carried out proved very shoddy.[88]

One by one the brood left their spacious nest, improving William's finances to a point where he felt able to accept the challenge of contesting Sudbury at the general election of 1831.[89] Even at the crisis of the Reform Bill, an election in this borough was just another opportunity for the electors to demonstrate their renowned venality, before long found so outrageous that Parliament disfranchised them altogether. Sudbury might have served as a model for Eatanswill, and although Windham, toughened by years at sea and blooded in the Norwich elections of the 'nineties, was well up to the rough and tumble, it soon became clear that the reforming position he took was anathema to the town and he withdrew from the contest.[90] Within eighteen months he was dead, and since his widow was already provided for he left his goods to his eldest son, William Howe, on whom Felbrigg was already entailed.[91]

Like the previous Mrs. Windham, Anne sought the comforts of a genteel watering place, in her case Leamington Spa, and lived another sixteen years, leaving her property carefully distributed among the children most in need.[92] The new owner of Felbrigg farmed enthusiastically after the best Holkham models and became MP for East Norfolk, though he made no mark and was perhaps none too disappointed when the resurgent Tories ousted him in 1835. He had no pretensions to refinement or intellectual distinction and neither his exiguous political services nor his marriage connection with the Herveys of Ickworth gave enough substance to his optimistic claim to a peerage.[93] In view of what was to follow that was all to the good.

William Howe Windham had just one son, but that one (William Frederick) was more trouble than all his grandfather's dozen children put together. The eccentric Hervey blood[94] mingled with the Lukins'- which itself produced notably choleric men like William Howe and his brother Charles- in a child who combined animal high spirits, an unruly temper and a feeble intellect in a repellent mixture.

Eton could beat no sense into him, nor could a sorry succession of tutors insinuate any. If ever an estate needed a protective trust it was this, but even the entail had been barred, leaving the master of Felbrigg free to do as he pleased.[95] What 'Mad Windham' liked best was playing with trains- real trains- but it was all too predictable that once he grew to manhood he would fall easy prey to the first unscrupulous woman to captivate him. So it proved: he found himself married to a high class prostitute, Agnes Willoughby, and the already mortgaged estate was mercilessly plundered by this harpy and her unsavoury companions while the titular owner induged his caprices unrestrained and unguided.[96] There could be only one roadblock on the road to ruin- a commission of lunacy- and the return of William's uncle Charles from India precipitated it.

Charles Ash Windham had once been a popular hero, 'Redan' Windham of the Crimea; but today's hero is tomorrow's scapegoat and his failure to hold Cawnpore during the Indian Mutiny, not openly censured but generally known to be regarded as `disappointing', blighted his prospects and marred his reputation.[97] Now he was at the centre of a vivid, titillating drama which played out a Victorian nightmare, the dread of incarceration in a madhouse. [98] William's advisers adroitly portrayed Charles as the wicked uncle and after the longest ever inquisition `Mad Windham' was declared sane.

The jury was probably right. He was no danger to himself or others, rational enough when it suited him, but utterly irresponsible. In the short life that remained to him he lost the rest of his fortune, sold Felbrigg to a man who had made his pile supplying the army in the Crimea and became the best born stage coach driver in England.[99] Plenty of Windhams remained to carry on the name and restore the family pride, but they never returned to Felbrigg.[100]

Augusta Thellusson's descendants had no such scandals, living rather in blameless respectability. After de Crespigny's early death she remained a widow until past fifty, then, with her own daughter married, she took as her second husband Sir Joseph Whately, a dozen years her senior.[101] Not much is known of Whately, a Somerset man, a modest benefactor of his old college and, from 1831 a K.C.H. and Groom of the Bedchamber.[102] He had a house near Egham, where they lived, and some property in Bristol, but no close relatives and when he died Augusta shared his estate with two distant relations.[103] Adding this to her marriage settlement and the annuities granted for the joint lives of the sisters, of whom she was the last survivor, Augusta became quite prosperous. She died in 1853, the last of her generation of Thellussons.[104]

She will have been gratified that her daughter, also Augusta, was securely placed in good society. Like her mother she married twice, each time with a Worcestershire family. Her first husband, Colonel Thomas Henry Hastings Davies, was given his third name in honour of the great Warren Hastings, a bosom friend of his father, Advocate- General to the E.I.C., who left Thomas heir to the sort of fortune most of Hastings' friends made in India.[105] Thomas saw action in the peninsula, was with the Foot Guards at Waterloo and then abandoned soldiering for politics, spending £12,000 to secure his seat in Abraham Robarts' old constituency of Worcester. Despite some expensive contests he held it for twenty-three years apart from a brief hiatus between 1835 and 1837, and as an enthusiastic seconder of Joseph Hume's unending proposals for economies in government spending, earned the nickname 'Smollett', after the continuator of the other Hume's famous *History*.[106] While canvassing in 1834 he was thrown from his carriage and paralysis set in, leaving Augusta with an invalid on her hands for some years before his death.[107]

Davies gave her a life interest in his ample real estate[108] and she soon married a neighbour, Sir John Somerset Pakington, middle- aged himself and a rising politician. Like William Lukin, Pakington had had the luck to be adopted by a childless man to take his name and his lands; in his case it was an uncle, who died in 1830 leaving a will described as 'in some respects like Mr. Thellusson's', by which he sought to make his lands descend to the eldest son of his nephew's four year old son. This clearly infringed the rule against perpetuities, so the nephew and the widow shared the estate under intestacy rules.[109]

Pakington, formerly Russell, entered Parliament after the Reform Act and eventually found a constituency, Droitwich, prepared to return him at election after election for thirty-seven years. He joined the protectionists in 1846, certainly the best avenue to office for a man of mediocre talents, and became Secretary for War and Colonies in Lord Derby's 'Who? Who?' administration of 1852. He was First Lord of the Admiralty in the equally transient ministry of 1859, had the same posts in the 1860s (though his interests lay more in education), and when the Droitwich electors finally tired of him in 1874 he was raised to the peerage as Baron Hampton of Lovett.[110] He was an uxorious man, with a son by each of his first two wives, and he and Augusta had a long and happy union. He died in 1880 and she went on to the great age of ninety-one, outliving Peter's other grandchildren as her mother had outlived his children, but she had no descendants.[111]

3. George's Descendants

George Woodford Thellusson's death in 1811 threatened to complicate further the dispute about the meaning of the `eldest male lineal descendants', for he had only daughters and while females were clearly excluded, it was certainly arguable that a male descended through females qualified and equally clear that his claim would not be admitted by the other branches, represented by persons claiming through males. This possibility made Marianne and Georgiana important figures in the family. However Marianne, the elder by four years and already of marriageable age when her father died, confounded expectations by remaining a spinster, living with her mother in the house at Otterspool which they rented after Wall Hall was sold.[112] The widow died there in 1844 and Marianne lived alone for the remaining eight years of her life, but though single, she was not solitary and evidently enjoyed the company of her sister's growing family, to whom she gave generous legacies.[113]

Any hopes that George's line would die out completely were shortlived, however, since Georgiana not only had a son but took a solicitor as her husband, making contention all the more likely. Fifty years earlier, such an alliance would have been a social disgrace, and among the 4,000 attorneys and solicitors up and down the land were still many with no claims to respectability at all and many others whose pretensions would be scorned by society. It was still almost a reflex among writers to preface `attorney' with the adjective `pettifogging' and not only the bar but judges like Thurlow and Kenyon went out of their way to disparage the junior branch at every opportunity. But neither snubs from bench and bar nor the contamination of low and unscrupulous fellow practitioners could keep down the more prosperous solicitors.[114] In country towns where they were indispensable as moneylenders and investment middlemen as well as conveyancers and drafters of wills and settlements they were more readily accepted than in London, but even there the likes of Dickens' Mr.Tulkinghorn, practising in the sedate atmosphere of Chancery rather than the hurly burly of Westminster Hall, and making a very good thing of it too, were inexorably

330

raising themselves in the social scale. Members of the Association of Gentlemen Practisers, that curious mixture of dining club, lobby and proto-professional organisation, were the cream of metropolitan solicitors, certainly fit to mix in good society and not to be dismissed out of hand as husbands.[115]

Henry Hoyle Oddie was such a man, partner with John Forster in a leading firm with its office in Carey Street.[116] They had acted for G.W. Thellusson for a good many years[117] and Oddie's son and namesake had by now joined the firm. As the only son, Henry Hoyle II could obviously expect a good inheritance. At thirty- four he was about twice Georgiana's age, but late marriage for middle- class men was a growing trend and so wide an age gap was not uncommon.[118] Georgiana was comparatively poor, but as well as any personal attractions she may have had, she might be the key to an immense fortune for her son.   They married in February 1813 and a daughter was soon followed by a son, Henry Hoyle III.[119] His prospects were veiled in obscurity while the `lives' lasted, which might be seven years or seventy. In 1820, however, the chance came to force the Chancellor into giving a judgment on the leading issue which, if not actually determining the eventual outcome, would provide the winners with a most potent argument. The perpetual curate of Butley resigned[120] and this being one of the five livings whose advowson, or right of presentation, belonged to the trust, it was for the trustees to choose a successor in accordance with the terms of Peter's will.[121]

Thellusson had taken care to insert express provisions for vacancies in the advowsons, directing that they be filled in rotation by each son or his eldest male lineal descendant `if he be capable by law of making such nomination, when the church becomes vacant', otherwise passing to the next in rotation. Rotation was by seniority and the most recent vacancy, the fourth, had been uncontentiously filled by the second Baron Rendlesham.[122] The next, therefore, belonged to G.W. Thellusson's eldest male lineal descendant (if he had one), and Henry Hoyle Oddie III was the only person with any claim to answer that description. Since the same phrase described the persons entitled to the accumulation itself, his claim could not be admitted without

331

weakening resistance to a subsequent claim to a share in the residue and so it fell out that this trivial dispute had to be fought out as though the fortune itself were stake. No- one knew the real stakes better than the Chancellor, whose dismay at the momentousness of his decision is almost comical. He practically insisted that his decision be taken to the Lords, answering the obvious objection that `while the Chancellor is Speaker, [it] is mere form' with the doubtful comfort that `in whatever way you may think proper to reconsider this, if you think I am wrong, it will create no difficulty, as I shall look at the question as if I had not heard a single word on this will'.[123] He longed to wriggle out of the decision by holding that Oddie's infancy disabled him from nominating or, failing that, that the terms of the will precluded an infant from doing so, but there was authoritative precedent against the former and only a strained construction could support the latter: there was no escape that way.[124]

Eldon therefore had to interpret the key phrases in the will. While having `a strong inclination to think that more might have been made of the argument of uncertainty than had antecedently been made of it'[125] he felt bound by the judges' views in *Thellusson v. Woodford*, that they did have a clear meaning and when obliged to tease it out, he almost lapsed into a self-parody of the `cunctative habit' in this striking passage:

`Now if Mr. Justice Buller was of opinion that there was no difficulty in this construction; if Lord Alvanley was of opinion there was no difficulty; if Lord Loughborough was of opinion there was no difficulty, in every way in which he could put the case to himself, I certainly have the more to lament, that it falls to my lot to decide; because, though I have formed an opinion upon it, and must act on my opinion, I cannot say this is not a case of considerable difficulty'.[126]

Essentially it came to this: should the phrase `eldest male lineal descendant' be construed as `the eldest male who is a lineal descendant', or `the eldest male who is descended exclusively through males'? In other words, should `male lineal' be treated as hyphenated to form a single phrase, or as two discrete adjectives? The latter construction made `lineal' redundant and Eldon took it to be `one rule in the

332

construction of a will, that you are not to impute to a testator, unless the context requires it, that he uses additional words except to some additional purpose'.[127] That Thellusson had used the phrase over and over again suggested that it was indeed meant to carry some special meaning, which must be the one contended for by the trustees. Against that construction was the fact that in choosing his measuring lives the testator had included any issue- unrestricted by sex- of one of the sons born in his lifetime, creating the possibility (unrealised as it happened) that the accumulation might continue during the lifetime of a female even after it had become clear that there would be no male claimant tracing descent solely through males[128]. Unless descent through females was permissible, the accumulation would then be running to no other purpose than to pile up money for the relief of the national debt, an implausible intention.[129]

The other view, however, is even more implausible. Suppose in George Woodford's case that he had had a son, his third child, whom we will call George for convenience, and suppose further that his children married and had sons in this order: (1) Marianne, (2) Georgiana, (3) George, (4) Marianne, (5) Georgiana, (6) George; according to the will, the eldest male, Marianne's first son, takes an estate tail and similar estates are limited to the second, third, fourth etc. male lineal descendant then living, so that those of the testator's great- grandsons whose descent is derived through males rank respectively third and sixth in the pecking order. Alternatively, suppose Marianne to have a son while her father still has none, but that he subsequently fathers one: does it fulfil the testator's intentions that the great- grandson precedes his grandson? The sort of conveyance which might become necessary was one which 'neither Mr. Butler, nor Mr. Sugden, nor Mr. Preston nor any conveyancer ever saw';[130] whatever Thellusson's peculiarities, he was unlikely to have wanted something so arbitrary.[131]

In the end, therefore, on a balance of improbabilities, the Chancellor endorsed the view favoured by his predecessor, granting however an injunction against any presentation before an appeal had been heard in the Lords.[132] In fact they faced a cross-appeal too, for Eldon can hardly have been surprised that Rendlesham's lawyers latched onto what was virtually an invitation to revive the argument upon uncertainty. As usual, there was a lengthy delay, but the judges, in an opinion given by Baron Alexander, were emphatic that there was no uncertainty and that Eldon's tentative view of the meaning of the contentious phrase was correct; whatever lingering doubts Eldon entertained, he could hardly press them in the face of that opinion and four years after the question was started it was laid to rest, the Oddies having to resign themselves to being excluded from any share in the fortune.[133]

When not in their town house in Portland Place, Georgiana and her husband lived in a small manor house near Hemel Hempstead,[134] but their household rapidly outgrew it and with Henry's father dead, they were able to afford something bigger and grander.[135] They found it in Colney House, a dignified classical mansion in 150 acres of parkland not far from St. Albans, rebuilt by a nabob fifty years earlier and imposing enough to feature in the drawing room albums of the day.[136] Colney became home to the Oddies and at least a dozen children, most of them girls, who were in due course bestowed on a conventional mixture of lawyers, clergymen and minor gentry.[137]

When Henry Hoyle II died in 1847 his widow and children placed a stained glass window in Shenley church *in memoriam*.[138] His eldest son, Henry Hoyle III, showed no enthusiasm for the law, so the family connection with the firm of Oddie and Lumley (as it had latterly become) was severed, though a younger son and his son did perpetuate the legal tradition.[139] The heir, who had all his father's lands (subject to Georgiana's right to live at Colney rent free), became a prosperous wine merchant with a country house in Sussex,[140] while the younger children had portions of £10,000 in the Funds to ensure them a comfortably genteel existence.[141] Though Georgiana died in 1866 and Henry Hoyle III three years after, some traces of the Thellusson connection remained; Edward Oddie was tenant of Piggott's Manor; the husband of one of Georgiana's daughters was incumbent of Aldenham, presented by Lord Rendlesham; and one of George Oddie's sons was hopefully baptised Arthur

Thellusson Oddie. But the Oddies went gently down in the world, Colney was sold in 1871 and soon they have to be traced in *Crockford* and local directories rather than *Burke* and its imitators, still gentlemen but no longer gentry.[142]

4. Charles and his Family

Charles Thellusson left his infant children (three boys and a girl, Adeline Maria) in John Mansel's care. They were left badly provided for and had to look to their mother's family for assistance. Their maternal grandfather left £8,000 to be invested for them[143] and through the influence of their uncle Abraham Wildey Robarts two boys were found places in India, where Alexander, an assistant magistrate in Calcutta, soon succumbed to climate and disease.[144] Thomas, who was in the Bengal army, married the daughter of an Indian judge and took his passage home before the same fate could befall him.[145]

Their elder brother Charles left Cambridge without a degree and is next heard of getting married to Mary Grant in Paris.[146] Since her elder brother had been obliged to elope with *his* bride, the Grants were presumably not a rich family. Mary's father was a Scotsman who had married into minor Norfolk gentry called Foster,[147] and as little money could be expected from her parents, the young couple would need to make prudence their watchword.

Unfortunately that word was not in Charles's vocabulary. He inherited from his father both a fondness for country sports and a friendship with George Osbaldeston, the sportsman *par excellence*. 'The Squire', as Osbaldeston was universally known, was a dangerous man to know if you had a weak character and a short purse, for if his passion was sport in all its forms, his vice was extravagance. He brought to sport the single-minded, all absorbing appetite that men like Peter Thellusson gave to business. He played cricket with invigorating and impetuous boldness until, overreaching himself at single-wicket, he flew into a rage, scratched his name from the M.C.C. books and forsook Lords for good. But cricket had never been more than a sideshow:

hunting, riding and shooting were the real sports, for which his appetite was inexhaustible and which made him legendary as the embodiment of John Bull's virile philistinism.[148] Others who rivalled his fame were more prudent, like Edward Hayward Budd, who gave up his post in the War Office when it interfered with his sporting life[149], or very wealthy, like Thomas Assheton Smith.[150]

Charles Thellusson was neither prudent nor wealthy. His courage was equal to the dangers he courted with the Squire[151] but his purse was unequal to the expense. For they betted incessantly. They were not gamblers like the habitués of White's and Brooks', but found racing, cricket and shooting unthinkable without a stake. Only hunting was free of the gaming mentality and that was costly enough without. The Squire had his first pack of hounds while an undergraduate,[152] was M.F.H. with one pack after another for thirty-five years and rapidly got through a large inheritance, summing up his career thus:`bred up in luxury and extravagance from the age of six years with the prospect of large estates to come into my possession at twenty-one, I became reckless and thoughtless of the future, and trusted to men who proved untrustworthy. Mine has been a life of plunder; no man has been so persecuted, robbed and cheated, by stewards and gentlemen who professed to be friends, by trainers, jockeys and betting men...'[153] Osbaldeston moved in that murky milieu so brilliantly described by Surtees,[154] where a man would be mercilessly `plucked' unless he had sharp wits and shrewd judgment. Thellusson had neither, and also had a family to provide for, Charles Sabine Augustus being followed by Alexander Dalton(1824), Frederick George(1825), Seymour Stuart(1827) and Ernest(1830).[155] These boys were potential heirs to a fortune, but their father was so straitened that he could not afford them the education to fit them for it. Lord Chancellors were usually sympathetic to petitioners in this plight but it was a major interference with testamentary freedom and property rights to decree that property which belonged only contingently to a beneficiary could be appropriated to his use. If all those who stood to lose could be ascertained and were prepared to consent it might be done, but more often an infant or unborn beneficiary was an obstacle and in the Thellusson case the

336

range of potential beneficiaries was too wide, and the direction to accumulate too positive, for an application to have much chance.

Only Parliament could vary a trust, through a private act, a procedure which was `cheap, expeditious and very effective',[156] a glaring contrast to Chancery in fact. Many families made use of estate acts, which supplied all manner of deficiencies in the original settlement, for instance enabling land to be sold to meet charges, or powers to be exercised when the life tenant was incapable.[157] The procedure was to petition the Lords, who referred it to a couple of judges, the promoters furnishing them with a draft report in the bill's favour. The judges usually did approve, making only verbal changes to the draft, and although Parliament gave it careful scrutiny and frequently made changes, it seldom rejected a bill.

In 1827 a petition was duly presented on behalf of the infant Charles, seeking to empower the court from time to time to make payments out of the fund for the boys' maintenance, education or support. It was referred to two judges and nothing more was heard of it that session. Next session it was presented again and this time Bayley and Littledale did report, but drew attention to the fact that Peter had clearly not intended maintenance out of the fund and that Charles Sabine's interest was precarious, `leaving it to your Lordships' consideration and wisdom whether the same should be passed into law'.[158] Leave was given to bring in a bill and the draft is among the House of Lords manuscripts, but the *Journal* falls silent and no further proceedings can be traced.[159]

It is not hard to guess why the bill foundered. To be successful it needed the backing both of the Rendlesham branch and the trustees and Charles was already at odds with the latter over the use of Brodsworth. It was simply a conflict of interests, for Charles wanted to follow his father in having it for his residence, while Flint was not disposed to relinquish the perquisite of a free country house for several months a year. Charles challenged him in court and started promisingly, Hart VC being persuaded to refer to the Master the question whether it would be for the benefit of the trust that Charles should reside there.[160] On appeal there was a full dress hearing before Lord Lyndhurst, the Seal having at last been prised from Eldon's grip, and although three future Chancellors[161] put Charles's argument, that `sons' in the clause dealing with the future of Brodsworth should be read as including grandsons, thirty-three could not have made it persuasive.[162]

Any doubt whether there was genuine ill-feeling between the two men is quelled by the sequel, for Charles forthwith launched a new petition, this time simply aiming to deprive Flint of the fruits of his victory by arguing that just as only the sons could avail themselves of Brodsworth, so it was only the original trustees who were entitled. This was dog in the manger and no more successful than the first claim;[163] Charles considered appealing to the Lords but thought better of it, perhaps being advised that Lyndhurst would be none too pleased to see it again. The attack on Flint did make some impression though, for Lyndhurst's surprise at the scale of the establishment at Brodsworth led him to direct that it be reviewed.[164] The trustees had no problems in getting the tenants to support their opposition to any letting, but economies were ordered which reduced the annual expense from £540 to £387;[165] more importantly, the Chancellor was clearly suspicious that the trust was being run largely for the benefit of the trustees.

While this dispute was going on the absent trustee, Ralph Woodford, was on his way home from Trinidad, his health ruined by the climate.[166] Sadly, he died on the voyage, and being unmarried left most of his possessions to his sister Vicomtesse Rosmordue and her children by her first marriage, to the London banker John Hammet.[167] It was the eldest of these, John Athol Hammet, whom Flint proposed to succeed Woodford and it comes as no surprise that Charles Thellusson put up a rival candidate of his own.[168] This was even less hopeful than the earlier challenge to Disney, since it was made by only one part of the family and Charles obtusely proposed Osbaldeston, perhaps the least suitable trustee who could have been found in good society. Even if it was justifiably suspected that Hammet would be Flint's creature, the challenge was foredoomed.[169]

Meeting Charles in Brighton while he had hopes of getting a free house, some

338

money or a friendly trustee, the Comte de la Garde had found that he was 'vif et épanoui, réfléchit toute la gâité du bonheur et de l'insouciance' [lively and beaming, reflecting all the cheerfulness of good fortune and freedom from care][170] but before long he was forced to adopt the familiar expedient of the embarrassed English gentleman, going abroad to the Low Countries, where living was cheap, old creditors could not follow and new ones might be tapped. There was no want of society- his cousins the Daltons were there already- and if some of it was raffish and shifty, still it was better than a debtors' prison. But whatever Charles gained from his exile it was certainly not solvency, for he noted when beginning his diary for the year 1838: 'I began the year owing £5,200 and £5,100 and £2,600. In all £12,900.'[171] Taking the interest at 5%, it would cost £650 a year just to service the loans and Charles had better things to do with his money than that. The life disclosed in these brief entries is very melancholy, a restless peregrination from one dull town to another, fitful news from home of births, marriages and deaths, occasional visits from friends, relations and lawyers and the sporadic excitements of duels that broke out too readily within a community in which many had things to hide or gloss over. Some men courted challenges and young Charles Sabine was twice close to fighting one of them, Colonel Nightingale.[172]

The three eldest sons all had to be provided for, which meant money had to be borrowed and connections exploited. In particular the Robartses, who had embedded themselves snugly into the City establishment, were targeted and by their means army commissions were bought for the two eldest.[173] Getting their father out from beneath his mountain of debt was another matter though.

Charles awaited the coming of age of his heir with growing impatience. The common law denied remedies to a person seeking to enforce a contract against a minor, and equity spread its protective umbrella wider, keeping a sceptical eye on bargains with expectant heirs (like Charles Sabine) even when they were adults.[174] Lending to such persons, who had no property but only the expectation of receiving it under a will or trust, was a risky business and a specialised market developed, inhabited by venturesome and often unscrupulous lenders. `Post-obit' bonds became common, wherein the borrower needed to repay only the advance unless he came into a specified inheritance, when he must pay a further sum, often very large indeed. Equity would relieve the borrower from honouring such `catching bargains' unless the lender could convince the court that he was receiving only market value and that there was no element of overreaching or unconscionability involved; it was no defence that the young man's father approved the arrangement either, for there were many fathers like Charles, desperate to relieve their own plight.[175]

It is unlikely that Charles Sabine Augustus would have allowed his father to persuade him to anything really disastrous, for he had grown up in a hard school, watching Charles flounder ever more helplessly. Charles owed money all round, but especially to his in-laws and their bank and since Robarts had become a trustee he now had a powerful voice in any of Charles's attempted manoeuvres. He sent Charles to a hard-headed London solicitor, M.A. Reyroux, who was adamant that no money could be raised on the heir's expectations except on `positively ruinous and destructive' terms. Reyroux urged his client, `give up this idea at once for it cannot be accomplished and turn to the other view of the matter as a compromise or any extremity rather than attempt this ruinous plan of anticipation.'[176]

Like so many debtors, Charles was sanguine about his prospects, talked airily of raising £20,000, derided the obstacle presented by his brother Thomas's claims(`Sir Edward Sugden and all the lawyers quite laughed at it and assured me it was perfectly absurd'[177]), was full of optimistic calculations and had even succeeded in borrowing £2,300 more to pay off pressing debts, this sum to be repaid as soon as Charles Sabine came of age. Robarts would not hear of such schemes and through his son handed down a lecture on retrenchment: `in fact, however pinching or inconvenient to you, he says these [expenses] necessarily *must* be limited, as he cannot and will not continue to fuel your expenditure, which at the rate it has hitherto been going on, must involve him and the House in advances which cannot be justified'.[178]

340

Evidently Reyroux managed to come up with something which enabled Charles to return to England without landing himself in a debtors' prison and without jeopardising his son's inheritance. He settled himself rather incongruously in decorous Worthing, in a house ominously called `The Casino', and his diary records a drowsy round of billiards(he usually lost), social calls and drives with ladies of unimpeachable respectability, often the Whitters, one of whom was to marry his son Frederick. His overdraft steadily increased[179] and so did his girth, his enormous bulk putting a painful burden on his legs.[180] Entries relating to the Turf become steadily more prominent, while there is almost nothing in the diaries- admittedly very sketchy ones- about his wife; perhaps they lived apart, certainly they seem to have done little together.[181]

The boys came and went on visits. Alexander had a commission in a highland regiment, Frederick was in India with the Bengal Lancers and Seymour sailed for the West Indies in 1848, leaving Ernest most regularly at home.[182] Charles seldom lacked company, for a well-mannered, courtly gentleman, always available, always obliging, was sure to be in demand in a small seaside resort; all the same there is something rather pathetic about his existence.

Charles's way of life was quite different from his cousin Lord Rendlesham's, but as the trust approached its half century there was a certain symmetry about the family: two male branches, each headed by a man in his late forties in indifferent health, each with a son to inherit, each with a younger brother to contest that inheritance. By now, however, it was painfully clear that the inheritance would fall far short of all predictions.[183]

NOTES

1. William Manning (1763-1835) was the father of Cardinal Manning. His own father founded the great West India house of Manning and Anderdon and William made his fortune in the heyday of the Caribbean trade. Entering Parliament in 1794, he sat (at one time for Evesham with Charles Thellusson) for thirty-six years. His first wife was a sister of the banker Robert Smith, Lord Carrington, and in 1810 he was making £25,000 p.a. In the 1820s his prosperity waned and in 1831 he was bankrupted and ended his life in obscurity: V.L. Oliver, *The History of Antigua* (3 vols., London, 1884-99), vol. III, p.439; W.R. Williams, *The Parliamentary Representatives of the County of Worcestershire* (Hereford, 1897), p.155; E.S. Purcell, *The Life of Cardinal Manning* (2 vols., London, 1895), vol. I, pp.3-8, 71; W. Manning to Mary Sergent, 20 Aug. 1831, Manning Mss, Bodleian Lib. Ms. Eng. Litt. C65/1, f. 402.

2. Samuel Heywood (1753-1828), son of a unitarian banker at Manchester and Liverpool, was at Trinity College, Cambridge before entering the law via the Middle Temple. He became a serjeant in 1794. A staunch adherent of Fox, he was disappointed when no place was found for him under the Talents, and was eventually fobbed off with a Welsh judgeship. For the rest of his life he was Chief Justice on the Carmarthen circuit. His private life was saddened by several bereavements. In 1828 Heywood was stricken with paralysis at Haverfordwest and died a fortnight later. *D.N.B.*, vol. XXVI, p.338; H.W. Woolrych, *Lives of Eminent Serjeants at Law* (2 vols., London, 1869), vol. II, pp.701-33.

3. Son of a Lt.Colonel in the 1st Foot, Samuel Dickens was commissioned in the Royal Artillery in 1779 and acted as C-in-C at Gibraltar. After service with General Abercromby, he fetched up in Malta for the rest of the war. Maria was his second daughter. He was knighted and made a K.C.H.: *Gents. Mag.* 121 (1847), 658.

4. Autobiography of G.W. Norman, Norman Mss KAO U310 F69, f.196; Flaxman Mss, B.L.Add.Mss. 39,791. The verses begin, `ascend in peace, sweet spirit, spotless, blest' and continue in the same vein. Maria had given some plate to the church: *Gents. Mag.* 91 (1821), 91.

5. Autobiography, Norman Mss KAO U310 F69, ff.151-2. Norman's first visit to Rendlesham proved embarrassing, for he shot a keeper in the thigh when aiming at a hare.

6. *Ibid.*

7. None of the London trade directories gives a more exact description, nor does his will (PRO PROB 11/1715, f.405) assist. He lived first in Aldermanbury, then in Bedford Square, and was still in the directories in the late 1820s. He followed a common pattern in removing first to

Cheshunt, in the inner ring of home counties, then further afield.

8. Edward Fuller of Carlton Hall, where one of the Thellusson trustees, Edward Simeon, later lived: A. Page, *A Topographical and Geographical History of Suffolk* (Ipswich, 1847), p.246; A.Suckling, *History and Antiquities of the County of Suffolk* (2 vols., London, 1846-8), vol. II, p.446.

9. The trustees of the marriage settlement held £16,666 13s. 4d. 4% Bank Annuities and £6,430 3 1/4% Long Annuities: Ann Sophia's will, PRO PROB 11/2240, f.787.

10. *Rendlesham v. Pasmore*, PRO C 13/ 1691/15, *v. King*, C 13/1694/43 and *Rendlesham v. Davies*, PRO C13/1740/1.

11. The last entry in the order books is one of 1820 (PRO C 33/674, f.1019) in *Davies*, ordering him to produce the documents. Rendlesham also made use of procedural points to delay actions at common law: *Davis v. Lord Rendlesham* (1817) 7 Taunt. 679.

12. *Gents. Mag.* 87 (1817), 361.

13. *Gents. Mag.* 89 (1819), 86. She was baptised at Leiston: PRO TS 18/1501.

14. *Gents. Mag.* 91 (1821), 175; Norman Mss. KAO U310 F13, f.142.

15. Ain, *Les Thellusson*, p.333.

16. *Gents. Mag.* 92 (1822), 94; Norman Mss KAO U310 F 13, ff.140-2.

17. Norman Mss KAO U 310 F 13, p.142.

18. H. Davy, *Views of the Seats of the Noblemen and Gentlemen of Suffolk* (Southwold, 1827).

19. *Gents. Mag.* 88 (1818), 470.

20. See *supra*, pp. 220-2, and order of 11 Aug. 1813, PRO C 33/602, f.1449.

21. Orders of 23 Jul., 14 Dec. 1813 (PRO C 33/601, f.1055; C 33/607, f.187); 21 Jul. 1815 C 33/618, f.1460); 22 Mar., 14 Jun. 1817 © 33/638, f.631; C 33/639, f.1066). Final accounts between Rendlesham's estate and the trust are detailed in the order of 24 Dec. 1818, C 33/661, f.625.

22. W. Dowding to G.W. Norman, 13 Feb. 1824, Norman Mss KAO U310 C144.

23. *Ibid.*, W. Manning to G. W. Norman, 22 Jul. 1824.

24. Statement of Assets and Claims on the late Lord Rendlesham's Estate, December 1824, Norman Mss KAO U310 B34.

25. *Williams on Wills*, pp. 813-15. The ecclesiastical courts originally had exclusive jurisdiction over legacies but the courts of equity encroached with increasing vigour and were applying abatement rules as early as 1626: Holdsworth, *History of English Law*, vol. V (3rd edn., 1945, repr. London, 1966), pp.318-20.

26. Until 1833 real property was not considered as 'assets' of the deceased in the legal sense and therefore not liable for payment of his debts either. However, if the testator left his residue as

one undifferentiated mass of realty and personalty, recourse might then be had to the realty to make up a shortfall once the personalty was exhausted: *Greville v. Browne* (1859) 7 H.L.C. 689. Rendlesham had not done this, nor given any indication that the general rules were not to apply. The privileged position of realty was finally ended in 1925: E.C.Ryder, The Incidence of General Pecuniary Legacies, *Cambridge Law Journal* 14 (1956), 80-100.

27. W. Dowding to G.W. Norman, 13 Feb. 1824, Norman Mss KAO U310 C144.

28. Rendlesham to `my dear brothers' (copy), 1 Jun. 1825, Norman Mss KAO U310 C119.

29. *Ibid.* See also Norman Mss KAO U310 B34 and PRO IR 26/1299.

30. Cussans, *Hertfordshire*, vol.II, p.243; *Alumni Cantabrigienses, 1752-1900*, vol. VI, p.147; *Complete Peerage*, vol. X, p.765. Frederick was on the half- pay list from 1820, having joined the 12th Lancers as a cornet in 1816.

31. He had been appointed in 1817, with Tatnall and Benbow as sureties: report of 21 Jan. 1817, PRO C 38/1130. His commission did not exceed £500 in most years, but as receipts had to be paid in only annually, he had the interest on outstanding balances.

32. PRO PROB 11/1715, f.465. Tatnall left personalty sworn under £14,000 but gave Rendlesham a legacy of £500: PRO IR 26/1104, f.626.

33. PRO PROB 11/1808, f.719.

34. *Annual Biography and Obituary* 17 (1833), 452. *Cf. Ipswich Journal*, 7 Jul. 1832.

35. Davy, *Seats of Suffolk*, includes an engraving and gives the dimensions of the principal rooms. See also *Ipswich Journal*, 6 Feb. 1830.

36. *Ipswich Journal*, 6 Feb. 1830.

37. The damage was estimated at £100,000: W.A. Copinger, *The Manors of Suffolk* (7 vols., London, 1905-11), vol.IV, p.320.

38. The *Ipswich Journal* (7 Jul. 1832) rather quaintly states that he went to Paris `for the benefit of his health'.

39. *Annual Biography and Obituary* 17 (1833), 452. He named as his particular `dear friends' his brothers and sister, George Barclay, Edward Dawkins, John Benbow and the Fullers: PRO PROB 11/1808, f.719.

40. *Gents. Mag.* 137 (1856), 524. She left considerable property to her daughters.

41. *Ipswich Journal*, 13 Sep. 1839; *Gents. Mag.* 109 (1839), 420.

42. W. Le Hardy and G. Ll. Reckitt (eds.), *Calendar of the Hertfordshire Session Books*, vol.9 (1799-1833), (Hertford, 1939), p. 372; Cussans, *Hertfordshire*, vol. V, pp. 262-70; Langford, *Public Life and the Propertied Englishman*, pp.410-20.

43. *Burke's Dictionary of the Landed Gentry*, vol.II, p.1065.

44. *Ibid.* Her father's will (PRO PROB 11/1895, f.340) shows that by 1838 only three other children

344

were married.

45.   PRO PROB 11/1895, f.340. The settlement is among the Pratt MSS (bundles PRA 620, 621).

46.   W. Manning to G.W. Norman, 6 Aug. 1832, Norman Mss KAO U310 C 183. They thought it would take six or seven years. Nevertheless he had been able greatly to enlarge the vicarage: *Aldenham Parish Registers*, p.340.

47.   Lady Granville to the Duchess of Devonshire, 12 Jun.1837, F.L. Leveson-Gower (ed.), *Letters of Harriet, Countess Granville*, (2 vols., London, 1894), vol. II, p.233. He gave up his living to Edward Benbow in December 1833: Cussans, *Hertfordshire*, vol. V, p.273.

48.   PRO TS 18/1501.

49.   PRO PROB 11/1919, f.712.

50.   See, for example, the £5,000 worth of 'terrible jointures' burdening the Ailesbury estate in the 1880s: Thompson, *English Landed Society*, p.314.

51.   1820-37, 1841-7. He was a Whig 'with very liberal tendencies': G. Wilks, *The Barons of the Cinque Ports and the Parliamentary Representation of Hythe* (Folkestone, 1892), pp.119 ff.

52.   *Ibid.*; *Complete Peerage*, vol.XII (2), p.85, *sub* Tweedmouth of Edington. A brother, Edward, was a partner in Coutts Bank for over seventy years whose son, ennobled in 1881, left gross personalty of over £714,000.

53.   *Gents. Mag.* 134 (1854), 671.

54.   He did keep a London house, though, and was a member of White's and the Travellers': Mrs. Arbuthnot to Lady Shelley, 15 Sep. 1833, R. Edgecumbe (ed.), *The Diary of Frances, Lady Shelley* (2 vols., London, 1913), vol. II, p.228; Norman Mss KAO U310 F69, f.503.

55.   James, born 1831, was captured at Inkerman; he was MP for North Norfolk from 1876 till his death two years later. Alfred, born 1833, was in the navy and died unmarried in 1857. A. and H. Taylor, *The Book of the Duffs* (2 vols., Edinburgh, 1914), vol.II, pp.506-31.

56.   For the Prescotts see Cussans, *Hertfordshire*, vol.III, pp.210-14 and G.E.C., *Complete Baronetage*, vol.V, p.293. Eliza's sister Louisa married Sir Edward Gooch, Frederick's fellow MP for East Suffolk.

57.   The wedding was in 1826 (*Gents. Mag.* 97 (1827), 638) and Duff, whose home was in Elgin, died at Leamington in 1836, aged thirty-three, leaving all his property to his widow: PRO PROB 11/1879, f.444. There is an unrevealing entry on James Duff senior in the *D.N.B.*, vol. XV, p.129, but *The Book of the Duffs* is more enlightening and includes interesting details on his family life, as well as an enigmatic reference to the Thellussons from 1802 (p.514).

58.   *Gents. Mag.* 108 (1838), 320.

59.   *Gents. Mag.* 110 (1840), 426; *Gents. Mag.* 111 (1841), 220; PRO TS 18/1501.

60.   Norman Mss KAO U310 F69, f.503. Compare the characters given by Trollope to the Duke of

Omnium and his heir Plantagenet Palliser (`Planty Pall') in his `Palliser' novels.

61. C.R.Dod, *Electoral Facts 1832-53 Impartially Stated*, (reprint, ed. H.J. Hanham, Hassocks, 1972), p.299 and *Dod's Parliamentary Companion* (1847 edn., London), p.226.

62. For a general summary see R.J. Olney, The Politics of Land, in G.E. Mingay (ed.), *The Victorian Countryside*, vol.I (London, 1981), 58-70.

63. The summary of Rendlesham's views given in *Dod's Companion* includes opposition to the duties on malt, tea, hops and tobacco, to Roman Catholic emancipation and to the funding of highways and asylums from the consolidated fund.

64. See the examples given in J.E. Thirsk with J. Imray, *Suffolk Farming in the Nineteenth Century* (Ipswich, 1958) and the obituaries cited in ch. 15 *infra*.

65. K. Jones, *A History of the Mental Health Services* (London, 1972), W.L. Parry-Jones, *The Trade in Lunacy* (London, 1972) and R. Porter, *Mind-Forg'd Manacles* (London, 1987) offer differing judgements on the private and public asylums.

66. Jones, *Mental Health Services*, pp.54-152.

67. *Gents. Mag.* 130 (1852), 514; *Fifth to Ninth Annual Reports of the Suffolk Lunatic Asylum* (Woodbridge, 1843-7).

68. *Journal of the British Archaeological Association* 9 (1854), 101.

69. To G.W.Norman, 4 Dec. 1851, Norman Mss KAO U310 C125.

70. On 3rd Jan. 1826, *Gents. Mag.* 96 (1826), 80. They lived first at Ribbersford (Worcs.), then near Reading, with a town house in Eaton Square.

71. *Burke's Landed Gentry* (1845-9), vol.I, p.238; Ain, *Les Thellusson*, p.334; R.H.Codrington, A Memoir of the Family of Codrington, *Transactions of the Bristol and Gloucestershire Archaeological Society* 21 (1898), 301-45.

72. A.J.B. was born in 1826 and sent to Eton, joining the Coldstream Guards straight from school. Arthur also had four daughters, one of whom died young.

73. Order of 21 Jan. 1818, PRO C33/649, f.617. Maria's portion had, of course, been paid over when she married.

74. Printed in *Thellusson v. Woodford* (1819) 4 Madd. 420.

75. *Williams on Wills*, vol.I, pp.441-50.

76. *Debeze v. Mann* (1787) 2 Bro.C.C. 165; *Ellison v. Cookson* (1789) 3 Bro.C.C. 60. In *Trimmer v. Bayne* (1802) 7 Ves. Jun. 508, counsel on both sides seem rather to deprecate the presumption.

77. The presumption is confined to a parent or person *in loco parentis* and the testator is rebuttably presumed to be aware of its existence, though in *Trimmer v. Bayne* Lord Eldon, discussing *Ellison v. Cookson*, drew on his personal knowledge of the family, maintaining that `it was

346

impossible to talk to the family upon the subject, in terms which they could understand' (at 517).

78. *Trimmer v. Bayne* at 513.

79. Sir John Leach VC summarised the case law in *Weall v. Rice* (1831) 2 Russ.& M. 251.

80. *Thellusson v. Woodford* (1819) 4 Madd.420 at 429. His report took fifteen months to produce.

81. Counsel argued that it was contradicted by Augusta's affidavit in which she declared that her father had substituted the stock for their personal allowances and never told her that it was other than a pure gift. Leach's judgment ignores this evidence.

82. Hart and Phillimore appeared for the daughters, Bell and Shadwell for the trustees.

83. *Thellusson v. Woodford* (1819) 4 Madd. 420 at 436-7.

84. *Ibid.*, at 427.

85. Ketton Cremer, *Felbrigg*, pp.221-34.

86. On 5th May 1824. Lukin was then fifty-six.

87. Required by the terms of William Windham's will: PRO PROB 11/1514, f. 446. Such clauses were very popular: W.T. Gibson, 'Withered Branches and Weighty Symbols': Surname Substitution in England, 1660-1880, *British Journal for 18th Century Studies* 15 (1992), 17-33.

88. Ketton Cremer, *Felbrigg*, pp.221-34.

89. One daughter, Cecilia, was married to Henry Baring, a scion of the great banking house. Two others intermarried with the Hare family, one of them, Maria, subsequently taking the Earl of Listowel as her second husband. *Burke's Dictionary of the Landed Gentry*, vol.I, p. 1612; *Complete Peerage*, vol.VIII, pp. 83-5 (Listowel).

90. A.R.Childs, *Politics and Elections in Suffolk Boroughs during the late Eighteenth and early Nineteenth Centuries* (M. Phil. thesis, Reading, 1973), pp.157-60, 184-7. The poll cost Windham several thousand pounds. When Sudbury was disfranchised, Lord Rendlesham unsuccessfully tried to persuade Peel to give Woodbridge the seat : 5 Jul. 1844, Peel Mss, BL. Add. Mss. 40,548, f.90.

91. PRO PROB 11/1813, f.195.

92. PRO PROB 11/2090, f.239. One son, Robert, was vicar of Felbrigg, another (Henry) a naval captain. Neither married. A third, Joseph, was an army captain.

93. Ketton Cremer, *Felbrigg*, pp.235-48.

94. For the Herveys of Ickworth, Marquesses of Bristol (curiously memorable for the Hotel Bristols that figure in many European cities) see *Complete Peerage*. They were already distant kin of the Windhams through Maria Thellusson (Phipps)'s mother- in- law, Lepel Hervey.

95. Just deserts perhaps, since William Howe and his sister Maria had contrived the deathbed barring of another entail in very suspicious circumstances to deprive Maria's sister-in-law of her inheritance: Ketton Cremer, *Felbrigg*, pp.241-2.

96.   *Ibid.*, pp. 249-55.

97.   *D.N.B.*, vol.LXII, pp.170-2. For a dispassionate account of Windham's actions see W. Baring Pemberton, *Battles of the Crimean War* (London, 1962).

98.   The best known fictional exploitation of this theme is in Wilkie Collins' *The Woman in White*, published in 1860.

99.   Ketton Cremer, *Felbrigg*, pp.257-66. Charles Ash Windham went out to Canada as Commander- in- Chief, where he died in 1870.

100. Some of the later Windhams are described in Commander Sir Walter Windham's *Waves, Wheels, Wings* (London, 1943).

101. 3 Feb. 1827. In the settlement she transferred all the property held in her account in Chancery, amounting to some £8,000 in various stocks, to trustees: order of 26 Jul. 1827, PRO C 33/760, f.1454.

102. W.A. Shaw, *The Knights of England* (4 vols., London, 1906), vol. I, p.457, vol. II, p. 330; *Alumni Cantabrigienses, 1752-1900*, vol.VI, p.421.

103. PRO PROB 11/2006, f.795. He died at his house in Hill Street, leaving his entire wardrobe to his butler.

104. *Gents. Mag.* 133 (1853), 324. Her will (PRO PROB 11/2177, f.646) gave £500 apiece to Lord Rendlesham and Thomas Robarts Thellusson and smaller legacies to others in the family, among them relatives by each of her marriages. The residue was left to her daughter.

105. Habbakuk, *Marriage, Debt and the Estates System*, pp.448-53.

106. *House of Commons, 1790-1820*, vol.III, p.573; *Burke's Dictionary of the Landed Gentry*, vol.I, p.313; Williams, *Members for Worcestershire*, p.108.

107. Williams, *Members for Worcestershire*, p.108; *V.C.H. Worcestershire*, vol. III (London, 1971), pp. 339-41.

108. PRO PROB 11/2050, f.115. It then passed to Davies's brother Warburton.

109. *Gents. Mag.* 100 (1830), 289. *V.C.H. Worcs.*, vol. III, p.155, *Complete Peerage*, vol.VI, p.289 and *D.N.B.*, vol.XV, p. 94 do not mention the will, which is at PRO PROB 11/ 1774, f. 462.

110. *Complete Peerage*, vol.VI, p.289.

111. *Ibid.*

112. Cussans, *Hertfordshire*, vol.V, p.251. Sir C.M. Pole bought the freehold of Otterspool in 1826 and granted the Thellussons a new lease in the following year at £100 p.a.: Herts.CRO D/EWh T6.

113. *Gents. Mag.* 115 (1844), 107; 132 (1852), 635; PRO PROB 11/2153, f.447.

114. R. Robson, *The Attorney in Eighteenth Century England* (Cambridge, 1959); M. Birks, *Gentlemen of the Law* (London, 1960), pp. 181-205; H. Kirk, *Portrait of a Profession* (London,

1976), pp.168-215.

115. *Ibid.* The term 'solicitor', originally confined to Chancery practitioners, had not acquired the opprobrious connotations of 'attorney', and was increasingly preferred by those with social pretensions, which attracted derisive comment from their detractors.

116. Forster was originally in practice with Bargrave, starting in 1774. He gave evidence to the Chancery Commission in 1824: *PP* 1826 (143) XVI, App. A 16. The Oddies were connected by marriage to the Nicoll family, one of the dominant practitioners in Doctors' Commons: *Burke's Dictionary of the Landed Gentry*, vol. I, p.1845; E.O. Walford, *County Families of the United Kingdom* (1888 edn., London), p.776 and G.D.Squibb, *Doctors' Commons* (Oxford, 1977), appendix III. There are many references to the Hertfordshire branch in Cussans, *Hertfordshire*, vol.I.

117. See various estate documents in Herts.CRO D/EWh/T3.

118. Leading to complaints about the selfishness of bachelors: M.F. Brightfield, *Victorian England in its Novels* (University of California, 1971), vol.4, pp.84ff.

119. On 31st Jan. 1815. They married in February 1813 and their daughter Georgiana was born in 1814: order of 15 Jul. 1817, PRO C 33/641, f.1682.

120. Butley went with the lands purchased by Peter Isaac for the trust: Page, *History of Suffolk*, p.87.

121. On the role of advowsons see Evans, *Contentious Tithe*, pp. 1-6 and Langford, *Public Life and the Propertied Englishman*, pp. 18-20. The legal position is summarised in *Halsbury's Laws of England* (4th edn., vol.14, London, 1975), paras. 399-434.

122. *Oddie v. Woodford* (1821-25) 3 My.& Cr. 584, at 590, 594-5. The report is taken from a shorthand note the Oddies obtained and for which they were reimbursed on appeal from the Master. In all, the case cost the estate some £200: order of 4 May 1822, PRO C33/699, f.1117.

123. At 624-5, and *cf.* pp. 598, 605.

124. At 604-9, the case being *Arthington v. Coverly* (1733) 2 Eq.Cas.Ab. 518, a decision of Lord King LC given added weight by having been argued by the foremost equity lawyers of their day, Yorke and Talbot. It is the only case mentioned in the judgment.

125. At 598.

126. At 609.

127. At 614.

128. At 610-11. It was not a remote possibility either, since the eldest grandson, John, was ten when the will was made and Peter might easily have lived another ten or fifteen years.

129. At 621-2.

130. At 622. This reference must have been flattering for Butler, who was appearing for Oddie; Sugden appeared in the appeal to the Lords.

131. Other arguments were put forward, notably the significance of the `name and arms' clause, but were given little weight.

132. *Oddie v. Woodford* (1821-25) 3 My.& Cr. 584, at 628-31.

133. There is no report of the Lords' judgment other than the formal record in *House of Lords Journals* 57 (1825), 1102, but there is a copy of the appellants' case in Herts.CRO D/P3 29/11. Needless to say, costs were in the cause: order of 1 Jul. 1825, PRO C33/735, f.1404. In *Thellusson v.Rendlesham* [1858-59] 7 H.L.C. 429 at 503-4, Sugden (Lord St.Leonards) criticised this `very irregular' petition of Lord Rendlesham.

134. *V.C.H. Hertfordshire*, vol. II (London, 1908), p.225.

135. The father's will (PRO PROB 11/1775, f.515) expressed `great confidence in the punctuality of my son', and on that account the £450 annuity to his widow was not charged on the testator's property but simply secured by the son's bond. Oddie died in 1830 at Barnwell in Northamptonshire aged eighty-seven. *Gents. Mag.* 95 (1825), 571; 100 (1830), 189. Oddie's personalty was sworn at under £100,000 and the residue was £86,000: PRO IR 26/1237, f.466.

136. Cussans, *Hertfordshire*, vol.V, p.31; *V.C.H. Hertfordshire*, vol.II, pp. 225, 269.

137. Two daughters married into the Royds family, while a son and daughter of a Sussex rector, Robert Gream, who also owned Frogmore Lodge in Hertfordshire, married Isabell and Henry Hoyle Oddie respectively. Mary Anne Oddie married her cousin, Henry Iltyd Nicoll, George Oddie the daughter of the Reverend Venables, Fanny a widowed clergyman named Wood and Georgiana the son of Sir Francis Freeling, who had made his fortune as Postmaster General.

138. Cussans, *Hertfordshire*, vol.V, p. 317. Henry died at Scarborough but was buried in Shenley churchyard, which contains the graves of his daughter Ellen Chetwynd-Stapleton, his son Henry Hoyle (d.1869) and his daughter-in-law Louisa (d.1864). It also has the tomb of Nicholas Hawksmoor.

139. G.A. Solly, *Rugby School Register Annotated, 1675-1857* (Rugby, 1933), p.447; L.S. Milford (ed.), *The Haileybury Register, 1862-1910* (Bungay and London, 1910), p.156. Edward's son practised in Watford.

140. Presumably inherited from his father-in-law. H.H. Oddie was a Cambridge cricket `blue' in 1836, having gone up to Trinity from Eton. He had at least three sons of his own.

141. PRO PROB 11/2065, f.865. Three codicils reflect his meticulous estate planning to allow for changes in the children's circumstances.

142. *V.C.H. Hertfordshire*, vol.II, p.158; Cussans, *Hertfordshire*, vol. V, p.273. A.T. Oddie later changed his name to Whyte-Venables on inheriting an Irish estate: *Alumni Cantabrigienses, 1752-1900*, vol.IV, p.580. Colney burned down some years later and a convent was built on the site.

143. PRO PROB 11/1587, f.636. His wife, their aunt, left them only token legacies, pointedly giving nothing at all to their father: PRO PROB 11/1823, f.656.

144. *Gents. Mag.*, 91 (1821), 475.

145. *Foster's Peerage*, p.411, *sub* McNaghten. Francis McNaghten (1763-1843) was knighted in 1809 on his appointment as a judge at Madras. Transferring to Calcutta in 1815, he retired in 1825 and was made a baronet on his return home. He had fourteen children by the daughter of another Indian judge: *Alumni Cantabrigienses, 1752-1900*, vol. VI, p.147; M.G. Dauglish and P.K. Stephenson, *The Harrow School Register, 1800-1911*(London, 1911).

146. *Gents. Mag.* 91 (1820), 464. None of the family were witnesses: PRO TS 18/1501.

147. *Burke's Landed Gentry* (1952), *sub* Grant-Dalton. Mary had two unmarried sisters. The hyphenated surname was imposed by her brother Robert's reluctant father-in-law as a condition of inheritance of his lands in Somerset: *V.C.H Somerset*, vol.IV(Oxford, 1978), p.13.

148. Osbaldeston's own autobiography (E.D. Cumming, *Squire Osbaldeston: his autobiography* (1926 edn., London)) can be supplemented by the *D.N.B.*, by the incongruous entry in *House of Commons, 1790-1820* and references in many books of sporting reminiscences.

149. Budd was a relation of the solicitor T.W.Budd, who was prominent in the Thellusson case and who procured him his War Office place from Windham. His exploits, and some of Osbaldeston's, are featured in C.A. Wheeler (ed.), *Sportascrapiana* (London, 1867).

150. Sir J.E. Eardley Wilmot, *Reminiscences of the Late Thomas Assheton Smith* (London, 1860).

151. As when he had to leap from Osbaldeston's gig when it went out of control on their way back from some snipe shooting in Lincolnshire: *Squire Osbaldeston*, p.86.

152. *Ibid.*, p.2. As a writer in the *Gentleman's Magazine* remarked, `it is needless to add that his name does not appear in the list of those who took their B.A. degree, much less among those who obtained honours': 148 (1866), 419.

153. *Squire Osbaldeston*, p.2.

154. The best evocation of this world is in *Mr. Sponge's Sporting Tour* (1853).

155. Since none of the other births found mention in the periodical press, it is uncertain whether they, like Charles, were born abroad.

156. Lambert, *Bills and Acts*, p.110.

157. *Ibid.*, pp. 84-128. According to E.H.Scammell, The Settled Land Act 1925, *Current Legal Problems* 1957, pp.152-67, there were over 700 such Acts between 1800 and 1850, one family alone requiring six.

158. HLRO main papers, no.114 of 1828: judges' report, f.23. This passage is interpolated in a different hand, probably Bayley's, and the judges also removed a reference to estates `of vast magnitude'. The draft bill was also altered, deleting any reference to George Woodford

Thellusson's descendants.

159. *House of Lords Journals* 59 (1827), 176; 60 (1828), 58, 211, 325. William Mitchell was examined, though it is not clear why.

160. Orders of 7 Aug., 3 Dec. 1827 (PRO C 33/761, f.1985, C 33/770, f.92); 21 Jun. 1828, C 33/776, f.2064.

161. Sugden (Lord St.Leonards), Pepys (Lord Cottenham) and Campbell. Bickersteth and Ellison represented the trustees.

162. *Thellusson v. Woodford* (1828) 5 Russ. 100. Lyndhurst's judgment on the first question is very brief indeed.

163. *Ibid.*, at 109-11.

164. Order of 19 May 1831, PRO C33/819, f.1324.

165. *Thellusson v. Woodford* (1828) 5 Russ. 100 at 111; order of 11 Apr. 1830, PRO C 33/806, f.2569.

166. *Gents. Mag.* 98 (1828), 373; *Annual Biography and Obituary* 13 (1829). Woodford was a resourceful and respected governor, not afraid to incur unpopularity in re-establishing the authority of his office, but displaying more tact than the choleric Picton. Well regarded by historians writing from a British colonial perspective (G. Carmichael, *History of the West Indian Islands of Trinidad and Tobago* (London, 1961), pp. 105-53 and L.M. Fraser, *A History of Trinidad* (vol. II, 1814-39, Port of Spain, 1896), pp. 1-213), he earns the grudging respect of Eric Williams in his very different *History of the People of Trinidad and Tobago*,(Trinidad, 1964), pp. 75-6.

167. PRO PROB 11/1748, f.682. One servant received £500, two others a full year's wages and the only slave he owned was freed with £20. A painting of Charles I and his queen was offered to the King, who had once expressed an interest in it, and Flint was left £200 to erect tablets to Woodford's father and mother, in Cheltenham and London churches respectively.

168. For Hammet see *infra*, PP. 349, 355. The Duke of Atholl was a friend of Woodford and, presumably, of the Hammets also, hence the Christian name.

169. Order of 22 Jan. 1829, PRO C33/787, f.524.

170. De la Garde, *Brighton*, p.310.

171. West Yorks RO DD 168/15. Diaries survive only for 1831, 1838, 1848-50, 1852 and 1854-55.

172. C.S.A. Thellusson to -.Mansfield, n.d., *ibid.*, DD 168/16d. Other letters make it clear that there had been an earlier quarrel and that Nightingale was well known for this sort of conduct, while Charles's diary for 23 Feb. 1838 has the laconic entry: `Duel: Nightingale and Smith'. Although readers of Dickens's early novels (*The Pickwick Papers* and *Nicholas Nickleby*) may receive the impression that duelling was still common in England in the 1830s, the fullest account suggests

about 10 to 20 duels a year and it seems finally to have expired in 1852, hastened by changes in the military code. D.T.Andrew, The Code of Honour and its Critics, *Social History* 5 (1980), 409-34 and A.E. Simpson, Dandelions on the Field of Honor: Dueling, the Middle Classes and the Law in Nineteenth Century England, *Criminal Justice History* 9 (1988), 99-156.

173. C. Thellusson to M.A. Reyroux, 14 Mar. 1843, West Yorks RO DD 168/16b.

174. J.B. Story, *Commentaries on Equity Jurisprudence* (10th edn., 2 vols., Boston, 1870), vol.I, pp. 331-45; G.W.Keeton, *Equity* (2nd edn., London, 1976), pp.244-7. Similar relief was given to common sailors on account of their proverbial improvidence.

175. The classic judgment on a post-obit bond is Lord Chancellor Hardwicke's in *Earl of Chesterfield v. Janssen* (1750) 2 Ves. Sen. 125. See also *Shelly v. Nash* (1818) 3 Madd. 232.

176. Letters of 24 Mar., 4 Mar. 1843, West Yorks RO DD 168/16b. Reyroux was the Robarts' family solicitor. Robarts warned Charles that he `would have nothing to do with Jews or professed money lenders' and Charles replied that he `could not hold them in greater abhorrence than I do'.

177. To Reyroux, 4 Mar. 1843.

178. 31 Mar. 1843, *ibid.*. He added that his father was confident that Charles's wife would lend her assistance.

179. The entry for 19 Jan. 1849 shows his overdraft at £8,279 16s 11d, *ibid.*:DD 168/15. Later in the year Robarts advanced £1,500 to buy Alexander a promotion.

180. He weighed twenty-one stone in 1843.

181. There are many fewer references in the late 1840s than in 1831, though he was still on good terms with his wife's family.

182. Charles's brother Tom crops up occasionally in the diaries. His only sister, Adeline, was living abroad at Verneuil, where she may have died.

183. There remains one Thellusson who is a complete mystery. The registers of St.Mary-le Bow, Cheapside record the calling of the banns for the wedding of Benjamin Middleton, bachelor, and Portsmouth Frances Thellusson, described first as a widow, but later as a spinster, both of the parish (*Registers of St. Mary Le Bow, Cheapside* (Harleian Society Registers 45 (1915), entries of Sep. 1828- Sep. 1829). This lady occurs in none of the other records I have seen, nor is any other family of the same name known. She may have been the bastard daughter of one of Peter's sons or of his grandsons John or George; John, the elder and later known for loose living, is the likelier.

CHAPTER 14

ESCAPING THE CLUTCHES OF THE HUNGRY SLOTH

1. The Thellusson Estate Act

As we saw, Charles Thellusson's unsuccessful Chancery foray did have one good effect: it impressed Lord Lyndhurst with the profligate management of the estate by the trustees.[1] Though he went into opposition soon afterwards, Lyndhurst did not lose sight of this Chancery scandal and he conceived a bold plan to assist the family which came as near to breaking the trust as could be broached with any hope of success. In this he seems to have been quite disinterested, for he had no personal connexion with the Thellussons;[2] perhaps his sympathy stemmed from a fellow feeling, for Lyndhurst was notoriously in perpetual want of money and his political cynicism was often attributed to mercenary motives.[3]

What he proposed was a private estate bill of an unusually radical kind. It was one which, because it proposed to vest extensive powers in the head of the Thellusson family, could not plausibly be promoted while that person was a man of doubtful financial and moral character, but John's unexpected death and the succession of William, a clergyman of unblemished reputation, enabled Lyndhurst to bring it forward in July 1833.

There was however a procedural obstacle. To guard against fraud standing orders in the House of Lords, where estate bills began, required a petition in favour of the measure signed by all those with a financial interest who had legal capacity, plus a report from the judges assigned to the bill.[4] Frederick however was living in Florence and would not journey home for this purpose,[5] so in order to meet the parliamentary timetable Lyndhurst had to seek the suspension of the standing orders. Not surprisingly, this cavalier approach met strong objections and since the House would not dispense with a petition Lyndhurst had to try again, this time with Frederick signing by his attorney.[6] Even then it was endorsed by only one trustee(Sir John Woodford), for although Lyndhurst had initially affected to believe that they were `men of the highest honor and character; and I am quite sure they will allow no petty interests of their own to interfere with this act of justice',[7] the others in fact delivered a counter-petition through Lord Eldon.[8] Since it was much too late by now to get the judges' report before proceeding with the bill, Lyndhurst had once again to propose the suspension of standing orders and this time succeeded, but only after a lively debate which disclosed considerable opposition to the measure itself, extending to a note of dissent entered in the *Journal* by three peers.[9]

Lyndhurst had foreseen that his proposal would meet resistance and in order to disarm its opponents he had commanded a whole battery of returns from Chancery itself to support his claim that the testator's outrageous design had failed utterly and that, so far from presenting any danger to the commonweal, the fabled accumulation was a pathetic affair, barely capable of sustaining itself, let alone swelling.[10] The returns showed a gross income in 1803 of £23,929, remaining almost unchanged in 1832 at £24,165,[11] and Lyndhurst ironically attributed this astonishing negation of the power of compound interest to `the power...possessed by the Court of Chancery to arrest such accumulations'.[12] The net rental stood at only £14,200 and taxed costs averaging more than £3,000 p.a. reduced the amount available to fuel the accumulation to a miserable £11,000 p.a.[13] Other returns showed in devastating detail how profitable the estate was proving to the several firms of solicitors, to the surveyor, to the receivers and to the court of Chancery.[14] The Thellusson trust had been proverbial for its relentless accumulation and as recently as 1828 the bride-hunting Prince Puckler-Muskau, meeting Charles Thellusson at Brighton, had written home of his son, the `pretty boy of eight', who was likely to inherit £12 millions.[15] Now the great fortune was exposed as a myth, the unconscionable project of Peter Thellusson thwarted by the greater rapacity of the court of Chancery.

Lyndhurst dismissed the possibility of substantially increasing the rental yield or of diminishing the costs which already stood at £176,000 and might ultimately amount to between £200,000 and £300,000 pounds.[16] He argued that so long as the current level of net income continued to be appropriated to the accumulation, with a proportionate addition from future purchases, the settlor's wishes would in essence be respected; the remaining income, currently wasted on receivers' poundages and on expenses 'incurred to a great extent for mere purposes of form',[17] might be put to better use in the hands of the Thellussons, since 'the heads of the family were at present in great distress' and 'it was out of their power to support or educate their children in a manner suitable to their rank and condition in life.'[18]

The remedy proposed was disarmingly simple and drastic. The trust estates should be leased to Lord Rendlesham for life at a rental equal to their current net yield, which he would pay straight into the Accountant-General's office. The rest of the rental income, which hitherto had gone to feed the court, the lawyers and the receivers, would be distributed among the family. Rendlesham would also have the power, subject to the approval of the court, to decide on future purchases as well as improvements to the properties, reducing the trustees to figureheads.[19]

Lyndhurst did not spare the court of Chancery and he did not spare the trustees either. While careful to stop short of alleging actual breaches of trust (for which there was a remedy in the court), he roundly criticised them, especially Flint, for the extravagances of the Brodsworth establishment, for since Flint and Hammet were opposing the bill anyway there was nothing to be gained by trying to appease them.[20] Flint, he said, was there for three months a year, with a steward, a housekeeper, a cook and three housemaids ('three housemaids, my lords, and only one trustee'), a man to carry coats, two gardeners and two women or boys to work in the garden, a man to keep the pleasure grounds and a gamekeeper - 'pray take note of this; the manor, as I understand, might be let to great advantage; but no, it remains unlet, and a gamekeeper is employed for the amusement of Sir Charles Flint'.[21] Lyndhurst went too far in alleging that the trustees had a policy of making many small land purchases to serve the interests of their own solicitor,[22] but it was a swingeing and effective attack. Nevertheless he was at pains to stress that such a very drastic alteration of the trust was justified by its unique nature and so could not become a precedent.[23]

It was predictable that Eldon would lead the opposition, but he was no longer the formidable figure he had once been [24] and a fatuous remark that he had never heard any complaints about the cost of the suit while he held the Seal was greeted with derision; the Lord Chancellor, Brougham, sarcastically retorted that since the master's office alone was making £700 to £800 a year from the trust, criticism was hardly likely to be forthcoming from that quarter.[25] Nevertheless Eldon had a good case and it was entered in the *Journal* as a further dissent.[26]

First, he argued that the potential of the accumulation (which might still have many years to run) would be artificially restricted, thereby denying the ultimate beneficiaries potential benefits. Second, `any Charges that can justly be complained of have resulted from the ordinary Practice and course of Proceeding of the Court [and] it became the Duty of the Legislature to reform such Practice generally, rather than to enact a partial Law giving Relief in one Particular Case only, in which Case, from the magnitude of the Property the Burthen must be comparatively light, whilst the Evil (if any) is allowed to operate with full Force in the numerous other Cases in which Property falls to be administered under the Court of Chancery'. Thirdly, although there may be no other testamentary accumulations of this length, there will certainly be other capricious wills creating other funds in Chancery and this unprecedented interference with their operation will be a standing temptation to tamper with those out of sympathy for the disappointed kin. Finally, `even if the Provisions enacted by this Bill were Improvements upon those created by the Testator... we should [not] be justified in making, in Effect, a will for a Testator, which he would not himself make, as to the Disposal and Management of his Property after his death, and which the Law of the Land authorised him to make.'[27]

It was magnificently hypocritical of Eldon to claim that the remedy for

Chancery's depredations lay in that very general reform which he had implacably resisted for so long, but his arguments had merit for, as Tooke pointed out in the lower house, it was 'unjust to be constantly referring to abuses which they took no pains to remedy'.[28] No-one but William Brougham, one of the masters, defended the court in the Commons, where the Solicitor-General, Sir James Scarlett, acknowledged that it had 'sweated' the estate.[29] Chancery, in Daniel Whittle Harvey's outlandish metaphor 'might be said to cling to this estate, as the hungry sloth clings to the luxuriant tree, upon which to make a similar, gluttonous repast',[30] but the foundering of his project in no way softened MPs' view of Peter Thellusson- even the normally unimpassioned Sir Robert Peel referred to 'such an extraordinary, such an unnatural, he would almost say such an insane exercise of the testamentary power'.[31] Even so, several members were uneasy about making such large inroads into the principle of testamentary freedom.

Unusual in being debated at length and in producing dissents in the *Journals*, the bill nevertheless won comfortable majorities.[32] It gave Rendlesham a lease on the standard terms for agricultural estates, including the right to grant underleases for up to twenty-one years (limited to seven years for Brodsworth Hall). Further purchases were to be demised to him on the same terms and, save for a reservation to them to cut timber, he would 'in all respects stand in place of the ...Trustees.' For this he would pay £11,500 p.a. in half-yearly payments, plus rent for the new purchases as determined by the court. The costs of the Act itself, of the leases drawn up to implement it, of purchases and improvements (but not repairs), were to be charged to the trust fund. When William died a fresh lease on the same terms was to be offered to the next Lord Rendlesham for the period of the life of the last survivor of the nine lives, i.e. Frederick or Charles.[33]

The alteration to Peter's scheme was also notable for abandoning his equal treatment of his sons in favour of the aristocratic principle of primogeniture. The leases were to be confined to the senior branch even though there might be an older representative (Charles) of the junior, who might indeed be of an older generation than the next Lord Rendlesham (if Frederick predeceased William and either had a son).[34] But Charles was in no position to object and could scarcely claim that he had the qualities to be a competent estate manager. In the distribution of the income however he came off better than his cousin Rendlesham. No trusts appeared in the Act, nor were any questions asked in Parliament about the destination of the money saved from Chancery, but the family executed a separate deed whereby the moiety allocated to the senior branch was split equally between William and his younger brother Arthur, while the other moiety was divided between Charles (or rather, two trustees for his creditors) and his younger brother Thomas in the proportion 5:3.[35] The difference, doubtless the outcome of some rather touchy negotiations, reflected the difference in their situations. William was childless, as was Frederick his twin, so Arthur had a good chance of claiming the spoils without a contest when the accumulation ended; in addition he still had his claim to be entitled ahead of any son of the twins. That argument, which would require the courts to hold that *Oddie v. Woodford* [36] was wrongly decided, was also open to Thomas, but because Charles already had four sons, his chances were effectively much poorer than Arthur's.[37]

It is not certain how much they actually received. In 1843 Charles claimed to have `something under £3,000 a year', which suggests a total of around £9,000, while a return of 1852 suggests a slightly lower figure.[38] Split four ways it hardly transformed their finances, but for William, Charles and probably Thomas, it did make an appreciable difference. And whatever violence the arrangement did to Peter's intentions, they had already been so distorted by a litigious family, unscrupulous trustees and the hungry sloth that it is unlikely that he would have found this salvage operation objectionable.

Just as the Thellusson trust was prised loose from its hungry grasp, the reform of the court of Chancery got under way. Though Eldon had been able to silt up the Chancery Commission, diverting the broad channel of reform into a delta of small, sluggish channels, it did make numerous recommendations for change and Lyndhurst had implemented some of them by orders.[39] His efforts were continued by successive

Chancellors, but though the unreformed court had few defenders after Eldon, its powers of inertia and passive resistance remained impressive. It is, for example, significant that an act of 1833 explicitly empowered the Chancellor to make rules and orders 'not being inconsistent with the enactment and provisions of the Act... for simplifying, establishing and settling the course of practice...of the Court',[40] although he already an inherent power to do so. That act, like Lyndhurst's orders, covered a miscellany of practices and abuses; gratuities and the insistence on the suitor taking (or at least paying for) office copies were ended; a handful of offices was immediately abolished and the six clerks phased out;[41] the allocation of business between judges and masters was rationalised.[42] Yet the most serious problems- the shortage of judges and the costs and delays of proceedings in the masters' offices, were not really touched; indeed by trying to alleviate the former by sending interlocutory matters to the masters, the latter was aggravated.[43]

These reforms were not without value. It was especially worthwhile to remove bankruptcy business from the Lord Chancellor, to have the Master of the Rolls sitting continuously and to reduce some fees and amalgamate others. Nevertheless, they fell well short of what was needed, and it only wanted a judge to fall sick, as Lord Chancellor Cottenham did in 1839, for arrears to mount alarmingly.[44] Even when two extra Vice- Chancellors were created after the abolition of the underused equity side of the Exchequer in 1841, causes still languished in a way the railway age found intolerable.[45]

Furthermore, in the lower reaches of the court it was one thing to decree a reform and quite another to enforce it. One of Lyndhurst's useful orders to simplify the antiquated mode of dealing with accounts was so narrowly construed by the officers as to be virtually useless,[46] while even the positive instruction in Brougham's Act that 'unless the court shall otherwise specially direct, no recitals shall be introduced in any decree or order', was often ignored.[47] Things could not go on like this. The reports of 1833 and 1848 made it clear that it was no longer acceptable that officials should live directly off suitors' fees,[48] and though the Treasury insisted, despite the arguments of the Benthamite Master of the Rolls Lord Langdale, that suitors must pay for the entire running costs of the court, including the salary bill and compensation to displaced officers, fixed salaries gradually became general.[49]

For the most part, the great lawyers of the post-Eldon generation were not dogmatic defenders of the *status quo*. It is instructive to compare the proceedings of the 1824 commission with its successor of 1851, which had Samuel Romilly's son as chairman and included among its members Bethell, Turner, Page-Wood, Crompton and James. This latter inquiry scarcely needed the evidence furnished by solicitors and brushed aside officers' defences of long-established practices.[50] Measures based on their report were indeed criticised for timidity,[51] but they really marked the end of the old system. In particular, the masters were swept away, leaving the business formerly referred to them to be dealt with by the judges in chambers.[52] It was this business which made protracted administration suits so costly and tedious, but by the time it was changed the Thellusson suits were drawing to their close at last. Lyndhurst had been pessimistic but correct in discounting the possibility of any substantial reduction in court costs so long as the suit remained on its old footing.[53] It was one of the misfortunes of that ill-fated family that their engagement with the sloth came at precisely the time when it was performing at its most greedy and slothful.

After 1833 the trust was still to feed the hungry sloth, but on a controlled diet. The rapacious trustees however were to be deprived of most of their functions and the perquisites which they were felt to have abused. A less thick-skinned man than Flint would have resigned after the slurs cast on his stewardship, particularly when Lyndhurst gave wider publicity to the fact that during Charles Thellusson's unsuccessful application Flint had written him a private letter 'to influence my judgment on the subject, and I expressed my opinion upon such conduct in the court of Chancery, and said that it was highly reprehensible and improper',[54] but in any event death carried him off a few months after the passage of the Act. Not surprisingly none of the Thellussons benefitted from his will, in which a specific bequest of his gun bore testament to his fondness for shooting.[55] His replacement was an obvious candidate, Abraham Wildey Robarts. Head of the big bank of Robarts Curtis, son of Charles Thellusson's father -in law and MP for Maidstone, he was typical of many of his class at that time: 'a Reformer, and supports all Whig and reforming Governments, but he does so (like many others) from fear. What he most dreads is collision, and most desires is quiet, and he thinks non-resistance the best way.'[56] Robarts was the opposite of Frederick, the fourth Baron Rendlesham, in this, the banker supporting change for fear of revolution, the landowner resisting it for fear that his class would be eclipsed.[57] Robarts was a cultivated man with a fine art collection at his Mayfair town house,[58] and though no special friend to the Thellussons he could be depended upon for strict integrity. Within a few months Flint's feeble sidekick Hammet was begging to be released from trusteeship on the grounds of ill-health and disappears into obscurity.[59] Perhaps a conscious effort was made to balance a marriage connection of Charles's line with someone from the Rendlesham side. A sister of Peter Isaac's wife Elizabeth Cornwall had married a Chancery master, Sir John Simeon, and among their six children was Edward, briefly a contemporary of John Thellusson's at Eton.[60] Recently widowed, he later came to live in Suffolk, not far from Rendlesham Hall but there is nothing to indicate why he was regarded as especially suitable to be a trustee.[61]

The continuing trustee, John George Woodford, is the most colourful and eccentric of all of them. While his brother Alexander- to whom he wrote daily- successfully pursued a wholly conventional career in the peacetime army,[62] John was a humane, impulsive man whose many virtues were marred by a total inability to conceive that he might be wrong on any question. He made it his business to improve the lot of the common soldier, and not content with promoting temperance and advocating more comfortable and durable uniforms, he also began to liberalise punishments and became a passionate opponent of flogging. No respecter of opinions or persons, this brought him repeatedly into clashes with the king and the Iron Duke and being unwilling either to moderate his views or to keep them to himself, he grew frustrated with the army.[63] A second windfall in 1837[64], this time the beautiful

Derwent Bay estate in the Lake District, enabled him to throw up his commission but he stayed on the army list until 1840 when he obstinately declined the offer of a foreign command unless the destination were first disclosed to him. He impetuously resigned only to discover that he had been destined for China, the one command he really coveted.[65] He had already withdrawn from society and from the trust (November 1837) and spent the rest of his life- nearly forty years- in rustic, reclusive isolation. His place was taken by Cornwallis Maude, third Viscount Hawarden, who seems to have had no links with the family nor any obvious connection with the trustees.[66]

Drawing up the lease for Lord Rendlesham took an unconscionable time. It was always a leisurely process, and the parties were usually content to carry on under their agreement while the lawyers dawdled.[67] Anything that took a long time out of court took longer in court and it is no surprise that Master Roupell and his successor Master Lynch did not have the lease ready until 1838.[68] There were however genuine obstacles to be overcome, for the Act did not explain how a fifty year lease could be granted out of copyhold manors where custom did not permit it, and since their stewards held divergent views it took much patient negotiation to achieve the desired end. In fact copyholds were proving a thorough nuisance to the trust at this time, for arguments also arose over the entry fines to be charged on the installation of new trustees. These were complicated by the fact that one manor, Bawdsey Butley, was itself in Chancery and the two masters took directly opposite views of the law.[69] Since they could not agree, a special case had to be sent to the common law judges, where Chief Baron Abinger found against the trust; this proved a costly business, for in addition to the claim of £1302-11s-8d there were legal costs which somehow mounted up to at least £1550.[70]

2. The Estates under the Leases

For almost twenty years the third and fourth Lords Rendlesham had the management of the trust estates. One effect of the reforms to Chancery was to condense the recording of orders and reports, making it impossible to examine their stewardship in full detail, but the crucial years of the accumulation were now past and their decisions had a relatively small impact on the final distribution. It is, however, instructive to see whether they made significant changes.

William was rather inactive in the land market, making a solitary purchase of 1,500 acres in Suffolk in 1836,[71] and regular acquisitions did not recommence until 1842, by which time there was £130,000 available. In fact the fund continued to increase, rising to £170,000 by the end of 1847 despite an outlay of £35,000 for 1,100 acres at Leiston.[72] From then on, however, Frederick was much more active and made three sizeable purchases as well as smaller ones. All told the lessees spent over £220,000 in buying some 6,200 acres, the price in years' purchase varying from twenty-seven to thirty-seven.[73] The striking feature is that they were concentrated in Suffolk. Apart from one very small piece at Aldenham there were none at all in the home counties or midlands and only 1,300 acres in Yorkshire, accounted for mostly by 813 acres at Barnby Dun bought in 1847.[74] While small plots which were intermixed with the trust estates were acquired when they came onto the market, there is less sense of a purposeful policy of seeking to round off the estates. Whether from indifference or a positive decision to save the funds for bigger purchases, there was always a substantial balance in hand and after the lease fell in the trustees allowed this to increase still further, limiting themselves to opportunities too obvious to be neglected, even so small as thirty perches at Amotherby for the grand sum of £31 10s.[75]

The largest of these late purchases was 300 acres bang in the middle of Brodsworth which Peter Thellusson had held on lease from the dean and chapter of York. The lease had been renewed in 1818 but a further renewal was refused;[76] instead the freehold could be acquired for £7,300, burdened with a hefty rentcharge in favour of a neighbouring landowner, but when the title was referred to the conveyancer Brodie, one of the `forty thieves', he pronounced it defective and it was with difficulty that the Master of the Rolls was persuaded to authorise the purchase.[77] It is quite surprising that this was the only defective title, though sixty acres of leasehold had to be removed from one purchase[78] and several vendors could only offer to sell subject to restrictive stipulations on proof of title. But conveyancers knew that even a clear paper title was no guarantee against hostile claims, and two of these surfaced on the trust estates. First the alleged owner of King's Langley manor started up a claim to free warren and hunting, and by purporting to lease shooting rights forced the tenant farmer into bringing claims to trespass which the trust had to support. The deeds went back to 1676 with no reference to such a claim, but it was mentioned in a county history.[79] The second claim was one manifestation of the activities which brought William Dimes a lasting legal fame and stemmed from his attempt to recover the costs of a new bridge from the tenants of Rickmansworth manor.[80]

Exploitation of dormant or doubtful manorial rights by men like Dimes made copyhold an undesirable tenure. Entry fines were expensive- the trust had to pay more than £10,500 when a new trustee was appointed in 1853-[81] but fines, quit rents and regular incidents were taken into account in the market price, whereas these other demands were an unlooked- for aggravation. The Real Property Commissioners had wanted to see an end to copyhold, but the first statute was a feeble affair. However in 1852 enfranchisement became obligatory at the instance of either lord or tenant[82] and the trustees lost no time in seeking sanction for the wholesale enfranchisement of their extensive copyholds. These were mostly in Suffolk, where they included parts of twenty-four separate purchases, held of thirty-eight different manors.[83] The 1852 Act prescribed a standard formula from which a valuer was to make a computation which included compensation not only to the lord but to his steward, an often highly lucrative sideline for a local attorney.[84] It proved a costly business, the trust spending over £8,000, but well worthwhile as long term investment.[85]

After 1833 the management of the trust estates became, if anything, less progressive despite Frederick's keen interest in matters agricultural. There was no longer a London surveyor on the lookout for new properties and reporting on existing ones and most of the routine work of inspection and suggesting repairs and improvements fell on Rendlesham's own surveyor James Hillen (who was paid a salary of £100 p.a. rather than a percentage like Shaw), supplemented by local land agents and surveyors as needed.[86] The grand scheme to put all tenants on long leases was not revived and, with the notable exception of lands bought from Henry Edwards in 1836 and leased back to him for twenty-one years,[87] the power to grant medium term leases was seldom used other than for sporting rights.[88]

Since the new purchases were all either near to trust lands or actually intermixed with them they should have afforded opportunities to rearrange the farms into more efficient economic units. Following one such purchase in Yorkshire three farms were consolidated into one, and a few years afterwards, in 1854, a more ambitious re-organization was carried out involving over 2,700 acres.[89] The overall impression, however, is that there was no real drive to improve layouts or enlarge farms, though this does not necessarily imply an unambitious or conservative outlook since the ideal size of farms was hotly debated and the merits of enlargement were not uncontested.[90]

Better evidence of unadventurous management is provided by expenditure on repairs and improvements. The estate Act required that underleases imposed a duty to repair on the tenants, while enabling the costs of 'improvements' to be charged to the trust. This was a difficult distinction to draw in any case and it causes no surprise to find that major expenditure on buildings was invariably described as a 'substantial and permanent improvement and a benefit and advantage'; no such application was rejected by the master.[91] Reports in the suit generally speak of an allowance of 8% p.a. for repairs, which unless intended to encompass improvements is on the high side.[92] Even so, the outlay on purely physical improvements (excluding, for example, tithe commutation and copyhold enfranchisement) fell well short of some progressive landlords. On the Duke of Bedford's estates in the home counties (admittedly with a rental of £300,000 plus, they were much bigger than the Thellussons') around half the gross rental was being spent in this way and the Leveson- Gowers were almost equally lavish; with expenditure on that scale it is no wonder returns from land were

367

sometimes disappointing.[93] The court records show only £35,000 (about £1,500 p.a.) on a rent roll which rose from £23,500 to £36,000. This is a rate of 5 to 6%, right at the bottom of the range of reliable estimates and especially low for a landlord who might be expected to take a long term view;[94] it would be understandable however if the family, most of whom were hard up, preferred to put their immediate needs first.

These figures conceal significant variations over time and place. Spending was appreciably higher in Suffolk and Yorkshire, what might be considered the core of the estate, and decidedly low in the home counties. This may reflect the need to bring the new purchases up to scratch and it may also suggest that earlier efforts had left the home counties farms in better condition or, less probably, that the trust was more successful in persuading farmers in that region to take up the burden. The likelihood is, however, that it denotes a policy of favouring the estates which their ultimate owners were likely to wish to retain. The time shift is also interesting, for after laying out less than £10,000 in the decade after 1834, Rendlesham became noticeably more liberal and the pace quickened further (particularly in Yorkshire) once a receiver was in place again after 1852.

One reason for the modest spending was that the Rendleshams were not seduced by the vogue for drainage, even when tiles were displaced by pipes and the government offered loans.[95] Moreover, while the lands in the Don valley were wet and soggy,[96] on some of the light Suffolk soils erosion was more of a problem than waterlogging, but many Suffolk farmers made good use of the cheapness of labour to insert old-fashioned 'bush' drains.[97] Whatever the reason, the trust's abstention from drainage projects was probably the best course, for many landowners almost literally sank money into the ground without deriving a commensurate return from increased rents.[98]

On the other hand, substantial sums were spent on farm buildings. In the mid-century a positive 'rage for rebuilding'[99] farmhouses afflicted the great estates, with new ones springing up in every style and fashion, old ones modernised and the very worst downgraded to mere labourers' cottages. Sometimes they were removed to a

368

more convenient location, often their internal layout was made more commodious and logical after the models publicised by the Board of Agriculture and the experts of the day, and usually they were a great improvement.[100] But Caird bemoaned instances of money lavished to little purpose (Holkham is one case where the results were more imposing than practical) and, as John Jorrocks found, farmers were often ungrateful.[101] On the trust estates about a dozen farmhouses were rebuilt completely or substantially, mostly for between £400 and £700, and reading their descriptions, especially of those around Amotherby, with their leaking roofs, damp walls, rotten timbers and cramped kitchens, is a reminder of how much the conventional image of the `traditional' farmhouse, snug, spacious and comfortable in brick or stone, owes to these undertakings of the `high farming' era.[102]

Farming efficiency also required outbuildings of a better quality than existed in most places. Barns, waggon sheds and cattle sheds were not very expensive where there was timber to hand and the farmer could himself supply transport and labour. Nevertheless tenants were constantly asking their landlord to pull down old and ramshackle structures and replace them with something better.[103] When the trust agreed to do so the result was sometimes that the farmer's cows were better housed than his men. The `hungry forties' burned themselves into folk memory and never was sordid reality further from rustic idyll than in Suffolk, where farm wages were the lowest in the country [104] and hunger, poverty and misery found outlets in drunkenness, poaching[105] and, more sinisterly, in arson. Incendiarism in parts of East Anglia reached `epidemic proportions' [106] in the 1840s yet curiously no fire is recorded on the Thellusson estates in Suffolk and the only three fires of any sort (none of them arson) broke out in the midlands and home counties.[107]

The uncompromising testimony of official and private investigations forced the labourers' plight before the public and put pressure on landlords and farmers to meet one of the biggest grievances, the lack of decent housing, cottages of any sort being in short supply and many of those which existed being insanitary and wretched.[108] The Thellusson estates were not above criticism in this regard. One cottage in the village of Brodsworth was condemned as a public nuisance by the local board of health and ordered to be pulled down, and it was not the only one that deserved it; those at Pigburn had never had a privy or a bakehouse, nor even a proper drain, while at Delrow (Herts.) one cottage was so rickety that it was liable to be blown to pieces in the next gale.[109] Tenant farmers, having to Cobbett's eloquent disgust ejected their labourers from their own farmhouses,[110] were often unwilling to provide them with cottages; the labourers were often too poor for speculative builders to find rural housing a worthwhile investment, and the contraction of waste and commons deprived them even of the opportunity to build their own. At the back of the rural housing crisis lurked the new poor law and the determination of selfish ratepayers to restrict settlement in their own parishes, even if that meant the labourers had to trudge extra miles to and from work.[111]

Shame, fear and philanthropy drove many landowners to build cottages, occasionally by the hundred but more often, like the trust, in their tens. On the trust estates they usually cost between £100 and £150 for a semi-detached pair and often simply replaced decayed hovels, though some were in new locations more convenient for the farmworkers.[112] The modest provision does not suggest that the trust in this later phase was in the van of enlightened landlordism and any favourable impression is weakened by the fact that the schoolhouse at Brodsworth which, from its 'proximity to an open drain and the floor of the schoolroom being very low and frequently covered with water from the overflow of the said drain...is at all times damp and unhealthy for the children', was reconverted into cottages when a new one was built in 1845.[113]

The new schoolhouse, on rising ground more central to its catchment area, was considered to come within the definition of 'improvements' which the private Act authorised to be met from the trust fund, although Lord Rendlesham met its running costs out of his own pocket.[114] The Act was also held to authorise money spent on the spiritual life of the community. Besides a small contribution to the rebuilding of Leiston church,[115] the trust spent £740 on a curate's house at Marr (Yorks.) and shared with Queen Anne's Bounty the cost of another at Butley.[116] The original proposal had been to rehabilitate Butley Abbey (whose ruins the first Lord Rendlesham had plundered for stone) 'without its general character being altered'; costed at £653, this was probably abandoned as too expensive.[117]

The trust also essayed one purely commercial speculation in the building line. This was the construction of a new inn at Amotherby to serve the Malton and Thirsk railway, which had just provided a station there.[118] Unlike other landowners, the trust tried neither to divert the iron road from its lands (though it withdrew from negotiations to give the North-Eastern Railway extra land at Barnby Dun when brickearth was found on the site[119]), nor actively to encourage it. Nevertheless the spreading of the railway network did inevitably bring in a few windfalls. First the Oxford and Rugby, then the Birmingham and Oxford Junction Railway drove their tracks across the midlands estates, paying between them over £2,300 for the privilege; the London and Northwestern struck out through Hertfordshire, the North Eastern through Yorkshire and the East Suffolk pottered down to the North Sea, each bringing in a few hundred pounds and none, seemingly, causing any great concern.[120]

A further indication, besides his inactivity in purchases and repairs, that the third baron was a rather indolent manager, comes from the handling of the timber on the estates. After the grant of the lease at least one of the woodreves (for the home counties) had ceased to be employed, and nothing was done in that part until 1847, when a local man was engaged to examine the woods and auctions were held, followed by a sale in the midlands, which had also been neglected.[121] Things were better in the north, where the woodreves had been kept on, but sales were only resumed in the 1840s and after one especially disappointing auction the trust turned to private sales, mostly to George Guest, described as a wheelwright but evidently a pretty substantial businessman.[122] Curiously, there were no sales in Suffolk, though the lands bought from De Horsey were well wooded,[123] but as elsewhere considerable quantities were used in repairs and new buildings. Overall, timber sales netted about £300 p.a., which at 2% of the gross rental was well short of some big estates;[124]

moreover, so far from any new planting being done, a few woods were grubbed up.[125]

There was one other source of casual profits from land which deserves mention. Around 1850 coprolite - fossilised dung rich in phosphates- was found on the Suffolk estates and being in vogue as a fertiliser had considerable commercial value.[126] In law mineral deposits belonged to the freeholder, but Rendlesham followed the local custom of encouraging the tenants to excavate it from shallow pits in return for an equal share in the profits. In the first few years of the diggings, from which the fertiliser was mostly exported through Ipswich, these came to some £500 in all and the amount later increased.[127]

The court records show only three instances where objections were raised by the other branch of the family to the Rendleshams' management of the estates. In 1845 Charles was unhappy with at least some aspects of the proposal to spend upwards of £1,000 on repairs and cottage building in Yorkshire[128] and in 1847 his son demurred to the purchase of over 500 acres at Cretingham (Suffolk) for £30,000 plus. In both cases the master overruled the objection.[129]

The most stoutly maintained quarrel was over Brodsworth Hall. Charles claimed that during the negotiations over the Act in 1833 he had insisted on a limit of seven years to any lease of the house, coupled with an option for him to have a tenancy from year to year when a vacancy occurred and if he were then in a position to take it up. By his account this was inadvertently omitted from the deed of settlement which embodied the agreement about the division of the surplus rental and he only executed it on the faith of verbal assurances from the other signatories (including the solicitor John Benbow as attorney for the absent Frederick). Charles was able to return to England soon afterwards and asked Frederick to implement the arrangement when the current lease expired, which would be in December 1844. Frederick, however, refused, coldly explaining that Benbow had gone farther than he would have wished and insisting on the letter of the deed.[130]

If Charles had been sensible he would have given up at that point, but his longing for Brodsworth overcame what little prudence he possessed and in November

1844 he began Chancery proceedings against his cousin for an injunction to restrain the granting of any new lease and for a declaration that he was entitled to the benefit of the option. Predictably, he did not get very far. Ignoring Robarts, who counselled him against seeking by litigation `redress for your imaginary grievances which...will only involve you in useless and idle expense and will in the end prove altogether unavailing'[131] he had his day in court and saw Shadwell VC uphold Rendlesham's demurrer to the bill on the ground that `there appears to me so much vagueness and uncertainty about the terms of this [alleged] agreement as to make it impossible to be performed.'[132] He had succeeded only in annoying his cousin and incurring legal costs to him, to the new tenant and to his own solicitor Beaven, though the last named had to wait many years for his.[133] Since a demurrer lacks the circumstantial detail of an answer it is impossible to guess how much truth there was in Charles's version, but while it is perfectly possible that he did seek an option, seven years was in any event the usual term for leases and any competent solicitor would have advised him that he would be unable to rely on oral undertakings. Charles Thellusson was not a bad man, but he was a very foolish one.

NOTES

1. *Supra*, p. 331.

2. *Mirror of Parliament* 1833(3), 2998.

3. D. Lee, *Lyndhurst: the Flexible Tory* (London, 1994).

4. Supra, p. 330. The orders were SO. 95, 99.

5. He sent a letter urging his friends to support the bill: *Parl. Debs.*(3rd s.) 19 (1832-3), col.556. He was still in Florence in September: *Diary of Lady Shelley*, vol.II, p.228.

6. Debates of 4 and 5 July, *Mirror of Parliament* 1833 (3), 2733-5, 2763-6; *Parl. Debs.*(3rd s.) 19 (1832-3), cols.111-14, 146-54. The Prime Minister, Lord Grey, `never felt himself in greater difficulty' (col. 152) and all the leading politicians in the House participated in the debate.

7. *Mirror of Parliament* 1833(3), 2735.

8. *Ibid.*, 2929; *Parl. Debs.* (3rd. s.) 19 (1832-3), col.556.

9. *Mirror of Parliament* 1833(3), 2929-31; *Parl. Debs.* (3rd s.) 19 (1832-3), cols.556-60; *House of Lords Journals* 65 (1833), 493.

10. The first batch was called for in May: *House of Lords Journals* 65 (1833), 343, 387, 423-4, 432, 446, 449, 452, 455, 466-9.

11. The returns are in *House of Lords Sessional Papers* 1833, vol. 11.

12. *Parl. Debs.* (3rd s.) 19 (1832-3), col. 112.

13. *House of Lords Sessional Papers* 1833 vol. 11, nos. 70, 92.

14. *Ibid.*, nos. 92, 114.   15. E.M. Butler, A Regency Visitor: The English Tour of Prince Puckler-Muskau, 1826-8 (London, 1957), p.294. For a similar reference, in 1818, see Historical Manuscripts Commission, *Report on the Manuscripts of Earl Bathurst preserved at Cirencester Park* (London, 1923), p.461.

16. *Parl. Debs.* (3rd s.) 19, cols. 111-13; *Mirror of Parliament* 1833(3), 2733-4.

17. *Parl. Debs.* (3rd s.) 19 (1832-3), cols. 112-13.

18. *Ibid.*, cols.113-14.

19. *Ibid.*, col. 557.

20. *Mirror of Parliament* 1833(3), 2929.

21. *Ibid.* Apparently it became a local tradition that `these gentlemen interpreted literally the clause empowering them "to manage the estates as if they were their own"': W. Sykes, *Notes and Queries* (9th s.) 1 (1896), 97.

22. *Mirror of Parliament*, 1833(3), 2988.

23. Parl. Debs. (3rd s.) 19 (1832-3), col. 112.

24.   R.A. Melikan, *John Scott, Lord Eldon, 1751-1838, The Duty of Loyalty* (Cambridge, 1999), p.348.

25.   *Parl. Debs.*(3rd s.) 19 (1832-3), cols. 147, 149.

26.   *House of Lords Journals* 65 (1833), 513, entered on the third reading. It was drawn up by Eldon and signed also by Lords Abingdon, Bexley, Kenyon, Mansfield, Shaftesbury and Wharncliffe. A dissent by some of these at an earlier stage is at p.493.

27.   *Ibid.*

28.   *Parl. Debs.* (3rd s.) 19 (1832-3), col. 190 (31 Jul.).

29.   *Ibid.*, cols., 189, 185. Scarlett was a friend of the Thellusson family: P.C. Scarlett, *A Memoir of James Scarlett, 1st Lord Abinger* (London, 1877), p.134.

30.   *Ibid.*, col. 187.

31.   *Ibid.*, col. 189. Daniel O'Connell said that to use Chancery to settle property disputes was `like setting up a steam engine to crush a fly' (col. 188).

32.   In the Lords by 57-13 on suspending the standing orders; 87-20 on the third reading (an impressive turnout for a private bill). The Commons did not divide and made only technical amendments to the bill (*House of Commons Journals* 88 (1833), 634, 640, 646, 671), which passed on August 14.

33.   3 & 4 Will. IV c. xxxxiii.

34.   s.3.

35.   No copy of the deed seems to have survived, but its contents are given in the bill in *Thellusson v. Lord Rendlesham*, 1 Nov. 1844, PRO C 14/310/T59.

36.   (1821) 3 My & Cr. 584.

37.   The last of the four, Seymour, was born in 1827.

38.   Thellusson to M.A. Reyroux, 4 Mar. 1843, Brodsworth House Mss DD168/16b; account for 1852, *ibid.*, DD 168/1.

39.   *PP* 1826 (143) XVI. Lyndhurst had called upon Bickersteth and three others to suggest reforms: *Select Committee on Fees in Courts of Equity, PP* 1847-8 (158), XV, q.1489. His own bill of 1827 had foundered on the vexed question of compensation.

40.   3 & 4 Will. IV c. 94 ss. 22-3.

41.   They were finally removed in 1842 by 5 & 6 Vict. c. 103.

42.   The Act was based upon the report of a select committee (*PP* 1833(685) XIV), which included such strong critics of Chancery as M.A. Taylor and D.W. Harvey, as well as the archpriest of economy Joseph Hume, both law officers, Peel and John Romilly. William Vizard told the committee (qq.4,5) that Brougham had followed Lyndhurst's example in setting up a small group to consider Chancery subjects.

43. C.S. Bowen, Progress in the Administration of Justice in the Victorian Period, in *Select Essays in Anglo-American Legal History*, vol. I (reprint, London, 1968), 516- 57, at 528-9.

44. J.B. Atlay, *The Victorian Chancellors* (London, 1908), vol.I, pp. 410-16.

45. The returns in *PP* 1836 (370) XLIII are useful. Bills in Chancery failed to match the growth of company promotions and railways simply because the intolerable delays discouraged potential suitors: evidence of J. Wigram to the select committee on the Administration of Justice Bill, quoted in A.H. Manchester, *Sources for English Legal History, 1750-1950* (London, 1984), p.134.

46. Report of Chancery Commission, *PP* 1852 (1437) XXI, pp.33-4.

47. 3 & 4 Will. IV c.94 s.10. Report of Select Committee on Fees in Courts of Equity, *PP* 1847/8 (158) XV, qq. 161-3 (R.H. Leach).

48. As the Chancery Commission of 1852 pointed out (*PP* 1852 (1437) XXI, at 26-30), much of the court's procedure lost its rationale when divorced from its fee- generating function.

49. Since offices could only be abolished if their holders were fully compensated for the loss of income they would have enjoyed for the rest of their lives, the Treasury insistence that suitors must pay for the running costs of the courts- including this compensation- was a distinct brake upon desirable improvements. Hence the Chancery judge who, to Dickens' mock incredulity, blamed many of the ills excoriated in *Bleak House* on 'a parsimonious public' (preface to 1st edition, August 1853).

50. They already had the evidence of the select committee of 1847/8.

51. *Parl. Debs.*(3rd s.) 122 (1852), cols. 109-12. There was a particularly spiteful attack by Lyndhurst upon Sir John Romilly.

52. The Acts were the Improvement of the Jurisdiction of Equity Act (c.86), Suitors in Chancery Relief Act (c.87) and Masters in Chancery Abolition Act (c.80). According to Augustine Birrell, 'the year 1852 may be fairly taken as an epoch in the history of the old Court of Chancery', Changes in Equity Procedure and Principles, in *A Century of Law Reform*, (London, 1901), 177-202, at 198.

53. Lord Cottenham's general orders of 1850 brought some improvement: *PP* 1852 (1437) XXI, 10-15.

54. *Mirror of Parliament* 1833 (3), 2930.

55. PRO PROB 11/ 1827, f.86; PRO IR 26/1351, f.64. He died on 19 Jan. 1834. The value to him of Brodsworth is indicated by the fact that his personal estate was sworn at under £8,000. The obituary in *Annual Biography and Obituary* 18 (1834), 416, is curiously unrevealing. Interestingly, Charles Thellusson seems to have remained on visiting terms with Lady Flint: diary, 1849, Brodsworth House Mss DD168/ 15.

56. *The Greville Memoirs*, ed. H.Reeve (8 vols., London, 1888), vol. 3, p.190. His prudence cut no ice with the venal electors of Maidstone, who rejected him at successive elections in 1837 and 1838, causing him to abandon politics.

57. *The House of Commons, 1790-1820*; F. R. Boase, *Modern English Biography* (6 vols., Truro, 1892-1903), vol.III, p. 190.

58. G.F. Waagen, *Galleries and Cabinets of Art in Great Britain* (London, 1857), pp.158-65.

59. PRO C 33/862, f. 1095. Lords Segrave and Lyndhurst had queried Hammet's capacity in the debates on the private bill, alleging that extreme mental and bodily infirmity had made him incapable of transacting business for years: *Parl. Debs.*(3rd s.) 19 (1832-3), col.556; *Mirror of Parliament* 1833 (3), 2929. I have been unable to trace a will or an obituary.

60. *Alumni Cantabrigienses, 1752-1900*, vol.V, p.510; *Burke's Dictionary of the Landed Gentry*, vol. II, 1064.

61. He was living at Carlton Hall in 1843. His will (PRO PROB 11/2142, f.890) offers no assistance.

62. Boase, *Modern English Biography*, vol.III, pp.1481-2; Crosthwaite, *Memoir of Sir J.G.Woodford*, p.56 and app. 1.

63. Crosthwaite, *Memoir of Sir J.G. Woodford*, pp.35-41.

64. For the first, see *supra*, p. 201.

65. *Ibid.*

66. *Complete Peerage*, vol.VI, p.411. An Irish representative peer from 1836, he was made a Lord in Waiting by Peel and voted with him on the Corn Laws. He became a trustee on 19th December 1837: PRO C 38/1684.

67. A situation which produced conflicts between law and equity, leading to the landmark case of *Walsh v. Lonsdale* (1881-2) 21 Ch. D. 9.

68. Reports of 16 May 1835, 13 Dec. 1837, 31 Oct. 1838, PRO C 38/ 1632, 1684, 1713.

69. *Ibid.* This was not the only private act to encounter this difficulty: F.A. Sharman, Feudal Copyholder and Industrial Shareholder: the Dimes Case, *Journal of Legal History* 10 (1989), 71-90.

70. Reports of 31 May 1838, 19 Jun. 1840, PRO C 38/1716, 1739; order of 23 Jun. 1838, PRO C 33/887, f.717; *Sheppard v. Woodford* (1839) 5 M. & W. 608, 9 LJ Ex. 90. 71. Report of 13 Dec. 1837, PRO C 38/1684.

72. Report of 8 Aug. 1844, PRO C 38/1891.

73. PRO C 38, *passim*. Fourteen purchases in all, the smallest of twenty-six acres; two were from estates in Chancery, two others (costing £37,000) from Spencer Horsey de Horsey.

74. Report of 13 Jan. 1848, PRO C 38/2045.

75.   Order of 8 May 1854, PRO C 33/1022, f.886.

76.   Petition of 16 Apr. 1853, PRO TS 18/1501.

77.   *Ibid.*, crown brief, 22 Apr. 1854; report of 10 Nov. 1854, PRO C 38/2260. The self-styled `forty thieves' were the eminent conveyancers retained by the court.

78.   Report of 4 Aug. 1847, PRO C 38/2205.

79.   Report of 9 Dec. 1845, PRO C 38/1930. It was agreed that the case, *Parsley v. Cooper*, should be defended, but it is not reported.

80.   Dimes' activities, culminating in a pyhrric victory over Lord Chancellor Cottenham, whose death it is said to have hastened, are recounted in Sharman, *Copyholder and Shareholder*. It was agreed to defend the action over the bridge: report of 20 Nov. 1834, PRO C 38/1604.

81.   Crown brief, 1854, PRO TS 18/1501.

82.   Holdsworth, *History of English Law*, vol. 7, pp. 309-12.

83.   Crown brief, 1854, PRO TS 18/1501; order of 1 Mar. 1853, PRO C 33/1014, f.495. The only Yorkshire copyhold was one that had been bought in 1848.

84.   J. Scriven, *A Treatise on the Law of Copyholds* (7th edn., by A. Brown, London, 1896), pp. 326-73. The Act (15 & 16 Vict. c.51) applied from the next admission after 1 July 1853. Copyholds were finally abolished by the Law of Property Act 1922.

85.   Reports of 30 Jun., 8 Aug. 1855 (PRO C 38/2301), 14 Mar., 18 Apr., 19 Jul. 1856 © 38/2345), 12 Dec. 1856 © 38/2346). The trust owned several manors, and a few Hertfordshire tenants enfranchised their copyholds, notably H.H. Gibbs (Lord Aldenham), who paid them £741: order of 8 Dec. 1856, PRO C 33/1045, f. 184.

86.   Report of 25 Jul. 1853, PRO C 38/2323. Salaries were still commoner than percentages, at least in east Yorkshire: English, *Patterns of Land Management*, 29-48.

87.   Report of 13 Dec. 1837, PRO C 38/1684. Seven of the nine Suffolk tenants who were given rebates in 1853 held from year to year: report of 26. Jul. 1853, C 38/2230.

88.   Shooting at Butley was leased for seven years, determinable on six months' notice, after Charles Thellusson's death (order of 21 Jul. 1854, PRO C 33/1024, f.1304), and that at Barnby Dun for twenty years determinable after ten (report of 15 Feb. 1854, C 38/2260).

89.   Reports of 20 Jun. 1851 (PRO C 38/2163), 15 Feb. 1854 © 38/2260).

90.   J.V. Beckett, The Debate over Farm Sizes in 18th and 19th Century England, *Agricultural History*, 57 (1983), 308-25.

91.   See e.g. report of 23 Nov. 1843, PRO C 38/1858.

92.   Report of 12 Nov. 1846 (PRO C 38/1969), 19 Apr. 1849 © 38/2046) .

93.   J.V. Beckett, Landownership and Estate Management, *Agrarian History*, vol.VI, pp. 545-640, at 601-7; Richards, *The Leviathan of Wealth*.

378

94. PRO C33, C38, *passim*; Holderness, *Landlords' Capital Formation*, 434-47.

95. J. Brown and H.A. Beecham, Farming Techniques, in *Agrarian History*, vol. VI, pp.284-5; Chambers and Mingay, *Agricultural Revolution, 1750-1880*, pp.175-7. Surtees in *Hillingdon Hall* (1845) cast a sceptical eye over the whole craze.

96. Thus the report on Dormers Green notes that `this is higher, less flooded ground, so very useful': report of 9 Feb. 1848, PRO C 38/2045.

97. The French visitor de Rochefoucauld had described the sandy soils around Woodbridge: J. Marchand (ed.), *A Frenchman in England* (Cambridge, 1933), pp.177-80. See the map on p. 125 of H.M.E. Holt and R.J.P. Kain, Land Use and Farming in Suffolk c.1840, *Proceedings of the Suffolk Institute of Archaeology and History* 35 (1984), 123-41. On bush drains see Martins and Williamson, *Labour and Improvement*, 275-95.

98. *Agrarian History* vol. VI, pp.604-9.

99. B.A. Holderness, Agriculture and Industrialization, in Mingay (ed.) *The Victorian Countryside*, vol.I, 227-43 at 241.

100. *Ibid.*, 241-3; Harvey, *History of Farm Buildings*, pp.71-90; A.D.M. Phillips, Landlord Investment in Farm Buildings in the English Midlands in the Mid-Nineteenth Century, in B.A. Holderness and M. Turner (eds.), *Land, Labour and Agriculture: Essays for Gordon Mingay* (London, 1991), pp. 191-210.

101. *English Agriculture in 1850-51*, 491; and *cf.* p.152, where it is said that in Suffolk the tenants usually did the rebuilding; Surtees, *Hillingdon Hall*.

102. Report of 22 Nov. 1853, PRO C 38/2231.

103. Phillips, *Landlord Investment*, p. 200. Examples abound in PRO C 38, for instance report of 29 Jan. 1847, C 38/2005.

104. P. Clarke with K. Langford, Hodge's Politics: The Agricultural Labourers and the Third Reform Act in Suffolk, N. Harte and R. Quinault (eds.), *Land and Society in Britain, 1700-1914* (Manchester, 1996), 119-36, at 127; Martins and Williamson, *Labour and Improvement*, 283.

105. *V.C.H. Suffolk*, vol.2, pp.366-7, F.S.Corrance's recollections including `desperate affrays', notably at Campsey Ash.

106. D. Jones, Thomas Campbell Foster and the Rural Labourer, *Social History* 1 (1976), 5-37 at 6.

107. Reports of 21 Jul.1840 (PRO C 38/1769), 29 Jan. 1847 (C 38/2005), 29 Jun. 1850 (C 38/2125).

108. Jones, *Foster*; E. Gauldie, Country Homes, *The Victorian Countryside*, vol. II, pp.531-41.

109. Reports of 29 Jun. 1850 (PRO C 38/2125), 23 Nov. 1843 (C 38/ 1858), 19 Dec. 1848 (C 38/2046).

110. *Rural Rides* (1912 edn., London), vol.I, pp.265-6; Martins and Williamson, *Labour and Improvement*, 282-3.

111. Jones, *Foster*; Gauldie, *Country Homes*. While the clear dichotomy between `open' and `closed' parishes, especially as described in D.R. Mills, *Lord and Peasant in Nineteenth Century Britain* (London, 1980), has been questioned (e.g. by S. Banks, Nineteenth Century Scandal or Twentieth Century Model? A New Look at `Open' and `Closed' Parishes, *Economic History Review* (2nd s.) 41 (1989), 51-73), there is no doubt that the new poor law did distort the provision of accommodation. According to W.H. Raynbird, *On the Agriculture of Suffolk* (London, 1849), `landlords will not build cottages' (p.281). Lord Rendlesham was one of the subscribers to this book.

112. E.g. the two at Newton Hanzard, report of 22 Nov. 1847, PRO C 38/2006.

113. Report of 22 Nov. 1845, PRO C 38/1930.

114. *Ibid.*

115. Report of 25 Jul. 1853, PRO C 38/2230. His sister Adeline was a more generous benefactor to the church, helping to raise the funds which enabled E.B. Lamb to exercise his peculiar talents for restlessly original churches: A. Raikes, *Victorian Churchbuilding and Restoration in Suffolk* (Woodbridge, 1982), p.419.

116. Report of 7 Aug. 1857, PRO C 38/2388; C 33/934, ff. 172, 265.

117. Report of 13 Aug. 1841, PRO C 38/1798.

118. Report of 22 Nov. 1853, PRO C 38/2231.

119. PRO C 33/1038, f.617. F.A. Sharman, The Influence of Landowners on Route Selection, *Journal of the Railway and Canal History Society*, 26 (1980), 49.

120. Orders of 29 Jul. 1846 (PRO C 33/957, f.1524), 10 Nov. 1847 (C33/974, f.69), 1 Aug. 1856 (C33/1040, f.1875).

121. Reports of 15 Mar. 1841 (PRO C 38/1797), 25 May 1847 © 38/2005), 17 Feb. 1848 © 38/2045), 30 Jan. 1852 © 38/2202), 24 Jun. 1856 © 38/ 2345).

122. Reports of 15 Mar. 1841 (PRO C 38/1797), 10 May 1844 © 38/1891). Sales to Guest began in 1842.

123. Reports of 9 Mar. 1848 (PRO C 38/2045), 25 Jan. 1850 © 38/2125).

124. *Cf.* the figures in the *Agrarian History*, vol.VI, pp.625-6.

125. Reports of 5 May 1851 (PRO C 38/2163), 22 Nov. 1853 © 38/2231).

126. Report of 25 Jul. 1853, PRO C 38/2230; W.G. Arnott, *A Suffolk Estuary*, (Ipswich, 1950), p.107.

127. R. Grove, Coprolite Mining in Cambridgeshire, *Agricultural History Review* 24 (1976), 36-43. The Suffolk pits were all defunct by c.1890: A. Jobson, *Victorian Suffolk* (London,1972), p. 47.

380

128. Report of 22 Nov. 1845, PRO C 38/1930.

129. Report of 4 Aug. 1847, PRO C 38/2005.

130. *Thellusson v. Lord Rendlesham*, PRO C 14/310, T59.

131. A.G. Robarts to C. Thellusson, 31 Jan. 1844, Brodsworth Hall Mss DD 168/16(a).

132. *Thellusson v. Lord Rendlesham* (1846-7) 8 *LT* 463.

133. PRO C 14/310, T59.

134. Reports of 16 Jan., 5 Jul. 1847, PRO C 38/2005.

CHAPTER 15

THE FINAL ROUND

In the year of the Great Exhibition, when Dickens began *Bleak House*, Frederick's health, never good, began to fail. Neither a course of `steel' nor the air of fashionable Folkestone did much good and next spring, on 6th April, he died of kidney failure and water on the chest.[1] The title passed to his only son, Frederick William Brooke, a boy of twelve about to go to Eton.

The lad's uncle Arthur lived close by at Aldeburgh but was passed over as guardian for him and his thirteen year old sister in favour of Francis Capper Brooke of Ufford Place.[2] Frederick's third christian name suggests that Brooke was a close family friend, and he had recently re-married with Louisa Duff, the children's twenty-two year old half-sister.[3] Brooke and another local landowner, Charles Austin of Blundiston Hall, were the executors of Frederick's will, a brief deathbed document which discloses that he owed several hundred pounds to his own valet. Practically everything he had to leave went to his daughter, a power given him by his father's will enabling him to charge the entailed estates with £10,000 in her favour.[4] Arthur took umbrage at Brooke's appointment and tried his hand at mischief making, complaining that Brooke estranged the boy from his family and mismanaged his affairs, but since he evidently failed to convince the trustees of the Rendlesham settled estates that there was anything in his allegations, it seems unlikely that they were more than the product of a disgruntled and underemployed mind.[5]

As a rival claimant to the Suffolk branch's half of the fortune Arthur was in a position to be more troublesome when it was proposed to petition Parliament for the leasing arrangement, which fell with Frederick's death, to be renewed in favour of his son, for whom Brooke and A.G. Robarts would hold it in trust until he came of age. His opposition so delayed matters that by the time a revised proposal, confined to the Yorkshire estates and operating only on the share of the cadet branch, had been settled, the promoters had run out of time. When the new session of Parliament began, Charles Thellusson's life, the thread by which the whole accumulation now hung, was so uncertain that the idea was dropped.[6] The old position was therefore restored, the trustees resuming their responsibilities and installing sundry Thellussons as receivers- Charles Sabine in the north, Thomas in the midlands and home counties, Arthur in Suffolk.[7] This immediately increased management costs and more expense was incurred in the replacement of Edward Simeon, who had died in October 1851.[8] Edward Dawkins, who had been *chargé d'affaires* in Florence in the 1820s and was an old acquaintance of the family, took his place. Related by marriage to another trustee, Lord Hawarden, he was a man about town, personable, respected and unobjectionable even to Arthur Thellusson.[9]   All were now marking time, waiting for Charles to die. He bore this invidious position with some dignity, struggling against sickness and debts, for, as he wrote, `in perfect health and spirits it is no easy or pleasant task to live by one's wits, but when suffering from illness and unable to get about, as is my case at this moment, it is extremely difficult to keep the head above water.'[10] He certainly showed plenty of resource in exploiting what limited credit he had, his debts exceeding £50,000 when he died,[11] but making economies he found much harder[12] and though he luckily had no daughters to marry, his wife had little money of her own and his four younger sons had to be set up.[13] The soldiers, Alexander and Frederick, came safely through `that fatal Crimea',[14] Seymour found employment in the civil service[15] and Ernest, married young to the only daughter of a London solicitor, decamped to county Down to start a family and later fetched up in the Isle of Man.[16]

Among Charles's many creditors the Robartses were the least exigent and most of the other big ones either came to accommodations, taking what security they could, or resigned themselves to hoping that Charles Sabine would pay when his father died. It was the small men who were most importunate, less able to wait for their money- like his doctor, who was driven into bankruptcy by Charles and patients like him;[17] they were convinced that he could discharge their `little bills' even though the bigger ones were hopeless. So money was paid on account, law suits were started, and settled, Peter was robbed to pay Paul- all the usual shifts and evasions were resorted to.[18] The ignominy and humiliations were all the harder to bear with the great accumulation so tantalisingly close and as well as being exposed to bullying from the creditors, Charles had to put up with lectures from his own solicitor, Thomas Gill. Gill was an insolent vulgarian who told him home truths: `you are a sad bungler in these affairs', and `you must not grumble to pay the expenses I have charged'.[19] Many solicitors in the great suit, men like Benbow, Freshfield, Reyroux and Budd, were thorough gentlemen who would never have used such familiarity, but Gill was another sort altogether, and for all his coarseness may have served his client well.

Charles's main source of regular income vanished when the trustees resumed management of the estates, but he found relief, if not salvation, in a quarter where many others met their ruin- on the Turf. With the coming of off-course betting in the wake of the railways, horse racing grew in popularity, but although the efforts of Lord George Bentinck, Admiral Rous and others had raised it from its lowest depths of corruption and iniquity, it remained a prey to cheats and crooks of all descriptions.[20] Charles knew all about its seamy side, having acted for Osbaldeston in a murky affair many years before,[21] but although pronounced `one of the best judges of horseflesh in the kingdom',[22] he lacked the means to back his judgement. But not all devotees of `the national pastime' were crooked, and it was through one shining exception that his last years were made bearable.

John Theobald was a noted racehorse breeder from whose stud at Stockwell, long since swallowed up in the march of the London suburbs, came some fine horses, the greatest of them Stockwell, `the emperor of stallions', whose fame poor Theobald did not live to see.[23] To use the language he loved, Theobald was by Jorrocks out of Pickwick: a huge man, not a grocer like Jorrocks but, as a hosier of Skinner Street, just as much a `Cit'. His passion was horses, but racing rather than hunting; `his highest ambition was to have the best of everything, cost what it might',[24] and every so often he would take off for Newmarket to be, like the grocer of Coram Street, `the death of a five pun note'; of a good many in fact, for rumour said he was worth half a million and if rumour exaggerated, it did not wholly invent.[25] In his youth he aped the dress of the Prince Regent, but unlike Mr.Turveydrop, he made no attempt to preserve it beyond the death of `the first gentleman of Europe', relapsing instead into an altogether individual style which earned him the nickname `Old Leather Breeches'.[26] He was Pickwickian in his generosity to servants and the poor and in his hospitality, but needed no Sam Weller to keep him out of trouble.[27]

Theobald's son William was quite another sort of man, a collector of fine china and *objets d'art*, so when the Theobalds and the Thellussons became friendly it was with Theobald *fils* that Charles Sabine had things in common. More important, William had a daughter Georgiana, a strikingly handsome brunette.[28] In the autumn of 1849 old Theobald died suddenly (so robust that even at eighty-five his passing was unexpected), and though his personal estate was sworn at less than £60,000, he left a good deal of land at Ludgate Hill and Brixton, ripe for development. His son was already prosperous and a few months later, Georgiana and Charles Sabine were married.[29]

While Theobald put a quantity of his valuable lands into the marriage settlement, Thellusson had nothing to give. Instead, the groom promised that if he inherited under the great will, he would settle land worth £5,000 a year and give Georgiana a jointure of £2,000 p.a. In other respects the settlement was a conventional strict settlement.[30] Within two months of the wedding William Theobald died, leaving handsome legacies to nieces and nephews, £5,000 to his only son (probably the recipient of large lifetime gifts) and the rest to Georgiana.[31]

The stud had been broken up on old Theobald's death. The best stallion, The Baron, went to France for 1,010 guineas, but Charles Sabine had bought Stockwell's mother, Pocahontas, for just 260 guineas. She was in foal again, and on the morning that William Theobald died, Rataplan was born.[32] Charles Sabine gave the colt to his father, who had aspirations to race horses,[33] and it quickly became clear that Rataplan had real potential. He was a big, dark chestnut with a mighty chest; an immensely powerful horse, no beauty and not particularly quick over the ground but when roused- he could be indolent- he had an abundance of courage and staying power.[34] These qualities were shrewdly developed by his trainer, Charles Parr, a quondam tea-pedlar and one of the great curiosities of the turf, a man so hopeless with money that he spent much of his time in hiding from his creditors but a gifted trainer for all that.[35]

By 1853 Rataplan was a force to be reckoned with and though he failed to emulate Stockwell by carrying off the St. Leger, run virtually in the Thellussons' own backyard at Doncaster, he won over £1,100 in prize money.[36] Even so, Charles found the cost of racing horses beyond his pocket and, needy as ever, borrowed £1,000 from Parr, who gained the right to race Rataplan in his own colours and keep his winnings; these reached £3,700, including the £1,000 Tradesmen's Cup at Manchester.[37] At the end of the season the two men quarrelled and parted, Parr sending in an inflated bill which Charles referred to Admiral Rous, the great authority on all racing matters. Rous advised him to pay up, cautioning that Parr ʻis a wonderfully clever man and may hold his own at a wrangle- all I can recommend to you is to have nothing more to do with him'.[38] Charles had already decided to be done with Parr, and despondently sought to sell Rataplan too, offering him to Osbaldeston for 3,300 guineas.[39] The price was too high, so ignoring the advice of the vicar of Doncaster to give up racing and prepare his soul for the next world,[40] he sent the horse to be trained by one of the Dawsons, even more uncouth than Parr but well reputed and rather more dependable.[41]

So ʻold Ratty' was seen again in the Thellusson colours, red with a green cap, usually with John Prince in the saddle.[42] He was indeed his owner's liferaft. For several years he had been ʻliving on the horses'[43] and in this, his last summer, he lived off Rataplan. The railways had revolutionised racing, turning meetings into national rather than local affairs and making it feasible to send a horse from one meeting to another month in and month out.[44] Few owners, before or since, have exploited that potential so ruthlessly as Thellusson: from Newcastle and Carlisle to Bath and Plymouth Rataplan went, sometimes to race several times in one meeting, in big races and, more often, in small, as odds-on favourite and rank outsider. When he turned out at Goodwood, Gill bluntly told his client, `it was disgraceful on your part to have run him and a sense of decency and humanity ought to have prevented your doing so.'[45] By the season's end the old horse had run thirty-three times- four more than in 1854- winning twenty races and nearly £3,000; appropriately, one of his last successes was in the Doncaster Cup. The previous December, after Parr had squeezed all he could out of him, Rous had explained when asked about a possible sale that `people naturally imagine that a horse must be very dry and unprofitable after being out twenty-nine times in one year, that he is not likely to have much more running in him';[46] Rataplan had confounded the pundits, but his race was almost run. His portrait hangs in the billiards room at Brodsworth and he deserves his place, for he worked much harder for the Thellussons than most of them did for themselves.[47]

Charles's own race was nearly over too. Doctors punctured his swollen legs, prescribed cabbage leaves externally and vichy water internally, but nothing helped and on 5th February 1856 he died in Brighton.[48]

With the death of Charles the great accumulation, begun almost sixty years before, came to a stop. Rents would continue to be collected and dividends would come in but no more land would be bought. Of the Thellussons whose lives determined the length of the accumulation, one met a premature end in battle, one died in childhood and seven came of age and died of natural causes; all of those seven reached forty yet none made sixty, Charles being the longest lived at fifty-nine. In the two generations spanned by the accumulation just one male lived to what may be called old age, Thomas, the third son of Charles senior (sixty-eight), whereas of the six females all but Frances, who died a child, passed sixty.[49]

Given that he had little to leave but his debts, it is not surprising that Charles made only a short will, appointing his long suffering wife his executrix and a leaving her a life interest in whatever he did have, with remainder to his sons. At his request he was buried in Brodsworth church, hard by the house he always felt should have been his to inhabit, if not to own.[50]

And so on 4th June 1856 twenty counsel learned in the law, half as many solicitors and all the spectators who could find space crammed into the Rolls court, though everyone, not least the Master of the Rolls himself, knew that whatever the verdict, it was no more than a formal prelude to the real business in the House of Lords. It was in everyone's interests, other than the lawyers', to expedite that process and no sooner had Roundell Palmer,[51] opening for Lord Rendlesham, got comfortably into his stride recounting the past hearings than Romilly seized on his reference to *Oddie v. Woodford*[52] to interrupt, explaining that he felt doubtful whether he was not bound to follow Eldon's considered judgment and its affirmation by the Lords. The concern he went on to express for the proper use of `public time' and for the queue of Chancery suitors marks the distance Chancery had travelled since the palmy days of Lord Eldon, when time hung suspended while perfect justice was divined, but his intervention also permitted the framing of a decree which would take the case directly to the Lords, by-passing the recently established Court of Appeals in Chancery.[53]

It also gave the rival claimants a last chance to settle out of court. Given Arthur's antagonism to his nephew's guardian, there was never much chance of an accommodation on that side,[54] but Charles Sabine's uncle Thomas was hard up and might be disposed to bargain. However, he had already turned down an offer of £30,000, which was rash given that the usually well informed Charles Greville reckoned the odds against him at 100-1. Greville let himself be persuaded to take a hand and sought to enlist A.G. Robarts to persuade Charles Sabine to renew that offer. Whether he refused or whether Thomas confounded Greville's view that he would `not be such a fool as to decline'[55] is not known; at any rate, the negotiation came to nothing and when Thomas later had the effrontery to ask his nephew for money, he was sharply upbraided and told that he had `resorted to every possible means of opposing my claims- have put me to the expence of many thousands of pounds, -have kept me out of possession of the estates for three years, thereby caused my mother and father to be pennyless during that period, as well as have deprived me of the opportunity of assisting other branches of the family who were in need of help, to say nothing of myself who would have been in a similar position but for my wife's property'.[56]

As Charles Sabine wrote, his offer would have made Thomas and his family comfortable for life, but an extra £1,500 a year hardly amounted to affluence, and Thomas had set his sights on at least double. He was playing for large stakes and was now left to contemplate the long odds against success.

It took another two years to reach the last big scene in the drama but the long wait did ensure that it took place before a court which no longer merited Bethell's savage criticism that its `judicial business was conducted...in a manner which would disgrace the lowest court of justice in the kingdom'.[57] The complaint had once been that equity appeals were merely a rehearing by the Chancellor of his own decrees, but more recently the tribunal had comprised three past and present Chancellors in a combustible mixture which frequently generated more heat than light. A maladroit proposal to stabilise the House by introducing eminent judges as life peers had only generated a minor constitutional crisis and in the confusion of parties and the feuding of powerful lawyers all reforms fell to the ground. Luckily the ministerial merry-go-round and the creation of a few new judicial peers diluted the animosities and restored dignity and some authority to the proceedings, and for the Thellusson case three ex-Chancellors were available, along with Lord Wensleydale and the new Chancellor, Lord Chelmsford.[58] Notwithstanding this formidable body of learning, eight of the common law judges were called upon for their advice, which ought to have been to the appellants' advantage, as they were less steeped in conveyancing lore and less likely to stand in awe of Lord Eldon's judgments.[59]

Counsel in the case were formidable too. Of the principal antagonists, Bethell[60] and Palmer, were future Chancellors, as was Cairns, who led the next-of-kin's forlorn

390

hope.[61] In fact, of the fifteen men who held the Great Seal between Thurlow's dismissal in 1792 and Halsbury's appointment in 1885 all but Wilde, Lord Truro, appeared in the cause either as counsel or judge or both, a record few suits can match.[62] Among the other counsel, John Rolt (for Charles Sabine) was a future Lord Justice and others, such as C.J. Selwyn, Markham Giffard and Chapman Barber, were all men of distinction.[63] However, Bethell, in particular, seldom gave much scope to his juniors and Palmer, if less brusque, was justifiably confident in his unaided powers.[64]

So the stage was set for a grand spectacle, with an all star cast in what the newspapers called `The Great Thellusson Case'. The script, however, was poor. Millionaires were no longer the rare birds they had been in the 1790s, and the size of the Thellusson fortune was less than half what had been at stake in the Bridgwater case a few years before;[65] furthermore that case had been one to decide a significant point of public policy, and that element was missing from the Thellusson case now.[66] When heard by Loughborough all those years before it had been a fight over the direction of the law in an area of great significance to the propertied classes; now the best legal brains in the country were gathered before its highest tribunal to do no more than argue about the meaning of a single phrase in an old will. What is more they all knew the arguments by heart, had argued it among themselves in exercises as pupils, had heard it expounded by their seniors, had read the judgments; no wonder it makes dull reading, this forensic sledgehammering of a tough old legal nut.[67]

The appellants' main argument ran thus.[68] The meaning of `male lineal descendant' had been authoritatively decided in *Oddie v. Woodford*[69] but any comments of Eldon's about the meaning of `eldest' were *obiter* and therefore not binding. `Eldest' had to be construed as a single adjective describing the compound phrase `male lineal descendant' and should be approached without preconceptions as to what a conveyancer would expect to find in a will since it is not a term of art. The correct approach is that suggested by Sir James Wigram in his treatise, *viz.*:

`that when there is nothing in the context of a will from which it is apparent that a testator has used the words in which he has expressed himself in any other sense than their strict and primary sense, and when the words so interpreted are sensible with reference to extrinsic circumstances, it is an inflexible rule of construction that the words in the will shall be interpreted in their strict and primary sense, and in no other, although they may be capable of some popular or secondary interpretation.'[70]

The 'strict and primary' meaning of eldest, as shown by the dictionaries, is 'oldest in years' and nothing in the will indicates that the testator intended the word to bear any secondary meaning; indeed, there are indications both in the advowson clause and in a parenthetical phrase repeatedly used in the limitation of estates in tail which support the primary meaning.[71] Decided cases are of no assistance in construing so unusual a will and the fact that the result of applying these propositions is unexpected or at variance with normal conveyancing practice is of no significance, especially as this testator was attempting something quite novel.

On the other side it was urged[72] that Lord Eldon's considered *dicta* were at least entitled to some persuasive authority and that since the will was evidently professionally drafted it was certainly proper to consider the meaning a word or phrase commonly bore in conveyancing practice. The interpretation which had been given to 'male lineal' as a compound adjective did not preclude the expansion of the compound to incorporate 'eldest', the whole phrase then qualifying 'descendant'. The primary meaning of eldest may indeed be oldest in years, but in a legal context it is just as likely to mean 'first', this reading being strongly supported by the presence of a series of limitations in the will which refer successively to 'the eldest', 'the second', 'the third' and so on.[73] Further support comes both from the parenthesis and the advowson clause; moreover, while the appellants' construction yields a capricious and unusual result, the respondents' gives, in effect, an ordinary series of entails preceded by an admittedly novel accumulation; it was only the latter that was intended as an innovation.

Two of the common law judges, Barons Martin and Bramwell, succumbed to the appellants' arguments. Martin has the lesser reputation[74] but his opinion is painstaking and solid, he deals carefully with the arguments about the alternative phraseology available to the draftsman, with the advowson and parenthesis, and with the effect of Eldon's judgment, concluding that the context gives no clear guidance. That being so, any deviation from the primary meaning of eldest is an unjustifiable embroidery of the will's language.[75]

Bramwell was a great judge but he was never at his best with the sophistries of equitable jurisprudence and the refinements of the conveyancer's art.[76] His opinion is a poor specimen of his talents, employing an unconvincing analogy with a `Scotch iron bridge', asserting that Eldon's argument had an `elaboration and ingenuity...which to my mind makes it suspicious' and describing the respondents' construction as `unnatural and forced'.[77] It is all rather superficial, as though he undertook the exercise reluctantly and was impatient to be done with it.

That two judges *were* convinced is a tribute to Bethell's powers, for none of the other six had much doubt. Willes expounded the grammar with a felicity that makes Bramwell seem clumsy;[78] Byles stressed that `the capital fallacy in the Appellants' argument' was to ignore that the will was `penned by a lawyer...addressed to lawyers, and intended to be understood by lawyers in a legal and technical sense';[79] Watson and Wightman, Crompton and Williams wove variations around the same themes at greater or lesser length.[80] They can be forgiven some impatience at being summoned at all, since they must have suspected that the heavyweights who would be reading their opinions were unlikely to give them much weight; nor, despite the conventional gestures of thanks, is there much in their lordships' speeches to suggest that they found them of great help.[81]

The judges were unanimous on the other question they had been asked, whether the will was void for uncertainty, and the only point on which the Lords differed seriously among themselves was whether it had been proper to consider that question at all, or whether it had not been conclusively determined by the House in the course of previous rounds in the litigation. Lord St. Leonards thought it had, and said so at length, but Lords Chelmsford and Cranworth would not submit to his dictation; the report ends with a bad tempered little squabble, St. Leonards insisting on saying the last word even if he could not have it.[82]

On the main question Brougham made a short, insignificant speech   to put himself on the record even though he had missed some of the argument.[83] Wensleydale's deals admirably with the arguments.[84] Both he and Cranworth accepted the correctness of the rules of construction put forward by Bethell but found indications in the will that eldest *was* to be used in a secondary sense, especially since `the words to be interpreted are not...words which can be said to have any ordinary popular sense. They are eminently technical; the words, not of the testator himself, but of his lawyer, dealing with a matter of a peculiarly technical nature.'[85]

All the Lords found the appellants' approach flawed by artificiality, requiring the judge to close his mind to all that he knows of the common practice of settlors and conveyancers and to grope his way towards a conclusion which will not only be surprising but wildly improbable. If a word is to be given its commonest meaning, that is simply because it is the meaning which, in the absence of any other evidence, the testator is most likely to have given it. But it is hardly consistent to assume that the testator intends a single word to have the commonest usage while not being prepared also to assume that he intends his dispositions, in the absence of contrary evidence, likewise to conform to the usual practice. Testators are entitled to be capricious with their dispositions as they are entitled to play Humpty-Dumpty with the meaning of words, but it is a curious rule that bids a judge make use of probabilities in construing words, while denying him the same assistance when considering the outcome of rival constructions. It is also one thing to ascribe the commonest meaning to a word occurring in isolation, quite another to do so where it evidently forms part of a phrase which, even if it has no accepted technical meaning, never appears in common speech at all.[86]

Cranworth's speech along these lines is a colourless, competent affair, typical of the man. The speech of Lord St.Leonards, by contrast, is that of a man in love with his subject, for whom wills and settlements were as fascinating as pleadings were to

Wensleydale. It is masterful and vivid, from his almost comical horror at being asked `to divest myself of my knowledge of law, and to come to [the will] with a naked mind and to consider it without these means',[87] to his evident pleasure in the craftsmanship of the will itself. The draftsman who had had to endure Buller's scornful assertion that he did not know how to draw up an entail should have been there to hear St.Leonards praise his `great learning and great accuracy', which had enabled the will to withstand every assault.[88] At one point he dons the mantle of Mr. Podsnap: `we all know countries in which, at the moment of the division of the property, they would collect all the heirs of the ancestor into a room, and call for baptismal certificates, and call out for the eldest male, without reference to the particular branch or line he represented, preferring the oldest man in age to the younger man of the elder branch. Well, that may do very well in Egypt, but it will not do in England.'[89] At another point he gives his fellow judges a gratuitous lecture on the drafting of settlements,[90] and he exhibits throughout all that dogmatic self-assertion of which his enemies complained; still, whatever the tone, it is hard to fault his reasoning.

Their Lordships were unanimous[91] that the two younger men, Lord Rendlesham and Charles Sabine Augustus Thellusson, were to share their great- grandfather's inheritance. It was the conclusion everyone had expected and it was surely the correct one: it is just unfortunate that it could not have been conclusively arrived at sixty years earlier, saving the family much dissension and the ultimate beneficiaries the loss they sustained through the expense of the later litigation.

Arthur Thellusson had been spared the dissolution of his hopes, for he died in the week before the Lords began their hearing, the ninth and last surviving of Peter Isaac's nine sons and at fifty-six the longest lived. His son, a veteran of the Crimea, took his place for the final stages of the suit. However much they contributed to their misfortunes by their own litigiousness, the Thellussons were certainly an unlucky family: in the senior branch the single life of Frederick's young son had kept the destination of their half of the fortune in doubt, while in the junior branch the obstacle was Thomas, who had no son to inherit his claim and who lived a good ten years longer than his elder brother or any of his male cousins. Ironically, it was only among George's descendants, had they been held entitled to a share, that there would have been a single, undisputed claimant.[92]

The Lords' decision resolved the destination of the property, but it could not be prised from Chancery's grasp immediately. It had first to be divided and even then the Rendlesham share could not be distributed, for the owner was still in his teens, having recently returned from an extended grand tour. A commission of partition had been appointed after the hearing at the Rolls and found their task quite straightforward: Suffolk to the senior branch, Yorkshire and the midlands to the junior, the home counties parcelled out between them.[93] Since Hawarden and Robarts had both died during the final bout of litigation, the last surviving trustee, Dawkins, was left to execute the conveyances alone.[94]

Brooke continued to manage the Rendlesham estates, both those derived from the young peer's grandfather and those he acquired from the partition, but repairs on the latter had still to be approved by Chancery, and these, together with sales to railway companies and the purchase of a small plot at Aldenham, ensured that there was still a steady trickle of routine orders in the suit.[95] Even when the heir came of age, celebrated in a great firework display at Rendlesham,[96] it did not dry up immediately, but there was nothing to match the great scene at the end of *Jarndyce v. Jarndyce*, where `presently great bundles of paper began to be carried out- bundles in bags, bundles too large to be got into any bags, immense masses of paper of all shapes and no shapes, which the bearers staggered under, and threw down for the time being, anyhow, on the Hall pavement, while they went back to bring out more.'[97] This, however, was not due to any lack of papers, the title deeds to the various properties belonging to the trust alone being so numerous and bulky that they had overflowed the master's chambers.[98] A glance at the documents preserved among the records of the Treasury Solicitor, covering only the last few years of the suit and no more extensive than was necessary to brief the crown's lawyers in a cause in which it had only the most peripheral interest, gives some idea of the mass of material which the solicitors for the main parties must have accumulated.[99]

There was no grand exit, the great suit which had been part of the court's business for half a century slipped unobtrusively away in a series of minor hearings and orders in which money lurking in odd accounts was extricated; it included proceeds of railway sales and copyhold enfranchisements by tenants of the trust's manors,[100] a few hundreds belatedly discovered by Smith, Payne, Smith[101] and £500 representing Long Annuities once in the names of the first trustees and later held by the National Debt Reduction Commissioners. Last of all, there was the money set aside to meet the West Indian annuities, finally freed in 1862 on the death of the last holder, the Nottingham banker Ichabod Wright, at the venerable age of ninety-five.[102] Even then one-sixteenth had to be held back to meet the claims of the heirs of John Cossart and was not removed from the list of dormant funds until the last years of the century.[103] Only then, after a hundred years, the ghost of Peter Thellusson at last ceased to haunt the court of Chancery.

The very last order in the suit proper was made by the Master of the Rolls, Sir John Romilly, on 23rd May 1863.[104] The four visits to the House of Lords and the major decisions in Chancery which the reporters included in their collections form the tip of a vast iceberg of decrees and orders, hearings and reports, more than 950 orders and at least 780 reports, including many concerned solely with costs.[105] *Thellusson v. Woodford* and its offspring were part of Chancery lore and few leading lawyers did not at some stage of their careers make an appearance in it. Like *Jarndyce v. Jarndyce* there were lavished on it, in Conversation Kenge's words, `the flower of the Bar and...the matured autumnal fruits of the Woolsack'.[106] Besides Lord Chancellors, every Master of the Rolls from Arden to Romilly[107] and most of the Vice-Chancellors were engaged in it.[108] It was in the office of five masters, lodging twenty-five years with Master Cox alone.[109] At least a hundred counsel appeared, some almost unknown today, others of great eminence; among their number are a dozen who became judges and others who became Chancery masters and law officers of the crown, as well as men who never held high public office but who were nevertheless held in the highest esteem at the bar, men such as Francis Hargrave and Charles Butler, Samuel Romilly, Richard Preston, George Heald and Arthur Hobhouse.[110]

Naturally, all this legal talent did not come cheap and the costs of the suit are legendary. As we have seen, they have also been exaggerated and never came near to swallowing up the fund,[111] but they are enormous all the same. Taking the figures given to Parliament in 1833, which total just over £96,000,[112] and adding all the subsequent taxed costs I have been able to find, the total is almost £147,000.[113] Since these seem not to include the costs of the final excursion to the House of Lords, it is safe to say that sums paid to solicitors for their own charges, for barristers' fees and other disbursements, together with court costs, reached £150,000, an average of £2,500 a year; the firm of Hayes, Budd and Porrett, which acted for the trustees throughout, was paid taxed costs of £60,000. Lincoln's Inn should have drunk a standing toast to Peter Thellusson and his descendants.[114]

NOTES

1. Rendlesham to Norman, 5 May, 19 Nov. 1851, Norman Mss KAO U310/C125; PRO TS 18/1501, exhibit XC. Obituaries are in *Gents. Mag.* 130 (1852), 514 and *Journal of the British Archaeological Association* 9 (1854), 101.

2. A captain in the Grenadiers, Brooke inherited Ufford from his father in 1836. He owned most of the parish and built up a fine library. *Burke's Dictionary of the Landed Gentry*, vol. I, p.145; Page, *History of Suffolk*, p.158; W. White, *History, Gazetteer and Directory of Suffolk* (3rd edn., Sheffield, 1874), p.659.

3. The marriage was in January 1852: Taylor, *Book of the Duffs*, p.527. He had been a widower since his first wife died in Athens in 1840 after barely a year of marriage.

4. PRO PROB 11/2153, f.433; PRO IR 26/1942. The personal estate, sworn at under £14,000, was insolvent with a deficiency of over £13,000.

5. Caroline Boulton to Norman, 21 Feb. 1852; Arthur Thellusson to Norman, 22 Feb., 12 Jul. 1852, Norman Mss KAO U310/C125. Caroline was the boy's aunt, and her husband might have been considered as a guardian, but he had died in 1850: *Gents. Mag.* 127 (1850), 677.

6. Brief for motion on 23 Jan.1854, PRO TS 18/1501; papers in *Newland v. Thellusson*, Brodsworth Hall MSS DD168/7.

7. Reports of 8, 19 Oct. 1852, PRO C 38/2202.

8. *Gents. Mag.* 129 (1851), 667; PRO C 33/1014, f.595. None of the Thellussons benefitted from his will (PRO PROB 11/2142, f.890).

9. *Burke's Landed Gentry* (1906), *sub* Dawkins of Over Norton. He was the grandson of Henry Dawkins, MP for Southampton and for many years a Commissioner of Woods and Forests.

10. To Maria ----, 19 July ?1855, Brodsworth Hall MSS DD168/16(a).

11. Various calculations made by Charles are in the Brodsworth Hall Mss. One, of 1853, shows his debts at £37,000 but the account of those settled after his death totals £59,581. It shows £26,000 owing to Robartses, against only £14,000 in the earlier account.

12. See e.g. the bills in *Ibid.*, DD168/16(b).

13. It is not known where the sons were educated, but it certainly was not at any of the best known schools and none went to university.

14. Augusta Pakington to Charles, 10 Dec. ?1855, Brodsworth Hall Mss DD168/16D. Frederick, in the Bengal Lancers, also came through the Indian Mutiny, in which General Alexander Woodford lost his son.

15. First in the Colonial Office (1852-4), then in the War Office : J.C. Sainty, *List of Office*

Holders, Colonial Office (London, 1976). It may have been Seymour for whom Lady Rendlesham had sought the help of Peel, who replied, `a clerkship in one of the Revenue Departments is almost the only appointment in my disposal in which a young man without a profession can enter the Civil Service': 11 Oct. 1845, B.L.Add.Mss. 40,575, f.350. The public service in general, like the Circumlocution Office, still largely merited the jibe that it was a `system of outdoor relief for the aristocracy'.

16.   *Gents. Mag.* 130 (1852), 511. Two daughters were followed by a son, Ernest (b. 1858), who went into the church, something unusual for the Thellussons, who mostly preferred the army. The solicitor was Alfred Robinson, of Robinson and Haynes.

17.   Diary entry, 7 Jul. 1854, Brodsworth Hall MSS DD 168/15.

18.   Papers in *Ibid.*, DD 168/16(b) and (d), especially on *Jacobs v. Thellusson* and correspondence about debts due to R.W. Walker and the solicitor J.P. Beaven. He was also unscrupulous in his resort to legal quibbles: *Van der Donckt v. Thellusson* (1849) 8 C.B. 811; *Meeus v. Thellusson* (1853) 8 Exch. 636.

19.   Letters of 24 Jul., 24 Jan. 1855, *Ibid.* DD168/16(d). Gill was an assiduous correspondent and was himself a creditor for £700 at one time. He was well known in racing circles.

20.   R. Longrigg, *The History of Horse Racing*, (London, 1972), pp. 115-19; W. Vamplew, *The Turf, a social and economic history* (London, 1972), pp.17-37; T.H.Bird, *Admiral Rous and the Turf* (London, 1939).

21.   J. Fairfax-Blaneborough, *Northern Turf History* (London, 1950), vol III, p.313.

22.   *Gents. Mag.* 138(1856), 326.

23.   `Druid',[H.H. Dixon], *Scott and Sebright*, (London, 1862), p.66 and *The Post and the Paddock* (1856 edn., London), p.210; *V.C.H. Surrey*, vol.II, p.499; Fairfax-Blaneborough, *Northern Turf History*, pp.356-8; *Gents. Mag.* 126 (1850), 94.

24.   `Druid', *Scott and Sebright*, p.68.

25.   *Gents. Mag.* 126 (1850), 94. The `large family of grandchildren' mentioned in the obituary may also be an exaggeration, since his will (PRO PROB 11/2108, f.71) mentions only two.

26.   `Thormanby' [W.W. Dixon], *Kings of the Turf* (London, 1898), pp.31-2.

27.   *Ibid.*, which shows him getting the better of an exchange with the formidable John Gully. He had a manservant who drove him on these jaunts in a yellow chariot. For his `Dickensian' Christmases see *Gents. Mag.* 126 (1850), 94. He left his housekeeper an annuity of £150.

28.   *Gents. Mag.* 126 (1850), 552. The families were on dining terms by 1848: Brodsworth Hall Mss DD168/15. William's sister Mary called her house at Boscombe `Brodsworth House'.

29.   *Ibid.*, 657. PRO IR 26/1881, f.7.

30.   Brodsworth Hall Mss DD168/10.

31. *Gents. Mag.* 126 (1850), 552; PRO PROB 11/2120, f.707; PRO IR 26/1883, f.704. The will is one of the very few in this study to contain a substantial charitable bequest, £500 to the Hospital for Consumption and Diseases of the East at Brompton.

32. *Sporting Magazine* (3rd s.) 27 (1856), 133-4. Pocahontas was later sold to the Marquess of Exeter.

33. *Ibid.*, 132-8. Charles had other horses, notably a useful stallion called King Tom, but not all were successful. Gill advised him to give away Donna Sabine if he could not sell her: 17 Dec. 1855, Brodsworth Hall Mss DD 168/16(a).

34. *Sporting Magazine* (3rd s.) 27 (1856), 132-8. `Druid' was rather grudging about him: *Silk and Scarlet* (London, 1858), p.251.

35. Longrigg, *Horse Racing*, pp.126-7; Bird, *Admiral Rous*, pp.132-6; *Sporting Magazine* (3rd s.) 27 (1856), 132-8.

36. *Sporting Magazine* (3rd s.) 27 (1856) gives his full record to the end of 1855. According to Bird (*Admiral Rous*, p.136), Parr ruined Rataplan's chances of the St. Leger by racing him at York when he was unfit shortly before the Doncaster meeting.

37. Diary entry, 2 Jan. 1854, Brodsworth Hall Ms DD168/15. *Cf.* his complaint of the expenses of racing in a letter to Maria -----, 19 July ?1855, DD 168/16(a).

38. 22 Dec. 1854, *Ibid.*, DD168/16(a).

39. *Ibid.* Osbaldeston lost more than £200,000 on the Turf in all and having sold his estates in 1848 (receiving only £23,000 of the £190,000 they fetched) had lost his last hope of retrieving the wreck of his fortune when his horse Rifleman was beaten in the St. Leger. His wife now held the purse strings and he was eventually reduced to carting furniture from Ebberston Hall to the Grapes Inn to pay for drinks: Osbaldeston, *Autobiography*, pp. 7, 235; H. Montgomery-Massingberd, The Fight for Gulliver's House, *Telegraph Weekend Magazine*, 21 Oct 1989, 38-44.

40. 11 Nov. 1854, Brodsworth Hall Mss DD168/16(d).

41. Longrigg, *Horse Racing*, pp.150-1; M.J. Huggins, *Kings of the Moor, North Yorkshire Racehorse Trainers, 1760-1900* (Teeside Polytechnic, 1991). Gill described Dawson as `a robin roughhead': 8 Aug. 1855, Brodsworth Hall Mss DD168/16(b).

42. Prince's bill for 1855 came to £105 13s: Brodsworth Hall Mss DD168/16(b).

43. Undated note to Charles Sabine, *Ibid.* DD168/16(b).

44. Vamplew, *The Turf*, pp.29-37.

45. 8 Aug. 1855, Brodsworth Hall Mss DD168/16(a).

46. 26 Dec. 1854, *Ibid.*, DD168/16(a).

47. His complete record to the end of 1855 was 42 wins in 71 races, with prize money totalling

£7,907. At that time races for two year old were still uncommon and Rataplan ran only three of them.

48. Brodsworth Hall MSS DD168/15; *Gents. Mag.* 138 (1856), 326.

49. But other families were less fortunate in this regard. The Manners, Dukes of Rutland, were one such: B. Masters, *The Dukes* (London, 1977), p.351.

50. PRO PROB 11/2231, f.340.

51. The future Lord Chancellor Selborne. He had first appeared in the suit in 1852 but does not mention it in his copious memoirs.

52. (1821) 3 Myl. & Cr. 584.

53. *Rendlesham v. Robarts* (1856) 23 Beav. 321 at 324-5; order of 4 Jun. 1856, PRO C 33/1039, f.1390. Sir John Romilly, son of Samuel, the great law reformer, was noted for his concern to dispatch cases expeditiously: *D.N.B.* vol.XLIX, pp.186-7.

54. Arthur had protested when the curacy of Butley became vacant in 1853 and was filled by the trustees, but he was told it was of too little value to be worth fighting: affidavit of M.A. Reyroux, with brief on motion for decree, 1856, PRO TS 18/1501.

55. To Mrs. H. Baring, 9 Sep. 1857, A.H. Johnson (ed.), *The Letters of Charles Greville and Henry Reeve, 1836-65* (London, 1924) vol.I, p.255. Mrs. Baring was Cecilia Windham, mother of the great proconsul Evelyn, Lord Cromer.

56. Draft (no date), Brodsworth Hall Mss DD168/16D.

57. Quoted in Atlay, *Victorian Chancellors*, vol. II, p.73. Since Bethell was Solicitor- General it is not surprising that the Lord Chancellor (Cranworth) was furious.

58. Stevens, *Law and Politics*, pp.37-45; O. Anderson, The Wensleydale Peerage Case and the Position of the House of Lords, *English Historical Review* 82 (1967), 486-502.

59. As in 1799, suitable questions had to be framed, see *Thellusson v. Lord Rendlesham* [1858-59] 7 H.L.C. 429 at 447.

60. Richard Bethell, Lord Westbury, had first appeared in the suit in 1847.

61. Hugh McCalmont Cairns, Lord Chancellor 1868, 1874-80. He does not seem to have appeared in the suit before.

62. Truro was Lord Chancellor 1850-2. He practised mostly in the common law courts, was Chief Justice of the Common Pleas and held the Great Seal for only nineteen months during which, as it happened, the suit was unusually quiet.

63. Rolt's *Memoirs* (London, 1939) give interesting appraisals of his contemporaries, but he is unduly harsh on the Chancellors from a common law background.

64. Atlay, *Victorian Chancellors*, vol.II, p.252.

65. Rubinstein's *Men of Property*, p.219, table 2.1, gives twenty-two estates probated at between

402

£200,000 and £500,000 (which excludes realty) in 1858, as well as James Morrison's, a millionaire in personalty alone. See also Thompson, *Life after Death*.

66.   *Egerton v. Lord Brownlow* (1853) 4 H.L.C. 1. Succession to a great estate was made conditional on a peer (Lord Afford) acquiring a dukedom or a marquessate. The condition was held void as tending to influence a peer in the proper performance of his public duties.

67.   Bethell's biographer reports one witticism from the case, when one counsel proposed deferring a very minor point 'until the day of judgment'; Bethell objected with mock innocence, 'will not that day, Mr.----, be a *very* busy day?': T.A. Nash, *Life of Lord Westbury*, (2 vols., London, 1888), vol I, p.289.

68.   *Thellusson v. Lord Rendlesham* (1858-59) 7 H.L.C.429 at 435-9.

69.   (1821) 3 My & Cr.584.

70.   *Thellusson v. Lord Rendlesham* (1858-59) 7 H.L.C. 429 at 472.

71.   The phrase in that clause is 'with remainder to the second, third, fourth, and all and every other male lineal descendant or descendants then living(*who shall be incapable of taking as heir in tail male of any of the persons to whom a prior estate is hereby directed to be limited*)'...[my italics].

72.   At 439-44. Because the judges had to go on circuit the respondents' arguments were postponed and it was fully seven months before all the judges could be brought together again to hear them.

73.   As well as legal works such as *Jarman on Wills*, counsel had recourse to the works of Raleigh and the judges cited Dr. Johnson's dictionary to elucidate the meanings of 'eldest'.

74.   *D.N.B.*, vol. XXXVI, p.295.

75.   Pp.471-85, concluding with an apology for long-windedness.

76.   George Bramwell became a baron of the Exchequer in 1856. Described by Holdsworth as 'a common lawyer and nothing but a common lawyer': *History of English Law*, vol.15 (London, 1965), pp.493-505.

77.   Pp.454-60; the quotations are from pp.454, 456 and 460.

78.   Pp.460-3. Willes was much admired; he shot himself in 1872: Foss, *Judges*, vol.IX, pp.311-12.

79.   Pp.448-9.

80.   For these judges see the *D.N.B.*. Their opinions are at pp.463-71, 485-7, 487-94 and 452-4 respectively.

81.   In the eighteenth century the judges' opinions had usually been decisive and it was still uncommon for the Lords to depart from them, but they had done so in the Bridgwater case and were to do so more famously in the politically charged trade union case of *Allen v. Flood* [1898] A.C. 1: Stevens, *Law and Politics*, pp. 9-10.

82. Pp.502-4, 528-31. This was probably a trial of wills, the new Chancellor having no intention of submitting to St.Leonards' domineering ways.

83. Pp.527-8. This was not uncommon, at least for Brougham. In earlier decades the Lords had been even more cavalier, see e.g. *Wright v. Tatham* (1837) 5 Cl. & Fin. 670.

84. Pp.519-27.

85. P.498 (Lord Cranworth).

86. The appellants' contention, it should be said, drew considerable support from cases such as *Trevor v. Trevor* (1845, 1847) 1 H.L.C. 238. In that case, the words `in tail male' had been held by the Lords to be descriptive not of the issue but of their interest, and hence let in daughters. *Trevor*, however, was generally regarded as an unfortunate decision.

87. P.505.

88. P.509. It is curious that even Sugden, the great authority on conveyancing for half a century, did not know who the draftsman was.

89. P.506. Compare Mr. Podsnap's majestic retort to a question about how other countries do: `they do- I am sorry to be obliged to say it- *as* they do': *Our Mutual Friend* (1952 edn., Oxford), p.133.

90. Pp.508-9.

91. The Chancellor, then Frederick Thesiger, had been Arthur Thellusson's counsel before the Master of the Rolls and therefore announced that he would not give an opinion unless the other four were evenly divided. Both St.Leonards and Brougham had been counsel in earlier proceedings and felt no difficulty in taking part now, though the former had been advising Charles Thellusson about the suit as recently as 1854: diary entry of 16 Mar. 1854, Brodsworth Hall Mss DD 168/15.

91. *Gents. Mag.* 142 (1858), 202.

92. The eldest son of Georgiana, Henry Hoyle Oddie III, born 1815 and therefore forty-two when Charles died. He died in 1869.

93. Orders of 1 Oct. 1856, 29 Jan. 1858, PRO C 33/1040, f.1788; C 33/1054, f.556. There is a bound copy of the report in East Suffolk RO HB 416/F1. Each commissioner was paid £400 out of the estate.

94. Lord Hawarden died on 12th October 1856 and A.W. Robarts on 2nd April 1858, aged seventy-seven and seventy-eight respectively: *Gents. Mag.* 139 (1856), 663; *House of Commons,1790-1820*, vol.V, p.24. Dawkins' daughter married the 4th Lord Rendlesham's stepson, James Duff.

95. E.g. 28 Jul., 4 Aug. 1858, PRO C 33/1056, ff.1569, 1674; 19 Feb., 3 Jun. 1859, C 33/1062, f.841, C 33/1063, f.1766 (repairs); 21 Apr., 22 Dec. 1860, C 33/1072, f.883, C 33/1074, f.2593

404

(railways); 14 Jan. 1860, C 33/1071, f.79 (purchase).

96. R. Gowing, *Public Men of Ipswich and East Suffolk*, (Ipswich, 1875), p.131.

97. *Bleak House*, p.922.

98. Order of 19 Dec .1853, PRO C 33/1021, f.194; schedule of title deeds (3 volumes), East Suffolk RO HB 416. Volume one alone lists ninety-four bundles, including the Brodsworth estate bundle containing 575 items. Each estate's title deeds contained an average of forty documents.

99. PRO TS 18/1501. It comprises 121 documents on proceedings from 1852 onwards. In *Trustees of the British Museum v. White* (1826) 2 Sim. and Stu. 594 at 596, Sir John Leach VC said that no decision had yet taken place on whether the gift over for reducing the national debt infringed the Mortmain Act.

100. Orders of 22 Dec. 1860 (PRO C 33/1074, f.2593); 12 Jan. 1861 © 33/1079, f.144); 23 May 1863 © 33/1096, f.1018).

101. Order of 26 Nov. 1859, PRO C 33/1066, f.324.

102. Orders of 22 Dec. 1860 (PRO C 33/1074, f.2596); 24 Jan. 1863© 33/1095, f.176). Wright's obituary in *Gents. Mag.* 143(1863), 518, gives a short account of this interesting family.

103. *London Gazette*, lists of dormant funds.

104. PRO C 33/1096, f.1018.

105. Figures compiled from PRO C 33 and C 38. The indexes are generally reliable but either through omissions or my own inattention a few will probably have been missed. I have included those made in the suits which sprang from the main one, but not e.g. *Lord Rendlesham v. Norman*, which was concerned exclusively with the trusts of the first Baron's will.

106. *Bleak House*, p.923.

107. Grant (1801-17), Plumer (1817-24), Gifford (1824-6), Copley (1826-7), Leach (1827-34), Pepys (1834-6) and Langdale (1836-51).

108. The first Vice-Chancellor was Plumer (1813-17), followed by Leach (1817-27), Hart (1827), Shadwell (1827-50) and, after the abolition of the equity side of the Exchequer and the creation of two extra Vice-Chancellors, Knight Bruce (1841-52), Wigram (1841-50), Cranworth (1850-1), Turner (1851-3), Kindersley (1851-66), Parker (1851-2), Stuart (1852-71) and Page-Wood (1853-68). All are appraised by Sir Robert Megarry in The Vice Chancellors, *Law Quarterly Review* 8 (1982), 370-405 and, as he remarks, all but Stuart are in the *D.N.B.* I cannot find any record of Wigram, Cranworth, Turner or Parker hearing the cause as Vice-Chancellor, though the last two had appeared as counsel and Cranworth heard it in the Lords.

109. The others were P. Holford, G.B. Roupell, A.H. Lynch, N.W. Senior and W. Horne. This

excludes the taxing master P. Martineau.

110. Those who became judges are mostly in Foss, *Judges* and the *D.N.B.*.

111. See *supra*, pp. 347-9.

112. *House of Lords Sessional Papers* (1833) 11,(92), (114), pp.833, 839. These figures include payments made out of the estate before it reached the Accountant-General.

113. Figures from PRO C 33, C 38. There were annual taxations down to 1855 as well as separate ones for e.g. the private Act and the common law action over tithes.

114. The cost of going to law in the nineteenth century has not really been explored by historians, so there is no good yardstick against which to measure this suit. The famous Jennens case (see *supra*, p. 3) was rumoured to have cost £250,000 (almost certainly an exaggeration). Dickens put it at £140,000 in 1853 and the Day case, also still ongoing, at £70,000: *Bleak House*, pp.41-2.

CHAPTER 16

SPENDING THE FORTUNE

1. Rendlesham

The last fireworks faded from the sky, the villagers trudged homewards, guests departed and Frederick settled into his inheritance. The legends surrounding the famous will had cast a romantic aura about him,[1] enhanced by his early marriage to a young bride whose name- Egidia Montgomerie- fitted her for one of Meredith's heroines. Her father, the thirteenth Earl of Eglintoun, had a romantic past of his own, for his seat in Ayrshire had staged the mock tournament in 1839 at which `Young England' had disported itself in a bizarre (and extravagant) display of idealised medievalism.[2] Eglintoun's more prosaic middle age had seen him Lord- Lieutenant of Ireland in Lord Derby's threadbare Conservative administrations.

Though Egidia must have brought a handsome dowry,[3] Rendlesham was not spectacularly rich. His estates could not compare with the Duke of Sutherland's *latifundia* or the great acreages of several other dukes, nor was his personal fortune on the scale of commercial men like Morrison and Brassey.[4] With 20,000 acres, however, he was the biggest landowner in Suffolk, outstripping the Duke of Grafton, the Marquis of Bristol and that exotic implant the Maharajah Duleep Singh of Elvedon Hall.[5] But just as the Thellusson fortune fell short of expectations so the young peer could not live up the role of romantic hero. He was, in fact, rather dull. He had his house in town[6] and his estate in the country, fathered a large family, hunted and shot, grew a beard to the cut of the Prince of Wales's (an Eton contemporary)-in short did everything demanded by convention and nothing more.[7]

Even the rebuilding of Rendlesham Hall did not inspire him. Since the fire which had left the `White House' an appropriately picturesque ruin, his predecessors had quartered themselves in the steward's house,[8] but the size of his family and the state of his finances enabled Frederick to be more ambitious. Disappointingly, he called in the elderly William Burn, renowned as a provider of `sensible, hard-wearing country houses',[9] and what he got was a large house in fierce red brick dressed with white stone and topped with Flemish gables - uninspired, unremarkable and thoroughly conventional.[10]

Perhaps Frederick was more interested in the gardens than the house; indeed this was the only character trait of old Peter's to descend to his great- grandson. Besides the obligatory conservatory he had hothouses filled with orchids, peaches and tropical plants, while the five drives which led from the old gothick lodges to the new house were lined with exotic trees and shrubs.[11]

The rebuilding affirmed Frederick's intention to take his place in county society. At first no more had been expected of him than that he would patronise the local tradesmen and subscribe to local charities and institutions, and he lived down to expectations, evidently feeling that `the duties of property...were all very well for fellows who liked to take the trouble', but not for him.[12] Despite this, he was gradually drawn into local government, as magistrate, deputy lieutenant and high sheriff, began to show himself at public meetings on the topics of the day[13] and earned this description from a quizzical commentator: `we have Lord Rendlesham among us, doing the honours of Rendlesham Hall; hunting the county; a Steward of the Races; a landlord who has begun to talk about political questions in connection with the land after the manner of men who have given actual thought to the subjects; a country gentleman beginning to persuade himself that he ought to know something of agriculture and agricultural questions; a noble lord, in fact, who has been told that he ought to do something, till he almost begins to think he ought, and to fancy that, perhaps after all he could do these things as well as other country gentlemen and great landlords.'[14]

408

When it came to voting at Parliamentary elections, Frederick purchased (at considerable expense) a footnote in constitutional history by establishing that his Irish peerage disfranchised him, although by one of the constitution's endearing quirks, he was eligible to sit in the Commons as his uncle and grandfather had done.[15] Despite Disraeli's `leap in the dark', the county seats were still largely the preserve of the landed interest, the voters too numerous for effective party management[16] and in Suffolk at least notoriously conservative and susceptible to `the politics of deference'.[17] Standing with Lord Mahon for Suffolk East in the general election of 1874, Frederick comfortably saw off his Liberal neighbour Colonel Tomline, retaining his seat with a reduced majority in 1880 when Gladstone's Midlothian campaign gave an alarming glimpse of the shape of elections to come.[18]

Frederick found that he could quite comfortably reconcile his duties as an MP with the competing claims of the hunt, the shoot and the season. He was without political ambitions and his two speeches (if they may be so called) in ten years could scarcely have been more parochial; one was on postal services in the Lowestoft area, the other on the status of lunatic asylum attendants under the new Employer's Liability Act.[19] According to the standard Parliamentary handbook he was `a Conservative, but not opposed to well-considered progress',[20] and his chief concern was the repeal of the malt tax, a long cherished farmers' grievance which probably reflects his constituents' priorities rather than his own.[21]

This profoundly undistinguished political career closed in 1885 when he was beaten by a bare 168 votes (out of more than 10,000) in the first general election held after the third Reform Act, which swept away the county constituencies and did much to drive the country gentlemen out of Parliament.[22] That Frederick had few personal regrets is suggested by his refusal to stand when the seat was again contested a few months later and recaptured by the Conservatives; he had done his duty but had no taste for officious whips and importunate constituents.

When Egidia died in 1880 at the early age of thirty-seven he was left with eight children.[23] There were three boys; Frederick Archibald Charles, the eleven year old heir, Percy Edward (five) and Hugh Edmund (four), and five girls, ranging from Adeline (eighteen) down to Mariota (seven). It may be that their aunt Blanche, who never married and lived nearby, assisted with the girls' upbringing.[24]

Their uncle Arthur, son of the loser in the final round of the law suit, also lived not far away, at Aldeburgh. He had seven children by his first marriage to Henrietta Vernon - Wentworth, daughter of a wealthy landowner from the neighbourhood of Brodsworth. Three of the girls died young and the other three married, but the only son, another Arthur, followed the family tradition by entering the army and was still unmarried when he died from wounds received in the Boer War.[25] Later the same year (1901) his father also died, at least partly from grief, and with this double death the male line became extinct.[26]

Like his father and grandfather and like so many of his class, Lord Rendlesham much preferred sport to cultural pursuits,[27] though he was not a man obsessed, like the Duke of Beaufort with hunting or the Duke of Sutherland with shooting.[28] He interested himself in the volunteers and became chairman of the new county council for instance, but country sports seem to have been closest to his heart and his obituary fairly described him as 'a typical English country gentleman and sportsman'.[29] One of his first acts on coming of age was to acquire a pack of harriers, but he found Suffolk men preferred their game birds to their foxes so he soon gave that up. His connection with the Turf was more long lasting and his horses had enough successes to keep the crimson and black colours familiar to racegoers over thirty years; a steward of the Jockey Club and a member of the National Hunt Committee, Rendlesham left a lasting legacy to the sport in the form of the Rendlesham Benevolent Fund. He also had a taste for sailing, being a member of the Royal Squadron and at one time commodore of the Royal Victoria Yacht Club.[30]

Like so many men of his time, however, he was happiest with a gun in his hand. Suffolk landowners were especially lavish in spending money to rear and preserve game. The Rendlesham estate had natural advantages for shooting, lying on sandy heaths much favoured for the purpose, and what the first baron had begun was enthusiastically continued by his grandson; nature was improved by art, 25,000 trees and shrubs, among them many attractive species, being planted out to provide cover, though even then the attempt to introduce the red grouse was a failure.[31] While never quite rivalling Elvedon, the mecca for Suffolk sportsmen, his estates offered opportunities for mass slaughter on an almost comparable scale. Pheasants and partridges were the chief victims, 738 partridges falling to the guns in just three days in 1887. These shooting parties became progressively more 'scientific', less of a country pastime than a rich man's diversion, a singular and unattractive feature of Edwardian society.[32]

Unlike the grouse moors of Yorkshire and Scotland, however, Suffolk estates, Rendlesham included, remained essentially farming units with a comparatively small acreage given over to game. When Frederick took over the 'high farming' boom was at its height, buoyant cereal prices and high rents seeming to confound those, like his father, who had predicted ruin from the abandonment of protection. It is not surprising that the new owner was happy to rely chiefly on his rents. Suffolk farmers mostly grew corn, and especially wheat, and many of them that had come to regard decent prosperity almost as an entitlement.

The shock was all the greater therefore when the price of wheat plunged suddenly in the mid -1870s. Worse, it failed to recover, remaining depressed for the rest of the century, 28/- a quarter during 1895-9 against 55/- during 1870-4. Other cereals fared little better and wool shared in the collapse, which was the onset of what came to be known as 'the great depression' in English agriculture, a phrase which was fully justified in the arable counties of southern England at least.[33] By railway and steamship the produce of the American prairies, of Australia and India, flooded into Europe, undercutting English produce in all markets, even the homeland.[34] A return to protection being politically unthinkable, English corn growers faced a stark choice between improving their efficiency by lowering production costs or going over to livestock, fruit or market gardening, but few of them (and few of their landlords) perceived it soon or acted promptly.[35] The Duke of Bedford, a studious and conscientious landlord, wrote that 'no feature is more remarkable than the complete failure of the agricultural experts to recognise at the beginning of the period, the permanent character of the various forces then at work',[36] and since successive royal commissions (permeated by political prejudices) proved almost equally inept, it is hard to blame individuals for their sluggish and reluctant response.

Many landlords reinforced their tenants' obstinate conservatism by holding them to husbandry covenants, refusing to finance new buildings for livestock and only remitting arrears instead of re - negotiating rents,[37] understandably, for the English system of land tenure had proved its worth in cushioning the impact of short - term fluctuations. Nevertheless, the extent of their territorial dominance revealed by the 'Return of Owners of Land',[38] landlords came in for sustained and indiscriminate criticism.[39] Hard - headed pundits urged landlords to abandon sentimentally feudal attitudes in favour of 'landowning as a business'.[40]

Many were willing to do so, and eagerly assisted the critics of primogeniture and settlements in passing the Settled Land Act of 1882. Much more radical than previous measures, the Act enabled life owners to sell settled land, detaching the beneficial interests from the land and fastening them upon the proceeds of sale instead, with appropriate safeguards against embezzlement.[41] The Act struck a lethal blow at the traditional strict settlement which kept a permanent endowment of land in the family, but its impact was delayed for a generation because in the depressed land market of the 'eighties few buyers could be found.[42]

In the absence of estate accounts, the effects of the depression on Rendlesham's estates can only be guessed. It has been estimated that in badly hit areas gross rents fell by 41% between the mid -1870s and the mid - 1890s, but even within the same county the variations were very great.[43] On the one hand there is no sign of significant land sales[44] and the light soils of most of his Suffolk lands were less vulnerable than the heavy clays of his neighbours to the west; on the other, Suffolk farmers were reckoned among the least adaptable and his other farms were in the home counties, which suffered badly. The likelihood must be that the impact was serious, and there

412

was little that could be done to mitigate it. Tenants had *de facto* security and even the slovenly were safe as long as few could be found to take their places, especially when those who could be found were often hard - headed Scotsmen who knew how to drive a bargain with a desperate landlord. The only alternative was to take farms in hand, and that was seldom profitable.[45]

Landlords had to cut back on their outgoings and many found that hard to do. Rendlesham was luckier than others in that he was not heavily burdened with mortgages and family charges[46] but even though other obligations were only moral, it still it went hard to cut back on charities, churches and amenities when the labourers were also suffering the consequences of the depression.[47] Moreover the children made considerable demands as they grew. The sons had to be educated and that meant Eton,[48] though none went on to university. The younger sons would have their portions but there was income tax to be reckoned with now and many of these young men found the cost of an upper class lifestyle exceeded their investment income or allowance. Deprived of their privileged access to government posts, though the church and the army were still their preserve, they faced increasing competition from the products of lesser, Arnoldian public schools and found themselves coldly appraised as 'bright eyed, clean limbed, high minded, ready for anything and fit for nothing'.[49]

Luckily two of Rendlesham's daughters, the eldest and youngest, were married before the depression set in, Adeline to Lewis Jarvis, a famous Cambridge sportsman in his golden youth, then a partner in the family bank at Kings Lynn, Mariota to Arthur Grey, the only son of the fourth Earl of Wilton.[50] Two of the other sisters (Miriam and Ruby) did marry later,[51] and only Cecilia remained at home, nursing her father in his final illness. She was a forceful woman with very decided views on religion and although for some time the Thellussons had shown a preference for Campsey Ash over their local church, probably because the living was in their gift, Cecilia completed the rupture in most unseasonable fashion by resigning her superintendence of the choir on Christmas Day 1908 and carrying off the portable organ.[52]

This was exciting stuff for rural Suffolk, but it could not match the entertainment the Thellussons had unwittingly provided ten years earlier when Rendlesham Hall went up in flames once more. All the family but Ruby were in town on 8th May 1898 when a chimney fire was discovered. It did not seem very serious at first but became so when it took hold of the north wing and the house fire engine was found to have no hose long enough to put it out. Engines hastened from Woodbridge and other neighbouring stations, nearly a dozen in all, but the men could do little except help to remove paintings and furniture to safety, for the pitch pine roof burned furiously and one by one the ceilings collapsed. As the news spread spectators came from miles around and eventually they were joined by Lord Rendlesham and two of his sons, one of whom was nearly brained by a falling ceiling while emptying the strong room. The house was a ruin but the fifth baron had learned from his uncle John's imprudence and had it insured for £40,000.[53]

The house was rebuilt and things resumed their accustomed course until in the midst of the constitutional crisis of 1911 Lord Rendlesham fell sick. Blood poisoning set in and though a hand was amputated its progress was not arrested; in the autumn his condition grew rapidly worse and he died with all his family around him on 9th November.[54] Of all the descendants of Peter Thellusson he was probably the most fortunate; wealthy almost all his life, blessed with good health and an equable disposition, little troubled by wars and social upheaval, with a large family and several sons to continue the line. Life was never to be so good for his successors.

The shattering impact of the Great War has been amply documented. It was cruellest and most immediate upon the hundreds and thousands of wounded men and bereaved families, and while the landed classes as a whole lost a disproportionate number of their young men the Thellussons were more fortunate than most. It chanced that few of them, either in the Suffolk or the Yorkshire branch, were of military age, and of those who were, like the 6th Lord Rendlesham's younger brothers Percy (who became a minor `brass hat' at G.H.Q) and Hugh (DSO and Croix de Guerre for service in the Royal Field Artillery[55]), most came home safely,[56] though at least one found the enemy easier to cope with than his creditors.[57] Rendlesham himself, too old for active service, threw himself into training the Suffolk Yeomanry.[58]

Nothing would ever be the same again after the war, the life of the gentry least of all. The `servant problem' changed from how to find and keep trustworthy and reliable staff to how to find any staff at all as a great `revolt of the backstairs' took hold of the lower classes, and even when they *could* be found, their wages (now augmented by `the stamp') could not always be afforded. Farmers had done well out of the war, with incentives and guaranteed prices, but rents had been frozen, so landlords did not share in the benefits.[59] They shared with a vengeance, however, in the wartime burdens of high income tax and steep death duties and many family trusts no longer yielded a decent income from the narrow range of `authorised investments'.[60]

Land could now be sold and family after family acknowledged the truth of Wilde's much quoted aphorism: `what between the duties expected of one during one's lifetime and the duties exacted from one after one's death, land has ceased to be either a profit or a pleasure. It gives one a position and prevents one from keeping it up.'[61] An avalanche of land hit the market and, unlike the 1880s, there were buyers. The pages of the *Estates Gazette* chronicle sales on such a scale that it was reckoned that in the four years to the end of 1921 one- quarter of England had changed hands in what was plausibly called `a revolution in landownership'.[62] What made it revolutionary was that it was not just the displacement of old families by *nouveaux riches* but the dissolution of the old social order in the countryside. Only a minority of estates was sold intact, for many owners wanted to cling to the house, the park and the home farm and few buyers wanted a whole estate. In a buyers' market the less commodious, distinguished and convenient houses were hard to shift, and since many buyers were tenant farmers or speculators looking to make a quick resale to builders many were demolished; there was, after all, a limit to schools and institutions seeking spacious new premises.[63]

Though a man of conservative views with two brothers to succeed him,

Frederick, the 6th Lord Rendlesham, was among the sellers.[64] Perhaps his wife had some influence, for Lilian Manley came from Jamaica and may have seen few charms in the large, cold house in deepest Suffolk.[65] They were childless and certainly Percy, the heir expectant, gourmand and *bon viveur*, had no desire for the life of an impoverished landowner.[66] Accordingly the farms were sold in 1921, just before the boom ended; the expanding Forestry Commission bought up much of the woodland and the house became a Norwood Institution for the victims of drink and drug abuse.[67]

So the Rendleshams joined the swelling ranks of the landless aristocracy and decamped to Cornwall, where Frederick pursued his hobbies of horticulture, entomology and deep sea fishing, and in due course remarried.[68] When his body was brought back to Rendlesham church for burial in 1938 there was little to connect the family with the neighbourhood any longer. Percy, who had run up considerable debts after his wife died,[69] promptly sold the last remaining portion of the lands purchased out of the great accumulation, those around Watford,[70] but was still unable to leave his nephew Anthony, who came to the title while serving as a Captain in the Royal Signal Corps in 1943,[71] the means to sustain through the years of post-war austerity the leisured existence the public at large still seems to think accompanies a peerage.[72] The 8th Baron had to earn his living and lives quite modestly in London. His first marriage ended in divorce.[73] His second wife was Clare McCririck, a soldier's daughter who claimed descent from Rurik, the Viking founder of Russia. `A formidable voice in fashion for many years', disdaining age( and leaving it discreetly vague) as `a handicap to style', she brought a rare dynamism to the Thellusson family. Still in the throes of a successful and combative career in fashion she collapsed and died while walking down the King's Road in 1987. Since he has a son, Charles, and there are also collateral heirs, the title is no danger of early extinction.[74]

Rendlesham Hall, however, no longer exists. The war brought the U.S.A.F. to Suffolk to carve Bentwaters air base out of the forest, leaving the Hall empty and derelict.[75] In the immediate post-war period scores of old houses met their end. Suffolk lost more than most counties and Rendlesham was not among the most lamented.[76] Today two of the gothick lodges remain as picturesque reminders of the past. The bombers have gone and a plan for commercial aviation has not yet won permission, so the forest is mostly quiet again, a backwater notable only for relics of the past- the Sutton Hoo treasure was found on the banks of the Deben a few miles away-[77] and intimations of the future- one of the best attested U.F.O. sightings in Britain occurred there in 1975. If the Thellussons are there at all, it is as ghosts in the churchyard.[78]

2. Brodsworth

Although the two heirs to the fortune were of the same generation, they were very different. Charles Sabine Augustus Thellusson was twenty years older and able to enjoy his inheritance straight away; he was married with children; he had been denied the education fitted to his rank and never made a grand tour like his cousin. But while Frederick had been sheltered by his guardians from bad company and importunate kinsmen, Charles had knocked around in a hard school, dependent upon the charity of his uncle Robarts for his commission in the army and always short of the cash needed to cut a dash in that free spending profession.[79] Moreover he had had to defend himself not only from the usual predators but from the desperate schemes of the father who should have been his protector. Charles learned the value of money and keenly enjoyed having it to spend at last.

The inheritance, however, carried obligations with it. Besides paying his father's debts,[80] Charles was head of a family left badly off by the improvidence of two generations and with moral claims to share in his prosperity. He allowed his mother £1,000 a year and his four brothers £700 each;[81] more surprisingly, he gave one of his uncle Thomas's daughters £250 p.a. even during her father's lifetime, and continued it after she married. Still odder, her sister Sabine, whose means were probably more modest, had nothing.[82] All told, and counting irregular loans and advances, these family charges added up to between £3,500 and £4,000 a year.[83]

This made considerable inroads into Charles' income and although the division of lands was scrupulously equal, his was a less compact inheritance, with detached blocks of land in Durham, the North Riding, Northamptonshire, Warwickshire and Hertfordshire. Management costs were therefore higher and acre for acre the northern lands were likely to prove less valuable; the gross yield in 1858 was £14,840 and though the net was £12,067, spending on repairs etc. was unusually low that year.[84] It is not surprising that Charles soon began selling off the outlying farms, and between 1861 and 1864 sales brought him in £82,000, well over a third of it ploughed back into the land, some in overdue repairs and cottage building, the rest in modest purchases intended to rationalise the core estates.[85]

Charles continued to seek out suitable additions- he spent £7,000 at Amotherby in 1868 [86] - but he was keen to diversify too. In purely financial terms land was becoming an indulgence; the rental of the estates sold earlier was less than £2,000, a return of under 2½%, and when the Warwickshire farms were offloaded in 1872, the investments which replaced them yielded £2,975 against a net rental of just £1,780.[87] Admittedly some of the portfolio, which included a French government loan, U.S. government stock, debentures of the South-Eastern Railway Company and the New River Company, Russian railway bonds and various other railway stock, was riskier than consols or land mortgages, but the risks seemed worth taking.[88] By 1867, he had over £70,000 invested, giving a pre-tax income of £3,200, though land mortgages were still the biggest element, two of them accounting for £32,000. The *Return of Owners of Land* shows Charles owning less than 9,000 acres against Rendlesham's 24,000.[89] Being less dependent upon rents, and most of his lands being in the north, which escaped the worst of the depression, Charles's income held up better. Still, the impact was considerable, especially on the hitherto prosperous farms outside Yorkshire; rents from Rickmansworth dropped from £690 to £542 in a decade after 1878, those from Northamptonshire from £445 to £280.[90] Yorkshire did not escape either, for on the Earl of Scarborough's estate nearby rents in 1880 were at their lowest for sixty years, while Thellusson's gross receipts fell from £12,780 in 1878 to £7,738 in 1888.[91]

Charles liked to spend his money, and had the family fondness for sport, though his ruling passion was boats rather than horses. Like so many sports, sailing acquired in Victoria's reign a structure of government, rules, etiquette and events that are substantially intact today.[92] Clubs proliferated and the boatyards boomed, turning out boats of all classes. One of Charles' first actions was to join the Royal Yacht Club and his schooner *Aline* soon became a familiar and successful competitor.[93] He moved on to brand new and bigger yachts, *Guinevere* and *Britannia*,[94] and once past the age for scrambling about in small boats, invested in 'the most striking personal possession ever produced by man',[95] the steam yacht. Rare until the 1860s, they soon became all the rage, and though the *Icena* and her successor the *Albion* were not among the grandest of their day, they were luxurious and handsome craft.[96]

Unlike his cousin, however, Charles was a man with marked artistic taste as well as a sportsman. He bought pictures- Dutch landscapes and genre pieces- which were good enough to be made heirlooms,[97] but the best expression of his taste is Brodsworth Hall itself. It was a time when the shires echoed to the building and rebuilding of country houses on a scale unmatched before or since: houses cost anything from £10,000 to the £600,000 the Duke of Westminster spent remodelling Eaton Hall, the only sure thing being that the cost would exceed the estimate.[98] They came in every size, shape, material, colour and architectural style, though by the time the Thellussons set to building the classical 'cold Palladianism'[99] was quite out of favour and even Barry's flamboyant exercises in the Italian Renaissance had lost ground; gothic and Elizabethan seemed more in tune with the spirit of the age, culturally insular, religious and family centred.[100]

None of this bothered Charles Thellusson. He knew what he wanted and who could provide it, and neither was English. Born in Florence, he sought something redolent of Tuscany and the Renaissance, but with thoroughly Victorian standards of comfort, so to Tuscany he went for his architect, the Chevalier Casentini, architect and sculptor of Lucca. There is still much to be learned about the mysterious chevalier and

419

his part in the building of Brodsworth, and his role is complicated by the employment of a little known Englishman, Philip Wilkinson, to see to most of the details.[101] The employment of a foreign architect alone makes Brodsworth almost unique, for even the most eminent continental practitioners seldom received country house commissions.[102]

Among the three of them- for there is no doubt that the owner had a big say in the design and fittings - they produced a house which is both original and attractive. It is basically a rectangular block with the servants' wing forming a smaller rectangle at right angles to the main one and discreetly masked by shrubbery. A pillared *porte cochère* projects from one of the narrow sides and gentle protrusions from the long garden front mark the dining and drawing rooms. The roof is concealed by an ornamental balustrade, leaving the skyline perfectly free of the romantic collection of chimneys and towers many owners demanded, yet the exterior is anything but dull; rather it is assured, confident and delicate. The interior has much that would be regarded as typically Victorian; rich, heavy hangings, solid, dark furniture, a billiards room almost untouched in a century; but here too there is originality. It shows in the generous, rather quirky, flow of space along the central spine of the house from the porch to the stained glass of the library; in the successful incorporation of doors and chimneypieces from the old house; in the unconventional positioning of the kitchen which requires the breaching of the convention that food should not pass openly thence to the dining room. Above all it shows in the sculptures. Beyond doubt they represent Charles's own taste and he spent £2,750 on them, taking great pains with their correct positioning. The contemporary Italian pieces he liked have long been out of fashion, and some are too sentimental for most modern tastes, but a respected critic warns against any temptation to dismiss them as `a miscellaneous collection of lascivious junk by foreign nobodies'.[103] Whatever the verdict on their individual merits, they are highly effective in their setting, their white shapes reflected from mirrors and glimpsed through doorways, lending real distinctiveness and allure to the house.

By 1863 the new house was substantially complete,[104] the gardens gradually took on their intended form and the church was restored soon afterwards.[105] With four healthy sons, the family seemed firmly entrenched and Charles and Georgiana had twenty years of prosperity and comfort before her death in 1883. When Charles died three years later, in his sixty-third year, three of his brothers were still living.[106] Alexander retired from the army, having served with some distinction in the Crimea and elsewhere, remained single and lived to be over eighty.[107] Ernest, who lived on the Isle of Man, had two daughters who married well[108] but his only son, and namesake, who took holy orders and became vicar of High Melton, not far from Brodsworth, died without a son in 1913,[109] so it was only Frederick of all Charles's brothers whose descendants carried the Thellusson name. Even that descent was precarious, for in 1894 death claimed Frederick's elder son[110] and then Frederick himself,[111] but the younger son, Percy, had two boys and by the second marriage of the elder, there are Thellussons living, the only remaining descendants in the male line of old Peter's youngest son.[112]

By most standards Charles Thellusson was a wealthy man, who besides still extensive estates left nearly £160,000 in personalty.[113] The dispositions he made were deeply conservative, for after deducting the money needed to pay a few legacies and to fund the family annuities,[114] the residue and the lands were both brought into the same strict settlement that he and his wife had created for the Theobald lands under their marriage settlement.[115] He also made the usual provision of portions for his grandchildren, restricted to £40,000 in total, but could hardly have foreseen that there would be no portions, that while three of his sons would marry, not one would father a child, so that they would become life tenants in succession, leaving the property to pass ultimately to his daughter Constance (her sister, Aline, died young) and her issue. By that time, however, the neighbourhood of Brodsworth had undergone a transformation.

A great coal basin underlies the eastern flank of the southern Pennines, the coal bearing strata dipping gently eastwards beneath the Don valley. The field has been

421

exploited since medieval times, the scale of mining expanding famously during the Industrial Revolution, with the incentives of rising local demand from voracious blast furnaces and more distant markets made accessible by improved transport.[116] Heavier capital investment was required for deeper and bigger mines and while landowners might deprecate the blighted landscapes and social transformations that were an unpleasant by-product, many were more than ready to participate in exploiting their subterranean assets. A few, notably the Earls Fitzwilliam, were vigorous and successful colliery owners on their own account, but by the time the first attempts were being made to work the concealed seams around Doncaster, towards the close of the nineteenth century, the landowner's role was seldom more than that of passive rentier, drawing income from leasing the subsoil, from wayleaves and from royalties on the coal.[117] The Settled Land Acts enabled even life owners to grant mining leases up to sixty years and since most farmers were on yearly tenancies, their interests were seldom an obstacle.[118]

For landowners like the Thellussons, their rents depleted by the depression, commercial interest in their deposits was opportune. In 1892 the manager of the Rylands Main Coal Company told Peter that exploitation of the Barnsley seam ('undoubtedly the most valuable and remunerative seam ever worked in this district') could make Brodsworth 'one of the richest and most (valuable) estates in Yorkshire'[119] and by 1900 Herbert was negotiating leases with Hickleton Main Colliery.[120] Royalties started coming in soon after, the Brodsworth Main colliery itself began production in 1908 and within a few years the Doncaster district had changed dramatically, for by 1914 the south Yorkshire field was producing more than 12% of Britain's coal and this at a time when output was at an all-time peak.[121] There were fewer pits than the older fields boasted, but they were bigger, requiring more roads and railways, more houses and amenities for the tough and independent workforce.[122] The Thellussons enjoyed the profits and the lie of the land around Brodsworth limited the aesthetic intrusiveness of winding gear and colliery buildings, but the atmospheric pollution from the new power stations (which enabled electricity to be installed at the

422

Hall in 1908)[123] bit into the porous local limestone used in its construction and the subsidence that was inevitable with deep mining eventually gave rise to structural problems.[124]

Neither Peter nor Herbert lived long enough to see the full impact of these changes,[125] and their deaths in middle age left the third son, Charles, unexpectedly owner of Brodsworth. Like his aristocratic cousin Rendlesham, he was a typical country gentleman, listing his interests as yachting, shooting and fishing; yachting probably came first, for he was a member of three Torbay yacht clubs and spent the summers in Torquay.[126]

In September 1910 Charles and his wife Constance (youngest daughter of the rector of Brodsworth) celebrated their silver wedding anniversary in the expected style, laying on carefully graded hospitality on a descending scale for friends and family, tenants, villagers and their children. Thirty-eight waiters, twenty-nine bandsmen and six constables were hired for the occasion and the whole entertainment cost Charles £636 17s 3d, but there was already something incongruous about these quasi-feudal gatherings in such a neighbourhood and Brodsworth was never to see another like it.[127]

Charles succumbed to the Spanish influenza epidemic of 1919[128] and was succeeded by the youngest brother Augustus, a gouty bachelor who preferred his home at Broadstairs and visited Brodsworth only for the shooting.[129] He died at Broadstairs in 1931, leaving £25,000 to the woman who had been his companion and nurse for years and the residue of his quite substantial property not to the nephew who inherited Brodsworth but to his younger brother Stuart and another nephew, Frederick.[130]

The heir to Brodsworth was Constance's son, Charles Grant-Dalton. It was fitting that a Grant-Dalton should inherit, for they were the family of Mary Grant, long suffering wife of Charles Thellusson II. Her brother Robert, who lived much in Belgium, had three sons, the eldest of whom, Dalton(1812-90) was a keen yachtsman. This may have helped keep them on closer terms with the Thellussons than would otherwise have been the case, given that the Grant- Daltons were on the lower margins of good society.[131] Dalton had twelve children, including nine sons, and the fourth in seniority, Horace, married Constance Thellusson in 1883.[132]

The relatively early death of both parents orphaned two boys, Charles (born 1884) and Stuart (1886).[133] Both fought in the Great War, Stuart as a pilot (he went on to become an R.A.F. wing-commander) and Charles with the R.A.S.C.[134] When Charles married Sylvia West in 1916 (she was barely sixteen, he was thirty-two,[135]) he was almost certain to inherit the Thellusson estates if he survived his two uncles, but by the time that came about it was as well that the coal royalties were still coming in, for farming was once more in the doldrums after the abrupt withdrawal of the price support mechanism ('the great betrayal' to those in agriculture).[136]

The Grant- Daltons were by no means hard up. Charles could still sail his yacht, drive his beloved Bentleys and have enough ready money to enjoy a comfortable life.[137] He spent much of his time in Scotland however, and made substantial economies at Brodsworth, cutting the domestic staff and closing some of the rooms, including the great kitchen. Though requisitioned in the war it suffered little damage but by the time Charles died in 1952 it was clearly in need of substantial refurbishment and, to make it a suitable family home, thorough modernisation too.[138]

But it received neither. For the next thirty- five years Sylvia Grant- Dalton lived at the Hall, at first alone, next with her second husband, Charles's octogenarian cousin Eustace,[139] then as a widow once more. Her only child, Pamela, was married,[140] money was chronically short and staff for the house and its grounds were progressively reduced. Farms were sold and essential repairs carried out, but the gardens fell into picturesque neglect and what with the intruding damp rising, and the acid rain from three power stations visible from the house falling, plus the effects of mining subsidence, the house suffered far from picturesque damage to the fabric. The indomitable *châtelaine* regarded the Hall with a mixture of bemused affection and distaste but her long occupation, preserving so much of the furnishings and contents of a bygone age, served posterity remarkably well.[141] When she died in 1988, buried according to her wishes in the church alongside her husbands and in the company of most of the Hall's owners, her daughter made Brodsworth over to English Heritage, for whom it posed a novel (and expensive) challenge.[142]

To visit Brodsworth in its unrestored state was a curious experience. There were long views towards Doncaster from the eminence on which the house stands, and the Great North Road was clearly visible, but there was little noise and though the colliery winding gear could be seen, it was not an industrial landscape. With its original metal shutters down the house seemed to slumber on its lawn and some of its rooms, the billiards room in particular, had that same air of having fallen asleep in the last century. English Heritage took the enlightened decision to aim `at making everything reasonably clean and stable, whilst retaining the appearance of a well-worn country house'[143] and when it was opened to visitors in 1995 they found a strange mixture of the conventional and the original. It is a mixture which has proved very appealing. What old Peter Thellusson, who lies in the church close by the house, would think of the outcome of his audacious scheme we shall never know, but perhaps after all the condemnation and abuse heaped upon him, we can now absolve him at last and accept Brodsworth as his inadvertent gift to the nation.

NOTES

1.   Gowing, *Public Men of Ipswich and East Suffolk*, pp.130-1.

2.   *Complete Peerage*, vol. V, pp.17 -27; *D.N.B.*, vol. XIII, pp.750-1. Disraeli's fictional depiction of the tournament, at `Montfort Castle', in *Endymion* (1880) is `second-hand and inaccurate', according to Lord Blake, *Disraeli*, (London, 1966), p.171. It cost Eglintoun £30- to £40,000 against the original estimate of £2,000.

3.   The settlement is presumably the origin of the 190 acres Rendlesham owned in Ayrshire. It is referred to in his will (*Wills 1912, London*, 120).

4.   Rubinstein, *Men of Property*, especially tables 2.7, 7.1, 7.3.

5.   Bateman, *Great Landowners* (4th edn., London, 1883). The figures date from 1873 and by then Rendlesham had made some purchases.

6.   The house in Upper Belgrave Street may have been rented. By 1900 his only London addresses were his clubs, White's, the Carlton and the Marlborough.

7.   There is a photograph in C.A. Manning Press, *Suffolk Celebrities* (Leeds, 1893), with a sycophantic character sketch. Though he was never one of the Prince's `set', they were said to be on very friendly terms: *Ipswich Journal*, 10 Nov. 1911.

8.   Though White's *Suffolk Directory* describes it as a `large and handsome mansion of flint and stone'.

9.   Girouard, *Victorian Country House*, p.33. Burn is credited with creating the characteristic layout of these houses and had the biggest practice of this sort. He died in 1870, aged eighty, and this was one of his last commissions.

10.   J. Kenworthy-Browne *et al.*, *Burke and Savill's Guide to Country Houses* (London, 1981), vol.III, p.258. There is a photograph in H.R. Barker, *East Suffolk Illustrated*, (Ipswich, 1908-9), pp.392- 3.

11.   The Gardener's Chronicle, 6 Aug. 1881, 178-9.

12.   Gowing, *Public Men of Ipswich and East Suffolk*, p.132.

13.   Examples can be found in Thirsk, *Suffolk Farming*, pp.142, 148, 154.

14.   Gowing, *Public Men of Ipswich and East Suffolk*, p.135. It would be interesting to know whether Gowing was related to the famous poacher of the same name whose encounter with Rendlesham is related in D.E. Johnson, *Victorian Shooting Days: East Anglia, 1810-1910* (Woodbridge, 1981), pp.47-9.

15.   *Lord Rendlesham v. Haward* (1873-74) 9 C.P. 252. The position of the remaining Irish peers has become increasingly anomalous: S. Winchester, *Their Noble Lordships* (London, 1981),

pp.235-43.

16. H.J. Hanham, *Elections and Party Management* (London, 1959), p.251, reckons that a county seat cost about £3,000 a candidate in 1868.

17. The title of D.C. Moore's book (Hassocks, 1976). N. Gash, *Politics in the Age of Peel: a study in Parliamentary Representation* (London, 1953), pp.177-8. The Liberal success in 1885 suggested to H. Pelling (*A Social Geography of British Elections* (London, 1967), pp.102-3) that landlord control in East Suffolk was weak by that time. The secret ballot had been introduced in 1872.

18. Craig, *British Parliamentary Election Results, 1832-85*, p.461. The 1874 candidates were Rendlesham, whose grandfather was ennobled by Pitt; Tomline, a descendant of Pitt's first biographer, and Lord Mahon, who wrote a later biography of Pitt.

19. *Parl. Debs.*, 3rd s., vol. 245 (1879), col.8; 3rd s. vol. 258 (1881), col. 1651.

20. *Dod's Parliamentary Companion*. The description remained unaltered through successive editions.

21. *Ibid.* The Conservatives' failure to assist agriculture caused great dissatisfaction among farmers: T. Lloyd, *The General Election of 1880* (Oxford, 1968). Rendlesham's electioneering is mentioned on p.62n.

22. F.W.S. Craig, *British Parliamentary Election Results, 1885-1918* (London, 1977).

23. She died at Rendlesham (*The Times*, 15 Jan. 1880). When the couple had visited their French relations, Amable de Thellusson described her as `une jolie personne' (Ain, *Les Thellusson*, p.336).

24. There is a memorial to Ann Blanche in Rendlesham church.

25. *The Times*, 29 Jan. 1901. Arthur Wentworth William Augustus had seen service in near forgotten battles and sieges in the Sudan. He left nearly £30,000 to his sisters: *Wills 1901, London*, 239.

26. *The Times*, 21 Oct. 1901. In 1877, four years after Henrietta died, he married Augusta Heine in Heidelberg. The marriage was childless and she died in Switzerland in 1916: *Wills 1922, London*, 162. Arthur seems to have had several houses along the Suffolk coast at different times and died at `Little Casino', Aldeburgh.

27. C.M. Gaskell, The Country Gentleman, *The Nineteenth Century* 12 (1882), 460-73; A. Ponsonby, *The Decline of the Aristocracy* (London, 1912), pp.85-98.

28. See Masters, *The Dukes*, p.339 and the Duke's autobiography, *Looking Back*. George V's passion for shooting was also remarkable.

29. *The Times*, 11 Nov. 1911.

30. *The Times*, 11 Nov.1911; *V.C.H. Suffolk*, vol.II, pp. 380-3; F. Hussey, *The Royal Harwich*

427

Yacht Club, a short history (Ipswich, 1972), app.`A'; M. Guest and W. B. Boulton, *The Royal Yacht Squadron* (London, 1903), p.429.

31. Johnson, *Victorian Shooting Days*, pp.1-51; *V.C.H. Suffolk*, vol.II, pp.364- 70, 408-10. It is revealing that this volume of the *V.C.H.*, published in 1907, devotes more pages to sports than to agriculture.

32. J.G. Ruffer, *The Big Shots* (rev. ed., London, 1998). It is used rather portentiously by I. Colegate, *The Shooting Party* (1980) as a microcosm of Edwardian England.

33. T.W.Fletcher, The Great Depression, 1873-96, reprinted in P.J. Perry (ed.), *British Agriculture, 1875-1914* (London, 1973), 30-55.

34. *Ibid.*, especially the introduction and articles by Fletcher, Perry and J.T.Coppock (Agricultural Changes in the Chilterns, 1875-1900, 56-76). C.S. Orwin and E.H. Whetham, *A History of British Agriculture, 1846-1914* (London, 1964), pp.240-88.

35. Livestock prices also tumbled at the end of the century when refrigerated imports began to arrive.

36. Duke of Bedford, *A Great Agricultural Estate* (London, 1897), p.180.

37. Fletcher, *Great Depression*, and R. Perren, The Landlord and Agricultural Transformation, in *British Agriculture, 1875-1914*, 109-28, at 127-8.

38. Commissioned by Lord Derby's administration to confound the wild allegations frequently made about the aristocratic monopoly of land, the returns, when rendered intelligible by John Bateman, in fact furnished ammunition for more accurate, and scarcely less damaging, charges.

39. Orwin and Whetham, *History of British Agriculture*, pp.289-306; A. Offer, *Property and Politics, 1870-1914: Landownership, Law, Ideology and Urban Development in England*, (Cambridge, 1981), 317-400; D. Cannadine, *The Decline and Fall of the British Aristocracy* (rev. edn., London, 1992), pp.54-69.

40. The title of W. Bence Jones' article in (1882) *The Nineteenth Century*, 346-68.

41. Thompson, *English Landed Society*, p.298. The machinery was complicated and expensive and there were safeguards for the `principal mansion house'. The Settled Land Act 1925 somewhat simplified the procedure and the Trusts of Land etc. Act 1996 ended the power to create settlements in this form.

42. Thompson, *English Landed Society* cites the Duke of Marlborough's comment that `were there any effective demand for the purchase of land, half the land of England would be in the market tomorrow' (p.319). There were some major sales, however, at least two of them in Suffolk, where Sir Edward Guinness, ennobled as Lord Iveagh, bought himself a seat.

43. *Ibid.*, p.310. Figures are for gross rentals in corn growing areas. Examples of the experience of estates are in Coppock, *Changes in the Chilterns*, and J.J. McGregor, The Economic History

428

of Two Rural Estates in Cambridgeshire, 1870 - 1934, *Journal of the Royal Agricultural Society* (1937), 142-61.

44. Indeed he made small purchases, e.g. the manor of Wantisden in 1896: Copinger, *Manors of Suffolk*, vol.V, p.187. This was a year when according to Thirsk, *Suffolk Farming*, land in the county `could be given away to anyone who would take it' (introduction).

45. *British Agriculture, 1875-1914*, xxv-xxx; Orwin and Whetham, *History of British Agriculture*, pp.274-6. Even on the Bedford estate, `taking in hand' was a last resort: Bedford, *A Great Agricultural Estate*, pp.180-93.

46. A. Arnold, The Indebtedness of the Landed Gentry, *Contemporary Review* 47 (1885), 225-32; Cannadine, *Decline of Aristocracy*, 91-5.

47. See e.g. Bedford, *A Great Agricultural Estate*, pp.55-112 and the example given in Bateman, *Great Landowners*, introduction. Rendlesham, for instance, repaired and enlarged the village school: *V.C.H. Suffolk*, vol.II, p.291.

48. When Lord Francis Hope invoked the Settled Land Act in 1898 to sell the famous `Hope diamond', one of his sisters reluctantly consented because of the `opportunity it gave her to have her son educated at Eton, which she considered essential to his station in life': *In re Hope* (1899) 2 Ch 679 at 683. Rising costs of education, dress and hospitality were an anxiety for many landowners: Gaskell, *Country Gentleman*, 466.

49. S.H. Jeyes, Our Gentlemanly Failures, (1897) 67 *Fortnightly Review*, 387-98. Cannadine, *Decline of Aristocracy*, 236-96. Competition enhanced the advantages of an Eton schooling, with its private language and aristocratic role: R. Perrott, *The Aristocrats* (London, 1968), pp.88-9.

50. *Alumni Cantabrigienses, 1752-1900*, vol.III, p.553. Jarvis was a triple blue, at athletics, football and cricket. *Complete Peerage*, vol.XII(2), pp.722-7; *V.C.H. Lancashire* (London, 1911), vol.V, p.82.

51. Miriam (d. 1950) married Godfrey Williams; Ruby (d. 1955) married Lt. Col. Bernard Petre.

52. P. Ashton, *Rendlesham* (1975), p.12. Egidia and Frederick are both buried at Campsey Ash and Adeline had been married there. To the next generation Cecilia was an aunt of Wodehousian dimensions, whose departure for Dar es Salaam was something of a relief, for she ran up debts wherever she rented houses and insisted on marking her transient occupation by planting fruit trees in her wake. She died in Mombasa in 1948.

53. *Ipswich Journal*, 13 May 1898.

54. *The Times*, 11 Nov. 1911. In addition to the funeral, there were memorial services at Butley and Ipswich and Society turned out in strength. His will (*Wills 1912, London*, 120) is the first in this family to make specific provision for payment of death duties. The gross estate, excluding

settled land, was £174,000.

55. *Complete Peerage*, vol.VII, appendix F; *Army List*, 1918.

56. But Louis Jarvis was killed and among those wounded were Bernard Petre and the 8th Baron Walsingham, grandson of Emily Thellusson, the 2nd Lord Rendlesham's daughter.

57. The misfortunes of William Thellusson (1893-1967), son of Percy Sabine, are reported in *In re Thellusson, Ex p. Abdy* [1919] 2 K.B. 735.

58. C.C.R. Murphy, *The History of the Suffolk Regiment, 1914-27* (London, 1928), pp.111-19, 360-79.

59. E.H. Whetham (ed.), *The Agrarian History of England and Wales*, vol.VIII, 1914-39 (Cambridge, 1978), pp.89-107.

60. Cannadine, *Decline of Aristocracy*, pp.95-8. Thompson, *English Landed Society*, p.328, instances a Wiltshire estate where direct taxes were taking 30% of the rental in 1919, as against 9% before the war. The wills of the 6th and 7th Lords Rendlesham gave the trustees a wider discretion than that of the 5th Baron.

61. *The Importance of Being Ernest* (1895), Act One. Lady Bracknell is speaking.

62. F.M.L. Thompson, English Landed Society in the 20th Century: the new poor and the new rich, *Transactions of the Royal Historical Society* (6th s.) 1 (1991), 1-20.

63. *Ibid.*, 329-35; M. Beard, *English Landed Society in the 20th Century* (London, 1989), pp.38-54; H. Cox, Changes in Landownership in England, (1922) 129 *Atlantic Monthly*, 556-62. The most famous house to become a school was Stowe, formerly home to the Dukes of Buckingham.

64. Frederick Archibald Charles. His picture is in *The Illustrated London News*, 18 Nov.1911. So conservative was he that he brought an unsuccessful high court action to restrain the Hurlingham Club from discontinuing the live pigeon shoots which had been one of its original amenities: *Thellusson v. Viscount Valentia* [1906] 1 Ch. 480.

65. Daughter of the Rt. Hon. J. Manley. She died at Claridge's in 1931. Her husband gave a new pulpit to Rendlesham church in her memory.

66. Percy and his wife Gladys, whom he married in 1922 were a couple in tune with the Jazz Age, she listing her interests as music, golf, motoring and ballooning (*The Ladies Who's Who*, 1923, 594), he keeping a few horses at Epsom and being renowned for his expert knowledge of food and drink.

67. Ashton, *Rendlesham*, pp.10-11; *Kelly's Suffolk Directory* (1937), 383. By 1937 population in the parish had fallen from 355 to 266 in forty years.

68. *The Times*, 6 Jul. 1938. His second wife, Dolores Olga Salusbury-Trelawney, a widow with a son, was the daughter of a baronet (an old Cornish family). She died in Park Lane in 1959.

430

69. *Wills 1938, London.* This despite taking over the agency for the champagne house of Pommery from his brother. The lectern in the church is a memorial to him.

70. The family also owned land in the West Indies. The 5th baron's will refers to land in Trinidad, but those of his successors do not. The present family says that a West Indian island was sold to the U.S.A. for a military base in the last war, but I have been unable to identify it.

71. Percy was bequeathed £20,000 plus the residue by the 6th Baron, but left only £42,444 net, devising the Rendlesham estates (or the sale proceeds if, as happened, he had sold them) to his nephew Anthony for life, remainder to his eldest son. He left the residue to Anthony and his brother Peter: *Wills 1943, London.* The *Times* obituary (13 Dec. 1943) is disappointingly anodyne.

72. Perrott, *Aristocrats*, pp.129-49. Charles Anthony Hugh (b.1915) is the eldest son of Hugh Edmund (1976-1926) and Gwynydd, née Colleton. Hugh was never very affluent (the boys' Eton education was paid for by their uncle Frederick) and died of pneumonia in 1926.

73. His first wife was Margaret Rome.

74. *The Times,* 4 Feb. 1987. He also has three married daughters. His younger brother Peter (b.1920) is a widower with two sons: *Complete Peerage* (new edn.), vol.14 (1998), p.544.

75. In 1977 plans to build shelters for fighters in part of the forest designated an area of outstanding natural beauty were strenuously opposed by the district council: *Eastern Star*, 10 August 1977.

76. Suffolk lost at least twenty-six such houses in the first twenty years after the war: Beard, *English Landed Society in the 20th Century*, p.109. The nearby Bawdsey Manor was luckier: part of an 8,000 acre estate on the River Deben bought by the founder of the National Telephone Company, Sir Cuthbert Quilter, in the 1880s, it was bought by the Air Ministry in 1936 and became a secret radar and research station, not marked on Ordnance Survey maps. It was sold in 1991.

77. Local inhabitants had long known of the ship's existence: Arnott, *A Suffolk Estuary.*

78. Not, presumably the gowned clergyman sometimes seen there: Ashton, *Rendlesham*, p.12.

79. There is a portrait of him as a dashing young cavalry officer at Brodsworth.

80. See *supra*, p. 374..

81. Estate accounts, Brodsworth Hall MSS DD168/1. His will charged his property with continuing annuities to Frederick, Alexander and Ernest, along with £250 p.a to Frederick's wife Annie if, as happened, she survived him; presumably Ernest's family were not thought likely to be in need: *Wills 1885, London*, 891.

82. Sabine married Richard Greville of Godalming.

83. Brodsworth Hall MSS DD168/1.

84   *Ibid.* By contrast, in 1868 repairs alone came to over £3,900 and another £200 was spent on drainage; between 1859 and 1865 £25,000 was spent on repairs, improvements and new purchases.

85.   *Ibid.*, DD168/7/2. The rest was mostly invested in mortgages; in 1865 Charles's income from investments was £3,466.

86.   Account for 1868, *ibid.*, DD168/1

87.   Brodsworth Hall MSS DD168/6.

88.   *Ibid.*, DD168/6/7. The risks had been highlighted by the Overend Gurney crash of 1866, triggering the greatest stock market panic for forty years. Nevertheless within a few years huge programmes of railway construction around the globe were attracting vast amounts of British capital; the Vera Cruz railway is the fraud at the centre of *The Way We Live Now*, Trollope's mordant view of a society mesmerised by the promise of easy money.

89.   Although the figure given for Charles is marked 'correct' by Bateman, it makes the common omission of urban property, not showing the Theobald lands in Brixton. There is a plan of them in Brodsworth Hall MSS DD168 and an oblique glimpse of their development in *Thellusson v. Liddard* [1900] 2 Ch. 635.

90.   Brodsworth Hall MSS DD168/1.

91   *Ibid.*; Beastall, *A South Yorkshire Estate*, 40-4.

92.   Guest and Boulton, *Royal Yacht Squadron*, p. 283ff.

93.   *Ibid.*, pp.278-9, 440. Charles's first boat was the schooner *Georgiana*. The *Aline's* subsequent owners were an exclusive company- the Earl of Hardwicke, the Prince of Wales, the Marquis of Hastings and Prince Ibrahim Pasha.

94.   *Guinevere* was traded in for £8,000 and *Boadicea* cost £15,000. The family papers, especially DD168/7, contain much about these yachts.

95.   E. Hotman, *The Steam Yachts* (Lymington n.d.), p.3.

96.   Brodsworth Hall MSS DD168/7, DD BROD /14. Both yachts were bequeathed to his eldest son: *Wills 1885, London*, 891.

97.   Nine paintings were made heirlooms, including three Theobald family portraits, two Backhuysens and one apiece by De Hooch, Wynants, Wouvermans and Van der Neer. Brodsworth Hall MSS DD168/7 shows what he had given for the Dutch paintings, notably 650 guineas for the Backhuysen.

98.   Girouard, *Victorian Country House*, introduction, esp. pp.7-10.

99.   G. Scott's phrase, quoted in *Ibid.*, at p.53.

100.   *Ibid.*, pp.52-3; R. Dixon and S. Muthesius, *Victorian Architecture* (2nd edn., London, 1985), pp.33-46.

101. Girouard, *Victorian Country House*, pp.236-42; English Heritage, *Welcome to Brodsworth Hall* (London, 1995). The Brodsworth Hall MSS contain important material on the building process.

102. Two notable exceptions are Waddesdon for the Rothschilds (1874-89 by G.H. Destailleur) and what is now the Bowes Museum (begun 1869, by J-A.F -A. Pellechet).

103. B. Read, *Sculpture at Brodsworth*, (Victorian Society paper, London, 1990), p.6.

104. Work continued until about 1870, the eventual cost being about £60,000.

105. Brodsworth Hall MSS DD168/7.

106. The youngest brother, Seymour, died a bachelor in furnished lodgings at Brighton. His will (*Wills 1868, London*, 430) shows that he left very little money.

107. Alexander reached the rank of Lieutenant-Colonel and died in 1904.

108. Mary married Sir C.H. Morton, a prominent solicitor. Laura married twice; her second husband was one of the Wood family of nearby Hickleton Hall.

109. The living was in the gift of Laura's husband. Ernest had previously held livings in the Isle of Man. Ernest senior died in 1893.

110. He was in the Forestry Department of the I.C.S. and died in Rangoon, leaving a Belgian wife Gabrielle. Their only child, Frederick Eugene (b.1894) also married in Belgium but had to flee the German advance a few months later and was given a temporary commission in the British army in 1916 (*Army List, 1918*). Augustus Thellusson left him a legacy but the phrasing suggests he was uncertain whether he was still alive.

111. Frederick had been honorary consul at Ostend and since the Grant- Daltons had been in business in Belgium it is possible he had business connections with them.

112. *Burke's Landed Gentry, 1952*; Ain, *Les Thellusson*, p.328; app. 2.

113. *Wills 1885, London*, 891.

114. In addition to those mentioned earlier, there were smaller ones to the relics of Georgiana's brother and sister.

115. Brodsworth Hall MSS DD168/10.

116. G.D.B. Gray, The South Yorkshire Coalfield, (1947) *Geography*, 113-31; B.E. Coates, The Geography of the Industrialization and Urbanization of South Yorkshire, in S. Pollard and C. Holmes, *Essays in the Economic and Social History of South Yorkshire* (Sheffield, 1976), 14-27.

117. J.T. Ward, West Riding Landowners and Mining in the Nineteenth Century, in J. Benson and R.G. Neville, *Studies in the Yorkshire Coal Industry* (Manchester, 1976), 45-65.

118. *Wolstenholme's Conveyancing and Settled Land Acts* (9th edn., by B. L. Cherry and A. E. Russell, London, 1905), pp.338-55. Because mining deprived the settlement of an irreplaceable capital asset, the rents from such leases were apportioned between income, to which the life

tenant could lay claim, and capital, which belonged to the remainderman.

119. J. Parkin to P. Thellusson, 10 May 1892, Brodsworth Hall MSS DD 168/5.

120. *Ibid.*, DD BROD/4/5, 15, 21-44.

121. 121. Gray, *South Yorkshire Coalfield*; Coates, *Industrialization of South Yorkshire*; H.S. Jevons, *The British Coal Trade* (London, 1915), p.65 and app.II.

122. Gray, *South Yorkshire Coalfield*, 125-30.

123. Brodsworth Hall MSS DD BROD/13/6.

124. This led the Woods to abandon nearby Hickleton Hall and caused severe problems in Hickleton church: A.C. Johnson, *Viscount Halifax, A Biography* (London, 1941), pp.35-6.

125. Peter died in 1899, his widow Elizabeth in 1922. Alone among Charles' sons, Peter went up from Eton (1864-9) to university (Christchurch, Oxford). To judge from the surviving bills and receipts (Brodsworth Hall MSS.DD BROD 12) he seems to have been fond of travel, yachting and photography. Herbert had lived mostly in Shropshire until he inherited. After leaving Eton (1868-71), he had been an officer in the Guards and in the Hussars, resigning when he married in 1885. His wife died in 1900 and Herbert in 1903.

126. *Yorkshire Who's Who* (1912), p.395. The Torquay house had belonged to Horace Grant- Dalton (*Wills 1899, London*, 555), and was presumably bought by Herbert Thellusson, from whom Charles inherited it.

127. Brodsworth Hall MSS DD12/13/1/1. Constance was the youngest daughter of the rector of Brodsworth. Until Herbert's death they had been living at Riccall, in a manor house rented from Lord Wenlock.

128. He died on 25th March. Since Herbert had settled most of his property, it is not surprising that Charles' personal estate (£62,061) was much smaller. Constance was left the house in Torquay, the funds in their marriage settlement and a jointure of £2,000; legacies totalled about £15,000 and the residue was given to Augustus: *Wills 1919, London*, 1683.

129. English Heritage, *Brodsworth*.

130. *Wills 1931, London*; *The Times*, 25 Apr. 1931. He left £86,000 and settled property valued at £472,000.

131. This is suggested by their intermittent appearances in successive editions of Walford, *County Families*, between 1860 and 1914.

132. *Burke's Landed Gentry, 1972*. Most of the boys went to Marlborough: L.W. Jones, *The Marlborough School Register, 1843-1952* (9th edn., Marlborough, 1952).

133. Constance died in 1893, Horace, who was in the merchant marine, in 1899 on the eve of a voyage to Argentina. He left a modest estate (under £7,000) to his sons: *Wills 1899, London*, 555.

134. Stuart was sent to Uppingham and Sandhurst, Charles to Repton. Stuart's duties took him abroad in the 1930s and he later emigrated permanently: *Uppingham School Roll, 1824-1931* (6th issue, by J.P. Graham, London, 1932); *Wills 1952, London*.

135. Daughter of Reginald West of Christchurch, Hants. To judge from her will (*Wills 1988, London*), and materials at Brodsworth (Brodsworth Hall MSS 7099/49) she was a descendant of William `Waterfall' West (1801-61), who exhibited many landscapes (often featuring his trademark falls) at the Royal Academy: H.C. Mallalieu, *Dictionary of British Watercolour Artists up to 1920* (Woodbridge, 1976), pp.274-5.

136. *Agrarian History*, vol.VIII, pp.139-61.

137. Brodsworth Hall MSS DD BROD/11/and /14; Brodsworth Hall MSS 7099/9-14. One car is pictured in English Heritage, *Brodsworth*, but a Rolls Bentley had to be sold in 1951: *Wills 1952, London*.

138. Brodsworth Hall MSS, 7099/48. The last thorough refurbishment had been in 1906, when £10,000 was spent under an agreement between the life tenant and the trustees: *Wills 1931, London* (Augustus Thellusson). Charles Grant- Dalton's estate was valued at £427,500, which suggests his personal wealth was not very substantial: *Wills 1952, London*.

139. Son of Horace's brother Gerald. A soldier like his father Eustace, he `got into every war he could' (Sylvia Grant- Dalton, quoted in English Heritage, *Brodsworth*). His first wife had died in 1910 and he married Sylvia in 1959. He died in 1970 (*Burke's Landed Gentry, 1972*) having made Sylvia promise to maintain the Hall: *The Guardian*, 1 Apr. 1988.

140. To Ronald Williams in 1958.

141. She made a great impact in Lucinda Lambton's television programme on the Great North Road.

142. *Wills 1988, London*. Pamela died in 1994, shortly before the house was opened to the public.

143. English Heritage, *Brodsworth*. English Heritage paid £3,360,000 and it cost at least as much again to put it into a condition to be displayed.

Table of Cases

Duke of Norfolk's Case (Howard v. Duke of Norfolk)

    (1681) 3 Cas. in Ch. 1, 2 Swanst. 455   4, 166-8, 171

Noys v. Mordaunt (1706) 2 Vern. 581   225

Oddie v. Brown (1849) 4 De G. & J. 179   201

    v. Woodford (1821-5) 3 My. & Cr. 584   331-4, 389

O'Neill v. Lucas (1838) 2 Keen 313   211 n60

Pells v. Brown (1620) Cro. Jac. 590   186 n30

Planche v. Fletcher (1779) 1 Doug. 252   54 n17

Porter v. Fox (1834) 6 Sim. 485   211 n72

Protheroe v. Protheroe [1968] 1 W.L.R. 519   290

Purefoy v. Rogers (1671) 2 Wms. Saunders 380   165

R. v. de Mierre (1771) Burr. 2788   54 n13

The Rebecca (1804) SC Rob. 102   105 n58

Reeve v. Long (1694) 1 Salk. 247   188 n64

Lord Rendlesham v. Haward (1873-4) 9 C.P. 252   409

    v. Robarts (1856) 23 Beav. 321   389

    v. Woodford (1813) 1 Dow. 249   227

Robinson v. Hardcastle (1786) 2 Bro. CC 22   188 n58

In re Lady Rossyn's Trusts (1848) 16 Sim. 391   210 n49, 211 n59

St. Paul v. Heath (1865) 13 L.T.R. 271   210 n55

Scarisbrick v. Skelmersdale (1849) 17 Sim. 187   201

Scattergood v. Edge (1687) 1 Salk. 229   170

Shaw v. Rhodes (1835) 1 My. & Cr. 135   202, 210 n48

Shelly v. Nash (1818) 3 Madd. 232   353 n175

Shepherd v. Ingram (1764) Amb. 448   178-9

Sheppard v. Woodford (1839) 5 M. & W. 608   364

Stephens v. Stephens (1736) Cas. temp. Talb. 228   174, 178

Re Stone & Saville's Contract [1962] 1 W.L.R. 460   278

Tench v. Cheese (1855) 6 De G.M. & G. 453   210 n48

Table of Statutes

BIBLIOGRAPHY

1. UNPUBLISHED MATERIALS

1. Public Record Office, London

PRO BT   107/8 Register of shipping, 1787-9

C   12   Bills in Chancery, 1758- 1800
C   13   same, 1801-42
C   14   same, 1842-52
C   15   same, 1852-60
C   30   Receivers' accounts
C   33   Decrees and orders
C   38   Masters' reports

IR   12   Legacy Duty papers
    26   Estate Duty papers

PROB 6   Grants of Letters of Administration
    11   Probated wills

T   78/65,66, 267-8 Claims and awards in France, 1815-17
    93/8   Subscriptions for the Relief of Distressed French Clergy, 1792-5

TS   18/342 Bequest of Sir Joseph Jekyll
    1501   Treasury Solicitor's papers in the Thellusson case, 1852-9
    33/6   Pedigree of Peter Thellusson

PRO 30/8   Chatham papers
    30/9/31-2   Diary of Charles Abbot, Lord Colchester

2. British Library, London

Add Mss 35,540 Hardwicke papers
    37,912-9, 37,850-1 Windham papers

38,232 Liverpool papers
39,791 Flaxman papers
40,548-75 Peel papers

3. Hertfordshire Record Office, Hertford

D/P 3 Papers in *Oddie v. Woodford*
26183-4 Papers concerning Wall Hall
24244 Lease of land
24245 Enfranchisement of copyholds in Aldenham
5/20a Sale of property in East Barnet 1875
5119-20 as above
D/ EWh Deposited Estate Documents
T2 Various Leases
T3 Aldenham
T6 Otterspool
T8 Edge Grove
T16 Manor of Park

4. East Suffolk County Record Office, Ipswich

HB 416 Terriers of Thellusson Estates, c.1830
/F1 Report on the Division of the Estates,1857
F2 Accounts 1857-8 in *Rendlesham v.Robarts*
E3 Consignee's Accounts, Bacolet Estate, 1812-21
Schedule of Title Deeds

5. Yorkshire Archaeological Society, Leeds

Brodsworth Hall MSS
DD 168/1 Annual Estate Accounts, 1858-98
2,3 Papers re the building of the Hall,1861-4
4 Report on limestone quarry, 1853
5 Mining proposal, 1892
6 Sales of Warwickshire estate, 1872
7 Bills, letters and legal papers, 1850-92
10. Minutes of Thellusson settlements, 1850-65
15 Diaries of Charles Thellusson, 1831 -55 and betting books
16 Letters and papers of Charles Thellusson
DD 132 Deeds of Yorkshire estates

6. Kent Archive Office, Maidstone

Norman MSS KAO U 310

    F 13 G.W. Norman's autobiographical notes
    F 14 G.W. Norman's diaries.
    F 69 G.W. Norman's autobiography
    C 125/2 Papers on the estate of Lord Rendlesham, 1824-32.
    C 183 Correspondence with the Mannings
    B 34 papers on the Thellusson case.

7. Warwickshire County Record Office, Warwick

Newdegate Papers
CR 764/236-7 Correspondence from and testamentary matters re E.J.A. Woodford

8. East India Company papers, India House, London

L/AG 14/5   East India stock ledgers, 1756-96

9. Bank of England, Roehampton

AC 27/470-503   Stock Ledgers and Indexes, 1753-98

10. House of Lords Record Office, London

Main papers, no 114, 21 Feb. 1828, Papers concerning the private bill of 1827

11. Principal Probate Registry, Somerset House

Probated wills, 1837 onwards

12. National Register of Archives, London

17856   Report on Pratt Mss, Norfolk RO
41369   Report on Northbrook Mss

13. Bodleian Library, Oxford

Ms. Eng. Lett. C65/1   Manning Mss

14. Middle Temple Library

Lord Eldon's casenotes

15. Guildhall Library, London

Index to Entries in Parish Registers

16. Unpublished Theses

Connell E.J. *Hertfordshire Agriculture*, 1750-1860. M. Sc. Econ., London University, 1966.

Childs A.R *Politics and Elections in Suffolk Boroughs during the late 18th and early 19th centuries*. M. Phil. Reading, 1973.

O'Brien P.K. *Government Revenue, 1793-1815*. D. Phil., Cambridge, 1967.

Olphin H.K. *George Tierney*. M.A., London, 1933.

Wilkinson E. *The French Emigres in England, 1792-1802*. B. Litt., Oxford, 1952.

2. OFFICIAL AND PARLIAMENTARY PUBLICATIONS

House of Commons Journals
House of Lords Journals
London Gazette : Lists of Dormant Funds in Court, 1890-96

House of Commons Papers

Names and Descriptions of the Proprietors entitled to Dividends on Public Funds transferrable at South Sea House on or before 1780 and unpaid on 25 February 1791. HCSP (old series) vol. 81 no.4284.

Papers presented to the House of Commons, pursuant to addresses relative to Sir Charles Grey and Sir John Jervis, HCSP (old series) vol. 96, nos 4537-41; vol. 100, no. 4643.

Report of a Committee on a petition of merchants trading to Grenada and St. Vincent, HCSP (old series) 96, no.4549.

A List of the ...Subscribers to the Loan of £18 million for the Service of the Year 1797. HCSP (old series), vol. 104, no. 4736.

Report of the Select Committee into the Circumstances of the Loan, HCJ 51 (1797), p.329.

Report from the Committee on the Commercial State of the West India Colonies, PP 1807 (65) III.

Report from the Select Committee on Corrupt Practices in the Appointment and Nomination of Writers and Cadets, PP 1809 (91) II.

7th Report of the Commissioners for Military Enquiry, PP 1809 (3) V.

Reports of the Commissioners on the Law of Real Property, PP 1829 (263) X; 1830 (575) XI; 1831-2 (484) XXIII; 1833 (109) XXII.

Report on the Affairs of the East India Company, PP 1831-2 (735-1) IX.

Report of the Commissioners on the Court of Chancery, PP 1826 (143) XVI.

Returns relative to the Court of Chancery PP 1828 (73, 97, 259) XX.
Further Accounts of Money...in the Masters' Offices, and others, PP 1830 (23, 361, 428, 626, 671) XX.
Report of the Select Committee on Chancery Offices, PP 1833 (685) XIV.
Returns from the Court of Chancery, PP 1836 (370) XLIII.
Reports from the Select Committee on Fees in Courts of Law and Equity, PP 1847-8 (158, 307) XV; 1848-9 (559) VIII.
Return of Causes in which no proceedings have been undertaken since 30 June 1844, PP 1850 (384) XLVI.
First Report of the Commissioners on the Court of Chancery, PP 1852 (1437) XXI.
4th Report of the Law Reform Committee, The Rule against Perpetuities, Cmnd 18 of 1956-7.
The Rule against Perpetuities, Law Commission Consultation Paper 133 (1993).
The Rules against Perpetuities and Excessive Accumulations, Law Commission Report 251, HC 579 of 1998.

House of Lords Papers

Returns in the Thellusson Case, *HLSP* 1833 (70, 92, 101, 102, 114) vol. 11.

Reports of Debates

A Collection of the Parliamentary Debates(Torbuck), 1736.
The Parliamentary Register (Almon), 1784-80.
The Parliamentary Register (Debrett), 1780-1803.
The Senator, or Parliamentray Chronicle, 1791-1802.
The Parliamentary Debates (Woodfall), 1794-6.
The Parliamentary Debates (Cobbett), 1803-20.
The Parliamentary Debates (Hansard), 1821-.
The Mirror of Parliament (Barrow), 1828-40

Other

Craig F.W.S. *British Parliamentary Election Results, 1832-85*. London, 1977.
British Parliamentary Election Results, 1885-1918. London, 1974.
Dod C.R. *Electoral Facts 1832-53, Impartially Stated*. Repr. Edn. of 1972, ed. Hanham H.J.
The Parliamentary Companion. London, various edns.
Hoppit J. and Innes J. (eds.) *Failed Legislation*. London, 1997.

3. SERIAL PUBLICATIONS AND WORKS OF REFERENCE

Journals, Newspapers and Annuals

Bells' Weekly Messenger
Notes and Queries
The Gentleman's Magazine
The Annual Register
The Ipswich Journal
The Burney Collection of British Newspapers, British Library
The Times
The European Magazine
The Illustrated London News
The London Magazine
The Scots Magazine
The Sporting Magazine
The Royal Kalendar
The Army List
Crockford's Clergy List
The Law List

Collected Biographies, Registers etc.

Registers of St. Dunstan in the East, London, *Harleian Society Registers* 86,87 (1956/7).

Registers of St. George's, Hanover Square, *Harleian Society Registers* 2 (1886).

Registers of St. Mary Le Bow, Cheapside, *Harleian Society Registers* 45 (1915).

Brigg W. (ed.) *The Parish Registers of Aldenham, 1660-1812*. St.Albans, 1910.

The Parish Registers of Brodsworth, 1538-1813, Yorkshire Parish Register Society, Wakefield, 1937.

Armytage Sir G.J.(ed.), Musgrave's Obituaries, *Harleian Society Publications* 44-9 (1899- 1901).

Shaw W.A. (ed.), *Naturalizations and Denizations, 1700-1800.* Manchester, 1923.

Public Characters, 1799-1810. London, 1800-11.

The Annual Biography and Obituary, London, 1817-37.

Boase F. R. *Modern English Biography*. 6 vols., Truro, 1892-1903.

Haag E. and E. *La France Protestante*. 2nd edn., Paris, 1877-88.

Corbaz A.(ed.) *Dictionnaire Historique et Biographique de la Suisse*. Neufchatel, 1932.

Galiffe J. A. *Notices Genealoguiques sur les Familles Genevoises*. 3 vols., Geneva, 1829.

Stephen L. and Lee. S. *The Dictionary of National Biography and Supplements*. London, 1885-1959.

Who Was Who 1916-28, 1929-40.

Brydges, Sir E. *The Biographical Peerage of Ireland*. London, 1817.

Burke's Dictionary of the Landed Gentry. 3 vols., London, 1845-9.

Burke's Extinct and Dormant Baronetcies. London, 1838, 1844.

Burke's Landed Gentry. Various edns., London.

Burke's Peerage, Baronetage and Knightage. Various edns., London.

G.E.C[okayne] *The Complete Baronetage*. London, 1906

The Complete Peerage of England, Scotland, Ireland, Great Britain and the United Kingdom. New edn., 14 vols., London, 1910-98.

Brydges Sir E. *Collins' Peerage of England*. London, 1812.

Foster J. *Peerage, Baronetage and Knightage*, London, 1882.

Kelly's Handbook to the Titled, Landed and Official Classes. 1924 edn., London.

The Ladies Who's Who. London, 1923.

Lodge E. *The Peerage, Baronetage, Knightage and Companionage*. 81st edn., London, 1912.

Paul Sir J.B. *The Scots Peerage*. 9 vols., Edinburgh, 1904-14.

Sharpe's Genealogical History of the British Empire. London, 1833.

Shaw W.A. *The Knights of England*. 4 vols., London, 1906.

Walford E. O. *County Families*. Edns. of 1860, 1865, 1888, 1892, 1904, 1920, London.

The Yorkshire Who's Who. London, 1912.

Austen Leigh R. A. *The Eton College Register, 1753-90*. London, 1921.

Stapylton H.E.C., *The Eton School List, 1791-1850*. 2nd edn., London, 1894.

Old Etonian Association, *The Eton Register, 1871-80*. London, 1907.

Beevor E., Evans R.J., Savory T.H., *The History and Register of Aldenham School*. 8th edn., Worcester, 1948.

Gun W.T.J.(ed.) *The Harrow School Register, 1571-1800*. London, 1934.

Dauglish M.G & Stephenson P.K. *The Harrow School Register, 1800-1911*. 3rd edn., London, 1911.

Moir J.W. (ed.) *The Harrow School Register, 1885-1949*. 5th edn., London, 1951.

Jones L.W. *The Marlborough College Register, 1843-1952*. 9th edn., Marlborough, 1952.

Milford L. S. (ed.) *The Haileybury Register, 1862-1910*. London & Bungay, 1910.

Russell Barker G.F. & Stenning A.H. *The Record of Old Westminsters (to 1927)*. 2 vols., London, 1928.

Solly G.A. *The Rugby School Register Annotated, vol. I, 1675-1857*. Rugby, 1933.

Graham J.P. (ed.) *The Uppingham School Roll, 1824-1931*. 6th issue, London, 1932.

Holgate I.W. & Chitty H.W. *Winchester Long Rolls (1723-1812)*. Winchester, 1904.

Foster J. *Alumni Oxonienses, 1715-1886*, 4 vols., Oxford, 1888.

Venn J. and Venn J. A. *Alumni Cantabrigienses, 1751-1900*. 6 vols., Cambridge, 1954.

Whishaw J. *A Synopsis of the English Bar*. London, 1835.

Lincolns' Inn Admissions Registers, vol. I (1420-1799). London, 1896.

Namier Sir L.B and Brooke J. *The House of Commons, 1754-90.* 3 vols., London, 1964.

Thorne R.G. *The House of Commons, 1790-1820.* 5 vols., London, 1986.

Wilks G. *The Barons of the Cinque Ports and the Parliamentary Representation of Hythe.* Folkestone, 1892.

Williams W. R. *The Parliamentary Representation of the County of Worcester.* Hereford, 1897.

Wilson T. *A Biographical Index to the Present House of Commons.* Edns. of 1806, 1808, London.

Sainty [Sir] J.C. *Lists of Office Holders: the Colonial Office.* London, 1976.

Foss E. *The Judges of England.* 9 vols., London, 1848-64.

Acres W. M. Directors of the Bank of England, *Notes and Queries* 1940 (2) *City Biography.* 2nd edn., London, 1800.

Colvin H. M. *A Biographical Dictionary of British Architects, 1600-1840.* 3rd edn., London and New Haven, 1995.

Eden P. *A Directory of Land Surveyors etc.* Folkestone, 1975.

Hilton Price F.G. *A Handbook of London Bankers.* London, 1890/1.

Hodson, Major V.C.P. *A List of Officers of the Bengal Army, 1758-1834.* 4 vols., London, 1827-47.

Horn D. B. *British Diplomatic Representatives, 1689-1789,* Camden Society, 3rd s., XLVI, 1932.

Mallalieu H. C. *A Dictionary of British Watercolour Artists up to 1920.* London, 1976.

Marshall J. *Royal Naval Biography.* 12 vols., London, 1823-30.

O'Byrne W.R. *A New Naval Biography.* 3 vols., London, 1849.

Wood C. *A Dictionary of Victorian Painters.* 3rd edn., Woodbridge, 1995.

4. BOOKS, ARTICLES etc.

The Declaration of the Merchants, Traders and other Inhabitants of London made at Grocers' Hall, December 1795.

Reports of the Suffolk Lunatic Asylum, 1843-7. Suffolk Social History Pamphlets. Institute of Historical Research, London.

Agnew D.C.A. *Protestant Exiles from France in the Reign of Louis XIV.* 3 vols., London, 1874.

Ain G G. de l' *Les Thellusson.* Paris, 1976.

Albion R. G. *Forests and Seapower.* Cambridge, Mass. 1926.

Alger J. G. *Englishmen in the French Revolution.* London, 1869.

Allen R. C. The Price of Freehold Land and the Interest Rate in the 17th and 18th Centuries. *Economic History Review* (2nd s.) 41 (1988), 33-50.

Amyot T. *The Speeches in Parliament of the R.H. William Windham [with an account of his life]* 3 vols., London, 1812.

Anderson J. S. *Lawyers and the Making of English Land Law, 1832 -1940.* Oxford,

1992.

Anderson O. The Wensleydale Peerage Case and the Position of the House of Lords. *English Historical Review* 82 (1967), 486-502.

Andrew D. T. The Code of Honour and its Critics: the opposition to duelling in England, 1700-1850. *Social History* 5 (1980), 409-34.

Antonetti G. *Une Maison de Banque a Paris au XVIIIe Siècle, Greffulhe Montz et Cie (1789-1792)*. Paris, 1963.

Archer J. E. *"By a Flash and a Scare"*. Oxford, 1990.

Arnold A. The Indebtedness of the Landed Gentry. *Contemporary Review* 47 (1885), 225-32.

Arnott W. G. *A Suffolk Estuary*. Ipswich, 1950.

Ashton P. *Rendlesham: a brief history and guide*. 1975.

Ashton T. S. *Economic Fluctuations in England, 1700-1800*. Oxford, 1959.

An Economic History of England: the 18th Century. Repr., London, 1972.

Aspinall A. (ed.), *The Correspondence of George, Prince of Wales, 1770-1812*. 8 vols., London, 1963-71.

Atkinson C.T. Foreign Regiments in the British Army. *Journal of the Society for Army Historical Research* 21 (1942), 175-81; 22 (1943), 2-14.

Atlay J.B. *The Victorian Chancellors*. 2 vols., London, 1908.

Austen J. *Persuasion*. London, 1818.

Aydelotte W.O. *et al.*(eds.) *The Dimensions of Quantitative Research in History*. Princeton and London, 1972.

Baker H.B. *The London Stage*. 2 vols., London, 1889.

Banks S. Nineteenth Century Scandal or Twentieth Century Model? A New Look at "Open" and "Closed" Parishes. *Economic History Review* (2nd s.) 41 (1989), 51-73.

Barbour V. *Capitalism in Amsterdam in the Seventeenth Century*. 1963 edn., Ann Arbor.

Baring Mrs. H.(ed.) *The Diary of William Windham, 1784-1810*. London, 1866.

Barker H. R. *East Suffolk Illustrated*. Ipswich, 1908-9.

Barry H. The Duke of Norfolk's Case. *Virginia Law Review* 23 (1937), 538-68.
    Mr. Thellusson's Will. *Ibid.* 22 (1936), 416-37.

Bateman J. *The Great Landowners of Great Britain and Ireland*. 4th edn. repr., Leicester, 1971

Beard M. *English Landed Society in the Twentieth Century*. London, 1989.

Beastall T. W. A South Yorkshire Estate in the Late 19th Century. *Agricultural History Review* 15 (1965), 40-4.

Beckett J. V. *The Aristocracy in England, 1660-1914*. Oxford, 1986.
    The Pattern of Landownership in England and Wales, 1660-1800. *Economic History Review* (2nd s.)37 (1984), 1-22.
    The Debate over Farm Sizes in 18th and 19th Century England. *Agricultural History Review* 57 (1983), 308-25.
    Family Matters. *Historical Journal* 39 (1996), 249-56.

Gosfield Hall: a country estate and its owners, 1715-1825. *Essex Archaeology and History* (3rd s.) 25 (1994), 185-92.

Landownership and Estate Management, in Mingay, *Agrarian History of England and Wales* vol.VI, pp. 546-640.

Bedford, Duke of *A Great Agricultural Estate*. London, 1897.

Bence-Jones W. Landowning as a Business. *The Nineteenth Century* 11 (1882), 346-68.

Bendall A.S. *Maps, Land and Society, a History*. Cambridge, 1992.

Benson J. and Neville R.G.(eds.) *Studies in the Yorkshire Coal Industry*. Manchester, 1976.

Bertrand P. *Genève et la Révocation de l'Edit de Nantes*. Geneva, 1935.

Bindoff S. T. *Tudor England*. London, 1950.

Binney J.E.D. *British Public Finance and Administration, 1774-1792*. London, 1958.

Bird T.H. *Admiral Rous and the Turf*. London, 1939.

Birks M. *Gentlemen of the Law*. London, 1960.

Birrell A. Changes in Equity Procedure, in *A Century of Law Reform* (London, 1901), 177-202.

Blum J. English Parliamentary Enclosure. *Journal of Modern History* 53 (1981), 477-504.

Bolton G. C. *The Passing of the Irish Act of Union*. Oxford, 1966.

Bonfield L. *Marriage Settlements, 1601-1740: the Adoption of the Strict Settlement*. Cambridge, 1983.

Bordo M.D. and White E.N. A Tale of Two Currencies: British and French Finance during the Napoleonic Wars. *Journal of Economic History* 51 (1991), 303-16.

Bordwell P. Alienability and Perpetuity. *Iowa Law Review* 22 (1936-7), 437-60; 23 (1937-8), 1-23; 24 (1938-9), 1-65, 636-59; 25(1939-40), 1-31, 708-36.

Bosher J. F. *French Finances, 1770-1795, from Business to Bureaucracy*. Cambridge, 1970.

Huguenot Merchants and the Protestant International in the 17th Century. *William and Mary Quarterly* (3rd s.) 52 (1995), 77-102.

Bouchary J. *Le Marché au Changes de Paris à la Fin du XVIIIe Siècle (1788-1800)*. Paris, 1937.

Les Manieurs d'Argent à Paris à la Fin du XVIIIe Siècle. 3 vols., Paris, 1939-43.

Boulton W.B. *The History of White's*. 3 vols. in 2, London, 1892.

Bourne J. M. *Patronage and Society in 19th century England* London, 1986.

Bouvier J. and Germain-Martin H. *Finances et Financiers de l'Ancien Régime*. Paris, 1964.

Bowen C.S. (Lord), Progress in the Administration of Justice during the Victorian Period, in *Select Essays in Anglo-American Legal History*, vol. I, 517-559.

Bowen H. V. "The Pests of Human Society": Stockbrokers, Jobbers and Speculators in mid-18th Century Britain. *History* 78 (1993), 38-53.

Brewer J. *The Sinews of Power: War, Money and the English State, 1763-83*.

London, 1989.

Brightfield M. F. *Victorian England in its Novels (vol. I, 1840-70)*. California, 1971.

Brooke D. The Equity Suit of McIntosh v. the Great Western Railway; the "Jarndyce" of railway litigation. *Journal of Transport History* (2nd s.) 17 (1996), 133-49. Brydges Sir E. *The Autobiography, Times, Opinions and Contemporaries of Sir Egerton Brydges* 2 vols., London, 1834.

Buist M. G. *At Spes Non Fracta: Hope & Co., 1770-1815*. The Hague, 1974.

Burne A. H. *The Noble Duke of York*. London, 1949.

Butler E.M. *A Regency Visitor: The English Tour of Prince Puckler-Muskau, 1826-8*. London, 1957.

Cain P. J. and Hopkins A.G. Gentlemanly Capitalism and British Expansion Overseas, part one. *Economic History Review* (2nd s.) 39 (1986), 501-25.

Caird J. *English Agriculture in 1850-1*. London, 1852.

Campbell J. (Lord) *Lives of the Lord Chancellors and Keepers of the Great Seal*, vol. 6. London, 1847.

Campbell R. *The London Tradesman*. 3rd edn., London, 1747.

Cannadine D.E. *The Decline and Fall of the British Aristocracy*. Rev. edn., London, 1992.

Cannon J. *Aristocratic Century: the Peerage of Eighteenth Century England*. Cambridge, 1984.
  Parliamentary Reform, 1640-1832. Cambridge, 1973.

Carmichael G. *The History of the West Indian Islands of Trinidad and Tobago, 1498-1900*. London, 1961.

Carpenter K. *Refugees of the French Revolution: Emigrés in London, 1792-1802*. Basingstoke and London, 1999.

Carrington S. H. H. The American War and the British West Indies' Economy. *Journal of Interdisciplinary History* (1987), 823-50.

Carter A. C. Financial Activities of the Huguenots in London and Amsterdam in the mid-18th century, in *Getting, Spending and Investing in Early Modern Times*. Amsterdam, 1975.

Cellard J. *John Law et la Regence, 1715-29*. Paris, 1996.

Chambers J. D. and Mingay G. E. *The Agricultural Revolution, 1750-1880*. London, 1966.

Chandler G. *Four Centuries of Banking*, vol.I, London, 1964.

Chandos J. *Boys Together. English Public Schools, 1800-1864*. Oxford, 1985.

Chapman J. The Extent and Nature of Parliamentary Enclosure. *Agricultural History Review* 35 (1986), 25-35.

Chapman S.D. *The Rise of Merchant Banking*. London, 1984.

Chaussinand-Nogaret G. *Gens de Finance au XVIIIe Siècle*. Paris, 1972.

Checkland S. G. Finance for the West Indies, 1780-1815. *Economic History Review* (2nd s.) 10 (1957-8), 461-9.

Cherry B.L. and Russell A.E., *Wolstenholme's Conveyancing and Settled Land Acts*. 9th edn., London, 1905.

Chesterman M.J. *Charities, Trusts and Social Welfare*. London, 1979.
Family Settlements on Trust, in Sugarman and Rubin, *Law, Economy and Society*, 124-67.

Christie I.R. *British Non-Elite M.Ps., 1715-1820*. Oxford, 1995.

Clapham Sir J. *The Bank of England, A History*. 2 vols., London, 1944.

Clark J.C.D. *English Society, 1688-1832*. Cambridge, 1985.

Clark J. and Ross-Martyn J.G. *Theobald on Wills*. 15th edn., London, 1993.

Clark G. Land Hunger: Land as a Commodity and a Status Good, England 1500-1910. *Explorations in Entrepreneurial History* 35 (1998), 59-82.

Clarke P.K. with Langford K. Hodge's Politics: the Agricultural Labourers and the Third Reform Act in Suffolk, in Harte and Quinault, *Land and Society in Britain*, 119-36.

Clay C. M. The Price of Freehold Land in the Later 17th and 18th Centuries. *Economic History Review* (2nd s.) 27 (1974), 173-89.

Clayton H. *The Great Swinfen Case*. London, 1980.

Clutterbuck J. *The History and Antiquities of the County of Hertfordshire*. 3 vols., London, 1815-27.

Coates B.E. The Geography of the Industrialization and Urbanization of South Yorkshire from the 18th to the 20th Century, in Pollard and Holmes (eds.), *Essays in the Economic and Social History of South Yorkshire*, 14-27.

Cobbett W. *Rural Rides*. 1912 edn., London.

Cobban A. and Smith R.A. *The Correspondence of Edmund Burke*. 9 vols., Cambridge, 1958-78.

Codrington R.H. A Memoir of the Family of Codrington..., *Transactions of the Bristol and Gloucestershire Archaeological Society for 1898* 21, 301-45.

Cohen J. The History of Imprisonment for Debt. *Journal of Legal History* 3 (1982), 151-71.

Colchester, Lord (ed.) *The Diary and Correspondence of Lord Colchester*. 3 vols., London, 1861.

Collins E.J.T. The Coppice and Underwood Trades, in Mingay, *Agrarian History of England and Wales* vol. VI, pp.485-501.

Combe E. *Les Réfugiés de la Révocation en Suisse*. Lausanne, 1880.

Committee of Anglo-American Law Schools *Select Essays in Anglo-American Legal History*. Repr., 3 vols., London, 1968.

Cooper J.P. Patterns of Inheritance and Settlement by Great Landowners from the 15th to the 18th Century, in Goody *et al.*, *Family and Inheritance*, 192-327.

Cope S.R. The Goldsmids and the Development of the London Money Market during the Napoleonic Wars. *Economica* (n.s.) 9 (1942), 180- 206.

The Stock Exchange Revisited. *Economica* (n.s) 45 (1978), 1-21.

Walter Boyd, A Merchant Banker in the Age of Napoleon. Gloucester, 1983.

Copinger W.A. *The Manors of Suffolk*. 7 vols., London, 1905-11.

Coppock J.T. Agricultural Changes in the Chilterns, 1875-1900, in Perry (ed.), *British Agriculture, 1875-1914*, 56-76.

Corbaz A. Isaac Thellusson et les Emigrés, and Micheli du Crest et Isaac Thellusson. *Bulletin de la Société d'Histoire et d'Archéologie de Genève* 4 (1917-18), 193-4; (1918-19), 279-80.

Cornish W.R. and Clark G. de N. *Law and Society in England, 1750-1950.* London, 1989.

Cox H. Changes in Landownership in England. *The Atlantic Monthly* 129 (1922), 556-62.

Cox J. *Hatred Pursued Beyond the Grave: Tales of our Ancestors from the London Church Courts.* London, 1993.

Crosthwaite J.F. *A Brief Memoir of Major-General Sir John George Woodford.* Keswick etc. 1883.

Crouzet F. *Britain Ascendant: comparative studies in Franco-British Economic History.* Cambridge, 1990.

Britain, France and International Commerce. Aldershot, 1996.

Crowhurst P. *The Defence of British Trade.* Folkestone, 1977.

Cuming E.D. *Squire Osbaldeston: his Autobiography.* 1926 edn., London.

Curle J.S. *The Victorian Celebration of Death.* Newton Abbot, 1972.

Cussans J.E. *A History of Hertfordshire.* 6 vols., Hertford, 1870-81.

Davidoff L. and Hall C. *Family Fortunes: Men and Women of the English Middle Class, 1780-1850.* London, 1987.

Davies J. S. *A History of Southampton.* Southampton, 1883.

Davis N.Z. The Rites of Violence: Religious Riot in 16th Century France, in Soman (ed.), *The Massacre of St. Bartholomew: Re-appraisals and Documents.* The Hague, 1974.

Davis R. *The Rise of the English Shipping Industry.* London, 1962.

Davy H. *Views of the Seats of the Noblemen and Gentlemen in Suffolk.* Southwold, 1827.

de Castro J.P. *The Gordon Riots.* London, 1926.

de Crespigny Sir C. C. *Forty Years of a Sportsman's Life.* Rev. edn., London, 1925.

de la Garde Count A.C. *Brighton: Scènes Détachées d'un Voyage en Angleterre.* Paris, 1834.

de Lolmé J. *Observations on the power of Individuals to prescribe, by Testamentary Declaration, the particular future Uses to be made of their Property.* London, 1798 and 2nd edn., 1800.

Devas R.P. *The History of the Island of Grenada.* Grenada, 1964.

Dickens C. *Bleak House.* London, 1853.

Our Mutual Friend 1952 edn., Oxford.

A Tale of Two Cities 1970 edn., London.

Dickinson H.T.(ed.) *Britain and the French Revolution.* London, 1989.

Dinwiddy J.R. (ed.) *The Correspondence of Jeremy Bentham*, vol. 6 (1798-1801). Oxford, 1984.

Disraeli B. *Sybil, or the Two Nations.* 1926 edn., London.

Dixon R. and Muthesius S. *Victorian Architecture.* 2nd edn., London, 1985.

`Druid' [Dixon H.H.] *Silk and Scarlet*. London, 1858.

The Post and the Paddock. 1856 edn., London.

Scott and Sebright. London, 1862.

Duffy M. *Soldiers, Sugar and Seapower*. Oxford, 1987.

War, Revolution and the Crisis of the British Empire, in Philp, *The French Revolution and English Popular Politics*, 118-45.

Dugdale J. *The New British Traveller*. 4 vols., London, 1819.

Durston W. The Real Jarndyce and Jarndyce. *The Dickensian* 93 (1997), 27-33.

Eardley Wilmot Sir J. *Thomas Assheton Smith: The Reminiscences of a Famous Fox Hunter.* 6th edn., London, 1902.

Earle P. Age and Accumulation in the London Business Community, 1665-1720, in McKendrick and Outhwaite, *Business Life and Public Policy*, 36-63.

The Making of the English Middle Class. London, 1989.

Edgcumbe R. (ed.) *The Diary of Lady Shelley*. 2 vols., London, 1913.

Edwards A. *Half-a-Million of Money*. London, 1865.

Edwards J.R. *A History of Financial Accounting*. London, 1989.

Ehrman J. *The Younger Pitt, vol. I, The Years of Acclaim*. London, 1969.

Emery C.T. Do we need a rule against perpetuities? *Modern Law Review* 57 (1994), 602-10.

England S.L. *The Massacre of St. Bartholomew*. London, 1938.

English B. Patterns of Land Management in East Yorkshire, c.1840-c.1880. *Agricutural History Review* 32 (1984), 29-48.

and Saville J. *Strict Settlement, A Guide for Historians*. Hull, 1983.

English Heritage *Welcome to Brodsworth Hall*. London, 1995.

Erickson A.L. *Women and Society in Early Modern England*. London and New York, 1993.

Common Law and Common Practice: the use of Marriage Settlements in Early Modern England. *Economic History Review* (2nd s.) 48 (1990), 21-39.

Evans E.J. *The Contentious Tithe*. London, 1976.

Fairfax-Blaneborough J. *Northern Turf History*, vol.III. London, 1950.

Fearne C. *An Essay upon Contingent Remainders*. 10th edn., by J.W. Smith, 2 vols., London, 1844.

Finch J., Mason J., Masson J., Wallis L, Hayes L. *Wills, Inheritance and Families*. Oxford, 1996.

Fletcher T.W. The Great Depression 1873-96, in Perry, *British Agriculture, 1875-1914*, 30-55.

Fletcher D.H. Mapping and Estate Management in the Early Nineteenth Century. *Archaeologia Cantiana* 109 (1993), 85-109.

Fonblanque E.B.de (ed.) *The Life and Labours of Albany Fonblanque*. London, 1874.

Fortescue J.W. *A History of the British Army*, vol.IX. London, 1920.

Fournier E. *Chroniques et Legendes des Rues de Paris*. Paris, 1864.

Fox-Bourne H.R. *English Merchants*. 2 vols., London, 1866.

Francis J. *Chronicles of the Stock Exchange*. London, 1855.

Franklin J. *The Gentleman's Country House*. London, 1981.

Fraser L.M. *A History of Trinidad, vol.II, 1814-39*. Port of Spain, 1896.

Fulford R. *Glyn's, 1753-1953*. London, 1953.

    Royal Dukes. London, 1948.

Garlick K., McIntyre A.M. and Cave K. (eds.), *The Farington Diaries*. 16 vols., New Haven and London, 1978-84.

Garnett E. *John Marsden's Will*. London, 1998.

Gash N. *Politics in the Age of Peel: a Study in Parliamentary Representation*. London, 1953.

Gaskell C.M. The Country Gentleman. *The Nineteenth Century* 12 (1882), 460-73.

Gauldie E. Country Homes, in Mingay, *The Victorian Countryside*, vol.II, 531-41.

Gautier C. Un Investissement Genevois: La Tontine d'Irelande de 1777. *Bulletin de la Société de l'Histoire et de l'Archéologie de Genève* 10 (1951), 53-64.

Gibson W.T. "Withered Branches and Weighty Symbols": Surname Substitution in England, 1660-1880. *British Journal for Eighteenth Century Studies* 15 (1992), 17-33.

Ginter D.E. *Voting Records of the House of Commons, 1761-1820*. London, 1995.

Girouard M. *The Victorian Country House*. Oxford, 1971.

Glover R.K. *Peninsular Preparation*. Cambridge, 1963.

Goldsmith J. and Powell-Smith V. *Against the Law*. London, 1977.

Goody J., Thirsk J. and Thompson, E.P. (eds.) *Family and Inheritance: Rural Society in Europe, 1200-1800*. Cambridge, 1976.

Gower L.C.B. *Principles of Company Law*. 6th edn., by P.L. Davies, London, 1997.

Gowing R. *Public Men of Ipswich and East Anglia*. Ipswich, 1875.

Grassby R. English Merchant Capitalism in the late 17th Century: the Composition of Business Fortunes. *Past and Present* 46 (1970), 87-107.

    The Personal Wealth of the Business Community in 17th Century England. *Economic History Review* (2nd s.) 23 (1970), 220-34.

Gray D. *Spencer Perceval*. Manchester, 1963.

Gray J.C. *The Rule against Perpetuities*. 4th edn., by R.Gray, Boston, USA, 1942.

Gray G.D.B. The South Yorkshire Coalfield. *Geography* 1947, 113-31.

Green D.R. and Owens A. Metropolitan Estates of the Middle Class, 1800-1850: Probates and Death Duties Revisited. *Historical Research* 70 (1997), 294-311.

Grellier J.J. *The Terms of all the Loans*. London, 1812.

Grote Mrs. *The Personal Life of George Grote*. London, 1873.

Grove R. Coprolite Mining in Cambridgeshire. *Agricultural History Review* 24 (1976), 24-43.

Guest M. and Boulton W.B. *The Royal Yacht Squadron*. London, 1903.

Gwynn R.D. *Huguenot Heritage*. London, 1985.

Habbakuk Sir H.J. *Strict Settlement and the Estates System*. Oxford, 1994.

Hancock D. "Domestic Bubbling": 18th Century London Merchants and individual investment in the Funds. *Economic History Review* (2nd s.) 47 (1994),

679-702.

Hanham H.J. *Elections and Party Management*. London, 1959.

Hardcastle D. *Banks and Banking*. London, 1842.

Hargrave F. *Juridical Arguments and Collections*, vol.2. London, 1799.
Observations written in April 1800, on the Bill against Trusts of Accumulation. London, 1801.

Hargrave J.F. *A Treatise on the Thellusson Act etc.* London, 1842.

Hargreaves J.F. *The National Debt*. London, 1930.

Harling P. *The Waning of "Old Corruption": the Politics of Economical Reform in Britain, 1779-1846*. Oxford, 1996.

Harris R. The Bubble Act: its Passage and its Effects on Business Organization. *Journal of Economic History* 54 (1994), 610-27.

Harris R.W. French Finances and the American War, 1777-83. *Journal of Modern History* 48 (1976), 233-58.

Harte N. and Quinault R. (eds.) *Land and Society in Britain, 1700-1914*. Manchester, 1996.

Harvey N. *A History of Farm Buildings in England and Wales*. London, 1970.

Haskins G.L. Extending the Grasp of the Dead Hand. Reflections on the Origin of the Rule against Perpetuities. *University of Pennsylvania Law Review* 126 (1977), 19-46.

Hawkins A.J. and Ryder E.C. *The Construction of Wills*. London, 1965.

Hawkins L.M. *Memoirs, Anecdotes, Facts and Opinions, Collected and Preserved by Laetitia-Matilda Hawkins*. 2 vols., London, 1824.

Hayton D.J. *Underhill and Hayton , the Law Relating to Trusts and Trustees*. 15th edn., London, 1995.

Helleiner K.F. *The Imperial Loans*. Oxford, 1965.

Journals of the Hon. William Hervey...from 1755 to 1814. Suffolk Green Books 14. Bury St. Edmunds, 1906.

Hertfordshire Record Society. *The Hertfordshire Session Book*, vol. 9 (1799-1853), Hertford, 1939.

Historical Manuscripts Commission *Report on the Manuscripts of the Marquis of Lothian preserved at Blickling Hall*. London, 1905.
Report on the Manuscripts of J.B. Fortescue preserved at Dropmore. Vol.VII, London, 1910.
Report on the Manuscripts of the Earl Bathurst at Cirencester Park. London, 1923.

Hobsbawm E.J. and Rudé G. *Captain Swing*. London, 1970.

Holderness B.A. Agriculture and Industrialization, in Mingay, *The Victorian Countryside*, vol.I, 227-43.
"Open" and "Close" Parishes in England in the 18th and 19th Centuries. *Agricultural History Review* 20 (1972), 126-39.
Landlords' Capital Formation in East Anglia, 1750-1870. *Economic History Review* (2nd s.)25 (1972), 434-47.

The English Land Market in the Eighteenth Century: the Case of Lincolnshire. *Economic History Review* (2nd s.) 27 (1974), 557-76.

and Turner M. (eds.). *Land, Labour and Agriculture: Essays for Gordon Mingay*. London, 1991.

Holdsworth Sir W. S. *A History of English Law*. 17 vols., London, 1903-72.

Holt H.M.E. and Kain R.J.P. Land Use and Farming in Suffolk about 1840. *Proceedings of the Suffolk Institute of Archaeology and History* 35 (1984), 123-41.

Hoppit J.J. Financial Crises in Eighteenth Century England. *Economic History Review* (2nd s.) 39 (1986), 39-58.

Risk and Failure in English Business, 1700-1800. Cambridge, 1987.

Horsbrugh E.L.S. *Bromley, Kent*. London, 1929.

Horwitz H. Testamentary Practice, Family Strategies and the Last Phases of the Custom of London, 1660-1725. *Law and History Review* 2 (1984), 223-39.

"The Mess of the Middle Class" Revisited: the case of the "big bourgeoisie" of Hanoverian London. *Continuity and Change* 2 (1987), 263-83.

Hotman E. *The Steam Yachts*. Lymington.

Huggins M.J. *Kings of the Moor, North Yorkshire Racecourse Trainers, 1760-1900*. Teeside Polytechnic, 1991.

Hunter J. *South Yorkshire. A History of the Deanery of Doncaster*. 2 vols., London, 1823-31.

Hussey F. *The Royal Harwich Yacht Squadron, a short history*. Ipswich, 1972.

Hutchins J. *The History and Antiquities of the County of Dorset*. 3rd edn., 4 vols., London, 1861-73.

Hunt H.G. Agricultural Rent in South-East England, 1788-1825. *Agricultural History Review* 7 (1959), 98-108.

Hurt J.S. Landowners, Farmers and Clergy and the Financing of Rural Education before 1870. *Journal of Education History and Administration* 1 (1969), 6-13.

Jackson G. *Hull in the Eighteenth Century*. Oxford, 1972.

Jarman T. *A Treatise on Wills*. 2 vols., London, 1844.

Jennings R.M. and Trout A.P. *The Tontine: from the reign of Louis XIV to the French Revolutionary era*. Homewood, Ill., 1982.

Jevons H.S. *The British Coal Trade*. London, 1915.

Jeyes S.H. Our Gentlemanly Failures. *Fortnightly Review* 67 (1897), 387-98.

Jobson A. *Victorian Suffolk*. London, 1972.

John A.H. War and the English Economy, 1700-63. *Economic History Review* (2nd s.) 7 (1955), 329-44.

Johnson A.C. *Viscount Halifax, a Biography*. London, 1941.

Johnson A.H. (ed.) *Letters of Charles Greville and Henry Reeve*. London, 1924.

Johnson D. *Victorian Shooting Days: East Anglia 1810-1910*. Woodbridge, 1981.

Jones D. Thomas Campbell Foster and the Rural Labourer: incendiarism in East Anglia in the 1840s. *Social History* 1 (1976), 5-37.

Jones G. *A History of the Law of Charity, 1532-1827*. Cambridge, 1969.

Jones G. and Rose M.B. Family Capitalism. *Business History* 35 (1994), 1-17.

Jones K. *A History of the Mental Health Services*. London, 1972.

Kaplan S.L. *Bread, Politics and Political Economy in the Reign of Louis XV*. 2 vols., The Hague, 1976.

Keeton G.W. The Thellusson Will and Trusts for Accumulation. *Northern Ireland Legal Quarterly* 21 (1970), 131-74.

and Sheridan L.A. *Equity*. 2nd edn., London, 1976.

Kellock K.A. London Merchants and the pre-1776 American Debts. *Guildhall Studies* 1 no.3 (1974), 109-49.

Kenworthy-Browne, J. *et al. Burke's and Savill's Guide to Country Houses*, vol. III (East Anglia), London, 1981.

Ketton Cremer R.W. *The Early Life and Diaries of William Windham*. London, 1930. *Felbrigg; The Story of a House*. London, 1962.

Kindleburger C.P. Financial Institutions and Economic Development. *Explorations in Economic History* 21 (1984), 103-24.

Kingdom R.M. Reactions in Rome and Geneva, in Soman, *Massacre of St. Bartholomew*, 25-49.

Kirby J. *The Suffolk Traveller*. 1829 edn., Woodbridge.

Kirby M.W. *The British Coal Mining Industry, 1870-1946*. London, 1977.

Kirby R.S. *The Wonderful and Scientific Museum, or Magazine of Remarkable Characters*. 3 vols., London, 1803.

Kirk H. *Portrait of a Profession*. London, 1976.

Laborde E.D. *Harrow School, Yesterday and Today*. London, 1948.

Lambert S. *Bills and Acts*. Cambridge, 1971.

Langford P. *A Polite and Commercial People*. Oxford, 1989.

Public Life and the Propertied Englishman. Oxford, 1991.

Lee D. *Lyndhurst, the Flexible Tory*. London, 1994.

Leighton-Boyce J.A.S. *Smiths the Bankers, 1658-1958*. London, 1958.

Lemmings D. Marriage and the Law in the Eighteenth Century. *Historical Journal* 39 (1996), 339-60.

Leveson-Gower F. (ed.) *The Letters of Countess Granville*. 2 vols., London, 1894.

Lewis W.D. *A Practical Treatise on the Law of Perpetuity*. London, 1843.

Lewis W.S. (ed.) *The Yale Edition of Horace Walpole's Correspondence*. 46 vols., Oxford and New Haven, 1937-83.

Lhomer J. *Le Banquier Perregaux et sa Fille la Duchesse de Raguse*. 1926 edn., Paris.

Lieberman D. *The Province of Legislation Determined*. Cambridge, 1989.

Liverpool Lord and Reade C. *The House of Cornewall*. Hereford, 1908.

Lloyd T. *The General Election of 1880*. Oxford, 1968.

Lokke C.L. London Merchant Interest in the St. Domingue Plantations of the Emigres. *American Historical Review* 43 (1937-8), 795-802.

Longrigg R. *The History of Horse Racing*. London, 1972.

Lovelass P. *The Law's Disposal of a Person's Estate, who dies without Will or Testament*. 9th edn., London, 1798.

Lowe W.C. George III, Peerage Creations and Politics, 1760-84. *Historical Journal* 35 (1992), 587-609.

Lüthy H. *La Banque Protestante en France de la Revocation de l'Edit de Nantes a la Revolution.* 1961 edn., 2 vols. Paris.

Une Diplomatie ornée de glaces. La Representation de Gèneve à la cour de France au XVIIIe Siècle. *Bulletin de la Société d'Histoire et d'Archéologie de Genève* 12 (1960), 9-42.

Lynn R.J. *The Modern Rule against Perpetuities.* New York, 1966.

Lysons D. *The Environs of London,* vol.3. London, 1795.

Maddock H. *A Treatise on the Principles and Practice of the High Court of Chancery.* 2 vols., London, 1815.

Manchester A. H. *Sources for English Legal History, 1750-1950.* London, 1984.

Mansel P. *Louis XVIII.* London, 1981.

Marchand J (ed.) *A Frenchman in England (Metanges sur l'Angleterre of François, de la Rochefoucauld).* Cambridge, 1933.

Margrave-Jones C.V. *Mellows: the Law of Succession.* 5th edn, London, 1993.

Markland J.H. *A Sketch of the Life and Character of George Hibbert.* London, 1837.

Marshall G. *In Search of the Spirit of Capitalism.* London, 1982.

Marshall W. *On the Landed Property of England.* London, 1804.

Martin J. *Hanbury, Maudsley and Martin's Modern Equity.* 13th and 15th edns., London, 1989 and 1997.

Martin J.B. *"The Grasshopper" in Lombard Street.* London, 1892.

Martins S.W. and Williamson T. Labour and Improvement: agricultural change in East Anglia, c.1750-1870. *Labour History Review* 62 (1997), 275-95.

Masters B. *The Dukes.* London, 1975.

Mathias P. *The First Industrial Nation.* 2nd edn., London, 1983.

and O'Brien P.K. Taxation in Britain and France. *Journal of Economic History* 36 (1976), 601-40.

Maudsley R.H. *The Modern Law of Perpetuities.* London, 1979.

McCahill M.W. Peerage Creations and the Changing Character of the British Nobility, 1750-1830. *English Historical Review* 96 (1981), 259-84.

McGregor J.R. The Economic History of Two Rural Estates in Cambridgeshire, 1870-1934. *Journal of the Royal Agricultural Society* 98 (1937), 142-61.

McGregor O.R. and Blom-Cooper L. *Separated Spouses.* London, 1970.

McKendrick N. and Outhwaite R.B. (eds.) *Business Life and Public Policy: Essays in Honour of D. C. Coleman.* Cambridge, 1986.

McVeagh J. *Tradefull Merchants, the Portrayal of the Capitalist in Literature.* London, 1981.

Megarry R.E. The Vice-Chancellors. *Law Quarterly Review* 98 (1982), 370-405.

and Wade H.W.R. *The Law of Real Property.* 2nd and 5th edns., London, 1959, 1984.

Meister H. *Letters written during a Residence in England, translated from the French of Henry Meister.* London, 1799.

Melikan R.A. *John Scott, Lord Eldon, 1751-1838, the Duty of Loyalty.* Cambridge, 1999.

Merryweather F.S. *Lives and Anecdotes of Misers; or the Passion of Avarice Displayed.* London, 1850.

Middlemas R.K. *The Pursuit of Pleasure: High Society in the 1900s.* London, 1977.

Mills D.R. *Lord and Peasant in Nineteenth Century England.* London, 1980.

Milsom S.F.C. *Historical Foundations of the Common Law.* 2nd edn., London, 1986.

Mingay G.E. *English Landed Society in the Eighteenth Century.* London, 1963.

(ed.) *The Agrarian History of England and Wales,* vol. 6 (1750-1850). Cambridge, 1989.

(ed.) *The Victorian Countryside.* 2 vols., London, 1981.

Misra B.B. *The Central Administration of the East India Company, 1773-1834.* Manchester, 1959.

Mitchell H. *The Underground War Against Revolutionary France.* Oxford, 1965.

Moerikofer J. C. (trans. Roux G.) *Histoire des Refugies de la Reforme en Suisse.* Neuchatel and Geneva, 1878.

Moffat G. *Trusts Law: text and materials.* 2nd edn., London, 1994.

Montgomery-Massingberd H. The Fight for Gulliver's House. *Sunday Telegraph Magazine,* 21 Oct 1989.

Moody T.W. and Vaughan W.E.V. (eds.) *A New History of Ireland.* Oxford, 1986.

Moore D.C. *The Politics of Deference.* Hassocks, 1976.

Morgan K. Bristol West India Merchants in the 18th Century. *Transactions of the Royal Historical Society* (6th s.) 3 (1993), 185-208.

Morris G. (ed. Davenport B.C.) *A Diary of the French Revolution.* 2 vols., Westport (Conn.), 1939.

Morris J.H.C. and Leach W.B. *The Rule against Perpetuities.* 2nd. edn., London, 1964.

Murphy Lt.Col. C.C.R. *A History of the Suffolk Regiment, 1914-27.* London, 1928.

Muskett P. The East Anglian Riots of 1822. *Agricultural History Review* 32 (1984), 1-13.

Nash T.A. *The Life of Richard, Lord Westbury.* 2 vols., London, 1888.

Nicollier de Weck B. Calvin's Geneva. *Bulletin de la Société d'Histoire et d'Archéologie de Genève* 26 & 27 (1996-7), 57-74.

Newman A.(ed.) *Politics and Finance in the 18th Century: for Lucy Sutherland.* London, 1984.

Newmarch W. *The Loans raised by Mr. Pitt during the first French War, 1793-1801.* London, 1855.

Norman P. Notes on Bromley and its Neighbourhood. *Archaeologia Cantiana* 24 (1900), 139-60.

O'Brien D.P. (ed.), *The Correspondence of Lord Overstone.* 3 vols., Cambridge, 1971.

O'Brien P.K. The Political Economy of British Taxation, 1660-1815. *Economic History Review* (2nd s.) 41 (1988), 1-32.

Public Finance in the Wars with France, 1793-1815, in Dickinson, *Britain and* the French Revolution, 165-88.

Offer A. Farm Tenure and Land Values, 1750-1950. *Economic History Review.* (2nd s.) 44 (1991), 1-20.

Property and Politics, 1870-1914: Landownership, Law, Ideology and Urban Development in England. Cambridge, 1981.

O'Gorman F. *Voters, Patrons and Parties. The Unreformed Electoral System of Hanoverian England.* Oxford, 1989.

Oldfield T.H.B. *A History of the Boroughs.* 3 vols., London, 1792.

Olphin H.K. *George Tierney.* London, 1934.

Oldham J.C. *The Mansfield Manuscripts and the Growth of English Law in the Eighteenth Century.* 2 vols., Chapel Hill, 1992.

Oliver V.L. *The History of Antigua.* 3 vols., London, 1884-99.

Caribbeana. 6 vols., London, 1910-19.

Olney R.J. The Politics of Land, in Mingay, *The Victorian Countryside*, vol. I, 58-70.

Orwin C.S. and Whetham E. *A History of British Agriculture, 1846-1914.* London, 1964.

Page A. *A Topographical and Geographical History of Suffolk.* Ipswich, 1847.

Page W. *A History of the Manor of Wall Hall in Hertfordshire.* 1920.

Paget G. and Irvine L. *The Flying Parson and Dick Christian.* London, 1934.

Pares R. *War and Trade in the West Indies, 1739-63.* Oxford, 1936.

Park J.A. *A System of the Law of Marine Insurance.* London, 1786.

Parker R.A.C. *Coke of Norfolk.* Oxford, 1975.

Parkes J. *A History of the Court of Chancery.* London, 1828.

Parkinson C.N. *War and Trade in the Eastern Seas, 1793-1813.* 1966 edn., London.

Parry-Jones W.L. *The Trade in Lunacy.* London, 1972.

Peacock A.J. *Bread or Blood.* London, 1965.

Peignot G. *Choix de Testamens Anciens et Modernes.* Paris and Dijon, 2 vols., 1829.

Pelling H. *A Social Geography of British Elections.* London, 1967.

Perkins J.A. Tenure, Tenant Right and Agricultural Progress in Lindsey, 1780-1850. *Agricultural History Review* 23 (1975), 1-22.

Petré-Grenaillou O. *Les Negòçes Maritimes Frànçaises, XVIIe-XXe Siècle.* Paris, 1997.

Pemberton W.Baring. *Battles of the Crimean War.* London, 1962.

Perren R. The Landlord and Agricultural Transformation, 1870-1900, in Perry (ed.), *British Agriculture, 1875-1914*, 109-28.

Perrott R. *The Aristocrats: a Portrait of Britain's Nobility and their Way of Life Today.* New York, 1968.

Perry P.J.(ed.) *British Agriculture, 1875-1914.* London, 1973.

Pevsner N. and Cherry B. *The Buildings of England: Hertfordshire.* 2nd edn., London, 1977.

Phillips A. *et al.* Ecclesiastical Law, *Halsbury's Laws of England*, 4th edn., vol. 14 (London, 1975), paras. 399-434.

Phillips A.D.M. Landlord Investment in Farm Buildings in the English Midlands in the Mid-Nineteenth Century, in Holderness and Turner, *Land, Labour and Agriculture*, 191-210.

Philp M.(ed.) *The French Revolution and English Popular Politics*. Oxford, 1991.

Phipps H.R. *Notes on the Phipps and Phip Family*. Lahore, 1911.

Pitman F.W. *The Development of the British West Indies, 1700-63*. New Haven, 1917.

Pollard S. and Holmes C. (eds.) *Essays in the Economic and Social History of South Yorkshire*. Sheffield, 1976.

Polden P. John Reeves as Superintendant of Aliens. *Journal of Legal History* 3 (1982), 31-51.

Pollock F.M.(ed.) *The Table Talk of John Selden*. London, 1927.

Ponsonby A. *The Decline of Aristocracy*. London, 1912.

Pool B.J.T. *Navy Board Contracts, 1660-1832*. London, 1966.

Portalis Baron R. *Henry-Pierre Danloux, peintre de portraits et son journal durant l'Emigration (1753-1809)*. Paris, 1910.

Porter R. *Mind-Forg'd Manacles*. London, 1987.

Powell R.R. *Materials for a Course in Future Interests and non-commercial Trusts*. New York, 1929.

Press C.A.Manning *Suffolk Celebrities*. Leeds, 1893.

Preston R. *An Essay in a course of lectures on Abstracts of Title*. 2nd edn., 2 vols., London, 1824.

Price J.M.(ed.) *Joshua Johnson's Letter Book, 1771-4*. London Record Society, 15, London, 1979.

What did Merchants Do? Reflections on British Overseas Trade, 166-1790. *Journal of Economic History* 49 (1989), 267-84.

Transaction Costs: a Note on Merchant Credit and the Organization of Private Trade, in Tracy, *Political Economy of Merchant Empires*, 276-97.

Prior M. (ed.) *Women in English Society, 1500-1800*. London, 1985.

Puiz A-M. *Affaires et Politique: Recherches sur le Commerce de Genève au XVIIe Siècle*. Societé de l'Histoire et d'Archéologie de Genève, Memoires et Documents, 42 (1964).

Les Genevois de 1700, Ont-Ils une Opinione Economique? *Bulletin de la Société de l'Histoire et Archéologie de Genève*, 15 (1976), 6-23.

Purcell E.S. *The Life of Cardinal Manning*. 2 vols., London, 1895.

Purdue A.W. An Oxford College, Two Parishes and a Tithe-Farmer: the Modernisation of Tithe Collection. *Rural History* 8 (1997), 1-19.

Ragatz L.J. *The Fall of the Planter Class in the British Caribbean, 1763-1833*. New Haven, Mass., 1928.

Raikes A. *Victorian Churchbuilding and Restoration in Suffolk*. Woodbridge, 1982.

Randell H.E. *An Essay on the Law of Perpetuities and on Trusts of Accumulation*. London, 1822.

Rapp D. Social Mobility in the 18th Century: the Whitbreads of Bedfordshire, 1720-1815. *Economic History Review* (2nd s.) 27 (1974), 380-9.

Raven J. *Judging New Wealth: Popular Publishing and Responses to Commerce in England, 1750-1800.* Oxford, 1992.

Raynbird W. *On the Agriculture of Suffolk.* London, 1849.

Raynes H.E. *A History of British Insurance.* London, 1948.

Read B. *Sculpture at Brodsworth.* Victorian Society, London, 1990.

Redlich O. *The Molding of American Banking.* 1968 repr., New York and London.

Reeve H. *The Greville Memoirs.* 8 vols., London, 1888.

Richards E. "The Leviathan of Wealth": West Midlands Agriculture, 1800-50. *Agricultural History Review* 22 (1974), 97-117.

Richards G.C. The Creation of Peers Recommended by the Younger Pitt. *American Historical Review* 24 (1928-9), 47-54.

Rickword G.O. Exiled Royalties in Essex, *Essex Review* 49 (1940), 190-7.

Riley J.C. *International Government Finance and the Amsterdam Capital Market, 1740-1815.* Cambridge, 1980.

Roberts R. *Schroders: Merchants and Bankers.* London, 1992.

Robinson R.M. *Coutts', the History of a Banking House.* London, 1929.

Robinson W. *The History and Antiquities of the Parish of Hackney.* 2 vols., London, 1842.

Robson R. *The Attorney in Eighteenth Century England.* Cambridge, 1959.

Rogers N. Money, Land and Lineage: the big bourgeoisie of Hanoverian London. *Social History* 14 (1979), 437-54.

Rolt Sir J. *Memoirs of the R.H. Sir John Rolt.* London, 1939.

Rondot N. *Les Protestants à Lyon au Dix-Septième Siecle.* Lyons, 1981.

Rosebery Earl (ed.) *The Windham Papers.* 2 vols., London, 1913.

Pitt. London, 1891.

Rubinstein W.D. Businessmen into Landowners: the Question Revisited, in Harte and Quinault, *Land and Society in Britain*, 90-118.

Men of Property: the very rich in Britain since the Industrial Revolution. London, 1981.

Rudé G. *Hanoverian London, 1714-1808.* London, 1971.

Ruffer J.G. *The Big Shots.* Rev. edn., London, 1998.

Ryder E.C. Re King's Will Trusts: a Reassessment. *Current Legal Problems* 29 (1976), 60-73.

The Incidence of General Pecuniary Legacies, *Cambridge Law Journal* 14 (1956), 80-100.

St. André C. *Madame du Barry, d'après les documents authentiques.* Paris, 1909.

Saint-Ogen L. Les Metiers de L'emigration. *Nouvelle Revue* (n.s.) 32 (1905), 315-24.

Salmon A.G. The Most Famous Will in the World. *Solicitors' Journal* 118 (1974), 544-7, 560-2.

Sawers L. The Navigation Acts Revisited. *Economic History Review* (2nd s.) 45 (1992), 262-84.

Sayous A-E. Calvinisme et *Capitalisme: l'Experience Genevoise. Annales* de l'Histoire Economique et Sociale 33 (1935), 225-44.

La Haute Bourgeoisie de Geneve. *Revue Historique* 180 (1937), 31-57.

L'Affaire de Law et les Genevois. *Revue d'Histoire Suisse* 3 (1937), 310-40.

The Bourgeoisie of Geneva in the Age of the Reformation. *Economic History Review* 6 (1935-6), 194-200.

Scamell E.H. Reform of the Settled Land Act 1925. *Current Legal Problems* 10 (1957), 152-67.

and I'Anson R.C. *Lindley and Banks on Partnership.* 16th edn., London, 1990.

Scarlett P.C. *A Memoir of James Scarlett, 1st Lord Abinger.* London, 1877.

Schofield A.B. The Thellusson Millions, *Law Society's Gazette* 62 (1965), 613-4.

Schwartz L.D. Income Distribution and Social Structure in London in the Late 18th Century. *Economic History Review* (2nd s.), 32 (1979), 250-9.

Scoville W.C. *The Persecution of the Huguenots and French Economic Development, 1680-1720.* U. of California, 1960.

Scriven J. *A Treatise of the Law of Copyhold.* 7th edn., by A.Brown, London, 1896.

Shammas C. English Inheritance Law and its Transfer to the Colonies. *American Journal of Legal History* 31 (1987), 145-63.

Sharman F.A. Feudal Copyholder and Industrial Shareholder: the Dimes Case. *Journal of Legal History* 10 (1989), 71-90.

The Influence of Landowners on Route Selection, *Journal of the Railway and Canal Historical Society* 26 (1980), 49.

Shatto S. *The Companion to Bleak House.* London, 1988.

Sheridan R.B. *Sugar and Slavery: an Economic History of the British West Indies, 1623-1775.* Caribbean UP, 1974.

Sherrin C.H., Barlow R.F.D. and Wallington R.A. *Williams' Law relating to Wills.* 7th edn., London 1995.

Simes L.M. *Public Policy and the Dead Hand.* Ann Arbor, 1955.

Simpson A.E. "Dandelions on the Field of Honor": Dueling, the Middle Class and the Law in Nineteenth Century England. *Criminal Justice History* 9 (1988), 99-156.

Simpson A.W.B. *An Introduction to the History of the Land Law.* 2nd edn., Oxford, 1986.

Leading Cases in the Common Law. Oxford, 1995.

Sinclair Sir J. *The History of the Public Revenue of the British Empire.* 3rd edn., 3 vols., London, 1804.

Smith B.D.A. The Galtons of Birmingham: Quaker Gun Merchants and Bankers. *Business History* 9 (1967), 132-50.

Soman A. (ed.) *The Massacre of St. Bartholomew: Re-appraisals and Documents.* The Hague, 1974.

Sparrow E. The Alien Office, 1792-1806. *Historical Journal* 33 (1990), 361-84.

Secret Service, British Agents in France, 1792-1815. Woodbridge, 1999.

Spence G. *The Equitable Jurisdiction of the Court of Chancery.* 2 vols., London, 1846-9.

Spitz L.W. *The Protestant Reformation.* New York, 1985.

Spooner F.C. *Risks at Sea: Amsterdam Insurance and Maritime Enterprise, 1766-80.* Cambridge, 1983.

Spring D. *The English Landed Estate in the Nineteenth Century* Baltimore, 1963.

Spring E. *Land, Law and Family. Aristocratic Inheritance in England, 1300-1800.* Chapel Hill & London, 1993.

Squibb G.D. *Doctors Commons.* Oxford, 1977.

Statham F.P. *A History of the Family of Maunsell* 2 vols. in 3, London, 1917-20.

Stauffenegger R. *Eglise et Société: Genève au XVIIIe Siècle.* 2 vols., Geneva, 1983-4.

Stelling-Michaud S. Deux Aspects du Role Financier de Geneve Pendant la Guerre de Succession d'Europe. *Bulletin de la Société de l'Histoire et d'Archéologie de Genève* 6 (1935-6), 147-68.

Stevens R. *Law and Politics: the House of Lords as a Judicial Body, 1800-1976.* London, 1979.

Stone L. *The Family, Sex and Marriage* 1979 edn., London.
Country Houses and their Owners in Hertfordshire, 1540-1879, in Aydelotte, *The Quantitative Dimension in History*, 56-123.

Story J.B. *Commentaries on Equity Jurisprudence.* 10th edn., 2 vols., Boston, USA, 1870.

Suckling A. *The History and Antiquities of the County of Suffolk.* 2 vols., London, 1846-8.

Sugarman D. and Rubin G. R.(eds.) *Law, Economy and Society, 1750-1914.* Abingdon, 1984.

Sutherland L.S. The Accounts of an 18th century merchant: the Portuguese ventures of William Braund, in Newman, *Politics and Finance*, 366-85.

Sugden E.G. *The Law of Vendors and Purchasers.* London, 1805.

Supple B.E. The Great Capitalist Manhunt. *Business History* 6 (1963-4), 48-62.

Surtees R. *Hillingdon Hall.* London, 1845.
Mr. Sponge's Sporting Tour. London, 1853.

Taylor A. and H. *The Book of the Duffs.* 2 vols., Edinburgh, 1914.

Taylor G. V. The Paris Bourse on the Eve of the Revolution, 1781-89. *American Historical Review* 67 (1961-2), 951-72.

Taylor S., Connors R., Jones C. *Hanoverian Britain and Empire: Essays in Memory of Philip Lawson.* Woodbridge, 1998.

Temple Patterson A. *A History of Southampton, 1700-1914.* Southampton, 1966.

Thirsk J., with Imray J.(eds.) *Suffolk Farming in the 19th Century*, vol.I. Suffolk Record Society, Ipswich, 1958.

Thompson E.P. The Grid of Inheritance, in Goody *et al.*, *Family and Inheritance*, 328-60.

Thompson F.M.L. Business and Landed Elites in Society, in Thompson, *Landowners, Capitalists and Entrepreneurs*, 139-70.
(ed.) *Landowners, Capitalists and Entrepreneurs: Essays for Sir John Habbakuk.* Manchester, 1996.

English Landed Society in the Nineteenth Century. 1971 edn., London.

English Landed Society in the Twentieth Century. *Transactions of the Royal Historical Society* (5th s.) 40 (1990), 1-24; (6th s.) 1 (1991), 1-20; 2 (1992), 1-24; 3 (1993), 1-22.

The Fall of the Grenvilles, 1844-48. *Huntingdon Library Quarterly* 19 (1956), 154-90.

Life after Death: how successful nineteenth century businessmen disposed of their fortunes. *Economic History Review* (2nd s.) 43 (1990), 40-59.

The Land Market in the Nineteenth Century. *Oxford Economic Papers* 9(1957), 285-300.

Thoms D.W. The Mills Family: London Sugar Merchants of the 18th Century. *Business History* 11 (1969), 3-10.

'Thormanby' [Dixon W.W.] *Kings of the Turf.* London, 1898.

Thornton H. *An Enquiry into the Nature and Effects of the Paper Credit of Great Britain.* 1939 edn., London, intro. by Hayek F.A.

Thornton P.M. *Harrow School and its Surroundings* London, 1885.
Some Things We Have Remembered. London, 1912.

Timbs J. *The Book of Modern Legal Anecdotes.* London, 1874.
English Eccentrics and Eccentricities. London, 1875.

Todd B.J. The Remarrying Widow- a Stereotype Reconsidered, in Prior, *Women in English Society*, 54-92.

Tracy J. D.(ed.), *The Political Economy of Merchant Empires.* Cambridge, 1991.

Trollope A. *An Autobiography.* 1980 edn., Oxford.

Trueman B. E. S. Corporate Estate Management: Guy's Hospital Agricultural Estates, 1726-1815. *Agricultural History Review* 28 (1980), 31-44.

Tudor- Craig Sir A. *The Romance of Melusine and de Lusignan together with notes and pedigrees ...* London, 1933.

Twiss H. *The Public and Private Life of John Scott...* 3 vols., London, 1844.

Tyrell J. *Suggestions sent to the Commissioners appointed to inquire into the Laws of Real Property.* London, 1929.

Underhill A. Changes to the Law of Real Property in the Nineteenth Century, in *Select Essays in Anglo-American Legal History*, vol.III, 673-719.

Unwin R.W. A Ninteenth Century Estate Sale: Wetherby, 1824. *Agricultural History Review* 23 (1975), 116-38.

Vamplew W. *The Turf, a Social and Economic History.* London, 1972.

Van Doren C. *Benjamin Franklin.* New York, 1938.

Victoria County History of England
Berkshire, vol.III. London, 1923.
Buckinghamshire, vol.IV. London, 1927.
Hampshire, vol.III. London, 1923.
Hertfordshire, vols. II, III. London, 1908, 1912.
Lancashire, vol.V, London, 1911.
Middlesex, vols. I, V. Oxford, 1969, 1976.

470

Somerset, vol.IV. Oxford, 1978.

Staffordshire, vol.XX. Oxford, 1984.

Suffolk, vol.II. London, 1907.

Surrey, vol.II. London, 1905.

Worcestershire, vols. II (London, 1906), III(Oxford, 1971).

Vidalenc J. *Les Emigrés Français, 1789-1825*. Caen, 1963.

Ville S.T. *English Shipowning during the Industrial Revolution*. Manchester, 1996.

Waagen G.F. *Galleries and Cabinets of Art in Great Britain*. London, 1857.

Walford E.O. *Tales of our Great Families*. 1890 edn., London.

Ward J.T. West Riding Landowners and Mining in the 19th Century, in Benson and Neville, *Studies in the Yorkshire Coal Industry*, 45-65.

Warren J. Trusts for Accumulation of Income: the Wills of Benjamin Franklin and Peter Thellusson. *Proceedings of the Massachusetts Historical Society* 66 (1942), 346-56.

Warren S. *Ten Thousand a Year*. London, 1839.

Watson C. *Snobbery with Violence*. London, 1971.

Weber M. *The Protestant Ethic and the Spirit of Capitalism*. 1976 edn., London.

Weiner M. *The French Exiles, 1789-1815*. London, 1960.

Weir D.R. Tontines, Public Finances and Revolution in France and England. *Journal of Economic History* 49 (1989), 95-124.

Wells R. *Insurrection, the British Experience*. Gloucester, 1983.

Westerfield R.B. *Middlemen in English Business, 1660-1760*. New Haven, 1915.

Wheeler C.A. *Sportascrapiana*. London, 1867.

Whetham E. *The Agrarian History of England and Wales*. Vol.VIII (1914-39), Cambridge, 1978.

Whiteman A., Bromley J.S., Dickson P.M.G.(eds.) *Statesmen, Scholars and Merchants: Essays in 18th Century History, presented to Dame Lucy Sutherland*. Oxford, 1973.

Wilkes A.R. Adjustments in Arable Farming after the Napoleonic Wars. *Agricultural History Review* 28 (1980), 90-104.

Williams E. *History of the People of Trinidad and Tobago*. Trinidad, 1964.

Williams T.D. A Pattern of Land Accumulation: the Audley End Experience, 1762-97. *Transactions of the Essex Archaeological Society* (3rd s.) 11 (1979), 90-110.

Willis R. Pitt's Resignation in 1801. *Bulletin of the Institute of Historical Research* 44 (1971), 239-57.

Wilson C. *Anglo-Dutch Commerce and Finance*. Cambridge, 1941.

England's Apprenticeship. London, 1963.

Wilson H. *Wonderful Characters*. London, 1821.

Wilson P.W. (ed.) *The Greville Diary*. London, 1927.

Winchester S. *Their Noble Lordships. The Hereditary Peerage Today*. London, 1981.

Windham Sir W. *Waves, Wheels, Wings, an autobiography*. London, 1943.

Woolrych H.W. *Lives of Eminent Serjeants at Law*. 2 vols., London, 1869.

Wordie J.R. Rent Movements and the English Tenant Farmer, 1700-1839. *Research in Economic History* 6(1981), 193-244.

Wright C. and Fayle C.E. *A History of Lloyds*. London, 1926.

Wrightson K.W. The Family in Early Modern England: Continuity and Change, in Taylor, Connors and Jones, *Hanoverian Britain*, 1-22.

Wrigley E.A. and Schofield R.S. *The Population History of England, 1541-1871*. London, 1981.

Yale D.E.C. *Lord Nottingham's Chancery Cases*. Selden Society, vol. LXXXIII, London, 1954.

Yorke O. Miserrimus, or the Thellusson Job. *Fraser's Magazine* 7 (1833), 730-1.

Yorke P.C. (ed.) *The Diary of John Baker*. London, 1931.

Young G.F. Noddy Boffin's Misers. *The Dickensian* 43 (1956-7), 14-16.

Ziegler P. *The Sixth Great Power: Barings, 1762-1929*. London, 1988.

Index

476

Martin, Sir Samuel 392-3
Martinique 112, 113
Massacre of St. Bartholomew 12-13
Maxwell, Charles 46
McCririck, Clare (Lady Rendelsham) 416
McWilliam, John 270-1
Meister, Henry 64
Merchants 7; Dutch 49, 53; French 49; English, specialisation by 51-2; Russia 68; marriage patterns 70; inheritance among 130; West India 111-12; in Parliament 110-11, 191-2; peerages 118-20; attitudes towards 195-6; fortunes 195; houses 63-4
Micheli, J.L. 95; Jules 105n56, 261
Michelistes 24, 27
Midhurst 111-113
Middlesex hospital 261
Middleditch, Joseph 49
Midlands, trust estates in 273, 274, 275, 299, 305, 306, 371, 384, 395, 417
Misers 144-5
Mississippi bubble 19-20
Mitchell, William 221, 242, 254n152, 352n159
Montagu, Viscount 111
Montgomerie, Egidia (Lady Rendelsham) 407, 409
Montserrat 48, 268
Montz, J-M. 86, 91
Morgan, Dr 194, 258, 262
Mortmain 128-9
Mulgrave, Lord 52, 71
Muilman, Robert 86
Mundon 70

Nabobs 195
Naturalization 36-7
Naville, Pierre 27, 44

Neate family 241
Necker, Jacques 22, 43, 51, 83, 93; Louis 51
Negatifs 24
Newland, Abraham 98, 209n41
New Farm 295
Newton Hanzard 225, 273, 274, 292, 304, 380n112
Nightingale, Col. 339
Norman, George 92, 316; Charlotte 316; George Warde 41, 65, 316, 317, 322
Northamptonshire, trust estates in 417, 418
North Weston estate 274, 279
Northumberland, Dukes of 289
Nottingham, Lord 4, 5, 166-7, 169, 170, 188, 224

Oddie, Henry Hoyle I 292, 331; Henry Hoyle II 331, 334; Henry Hoyle III 331-2, 334, 404n92; family 334-5 331, 349n116
Oddie, John 201
Okehampton 228
Oldfield, T.H.B. 111
Old Parkbury Farm 306
Osbaldeston, George 335-6, 338, 385, 387
Otterspool 241, 242, 243, 330

Page-Wood, W. 362, 405n108
Pakington, Sir J.S. (Lord Hampton) 329
Palmer, Thomas 2
Palmer, Roundell (Lord Selborne) 204, 389, 390, 391
Paris 11, 12, 21, 22, 24-5, 81, 82, 85-6, 320, 321, 328
Park manor 274
Park Place, Henley 110, 195
Parliament, merchants in 110-11;